OKANAGAN COLLEGE LIBRARY

P9-ECU-406

Social Psychology and Discourse

OKANAGAN COLLEGE
LIBRARY
BRITISH COLUMBIA

Social Psychology and Discourse

Andrew McKinlay

and

Chris McVittie

WILEY-BLACKWELL

A John Wiley & Sons, Ltd., Publication

This edition first published 2008
© 2008 Andrew McKinlay and Chris McVittie

Blackwell Publishing was acquired by John Wiley & Sons in February 2007. Blackwell's publishing program has been merged with Wiley's global Scientific, Technical, and Medical business to form Wiley-Blackwell.

Registered Office
John Wiley & Sons Ltd, The Atrium, Southern Gate, Chichester, West Sussex, PO19 8SQ, United Kingdom

Editorial Offices
350 Main Street, Malden, MA 02148-5020, USA
9600 Garsington Road, Oxford, OX4 2DQ, UK
The Atrium, Southern Gate, Chichester, West Sussex, PO19 8SQ, UK

For details of our global editorial offices, for customer services, and for information about how to apply for permission to reuse the copyright material in this book please see our website at www.wiley.com/wiley-blackwell.

The right of Andrew McKinlay and Chris McVittie to be identified as the author of this work has been asserted in accordance with the Copyright, Designs and Patents Act 1988.

All rights reserved. No part of this publication may be reproduced, stored in a retrieval system, or transmitted, in any form or by any means, electronic, mechanical, photocopying, recording or otherwise, except as permitted by the UK Copyright, Designs and Patents Act 1988, without the prior permission of the publisher.

Wiley also publishes its books in a variety of electronic formats. Some content that appears in print may not be available in electronic books.

Designations used by companies to distinguish their products are often claimed as trademarks. All brand names and product names used in this book are trade names, service marks, trademarks or registered trademarks of their respective owners. The publisher is not associated with any product or vendor mentioned in this book. This publication is designed to provide accurate and authoritative information in regard to the subject matter covered. It is sold on the understanding that the publisher is not engaged in rendering professional services. If professional advice or other expert assistance is required, the services of a competent professional should be sought.

Library of Congress Cataloging-in-Publication Data

McKinlay, Andrew.
Social psychology and discourse / Andrew McKinlay and Chris McVittie.
p. cm.
Includes bibliographical references and index.
ISBN 978-1-4051-4658-6 (hardcover : alk. paper) — ISBN 978-1-4051-4657-9 (pbk. : alk. paper)
1. Social psychology.   I. McVittie, Chris.   II. Title.

HM1033.M359 2008
302—dc22

2007045479

A catalogue record for this book is available from the British Library.

Set in 10.5/12.5 Dante MT by Graphicraft Limited, Hong Kong
Printed in Sinagpore by Markono Print Media Pte Ltd

1   2008

Contents

Preface

Our aim in writing this book was to provide readers with a modern overview of how discursive research has contributed to social psychology. To do this, we have deliberately chosen to organize the book around central themes in social psychology, rather than organizing the book around different aspects of discursive research. We hope that by doing this readers will immediately be able to see the relevance of discursive research to academic social psychology and to social life in general. As far as we know, this is the first general book on social psychology and discourse that adopts this approach. Other texts on discursive research in social psychology have tended to use the different "varieties" of discursive study as an organizational principle. Our view is that while this is useful in explaining important theoretical and methodological differences within the field, it runs the risk of confusing the reader by concealing the important contributions that discursive research makes to understanding our social world.

Readers will also note that, unlike other texts, this book does not begin by offering a "defense" of discursive methods. Our view is that discursive research is a mature enough discipline to no longer require pleas for acceptance from other branches of psychology. Our claim is that discursive research informs our understanding of the social world as well as, or better than, other approaches to social psychology. Having read this book, it will be up to readers to decide whether this is a valid claim.

The book is intended to convey current research findings within social psychology which arise out of discursive research. However, we hope that the book will also encourage readers to think and reflect more generally on how our social life is built up from, or conditioned by, the discursive processes that surround us. To this extent, the book is aimed not only at specialist social psychology students but also at all those who have a lively interest in the way that interactions with other people influence the self. To this end, we have drawn our examples from a wide range of studies in which real people talk about real aspects of their social life.

Anyone who has written a book of this sort knows the difficulty associated with the selection process in which some favored research paper has to be omitted. Our intention was that this book should offer a modern account of contemporary research. For that reason, many well-cited but now relatively elderly research articles are not included here. However, we have tried to give readers a grasp of discursive research's historical development by including in each chapter one or more descriptions of "classic texts" which demonstrate contemporary discursive research's historical legacies.

We have adopted an international perspective in writing this book. Much of the development of discursive research can be traced back to Europe and to the United States. However, researchers from across the world have used discursive techniques in pursuing their own research goal. We have reflected this in the breadth of the examples of research that we have selected.

Advantages for the Student

The design of the book is intended to aid student readers in their studies. Each chapter is structured around clearly "signposted" themes which are also presented on the title page of each chapter. Where appropriate, we have also included summary sections within chapters which recapitulate those themes. At the end of each chapter there is a "Chapter Summary" box in which the major issues raised within the chapter are briefly reviewed. There is also a "Connections" box for each chapter in which readers are offered guidance about the ways in which issues that arise in that chapter are picked up in other chapters. In addition, each chapter concludes by identifying several "Further Readings," which are accompanied by brief descriptions that allow readers to see their relevance. In any field, jargon can be a problem. To help with this, each chapter includes text boxes at the foot of the page where potentially difficult terms are spelled out in an accessible way. In each chapter, we have interspersed "technical" discourse research terms with terms associated with the chapter's main theme, in the hope that this will provide a user-friendly way of coming to grips with discursive research terminology. These terms are usually introduced on their first occurrence in the text, unless they are dealt with substantively later in the book. The contents of these text boxes are also organized alphabetically in the book's "Glossary" section.

Advantages for the Teacher

We have made sure that each chapter of the book is a "stand-alone" text which could form the basis for one or several lessons in its own right. The clearly structured nature of each chapter should allow the teacher to develop lessons of this sort with the minimum of effort. Teachers will also benefit from the "Connections" boxes provided for each chapter in which links between that chapter and other chapters within the book are made clear. The best form of teaching involves students in active learning as well as passively receiving information in a lecture format. Accordingly, at the end of each chapter we have included an "Activity Box" which spells out an idea for how students could practically examine one or more of the themes that arise in the chapter, for example, through student projects or student-led seminars.

Chapter 1

Introduction

Key terms
Archive research
Behavior
Case study
Cognitive
Context
Conversation analysis
Correlation
Critical discourse analysis
Dependent variable
Discourse analysis
Discursive action
Discursive psychology
Experiment
Focus group
Foucauldian discourse analysis
Grounded theory
Hypothesis
Independent variable
Interpretative phenomenological analysis
Interview
Linguistics
Narrative analysis
Naturally occurring talk
Norm
Observation
Operationalization
Positivism
Qualitative data
Quantitative data
Rhetorical psychology
Science
Social constructionism
Social psychology
Sociology
Survey
Theory
Variable

This book is about social psychology. It is also about discourse, understood as spoken talk or written texts, and its relationship to social life. Unlike most social psychology texts, we will focus in this book on the findings of qualitative rather than quantitative research. We will introduce readers to a wide variety of up-to-date, interesting, and informative findings from contemporary qualitative social psychological research in areas as diverse as identity, relationships, prejudice, the law, and health. The aim of this book is quite different from that of most other qualitative social psychology texts. Most of those texts are designed to explore the differences in theoretical and methodological perspectives that arise among the different varieties of contemporary qualitative social psychology. Although we do review and discuss these differences towards the end of this book, the main aim of this book is, instead, to provide readers with a survey of qualitative research findings across a number of different social psychology topic areas. To achieve this, the book follows a structure that will be familiar to anyone who has looked at quantitative social psychology textbooks. Each of the book's chapters focuses on a single, broad topic drawn from the area of social psychology and discusses the contributions which qualitative research has made in those areas.

But before describing in detail what these research findings are, we want to begin by "setting the scene" for readers. To do this, in this chapter we begin with an account of what social psychology is and how social psychologists carry out their research. By providing this background, we hope to present readers with a useful way of locating qualitative social psychological research within the wider framework of social psychology in general. However, readers should be aware that this book is about qualitative research, not experimental research. The material on experimental methods presented in the first section of this chapter is only intended to allow readers to draw a contrast between experimental social psychology and research which uses qualitative approaches. In particular, we would like to emphasize that in placing this material at the

very beginning of the book, we are not suggesting that this is the "primary" or "most important" way of thinking about social psychological issues. So readers should be aware that the brief description of experimental social psychological research which follows is merely a background against which qualitative research can be contrasted. Against this background, we will then go on to present some "thumbnail sketches" of the different varieties of qualitative research which appear throughout this book.

What is Social Psychology?

The nature of social psychology

The psychologists' goal is to provide scientific explanations for people's behavior in terms of the mental processes which underlie, or are associated with, that behavior. **Social psychology**, as a branch of psychology, is the field in which the nature and causes of people's behavior are considered in relation to social situations. This means that social psychologists want to understand behavior as it is influenced by other people. Social psychologists want to understand how being in a social group or some other aggregation of individuals influences the way an individual member behaves. If someone takes part in a riot, for example, the social psychologist wants to understand how that individual person's actions were influenced by other members of the crowd. But this does not mean that social psychologists only study people when they are actually interacting with one another. Even when we are alone, the way we think about ourselves and others, and the way we make sense of actions and events in our lives, is influenced by other people in a number of ways. For example, we are aware of the opinions of those close to us, and that can influence our own opinions; we sometimes know how other people would react to what we say and do, and this may influence our actions even when we are by ourselves. So even though the social psychologist is trying to explain human **behavior**, and any specific item of

---

Social psychology The study of how what people say and do is influenced by social interaction

Behavior What people do, including the production of verbal utterances

human behavior is produced by a single individual, the focus of social psychology is always on understanding the ways in which that item of behavior was influenced by other people.

One basic way in which other people influence us is through language (though this is not to suggest, of course, that language use is essentially, or even primarily, about influencing others). Even when we are alone, at the most basic level the way we use language to form our thoughts is determined by the way we use language when we are with other people. Someone from an English-speaking culture, for example, will probably employ English language expressions when expressing his or her thoughts or feelings to himself or herself in words. But much more than this, the elements of language which we rely on to make sense of our social world are also influenced by others. Suppose we notice that when we think about other people we use particular categories or distinctions. We might, for example, tend to think of some people as "fellow countrymen" and other people as "immigrants." When we do this, it is likely that the precise meaning we give to those category terms is influenced by the ways in which other people within our social background give meaning to them. Indeed, it may be that the very categories themselves derive from that background. So people from some social backgrounds might routinely use categories like "novice" and "expert" to make sense of others, while people from a different social background might not. In other words, the influence which other people have on us is buried deep within the ways in which we think about ourselves and those around us and in how we understand the actions and events which we and others become involved in. It is this influence which the social psychologist seeks to understand.

Related disciplines

Some of the interests of the social psychologist are shared by researchers from other areas. Social psychologists want to understand the nature and effects of social interaction. Since social interaction involves individual people engaging with each other, it is not surprising that social psychologists and those who study the psychology of individual differences (or dif-ferential psychology) sometimes find themselves trying to explain the same phenomena. Where prejudice arises, for example, researchers from both fields will attempt to explain it. The individual differences researcher will focus on the particular characteristics of the prejudiced individual such as personality or intelligence. The social psychologist, on the other hand, will focus on the social relationships which influence the prejudiced person in the formation and maintenance of his or her prejudiced views. So the social psychologist might want to discover, for example, whether a person holds prejudiced views because all of his or her friends do. Staying within the realm of psychology, social psychologists also formulate theories which are related to theories in cognitive psychology. Cognitive psychologists are interested in the structure and function of the mental processes which underlie behavior. This is similar to the interests of some social psychologists, who seek to understand the structure and function of mental processes underlying *social* behavior. So, for example, some cognitive psychologists explain our representations of the physical world in terms of schemata (Rumelhart, 1980), which are mental structures which picture or otherwise represent specific aspects of the world through the use of categorization. According to this theory, we make sense of the complexity of the world by assimilating our experiences to these schemata. Your schema for movie theaters might include comfy seats and popcorn, while your schema for dogs might include four-legged-ness and woofing. Social psychologists have drawn on this construct in the development of the theoretical notion of stereotypes (Fiske, 1998), which can be thought of as schemata for social objects such as groups of people. The main difference here is that the social psychologist, unlike the cognitive psychologist, is solely concerned with the mental constructs we employ in making sense of social phenomena. More recently, some social psychologists have also become interested in biological psychology, and attempt to explore whether these sorts of mental processes can reliably be identified with corresponding processes in the brain (Heatherton, Macrae, & Kelley, 2004).

Beyond the realm of psychology, social psychologists acknowledge shared interests with other research fields. **Sociology** is the study of how people organize themselves into collectivities such as groups or societies or nations. Sociologists want to understand why these social organizations exist, how they develop, and how they change. So a sociologist might be interested in how a particular society becomes stratified into different levels, or in the question of why some members of that society come to be regarded as deviant or as outsiders. Given the emphasis which social psychologists place on the importance of social interaction, it is clear that they have much in common with the sociologist. Indeed, some areas of social psychology, especially those which employ qualitative methods of study, are hardly distinguishable from some areas of sociology. On the other hand, social psychologists who rely upon techniques related to those of the cognitive psychologist will draw clear distinctions. In these cases, social psychology can be distinguished from sociology because social psychology, unlike sociology, places an emphasis on understanding the structure and function of individualistic mental phenomena such as social perception and social categorization. There are analogous similarities and differences between social psychology and social anthropology, which is that branch of anthropology dealing with human cultures.

Some forms of social psychology also display overlaps with the concerns of **linguistics**. For example, the sub-area of linguistics known as sociolinguistics is the study of how language is influenced by social and cultural phenomena such as gender, race, or class which social psychologists (like sociologists and social anthropologists) also study. This means that where social psychologists have a particular interest in language, social psychology may draw upon or inform the theoretical perspectives of the sociolinguist. Social psychologists of this sort are also likely to display an interest in some of the findings of linguistics in general. Linguistics is the scientific study of language, and those social psychologists who study language may find themselves considering the same sorts of questions as the linguist, such as the way in which the linguistic structure of everyday talk carries implications for what people understand by that talk.

Social psychology as a science

Science is an approach to understanding which relies upon systematically gathering accurate information in an open-minded fashion. Scientists use research questions to guide their work, but rely upon empirical evidence in order to establish the answers to those questions. This differs from other forms of understanding. Some non-scientific approaches to understanding such as philosophy rely upon a priori argument to establish whether someone's claims are acceptable or not. Other non-scientific approaches such as some forms of religion rely upon dogmatic appeals to authority to settle the issue of whether a claim is correct or not. Although non-empirical forms of study have been very influential in determining our current ways of thinking about the world, science has also made important contributions to our current understanding of nature and our place within it. For this reason, social psychologists locate themselves firmly in the scientific camp.

Scientific study is guided by the use of theories. A **theory** is the researcher's attempt to provide an abstract model of the world. The theoretical model is made up of a set of components, such as abstract symbols, representing phenomena in the real world and also representing relationships between or among those phenomena. The purpose of a theory is to explain observations of the world in terms of the theoretical components and their theoretical relationships. A psychological theory, then, is an abstract model in which human behavior is explained in terms of theoretical entities and their relationships with one another. According

---

Sociology The study of people interacting in social groupings and other social formations

---

Linguistics The scientific study of the system and structure of language

---

Science The method of studying our world which relies upon the systematic, theory-led gathering of data

---

Theory An explanatory model used to explain a phenomenon by positing relationships between or among the theory's constructs

to one influential view of science, theories are related to the researcher's research questions in a very specific way. Since the theory is meant to be explanatory, it can be used by the researcher to make predictions about events which have not yet occurred. It is these predictions which comprise the researcher's research questions, which are framed as **hypotheses**. As long as a theory yields hypotheses in this way, it can be considered to be "testable." The hypotheses generated by the theory will, once the appropriate data have been collected, be shown to be supported or unsupported by the data. In other words, collecting data in order to establish whether a hypothesis is supported or not is a means of testing the value of the theory itself. A theory which does not yield hypotheses which are supported by data is usually either abandoned or revised. This approach to science is often referred to as "**positivism**." On the other hand, it is interesting to note that some philosophers of science, influenced by Popper (1959), often point out that theories cannot be proven to be true even if many hypothetical statements derived from the theory are supported by evidence. Since theoretical statements are universal in nature, and since no researcher can ever test every single example of a universal claim, the best that can be said for theories is that they are supported, or warranted, by the evidence.

The role of theory in social psychology is less clear cut. While most social psychologists would identify with one theoretical position or another, they may differ in the way in which they view the relationship between theory and empirical data. Many social psychologists are broadly in agreement with the general account provided above, and rely upon the hypothesis-testing approach. But other social psychologists are critical of the positivist's assumptions and argue that social psychology must focus on the meanings which participants themselves attribute to actions and

events. This means that the positivist emphasis on devising scientifically measurable variables as a means of "**operationalizing**" a hypothesis is replaced with an emphasis on gathering more or less naturally occurring verbal (and sometimes nonverbal) data. The reason for this is that the measurable variables which a positivist might use will have been defined by the researcher and therefore may not reflect the common-sense understanding which the participants in the study themselves rely upon. So instead of using researcher-defined constructs, the non-positivist researcher reproduces as data the utterances (usually vocal or written) of the participants themselves and analyzes these without recourse to hypothetical variables. For these researchers, the link between theory and data is made by using empirical findings to demonstrate that the proposed theoretical elements and their relationships are instantiated in the data. Readers who are interested in understanding this debate between positivists and non-positivists can find a discussion of this issue in the last chapter of this book.

Social psychology: Its methods and data

The social psychologist has access to a range of scientific methods. Perhaps the most commonly used method in contemporary social psychology is the experimental method. The basis of the **experiment** is that scientific **variables** are deployed in a specific fashion. At least one variable, the "**independent variable**," is systematically changed by the experimenter and the effects of this change on the other variable (or variables), the "**dependent variable**," is observed. Sometimes, the experimenter's manipulation of

---

Hypothesis An empirically testable statement about relationships among theoretical entities

Positivism The view that explanations of empirical events must be scientific

Operationalization The process of identifying variables within a hypothesis with measures of observable events

---

Experiment A set of observations collected under controlled conditions in order to test a hypothesis

Variable A changeable property of the experimental context

Independent variable A variable whose different levels are assigned to experimental participants by the experimenter

Dependent variable A variable whose values are compared by the experimenter across the levels of the independent variable

an independent variable involves an intervention, such as giving some participants a particular treatment while withholding the treatment from other participants. In other cases, the independent variable occurs "naturally" (e.g., gender) and the experimenter's manipulation involves allocating the different levels of the independent variables (e.g., men and women) to different experimental conditions. If movement from one of the levels of the independent variable to another is associated with changes in the dependent variable, then the social psychologist will, with caution, infer that the difference which constitutes the different levels in the independent variable caused the changes observed in the dependent variable. The "with caution" part of the story derives from the fact that experiments, like rare plants, require careful cultivation. Experimenters are careful to ensure that experimental participants are randomly assigned to the different levels of the independent variable. They also try to make sure that all other factors which might have a potential effect on the dependent variables are kept constant. They also try to ensure that the measures they use to identify changes in the dependent variable are as accurate, reliable, and valid as possible. Experiments are often conducted within laboratory settings, although less often they may be conducted within naturalistic settings outwith the laboratory.

In addition to the experimental method, social psychologists rely upon a range of other approaches. One nonexperimental method is the use of **observation**. In one sense, scientific observation is the same sort of thing that we all routinely carry out when we observe the world around us. However, the scientist lays greater emphasis on being systematic and accurate in measurement. The scientist may, for example, carefully log the frequency of occurrence of the sort of behavior that he or she is interested in. And this may rely upon the use of previously prepared behavioral coding strategies in which different varieties of behavior can be systematically allocated to one specific category or another. The main difference between the observational method and the experimental method is that in the former

the researcher explicitly tries to avoid having any influence on the variables under observation, while in the latter the essence of the technique is that the experimenter seeks to manipulate an independent variable.

Another non-experimental approach in the social psychologist's scientific arsenal is the **correlational** study. The basis of this method is that the scientist attempts to measure people on at least two different variables and then seeks to discover whether participants' scores on one variable are related in some regular fashion with their scores on the other variable. If they are, the researcher will claim that the two sets of scores are correlated. Typically, researchers are interested in the strength of this correlation, which is standardly assessed as falling somewhere between -1.00 to 0 in the case of negative correlations and between $+1.00$ and 0 for positive correlations. Correlational studies differ from experimental studies in that there is no attempt to manipulate either variable. In consequence, correlational studies do not usually claim to have produced evidence of causation. So while the experimenter claims that changes in the independent variable cause changes in the dependent variable, the correlational researcher normally only reports that changes in one variable are associated with changes in the other variable. (Of course, there are exceptions. If a correlational study reveals that height is associated with age, the researcher may claim that change in age caused the change in height, but not vice versa.)

Another non-experimental technique which is common in social psychology research is the **survey**. The essence of the survey approach is that the researcher prepares a carefully constructed interview implement, which is often in the form of a written list of questions arranged in a specific order. These questions may be "closed" in that they allow the participant only to select from a pre-set range of answers (e.g., "Yes" or "No" or "Always," "Sometimes," "Never"), or the questions may be "open" in that they allow

Correlation The strength and direction of the relationship between two variables

Observation Collecting and recording empirical data to answer a research question

Survey The collection of data via interview or questionnaire from a sample of a population

participants to phrase their answers in their own words.

One similarity across experimental, correlational, and observational approaches is that they often rely upon gathering **quantitative data**. Dependent variables and correlational variables are often measures of something which allow the experimenter to place each participant at a particular point on a numerical scale. Similarly, observational measures often rely upon measures of frequency or duration of occurrence of the categories of behavior of interest. Quantitative data are amenable to numerical analysis. At its simplest, this might involve examining whether the numerical value of participant scores in one experimental condition is larger than the numerical value in a second experimental condition. More usually, a range of statistical techniques is involved in making decisions of this sort. But no matter how simple or complex the statistical analysis, the researcher is usually in a position to determine whether his or her hypothesis is supported or not by merely inspecting the numerical outcome of analysis.

Qualitative data

Although quantitative data have been of great importance to the social psychologist, many non-experimental approaches in social psychology yield data which are **qualitative** in nature. One basic difference between quantitative and qualitative data is that quantitative data are reported as a set of numbers, and qualitative data are not. This is not to say that non-numerical data cannot be transformed into numerical data. For example, it was noted above that survey techniques sometimes require that participants provide a verbal response to closed questions such as "Always," "Sometimes," or "Never." However,

usually such responses are "recoded" to yield numerical values so that "Always" might be recoded as "3," "Sometimes" as "2," and "Never" as "1." (To avoid confusion, it is useful to note that quantitative data are often separated out into "interval," "ordinal," and "nominal" levels of measurement; recoding from a verbal categorization to a numerical categorization does not alter the level of measurement.) Even in the case of open-ended questions, the survey researcher often analyzes the relevant responses as falling into particular categories and then reports, in numerical form, the frequency of occurrence of each category. So it is only if the researcher gathers information which is neither numerical, nor transformed in this way, that we refer to the data as "qualitative."

Qualitative data can be gathered using most of the social psychologist's empirical techniques. Survey researchers, for example, sometimes refrain from recoding open-ended questions and instead try to deal with the resultant data in a non-numerical fashion. Other techniques which generate qualitative data (sometimes in conjunction with quantitative data) include observations, **case studies**, **archive research**, **interviews**, and **focus groups**. Observations may yield researcher-generated descriptive summaries of the activities observed, or they may yield actual audio or video recordings of what participants themselves have said and done. Case studies may include qualitative descriptions of the settings and circumstances which are unique to that study. Archive research involves the researcher in collecting material from locations such as newspaper archives or institutional records. The qualitative researcher can use resources such as these to gather examples of the way in which individuals have written descriptions of social phenomena as they understand them. Interviews

---

Quantitative data Observations which are represented by numerical values

Qualitative data Observations (often verbal material) which are not represented by numerical values

Case study An in-depth observational study of a single event or context

Archive research The collection of data from existing sources such as official records

Interview An interaction between a researcher and a participant in which the researcher asks questions relevant to the research topic

Focus group A group organized by a researcher to discuss issues relevant to the research topic

and focus groups often allow participants to provide verbal responses to the researcher's questions or probes in a naturalistic fashion using everyday speech.

Since qualitative data are non-numerical, the researcher cannot merely inspect the outcome of analysis and determine, for example, whether a particular test statistic has reached a criterial level. Instead, the researcher relies upon interpreting the data without the use of numerical analysis. It is important to point out that for many researchers this rejection of numerical analysis in favor of other means of interpreting data is a, or even the, major advantage of qualitative research over quantitative research. As the rest of the chapters in this book will demonstrate, qualitative data analyzed in this way are capable of shedding light on a wide range of social issues. The extent to which this form of analysis is superior to, or merely complementary to, numerical analysis of quantitative data is explored further in the last chapter. In this chapter, however, we want to turn to a discussion of the variety of ways in which this task of interpreting qualitative data has been approached.

What is Discourse?

The nature of discourse

The task of interpreting qualitative data is a difficult one, and it has been approached from a variety of different perspectives. In the rest of this book, we are going to focus on qualitative research which lays its primary analytic emphasis on understanding discourse. In order to make clear to the reader that this is just one of the ways in which qualitative research is conducted, from now on we will use the term "discursive research" to identify this broad approach.

Discursive researchers, as this term implies, are interested in discourse. We said at the start of this chapter that "discourse" can be taken to refer both to talk, i.e., spoken utterances, and to text, i.e., written utterances. What makes discursive research distinctive is that it treats discourse as a topic in its own right. This means that discursive researchers do not view discourse merely as a medium through which the researcher can discover something about research participants'

inner, mental worlds. Instead, discourse is viewed as a phenomenon which has its own properties, properties which have an impact on people and their social interaction. One important aspect of this approach is to emphasize the way in which participants themselves have an at least implicit understanding that discourse has these properties. In using discourse, participants often rely on some of its properties to accomplish a specific social action.

In many forms of discursive research, this foregrounding of discourse is viewed as much more than the social psychologist merely switching attention from topics such as cognitive states like attitudes or stereotypes to the topic of discourse. Instead, it is viewed as a theoretical sea-change. From this perspective, understanding social actions and interactions is just understanding the ways in which people use discourse to accomplish these actions and to engage in these interactions. And so the experimental social psychologist's panoply of mental or cognitive states like stereotypes and attitudes is abandoned in favor of directing attention to the structural and functional properties of discourse.

It is important to be aware, however, that there are a number of differences among the varieties of discursive research. Some discursive researchers view discourse as a monolithic, though not unchanging, entity which determines the way in which we think and act. From this perspective, social settings such as the lawcourt or the hospital are arenas in which participants' understanding of their experiences and actions are conditioned by the ways in which legal discourse or medical discourse represents those experiences and actions. Other discursive researchers view discourse as a routinized way of talking which has a similar effect, although it is not bound up with any particular social structure or organization. From this perspective, for example, when we talk about men and women we may reflect the influence of broader social views because we perform that talk through discourses of "masculinity" or "femininity." Yet other discursive researchers take a different view by emphasizing the dynamic nature of discourse. From this perspective, discourse should not be characterized as a broad social entity like "legal discourse" or "masculinity discourse." Instead, it should be seen as an activity in which descriptions of legal matters or of men and women are developed in an ongoing fashion as the discursive interaction unfolds.

These differences of perspective among discursive researchers have often generated intense debate. For example, some discursive researchers argue that discursive research should mainly focus only on **naturally occurring talk** of the sort that occurs in everyday conversations. Other researchers argue that the sort of talk that arises from studies in which a researcher interviews participants or conducts a focus group is equally amenable to discursive analysis. Discursive researchers also disagree with each other on the extent to which extra-linguistic **context** is important to the analyst. Some researchers claim that social phenomena such as status and power are only relevant to an analysis if the participants themselves can be seen to be attending to those issues in what they say. Other researchers claim that even if participants themselves do not display a concern with such issues, the analyst certainly ought to. Since there is such a wide variety in perspective among discursive researchers, it is useful to provide a basic introduction to some of the "flavors" of discursive research that arise throughout this book. Readers who are interested in a more detailed exposition of the debates that are internal to discursive research can find a discussion of a number of these issues in Chapter 12, although some of these issues are also addressed as they arise within earlier chapters.

Readers should also be aware that the flavors of discursive research are a bit like the flavors of ice cream. An ice cream shop might sell chocolate, strawberry, and banana flavored ice cream. So, in one sense, these flavors are easily distinguishable because each ice cream tub is clearly labeled. However, different ice cream sellers may use different recipes, and so they may disagree as to what exactly constitutes "chocolate" ice cream or "banana" ice cream. Moreover, the customer

will often order more than one flavor in the same dish, only to find that within minutes the different flavors have begun to melt into one another. Discursive research is a bit like this. Two researchers may agree in describing their research as, say, "discourse analysis," but disagree as to the recipe they are following. Or a specific researcher may begin by selecting from more than one flavor, but then go on to mix those flavors in a way which draws upon different elements of the different perspectives. Whether this practice works as well for the researcher as it does for the ice cream eater is quite a different matter. While a number of discursive researchers are happy with this sort of eclecticism, others have argued that, depending on which elements are being combined, it leads to "a recipe for incoherence" (Potter, 2003a, p. 785). Readers should bear these thoughts in mind when examining the descriptions that follow.

Conversation analysis (CA)

Conversation analysis (Sacks, 1992; Hutchby & Wooffitt, 1998; ten Have, 1999) grew out of the work of Harvey Sacks and the theoretical and methodological interests of the ethnomethodology movement, especially the work of Harold Garfinkel (Heritage, 1984). Conversation analysis was also influenced by Erving Goffman's work on the social structures of everyday life (Goffman, 1959; Schegloff, 1988). Sacks was one of the first sociologists to display an interest in treating naturally occurring talk as sociologically interesting in its own right, rather than viewing talk as a semi-transparent medium through which sociological phenomena such as social stratification made themselves apparent. Ethnomethodologists are concerned to understand the everyday skills and abilities which underlie social practices. They view social interaction as the outcome of participants' own understandings of what they are doing. Often these understandings are implicit in that participants themselves might be in a position to articulate the sorts of skills and competencies

---

Naturally occurring talk Talk between or among people which is unprompted but recorded by the researcher

Context The setting, surroundings, and other background elements relevant to the data that are being collected

Conversation analysis The collection and analysis of naturally occurring talk, emphasizing its sequential properties and the actions performed

which they deploy. Drawing on the early work of Sacks and Garfinkel, conversation analysis focuses on the social actions which people perform in naturally occurring interactions. Its emphasis is on the way that sequences of utterances are organized and it examines how utterances are designed to accomplish specific actions. The locus for these social actions is sometimes referred to as "talk-in-interaction," and the conversation analyst will often be concerned with analyzing talk-in-interaction in terms of "**discursive action** sequences." Action sequences are patterns of interaction which have regularly identifiable structural properties that are consistently associated with specific actions. Conversation analysis identifies action sequences with particular normative expectations which any competent speaker can be expected to display. For example, in a question sequence a relevant normative expectation that competent speakers are taken to understand is that questions from one speaker are normally followed by answers from a different speaker. The issue of **norms** here lies in the fact that if a question is not followed by an answer, the participants are likely to display some sensitivity to this by, perhaps, offering an explanation as to why an answer is not produced. This example highlights another aspect of the conversation analytic approach. Particular contributions to an interaction are influenced by the immediate conversational context and often this means that a "turn" in a conversation is often designed in response to the immediately prior turn. This property of conversations allows the analyst to make claims about the way that participants themselves orient to the social actions that are being performed. Because a succeeding conversational turn is shaped by the context of what was said before, if a participant produces an answer to a question, then this displays that he or she is orienting to a previous turn as though it was a question. Similarly, if he or she produces a rejection of a request, then he or she is orienting to a preceding

turn as though it was a request. It is this public aspect of the way participants understand each others' talk which underpins the conversation analyst's analytic claims. The analyst does not infer something about the underlying psychological properties of the participants. Instead, he or she merely draws attention to the public display of understanding which the participants provide for each other.

Discourse analysis (DA)

Discourse analysis (Potter & Wetherell, 1987; Potter, 1997; Wetherell & Potter, 1998) draws in part on the work of sociologists from the sociology of scientific knowledge tradition. Sociology of scientific knowledge is an attempt to understand the ways in which social phenomena impinge on how science in done. Some researchers in this area have argued that the proper way to analyze the effect of sociological factors on science is to focus on scientists' discourse. Gilbert and Mulkay (1984), for example, demonstrated that scientists produce discursive accounts of their own work and of the work of their scientific colleagues and competitors which display interesting properties of variability and flexibility. "Variability" means that different sorts of accounts might be generated in order to accomplish different effects. "Flexibility" means that the same sort of account could be used to perform different social actions on different occasions. The study of these sorts of accounts gave rise to a more general interest in how flexible and variable accounts might be designed to perform specific functions within specific contexts, and this formed one of the bases for the social psychologist's interest in discourse analysis.

In order to avoid confusion, it is helpful to remember that social psychology has sometimes drawn on studies in linguistics, and that some linguistics researchers have identified an interest in what they term "discourse analysis." But despite the confusing similarity in title, the social psycho-

---

Discursive action That which people do or accomplish through talk

Norm A standard or rule which applies to human behavior

Discourse analysis The collection and analysis of verbal material, spoken or written, which emphasizes properties such as structure and variability and focuses on action

logical version of discourse analysis is different from the linguist's version of discourse analysis. The latter has a much greater interest in the formal structural properties of language (Brown & Yule, 1983). Linguists working in this area have, though, displayed a lively interest in explaining the way that linguistic items such as referring terms function by reference to the actions which people are trying to accomplish within particular discursive contexts. In this respect, some of the discourse analytic concerns of the linguist are not too dissimilar to those of the social psychologist. More generally, the genesis of the social psychological version of discourse analysis is attributable to linguistics insofar as the formulation of discourse analysis as a field of study relied, in part, upon work done in the field of semiotics. Ferdinand de Saussure (Saussure, 1983), for example, distinguished between *langue*, the linguistic framework or system which provides structure for an utterance, and *parole*, the actual utterances people produce in specific situations, and this reliance on examining actual utterances is seen in contemporary discourse analysis.

Many social psychologists were introduced to these issues through Potter and Wetherell's influential book *Discourse and social psychology: Beyond attitudes and behavior* (1987) and through a series of papers in which Edwards and Middleton began to criticize, from a discourse analytic perspective, social psychology's emphasis on cognitive psychological explanation (Edwards & Middleton, 1986, 1987, 1988). At the heart of these critiques was a rejection of the idea that **cognitive** phenomena such as "stereotypes" or "attitudes" are explanatory constructs to which the social psychologist should refer in explaining social interaction. Instead, it was argued, the researcher should emphasize the way in which language is used to perform a variety of social actions. This in turn leads to a concern with examining similarity and variation in the accounts which people produce. This switches the emphasis away from viewing language as a medium through which supposed explanatory constructs such as attitudes or stereotypes are expressed. Instead, the analyst attempts to show how language is used in everyday life to accomplish the "construction" of "versions" of actions and events. For this reason, discourse analysts often refer to themselves as **social constructionists** because they wish to examine how people deploy variable accounts in producing or constructing a particular version of an action or event.

So the focal point of discourse analysis is the study of language in use. The discourse analyst is likely to be interested in the way particular types of account are deployed to particular effect. Sometimes, this involves codifying types of account into categories of "discourses" or "repertoires" (Edley, 2001). So, for example, the discourse analyst might be interested in how a phenomenon such as "homosexuality" is socially constructed in people's discursive practices through the use of repertoires or discourses of masculinity and femininity. These are viewed by the analyst as identifiably coherent ways of talking about a subject which participants draw upon in offering accounts of what it is like to be a man or to be a woman. In other cases, the discourse analyst's work does not make specific reference to identifiable discourses or repertoires. Instead, the discourse analyst draws attention to accounts which are more specific to the immediate conversational context than discourses or repertoires are usually taken to be. However, the main analytic thrust remains the same: that of identifying the social actions which participants are accomplishing in generating such accounts. Discourse analysts often display an interest in the fine-grain detail of how accounts are constructed, and draw upon some of the terminology of conversation analysis to do this. However, one difference between discourse analysis and conversation analysis is that the discourse analyst may examine single turns in a conversation in which the participant produces an account, whereas the conversation analyst

---

Cognitive Pertaining to states of cognition such as beliefs

Social constructionism The view that social phenomena are best understood as the outcome of discursive interaction rather than as extra-discursive phenomena in their own right

usually focuses on multiple turns and their sequential properties.

Critical discourse analysis (CDA)

As the title suggests, **critical discourse analysis** (Fairclough, 1995; Meyer, 2001; van Dijk, 2001b; Wodak, 2001b) seeks to examine the way in which people's talk instantiates forms of social or political inequality. So a critical discourse analyst will, for example, be interested in how dominant ideologies are manifest in language (or, less often, in non-linguistic phenomena such as images). The critical discourse analyst is interested not only in understanding how social inequalities get to be produced and reproduced in language, but also in the question of how these social problems can be challenged. This is sometimes referred to as the emancipatory aspect of CDA. For many critical discourse analysts, the social phenomena they seek to explain are thought of as real social objects, rather than the "social constructions" of the discourse analyst. Critical discourse analysts do draw attention to the way in which changes in discursive practices are related to changes in non-discursive elements of the social world. But they point out that the patterns of allowance for change and resistance to change which different social entities display mean that it is often misleading to consider them as the socially constructive output of discursive processes. Like discourse analysts, critical discourse analysts are concerned to demonstrate the sorts of actions which people accomplish through language. However, their analyses make explicit reference to wider contextual issues which may have an important bearing on questions of ideology and power, such as the setting in which the discursive event takes place. In addition, unlike discourse analysts some critical discourse analysts make use of the sorts of grammatical analysis which are found in linguistics. In particular, some CDA researchers draw heavily upon Halliday's (1985) systemic functional linguistics. This approach to linguistics emphasizes the way that language functions by allowing people to exchange meanings. It emphasizes the range of choices which people do and do not make in producing utterances in particular contexts, rather than focusing on the grammatical properties which other linguists take to lie beneath the surface of those utterances.

Foucauldian discourse analysis (FDA)

Foucauldian discourse analysis (Parker, 1992; Burman & Parker, 1993) draws its inspiration from the work of Michel Foucault (1980, 2002), although it also makes reference to other perspectives such as poststructuralism and psychoanalysis. In particular, it makes use of Foucault's idea that language structures display a historical nature in that they change over time and, in the changing, shape and reflect social and institutional practices. Because of this intertwining of discourse and practice, discourses are determinative of the ways in which we perceive and act within the world. In this respect, the Foucauldian discourse analyst shares similar concerns with the critical discourse analyst, because dominant or hegemonic ways of perceiving actions and events in the world tend to derive from existing power-relations within the world. However, unlike the critical discourse analyst, the Foucauldian discourse analyst does not necessarily view such power-asymmetries as the ideological outcome of class-based inequalities. In this sense, although the "common-sense" way of viewing the world just is the way that those in power see it, the critical discourse analyst's appeal to overweening ideologies is replaced by Foucault's more context-sensitive notion that particular social phenomena, e.g., the treatment of the ill or of criminals, display particular historical-ideological features. Moreover, unlike many critical discourse analysts, the Foucauldian discourse analyst shares with the discourse analyst a strong claim about social construction. Discourses produce "subject positions" which, if adopted, carry implications for how an individual will construe experience.

Critical discourse analysis The analysis of discourse with an emphasis on the way it is affected by power and ideology

Foucauldian discourse analysis A form of discourse analysis which relies on the work of Foucault and emphasizes the historical and ideological aspects of discourse

Medical discourses, for example, offer the subject position of "patient" and if someone takes up that position then this implies normative constraints on the extent to which that person can be an active agent as opposed to a passive recipient of health care. More generally, the Foucauldian discourse analyst views discourse as a locus where social objects are constructed, although the proper analysis of such constructive phenomena is understood to involve reference to extra-linguistic matters of power and material relations within society at large.

Discursive psychology (DP)

Discursive psychology (Edwards, 1997, 2005a; Edwards & Potter, 2005; Potter, 2003a) is a relatively recent addition to the discursive field and was introduced through the work of Jonathan Potter and Derek Edwards. There are many similarities between discursive psychology and other discursive approaches, especially conversation analysis. Like the other discursive approaches already discussed, discursive psychology emphasizes the importance of an action-orientation to the study of discourse. Discursive psychology also focuses on the sequential unfolding of talk, and has an interest in looking at "deviant" cases where participants display awareness that some of the normative expectations of talk within the local context have not been met. One difference between discursive psychology and other discursive approaches lies in its critical reflection on the theory and method of cognitive psychology. The cognitive-oriented social psychologist studies features of psychology such as perception or memory or problem-solving by positing the existence of internal mental states and then looking for external behavioral evidence for the way that these states are structured and function. The discursive psychologist examines instead the way that memories or states of thought are made relevant in talk and the actions which are accomplished by that process within the local discursive context. Another difference between

discursive psychology and other discursive approaches is that there is a greater emphasis on the way in which people display sensitivity to what might be inferred about their own psychological state from what they say. Thus, for example, the management of stake and interest becomes especially relevant for the discursive psychologist. We are all aware that on occasion people may interpret what we say in terms of the stake which we might have in the claim which is being made. Consider the batter in a baseball game who criticizes an umpire for calling a strike, accusing him or her of being half-blind. The crowd might consider that the batter's criticism derives more from his or her stake in staying at the plate than it does from his or her belief that the umpire needs assistance from an optician. Discursive psychologists are especially interested in those occasions where people orient to what they say as though inferences about stake of this sort might be drawn by others who are listening to what they say. More recently, discursive psychologists have extended their interest from critical reflection on cognitive psychological explanation to apply the perspective to real life situations such as relationship counseling.

Rhetorical psychology

The modern social psychological study of rhetoric can be traced back to Michael Billig's influential book, *Arguing and thinking: A rhetorical approach to social psychology* (Billig, 1987). In this book, Billig explores the history of persuasive talk and then produces a number of analyses of the way that everyday argumentation relies on implicit rhetorical skills. For example, he draws attention to the way that ordinary processes of categorization are often produced in talk alongside processes of particularization in which people provide argumentative counter-examples to general claims. Similarly he points out that common-sense phrases and maxims often occur in contradictory pairs. Because of this, **rhetorical psychology** construes thinking processes as essentially

Discursive psychology The use of discursive techniques to analyze talk of psychological states and the application of those analyses to real world settings

Rhetorical psychology The application of discursive techniques to the study of persuasive language and, more broadly, the view that talk is inherently argumentative dialogical, and views the expression of attitudes or opinions as at least implicitly encompassing a debate among alternative viewpoints. The creativity which can be observed in everyday moments of conversational activity is better explained, according to the rhetorical psychologist, by thinking of people as influenced by ongoing processes of formulation and reformulation of ideas rather than as behaving in response to internal mental states. Rhetorical psychology has a number of overlaps with other forms of discursive research. In particular, discourse analysts and discursive psychologists have displayed an interest in examining the argumentative and persuasive elements of everyday talk by looking, for example, at processes of fact-construction and the ways in which people present what they say as though it is the natural outcome of the way the world happens to be, rather than an individualistic point of view.

Narrative analysis

Narrative analysis (Daiute & Lightfoot, 2003) stems in part from the work of William Labov (Labov, 1972). Interest in narratives derives from the fact that people can be seen to rely upon narratives in trying to make sense of their own experiences and to report on the important aspects of their lives. Narratives can be thought of as extended portions of talk which have an identifiable, story-like structure such as having a beginning, middle, and end. Often this structure is identifiable through the participant's use of temporally ordering phrases. Much of the narrative analyst's work involves identifying the type and function of clauses which comprise the narrative as a whole and to separate out those elements of a narrative which are evaluative upshots on the consequences of the event described in the narrative.

Other forms of qualitative study

The varieties of qualitative research described above all share a common interest in treating discourse as the main focus of the analyst's concerns.

> **Narrative analysis** The analysis of talk in terms of its story-like elements

However, it is worth mentioning that there are other forms of qualitative study which adopt a different tack. These approaches will not feature in the chapters which follow, but the reader may find it interesting to compare these approaches to the ones described above. Some researchers rely upon discourse as data to develop an idea of what the individual thinks about a given social phenomenon. In this view, what an individual says can be thought of as reflecting his or her interior mental states. For example, **interpretative phenomenological analysis** (IPA) draws on the work of the phenomenological philosophers, notably Edmund Husserl (Welton, 1999). Husserl stressed the importance of examining particular phenomena as they are experienced by us. Some psychologists (e.g., Smith, 1997) have utilized these ideas in developing an interpretative approach to the analysis of what participants say during semi-structured interviews. The essence of the technique is to enable participants to share their personal experiences of the phenomenon under consideration. The analyst's job is to organize these reports into a structured thematic report on what the participant said in order to represent what that experience was like for him or her.

Other forms of qualitative analysis rely on a similar process of developing thematic categories which summarize what participants have said. For example, **grounded theory** is an approach which was developed by Glaser and Strauss (1967). The analyst's task here is to identify categories of meaning from the data. This involves attempting to identify important or relevant categories and also the attempt to integrate further examples into this categorical framework through a process of comparative analysis. One of the consequences of this comparison is often that an initially proposed categorical framework is revised in the light of new examples. This iterative process concludes at a point which grounded theorists refer to as "theoretical satura-

> **Interpretative phenomenological analysis**
> A research method focusing on participants' experiences as they interpret them

> **Grounded theory** A method of categorizing qualitative data in which categories are developed out of the data

tion" where succeeding examples provide no further impetus for the refinement of the categories in use. The process of identification of categories from data has, however, been a matter of debate in recent years. The founders of grounded theory, Glaser and Strauss, have diverged as to what actually constitutes the emergence of categories and their relationships to the theories that emerge (Glaser, 1992; Strauss & Corbin, 1990). Following these differences between the originators of the method, Charmaz (2006) argues that grounded theory requires not so much the identification within the data of preexisting categories but rather the construction of an analytic framework that provides understanding of the data as a result of the engagement of the researcher with the dataset. In practice therefore, grounded theory as used often comes to reflect a somewhat more constructionist and reflexive method of working with verbal data than that originally envisaged.

Summary

It is clear, then, that discursive social psychology encompasses a range of theoretical notions and methodological techniques. Sometimes this variety has been described in terms of a continuum from "bottom-up" approaches that concentrate on the fine-grain detail of small fragments of interaction to "top-down" approaches that take, as a central concern, ideas about large-scale social phenomena such as ideologies or political power. Another descriptive continuum that is sometimes employed here is the idea of researchers differing in the extent to which they are "data-driven" as opposed to "theory-driven." Yet another differentiation which has been employed has been to characterize discursive research by evaluating the extent to which it aims towards sociopolitical change as opposed to detailed description and explanation of interactions considered in isolation from wider social concerns. In this book, we are less concerned with developing typologies of discursive research of this sort than with discussion of the results which such research generates. Accordingly, throughout the rest of this book we will employ the term "discursive researcher" to refer to those who work in any of these areas. This term is intended to convey both the discursive aspect of such work and the fact that, unlike other approaches,

the research presented in this book has a special emphasis on analyzing discourse. It is worth emphasizing here that we intend, through this phrase, to refer to conversation analytic research and to rhetoric studies and to narrative analysis in addition to the varieties of discourse analysis described above.

A Note on Ethics

As in other branches of science, social psychologists must attend to ethical questions in their research and ensure appropriate ethical guidelines are respected. Participants in a social psychological study should be in a position to give their informed consent to taking part in a study. This means that they must understand the purposes and nature of the research and be given the opportunity to agree or disagree to take part. This can cause problems for experimental studies, since many of these involve some degree of deception. The experimentalist's response to this is that the forms of deception in use (e.g., telling participants a study is about memory when it is really about social perception) are of a trivial nature. While discursive research usually does not rely on this sort of deception, researchers are often keen to be less than explicit about their research questions, largely because of a concern that what they say will influence how participants talk about the social phenomenon that is the object of study. Both quantitative and discursive forms of research also must meet the requirement that participants be in a position to withdraw from the study at any time. However, in discursive research there may be practical limitations on participants' right of withdrawal. If naturally occurring discursive data are collected in the workplace, for example, it may be more difficult for participants to retain an awareness that what they say and do are being recorded for research purposes than is the case where participants are located in the unnatural confines of the psychology laboratory. In addition, the properly designed study will ensure that the anonymity of participants is guaranteed. It should be noted, though, that some discursive studies, especially those which draw on public archives such as studies of news media reports, are often not in a position to meet this goal. In particular, some forms of analysis rely upon establishing the formal position or hierarchical status of the participants, and this may require that people such as politicians are identified by name. In these cases, the discursive researcher takes the view that since the material under discussion is already a matter of public record, normal expectations of right to privacy have been rescinded. Social psychologists also emphasize the importance of "debriefing" participants by informing them of the outcomes of the study.

About this Book

As we said at the start of this chapter, this book is thematically organized around a set of key social psychological topics. The aim here is to present the reader with an up-to-date survey of the ways in which qualitative researchers have contributed to our understanding of central areas of social psychology. To do this, we have, wherever possible, focused the structure of each chapter on the substantive social psychological topic and have tried to avoid drawing comparisons across different forms of discursive research. However on occasion, the perspective on that topic adopted by one set of discursive researchers, e.g., critical discourse analysts, varies from that adopted by other researchers, e.g., conversation analysts. Where this occurs, we have tried to aid readers' comprehension by separating out those views within the relevant chapter. Each of the following chapters contains a range of transcription extracts drawn from research articles. Wherever possible, we have tried to retain the original author's line-numbering scheme. However, the typographical layout of this text differs from that of many academic journals. For this reason, readers will note that on some occasions, where an extract uses line numbering, text which spreads across more than one line is denoted by a single line number. In addition, where we have thought it helpful, we have included the original author's foreign language transcription along with the translation into English.

The next chapter, Chapter 2, will provide an introduction to the way that discursive researchers have dealt with the issues of self and identity. The emphasis here will be on explaining how selves and identities can be understood as social constructions, and how such constructions are developed, maintained, and challenged through discourse. The chapter begins by considering the ways in which identity talk is sensitive to context, by looking at identity talk as it arises in conversation, and then considering the cultural aspects of talk about identity. The idea of the self as an underlying "core" element which can be perceived or inspected will be seen to contrast sharply with the social constructionist view of selves as variable constructive achievements that are accomplished to meet local interactional concerns. The chapter then moves on to consider national identities and the ways in which time and place become relevant when one talks of oneself and others. Another important aspect of identity is the notion of the social group, and here we will look at the ways in which discursive accomplishments of identity are sensitive to notions of gender and ethnicity. Because the Internet has become such a pervasive feature of social life, we also consider the question of "virtual" identities. Finally, we examine the ways in which discourse represents a locus for action in looking at the ways in which people display resistance to identity ascription.

Chapter 3 looks at the variety of discursive phenomena which arise when small groups of people interact. The chapter looks at different sorts of group, from informally arranged small groups to more formally structured groups such as self-help and other support groups to large-scale social groups such as nationalities or religious affiliations. The chapter begins by examining how group membership affects the way that people represent the world around them. It then considers the extent to which group membership influences the way we think about ourselves and others. The chapter then moves on to discuss the way that properties of groups are worked up in discourse. One important issue here is the extent to which group members feel that they belong to a unified or cohesive social group. The chapter then considers aspects of group structure and function. It discusses how people use discursive strategies to develop notions of group homogeneity and heterogeneity. The chapter also examines the ways in which group roles and discursive processes influence one another. The chapter moves to a close by examining two aspects of group function: the establishment of group norms and the performance of group tasks.

Chapter 4 moves on from the consideration of selves and groups to examine how people develop close relationships and then interact within them. The chapter is arranged around several thematic areas: attraction, marriage, and partnerships; parenthood, the family, peers, and friendships; and relationship troubles and breaking up. Discursive researchers have shown a keen interest in understanding how people negotiate attraction, including sexual attraction, and how relationships are constructed throughout everyday life. The chapter looks also at how children acquire social competence, through involvement with peers and friends in early years and within the context of the family. We consider finally the difficulties that can stem from potentially problematic relationships, such as those with neighbors, and the issues that arise when relationships break down.

Chapter 5 introduces the reader to the way in which discursive research has approached themes which are central to ideas of "social cognition" within the experimental tradition of research. The chapter begins by exploring the perspective which different discursive traditions have adopted to the notion of the "mental state." This is followed by an examination of how social memory processes are addressed through talk. The chapter then moves on to consider how these sorts of processes intersect with our everyday concerns of understanding and making sense of one another. Two themes are especially relevant here: impression management and attributions. The chapter concludes by discussing the ways in which discursive researchers have contributed to our understanding of processes of social categorization.

Chapter 6 introduces the reader to discursive research on two of the most central concepts within social psychology. The first section deals with attitudes and ranges from attitudes towards food to attitudes towards people with mental health problems. The section will allow the reader to explore some of the theoretical linkages between talk about attitudes and other discourses such as talk of opinions and ideologies. The second section in this chapter turns to the notion of persuasion. Here, we present an introductory exploration of the wealth of discursive research material on how people persuade through talk. One focus here is on rhetorical analyses of everyday and political discourse.

Chapter 7 explores the ways in which discursive researchers have studied prejudice. This is one of the most heavily researched areas in discursive research: the chapter aims to select an informative range of work on prejudice which typifies the discourse researcher's approach. The chapter begins with an account of the ways in which these researchers have approached the topic of racism. It examines how constructions of the other are woven in with talk in which people manage the potential inferences about themselves which their racist talk might make available. The second section moves on to a consideration of prejudice in respect of gender or sexual orientation by examining discursive analyses of sexism and heterosexism.

Chapter 8 presents the discursive researcher's perspective on understanding dispute and aggression. The chapter begins by considering those occasions in which disputatious talk can be seen to perform valuable social functions. It then moves on to consider why argument and dispute can result in interactional problems. In the next section, the chapter turns to the question of how people provide accounts of aggressive acts. Finally, the chapter looks at the question of how aggression is denied or, in extreme cases, made "invisible" in such accounts.

Chapters 9, 10, and 11 each present the findings of discursive research within an applied setting. Chapter 9 examines discourse within the legal setting. It begins with a study of the way that the police officer's interactions with the citizen display regular discursive features which underpin their relative positions as more and less powerful. The chapter then goes on to examine discourse as it arises in the courtroom, looking first at the role of lawyers and then at the roles of the witness and the judge. Chapter 10 turns to a consideration of discourse within health settings. Here we look at how people make sense of health and ill-health, particularly in their interactions with health professionals. We examine also how particular conditions, such as myalgic encephalomyelitis (ME), provide sites for the negotiation and contestation of different practices and constructions of illness. The chapter also looks at issues of support and at the meanings of health and illness in community settings. Chapter 11 concludes the applied section of the book by looking at discourse of organizations and work. In this chapter, we consider features of institutional talk and look at the interrelationship of organizational discourse and employment practices. The chapter also examines social elements of discourse in organizations, in terms of working relationships, organizational decision-making, job-related interviews, employment discrimination, and organizations' interactions with their customers. Finally, the chapter explores how, in the context of the family, children develop their understandings of organizations and work.

Chapters 12 and 13 switch emphasis from practical research to theoretical debate. The aim of chapter 12 is to provide a clear account of several of the areas in which discursive researchers find themselves in disagreement. The chapter examines three of these: the "external contexts" debate, the "membership categorization analysis" debate, and the "social constructionism" debate. In chapter 13, we broaden the compass of the theoretical discussion by considering the relationship between discursive research and experimental social psychology. This chapter sets out some of the philosophical and methodological differences between the two approaches. The chapter also presents two alternative perspectives on the relationship between experimental and discursive research. One of these, the "research independence" position, emphasizes differences between experimental and discursive research. The other, the "research integration" position, emphasizes their complementary aspects.

Chapter summary

- Social psychology is the study of how people behave in social interaction. Social psychologists view interaction with others as influential on how we think and behave even when we are by ourselves or in isolation.
- Social psychology has areas of joint interest with other disciplines both within and outwith the field of psychology. These other disciplines include sociology, social anthropology, and linguistics.
- Social psychology is a scientific enterprise. However, there is debate within the field as to whether positivism is the appropriate approach to the scientific study of people in interaction.
- Although some areas of social psychology collect quantitative data and rely on quantitative analysis, other forms of social psychology rely upon qualitative data and employ qualitative techniques of analysis.
- Qualitative social psychology employs a variety of different approaches. These include conversation analysis, discourse analysis, critical discourse analysis, Foucauldian discourse analysis, discursive psychology, rhetorical psychology, narrative analysis, interpretative phenomenological analysis, and grounded theory.
- Both quantitative and qualitative social psychologists hold themselves to be responsible to strict ethical guidelines in carrying out their research.

Activity

Suppose that you wanted to study the effect of prejudice on the way that a particular minority group is treated within your society. What advantages and disadvantages would there be in adopting a qualitative approach to this sort of study?

Further reading

Parker, I. (2005). *Qualitative psychology: Introducing radical research.* Maidenhead: Open University Press.

Rosenberg, A. (2005). *Philosophy of science: A contemporary introduction.* London: Routledge.

Wetherell, M., Taylor, S., & Yates, S. J. (2001). *Discourse as data: A guide for analysis.* Milton Keynes: Open University Press/London: Sage.

Wooffitt, R. (2005). *Conversation analysis and discourse analysis: A comparative and critical introduction.* London: Sage.

Appendix: A Note on Transcription

Throughout the following chapters, readers will find many transcribed episodes of talk which have been drawn from a number of different examples of discursive research. The transcription of talk is a complex affair. Most discursive researchers rely upon a form of notation developed by Gail Jefferson. However, transcription schemes vary, and readers will find that different researchers have their own transcription preferences. In order to aid readers in making sense of the transcribed examples presented in this book, we have produced below a table describing the way that special symbols are used in transcribing talk. The table summarizes some of the main features of Jefferson's transcription notation which is described more fully, together with explanatory examples, in Jefferson (2004b). Readers might also wish to consult two excellent online resources on transcription, which can be found at:

• www.sscnet.ucla.edu/soc/faculty/schegloff/ TranscriptionProject/index.html
• www-staff.lboro.ac.uk/~ssca1/ sitemenu.htm

TRANSCRIPTION NOTATION

[ ]	Overlapping talk is shown by square brackets, with "[" indicating where the overlap begins and "]" indicating where the overlapped utterance (or part of an utterance) stops.
=	An "equal to" sign "=" at the end of one line and another at the end of the succeeding line indicates that there is no gap between the two lines.
(.) (dot)	A dot in parentheses "(.)" indicates a very slight gap.
: (colon)	A colon ":" indicates that the sound immediately preceding the colon has been elongated, with the lengthening of the sound indicated by the number of colons.
↑	An upwards pointing arrow "↑" indicates that the speaker is raising pitch.
↓	A downwards pointing arrow "↓" indicates the speaker is lowering pitch.
Numbers	Numbers in parentheses, e.g. (0.3) indicate time elapsed in tenths of a second.
Underlining	Underlining of letters or words (e.g. "<u>Doh</u>") indicates that the speaker is stressing that part of the speech by increasing volume or raising or lowering pitch.

Upper case	Upper case indicates that the speaker's utterance is produced with a particularly high volume (e.g., "DOH").
Punctuation	Punctuation markers indicate the speaker's intonation. For example, the question mark "?" indicates a "questioning" intonation.
° (degree sign)	The superscripted degree sign "°" indicates unvoiced production.
< (left caret)	Placed before a word, a left caret "<" indicates a hurried start. Placed after a word it indicates that the word stopped suddenly.
> < (right/left carets)	Right/left carets "> <" surrounding an utterance (or part of an utterance) indicate the speech is speeding up.
< > (left/right carets)	Left/right carets < > surrounding an utterance (or part of an utterance) indicate the speech is slowing down.
– (dash)	A dash "–" indicates that an utterance is "cut off."
hhh	A row of instances of the letter "h" "hhh" indicates an out-breath.
.hhh	A row of instances of the letter "h" prefixed by a dot, ".hhh" indicates an in-breath.
( )	Empty parentheses ( ) indicate that the transcriber could not make out what was said or, alternatively, who was speaking.
(Doh) (word in parenthesis)	Placing parentheses around a word indicates that the transcription is uncertain.
(( ))	Doubled parentheses contain transcriber's descriptions.

Chapter 2

Self and Identity

Topics covered in this chapter

Identities in Context
Conversational identities
Identities in culture

National Identities
Nations and time
Nations and place
Other community identities

Social Groups
Gendered identities
Masculine identities
Feminine identities
Ethnic groups

Virtual Identities

Resisting Identities

Selves in Action

Key terms

Apartheid
Conversational identities
Cultural and interpretative framework
Evaluation
Feminism
Hegemonic masculinity
Ideology
Micro context
National identities
Place-identities
Sequencing
Turn
Virtual identities
Warrant

> "Shortly before four [on February 11, 1990], we left in a small motorcade from the [prison] cottage. About a quarter of a mile in front of the gate, the car slowed to a stop and Winnie and I got out and began to walk toward the prison gate.
>
> At first, I could not really make out what was going on in front of us, but when I was within 150 feet or so, I saw a tremendous commotion and a great crowd of people: hundreds of photographers and television cameras and newspeople as well as several thousand well-wishers. I was astounded and a little bit alarmed. I had truly not expected such a scene.
>
> When I was among the crowd I raised my right fist and there was a roar. I had not been able to do that for 27 years and it gave me a surge of strength and joy. We stayed among the crowd for only a few minutes before jumping back into the car for the drive to Cape Town. As I finally walked through those gates to enter a car on the other side, I felt – even at the age of 71 – that my life was beginning anew. My 10,000 days of imprisonment were over.
>
> The City Hall [in Cape Town] was surrounded by people on all sides. I raised my fist to the crowd and the crowd responded with an enormous cheer. Finally, when the crowd had settled down a bit, I took out my speech.
>
> I spoke from the heart. I wanted first of all to tell the people that I was not a messiah, but an ordinary man who had become a leader because of extraordinary circumstances."
>
> Mandela (1994)

In his autobiography *Long walk to freedom*, from which the above extract comes, Nelson Mandela describes the progress of a truly remarkable life. Born in Transkei, South Africa, on July 18, 1918, Mandela in 1944 joined the African National Congress (ANC), an organization that opposed the **apartheid** policies of the ruling National Party. After becoming leader of the armed wing of the by then outlawed ANC in 1961, he was arrested in 1962. Convicted initially of being the leader of a strike, and thereafter of being a saboteur and conspirator against the state, Mandela spent the next 27 years in prison until his release on February 11, 1990. Subsequent to that release, in 1993 he became the recipient of the Nobel Prize for Peace and in 1994 became the first democratically elected State President of South Africa.

What are we to make of the many possible identities that might be relevant to such a man? Should we accept Nelson Mandela's description of himself as "not a messiah, but an ordinary man?" Alternatively might we prefer the descriptions of him provided by others that appear to reflect his part in extraordinary events? How far is Mandela's identity bound up with those of other people, such as his captors, other ANC members, or South African electors? To what extent are possible identities related to contexts within which he found himself at different times? Do his identities reflect changes that occurred within the broader culture during his life? These are the sorts of questions relevant not just to his life but indeed to any of us. The issue of identity, of who we are, is a central one within social psychology and it is such questions that this chapter will explore.

Identities in Context

As we noted in Chapter 1, there is considerable debate within discursive research as to what precisely counts as context. One argument is that context should be viewed as the specific passage of talk within which any description is to be found. Applying this approach to identity, careful examination of the identity that is being

Apartheid A political and legal system of social separation based on race

described and of the surrounding turns will provide detailed understanding of the identity and of its immediate relevance. In the extract above, Mandela's statement that he is "not a messiah, but an ordinary man" would on this basis provide in itself sufficient information to understand who he claims to be at that precise moment. This description can be viewed as "doing modesty" and as downplaying the expectations that people would have of him should he instead claim to be a messiah. On other occasions, including those within the same book or even same paragraph, he will offer different descriptions of himself and these similarly can be examined for their consequences.

An alternative view is that, to make sense even of an apparently self-explanatory claim such as this one, we must apply knowledge that extends beyond these words in themselves. For example, can we make sense of the term "messiah" without some broader notion of what this description might include? Mandela himself does not spell out in any further detail what is being referenced here; instead it is left to the reader to draw the appropriate inferences. Identities, on this argument, should be understood within a broader context than one that is restricted to a specific passage of words.

Conversational identities

Influenced by the conversational analytic work of Sacks and colleagues (e.g., Sacks, 1992; Sacks, Schegloff, & Jefferson, 1974), many discursive researchers have examined identities in terms of the descriptions that people offer in specific instances of conversation. Identities are regarded as practical actions that are found in interchange with others who are engaged in similar issues of identity (McHoul & Rapley, 2001, 2005b). Accordingly, to understand who the participants are at particular times we have to consider how they negotiate their own identities within these interactions. We cannot assume that we have knowledge of them that goes beyond this as we cannot demonstrate that they necessarily share this knowledge or indeed that any additional information is relevant for them in their exchanges (Antaki, Condor, & Levine, 1996; Antaki, 1998; see also Wooffitt, 2005a).

Indeed, from a starting point of taking identities to be practical actions, we might ask about the sorts of **conversational identities** that allow social interaction to function effectively to any extent. Terms such as speaker, listener, conversant, and so on appear to be reasonably self-evident with regard to the possibilities that they carry in any interaction. We would not expect these identities to be fixed: someone who speaks at one point of a conversation might reasonably be expected to listen at a different point if the exchange is to be two-party rather than a monologue! For everyday talk to proceed in these sorts of ways, there are recurring conversational structures that offer participants possibilities of moving in and out of such identities. On more formalized occasions, such as a courtroom setting, the range of identities relevant to the interaction will be very different, including those of judge, counsel, witness, and accused. Again, however, these identities and the expectations that go with each will be marked out in the talk within the courtroom, as we will see in Chapter 9. Similar factors are found within other instances of talk, such as telephone conversations. Take, for example, situations where an individual calls an emergency services number. In such cases, the caller will usually be expected to state to the answerer the purpose of the call and problem that is relevant to the service that is being called. A caller's failure to do so will result in the person receiving the call relinquishing an identity of answerer and terminating the call (Zimmerman, 1998). Even a description of, say, television viewer relies upon the individual taking up a relevant identity within the immediate exchange (Dickerson, 1996).

How we present ourselves and who we present ourselves as being therefore have considerable impact upon the ways in which others will respond to us in the immediate context. Even, for instance, the language that we use says much about us. If two people share more than one language, the choice of language and alternation of languages within a conversation can point to the elements of linguistic and cultural

> **Conversational identities** Identities that individuals take up when interaction occurs

background that are of greater relevance at different times (Gafaranga, 2001). The language of interaction is equally, if not more, important where conversational parties come from different cultural backgrounds. In such cases, differences in background are likely to become particularly important when an individual shows trouble in understanding or hearing what is being said. Progress of the exchange will break down unless allowed to continue by the repeating or further explanation of what has gone before (Egbert, 2004). People such as migrants, with initial difficulties in conversing in what for them is a second language, often experience problems in effectively communicating their identities within interactions with institutions such as schools (Miller, 2000).

Of course, beyond choice of language, we may make more explicit claims about who we are. There are many contexts, such as that of the psychotherapeutic encounter, where offering precisely this sort of information about ourselves is taken to be a central part of activity; without information about the self, it is hard to see the process going very far. Disclosing information about ourselves, however, is equally found in other interactions. In, for example, a research interview, an interviewee might refer to attributes, actions, or qualities of the self in responding to specific questions or to the interview context in general (Bangerter, 2000). Across these contexts and others, for instance mundane telephone calls, people signal that they are introducing information about themselves that is personal and significant and that will exceed the expectations of a listener. Providing information in these ways takes account of what has gone before in the conversation and leads to it being accepted as new information regarding the identity of the provider of the information (Antaki, Barnes, & Leudar, 2005b).

Unexpected information about the self will not always be taken up in ways that are anticipated. In settings where information is to be produced in particular forms, an individual offering information that does not correspond to the expected form might be attributed with a somewhat negative identity. For example, Antaki (2001) observes that processes such as psychological assessment circumscribe particular forms of interaction between assessor and interviewee.

Where an interviewee provides responses that do not match the requirements of the interviewee identity, then he or she might well be taken to be socially incompetent. Commonly though as we tell stories about our lives to others, we emphasize our control over our experiences and our identities (Drewery, 2005). Equally, where groups are closely involved in the same range of experiences, much of the group interaction will revolve around the roles taken up by different group members and their relationships to past and future events (Georgakopoulou, 2002).

A broader range of identities can also be relevant in the immediate context of conversation. Let us consider, for example, the potential identity of being a gun-owner. In recent history, beyond the context of war, gun-related incidents are commonplace in many parts of the world and gun-related outrages have occurred in places as far apart as Scotland, Australia, and the United States. Owning a gun therefore, even in a country where gun ownership is legally permitted, might reasonably be viewed as problematic. Although all gun-owners are not necessarily violent or irresponsible, they do have in their possession and available for use a weapon that could be used to kill fellow human beings. McKinlay and Dunnett (1998), in a study of calls by gun-owners to a radio phone-in program, show how this potentially problematic identity can be managed in conversation.

1 BOB: give me an idea of when the NRA started and what are
2   its aims
3 TED: well the NRA was started back in the 1800's (em) (.) it
4   was originally started basically as a group for
5   competition shooters and it has grown from that into
6   the main protector of gun rights in the United States
7   (ah) they do lobbying they work with the legislatures
8   both state and national (.) (em) to try to protect the rights
9   that are guaranteed under the Constitution of the
10   United States for the the <u>average</u> citizen to be able to
11   own a handgun or a rifle
              (McKinlay & Dunnett, 1998, p. 38)

An association that has as its members gun-owners in the United States might be taken to represent extremist and socially dangerous elements. Ted's response to Bob's initial question in the extract above counters this inference and instead associates the NRA (National Rifle Association of America) with reasonable and responsible activities. McKinlay and Dunnett draw attention to the explicit reference within this extract to the status of gun-owners as people whose rights are legally recognized under the Constitution and the description of such people as "average." The description negotiates an identity for a gun-owner of being an average and responsible citizen. In later parts of the phone-in discussions, the callers contrast these average law-abiding identities with the identities of others.

116 CAROL:	well yeah a lot of women a lot of women are (.) more
117	and more women are finding the <u>need</u> to (.) protect
118	themselves because – (amm) the gun laws being what
119	they are – the <u>criminals</u> are the ones that are going to
120	disregard any kind of licensing laws and the criminals
121	and the gang-bangers are the ones that are gonna be
122	<u>carrying</u> (.)

(McKinlay & Dunnett, 1998, p. 44)

Here, the identity of gun-owner is not in evidence as Carol makes relevant a different identity, that of women who find the "need to protect themselves." This identity is contrasted with other group identities, namely "criminals" and "gang-bangers," which should be considered as comprising dangerous and law-infringing individuals. Owning a gun therefore is presented as a reasonable and necessary response to the potential illegal actions of others rather than a dangerous choice by those concerned. In these ways, the callers to the phone-in counter any possible inferences that might follow from their ownership of guns and construct themselves as reasonable and average US citizens.

Potentially, many broader elements of social awareness might be found in conversational identities. Gender is one such possibility. The study of

conversation itself can show how gender differences are reproduced within **micro contexts** of interaction (Stokoe, 1998, 2000, 2004) and how conversational structures work to reinforce **ideological** beliefs about women (Kitzinger & Frith, 1999; Ohara & Saft, 2003; Tainio, 2003). The extent to which these can be understood without any recourse to other social knowledge, however, is a contested issue and one to which we return below.

Identities in culture

Conversational identities can reflect immediate identities of speaker, listener, and so on, issues of how individuals present themselves and are conversationally treated, along with aspects of self that link into wider notions of social acceptance or not and social patterns. There remains, however, the question of how much, if any, social knowledge we have to apply in order to make sense of what is taking place in the close interaction. Do the unedited or unexpanded words of the individuals involved tell us all that we need to know of what is relevant, especially where social groupings are concerned? Consider the examples provided above. We might work out from phone-in calls that gun-owners find their stories difficult but we are left not knowing the source of the difficulty. Similarly, we might observe gender-related matters occurring within conversations but would these be sufficient for us to understand the effect of such talk? Many discursive researchers would suggest that the answers to these sorts of questions are "no" and encourage looking wider in our search to understand identities.

Let us start with an example taken from a study by Abell and Stokoe (2001). This study comprises an analysis of data taken from an interview between the late Diana, Princess of Wales, and the interviewer Martin Bashir, broadcast on British television in 1995. In the course of the interview, Diana is asked about and discusses her life before, during, and after her marriage to Prince

Micro context The immediate surroundings of an interaction, including time and place

Ideology An organized set of ideas which typifies the thinking of a group or society

Charles. Her response to one of Bashir's questions is seen below.

BASHIR: and what did you do
DIANA: I swam (2) we went to erm (.) Alice Springs (.) to Australia (2) and we went and did a walkabout and I said to my husband (.) what do I do now (.) and he said "go over to the other side (.) and speak to them" (.) I said I can't (.) I just can't (.) and – he said "well (.) you've got to do it" (1) and he went off and did his bit (1) and I went off and did my bit (.) and – it practically finished me off there and then (.) and I suddenly realized I went back to our-my hotel room (.) and realized the impact that (.) you know (.) I had to sort myself out (.) we had a six week tour (1) four weeks in Australia and two weeks in New Zealand and by the end (.) when we flew back from New Zealand I was a different person (.) I realized (.) the sense of duty (.) the level of intensity of interest (.) and (.) the demanding role (.) I now found myself in
(Abell & Stokoe, 2001, p. 424)

In this extract, a number of identities are potentially relevant for Diana. She refers at various points to "we," "my husband," "me," "myself," "a different person," and "demanding role" among other possibilities. These descriptions are accompanied by little detail, as are various other terms that she uses, such as "walkabout," "you've got to do it," and "sense of duty." However we as listeners/readers can readily make sense of how these descriptions tie together and of who Diana is claiming to be. For example, her reference to "a walkabout" is recognizable as a description of a royal practice of being seen by an expectant public, while "you've got to do it" refers to the actions as comprising a matter of duty rather than choice. These issues are not spelt out at length in the talk itself, nor do they need to be. Instead we as an audience can and are expected to apply our knowledge of royal identities and of the features that are associated with them. It is this cultural understanding that makes sense of what otherwise would be poorly defined terms. As Abell and Stokoe point out, "to understand the rhetorical thrust of Diana's use of naming

conventions, metaphors and the positioning of herself and others, the listener must engage in a wider understanding of the cultural and interpretative framework within which these become relevant" (2001, p. 433).

This argument has considerable implications for how we should understand identities. On this view, we cannot simply discover identities from confined passages of talk, except in a very narrow sense. Identities such as conversational speakers, listeners, and group members might remain reasonably clear. However to understand royals, gun-owners, identities in the changing conditions of South Africa, and so on, we have to engage with a broader understanding of the contexts in which these are located. Our knowledge of these contexts might of course be limited: what we know of the finer details of royal practices or of being confined to a South African prison is likely to be less than complete. However, what we do know about these and similar backgrounds will offer a better understanding of who people are than will paying insufficient attention to such matters.

All research is conducted against some background of cultural practices: it is impossible to conceive of any study (at least one worthy of the name) being carried out in a social and political vacuum. Accordingly numerous investigators draw upon their knowledge of this context in interpreting individual identities. The extent and basis of this knowledge, however, are not always made entirely clear in the findings that are reported and it is this absence that marks one area of disagreement between conversational and broader approaches to understanding identities.

Suppose that we return to the issue of gender and identity. As discussed above, issues of gendered identities and the ideologies that sustain them are to be found within conversational talk. This, however, leaves the question of how we make sense of those conversational matters without drawing on our knowledge of what constitutes gender. In addition, such knowledge as we have is likely to come from our own cultural frameworks. Whether such frameworks and the

Cultural and interpretative framework Broad social and historical context in which individual identities are located

knowledge that results from them are applicable to other contexts is a moot point. In short, it is unlikely that we can fully understand the consequences for individuals of social understandings of gender either simply from their talk or from our own standpoints. For example, talk about sexuality in the context of Korea we might reasonably expect to be rather different from that found in Western societies. In examining the effects of sexuality for Korean identities, Shim (2001) considers both current talk about sexuality and the historical context that has led to the discourse that is now found. She traces the development of notions of sexuality to the Confucianism of the Chosun dynasty, an ideology that continues to exert an impact on many aspects of Korean everyday life. More recent developments, though, include the emergence of a feminist movement that has challenged many of the tenets of Confucianism. Shim notes particularly the changing view of women that **feminism** has offered, moving from one of a woman as a sexual object to the more empowering view of a woman as a sexual subject. Confucianist ideas, however, have not been totally superseded, resulting in clashes in the ideas of identities now available for women within Korean society. It is the consequences of these two very different versions of sexuality, sometimes coinciding although often contradictory, that are found within female sexual identities in current Korean society.

Understanding the cultural frameworks of identities allows us to make sense of much discourse that surrounds identities in a range of micro settings. The effects of cultural notions of female sexuality on specific instances of discourse are not limited to Korea but can be seen in other countries, including the United States and Brazil. Indeed, social understandings appear to permeate even apparently innocuous contexts. Study of quizzes in teenage girls' magazines shows that such seemingly playful features reflect culturally based expectations of heterosexuality and promote behavior that is consistent with these expectations (Ostermann & Keller-Cohen, 1998). Other understandings, for example of music and improvisation, allow jazz practitioners to manage among themselves to shape individual identities as musicians (Wilson & MacDonald, 2005).

National Identities

Thus far we have examined how the identities of individuals require to be considered and examined in terms of the contexts in which they are found. One question that we might ask at this point is "what do we mean by cultural and interpretative frameworks"? If these are relevant, to any extent, in understanding how individual identities are presented, then a clearer view is needed of the broader context and how this operates.

A common part of this context is nationhood. When we speak of our nationalities, doing so appears to provide us with a distinctiveness that separates us from many other individuals and groups throughout the world. At the same time, it seems to provide us a sense of continuity that will endure, regardless of other social interactions that may come and go. National identities, however, do not need to have these elements; we have witnessed in recent times the births and rebirths of numerous nation-states in Eastern Europe and elsewhere. Changes such as these, to parts of our world that we commonly take for granted, lead us to question the idea of nation itself and of the construction of a national identity. Moreover, while national identity is something that we routinely accept as being self-evident, closer inspection shows that it is something of which we are constantly reminded. These reminders need not be obvious but often are presented to us in seemingly unremarkable ways, such as in weather forecasts, newspapers, and other inclusive references to "we," "us," and so on (Billig, 1995). References to nations and **national identities** therefore come to be seen less as straightforward descriptions of the world around us and more as discursive constructions of community that allow us to view ourselves as belonging to a distinctive location within an imagined social world.

Feminism The view that men and women should be treated equally

National identities Descriptions of individuals as members of distinct national communities

Nations and time

In describing a nation, a key element is time. Usually talk of a nation invokes some sense of a past, present, and imagined future that will be shared by those included within the description. In this, the length of time is rather less important than the inclusion of time in the description. For instance, we can speak about "old" nations, "young" nations, or others to very similar effect in that the reference suggests commonality and inclusion of a collection of people instead of diversity and individuality. Neither is it necessary to have knowledge of what is being described. A description of Greece as the birthplace of civilization will invoke imagined memories of a shared past, regardless of whether or not anyone now alive or indeed their ancestors were personally aware of this aspect of that country. Talk of the future works similarly. We do not know what will happen in times to come, but the image of sharing future experiences as a member of a collective body offers feelings of sameness and of connections with other people.

Findings from different studies suggest that such considerations are not unique to a specific nation or nations. A useful starting point is a study of Austrian national identity, in which Rudolf de Cillia and colleagues examine materials from political speeches, newspaper articles, posters and brochures, interviews, and group discussions.

> the State Treaty in 1955 is the most important event for me and I also think that actually (umm) for Austria -/ umm in -/ that / that that document is why you are conscious of being Austrian because really umm it is the foundation stone for the Second Republic. and I hope will stay that way. in it neutrality is anchored.
> [*Für mich is der Staatsvertrag von neunzehnfünfundfünzig das wichtigste reignis und ich mein auch daß eigentlich (ah) für Österreich -/ ah in -/ daß / daß das Dokument das das Österreich-Bewußtsein ausmacht. weil es eigentlich äh der Grundstein für die Zweite Republik ist. und ich hoffe auch bleibm wird. darin ist fixiert die Neutralität*]
> (de Cillia, Reisigl, & Wodak, 1999, p. 158)

The authors noted that across a range of contexts descriptions of Austria frequently included references to shared war experiences and political institutions, such as to the Treaty mentioned above. All such references suggested a collective history that was specific to Austria. In addition, the frequent use of collective pronouns emphasized the ongoing common aspects of experience.

> well I think: that the Austrian is somehow different: from anyone else otherwise we wouldn't be an own / otherwise we wouldn't be Austrians, would we? we just wouldn't all be one people, would we?
> [*also i glaub: daß si der Österreicher von jedn ondern irgndwie unterscheidet: sonst war ma ka eigen / sunst war ma net Österreicher net? war ma jo olle – kein ein Volk net?*]
> (de Cillia et al., 1999, p. 162)

Such references to shared historical achievements and of ongoing experiences that were common to all members of the proposed group functioned across a range of contexts to suggest a distinctive Austrian identity. The descriptions accordingly both presented an identity that was both enduring and unique in that it distinguished Austrians from individuals of other nationalities (see also Wodak, de Cillia, Reisigl, & Liebhart, 1999; Wodak, 2001a).

The relationship of time to national identity can assume particular significance where national identities come into conflict with other identities. If, for example, the rights of other groups vis-à-vis the nation are contested, such as those of the Maori people in New Zealand/Aotearoa, different constructions of time can be used to argue for or against indigenous status of the competing group and the rights to which they might be entitled (see also Taylor & Wetherell, 1999; Wetherell & Potter, 1992).

The issue, then, of what version of national history is told has a considerable bearing on how national identities are constructed. This is clearly exemplified in a study of American identity by Ricento (2003). From an analysis of texts publicly available in the United States between 1914 and 1924, Ricento identifies three rather different and competing versions of early twentieth-century Americanism that reflected varying histories of the development of the United States to that point. These versions of Americanism comprised a "conservative" discourse, a "liberal" discourse, and a "progressive" discourse. The "conservative" discourse highlighted the achievements of the American nation that far and emphasized the need for any migrants to America to become like native-born Americans through education and training. By contrast, the "liberal" discourse focused on the development of American values through the talents and cultures of people coming from many countries. On this argument, native-born Americans had a responsibility to welcome and to appreciate the strengths of migrants. The "progressive" discourse emphasized the importance of democracy in American history, uniqueness of individuals, and open debate. This view allowed all individual citizens the right to self-determination rather than requiring conformity to "typical" values that in any case might not be representative of the majority of Americans. These three contradictory versions of American identity all relied upon rather different histories of the United States and its values. Nonetheless, the three competing identities identified in the writings of the early part of the twentieth century, all invoking a history of the nation, continue to shape contemporary debates about immigration, American national identity, and related matters.

We have seen, then, how differing versions of development of a nation over time can be used to provide a range of national identities in a current context. What happens, however, when one readily available account of national history might lead to national identity being presented in a negative light? Condor (2000) found that when English people talk about England and English identities they display a sensitivity in doing so. In her study, (English) interviewees resisted being classified as English, avoided the topic of national identity even when responding to specific questions, and disavowed English national identities. The apparent explanation for this sensitivity and their reluctance to claim national identities is that, were they to do so, the interviewees would be associating themselves with problematic aspects of the development of that identity. Anglo-British identity would lead to connotations stemming from an imperial past, including expansionism, jingoism, separatism, and xenophobia. Claiming national identities in a current context might readily be taken as indicating prejudice on the part of the participants. Accordingly, for the interviewees, the avoidance of national identity removed possible accusations of prejudice and

resolved the potential difficulty. A similar sensitivity to English national identity has been found in interviews with soldiers serving in the British Army and Territorial Army (Gibson & Abell, 2004). The soldiers would talk about national identities in the context of a superordinate European identity but avoided references to nation in describing their reasons for joining the army. Although it is often assumed that the motivation for soldiers to join any national army is "serving one's country," the interviewees downplayed service as a possible motivation for them. Similarly to Condor's (2000) interviewees, the soldiers avoided such expressions of national identity and the historical associations that might accompany them.

Nations and place

Time, then, is an important element in the construction of national identities. It is not, however, the only one. To speak of any nation, as well as evoking the idea of an enduring group of people, commonly draws upon the notion of a shared and identifiable geographical location. On a map, for instance, one can point to an identifiably demarcated area such as Australia or China. It is then easy to assume that those individuals living in that area comprise Australians, Chinese, or other nationalities as the case may be. This assumption, however, is questionable in two ways. First, as we saw above, the identity entitlements of different individuals sharing the same space may be a matter of dispute depending on the narrated history of the group; identities of groups of indigenous peoples as compared with other groups of nationals are contested in many parts of the globe. Second, national identities commonly exclude individuals such as visitors, refugees, and asylum seekers among others. We are left therefore without an explicit sense of what the connection is between the space that is occupied and those who occupy it and who might be said to have a national identity.

Let us start by reconsidering the relationship between spaces and individuals. One view, perhaps a common one, of the connection between the two would be that spaces provide the arenas for individual and social action. In some sense then, places would be beyond individual actions and interaction, instead comprising parts of an external, physical world. This, however, is a rather minimalist and impoverished concept of place that would largely remove the study of place in itself from the realm of social psychology. An alternative view is offered by Dixon and Durrheim (2000) who argue that questions of "who we are" are often closely interlinked with questions of "where we are." The argument here is that descriptions of places, as with descriptions of individuals, events, and so on, can be provided in a number of ways. It is not that places exist in some neutral manner that is self-evident, but rather that they can be presented according to the requirements of the context within which the description is offered. Thus, different descriptions of individual identities and places are commonly combined when required. The connection between individuals, groups, and places can therefore usefully be understood in the form of "**place-identities**." "Place-identities" provide both a sense of spatial belonging for the person or persons being described and a **warrant** for social practices in relation to the place (see also Dixon & Durrheim, 2004).

An example that Dixon and Durrheim provide of exploring "place-identities" in this way relates to the desegregation of space within South Africa as it moved from apartheid to a post-apartheid era. Alongside political change came physical changes, including the desegregation of townships and beaches. The previously advantaged white residents and citizens often opposed such changes. To argue against change on racial grounds, however, would be taken to be prejudiced in a context where change was required on exactly these grounds. Arguments of those opposing changes accordingly relied extensively on particular descriptions of the places that were involved such as "squatter camps" and of the proposed changes as the destruction of "rural life." In this way, they provided not simply particular descriptions of the places that were referenced but in addition the relationships of individuals to these places ("squatter," "rural"). It is therefore these relationships and their meanings

---

Place-identities Constructions of places and of the relationships of individuals to these

---

Warrant An argumentative basis for a claim

---

for collective identities that are encompassed within the idea of "place-identities." The meanings of South Africa as a nation and individual national identities thus become closely interwoven through particular descriptions of the places concerned.

The value of using "place-identities" to understand national identities is further illustrated in relation to English/British identities. In a study of the arguments mobilized by the Countryside Alliance against a prohibition on foxhunting, Wallwork and Dixon (2004) found that these arguments relied heavily on the descriptions that they offered of England and Britain itself. Within these arguments, the site of the disputed activity of foxhunting became portrayed as natural and idyllic, in the form of the English countryside. By associating this space with essential elements of nationality, campaigners were able to claim that the proposed ban would run contrary to the essence of British national identity. Again, social activities and the place in which these occur can be seen to be closely interlinked with and descriptions of nation and identities of relevance.

Other community identities

As well as providing a useful account of the relationship of place to national identities, examination of people's descriptions of spaces has opened up for critical inquiry several related issues. For example, national identities can be emphasized not only through references to national spaces bit also to specific locations within that space. Where specific buildings are described as sources of national activities, such as government, these work to emphasize the national character of that activity and to contrast it with other possibilities (Higgins, 2004). Alternatively, accounts of spaces and of the activities to be associated with them can be used to mark out identities that are to be viewed as not national, such as tourists (McCabe & Stokoe, 2004). In this regard, a description of a space as an ecotourist area can emphasize the activities relevant to the place and so the identities of the individuals to be found there (Muhlhausler & Peace, 2001).

Recent work has shown that elements of place and time are found also in other identities of a community nature. For example, in relation to an island community residents can use differing constructions of time and of place-identity to argue for the relative standings of groups within that community (McKinlay & McVittie, 2007). Specific versions of island identities, such as "local" and "incomer," function to enhance the status of certain residents while downgrading the standings of others. Features similar to those found in the context of nationality can thus be found in local community settings where a shift from a lower-status identity to a higher-status one is a highly sensitive matter.

Social Groups

The issue of nation provides one part of the cultural and interpretative framework within which identities are managed. Nations, as we have seen, are neither unitary nor given but rather are constructed in many different and inconsistent ways according to the discursive context in which they are located. Of course, nations comprise only part of the broader context in which identity work is done. Within the social realm, there are many other considerations of potential relevance. Often society is viewed as including a wide diversity of social groups, marked out by differences in racial background, ethnic group membership, age, social class, and gender among others. Like nations however, social groups and their memberships cannot be simply taken as obvious or given but instead can be examined in terms of their construction and use.

Gendered identities

We will start this exploration of group memberships by returning to the question of gender. Earlier in this chapter, we noted in relation to female sexuality in Korea that historical ideologies had come to be reflected in present-day female sexual identities (Shim, 2001). Different views of sexuality from separate times continued to be in circulation throughout Korean society. These versions did not in themselves determine current identities; they did, however, provide part of the cultural backdrop against which Korean women now made sense of their lives.

In the historical emergence of Western societies, it is perhaps more difficult to point to a single

source of influence with an enduring strength similar to that of Confucianism. This however does not mean that these societies have an absence of cultural influences. Again, however, there is the question of the extent to which we should apply our cultural knowledge to the interpretation of individual identities. A number of writers (e.g., Kitzinger, 2000; Stokoe, 2004; Stokoe & Smithson, 2001; Speer, 2002) argue that to do so is potentially problematic and it is in any case unnecessary to look beyond the specific descriptions that individuals provide: these descriptions can in themselves offer sufficient information about gender as with other aspects of identities. Many researchers, however, use their understandings of prevailing social notions of gender to inform the investigation of individual identities.

Masculine identities

One point of agreement among discursive researchers is that gendered identities should not be accepted as self-explanatory or as straightforwardly reflecting biological differences between individuals. Wetherell and Edley (1999), for example, argue that masculine identities do not simply reflect essential gendered features but rather are matters that are negotiated in everyday talk and social interaction. For researchers such as Wetherell and Edley, this negotiation does not take place in a social vacuum but is part of a broader social and historical context: although enacted by individual men, the forms of masculinity that prevail within particular contexts and periods reflect social expectations of what these should encompass. Thus, for example, overt displays of emotion might be regarded as unmanly at some points in time while being accepted or even encouraged in other historical periods (Wetherell, 1996). The identities that are constructed by individual men accordingly will both acknowledge and reproduce the definitions of masculinity prevailing within particular cultures and time periods (Edley & Wetherell, 1995).

The form of male identity currently prevailing is one of macho masculinity, exemplified by male characters in contemporary cinema, in the media more generally, and appearing widely throughout our society (Connell, 1987, 1995). This ideal identity symbolizes male power and authority, epitomizing patriarchal society. It

CLASSIC STUDY: Negotiating masculinities

Nigel Edley and Margaret Wetherell over the course of a series of studies (e.g., Edley & Wetherell, 1995, 1997, 1999; Wetherell, 1998; Wetherell & Edley, 1999) examined how young men negotiated masculine identities. During 1992 and 1993, they conducted interviews with small groups (three people) of boys who were attending the sixth form of a single-sex, independent school in the UK. The group discussions were loosely structured, allowing the boys to talk about a wide range of topics including sexualities, images of men, feminism, and their own identities within the school. In their discussions, the boys proposed, challenged, resisted, and reworked versions of masculinities and their meanings.

Edley and Wetherell in one of their reports (Edley & Wetherell, 1997) show how the boys at times resisted versions of identity that reflected socially prevailing hegemonic masculinities and sought instead to negotiate

"new man" identities. At other points, however, the boys promoted hegemonic masculinities, claiming that they matched up to these more than other boys in the sixth form. In both cases, the participants compared their individual identities with those of other boys at the school and of men more generally. Edley and Wetherell argue that the boys' identities should be understood in terms of broader cultural views of masculinities. They argue also, however, that versions of masculinities are more variable, fragmented, and contradictory than is often suggested. To understand the meanings of masculine identities we need to study closely the everyday talk in which different versions of masculinities are found.

Edley, N. & Wetherell, M. (1997). Jockeying for position: The construction of masculine identities. *Discourse & Society, 8,* 203–217.

---

thus works to distance masculinities from other gender identities such as female identities. Alternative masculine identities do not draw upon the same notion of power or function to optimize male invulnerability and are accordingly presented as subordinate to the "hegemonic" one. Although unattainable in its extreme form, the ideal **hegemonic masculinity** acts to provide a yardstick against which alternative identities can be assessed. (See 'Classic Study' box above.)

The influence of hegemonic masculinity can be seen in male identities and actions across a range of settings. For example, it is viewed as masculine for men to display certain emotions, namely grief, joy, and anger, but only within prescribed contexts such as death and football matches (Walton, Coyle, & Lyons, 2004). In relation to health and ill-health, men commonly describe

both men in general and themselves as individuals as being invulnerable to illness, even when challenged with medical evidence to the contrary (Hodgetts & Chamberlain, 2002; McVittie, Cavers, & Hepworth, 2005; McVittie & Willock, 2006). Males who do not conform to expected employment patterns, by for instance taking time out of work for paternity leave, are viewed as "unmasculine" (Pleck, 1993). Conversely, where men are out of work but not through choice, unemployment or redundancy can leave them experiencing disempowerment in being unable to fulfill the socially expected male role of breadwinner (Willott & Griffin, 1997, 2004). Similar issues arise in relation to crime, where male criminals draw upon the social expectations of being a male breadwinner in order to account for their roles in committing crimes of which they have been convicted (Willott & Griffin, 1999; Willott, Griffin, & Torrance, 2001).

Hegemonic masculinity Socially prevailing view of ideal form of masculine identity

WILL: I mean that's why <u>we</u> go an' commit crime, so our kids don't have to do it.

You know what I mean. We want to provide for them, so they're not in the same situation as we grew up in.

[Neil, Shaun, & Jimmy repeat these arguments, partially inaudible.]

SHAUN: If my kids grow up and get into trouble, it'll break my heart.

JIMMY: Well I can't understand [inaudible] talking about the children, where does the government start? What are we talking about here paying out . . . if a man wants to stop in and he doesn't drink and he doesn't smoke so he can buy his children clothing, he shouldn't be taxed on things like that, he shouldn't have the tax taken out his wages. 'Cos that's what he's doing . . . The price of clothes, it's just the government I think, not just the villain. I think the price is so high it's ridiculous.

(Willott & Griffin, 1999, p. 453; extract abbreviated)

Sara Willott and Chris Griffin note how, in extracts like that above, working-class men use discourse of being a male breadwinner to account for the crimes of which they have been convicted. The idea of providing for their families, in terms of making available the necessities and of ensuring that other family members do not have to resort to similar means, ties in to traditional notions associated with male social roles. The men further account for their actions by describing ways in which the state has failed to meet its side of the "bargain" by enabling them to meet masculine expectations in legally accepted ways. Crime therefore is presented as the only way by which they can be breadwinners and fulfill the identities that are expected of them.

The sorts of masculine identity that men commonly assume therefore are strongly influenced by dominant social notions of who the ideal man should be. The identities consequent upon this ideal standard are by no means those that might be of greatest benefit to men themselves, especially when we consider issues of health and non-employment. As Wetherell (1996) observes, versions of masculine identity do of course change perceptibly over time. Men of younger ages can negotiate masculine identities in different ways from those of previous generations, drawing upon changing sets of linguistic resources and shared understandings of gender that in turn allow a changing set of social actions. However, the recurring use of hegemonic masculinity across a range of contexts suggests that it will not be given up easily or alternative forms readily adopted.

One possible future change in masculinities, signaled in men's health magazines, might be a greater social acceptance of "real men" identities, which promote informed knowledge rather than simple invincibility (Toerien & Durrheim, 2001). The extent to which such possible alternative versions of masculinity will in time come to influence individual identities remains to be seen.

Feminine identities

Expectations of feminine identities, like those of masculine identities, are commonly organized around socially prevailing forms. Qualities associated with being female have traditionally in Western societies been presented in opposition to the hegemonic attributes of masculine identities (Weedon, 1997). Typically, feminine identities have been understood to encompass aspects of beauty and appearance, slenderness, individuality and self-control, a propensity to nurture others, and heterosexuality (Burns, 2004; Holland, 2004; Lafrance & Stoppard, 2006). Such images of femininity continue to be commonplace, in women's magazines, on television and in films, and more broadly across Western cultures (Weedon, 1997).

Although such images do not of course determine feminine identities, they do constitute norms for "ideal" femininity (Burns, 2004). Increasingly, however, these descriptions of "ideal" femininity are found alongside alternative versions of identity. Some alternative versions of feminine identities can be seen in analyses of group conversations among female friends. For example, in examining the group conversation among female friends prior to a night out, Benwell and Stokoe (2006) show how participants shift between different femininities.

DAWN: We need to go in three quarters of an hour.

ELENA: Okay.

MARIE: Oh MAN I haven't even gone out and I'm sweating like a rapist!
(Laughter and horrified reaction)

MARIE: I'm really hot.
ELENA: You two have got to stop with that
        phrase.
MARIE: Has anyone – has anyone got any really
        non sweaty stuff.
DAWN: Dave has. But you'll smell like a man.
KATE: (Laughs)
MARIE: Right has anyone got any feminine non
        sweaty stuff.
KATE: I've got erm roll on.
                        (Benwell & Stokoe, 2006, p. 48)

In the above extract, we can see the speakers refer to matters involved in traditional forms of femininity, such as a concern with not appearing hot and sweaty and the importance of smelling feminine not masculine. These descriptions, though, are located alongside references to somewhat different identities. Marie's description of herself, for example, as "sweating like a rapist" suggests a more "laddish" form of femininity. This **turn** evokes from other conversational participants a response that appears to combine amusement and disapproval. Elena's challenge to the description ("got to stop") then suggests that two of the participants have invoked such identities on a previous occasion or occasions. What even this short extract points to is the range of potential femininities that might be available for negotiation by individual women.

Coates (1996) similarly examines how feminine identities are negotiated among groups of girls and/or women rather than reflecting a hegemonic ideal. In discussions among female friends, the use of overt compliments, references to wearing make-up, and positive **evaluation** of model-like attributes all present a traditional, appearance-related femininity. Other parts of their discussion, however, draw upon ideas that include references to feminism, love, maternalism, science, and medicine among other factors, reflecting a diversity of feminine identities of relevance to the group. In these ways, meanings of feminine

---

Turn The basic unit of conversation in which one speaker talks

---

Evaluation Talk which situates the relevant topic in a comparative frame indicating features such as levels of goodness or worth

---

identities can be seen as issues that are directly negotiated in conversational contexts where feminine identities are of immediate relevance for the participants.

Beyond the context of conversation itself, other expectations surrounding femininity and identity considerations come into play. For example, in US high schools an identity of "nerd girl" is not one that might be thought particularly desirable, being often associated with social and academic failure. This identity, however, can, like any other identity, be claimed and managed to best effect by those who identify with the description and who do not treat it as a negative outcome (Bucholtz, 1999). At a social level, feminine identities are implicated in readily recognizable identities such as mother. Here, transitions between feminine identities and other social identities like that of worker can often be challenging. In this respect, cultural resources in the form of books, magazines, and other literature can, potentially at least, provide support in effecting the transition and in dealing with the expectations that are associated with each identity (Gross & Pattison, 2001).

Again, our understanding of such identities has to be set within a cultural framework for these identities to make sense as being available to individual women. By way of contrast with the girls' discussions observed by Benwell and Stokoe (2006) and Coates (1996), consider the lives of Protestant women belonging to the Tzotzil community in Chiapas in southern Mexico. Traditionally, Tzotzil culture is organized around Roman Catholicism and ritual, and little authority or status is granted to female members of the community. Since the 1970s however, increasing numbers of Tzotzils have converted from Roman Catholicism to Protestantism, notwithstanding the fierce opposition of the remainder of the community. Many Protestant converts who have refused to take part in recognized Catholic practices have been expelled from the community and had their homes torched.

For a Protestant woman living in this community, her main concerns are unlikely to be a choice between one of adopting a feminine appearance by wearing make-up and that of aligning with a more progressive femininity using "laddish" descriptions. The feminine identities in circulation within Tzotzil communities are likely to be rather more limited. Baron (2004) notes, however, that other identity options might be available to individual women in such circumstances.

76 *Va., lajk'opankutik yos .un.*
   "So, then we prayed."
77 *Va.i, k'alal ya.i xa lajk'oponkutik yos .une, komo lajkalbe ti yose,*
   "Listen, when we prayed, then they heard it already, because I said to God,"
78 *"Kajval, ja . jech ti li .i, yu.un ja . li . ta xnupin ti kole,*
   "'My Lord, this is how it is here, because it's here my child is getting married,'
79 *xchi .uk ti jun xnich'on ti anich'on le . eke,' xkut ti kajvaltik xkaltike . . .*
   'with their one child, your child there, too,' I said to Our Lord as we say . . ."
80 *.i va. jech k'alal lajk'oponkutik yos .une.*
   "So that's how it was when we prayed."
   (Baron, 2004, p. 266)

Lucía, the female speaker in the extract above, is seeking to arrange the marriage of her son to the younger sister of an as yet unmarried girl. To do so, though, is problematic: a marriage of this kind would run counter to accepted Tzotzil traditions, and Lucía, as a female member of the community, has little authority herself to argue for such a breach of custom. By invoking religion, she is able to distance herself from the argument for the proposed marriage and instead appeal to a higher authority. As Baron (2004, pp. 249–250) observes, "evangelicals can manoeuvre to affect others by bringing God into a conversation. A speaker who highlights a religious identity from which she can draw greater authority renders gender immaterial." In ways such as these, Protestantism, while not offering practical authority within the community, does provide scope for women to have moral authority in their everyday lives. It accordingly opens up a potentially greater range of identity possibilities for Tzotzil women than would traditional discourse of Tzotzil femininity.

Ethnic groups

Although ethnic group memberships have long been of interest to social psychology, little social psychology writing has taken the question of membership as a prime topic of study in its own right. Instead, group memberships have been taken as a starting point for consideration of differences between groups and to what extent perceived differences might have any essential basis. Consideration of ethnic group membership thus becomes primarily a process of investigation of individual cognitive processes. An alternative focus has been on the processes that stem from memberships of different social groups, such as identification with the group and comparison with other groups. Although this latter approach does look to the wider social context rather than to individual cognitions, issues of who belongs to groups and indeed how groups are viewed as groups at all are left relatively unexamined.

In considering issues of comparison and of essential features of ethnic groups, we do so here in somewhat different ways than those adopted in the approaches outlined above. Given the present focus on understanding identities in context, we take questions such as possible group comparisons and group attributes not as psychological realities but rather as matters that arise in individuals' negotiations of identities that are meaningful for them. The negotiation of identities that orient to or potentially draw upon ethnic group membership is most commonly found in cultural contexts of migration, where group expectations and group entitlements are of most immediate relevance. Establishing an identity of this sort, and of its relationships to a majority ethnic group, might be viewed as an ongoing process of narrating memberships of both groups, as for example in the case of undocumented Mexican immigrants to the United States (Fina, 2000). It is in such instances that concerns about comparisons and group features are located.

Evidence shows that the identities that immigrants construct for themselves orient to a considerable extent to comparisons with other residents. Verkuyten (1997), for example, shows that Turkish inhabitants of an inner-city quarter in Rotterdam when discussing issues of identity draw upon many different comparisons between themselves, Dutch nationals, and other groups, including other Turkish inhabitants. These various descriptions provide a set of identities that immigrants can use to argue for or against maintaining distinctive ethnic migrant identities or seeking assimilation into broader Dutch culture. Similar comparisons of group identities are found in the descriptions of Chinese people living in the Netherlands (Verkuyten & de Wolf, 2002).

Identity comparisons moreover are not restricted to particular geographical contexts of immigration. In a study of two "Generation 1.5 Japanese" individuals who immigrated to the US early in their lives, Masataka Yamaguchi (2005) found that the interviewees compared their previous experiences of Japan and Japanese identities with their current identities in the United States.

1 MARCO: Yeah so it's just um um and you know I just realized I felt much more comfortable
2   interacting with *Japanese people in America*
3   because there I didn't have <u>this overwhelming societal sort of pressure to interact in a certain way</u> but I did *in Japan*
4 MASA: Oh I see
5 MARCO: You know *in Japan* you it's almost like **everyone** speaks in formulas, you know,
6   and what you say is not important. What you do is important. How you act is important.
7   How you ... **everything** is expressed nonverbally and it's <u>exhausting</u>. I mean it really is <u>exhausting</u>
                        (Yamaguchi, 2005, pp. 282–283, original emphasis)

As seen in the example above, the interviewees described their previous identities as individuals living in Japan in negative terms. These identities, and the expectations that they carry by way of behavior and speech, are presented as being undesirable in restricting forms of interaction with other individuals working within similar identity constraints. By contrast, the interviewees describe their current experiences, involving interactions with a different group ("Japanese people in America"), as positive or "comfortable." This comparison allows the interviewees to build up favorably their current identities as migrants living in the United States.

Descriptions such as these indicate that migrants can make a number of identity comparisons, including comparisons (favorable or unfavorable) with former fellow nationals. In this light it is indeed questionable whether ethnic group identities should be considered in any sense as homogeneous or as applying equally to all members of a potential group. Any comparison that is made has implications for the individual concerned and the identity that he or she is looking to manage in the broader context of migration.

As with comparisons, so too the issue of essential differences between groups forms a central element of the negotiation of migrant identities. Commonly it might be assumed that migrants would look to counter any argument for differences in order to reduce the likelihood of prejudice from majority group members on precisely those grounds. An interesting aspect of migrant identities, however, is that minority ethnic group members do not inevitably reject descriptions of difference, and indeed on occasions themselves claim that their group is essentially different from majority groups. Arguments of this type can be used to argue for preferential acceptance and the cultural rights that should accompany recognizably different identities (Verkuyten, 2003).

One specific ethnic identity that has received much attention of late is that of being Muslim. In the wake of the September 11, 2001 attacks on the United States and subsequent attacks across the globe, a Muslim identity has become highly politicized and controversial in many parts of the Western world. Nowhere has this been more so, apart from the United States, than in the United Kingdom where the bombings of public transport on July 7, 2005 and subsequent alleged terrorist conspiracies have been attributed to Muslim extremists. Muslim identities have therefore come under close scrutiny.

Studies of Muslim identities in the United Kingdom have shown widely divergent descriptions of what the identity encompasses and of the expectations that follow from it (Hopkins & Kahani-Hopkins, 2004a, 2004b). A primary concern for this identity is the issue of what membership is appropriate for individual Muslims. One version of Muslim identity, promoted by the Muslim Parliament of Great Britain among others, presents British Muslim identity as primarily sharing common interests with non-British Muslims elsewhere in the world. This identity provides for a geographically disparate group identified along ethnic and religious lines and one which is to be viewed as essentially distinct from majority groups in the UK and elsewhere. On such a view, British Muslims should not look to assimilate into British culture and should play no part in maintaining the institutions that reflect it, for example by not voting in parliamentary elections. An alternative Muslim identity, promoted for instance by figures within the UK Imams and Mosques Council, calls for common interest with both non-British Muslims and British non-Muslims. This view of identity allows for greater participation within British culture and for inclusion in parliamentary processes as elsewhere.

The wholly contradictory identities offered for British Muslims thus come into stark contrast: distinctiveness vs. commonality, non-participation vs. participation, non-acceptance vs. acceptance of British culture. Again, rather than being constant and fixed, these perhaps can more usefully be regarded as comprising a set of possibilities within which individual Muslims have to negotiate their identities in ways relevant to them. More than anything, however, they do perhaps usefully serve to highlight the difficulties that were outlined at the start of this section: the problems of understanding group memberships, the comparisons of relevance, and the extent to which features should be routinely associated with group memberships.

Virtual Identities

One context where there appear to be fewer constraints on the identities available to individuals is the Internet. The relatively recent history of the development of the Internet, together with absence of potential identity-related elements such as space, appears to offer a context that is unconstrained in many ways and which opens up the possibilities available for many individuals. In this, it seems to afford individuals a kind of virtual laboratory for exploring and experimenting with different versions of self (Turkle, 1995).

Despite the clear implications for the construction of identities, as yet there is relatively little research that has sought to understand such **virtual identities** from the viewpoint of discursive research.

An exception to this absence has been the context of support groups and discussion boards in which individuals provide versions of themselves in relation to other people who are considered potentially to have similar interests in the topic under discussion. One particular instance where virtual forms of communication have come to offer a prominent means of negotiating identities is that of health. As elsewhere, the identities that are on offer in such contexts can be jointly negotiated, contested, or otherwise negotiated according to the demands of the context and the responses of other users. For example, users can describe experiences of illness that draw upon recognizable shared elements and that potentially become less likely to be contested by non-users (Bulow, 2004). In other cases, however, the experiences that individuals describe online may be challenged by other users with consequences for the identities that are available to them (Giles, 2006). Such identities and their implications for health are examined in greater detail in Chapter 10.

The Internet also provides the opportunity for individuals to take up new and different forms of identity. One example of this is where individuals claim identities that differ from those that they take up in everyday lives. For instance, an identity of disability can be managed in everyday talk according to the context within which the individual is placed. Online, individuals can exercise a choice as to what personal information is revealed (Bowker & Tuffin, 2002) and thus can opt whether or not to disclose information about the self in a way similar to that commonly found in conversational talk.

There are, in addition, virtual identities that have a specific relevance to the Internet as a form of communication. Vallis (2001), in a study of talk in Internet chat-rooms, notes that participants often explicitly refer to the online status relevant

> **Virtual identities** Forms of identity that people take up in online communications and communities

to themselves and to others. Explicit categories thus include "ops" (operators or moderators), "founder," and "not an op." The characteristics to be associated with the identity "op" can be either positive or negative, according to the context of use. Thus, while an "op" might be considered someone who protects the integrity of the chat-room, the identity might alternatively be viewed as being primarily concerned with unnecessary control or obsession. The negotiation of this identity and its relations with other users there-fore come to be intrinsic features of the com-munication within the chat-room. Benwell and Stokoe (2006) point to other identities that are specific to Internet communication, those of "newbie" (newcomer), "Flamer," and "Troll" (troublemakers). In considering the identity of "newbie," the authors observe that within online communities commonly the identity is com-monly contrasted with that of "regular" or estab-lished community member. "Newbie" carries with it expectations of deference towards estab-lished users while "regulars" are expected to be tolerant of newcomers while maintaining the standards of the community. These identities accordingly function to preserve accepted order and set the context within which "newbies" can gain acceptance and in time progress towards identities as "regulars" of the online community.

Resisting Identities

So far, we have looked at the ways in which indi-viduals can claim certain identities, for example national identities, and how individuals move in and out of different identity possibilities, as in for instance different forms of ethnic identities. One point of note has been the forms of work in which individuals engage in order to present themselves as particular sorts of people. Identity work, however, clearly is not limited to the description and claiming of identities. By contrast, many of the potential identities that we have considered along the way could be very difficult for those concerned to manage. English national identity, as seen in Condor's (2000) study, is treated as an extremely sensitive issue and many of her interviewees did not readily align with it. Similarly a context of migration is one in which migrant identities and their features become

highly contestable, especially in relation to the majority group (e.g., Verkuyten, 2003). Ident-ities then are seen to provide a central orienta-tion for the individuals involved; at times people might claim identities, to manage the inferences that follow from an identity categorization or indeed to resist altogether the identity category that is on offer.

We saw above, in McKinlay and Dunnett's (1998) study of callers to a radio phone-in, that the identity of gun-owner is one that individuals treat as being highly sensitive and that they do not take up this identity without qualification. Although the callers in that situation identified with a description of gun-owner, they resisted the associations of the description with particular types of activities and attributes. Potentially, how-ever, many identities might not be amenable to being reworked in this way and will conse-quently be highly problematic for the individuals concerned should the identities be accepted. Just as identities can be taken up and managed within local conversational contexts, so too can they be resisted according to the requirements of the immediate interaction. Take, for example, the case of someone who is facing the description of having learning difficulties or learning dis-abilities. In social terms an identity such as this is commonly regarded as being extremely nega-tive, even "toxic" (Todd & Shearn, 1995, 1997). It is thus less amenable to renegotiation in favor-able terms than an identity such as that of being a gun-owner, an identity that can be managed to incorporate claims of normality. For a person therefore to avoid the negative inferences that a description of having learning difficulties makes available, he or she will very likely require to resist being described in these terms at all. The extent to which conversational resistance will be effective is, however, open to question. Indeed, in some contexts, resistance may be misinterpreted as acquiescence in acceptance of the identity on offer. Rapley and Antaki (1996) note that, in the structured context of quality of life assess-ment interviews, interviewees' responses can be reframed by the interviewer so as to indicate acceptance rather than rejection of the negative descriptions that are on offer. Nonetheless, care-ful examination of the ways in which individuals concerned do deal with potentially negative identity attributions such as having learning disabilities shows that these identities can variously be accepted, managed, or rejected according to the demands of the context within which the identity is proposed (Rapley, Kiernan, & Antaki, 1998).

Similar conversational variation is to be found in relation to other identities. For instance, much interaction is permeated by prevailing assumptions of heterosexuality and heterosexist identities (McIlvenny, 2002; Speer & Potter, 2000). Within conversation therefore lesbians often are confronted with heterosexist assumptions of sexuality. Analysis of lesbian conversational talk shows that such assumptions can be addressed explicitly or implicitly, or left unaddressed, according to the conversational contexts within which lesbians find themselves (Land & Kitzinger, 2005). One potential way of resisting the attribution of an unwanted identity is to explicitly distance oneself from the identity that is on offer. In doing so, the greater the distance that a speaker can introduce between himself or herself and the suggested category, the greater the likelihood is of avoiding that particular identity. Use of contrast between the self and the category can provide a means of resisting identity as a conversation unfolds (Dickerson, 2000).

Although resistance then is found at a conversational level, the question again arises of the extent to which the local context should be taken to reflect the social framework within which it is located. Negotiations of sexuality arguably can only be fully understood in terms of broader social understandings of gender and sexual identities. Similarly, descriptions of learning disabilities invoke normative expectations of abilities and comparisons across a diversity of contexts, encompassed within socially constructed labels and categories (Finlay & Lyons, 2005). Social understandings of identities and actions can also be seen in the accounts of women who have been abused in childhood. Within their accounts, those who have suffered abuse display awareness of and resistance to the social expectation that sufferers of abuse will become abusers themselves in later life (Croghan & Miell, 1999).

Resistance to identities is equally evident where the identity in dispute is one of membership of a social group. One example of such identity negotiations is provided by Dominican immigrants in Rhode Island who potentially might be classed as "black" or "African American" but who consider themselves to be Spanish or Hispanic (Bailey, 2000b). As with other elements of group identities, the issue of what features are relevant for group membership becomes particularly salient and a matter of resistance as the immigrants look to distinguish themselves from being categorized as "black" or "African American" and to claim alternative identities.

Selves in Action

A central argument of this chapter has been that identities should not be taken to be straightforward descriptions of who we are. As we have seen, identities are subject to claims, negotiation, resistance, and other management in contexts of interaction with other people and within the cultural and social contexts that we inhabit. In short, identities are not simply features or products of the individual, but rather should be viewed as practices within interactions with others and the outcomes of those interactions.

It is evident also that identity does not happen in the abstract but is inevitably implicated in social actions. Identities, whether viewed in a context of conversation or in the broader culture, have consequences for what will follow. Conversational identities have consequences for how social interaction proceeds and how individuals respond to conversational partners in the immediate context. (See 'Classic Study' box on p. 40.)

Interactions of course take place in a wider cultural framework that encompasses a multitude of understandings of gender, sexuality, and communities among other elements. In this regard, many discursive researchers argue that identities both reflect and make possible broad possibilities for action and require to be interpreted accordingly. National identities and group identities are contested in contexts where collective identities have particular consequences for category rights and entitlements and for intergroup relations. Thus, for example, the identities available to Tzotzil women or to British Muslims are inextricably linked to the actions of the individuals concerned. The identities therefore that individuals negotiate, whether through direct claims, management, resistance, or otherwise, have direct relevance for their everyday practical

CLASSIC STUDY: The language of youth subcultures

In August 1987 and August 1989, Sue Widdicombe and Robin Wooffitt interviewed 85 young people of distinctive appearance in a range of different locations, including rock festivals, street corners, alternative markets, and similar places. They conducted a total of 38 informal interviews, either with individuals or with small groups of people. The authors did not assume that the participants belonged to particular subcultural groups, for example punks, but were interested in examining how the young people themselves made sense of their identities.

Widdicombe and Wooffitt identified a number of ways in which the participants resisted aligning themselves with membership of subcultural groups. Commonly the young people described their appearance and behavior as being very ordinary, in developing identities as ordinary people. At times when they might be viewed as similar to other members of particular groups, for example in terms of appearance or musical preferences, the interviewees accounted for

these preferences as being the result of personal motivations and knowledge rather than of affiliation with a group. In addition to accounting for their appearance and actions in individual ways, the participants commonly avoided giving any definition of the proposed groups.

Widdicombe and Wooffitt argue that the strategies that the young people used in discourse provided a range of ways of resisting the identities that others might attribute to them. By doing so, the interviewees could present themselves as personally motivated and authentic individuals rather than shallow people who simply conformed to the expectations of group standards. The authors conclude that identities are thus inextricably linked to social action; identities are things that people use to accomplish outcomes.

Widdicombe, S. & Wooffitt, R. (1995). *The language of youth subcultures: Social identity in action.* Hemel Hempstead and New York: Harvester Wheatsheaf.

concerns and the social actions in which they are engaged. This, moreover, is a two-way process; descriptions of social actions and of the circumstances to which they relate impact upon everyday interactions with others and the identities that are available and ascribed to individuals within the broader social realm.

The actions that stem from identities, like identities themselves, might be viewed either as somewhat localized or as having somewhat broader effects. For example, the smooth **sequencing** of conversation can depend on the conversational identities accorded to the conversational participants. Participants can use their preference for one language over another, where a choice is available to all participants, to highlight

specific linguistic identities and so to increase or to reduce their affiliations with conversational partners (Torras & Gafaranga, 2002). Similarly, ethnic identities can be adopted or avoided to argue for or against the merits of a proposed charter school (Hansen, 2005).

The potential relationships between conversational contexts and wider cultural knowledge are evident in situations where individuals explicitly look to accept or to disrupt prevailing social assumptions. One example of explicit acceptance comes from the talk of criminals who are rehabilitated in Jewish religious academies. For them, the use a range of conversational elements that include religious utterances, tag questions, and passive voice suggests the identity of penitent and is more likely than other possibilities to meet social expectations and gain acceptance (Timor & Landau, 1998). Specific conversational features are, however, available also to disrupt and challenge

---

Sequencing The ordering of turns within a conversation

social presumptions of identity. In a study of gay males' conversation, Bunzl (2000) observes that participants frequently refer to other gay males using feminine terms such as "she" or "her." In these interactions, the use of feminine references works both to parody assumptions surrounding gay identities and to challenge socially prevailing notions of heterosexual masculinities.

Social identities, then, both make available and reflect possibilities for individual action in the broader social world. The identities that we take up, manage, and resist carry implications not just for us but also for our relationships with others and for broader patterns of social actions. We have already seen in this chapter a range of examples of the kinds of identity negotiation in which individuals routinely engage, pointing to the fluid nature of identities and the diverse possibilities that are open to people in the contexts in which they located. From this understanding of identities, it is evident that the identities that are relevant to individuals in the ebb and flow of their everyday lives cannot be assumed but instead must be considered in their own terms and in terms of what they accomplish by way of possibilities for action. Take, for example, collective identities. Above we noted that issues of group memberships and the contestation of intergroup rights and obligations commonly took place in contexts where group identities were in dispute: different versions of group identities can be developed, for example, to maintain group distinctiveness or to reduce distance between majority and minority groups. The relevance of particular group identities as the bases of claims, memberships, and the warranting of actions is negotiated according to demands of the interactional context.

Group-based identities, however, are open to the same negotiation as any other identities. The question of what groups might be relevant for making or resisting claims has to be viewed in context and potential identities need not be framed in terms of ethnicity, nationality, or similar features. One collective identity that has received increasing attention of late is that of citizenship. From an external viewpoint, the identity of citizen does not rely explicitly upon the description of group attributes or differences and consequently might be taken to be more socially inclusive than description in which these features are made explicit. Closer inspection, though, shows that

an identity of citizen, like all other identities that we have considered in this chapter, is open to negotiation in context, and further, it is linked to a range of social actions. Findings show that citizenship can be used to argue for or against commonality of interests with other individuals or groups. The question becomes one of when individuals would avow or disavow an identity of citizen and what the effects would be in either case. Studies of British Muslims, for example, indicate that the issue of citizenship is equally as problematic and ambivalent for individuals as are matters of group identities. While some Muslims argue for commonalities with British non-Muslims, others argue against the agreement that citizenship would suggest and the actions, such as electoral participation, that would come from acceptance of such an identity (Hopkins, Reicher, & Kahani-Hopkins, 2003; Kahani-Hopkins & Hopkins, 2002).

Citizenship alternatively can be used to exclude from common interests individuals or groups who do not conform to the actions that might be associated with this identity. One such case is that of new age travelers, whose entitlement to settle in a particular area is often the subject of complaint from neighboring residents. In an analysis of such complaints, made in letters to local council officials, Barnes, Auburn, and Lea (2004) show that local residents claim citizenship for themselves while excluding new-age travelers from any such membership. Deploying citizenship in this way allows the letter writers to present their complaints ostensibly on behalf of a local community and to call for action by the council to remove or prevent any further settlement by travelers in the local area. As with other collective identity therefore, citizenship can be used to define inclusion and exclusion in the community as defined and to provide a basis for claims to differential rights and obligations of individuals and groups. It offers but one example of the ways in which individual identities and actions are bound up with the broader social context within which they are to be found. It is these very considerations of who people are at various points, the consequences of their claims, and the understandings that we have of them that accompany individuals' claims, management, and resistance in their negotiations of identity throughout social life.

Chapter summary

- Certain identities (speaker, listener, telephone caller etc.) are necessary for interaction to happen at all.
- Discursive researchers disagree as to whether or not broader identities within talk, e.g., gun-owner, princess, mother, can be fully understood without taking account of the broader cultural context.
- Collective identities, particularly national identities, rely heavily on descriptions of time and place.
- Social groups and group memberships can be understood in contexts where these are of particular relevance, e.g., arguments for group rights, cultural possibilities available to women.
- A central part of virtual identities is disclosure or non-disclosure of information about the self.
- Individuals not only accept identities that are available, they also can manage or resist identities depending upon the demands of the contexts in which they find themselves.
- Identities do not happen in the abstract. Instead they are linked to possibilities for social action. Even apparently self-apparent identities such as citizen are open to negotiation and can be used to include or exclude others and to argue for appropriate actions and entitlements.

Connections

The links between identities and social action are relevant for understanding much, if not all, of the material covered in this book. See particularly the discussions of groups (Chapter 3), attraction and relationships (Chapter 4), social cognition (Chapter 5), prejudice (Chapter 7), health (Chapter 10), and organizations (Chapter 11).

Activity

Consider again the brief description of the life of Nelson Mandela given at the beginning of this chapter. How might we now more usefully understand his life and who he is, in the light of the contextual description offered, the broader (changing) context of South Africa, his membership of a particular group opposed to prevailing apartheid policies, and the possibilities open to him in terms of his various identities?

Further reading

Antaki, C. & Widdicombe, S. (Eds.) (1998). *Identities in talk*. London and Thousand Oaks, CA: Sage. This edited collection provides a useful introduction to the study of identities in talk and provides a range of examples drawn from a diversity of settings.

Benwell, B. & Stokoe, E. (2006). *Discourse and identity*. Edinburgh: Edinburgh University Press. An accessible and comprehensive guide to the study of identities from different theoretical perspectives. The authors include discussion of conversational and other identities, and of new and emerging forms of identities, such as "newbies."

Widdicombe, S. & Wooffitt, R. (1995). *The language of youth subcultures: Social identity in action*. Hemel Hempstead and New York: Harvester Wheatsheaf. A comprehensive introduction to the ways in which people use language to construct identities and the relationships between individuals, groups, and society.

Chapter 3

Groups

Key terms
Asymmetrical interactions
Conversational repair
Frame
Heterogeneity
Homogeneity
Noticing
Positioning
Reported speech
Second stories
Talk-in-interaction
Worked up

One of the features of social psychology in general which makes it distinctive from other forms of social psychology is its emphasis on the way that the notion of groups or collectivities is in a sense inseparable from the idea of the individual. Groups can be thought of as a collection of individuals who think of themselves, or who are thought of by others, as joined together in some sort of coherent collective. This might be because they share some "basic" social characteristic like nationality, gender, or race. Or it might be because they share some other property such as belonging to the same institution or sharing a particular preference, such as taste in music, or sharing a common fate, such as the inhabitants of a hospital. In these cases, the social group will probably be large in number and most members of the group will never come into contact with the other group members. In other cases, groups might be relatively small collections of people who are bound together by specific social relationships such as family connections or friendship or working relationships. In these cases, group members are likely to come into contact with the other group members and may face a future in which they have to interact with the other group members over extended periods of time.

Because groups are an almost unavoidable facet of social life, many discursive researchers have regarded consideration of group-related discourses as an important element of their analyses, whether this involves an explicit focus on groups as discursive terms in their own right, or a more general attention to the way that categorizations of people in terms of group membership are accomplished. We will see below that the study of groups merges with other central concerns of discursive research such as the study of self and identity and the explanation of prejudice. However, as this chapter unfolds, we will also see that there are other aspects of group structure and function which have drawn the attention of discursive researchers. As members of groups, we all display an interest in what it is like to belong to a group which goes beyond issues of what that group membership says about ourselves and about others. When we talk about and within groups, we can be seen to attend to questions about how similar or different from one another group members are: in other words, how homogeneous or hetero-geneous the group is. We also rely on notions of the specific roles which group membership bestows upon us. In addition to these sorts of structural issues, discursive researchers have also been interested in how groups function. We will pursue that theme here by looking later at two processes which are common in a wide range of group activities: the establishment and maintenance of norms and the discursive complexities of group task performance.

The Impact of Groups

Groups and social representations

For the discursive researcher the focus of interest, when considering social groups, is on how social groups and categories are represented in talk, and what such representations achieve. However, within the discursive research tradition there are a variety of ways in which this research focus is pursued. Some discursive researchers, notably those who adopt the critical discourse analysis approach, are especially interested in how group membership provides an interpretative or ideological framework for the group's members (van Dijk, 1998, 2006a). For the critical discourse analyst, the role of discourse here is in the way that such ideological frameworks are produced and reproduced, or challenged and changed, through talk. Other discursive researchers such as discursive social psychologists and conversation analysts are less willing to adopt the notion that ideological frameworks are useful analytic tools. Instead, they suggest that the way a group of people represents a social issue is, itself, an outcome or product of that group's discursive interactions, rather than a preexisting framework around which those discursive interactions coalesce. This difference in views within the discursive tradition about the impact of social groups on interindividual interaction will surface in later chapters of this book, notably in the chapter on attitudes. For the moment, however, the disagreement in perspectives between the different approaches to discursive research can be neatly encapsulated in the different way they treat the notion of "social representations."

The term "social representations" is best known through the work of Serge Moscovici

(Moscovici, 1984, 2000). Social representations can be thought of as mental constructs, analogous to attitudes or stereotypes, in which elements of a society's beliefs or knowledge about a particular topic are stored. Social representations are taken to have a historical aspect, in that they store previous socially determined ways of thinking about the world. However, they are also said to be open to change, in that changes in society can subsequently result in changes to that society's social representations. They are also assumed to have a prescriptive dimension in that a society's social representations constitute norms for thinking and behavior which the society's members are expected to follow.

Critical discursive analysts have a long-standing interest in the role of social representations. As far back as 1987, van Dijk proposed that such representations are the means by which the content of prejudiced representations of other people are schematically organized (van Dijk, 1987). Since then, social representations have been viewed as an important aspect of the way that societal ideologies are maintained and developed in social interaction (Tileagă, 2005; van Dijk, 1995, 2006a; van der Valk, 2003) In describing how social representations play this role, critical discourse analysts have suggested that in many respects they resemble cognitive schemas (Augoustinos & Walker, 1995; Augoustinos, Walker, & Ngaire, 2006).

Over more or less the same span of time, other discursive researchers have displayed a more critical stance towards social representations as theoretical entities (Condor & Antaki, 1997; McKinlay & Potter, 1987; McKinlay, Potter, & Wetherell, 1993; Potter, 1996a; Potter & Edwards, 1999). According to this latter view, the content of social representations is not independent of the ways in which such content features in **talk-in-interaction**. Representations such as those of race or nationality cannot be thought of as existing outside discursive practices and are, instead, merely one feature of the way that people utilize discourse in pursuing a wide variety of social goals and activities.

Recent research in this area, however, has tended to soften these sorts of theoretical distinctions. For example, Achugar (2004) has suggested, from a critical discourse analytic perspective, that although social representations are bound up with the construction of ingroup and outgroup identities, such representations can be challenged by the way participants use discourse in making sense of their social lives. One way to take this claim is to see it as locating the "dynamic" aspect of social representations in discursive processes. In another example, Drury and Reicher (2000) have illustrated how the idea of social representations can be deployed in discursive analysis of crowd events. This trend is well summed up by Durrheim and Dixon (2005b), who advocate what they describe as a more "relaxed" view to the discourse analyst's use of social representations as a theoretical and methodological tool.

Groups, self, and others

From the perspective of some discursive researchers, it is important to remember that talk of groups often occurs in contexts where a speaker might be pursuing other social actions, such as accomplishing a blaming or providing a warrant for a claim. The discursive researcher's goal is therefore not to divine the influence of social groups on an individual's discourse, but to analyze participants' own characterizations of themselves and others in terms of group memberships, and to reveal how those characterizations are bound up with the participants' other social goals within that local discursive context (Potter, 2003a). This marks out a difference between the discursive perspective and the way that experimental social psychologists such as social identity theorists view groups. For the experimental social psychologist, group labels pick out preexisting features of the social world, allowing the analyst to deploy such labels as independent variables. For discursive researchers such as conversation analysts and discursive psychologists, on the other hand, group labels or categorizations are best thought of as participants' resources which are modified, **worked up**, challenged, or negotiated

Talk-in-interaction Discourse which reflects and is constitutive of the local context of a particular social interaction

Worked up Designing what is said in order to achieve an interactional goal in episodes of talk, especially through categorization talk. One way in which this difference is sometimes expressed is that experimental social psychology views groups as "real" while discursive researchers view groups as "socially constructed."

So one key element to discursive research in this area is the assumption that descriptions of people in terms of the groups they belong to are produced at particular points in discourse for particular reasons. Two different discursive goals are of particular relevance to the discursive researcher. The first is the notion of constructing a sense of self or an identity through claiming membership of or affiliation with a specific social group, and the second is constructing a sense of "the other," especially in contexts of prejudice or discrimination. We saw in the earlier chapter on identity and self (Chapter 2) that one of the ways in which social groups arise in discourse is in the negotiation of identities such as gender or ethnic identities. In particular, the identities which people claim for themselves and others are closely bound up with the ways in which the characteristics of groups and their membership boundaries are worked up in talk. Later on, in the chapter on prejudice (Chapter 7), we will see that a central feature of the expression of discrimination is often the characterization of others as belonging to a group or category of people which is in some way deviant or typified by negative features.

As an example of the way that talk about social groups is bound up with issues of identity, we can turn to Bailey's (2000a), study of how Dominican Americans negotiate what it means to belong to this particular group in a context where Dominican Americans themselves associate this group membership with being "Spanish" or "Hispanic" while others associate it with being "black" or "African American." Bailey notes that in the Dominican Republic, being of African descent is not associated with explicitly racial identifications whereas in the United States, the same heritage is likely to produce identifications based on race. When Dominicans immigrate to the United States, they are therefore faced with a system of social categorization with which they may not be familiar. What this means, says Bailey, is that in everyday situations Dominican Americans find themselves involved

in challenging or resisting forms of racial group-based identification with which they do not agree. One of the ways that Dominican Americans manage interactions of this sort is to establish their ability to speak Spanish as a group membership criterion.

BB: Can you think of a specific time when someone thought you were Black?

JANELLE: I was in the gym, and usually in school I don't really talk in Spanish, and I was talking to some kid in English, and some girl, I guess she was listening, and I said a word in Spanish, and she goes, "Oh my God, you're Spanish." No she goes, "You know Spanish." She thought I was just a Black who knew Spanish. I was like, "I am Spanish." She's like, "Oh my God, I thought you was Cape Verdean or Black." I was like, "No." A lot of people think I'm Black. I don't know, it's usually just little things like that, just people be like, "What are you, Black?" I'm like, "No, I'm Spanish."

(Bailey, 2000b, p. 559)

Bailey argues that Dominican Americans, especially those from low-income neighborhoods, may in their appearance and dress be indistinguishable from local African Americans. However, in interactions where social group membership and identity become relevant, Dominican Americans are able to negate characterizations of themselves as "black" through their strategic use of multiple language varieties, including Spanish.

In the chapter on prejudice later in this book, we will explore in detail how talk of social groups can be interwoven into statements of prejudice about others. The issue is made more complex in that talk about large-scale social groupings such as gender (Peace, 2003) or race (Buttny, 1999) is deployed by the "targets" of the categorization process as well as by those outside the group so categorized. The sorts of things which we will look at there include the ways in which large-scale category labels are bound up with discourses which emphasize the negative properties of the members of that category of people. Thus Edley and Wetherell (2001) have shown how men's talk of women who are feminists veers across a continuum from **positioning** feminists as reasonable to positioning them as dangerous extremists. In another example, Leudar and Nekvapil (2000) looked at the way Romany people are represented in the media. Leudar and Nekvapil were concerned with examining which categories get ascribed to Romanies, how these categorizations are warranted, and how they result in particular features such as criminality and deviance being ascribed to Romany people. They concluded that the descriptions of Romanies produced by their participants were carefully designed both to implicate Romanies in negative activities and, at the same time, to establish that such views were reasonable conclusions from "the facts."

In another study which explored linkages between social group membership and prejudice, LeCouteur, Rapley, and Augoustinos (2001) examined speeches made by Australian politicians including the prime minister, John Howard. This study examined the way in which Howard used category membership discourse to develop and maintain specific social group categorizations. Howard's discourse arose in a context in which disputes had arisen between farming and mining interests in Australia and Aboriginal Australians, who felt that their native titles to tracts of land were being ignored. In 1996, the Wik people had tried to establish their native title claim, and this led to a period during which legislators tried to abolish such rights. LeCouteur and her colleagues describe the way in which Howard seeks to present the native title issue as a conflict between two main groups: the Aboriginal people and Australia's farmers and miners while, at the same time, constructing a version of his government as a neutral problem solver.

LeCouteur and her colleagues suggest that Howard uses his speech to promote the idea that native title to land should be abolished by establishing that these two categories of people are associated with different forms of activity. The category comprising the beneficiaries of the move to extinguish native title, the farmers and miners, is bound to positive, productive activities, while the category comprising the people who will

> Positioning Adopting a stance or voice normatively associated with a category of person

lose out, the Aboriginals, is bound with properties of obstruction, passivity, and dependency.

07 I think we probably also agree on some other things – for example,
08 the Aboriginal and Torres Strait Islander people of Australia have
09 been very badly treated in the past and we must continue our efforts
10 to improve their health, their housing, their employment and their
11 educational opportunities. And in doing that we should always
12 remember that the Aboriginal people of Australia have a very special
13 affinity with their land.
14 I think we would also agree on how important the rural and mining
15 industries are to the future of our country. Between them they
16 contribute 63 per cent of Australia's export income and that helps
17 generate a lot of wealth, which in turn enables us to help the less
18 fortunate within our community.
19 Australia's farmers, of course, have always occupied a very special
20 place in our heart. They often endure the heartbreak of drought, the
21 disappointment of bad international prices after a hard worked season
22 and, quite frankly, I find it impossible to imagine the Australia I love
23 without a strong and vibrant farming sector.
(LeCouteur, Rapley, & Augoustinos, 2001, pp. 43–44)

LeCouteur and her colleagues draw out a number of the discursive features in this extract of Howard's speech. An initial reference to two different socioeconomic groups, "rural and mining industries," is subsequently collapsed into one group label: "Australia's farmers." Those who are identified by means of these categorizations are depicted as active, and as contributing to the future. The group's output, a "lot of wealth," is constructed as being a prerequisite for the helping of Aboriginals. In contrast, the Aboriginals are constructed as passive recipients of treatment by others and as requiring effort from others to improve their health and welfare. Moreover, Howard's admission that Aboriginals have been badly treated in the past makes available the inference that they are not badly treated now. So whereas the group of people identified as "the farmers" is identified with activities useful to Australia's future, Aboriginality is associated with passivity. By producing descriptions of "farmers" and "Aboriginal people" which emphasize their differing levels of contribution to Australia, Howard was able to develop his argument that the farmers ought to be viewed as having rights and entitlements to land which Aboriginal people did not.

At this point, it is important to note three further features of the relationship between group membership and discourse. The first feature is that talk of one's own group membership and talk of other groups is often jointly accomplished within the same discursive context. The second feature is that characterizations of outgroups sometimes include positive elements as well as negative or discriminatory elements. The third feature is that even when discourse is discriminatory, such characterizations may be common across different groups which include both discriminators and the discriminated against.

Jointly accomplishing ingroup and outgroup characterizations

When speakers engage in the discursive construction both of their own groups and of "other" groups to which they do not belong, the establishment of a positive sense of self as reflected in one's group membership often goes hand in hand with the development of a negative evaluation of the "outgroup" other. For example, Oktar (2001) examines the ways in which secular and Islamist media discourses are used in the presentation of self and of the other within Turkey. Both secular and non-secular newspapers rely upon discursive constructions of their own group as having positive attributes such as being tolerant and modern, in the case of secularists, and being honest and having strong beliefs in the case of non-secularists. At the same time, both groups portray the other group as in some way negative. Hence secularists portray non-secularists as reactionary and a threat to the Turkish Republic, while non-secularists portray secularists as oppressive and tyrannical. Such processes are not restricted to the potentially contentious areas of religious faith or nationality. In a study of the

way that scientists view "ordinary" people in the context of discussing genetically modified foods, Cook, Pieri, and Robbins (2004) showed that scientists construct a version of the public which undermines their ability to contribute to the debate by questioning their rationality and objectivity.

A similar process can be observed in MacMillan and Edwards's (1999) study of press reports on the death of Diana, Princess of Wales, in a car accident in 1997. Following the death of the princess, a national debate arose in the United Kingdom over the extent to which press intrusion into the life of the princess was responsible for her accident. One of the points that MacMillan and Edwards make is that the British press were concerned with demonstrating that they were not culpable. However, the circumstances of the accident included the fact that the princess was apparently being hounded by press photographers at the time of the accident, which might be taken to imply that it was the actions of the press which led, in part, to the accident taking place.

1   At times she was confused
2   And the line became blurred.
3   But there was a standard of privacy and
4   Basic decency which did prevail
5   The same, we now know only too sadly, did not hold
6   for those photographers called "the paparazzi"
          (MacMillan & Edwards, 1999, pp. 156–157)

In this extract, taken from an article in the United Kingdom newspaper the *Daily Mirror* which was written by a British press photographer, the British press man attempts to draw a distinction between two groups of people: "regular" press photographers and the "paparazzi." The former group are identified as conforming to moral codes of privacy and decency. A contrast is then drawn between "we" on the one hand and "those" paparazzi on the other, with the paparazzi being positioned as outside the group which upheld "basic decency."

The inclusion of positive features in portraying the outgroup

In Oktar's study, the participants produced positive evaluations of their own groups and negative evaluations of the groups to which "the other" belonged. However, it is worthwhile noting that evaluative distinctions of this sort often arise in a more complex form. Holt and Griffin (2005) looked at the way that issues of social class differences arose in young, middle-class adults' talk about leisure activities and settings such as pubs, bars, and clubs. One of their findings was that their participants constituted the working class as "the other."

ALAN: : : :y'know when you go into the Banks's pub, an Ansells pub, a Firkin pub, y'know or an O'Neill's, you know what it's gonna be like because they control the, the atmosphere in there so precisely, basically it kills it, and um, and so because you go well, y'know I know some of these pubs, these y'know : : : there's the one round where I used to live, um y'know it's like it's just this, it's a prison basically [laughs], where all the inmates went y'know every Friday night and had a fight, and like you just didn't go in there, sort of thing, and when people did they got, they got thrown out before the fight started in case they got killed or something . . .

DAN: Where's that?

ALAN: : : :um it's just round, there's this housing estate just, just round the corner from where I used to live . . .

DAN: In [the city]?

ALAN: : : :in, yeah in um, in Harborne, Quinton area, which of course y'know, you get that kind of, you get that kind of thing in those pubs cos they're not controlled, they're not sort of, y'know there's no corporate . . .

TOM: There's no bouncers

ALAN: : : :exactly, there's no [laughs], in fact if there are, they're starting the fight, and so like y'know it's sort of an unknown quantity, you feel like "oh God, y'know what am I stepping into here," y'know, it's like a dangerous sport to go into these, into these places, um, but once you go in there and you find it's okay, then it's like such a much more rewarding experience than : : :

TOM: It's much more rewarding, but you have to make the effort in the first place : : :

ALAN: Yeah, yeah : : :

(Holt & Griffin, 2005, p. 261)

In this extract, Alan offers two different formulations of "pubs." One sort of pub is predictable but lacking in atmosphere. The other sort is described as being like a prison where fights break out. By specifying that this pub is located near to a housing estate (housing project), Alan is indicating that the pub's regular clientele are working-class people. Alan and Tom then jointly work up a characterization of the working-class pub as both dangerous and yet rewarding because of the absence of predictability, which is a feature of other pubs. In this way, say Holt and Griffin, the working class are characterized by Alan and Tom as both to be feared and yet also in some sense desirable.

Common discourses of discrimination

Holt and Griffin demonstrate that not only do members of a group offer positive assessments of their own group, sometimes people who are not members of that group also offer positive evaluations too. More surprising, perhaps, is the finding that just as people may seek to warrant or support discrimination against an outgroup, the same sort of discourse can be noted among members of the group which is the target of such discrimination. For example, in a study of discrimination in Holland, Verkuyten (2005a) has shown that both Dutch people and members of ethnic minorities rely upon similar forms of explanation for why discrimination exists in Holland.

1 HENK: I don't know what causes it. Well, I guess it's in people's nature. It, it's as
2 old as man himself.
3 INTERVIEWER: It's not typically Dutch?
4 HENK: That is, no.
5 GERDA: No, definitely no. I think it happens abroad, too.
6 HENK: Yes, it certainly does happen abroad.
(Verkuyten, 2005a, p. 80)

1 FATMA: But we discriminate, too, Turkish people against Dutch people.
2 NEZAHAT: Yeah, discrimination . . .
3 FATMA: Too, against the Dutch.
4 NEZAHAT: And, er, against Surinamese and Moroccans.
5 FATMA: We even discriminate among ourselves, among Turkish people.
(Verkuyten, 2005a, p. 84)

The first of the extracts presented above comes from an interview with Dutch people, the second from an interview with members of an ethnic minority. Verkuyten points out the way in which both extracts are organized around a common theme of discrimination being in some senses a universal human phenomenon and therefore something which people have to just accept.

Summary

Discursive researchers are interested in how social groups feature in discourse. One area of interest here is the question of how descriptions of social groups, and attributions of group membership, are used to establish a sense of self and to characterize others. Such characterizations are often bound up with other discursive goals such as presenting a positive sense of self or a negative sense of "the other." But discursive research reveals that evaluations associated with characterizations of one's own group and others' groups are not always this clear cut. The analyst's task is made more complex by the facts that often characterizations of "the other" are interwoven with characterizations of the self and that members of different groups often rely upon the same sorts of discursive strategies in their talk.

Group Cohesion

Because group membership has important consequences for the way that we see ourselves and others, members of groups can often be seen to engage in establishing the extent to which their group is perceived by its members to be a cohesive one. One of the features of discourse within groups which has been examined here is the way in which participants rely upon discursive strategies in order to establish or maintain group cohesion. For example, Barton (1999) examined the repeated use of slogans and sayings in a support group for parents of children with disabilities. The purpose of the group was to allow its members to gain information on special education law as it applies to public schools in the United States. Barton notes that one of the functions of repeating the group's slogans was to promote informational exchange. But in addition she notes that group members also used repetition of the

slogans as a means of promoting and enhancing group solidarity.

However, as we have already pointed out, discursive interaction often involves interweaving a number of different social goals or actions. This is well demonstrated in Jaworski and Coupland's (2005) study of gossiping. They note that gossip is used by group members as a means of promoting social solidarity and cohesion within the group. However, the way in which gossip is used to achieve this group cohesion is by a process of "othering" of the sort described above when we discussed Oktar's study of secularism and non-secularism in Turkey. They suggest that gossiping helps to reinforce group coherence and identity by negotiating the "fuzzy edges" of social categories through a process of criticizing those others who in some way or another fall outside the group's boundaries. This sort of talk functions to promote coherence and solidarity within the group by helping to establish who "we" are in contrast with who "they" are. An example of this is seen in the following extract fragment, where a group of friends are gossiping about a visit by a pest-controller to the flat of one of the speakers, Tom.

30	TOM:	he goes like (.) he goes ah you got to make sure you to fill in the
31		hole <u>properly</u> (.) cos if you leave a little hole like that (.) he said they can
32		<u>squeeze</u> <u>through</u> little holes like that see
		[
33		[loud laughter]
34	TOM:	cos they have a
	[	
35	JIM:	<u>big</u> rat like that
36	TOM:	[laughing] he goes he goes cos they haven't got any <u>bones</u>
37		[loud laughter]
38	TOM:	[high pitched] I said you <u>what</u>? [laughs] they haven't got any <u>bones</u> (.)
39		<u>course</u> they got bloody <u>bones</u> wouldn't be able to <u>move</u> otherwise like (.) .
40		and he goes [voicing] ^oh well they haven't got any <u>backbone</u>& ((3 syll))
41		[all laugh loudly]
42	TOM:	it's crazy and I went alright then mate
43	JIM:	[seriously] haven't they got a <u>backbone</u>?
44	TOM:	[splutters] <u>yes</u> course they have
		[
45	CHRIS:	course

CLASSIC STUDY: Discreet indiscretions: The social organization of gossip

Bergmann begins this text by outlining the importance of gossip as a social scientific area of interest. He moves on to a discussion of genres as an analytic concept and then applies this notion to gossip as a topic. As a communicative genre, gossip, like other forms of communication, can be thought of as a fixed or "routine" approach through which participants relate to and solve social problems. He points out that gossip as a form of talk relies upon specific social relations. For example, news about a woman's infidelity might count as gossip when it is passed between two of her neighbors, but not when it is passed from her husband to her husband's lawyer. Embedded within these relations, gossip incorporates a particular triadic structure involving the subject of the gossip, and its producers and recipients. Gossip can also be considered to be "socially embedded." It can arise in a variety of contexts from the "idle" group who have nothing better to do than attend to whatever counts

as newsworthy to the busy workgroup. However, gossipers are aware of the "idle" and indeed morally dubious nature of their actions, according to Bergmann, and so they tend to **frame** their gossip as something that "accidentally" arises out of other activities. As noted in this chapter, gossip may play a role in establishing group solidarity. But Bergmann argues that as a social phenomenon gossip transcends this single function. For the central contradiction in gossip is that while gossipers may display solidarity with one another, at the same time they may be discussing an absent acquaintance or friend in a way which might seem to display lack of solidarity. So gossip represents what can be thought of as a "moral balancing act": a "paradoxical" process in which loyalty structures are both maintained and yet questioned.

Bergmann, J. R. (1993). *Discreet indiscretions: The social organization of gossip*. New Jersey: Aldine Transaction.

46 JIM: why did he say that then?
47 TOM: cos he come from Cardiff and he's <u>thick</u>
           [laughing] that's why
                              (Jaworski & Coupland, 2005,
                                            pp. 679–680)

Jaworski and Coupland note that the "other" in this story, the pest-controller, is portrayed in a negative light as someone who is foolish. This is marked by the laughter which appears at a number of points in the sequence and by Tom's assessment at line 47 where the pest-controller is described as "thick" (stupid). The outgroup status of the pest-controller is also emphasized by Tom, who specifies that he derives from a particular city, Cardiff, to which the group members do not belong. In this narrative, the stupidity of the pest-controller is located in his apparent belief that rats do not have bones. However, at line 43, Jim implies that he is uncertain as to whether this is true or not. But whereas ascrip-

tion of this belief to the pest-controller resulted in his denigration, when Jim implies that he may hold the same belief, the other group members withhold criticism or ridicule, and treat Jim's question merely as a request for factual information. In this way, Tom and Chris are able to establish the "otherness" of the pest-controller while, at the same time, maintaining solidarity with Jim as a member of the group.

It is noteworthy that the episode of gossip described in Jaworski and Coupland's study involved Tom in recounting a narrative or story. It turns out that storytelling is an important resource in the formation and development of group coherence. Lehtinen (2005), for example, has looked at the way that the members of a Bible study group

Frame A term deriving initially from Goffman to indicate participants' organization of their experiences into recognizable activities

relied upon second stories in order to demonstrate similarity between their own experiences and those of other members of the group. **Second stories** are interactional turns which follow on from a preceding story and are designed to be recognizably relevant to that preceding story. In the Bible study group, participants designed their contributions so that they were hearably addressing issues which were associated with the contents of the Bible and were also categorizable as matters of importance to their fellow group members. In another study, Arminen (2004b) examined the ways in which members of an Alcoholics Anonymous self-help group used storytelling as a means of building and developing their interrelationships. In particular, he looked at the ways in which second stories were used by the group members to provide support for prior speakers. The following extract occurs at a point where the speaker, Ari, has been telling a second story about experiencing hallucinations in response to a prior story recounted by Mari about a family accident occasioned while she was drunk.

25 .hhh u:h (.) <u>i</u>t was something wholly (0.8) horrible.
26 (.) >I've'n't<ever (0.2) b<u>e</u>fore <u>e</u>xperienced such a thing
27 .hhh and ↑at th<u>a</u>t point (0.2) when Mari (.) told about the
28 (.) .hhh agony of s<u>ou</u>l (1.0) so I e– realized that
29 .hhh Mari meant thi:s point, (.) also (0.7) and I<identified>
30 with that. (1.0) .hhh It i::s (0.2) u:hhh the kind of condition, (0.5)
31 .hhh that you can't really (0.6) describe with w<u>o</u>rds.(1.5)
32 There's only one <cha::nce>.(0. 5) to <u>e</u>xperience, (1.0)

(Arminen, 2004b, p. 327)

The extract begins at the point where Ari has concluded his story with the upshot that his experience was "wholly horrible." Although Mari's story was about a family accident, and Ari's story was about having hallucinations, Ari implies that their experiences were similar because of their

unpleasant nature. This is stressed through his use of the phrase "agony of the soul" and by his claim at line 29 that Mari meant the same thing as he did by his story. In this way, Arminen concludes, Ari relies upon the second story device to display empathy for and solidarity with Mari both through the act of aligning his story to Mari's and by suggesting that they share a commonality of experience. This idea that group interaction is a context in which shared understandings of the world can be developed and explored is also shown in Bulow's (2004) study of group discussions among sufferers of chronic fatigue syndrome. Bulow shows how the patients in his study used joint co-narration (Norrick, 2004) to produce "collectivized" stories which reproduced shared elements of their experiences of suffering from the illness.

Of course, just as group cohesion can be thought of as a discursive accomplishment, so can its opposite, group fragmentation. A number of discursive studies have examined the ways in which interactions within groups lead to the temporary formation of sub-groups or "teams" of group members who discursively work together as a group discussion unfolds. For example, in a study of "supportive alignment" in conversation, Gordon (2003) identifies a number of ways in which sub-groups of conversants within a group context can supportively align their conversational contributions with one another such as sharing in the construction of conversational turns or producing a sequence of turns which are all based on the same background of implicit or shared knowledge. Of particular relevance here is the fact that these sorts of alignment practices can lead to opposition within groups. In a study of committee meeting talk, Kangasharju (2002) shows how such oppositional alignment practices arise.

```
01 MARJA A  ((looks at her watch))
02          We've been here half an hour and
03          got nothing done.
04 EEVA B   °Well we've gone°
05 SIRKKA C Well we've
06          g[one through these (.) timetables so
            that]
[ ]
07 LEENA D  [We've got a lot done ]
08          (that's already a little) (–)
```

> **Second stories** Conversational turns which have a narrative element and which follow on from, and are oriented to, stories produced in preceding turns

09 (1.8)
10 MARJA A °.Yeah° .Hhh
(Kangasharju, 2002, pp. 1452–1453)

Marja's initial turn can be heard as a complaint, possibly targeted at the chair of the meeting, Leena. The subsequent turns of Eeva, Sirkka, and Leena are co-constructed, in that Eeva and Sirkka jointly produce a claim about having gone through timetables, which Leena then glosses as the claim that they have got a lot done. Kangasharju notes that Marja subsequently appears to back away from her original complaint, and concludes that in this instance the "team" which arises out of the alignment of Eeva, Sirkka, and Leena has therefore accomplished its local goal within this part of the conversation.

Summary

One of the concerns that people display in their group interactions is the idea that the group should be cohesive. Group members may overtly display this through the joint use of discursive items like slogans. However, examination of the detail of conversational interactions within groups reveals that group members also design their utterances in part as a display of solidarity or empathy with other group members. However, such displays can prove to be a "double-edged sword," because the solidarity and support which such discursive techniques achieve can sometimes be limited to sub-groups within the group as a whole.

Group Structure

The ascription of positive or negative evaluations and the establishment of group cohesion are not the only forms of group-related interactional business in which speakers engage. Discursive researchers have also examined the way participants negotiate structural properties of the group, such as group homogeneity and group roles. However, just as the examination of self- and other-evaluations demonstrated that social groups can be thought of as socially constructed, so too researchers in these other areas have shown that the social properties ascribed to groups such

as homogeneity may likewise be the result of discursive formulation and negotiation.

Homogeneity and heterogeneity

The idea that members of a group should somehow be **homogeneous** – similar to one another – is an important element in the way we think of ourselves as group members. Blommaert, Creve, and Willaert (2006), for example, have described the sorts of pressures which immigrants face to assimilate to a different culture when they reach their new home. In a study of immigrants in Belgium, they showed that immigrants are socially judged on the extent to which they entered the homogeneous culture of the Dutch speaker. They point out that these immigrants were practically treated as illiterate if they were unable to cope with spoken and written Dutch, even if they were highly proficient in a number of other languages.

In this study, there was a clear dimension, the ability to use the Dutch language, along which group homogeneity could be established. However, Bishop and Jaworski (2003) have pointed to the way in which a group's homogeneity can arise out of talk about the group as a constructive achievement. They examined press coverage of a soccer game between the national teams of England and Germany during the European Football Championships in 2000. They noted that football supporters who were engaged in civic disturbances were "othered" in that they were distinguished from "normal" English supporters and marginalized as problematic and different. But this effect was achieved within a context in which the press constructed a sense of the entire nation engaging with these sporting events by formulating a version of the nation as a single, unified, and homogeneous collective. This was achieved by means of a variety of discursive devices, such as the invoking of national stereotypes and shared history and the evocation of the nation as a timeless entity stretching from the past into the future.

> **Homogeneity** A term used to describe a collection or group of people or things whose members are similar

LET'S WELLY THEM KEV!

England stay in Waterloo 185 years after Iron Duke's win

Kevin Keegan's lionhearts will be roaring into battle against Germany today – after spending the night at WATERLOO.

The England squad checked into the plush Grand Hotel at the historic Belgium town made famous by the Duke of Wellington's stunning defeat of Napoleon in 1815.

And they will take to the field at nearby Charlerois almost 185 years to the day after the Iron Duke led his troops to victory.

(Bishop & Jaworski, 2003, p. 252)

Bishop and Jaworski suggest that the pronominal use of "us" (in "let's," a contraction of "let us") and "them" helps to distinguish and make exclusive the English as the assumed reader's ingroup and the Germans as an outgroup. In addition, English national history is invoked in the headline and the sub-headline, both of which make reference to a famous military victory in which the English Duke of Wellington defeated the French Napoleon, and this militaristic language is continued in the body of the text through the description of Keegan's England team acting as "lionhearts" who will be "roaring into battle." Bishop and Jaworski further note that by utilizing a reference to a military victory, the author also seeks to address the reader's sense of national pride, which is supported by the description of that victory as "stunning." What this shows, say Bishop and Jaworski, is that press reports of this sort rely upon common-sense notions of uniformity and conformity in which the formulation of national identity, implicitly ascribed to the reader, is one which emphasizes the ingroup's homogeneity.

Just as group homogeneity can be considered to be a discursive achievement, so can its opposite, group **heterogeneity** (the idea that members of a group are dissimilar). In a study of how

political groups are represented in the media, Lauerbach (2006) looked at the way television commentators rely upon **reported speech** formulations in order to imply that political parties contain divisions within them. His data are drawn from television commentary on the night of the 1997 British general election. The British Labour Party at that time was typified by strong party discipline, and as the election results came in, it was apparent that the party was heading for a landslide political victory. Accordingly, there were few critical or dissenting voices within the party. However, the television interviewer was able to use reported speech devices to imply that, nevertheless, dissent did exist. In identifying these devices, Lauerbach draws in particular on Goffman's (1974) notion of "ventriloquizing," which he describes as a form of "mock-representation." Ventriloquizing will be a familiar phenomenon to the parents of prelinguistic infants or to the owners of pets. For example, suppose someone, AMcK, owns a dog called "Truffle." If AMcK wishes to avoid walking the dog, he might say to his wife, "Truffle says 'It is too rainy to walk today.'" In this example, AMcK is ventriloquizing by formulating a claim he wishes to make as though it has been uttered by his dog. Lauerbach notes that this sort of ventriloquizing is also put into use by television journalists as a vivid way of "enacting" one's own discourse through someone else.

> JD But your/your people (.) Ha/ Harriet Harman in/in your area which is a very (.) uhm deprived area of London, one **might** expect that they would be **frustrated** by New Labour and might say
> "'Why can't we have (.) more taxes in order to fund better services, why can't the rich be socked (.) so that we can have more resources here'" and you're not/you don't get that at all?
> (Lauerbach, 2006, p. 208)

In this fragment of an extract, the television interviewer, JD, is suggesting that the Labour politician who is being interviewed, Harriet

---

Heterogeneity A term used to describe a collection or group of people or things whose members are not similar

Reported speech Discourse in which the speaker deploys actual (or apparent) literal repetition of previously made statements

Harman, faces dissent among her own constituents. One of the advantages of ventriloquizing, says Lauerbach, is that it allows the speaker to invent quotes which are nevertheless presented not merely as inventions, but rather as the sort of thing which some other person or agent might say or think. In the present case, JD relies upon this device to suggest that his own criticism is in fact one that might be raised by Harman's "own people." In this way, the interviewer was able to imply that Harman's Labour supporters were more heterogeneous in their views that the landslide Labour victory might otherwise have suggested.

Roles within the group

One noteworthy feature of group interactions is that the nature of a participant's contribution to the group may be influenced by that participant's role within the group. Possession of particular types of roles can provide the role holder with certain rights and entitlements which other group members do not have. This relationship between group role and interactional contributions is noted by Jingree, Finlay, and Antaki (2006), who examined verbal interactions between care staff and people with learning disabilities. The occasions in which these interactions took place were a set of residents' meetings in a residential center. The official rationale for such meetings included empowering clients and allowing them to have a say in the running of their own lives by attempting to involve people with learning disabilities in decision-making about their own lives. However, the authors note that in practice such interactions are often **asymmetrical**, due to power differentials arising out of status differences and imbalances of knowledge and communicative abilities. One of the ways that power differentials were manifested in the meetings centered on the way that staff negotiated group roles such as acting as chair of the meeting or engaging in a teaching role. These sorts of roles are, of

Asymmetrical interactions Episodes in which participants differ in socially relevant ways, e.g., formal position or status

course, associated with interactional requirements such as getting through the agenda and checking that everyone has a say, and checking and rehearsing residents' knowledge. However, Jingree, Finlay, and Antaki found that such leadership roles meant that the actual conversational practices within the group were at odds with the official rationale. As one example of this, they noted the way in which staff members used the residents' meeting interactions in order to produce affirmations of the service philosophies which underlay the work of the center. One of the ways the staff members achieved this was by asking the residents questions and then offering up to the residents candidate answers.

375 ANN What's your relationship with your care
         worker Natalie?
376 NAT Ees er I dunno
377 ANN What's ee there for?
378 KAT Help
379 ANN: um
380 KAT HELP
381 ANN talk to
382 NAT yeah
383 ANN and do you go and talk to him?
384 NAT talk to her
385 ANN t her
386 NAT yeah
387 MEL What kind of relationship do you have
         with her, dear?
388 NAT Alright
389 MEL umm?
390 NAT Sh [e she she's alright
391 TIM [coughs
392 MEL She's alright.
393 NAT Yeah
394 ANN so she's a friend
395 NAT yeah she's a [friend
               (Jingree, Finlay, & Antaki, 2006, p. 223)

In this extract, Natalie, one of the residents, is the speaker who has been nominated by a staff member to talk about the relationship between residents and their key workers. Jingree, Finlay, and Antaki point out that the contribution of one of the other residents, Kathy, is ignored by the staff member, Ann, who instead focuses attention on Natalie. When Natalie does not produce a response, Ann offers up a candidate response, that key workers are there for residents to "talk to," with which Natalie agrees. When Natalie is asked by one of the other staff to describe her relationship with her key worker, her description of her as "alright" is upgraded by Ann to "she's a friend," with which Natalie then agrees. What interactional sequences of this sort reveal, say Jingree, Finlay, and Antaki, is that the official rationale of the center, which is one of empowering residents and allowing them to have their own say, is subverted by the actual practices by means of which this rationale is meant to be carried out.

However, the influence of roles on group interaction is not limited to those which are bestowed on group members as a function of their membership of the group. For example, in a study of rural agricultural collectives in Zanzibar, Hanak (1998) has shown how the organizational role of chairwoman was used by one of her participants to control the topics under discussion as well as to allocate interactional turns. But Hanak also shows that this sort of organizational position is not the only relevant role in group discussion. In one of the collective's discussions, the chairwoman's role was usurped by a visiting government official, a fact which was reflected in the adoption by the chairwoman of more "powerless" forms of speech. So the contribution of roles to the unfolding of group interactions turns out to be a complicated affair in which roles associated with position within the group may come into conflict with other roles which derive from a speaker's wider societal position. This is also reflected in a study by Abu-Akel (2002), who has examined the way that conversational topic is controlled during family dinnertime interactions. He suggests that the question of which topics are adopted and developed, and which topics introduced but abandoned, is determined in part both by power relations within the family and by wider societal norms associated with gender roles.

In some instances of group interaction, then, what participants say and how they say it is influenced by the sorts of roles which are bestowed on them by their membership of the group. But it is important to note that in many forms of group interaction, the nature of group roles is, in itself, a discursive outcome of the group's talk. For example, Thornborrow (2003) examined the way in which a group of schoolchildren, comprising older children, aged 10 or

11, and younger children, aged 7 or 8, collaborated on an educational task. Thornborrow points out that during these interactions the children used task-based interactions to manage shared understandings about normative issues within the school context and to negotiate locally relevant identities, such as the distinctions between older boys and younger boys in terms of what they might be expected to understand. However, Thornborrow also notes that the older children adopted specific group-relevant roles by aligning themselves as "instructors." They accomplished this by adopting ways of talking that are typical of the way that teachers routinely talk to schoolchildren, which allowed them to "instruct" the younger children on both the task itself and on wider social issues. One example of this was the use of **conversational repair**. MacBeth (2004) has argued that in the classroom, repair is often used in order to establish that all of the participants share a common understanding of what is being talked about. In the present case, Thornborrow shows how conversational repair of this sort is bound up with establishing the roles which group members are currently adopting:

```
211  FRED:  okay, I'm doing this one (.)
212         'kay this is call (.) the (.)
213         °what does that say William°
214  JOSH:  (the)
215  FRED:  I think I could (.) huh
216  WILL:  the scheduling [section
217  JOSH:            [the scheduling [section ((reading))
218  FRED:                           [scheduling OY
219         (.)
220  FRED:  right
221         (.)
222  FRED:  you have some (.) parcels to take to the
             town                        ((reading))
                        (Thornborrow, 2003, p. 14)
```

In this extract, the boys are reading out some of the task instructions. The repair section begins with a request at line 213 from one of the older boys, Fred, which is directed to one of the other older boys, William. This is followed by

> **Conversational repair** An element of a conversational sequence which addresses problems of mis-speaking, mis-hearing, or misunderstanding

William providing information on how to pronounce the difficult phrase "scheduling section." But as William formulates his response, Josh, one of the younger boys, also begins to read out the phrase. Fred interrupts and halts Josh's turns by issuing the loud reprimand "OY" (a colloquial expression used in the United Kingdom indicating that someone should stop what he or she is currently doing). Thornborrow suggests that in this brief passage, Fred first adopts the position of instructor by reading out the task instructions. He then moves out of this role in order to direct a request for help from William, who then adopts the instructor position. But when the younger boy seeks to provide the requested information, Fred readopts the instructor role by stopping Josh from speaking and then moving on to read out the next element of the task.

Summary

The structural properties of a social group can often be thought of as discursive accomplishments. When people present a group as homogeneous or heterogeneous, for example, this is bound up with other local discursive goals such as establishing identity or formulating criticisms. Membership of a group can be associated with adopting or holding specific roles and these roles may have an influence on the way that the group interaction unfolds. However, like other properties of a group, the nature of the roles which group members adopt may itself be an outcome of discursive interaction within the group.

Group Function

Group norms

One of the features of group membership which distinguishes it from other forms of social life is the participants' understanding that being a member of the group involves one in following the group's explicit or implicit rules. For this reason, one important aspect of group function is the development and maintenance of the rules by which the group is regulated. Arminen (2004a) explored this notion in a study of the way that explicit institutional rules are negotiated. This study was based in a clinic in Finland whose

clients were undergoing substance addiction therapy. The clinic relied upon group discussion sessions in which clients were able to present their own stories and discuss the problems and opportunities which they faced. The group discussion sessions were organized by reference to a set of rules which dealt with the question of how participants should talk and behave within their therapeutic group. These rules, which were written out on tables hung on the clinic walls, included items such as a prohibition on food and drink being consumed during group sessions and the injunction that group members should only talk one at a time. The interactions observed within the study involved group therapy sessions in which the rules were being explained to newcomers to the clinic. Arminen found that as these rules were presented to the newcomers and discussed by the group, some of the rules were formulated as rigid and non-negotiable. Others were described in such a way that they were presented as open or susceptible to negotiation. In the following extract, a senior group member, S, is explaining to a newcomer, T, the rule that only one person should talk at a time:

```
1    S:  that's y'know is somewhat clear though
2        t[hat,
3    T:  [Of course yeah,=
4        [T turns towards table of rules
5    S:  =.hhhhh Erm (0.3) we'll talk one at a time,h
6        (0.5)((T turns towards S))
7    S:  of course °and,° hhh
8        (0.7)((T nods))
9    S:  ↓No one I guess has
10       become mad here if someone has commented on things.=
```
                              (Arminen, 2004a, pp. 689–690)

Arminen notes that at lines 9 and 10, the senior group member introduces a context in which group members might comment on one another's contributions. By phrasing this in terms of the past tense, the senior member implies that such events have, in fact occurred. Moreover, his use of "I guess" indicates that obeying the rule is, in any event, a conditional event and that there is some doubtfulness attached to whether the rule is or is not followed. In addition, the senior group member's description of this potential rule transgression as something that "no one" would become mad about carries the inference that such transgressions are sanctioned by the group as a whole. So even where group rules are explicit and publicly represented, Arminen concludes, the nature of group interactions is such that a group's rules are on many occasions susceptible to reformulation and renegotiation as the business of such interactions unfolds. It is worth noting here that this respecification of group norms was accomplished by a senior member of the group, whose role as senior member offered him particular rights and entitlements. This is an example of the way that group function is sometimes influenced by group structure.

Group tasks

Some of the groups we have considered above, such as ethnic or religious groups, could be classed as "large" groups, while other groups we have examined might be thought of as "small" groups such as committee meetings or self-help groups. Of course, as we saw in the discussion of group roles, the properties of the large-scale groups sometimes impinge on the nature of the interaction within small groups. Thus small group interaction may be influenced by large group, societal power relations grounded in gender or familial roles of the sort discussed by Abu-Akel (2002) or in institutional roles of the sort discussed by Jingree, Finlay, and Antaki (2006). However, one of the distinctions between large, social groups and small groups is that the latter can often be thought of as functioning to perform specific, group-related tasks. For this reason, discursive researchers who have examined the workings of small groups have been especially interested in how those groups manage their talk in relation to the task at hand.

In a conversation-analytic study of small group task coordination within the school room, Szymanski (1999) observed third grade students who were arranged into groups of four and who were involved in common reading and writing tasks. Szymanski notes that their conversational interactions displayed a clear orientation to the task in which they were engaged, with the students alternately conversing together and then lapsing into periods of silence as they each performed their individual elements of the task. In particular, the students could be seen to deal with two inter-

actional issues: how to accomplish reengaging in talk after a lapse, and how to end periods of talk to generate such lapses. Reengagement in talk was managed by speakers in a number of ways, such as asking questions or "**noticing**" something about the environment, which made relevant a response from others such as an answer or an agreement. Disengagement, on the other hand, was accomplished by the production of sequence-completing actions which left open the possibility that a next action might not be produced. For example, one of the ways in which lapses in conversation arose was when students returned to their individual tasks. So one of the ways in which the participants managed disengagement was to introduce comments which made the group's task relevant, and thereby established the possibility that speakers might not engage in a next conversational turn, but instead allow the conversation to lapse by returning to the task.

```
1     ((Y and D are writing))
2  G: who invented electricity,
3  S: she did.
4  Y: ((to D)) what are: (.) you doing,
5  G: ((shakes head "no")) Abraham Lincoln
6     ((G laughs then S laughs))
7  S: [Abraha:m Lincoln
8  Y: (R.>) but [their bodies (<R)
9     ((Teacher stands across room, watching
10    table, she hesitates then starts walking
11    toward table))
12    (.)
13 Y: (R>) WERE [(.) not intelligent. (<R)
14 G:       [you're finished?
15    (1.0) ((Teacher turns away from their table))
16 S: ((looks at papers in front of her))
17    I have to check something=
18 G: =y' have to wait for us ((reorients to work))
                              (Szymanski, 1999, p. 14)
```

Szymanski notes that in this extract, G and S laugh at G's non-serious response to his own question about the inventor of electricity. Their laughter draws the attention of the teacher who moves towards them. However, G then introduces talk about the task by referring to S's position

Noticing Making some feature of the environment salient or relevant to the present discursive context in the task. The importance of this move, says Szymanski, is that a turn which comments on someone's position within the task evokes the group as a collective of people working independently on a joint task. And formulating someone's position in the task makes the other participants accountable for their own positions within the task. So one way for participants to produce conversational disengagement and a return to the task is to make precisely these sorts of "position-in-the-task" comments.

In the extract from Szymanski's study, there was a neat division between "on-task" talk and "off-task" talk, with "on-task" talk being used to guide the participants' actions back to performance of the task. However, other studies have shown that the relationship between "on-task" talk and "off-task" talk can be more complex than this, and that these forms of talk can have more complex roles to play than in merely separating out actions which are task related from those that are not. For example, "on-task" talk and "off-task" talk are sometimes bound up with structural issues of group cohesion and with functional issues of maintaining group norms. In a school-based study by Davies (2003), the forms of talk arising out of collaborations among members of all-boys or all-girls groups were compared. We saw earlier that on occasion group members will rely upon narratives or storytelling as a means of establishing group coherence. In her study, Davies notes that participants in the all-girls groups could be seen to participate in the collaborative co-construction of narratives and other forms of "friendship talk" in order to display a shared sense of common goals while accomplishing tasks. Davies notes that this form of collaborative achievement was replaced in all-boys groups by "distancing tactics" in which the boys used off-task comments to police contributions in order to assess the extent to which they complied with the norms of "masculine" behavior. In particular, among the boys a high level of perceived commitment to school expectations on task performance was often criticized as not being sufficiently masculine.

242	ANDY	What are we on?/
243	PIERRE	Part three/<high voice>
244	KIRK	<u>Ooooh</u>/ <two tone high pitch in mockery of Pierre>

245	PIERRE	The sun dazzling through the leaves [like orange -/
	KIRK	[Pierre Pierre
246	PIERRE	[**and things it's gorgeous/**
	KIRK	|shut up/I'm not bothered/<high pitched mimicry>
247	PIERRE	And the yellow gold/
248	KIRK	You're just stupid you/
249	PIERRE	And a GOLDEN GALAXY/erm/
250	KIRK	Shut up Pierre/
255	ANDY	Listen to him/Listen to him/oh God/
256	KIRK	**He'll shut up now cos he's gonna smell it/**
257	ANDY	**Oh God!/**
258	KIRK	Oh [God
	PIERRE	[**Like crystals like with all colours coming out of it/**
259	KIRK	See?/do you HAVE to speak like that and moving your hands about like a queer?<laughs>/

(Davies, 2003, pp. 126–127)

The boys in this extract have the task of discussing a poem. Pierre's contributions deploy a sophisticated vocabulary to describe the poem's contents. However, his descriptions are interrupted by Andy and Kirk, and Kirk then concludes by offering an assessment of Pierre which questions his allegiance to heterosexual, masculine norms of behavior. In this way, Davies concludes, the boys were able to use discourse rising out of the task at hand in order to display gender allegiances, just as the girls were able to demonstrate ingroup allegiance by means of their collaborative behaviors.

Another element of group structure which can arise in task-related activities is the negotiation of group roles. For example, in the Thornborrow study (2003) above, Thornborrow describes the way in which the children indulged in off-task talk as well as talk focused on the task itself as a means of organizing group roles:

31	WILL:	'kay right (.) route one
32	??:	wait
33	WILL:	route route one
34		leave the headquarters [building by the front [exit
35	JOSH:	[route [route one?
36	WILL:	route one.
37	JOSH:	huh? (.) there's a shop called route one (.)
38		that sells rally (clothes) (.) and

39   (1.2)
40   FRED: don't worry about that [you fool
41   WILL: [(>c'mon hurry up 'kay<)
42   WILL: leave the (.)
43   ??:   ssh=
44   WILL: =headquarters building by the front
             entrance

                                    (Thornborrow, 2003, p. 18)

In this extract, the boys are engaged in a group
task. Thornborrow notes that the extract
begins with Will, an older boy, issuing instructions about the task, but that at line 37 Josh,
a younger boy, introduces some off-task talk
about a rally shop. However, in the next turn, Fred,
another older boy, issues a mock-serious reprimand (which Thornborrow notes was voiced
in a deep, mock-adult key). In this way, Will and
Fred combine together to deal with a potential
disruption from task completion. However, in
doing this, they both co-align in adopting an
instructional role in which they, as older children,
adopt the position that adult teachers might
adopt of instructing the younger boy.

Summary

In this section, we have examined group function
as represented by two common group tasks:
establishing group norms and performing group
tasks. Arminen's study shows that even in circumstances where group norms are explicit and
publicly available for inspection, group interaction provides a basis for such group norms to be
renegotiated. Discourse within groups can also be
seen to be interwoven with task activities. Talk
within the group can be used to manage the
switch from other activities to task performance.
But the distinction between "on-task" talk and
"off-task" talk involves more than this. By managing the interplay between these two forms of
talk, group members are able to address other
functional and structural group concerns such as
participants' roles and group cohesion and the
maintenance of group norms.

In Conclusion

It is not surprising that social psychology,
including discursive research, has displayed such

interest in the social group, because a concern
with the way individuals act within and are
influenced by collectivities of others is central to
social psychological explanation. Social groups
are bound up with a sense of self and also with
a sense of other people. These are themes which
were pursued in the previous chapter on identity
and which will be taken up again at later points
in this book, especially in the chapter on prejudice. However, discursive researchers' interest
in the group has not been confined solely to
these sorts of group characterizations. Talk
about or amongst group members can also be
seen to address itself to the structural properties
of groups and to the functions which those
groups pursue. In following those other research
themes, it becomes apparent that discursive
research is especially useful in the study of
groups. By addressing both large-scale social
groups and small-scale groups as discursive
entities, discursive researchers are especially well
placed to examine the interstices between society-
wide categorizations such as gender or race and
the minutiae of how small groups carry out their
business.

We have tried to be relatively inclusive in
this chapter, and have included research which
addresses questions involving "large-scale" social
groups as well as smaller-scale groups such as
families, committees, and the classroom. However, finally, we should point out that there is a
range of other group-related themes in discursive
research which are not presented here. We have
not, for example, looked at the ways in which discursive researchers have sought to explain the
phenomenon of crowd behavior (Drury, 2002).
Nor have we explored the ways in which studies
of nonverbal behaviors have contributed to
our understanding of small group activities
(MacMartin & LeBaron, 2006; Matoesian &
Coldren, 2002). Nor has there been space in the
present chapter to consider applications of the
discursive approach to the study of group
decision-making (Priola, Smith, & Armstrong,
2004). Nevertheless, we hope that the brief overview presented in the chapter will have provided
readers with a clear understanding of the way
in which the study of discursive processes can
provide essential insight into the role of social
groups in social life.

Chapter summary

- The term "social group" encompasses a range of different collectivities of individuals. Some groups, such as races or genders, can be thought of as social groups because their members are perceived, by themselves and/or others, as sharing a particular social characteristic. Other, smaller groups such as families or committees can be thought of as collections of individuals who share a common fate or purpose.
- Critical discourse analysis uses the theoretical notion of social representations as a means of capturing the way that group membership influences the way we think. Other forms of discursive research are less willing to adopt this idea, and view such representations as merely one aspect of discursive social construction.
- Some discursive researchers are interested in the way that group membership is bound up with sense of self and with the way in which we think of others.
- Discursive researchers have also been interested in other properties of groups, such as their structural and functional features.
- The studies described here indicate that the cohesiveness of a group is something which group members establish through a variety of discursive practices. One important practice here is the use of storytelling in which the narrator displays empathy and solidarity with other group members.
- Evidence suggests that group homogeneity and heterogeneity are also features of groups that are worked up in discourse.
- The roles which people adopt, or are given, in groups influence the way in which they interact with other group members. However, like group homogeneity, group roles may themselves be the output of discursive negotiation.
- One important function of groups is to establish and maintain the group's rules and norms. Even explicitly formulated rules can be seen to be "worked up" during intragroup interactions.
- Another aspect of group function is the performance of group tasks. "On-task" talk and "off-task" talk are sensitively deployed by group members in order to accomplish a variety of goals. Such goals include switching from task behaviors to non-task behaviors. But they also include more subtle aims such as the establishing of group cohesion and the "policing" of group norms.

Connections

One set of major links between the current chapter and other areas of the book centers around the way that references to social groups are used in making sense of the self (Chapter 2) and of others (Chapter 7). Aspects of group membership are also relevant to the working of support groups of the sort discussed in Chapter 10. Group membership issues of the sort discussed here are also important within organizational contexts (Chapter 11).

Activity

Think of a small group to which you belong, e.g., a classroom group or a friendship group. Can you describe the rules that guide the behavior of the group members? Can you think of any episode in which those rules were upheld, modified, or ignored? Thinking back to that episode, how did you and your fellow group members manage the event?

Further reading

Blommaert, J., Creve, L., & Willaert, E. (2006). On being declared illiterate: Language-ideological disqualification in Dutch classes for immigrants in Belgium. *Language & Communication, 26,* 34–54. In this study of immigrants in Belgium, the authors demonstrate the social pressures to assimilate which minority group members can face. One of the features of interest in the paper is the use the authors make of reproductions of participants' written text as a means of showing how certain forms of writing are excluded from the realms of what counts as acceptable literary performance.

MacMartin, C. & LeBaron, C. D. (2006). Multiple involvements within group interaction: A video-based study of sex offender therapy. *Research on Language and Social Interaction, 39,* 41–80. For reasons of space, we have omitted discussion of the contributions of nonverbal studies within discursive research on groups. However, if readers wish to understand the way in which nonverbal issues impinge on discourse within the group, this paper makes a good starting point. In this study of group therapy for sex offenders, the authors make use of photographs of group interactions to show how factors such as bodily orientation play a role in group interaction.

Chapter 4

Attraction and Relationships

Topics covered in this chapter

Attraction
Achieving attraction
Sexual attraction and desire

Partnership and Marriage
Marriage
Partnerships
Being single

Parenthood
Parenting in families
Parenting and society

Family Relationships
Collaborative competence
Family dynamics
Caring in families

Peers and Friends
Collaboration among peers
Teasing and exclusion

Troubles and Breaking Up
Neighbor disputes
Family and relationship troubles

Key terms

Accountability
Agony aunt
Collaborative identification
Confabulation
Conversational power
Double standard
Invited guessing
New father
New woman
Patriarchy
Role-play
Undermining

HAPPY, easygoing, attractive, 31-yr-old female, 5ft 6in, slim, genuine, honest, caring, WLTM genuine male, 25–32, for friendship, possible relationship.

VERY RESPECTABLE, well-dressed, honest guy, solvent, GSOH, looking for a decent female, under 40, for fun, leading to a possible, serious relationship.

Metro People, *Metro* (March 21, 2007), p. 38.

The two advertisements above come from the personal dating columns of a UK daily newspaper. Newspaper columns such as this, together with an ever-increasing diversity of Internet sites, offer a wide range of opportunities for people to initiate new contacts and possibly new relationships with others. The advertisements above assume familiarity with this form of contact on the part of readers; abbreviations such as WLTM (would to like to meet) and GSOH (good sense of humor) assume that readers will be able to decode the message by applying knowledge of common descriptions used in such instances. The structure also follows a familiar pattern, providing a description of the advertiser, the aim, the target respondent, and the desired outcome. Although advertisers can construct their advertisements in any manner that they choose; in practice they routinely rely upon descriptions of a kind that will be readily recognizable to the target audience (Coupland, 1996).

Outcomes of such advertisements of course remain unknown. Unsurprisingly, advertisers usually list personal attributes that others might consider attractive, and indicate the qualities or characteristics that they would be looking for in another. As with the structures used, the descriptions found in personal advertisements recur frequently. Adjectives such as "easygoing," "honest," and others appear to reflect a shared sense of the features that constitute attractiveness. This is not to say that the descriptions will be taken up in this way in any one case; people might disagree as to what comprises attraction, or to what extent an individual matches up to the suggested description. Attraction and (possible) relationships are two-way processes in which those involved negotiate their own understandings. This negotiation nonetheless takes place against a backdrop of expectations as to the form that such processes commonly take and what occurs within them.

Attraction

Attraction, in a broad sense, is not limited to contexts of personal dating or sexual attraction. There are many contexts in which individuals communicate in ways that are designed to promote relational affinity between themselves and other people. Insofar as attraction occurs, it depends as much upon the response of the recipient of the communication as upon the initial speaker. Although beauty might not lie entirely in the eye of the beholder, it depends very much on the response of the beholder. Attraction is a joint achievement.

Achieving attraction

As an illustration of the collaborative accomplishment of interpersonal attraction, let us consider an example provided by Sun (2002). The extract below comes from the opening sequence of an informal telephone conversation between two Chinese participants who are well known to each other. In similar calls between North American or UK participants the common practice is that the caller and recipient do not specifically refer to identity except in cases of doubt. For Chinese participants, identification assumes a more explicit role, as seen in the common practice of **invited guessing**.

1   A: Hello.
2   C: Hello. ?
       kang yue ma
       name Qtg
       "Hello. Is this Yue Kang?"

Invited guessing Overt request that a listener correctly guesses information known to the speaker

3   A: *ei*
     "Yes."
4   C: *hei ni hui lai la*
     hi you return Qtg
     "Hi, so you are back."
5   A: *hui lai le*
     return ASP
     "Yeah."
6(a) C: *wo jiu lai shi shi*
      I just come try try
      "I'm just calling to see if you are back."
6(b)→   *ni zhi dao wo shi shui ma*
        you know I am who Qtg
        "Do you know who this is?"
7   A: *li xiao li shi ma*
     full name is Qtg
     "Isn't this Xiaoli Li?"
8→   C: *ei ya ni ting chu lai le*
      wow you hear out ASP
      "Wow, you can recognize my voice."
            (Sun, 2002, pp. 92–93; A = answerer,
                                C = caller)

In such opening sequences, identification of caller and recipient becomes an extended part of the telephone conversation, in which both parties are expected to guess (correctly) the identity of the other. This sequence provides for **collaborative identification,** instead of the implicit identification found in telephone conversations between people of other cultures. The number of conversational turns and collaborative effort provide a conversational space and opportunity for both individuals to display interpersonal engagement and so to promote the affinity between them (Sun, 2004). Interpersonal proximity is more relevant to some exchanges than to others: in formal conversations with people not previously known to the caller, or in conversations with elders, interpersonal proximity will be less relevant and the opening sequences of such calls will include more one-sided forms of identification. When, however, participants seek interpersonal affinity, collaborative identification provides one conversational way of enhancing that affinity and displaying it to each other.

> **Collaborative identification** Identification of an individual through the turns of two or more people

In other situations, introductory sequences may enhance the attraction of a third party rather than that of the person initiating the introduction. Take, for example, the introduction of a performer to an audience. Usually, for a performance to be successful, the performer delivers material that is designed to be attractive and the audience accepts that material in appropriate ways: musicians who play enjoyable music are applauded, humorous comedians provoke laughter, and so on. Commonly, as Rutter (2000) notes, introductions of comedy routines are organized to promote the desired attraction between comedian and audience.

1   RM: >I wan you t show< Huge ↓love an appreciation for awl
2   the ↑acts as they come on tonight particularly for (the next
3   man) who's doing a short spot for you.
4   He's ↑POPin in on his way UP to Edinburah >just to keep
5   the Edinburgh (theme) going<
6   Aud 1:   YAA:::
7   RM: Way:::
8   Aud: hahhhhhhhhhh
9   RM: So ↑you'll be
10   >able to understand him< (which is nice).
11 Aud: hahahahhhhhahhhh
12 RM: Please
13   welcome (.) O::n t the stage. All the way >from over there<
14   The excellent (.)
15   Graham Swanson.
16   Y – roundov applause please.
17 Aud: x-XXXXXXXXXXXXXxxxxxxx-x-x
                              (Rutter, 2000, p. 465)

In this extract, we see the compère of a stand-up comedy venue introducing to the audience a comedian who is about to perform. A typical introduction includes some contextualization or background description of the comedian; a framing of the response that is expected from the audience; an evaluation of the comedian; a request for action (usually applause); an introduction of the comedian; and audience applause. These elements recur independently of specific compères, comedians, or venues involved. The introductory sequence is immediately recognizable both to compère and audience, and is designed to promote affinity between the comedian and the audience in the performance to follow.

The initial communication of attraction, of course, does not always succeed. Invited guessing in Chinese telephone conversations might fail to result in successful collaborative identifications, leading to renewed conversational efforts and potentially to eventual disappointment for caller and recipient (Sun, 2002). In a similar way, most of us will have witnessed, at one time or another, performers who failed to deliver attractive entertainment, regardless of the apparent promise of the introduction. Personal advertisers will not necessarily receive the responses that they seek to their advertisements. When attraction is achieved in any instance, it results as much from the response to the initial communication as from that communication itself, and upon the ongoing negotiation of meanings between those who are involved.

Sexual attraction and desire

Sexual attraction is in some ways little different from other forms of attraction. Like interpersonal attraction more generally, sexual attraction is necessarily collaborative, involving initial communications and subsequent responses. Moreover, the responses that individuals give proceed on the basis of their understandings of the earlier communication. In this respect, however, the communication of sexual attraction differs markedly from other possible descriptions of attraction. Common understandings of the communication of sexual attraction vary according to who is expressing the attraction, specifically the gender of the communicator and the way in which sexual attraction is presented.

Expressions of sexual attraction and desire are closely linked to possible actions that might result from that attraction. However, social understandings of sexual behavior, and consequently of expressions of sexual desire, diverge greatly for men and for women. For men, serial involvement with many female sexual partners is commonly understood to be the consequence of a naturally occurring biological drive. Such behavior, and the explicit expression of attraction or desire, thus comes to be regarded as natural in itself and morally acceptable. By contrast, multiple serial

sexual encounters by women are not taken to be the outcomes of a natural female drive but instead are viewed as matters of choice, indiscriminate choice at that. Female sexual behavior of this kind accordingly is often viewed as morally culpable, and statements of explicit sexual desire are taken to be indications of loose individual morals and blameworthy. Sexual behavior and desire in men and women are therefore understood in terms of a **double standard,** being evaluated differently solely on the basis of the gender of the individual involved in the sexual behavior or expression of attraction. As Jackson and Cram (2003) note, it is difficult for young women to resist these negative evaluations.

SUE: So she gets called a slag and a slut – what happens if it's the guy that's doing the flirting?

NINA: He's a stud. [several agree, saying "yeah"]

HAVILLA: Staunch.

SALA: Oh sometimes "you sleaze," especially – [several girls talking at once].

IOLI: But the guys are studs.

KIRI: It's the first time they've done it and stuff – it's like, God –

HAVILLA: The girls label guys like them "a bastard." [laughs]

IOLI: Sleaze ball.

HAVILLA: "You keep away from me."

SUE: But amongst guys is it amongst guys then that=

MAREE: =It's studly among guys and it's slutty amongst girls.

IOLI: Shucks yeah.

HAVILLA: But it can be studly around us if we sort of like think in their way. [laughter]. You know what I mean?

                    (Jackson & Cram, 2003, p. 117)

In the discussion above, the young women evaluate male displays of sexual attraction positively, using terms ("stud," "studly") that reflect male sexual prowess. They also evaluate possibly similar behavior by women negatively, through

Double standard Evaluation of behavior that differs according to the actor rather than the behavior

the use of recognizably derogatory terms ("slag," "slutty"). The participants, however, do not passively accept these contrasting evaluations of male and female sexual behavior, and attempt to rework female desire in potentially less negative terms. The double standard, though, provides the focus for the discussion and indicates the difficulties that women face in displaying sexual attraction in similar ways to men. These difficulties resurface when the young women discuss sex itself.

RACHEL: I dunno, girls these days seem to have no morals left in society really, like chastity has gone out the window sort of thing. I don't know, sex seems to be just one of those things these days, it's not really that special any more.

OLIVIA: I think it can be. I think that there is definitely a distinction between making love and having sex, and often having sex is just something you need to do, you know. If you feel like having sex, you have sex whatever, but there's a huge distinction between making love and having sex. There's time when=

SARA: =Making love is special=

OLIVIA: =Yeah, making love is special.

CARLA: Having sex is just like having fun basically. [laughter and several talking at once]

LILLY: It's like if you have sex then later on you go "oh yea we had sex" but when you make love you go "oh wasn't that beautiful."

OLIVIA: Yeah you hold that moment.

JENNI: You don't go "wow, sex!"

OLIVIA: Well you do, you say that's great sex and that's just part of life and then there's making love which is a bit more special.
(Jackson & Cram, 2003, p. 122)

The issue of morals again is highlighted as a problem. Here, the women attempt to avoid negative moral judgments in various ways, particularly by reframing female sexual activity as being romance or love rather than simply sex. Their tentative descriptions, however, point to the problems for women in making sense of female sexual desire and behavior in ways that will not be understood to be morally culpable, in terms of common constructions of sexual behavior.

The effects of the double standard are found across many contexts. One example is that of teenage magazines targeted at a female readership. Many of these magazines provide space for readers to write in with personal concerns and to receive advice from a person, often described as an "**agony aunt**," engaged by the magazine to respond to their letters. Given that much of the content of the magazines addresses sexual topics, it is unsurprising that readers' letters frequently raise issues of sexual attraction. Paradoxically, however, the advice that is given typically reworks expressions of female sexual attraction in familiar ways and undermines explicit descriptions of female desire. Even in such contexts, female sexual desire is rarely, if ever, constructed as being positive (Jackson, 2005).

Moreover, it is not only female sexual attraction that brings difficulties for women in close interpersonal encounters. There is also the issue of how to respond to expressions of male sexual attraction. To accept all suggestions of sexual activity is to run the risk of being constructed in morally blameworthy terms; refusal of unwanted sexual advances is no straightforward matter either. Various initiatives have encouraged women to be direct and explicit in refusing unwanted sex, offering the message "Just say 'no'" or a similar one. Although direct messages of this kind appear to be unambiguous, they give rise to two problems in a sexual context (Kitzinger & Frith, 1999). One problem is that insistence upon direct refusals might cast doubt upon less explicit refusals. In everyday talk, individuals can refuse invitations and suggestions in various ways that include hesitancies in responses, accounts of circumstances that preclude acceptance, and so on. A construction of direct rejection as the only effective means of refusing unwanted sexual advances potentially negates other more common but less direct forms of refusal. A second problem of requiring direct refusal is that sexual refusals would be marked out as difficult to accomplish and different from usual everyday expectations. However, young women (Kitzinger & Frith, 1999) and young men (O'Byrne, Rapley, & Hansen, 2006) recognize sexual refusals that take

Agony aunt Person employed by magazine or similar to respond to readers' personal letters

the form of refusals of any other kind. To suggest therefore that women can refuse sex only in highly prescribed and explicit ways is to introduce an understanding of sexual behavior that is neither commonplace nor consistent with other understandings of social practices.

In the light of the difficulties that women encounter in relation to understandings of male and female sexual activity and desire, it is perhaps unsurprising that the accounts they give of sexual behavior can appear highly formulaic, and scripted in following particular patterns. By providing accounts that make sense of sexual behavior in terms of prevailing understandings of male and female sexual desire, women potentially can avoid being held accountable for individual difficulties in relation to sexual behavior, and thus avoid the negative evaluations that would otherwise follow (Frith & Kitzinger, 2001).

Partnership and Marriage

Let us return for one moment to the two advertisements with which we began this chapter. One question that we might ask is why participation in dating forums, including personal columns, Internet sites, and options such as speed-dating meetings, has become so popular in recent times. To the question, there are (at least) two answers

that we can usefully consider at this point. One answer is that romantic relationships are presented to us as routine states of involvement with other people, both as spaces for the construction of meanings and understandings between partners (Staske, 2002), and as the basis for many social arrangements, for example invitations to attend social events. A second (and connected) answer is that being single, in adult years, is viewed as being problematic. Singleness is regarded as being a temporary state, for which one has to account, except perhaps in particular circumstances such as bereavement. Here we examine each of these answers in more detail.

Marriage

Marriage continues to be presented as the most valued form of romantic relationship, notwithstanding that recorded rates of marriage are decreasing in many countries. Wedding ceremonies usually are very public occasions of celebration that mark the beginning of a particular relationship between two people. Further, these ceremonies function to connect an individual marriage to cultural practices that shape how the relationship is to be understood in broader society. Consider the following example of an invitation to a wedding in Jordanian society.

Opening	wa min ?aayaatihii ?an khalaqa lakum min ?anfusikum ?azwaajan litaskunuu ?ilayhaa wa-ja"ala baynakum mawaddatan wa-raHmah. ?inn fii thaalika la-?aayaatin liqawmin yatafakkaruun. (And among His Signs is this, that he created for you mates from among yourselves, that ye may dwell in tranquility with them. And he has put love and mercy between your (hearts): verily in that are signs for those who reflect.) (Surah Al Rum, verse 21)	
Heading	?afraaH 'asheerat [Name of groom's Tribe] (Weddings of [Name of groom's Tribe] and	wa 'asheerat [Name of bride's Tribe] [Name of bride's Tribe)
Identifying the inviters	?alhaaj [X] wa 'aqiilatuh wa (Hajji [X] & his wife	and ?aduktoor [Y] a'aqiilatuh Doctor [Y] & his wife)
Requesting the presence of others	yatasharafan bida'watikum liHuDuur Hafl zafaf . . . request the honor of your presence at the wedding ceremony of	
Identifying the bride and groom	Waladihi ?aduktoor (His son Doctor) (Ali)	kariimatih (His daughter)

Situating the wedding ceremony	Wa-thaalika bi-mashii?ati-allah fii tamaam ?asaa'ah ?athaaniyah min ba'di Sallati ?aljum'ah ?almuwafiq 15/5/2003 fii manzil waalid al'ariis fii shaari' ?ajaam'ah fiimadiinati irbid
	This (will take place) if Allah wills at two o'clock after Friday prayers 15/5/2003 at the residence of the groom's father, University Street, Irbid City.
Closing	daamat ?al?afraaH Haliifatu diyaarikum ?al'aamirah
	(May your inhabited homes be always full of happiness!)
Other optional components	MulaaHaDah: ?alfaardih ?asaa 'ah ?alkhaamisah
	(Notice: The escort of the bride is at five o'clock)

nawman hanii?an li?aTfaalikum
(Pleasant sleeping for your children)

(Al-Ali, 2006, p. 706)

In this invitation, we see various components that are commonplace in Jordanian wedding invitations. The invitation begins with a quotation from the Holy Qur'an, and continues with names of the tribes of each party, the names of the male guardians of the groom and bride, the names of the groom and bride themselves, and details of ritual, time, and place. The invitation is organized hierarchically so that the names of the tribes follow the quotation and are placed above the names of the male guardians, which in turn precede the names of two people who are to be married. Other than the bride, no mention is made of female family members.

Although many of the elements might appear unexceptional (particularly to Jordanians!), Al-Ali (2006) observes that the organization of details is carefully designed to be consistent with Jordanian understandings, not just of marriage but also of social practices. Religion (most commonly Islam) is given precedence over all other aspects of life, and this priority is marked by the initial quotation in the invitation. References to tribes and male guardians, along with the omission of female family members, in a similar way reflect and enact understandings of a society that is organized in terms of tribal origins and continuing **patriarchal** practices. The content of a particular invitation and order of presentation of detail thus locate an individual marriage within broader understandings of relationships and of the social order.

Patriarchy Set of social practices that favors men over women

Cultural understandings of marriage, and forms of wedding invitations, vary from culture to culture, perhaps providing for more or less detail than that seen in Jordanian society. The wedding ceremony itself, however, is not the only social marker of such a relationship. Often anniversaries of the ceremony provide occasions for further celebration, perhaps in public or in the company of family and friends with whom couples can share their experiences of being married. Anniversaries serve also to allow couples to share with others positive experiences of marriage, and to provide publicly positive evaluations of marriage as a form of relationship (Leeds-Hurwitz, 2006). The highly evaluated nature of marriage, thus, does not arise from the relationship itself, but is the outcome of recurring practices of celebration and public acknowledgment.

Marriage of course is not always a cause for ongoing celebration; divorce statistics in many countries point to the difficulties experienced by many couples, leading to the termination of their shared experience. One factor in the break-up of marriages is that couples cease to construct their shared experiences as being positive. For example, events that occur during the course of a marriage might be understood differently by each spouse and become matters of disagreement rather than agreement. When, for instance, a spouse loses his or her job, a couple might construct the impact upon their relationship as presenting a challenge or as an insurmountable problem. If a couple do not arrive at a joint understanding that the difficulty can be overcome and that the relationship should continue, then the future of the marriage will be in doubt (Conroy, 1999). Events such as these are unlikely to offer occasions for the celebration of meaning and experience in wider circles!

One group for which marriage has become less popular comprises those born after 1960, particularly in the UK and North America. Within this group, understandings of marriage appear somewhat mixed. Marriage is still understood as a romantic and enduring endeavor, within which spouses will be exclusively committed to each other. An alternative view, however, is that marriage as a relationship can simply wear out, and that it is unrealistic to expect that a relationship will be permanent and that spouses will be committed forever to unwavering fidelity (Lawes, 1999). Individuals born after 1960 thus understand marriage to be less positive, more inconsistent, and potentially more problematic than the highly valued relationship that is so frequently celebrated in public.

Partnerships

Although marriage appears to be less popular than previously, it is still commonly expected that individuals will be involved in some form of heterosexual relationship. Frequently, this understanding is found in everyday talk about other matters. Consider, for instance, the following excerpts of conversation that are taken from calls to talk-back programs on Australian radio.

> when I was married
> I just went with my boyfriend of the time
> (Rendle-Short, 2005, pp. 564–565)

In the two examples above, we see callers explicitly referring to their relationships, marriage in the first instance and heterosexual partnership in the second. Sexual relationships themselves were not a main discussion topic in any of the programs; topics covered included matters relating to tax, housing, friends as family, and surfing. Rendle-Short (2005) observes that in the course of making calls on such discussion topics, callers frequently described their relationship status. Further, these references implicitly described also the sexualities of the callers, heterosexuality in each case. By providing such descriptions, callers could in unremarkable

ways make known both their relationships with others and the forms of those relationships. There were, though, instances where the caller's relationship remained unclear after an initial reference.

1 C1: I'm the father of two kids.
2   'n we chose to have these children,
3   my wife and myself chose to have these children.
> (Rendle-Short, 2005, p. 567)

When the initial reference did not make explicit the sexual relationship of the caller and another person, that relationship and the caller's sexuality remained open to more than one interpretation. Recognizing this, the caller above provided more detail of his partner (wife) and thus implicitly of his (hetero)sexuality. Although more extended than the earlier examples, this reference also describes the caller's relationship in the course of discussion of other topics. In examples where an individual was not involved in a heterosexual partnership, a more direct description of the relationship was given.

> and I'm of course a lesbian myself.
> (Rendle-Short, 2005, p. 569)

None of the callers referred to gay or lesbian relationships. Studio guests, however, did refer to their sexualities and to gay or lesbian relationships in which they were involved By contrast with heterosexual relationships that could be inferred from references to wives or girlfriends, individuals describing non-heterosexual relationships had to make explicit their sexualities or the forms of their relationships. Involvement in a non-heterosexual relationship consequently was marked out conversationally as being different from, and more visible than, involvement in a heterosexual partnership, which was taken-for-granted as reflecting the assumed form of close relationships.

Being single

Being in a heterosexual relationship is taken to be a routine and unremarkable part of life, and can be included in the discussion of a vast range of everyday topics. When judged against this yardstick, being single and not being in such a relationship becomes problematic. To be single is to present oneself as lacking what is usually expected and potentially to indicate social failure. Singleness of itself, of course, need not be constructed negatively; it could alternatively be understood as indicating personal choice or independence. Describing it positively, however, throws up the question of why anyone would wish to lose the benefits of such status by seeking involvement with another. Single individuals who seek relationships accordingly have to negotiate dilemmatic and inconsistent expectations of current and future status (Reynolds & Wetherell, 2003).

Sandfield and Percy (2003) explored the negative associations of singleness, in a study conducted with women of between 20 and 48 years of age who were or had previously been single. The interviewees described single status as being undesirable in itself, and as being a temporary stage prior to involvement in an enduring relationship.

ANNA: That's nice. Do you feel that you are happier now?

TESS: Yeah. Sometimes I think to myself "Why wasn't I happy before?" but I know that I wasn't (.) I know that I was always very miserable and thought that I'd be forever alone and a spinster (.) end up half eaten by an Alsatian! [Tess and Anna laugh] which is a silly thing to worry about at the age of seventeen but I did (.) and erm also everybody else seemed to be in relationships and I didn't so I think that I'm happy.

(Sandfield & Percy, 2003, p. 482)

Although not all of the descriptions were as graphic as that above, the women's accounts clearly oriented to the difficulties of negotiating being single. In this instance, the reference to being "half eaten by an Alsatian" reflects the words of the fictional character Bridget Jones (Fielding, 1997, p. 20), a stereotypical single woman who is anxious to enter into a meaningful heterosexual relationship but is unable to do so. Miss Jones's despairing efforts to form a meaningful relationship are portrayed as exemplifying failure, which, if it continues, will lead to the exaggerated and humorous fate that is suggested. Tess in the extract above, humorously suggesting that she

might meet a similar fate, nonetheless does so in discussing the downside of being single and her concern at a younger age that she might fail to move on from this stage.

For some participants, the terminations of previous relationships were equally difficult.

MAGGIE: . . . because they've got all these other problems they drive people away, because I've been like (.) like depressed over the last 12 months, I think that's probably, well, I'm fairly sure that's probably the reason why we split up in the end (.) because he got fed up of seeing a miserable face . . . I mean (.) y'know everybody needs outlets, I mean even if you're married you still have to have outlets xxx I've probably made me dependent on him (.) too much (.) maybe that was the problem, maybe I was (.) stifling him.

(Sandfield & Percy, 2003, p. 483)

In such cases, the women described the ending of a previous heterosexual relationship as leading to the negative consequence of being single. The women sought to account for the end of their previous relationships, usually doing so by blaming themselves rather than attributing blame to partners or to the relationships. Attributing blame to themselves provided another source of failure for these women, compounding their constructions of failure at not forming subsequent relationships.

While therefore heterosexual partnerships might enjoy a valued and readily recognizable status as the socially accepted form of relationship, they do so at a considerable cost to other possibilities. Being single might be difficult in itself; being single and taking the blame for failure in previous relationships makes the negotiation of positive individual experience highly problematic.

Parenthood

Within traditional notions of parenting, parental roles and responsibilities were organized very much along gendered lines. Commonly mothers were expected to provide care and nurturing for children, while fathers acted as family breadwinners but had less involvement with children of the relationship. Recent evidence, however, has suggested that parental roles have been changing, with fathers becoming more fully involved in all aspects of the upbringing of their children, leading possibly to a more egalitarian division of responsibilities between mothers and fathers. Perhaps in response to changing perceptions of parenting, the UK government in April 2003 introduced for the first time legal entitlement to paternity leave for fathers. This entitlement is similar to rights of fathers found in other European Union states and elsewhere, all designed to respond to and to promote changing social expectations. Let us here consider the questions of whether and to what extent parental roles have noticeably changed in recent times, in the context of the family and in wider society.

Parenting in families

Much of the discussion of changing parental roles has focused on the idea of the **new father**. The new father is presented as an extension of the new man within the family context, someone "who begins by being present at antenatal classes and at the birth [...], continues by actively participating in the raising of his children, and generally shares with his domestic partner commitment to and responsibility for maintaining family life and the home" (Henwood & Procter, 2003, p. 337).

Constructing fatherhood in this way would mark a departure from previous understandings of fatherhood. Even until the early to mid-1990s, the advice being provided to parents very much reproduced traditional notions of parenting. Sunderland (2000) noted that the parentcraft texts that were readily available during that period offered primarily a message of "part-time father/mother as main parent." To the extent that parentcraft texts did specifically address fathers, they provided advice in very specific ways. Much of this advice focused on activities that could be viewed as the fun side of parenting.

The modern father ...] will spend time playing with [his children], showing them new things,

New father Father who participates actively in all aspects of parenting and domestic life

helping them with their hobbies, taking them with him when he enjoys his own [...] and will participate with reading stories, playing games and singing songs before bedtime.

(Sunderland, 2000, p. 262)

In contrast to guidance regarding enjoyment of activities with children, there was no mention of a father's responsibilities to help out with the more difficult but necessary elements of parental duties. Indeed, to at least some extent, fathers were constructed as being unskilled in such respects.

They [fathers] are often keen to be involved, but are not sure how to go about it.

(Sunderland, 2000, pp. 262–263)

Much of the father's responsibility, given his apparent lack of skill in the practical aspects of parenting, focused on acting as what Sunderland termed "line-manager" for the mother, who took on the main parenting role.

plan for the future. Get yourselves a stair-gate, put locks on all the low cupboards, protect electric wires and sockets

(Sunderland, 2000, p. 264)

In total, the guidance available to parents constructed fathers as having limited and clearly defined roles in the raising and care of children. Taken in themselves, these descriptions made up only a small part of a parentcraft text as a whole. That, however, is the point: the majority of advice presented mothers as being main parents and fathers having minor roles and having responsibility for the upkeep of the family in relation to the outside world.

The version of fatherhood found in these 1990s texts certainly seems at odds with how we might now understand fatherhood, and is clearly inconsistent with the idea of the new father. This is not to say, however, that this earlier version of fathering has been entirely superseded by more enlightened and egalitarian constructions. Indeed, evidence would suggest to the contrary. For example, Edley and Wetherell (1999) asked 17- to 18-year-old male students to imagine themselves in future roles of being fathers and to describe what fatherhood and parenting arrangements would be like for them. Those interviewed often described their imagined lives as including full and caring involvement with their children, and themselves as willing to be at home, full-time if necessary, to look after the children. In large part, this commitment appeared to reflect the ideals of new fatherhood. The students, however, also described themselves and their future partners as likely to have a clear division of parental responsibilities, whereby they would be primary income-providers and their partners would be primary child-carers. Such a division of responsibilities was rather less consistent with new fathering than with traditional parenting practices. One way in which the students resolved these dilemmas was by drawing a distinction between theoretical ideals and the practical necessities of parenting. The young men constructed mothers as being biologically predisposed to look after children, or themselves as being unable effectively to provide extensive child-care and carry out domestic responsibilities. These and other resolutions of the dilemmas worked to downgrade the expectations that might reasonably be made of fathers (see also Dixon & Wetherell, 2004) and to rework the ideals of new fatherhood in ways more consistent with previous understandings of parenting.

Similar findings come from a study by Henwood and Procter (2003), conducted with fathers over a period from before the birth of their child until their children were 4 to 9 months old. Many fathers described themselves as wanting full involvement with their children, and the commitment that new fatherhood would bring.

> I think you are a union or a cooperative, and everything gets mucked in and everyone does a bit of everything . . . So there is a sharing of roles, and I think that's quite important. I think it's important for children to see a father can do what has always been considered girlie roles, like the washing, like hanging the washing up, like doing the ironing. I think that's more important, I think everyone just does everything, there's no traditional role for anything as far as I'm concerned.
>
> (Henwood & Procter, 2003, p. 344)

The fathers, however, described themselves as being unable to fulfill these desires for full involvement with their children, due to factors such as the necessity of working away from home.

> I think there's an issue with me partner that, and we have touched on it, that I don't want all decisions made by her, I want it to be discussed, I want it to be fair. But obviously then what I've also got to appreciate, that if I'm a hundred miles away, as I am quite regularly, and although we can discuss things on the phone, she might have to make a decision quicker than that, in which case she makes the decision, doesn't she? So I'd be worried about not being involved in some decision-making.
>
> (Henwood & Procter, 2003, p. 349)

Again, the perceived conflict between theoretical and practical versions of fatherhood gave rise to tensions for fathers in making sense of their roles. Henwood and Procter argue that neither traditional nor new forms of fathering fully capture the understandings of men and couples who are working out the arrangements for looking after their children. Currently, fatherhood does not appear to reflect the clear division of parental roles that previously was widely accepted. However, fatherhood in practice has become a fragmented set of understandings and practices that have to be negotiated in and according to individual circumstances. The ideals of the new father are certainly in social circulation; these, however, have to compete with alternative models, and competing understandings of fathering provide tensions that remain to be resolved by individual parents and families.

Parenting and society

Much of the discursive research into parental responsibilities has focused on individual descriptions of parenting. Constructions of parenting, however, are commonly found in contexts beyond the family, such as governmental or legislative initiatives, that provide their own versions of parental rights and responsibilities. The understandings of parenting promoted in such instances might be inconsistent in themselves or might compete with the ways in which parents make sense of their responsibilities.

In Singapore, for example, the government has since the 1980s pursued a pro-fertility policy, exemplified by a "Family Life" advertising campaign. This campaign has twin aims of encouraging marriage among unmarried couples and promoting early parenthood to married couples. Within the advertisements, two conflicting versions of parenthood are found. One version is similar to the new father idea of parenting, suggesting egalitarian gender relations, and presenting fathers as caring and sensitive individuals who are as comfortable in the family as in the work environment. In this version of parenthood, there is found also a description of the mother as a **new woman**, someone who has a successful career while enjoying the rewards of family life. This version of parenthood, however, is set alongside an alternative version that reflects conservative gender relations, emphasizing fathering as being play and fun and pointing to the contribution that family life can make to a successful career. In this version, women are constructed as being responsible for facilitating their husbands' choices and careers. In consequence, should mothers wish to pursue careers of their own, it becomes their responsibility also to achieve a balance between work and family life. When these two conflicting versions of parenthood are presented together in the same advertisement, it is the conservative version that is prominent. Although identities such as new father and new woman are in wide circulation, these in themselves appear to have had little impact upon traditional parenting practices and responsibilities in Singapore (Lazar, 2000).

Rather than (ostensibly) promoting changes in parenting practices, policy measures may function to reinforce traditional arrangements. In the United States, recent reforms to welfare benefits have reduced the entitlements of mothers, encouraging them to seek paid employment instead of claiming social assistance. Such changes have been accompanied by measures designed to promote fatherhood and paternal obligations to families. In producing this legislation, Congress offered an ideal of parenthood and fathering that was somewhat different from any suggestions of parents as being a new father or new woman. Instead, ideal family life was presented in terms of traditional family structures, as Haney and March (2003) observe.

Young, low-skilled, unmarried, poor parents have their children before they are mature

---

New woman Woman who has full opportunities to enjoy a successful career and family life

---

enough to understand and manage a committed relationship and before they recognize the implications of unmarried, unprotected sex and childbearing.

(Jeffrey Johnson before the US Congress, Senate Finance Committee, in Haney & March, 2003, p. 468)

Within this version of family life, the role of fathers was presented primarily as one of being in employment and providing financial support.

Serious attention must be paid to building the capacity of low-income fathers to attain the economic sustainability necessary to maximize the potential for children to grow up free from poverty and dependence on the government. To accomplish this, we must give attention to increasing the ability of fathers . . . to become employable in the new workforce so they can contribute economically and emotionally to their children.

(Preston Garrison before the US Congress, Senate Finance Committee in Haney & March, 2003, p. 469)

These understandings of family life differed greatly from the expressed views of mothers who would be affected by the legislative changes. Haney and March contrast Congressional descriptions of fatherhood with alternative versions provided by low-income mothers in Baltimore.

As far as they [her children] know, Arnold is not their real father. He's daddy. He is not who made us . . . But he is daddy. He does everything for them. He has been in their lives since they were babies . . . So they call him daddy. They know nobody else as daddy. I know I will have to answer for it, come Judgment Day, but until I get to that point, all they will know is that their biological father is dead. If they see him on a bus, I wouldn't say, "That's your father."

(Haney & March, 2003, p. 471)

For these mothers the contributions of fathers to family life were taken to be more important than the structure of the family itself. Here we see fatherhood defined in terms of involvement with children and sensitivity to the children's needs and lives. Recognized family structures, by contrast, did not in themselves provide good fathering.

I get angry when I see all these studies that say there's something wrong with children because it's only one parent raising them ... I have two very positive children. One of them is Stephanie, who I raised as a single parent. And the other one, I was married and still raised [him] as a single parent ... My son and daughter are almost identical. Because a person being there and a person participating and being a father and a dad are two different things. He fathered him. He didn't discipline him. He didn't listen to him. He didn't help. He didn't do anything ... I can love my children enough for two. I can be a mother and a father if I have to, and I have been.

(Haney & March, 2003, p. 473)

What we see in effect, again, is a divergence between a theoretical model of parenting and parenting as practiced. Here, the versions of parenting proposed in theory and in practice are reversed from the fathers' descriptions that we saw above: the theoretical version proposes traditional family structures and responsibilities, practical parenting emphasizes involvement of fathers and has little regard for traditional structures. In large part, however, the outcome of competing constructions of parenting is similar, in that individual parents have to make sense of their own practices against a background of conflicting understandings of what it means to be a mother or father.

Constructions of forms of parenting, as we have seen, vary considerably. Other issues surrounding parenting, however, are perhaps less ambiguous. There remains a common expectation that women of appropriate ages, especially those in long-term relationships, will become mothers. Where couples do not otherwise have children, the use of IVF (in vitro fertilization) treatments to facilitate pregnancy has become increasingly common in recent times. Women who undergo such treatments, while acknowledging the social expectations on them to have children, present their individual choices to use IVF as one means of fulfilling a natural biological instinct to become a mother (Ulrich & Weatherall, 2000).

Although changes in patterns of relationships have made lesbian and gay parenting more common, many of the discussions relating to parenting proceed on the continuing (implicit) understanding that family structures will be heterosexual, involving one mother and one father. This understanding poses challenges for parents in families that do not correspond to the assumed model. Regardless of whether lesbian and gay parents construct themselves as being similar to other parents, or different in some respects from other parents, they are faced with the difficulties of negotiating their family understandings in social contexts that sustain traditional assumptions of heterosexual parenting (Clarke, 2002; Clarke & Kitzinger, 2004). Even contexts in which the sexuality of parents would not appear directly relevant, such as calls to after-hours doctor services, operate on assumptions of heterosexual families (Kitzinger, 2005b), and so maintain prevailing understandings of parenthood and of families.

Family Relationships

Family relationships provide a range of settings within which children can both acquire and display competence in communicating with other people. More than this, interactions with parents (and possibly siblings) offer opportunities for collaborative construction of meanings and thus for children to learn how to make sense of the broader social world in which they live. Not all family life, however, is necessarily harmonious; we will all be aware of times of disagreement, and of the dynamics of negotiating meanings of actions within the family. In addition, families bring their own expectations, including perhaps expectations of how other family members should be cared for in later life. Families accordingly comprise sites where local understandings and broader social understandings meet, and where individuals make sense of themselves and their actions in a network of social relations.

Collaborative competence

Commonly, interactions between parents and young involve many elements that we might expect to find, such as those of providing comfort, discipline, or other forms of interpersonal action. Within these interactions, usually the parent is more directive than the child in shaping the exchange and the eventual outcome. Such interactions, however, as well as providing for the construction of meanings in themselves, make available understandings that can later be revisited in other forms. In a detailed study of interactions between a mother (Janet) and her daughter (Natalie, aged almost 3 years), Gordon (2002) notes that everyday "real-life" episodes, shaped primarily by the mother, offer understandings that Natalie can rework in later **role-play** interactions with her mother. Below we see an example of an everyday real-life sequence in which Janet is comforting Natalie, following the loss of a friend and play-mate.

	Natalie (Child)	Janet (Mother)
14	Are you feeling angry about something?	
15	I'm feeling sad about something.	
16		You're feeling sad?
17		What– what's making you sad,
18		Hon.
19	(*sad*) That Annie went awa:y.)	
20		That's making you sad?
21	Yes.	
22		Yeah.
23	Yes.	
24		Well that is sad Honey when somebody moves.
25		I bet you'll miss playing with her huh?
26	(*sad*) I miss playing with her.)	

(Gordon, 2002, p. 687)

Similar reassurances and comfort can be seen in a subsequent interaction between Janet and Natalie. In this exchange, however, Natalie acts as the mother and Janet as the child.

	Natalie (Child)	Janet (Mother)
43	(*high-pitched*) what happened to Annie?)	
44	She moved away Sweetheart.	
45	(*high-pitched*) Why:?)	
46	She's not here anymore.	
47	(*high-pitched*) Will she come back→	
48	to the Burke School?	
49	She won't come back to the Burke School,	
50	because she moved awa:y.	
51	(*high-pitched*) Wh– Is she gonna go→	
52	to a different schoo:l?&	
53	She moved to another school.	
54	(*high-pitched, sad*) O:h.	
55	But I used to play with her.&	
56	Did you guys play babies,	

57	and– and you can't play babies anymore?
58	(*high-pitched*) Yeah,
59	who– who will be there to play babies→
60	with me.&
61	Sarah will be here to play babies with you.
62	(*high-pitched*) Sarah will play babies?)
63	Sarah will play babies with you.
64	(*high-pitched*) Oh that makes me happy.)

(Gordon, 2002, pp. 687–688)

Within this later interaction, through role-play, Natalie displays her understandings of comfort in two ways. First, her responses to her mother's turns are designed to meet the concerns that are expressed, and so to work towards collaborative construction of these constructions as matters that should be addressed in particular ways. Second, in doing this, Natalie orients to social expectations of what comfort should be about and how it is widely understood. Natalie's understandings, of course, closely resemble those found in the earlier exchange in which their roles were reversed. The two interactions therefore show how, within the course of the relationship, topics such as comfort are jointly managed to facilitate Natalie's acquisition of social competence in these respects.

The outcome of the role-play episode, of course, depends also upon Janet's participation in ways that take up and respond to her daughter's turns. Were she unwilling to be involved in role-play, the second exchange would take a rather different form. Janet's participation, however, can also be understood as part of a broader pattern of making sense of social expectations. For her, the expectations are somewhat different from those of understanding comfort. What the second exchange provides for Janet is an opportunity to display her understandings of mothering, specifically the form and content that interactions between mothers and daughters should have. Janet herself can rework the interaction on other occasions, recounting to friends as an example of her parenting understandings and skills (Gordon, 2006).

Interactions in early years thus allow young children to develop and practice social competence that will enable them to make sense of a range of shared social practices. Over the course of childhood, children become increasingly adept communicative participants, who not only rework

> **Role-play** Interactions in which individuals play roles that differ from their own identities

previous conversational material but also play a greater role in the selection of topics for discussion and in the shaping of family conversations. By mid-childhood many children, including those often assumed to be less conversationally competent, use narratives to introduce new topics. For example, high-functioning children diagnosed with autistic spectrum disorders can demonstrate the competence normally expected of a narrative storyteller, showing negotiation of shift in topic, continuity in theme, and responsiveness to the turns of conversational partners (Solomon, 2004). The communicative skills and social understandings that children develop within family relationships thus provide a basis on which they can interact successfully in other relationships that extend well beyond the immediate context of the family (Sirota, 2004).

Family dynamics

As we noted earlier, many families continue to be organized along traditional lines, with fathers assuming responsibilities as main income-providers and mothers taking primary responsibility for child-care and domestic arrangements. Such family practices usually are taken to reflect the patriarchal organization of the social order, in which power favors men rather than women. In the context of the family, perceived social power does not readily translate into power within family relationships. Turkish family patterns, for instance, are widely regarded as being strongly patriarchal and authoritarian. However, if we examine the interactions of Turkish immigrant families living in the Netherlands, we see a rather different pattern. Close inspection of family exchanges indicates that **conversational power**, in terms of conversational turns in exchanges between family members, is either equally distributed between parents or indeed favors mothers during the negotiation of family discussions on different topics (Huls, 2000). At least in some respects these findings might be unsurprising; where mothers are primary

> **Conversational power** Power to shape the progress of a conversation, such as in taking of conversational turns

child-carers and interact with the children to a greater extent in the domestic setting, we might reasonably anticipate that they will have major roles within family interactions.

Routine family activities, though, are frequently designed to negate the overt exercise of power and to elicit collaboration between family members towards the joint accomplishment of particular outcomes. Topics such as when a child should go to bed or carry out homework can be thorny subjects within families, as many parents will know! When parents appear directive on these matters, their statements can all too easily be taken to reflect asymmetrical parental power and be met with resistance from children, leading potentially to conflict between family members. One way potentially of achieving such outcomes without overt disagreement is for parents and children to engage conversationally in preliminary talk about the topic, a process that is more likely to lead to children subsequently accepting what is proposed and thereafter going to bed (Sirota, 2006) or carrying out the homework (Wingard, 2006).

One regular opportunity for the discussion of family matters and other issues is that of dinnertime. At such times, all family members are frequently co-present, even if not eating together. Dinnertime provides a space for family members to converse, to raise issues for discussion, and perhaps to promote cohesion and mutual co-operation (Kendall, 2006). Often, dinnertime discussions focus on issues of morality, whereby children become familiar with what is expected of them as members of a particular social order. Sterponi (2003) shows how dinnertime exchanges in Italian families often require members of the family to account for their behaviors during the day.

[Tanucci family: Mamma (Paola), Papà (Fabrizio), Marco (10.6 years), Leonardo (3.9 years)]

1   PAPÀ: Leonardo
2   (.) ((Leonardo looks at Papà))
3   PAPÀ: ascolta una cosa.
        listen to this
4→   come mai oggi hai graffiato a– a Ivan tu?
        how come you scratched Ivan today?
5   (2.5) ((Leonardo looks at Papà))
6   PAPÀ: eh?
7   (1.0)

8→ PAPÀ: come mai? che t'aveva fatto Ivan?
how come? what had Ivan been doing to you?

9   LEO: pe- pecchè ce stavo prima io di quello. VEro!
bec- because I was before that ((kid)). TRue!

10   ((Papà nods))
        [. . .]

(Sterponi, 2003, p. 84)

In the extract above, Papà constructs Leonardo's actions as problematic in calling for an account of why Leonardo acted as he did towards another boy. The requirement to account for this behavior is then reiterated, prior to Leonardo offering an account that appears to be accepted. It is not only parents who can seek accounts from other family members, however.

[Fanaro family: Mamma (Teresa), Papà (Silvano), Sergio (7.5 years), Stefania (5.5 years), Andrea (Sergio's friend: 7 years)]

1   STEFANIA: mamma::
              mom

2   MAMMA: dimmi.
           tell me

3→ STEFANIA: com'è che Sergio non si taglia mai le unghie?
how come that Sergio never cuts his nails

4→   ce l'ha tutte nere.
            he has them all black ((sic))

5   MAMMA: le unghie?
           his nails?

6   STEFANIA: eh.
              yeah

7→ MAMMA: e beh veramente gliele abbiamo sempre tagliate
well actually we have always cut them for him

8→   allora evidentemente non facciamo in tempo
            then it seems we don't have enough time

9→   a farle crescere.
            to have them grow ((sic))

(Sterponi, 2003, p. 94)

In exchanges such as that above, one of the younger family members (Stefania) raises an issue that can be heard as problematic, namely her brother Sergio's lack of personal hygiene.

Although Stefania addresses her complaint to her mother, the complaint suggests that her brother (Sergio) should account for this behavior. Her mother, however, instead of treating Sergio as accountable, provides an alternative account in terms of her duties as a parent.

What such sequences demonstrate is that matters of morality are treated, by parents and children alike, as issues that can legitimately be raised in the course of family dinnertime discussions. It is in such ways that the local family order reflects a broader social order of morality and **accountability**. By negotiating accountability and morality in interactions with family members, children become familiar with the social rules and the expectations of others that they will find in their interactions outside the family (Sterponi, 2003, 2004).

In considering issues of family dynamics, there is of course the question of who exactly count as family members: parents, children, other relatives, certainly, but should we also include family pets? Evidence suggests that people frequently talk to dogs in ways that to some extent resemble those in which they talk to infants: using short, direct turns, a high-pitched voice, and conversational features that are designed to attract the attention of the other. It is not altogether surprising, however, that talk to infants differs from talk to dogs in other respects, most noticeably that people treat infants as rather more conversationally competent than dogs (Mitchell, 2001)! Even when family members are not expecting a conversational response, talk to or about dogs in a family context provides scope for displaying values, resolving potential conflicts, or otherwise dealing with a range of issues that might arise (Tannen, 2004). In facilitating family dynamics in these ways, dogs (and possibly other pets) arguably might reasonably be regarded as central to many families.

Caring in families

Family relationships can be bound up also with other expectations of behavior and of morality.

Accountability Responsibility, especially in relation to the speaker's responsibility in providing a particular account

When older relatives require care in the context of a family, the provision of such care is commonly seen as a female activity, becoming a further element of the set of domestic-oriented responsibilities. More than this, offering the required assistance is usually viewed as a question of morality, with refusal or absence being understood as a failure on the part of the female family members responsible for providing it. Male family members, however, are not understood to be under a similar obligation, and when they do give help it is usually constructed as secondary rather than as primary caregiving. Caring for older relatives is thus a gendered activity, its morality being acted out and confirmed in the course of interactions between family members and others (Paoletti, 2001, 2002).

Communication between caregiver and recipient is a central element of many, if not all, care relationships. Form of communication, though, assumes a particular importance in contexts where the recipient is understood to have communicative difficulties, such as interactions with people with dementia. Successful communication within such relationships might well require conversational partners to structure their turns in ways that facilitate responses, and that allow the conversation to focus on topics other than communicative competence in itself (Shakespeare & Clare, 2005). As dementia progresses however, communications are likely to prove increasingly difficult. One outcome of progressive dementia is that patients **confabulate**, producing descriptions of the world or of the self that clearly do not correspond to other evidence but without any intention of deceiving. Challenging or resisting such descriptions can be challenging for even the most skilled conversational partners. Often, this constitutes a stage where caring at home is no longer effectively viable, and the care recipient moves to contexts where he or she communicates with professional carers and other sufferers. In such contexts, dementia sufferers can engage with each other in conversations that display internal logics but which have little relevance to changing external events and experiences (Orulv & Hyden, 2006).

> **Confabulation** An unintentionally false statement about the world, usually resulting from pathological disorder

Peers and Friends

Much of our lives are spent in relationships with friends. These relationships, more so than families, are ongoing choices that we make, and we usually expect that friends will be accepting of how we describe ourselves at different times and will respond to us in preferred ways. Friendships offer possibilities for working out who we are in terms of social identities (Kiesling, 2005), of making sense of major events that have taken place during our lifetimes (Schiffrin, 2002), or, more light-heartedly, of enjoying the company of others and sharing fun and pleasure (Coates, 2007). Accordingly, friendships are understood to be essentially collaborative and reciprocal relationships. We do not usually anticipate that friends, in their interactions with us, will pursue personal business interests to the extent of jeopardizing the collaborative elements of friendship (Kong, 2003).

Many friendships have their origins in and develop from our interactions with other individuals as peers. The progression from peer relationships to friendships does not always happen; there are instances where collaborative sharing of experiences may be taken to be sufficient in itself, such as participation in support groups (Pudlinski, 2005). However, often interactions with those who appear to have similar interests to ourselves, and who respond in ways that we expect, provide the basis for ongoing development of the initial relationship.

The distinction between peers and friends is particularly blurred in the early years of life when many of children's interactions are with those of similar ages to themselves. Children's interactions with their peers offer wide-ranging possibilities for the practice and acquisition of communicative and social competence (Blum-Kulka & Snow, 2004). By participating in early relationships with peers, children learn about the meanings of being in relationships and of engaging in joint activities. The shape and content of peer activities of course change over childhood; adolescents, even in collaborative interactions, are unlikely to express the same concerns as younger children. Later peer relationships allow children to display and to enact their developed understandings of relationships and of how collaboration or non-collaboration can be accomplished in such settings.

Collaboration among peers

To a large extent, children's interactions of choice with other children are centered around play. Sequences of play are creative situations, in which the participants can imagine and experiment with different social activities. Even play and game situations, however, require those involved to act and to respond in ways that allow the sequence to proceed (Blum-Kulka, Huck-Taglicht, & Avni, 2004), and thus necessarily involve the construction of identities and of actions that should go with these play identities (Butler & Weatherall, 2006). Play is commonly enacted in narratives, in which children explicitly describe who they are and what they are doing, and often make equally explicit how other participants should respond within the context of the developing sequence. In the play of preschool children in particular, we find numerous switches between talk about what the children are currently doing and descriptions of the children's understandings of real-world social relationships. In such ways, children creatively rework their understandings of social life in collaboration with their peers (Britsch, 2005).

Exchanges between young children, of course, differ in various respects depending upon the participants involved. Even where interactions involve joint activity, the focus of such activity can vary between joint meaning-making of social worlds and the act of mutual engagement itself. Katz (2004) provides examples of these differences from two sets of play interactions between 3-year-old girls, involving the same child Elizabeth and different relationship partners. Below we see an excerpt from an interaction between Elizabeth and Elena.

I. Getting Married

ELENA: I'll put my scarf on. (giggles) I need my hood because it's chilly.

ELIZ: It's chilly. I need one – Hey, maybe this could be mine.
[The girls are trying on dress-up clothes.]

ELIZ: I'm gonna put this on my head.

ELENA: This is how we marry us. Let's, this is how we marry us.

. . .

ELIZ: I have my hood on.

ELENA: I need my hood turned up.

ELIZ: Mine is chilly. When it's the summer time we will take our hoods off.

ELENA: Um, in the summer time, in the winter we have to take our, our coats off and, and brush it and put it on xx xx, and take it, my, our sleeves off in the, in the pool so we can do, put water on it, and xx on it.

ELIZ: It's summer time, let's take our hats off!

ELENA: No, it's still chilly, it's still chilly.
(Katz, 2004, p. 339)

Within such exchanges, the girls displayed a primary focus on joint narrative, incorporating talk about their current actions or intended actions (either contextualized or imagined). Topic provided a central element and allowed the girls to rework their understandings of aspects of social life, such as marriage in the excerpt above, and to construct interpersonal understanding through their collaboration. Elizabeth's exchanges with another peer, Nina, adopted a somewhat different focus, as in the excerpt below.

II. Looking for Jujus

NINA: [screams] Oh, lookit, a juju!
(Jujus, named by the girls, are fluorescent pink and green plastic tubes.)

ELIZ: Juju dropped her juju?

NINA: [laughing] I brought my juju!

ELIZ: Juju? Xx find my juju!

NINA: Xxx my juju. I found my juju.
(The girls are looking at each other and pretend-crying, making their voices high and squeaky and trying to pucker their faces, but still smiling.)

ELIZ: [yelling] Oh, I found my juju!
(Katz, 2004, p. 341)

In the exchanges between Elizabeth and Nina, the girls paid little attention to reworking marriage or other elements of broader social life. Instead, the interaction focused on the very act of conversation as a game, providing the girls with many instances of shared humor. This shared humor exemplified the interactions between the girls, displaying their enjoyment of the relationship itself and of their joint participation in the activities.

We should note that both sets of interactions succeeded in maintaining the close collaboration of the two participants. A recurring element of these exchanges was repetition, whereby each girl would repeat some of the preceding talk of the other. By doing so, the girls displayed their understandings of what their communication was about, in that their turns were designed to respond appropriately to their interactional partner and to facilitate continuation of the conversation. Regardless therefore of the topic (imaginary or real-life) of the conversation, these peer interactions allowed the girls to display their competence in communicating within relationships.

As we saw above, in the exchange between Elizabeth and Elena, one topic of the children's conversations is that of later relationships, particularly marriage. Even among children in this age group (3 years), marriage is constructed as a valued form of later relationship. As children progress through childhood, this understanding of marriage or heterosexual partnership potentially can come into conflict with the maintenance of friendships with peers. Attraction to or from members of the opposite sex opens up possibilities for jealousy or competition among peers, or possibly lack of effort into the continuation of previously established friendships. Pre-adolescents (9- to 12-year-olds) appear to deal with this potential difficulty primarily by resisting the efforts of others to attract them, especially where attraction is most likely to lead to troubles within existing relationships. Ongoing relationships with peers and friends thus are constructed as more valuable than potential involvements with members of the opposite sex (Walton, Weatherall, & Jackson, 2002). Such a strategy, however, might be less effective in later years, when the expectation that people will be involved in heterosexual relationships becomes all the greater.

Teasing and exclusion

The elements of play and of humor seen in early peer relationships often take different forms in later relationships, as children become adept social communicators. Sharing of topic or of humor can become less explicit, with collaboration often being achieved less explicitly and the interactions assuming greater familiarity with many aspects of social life. One common element of later peer relationships is that of teasing, talk which is marked as being playful or humorous but is directed at a particular participant or participants. Pichler (2006) notes that for a friendship group of 15- to 16-year-old Bangladeshi girls attending a school in London, teasing comprised a recurring element of their interactions.

1 ARDIANA did you see your man (–) didn't [you]
                                           that man over
  HELEN   [which] man is that
2 ARDIANA [the:re] [(xxxxxxxxxxxxxxx)]
  HENNAH [UH:::] [teasing] [(are you trying to)] say you have millions
  ?   [which man]
3 ARDIANA   [she's got **loads**]
  HENNAH [laughs]
  HELEN that's not^ e– exactly I've got **loads** [>you know what I mean<]
4 ARDIANA don't [you **know** she's got] loads <u>one</u> after o:[:ne] [teasing]
  HELEN   [I've got <u>(loads)</u>] [laughing] [staccato] [<u>I don</u>]'t
5 HELEN <u>need some ugly guy who whose</u> (.) <u>career is in giving</u>
6 ARDIANA   [laughs]
  HELEN <u>crappy food at schools</u>   uah:
                                      (Pichler, 2006, p. 240)

Here we see one group member, Helen, being teased by other members of the group on the basis of a purported romantic interest in another individual at the school. Helen resists this suggestion, in the course of an exchange that is marked by various expressions of individual rather than shared humor. The teasing found in this, and in other instances, nonetheless is treated as fun rather than conflict and offers the participants opportunities to demonstrate their verbal skills. Further, jocular references to topics that included boys and sex allowed the girls to approach topics that otherwise would not be taken to be consistent with Muslim Bangladeshi identities. Teasing, as Pichler (2006) notes, thus strengthened group cohesion while also allowing members of the group to make sense of a range of different discourses and identities.

Peer interactions, however, are not always sites of collaborative activities and communication. Negative comments in a group setting will not necessarily be treated as fun either by a speaker or by a recipient, and may be designed to exclude an individual from a group instead of promoting solidarity and cohesion (Goodwin,

2002a). Further, the cohesion and shared understandings of particular groups can serve either to promote alignment with other individuals or to maintain distance from other people. For example, terms such as "girl" or "look" might come to acquire group meanings that differ from their uses in everyday talk. Black women recently attending a US university used the term "girl" to demonstrate alignment and cultural affinity with other black women, while "look" described distance between themselves and others who were not black and female. The descriptive terms thus marked out the women's identities and those who might be regarded and treated as peers or not (Scott, 2000).

Of course, different descriptions of potential peers can be used to meet the demands of particular contexts. Negative descriptions of peers are commonly used to exclude such individuals from relationships, whereas positive descriptions offer the basis for seeking relationships with others. The version deployed in any setting, however, will be oriented to social action. Where some peers, such as asylum seekers, are evaluated very negatively, the possibilities of relationships with peers from different minority groups might suddenly become somewhat more attractive than they seemed previously (Verkuyten & Steenhuis, 2005).

Troubles and Breaking Up

We have already seen that matters of attraction and relationship do not always run smoothly. Attempted attraction can involve refusal as well as acceptance, marriages can be sites of dispute instead of agreement, and peer relationships can exclude rather than include. Certain relationships, however, often appear more prone than others to potential problems. Take the case of neighbors. We live much of our lives in close proximity to others with whom we have not directly chosen to become involved. Yet, this very proximity ordinarily requires some levels of reciprocal cooperation and understanding if our own life experiences are to proceed smoothly. The difficulties inherent in attempting to get along with neighbors who are totally idiosyncratic, or impossibly irritating, have provided unlimited material over the years for the writers of television situation comedies. Further, when neighbor relationships go wrong, it appears that they can go spectacularly wrong. Television documentaries, entitled *Neighbours at War, Neighbours from Hell*, or similar, serve to remind us of the problems that can all too easily surface between our neighbors and ourselves. We consider below issues that can arise in these relationships.

Other relationships, of course, present their own challenges. Given the frequency and interconnectedness of family interactions, it is not surprising that disagreements arise both within the family and sometimes in more public contexts. Often, however, such disagreements can be resolved without leading to direct confrontation (Laforest, 2002), and meanings can be renegotiated in order to focus on shared concerns instead of divisions (Tannen, 2006). Public displays of family disagreements often may more be more oriented to the negotiation of family dynamics and individuals' actions within these than to the publicizing of irreconcilable conflicts (Petraki, 2005; Sandel, 2004). Relationships with partners and spouses reflect some of these elements also. In such close relationships, however, the breakdown of shared understandings often puts into doubt the future of the relationship itself. Whether we understand such relationships as simply wearing out (Lawes, 1999) or as reaching a point where joint activities are no longer collaborative, termination of the relationship offers one way of resolving relationship problems in the longer term. Ending a close relationship, though, is interlinked with a range of other social and possibly legal practices, as we shall see.

Neighbor disputes

In a series of studies, Elizabeth Stokoe and her colleagues have examined some of the issues that potentially can arise between neighbors. One point of possible contention, as we might expect in disputes among people who live in close proximity to each other, is space. We all have a sense of our own spaces and understandings of what we can reasonably do within the limits of our own homes. Our constructions of space, however, inevitably must meet our neighbors' constructions of their homes and of what is reasonable for them. Boundaries can become the meeting points of two or more very different sets of expectations and actions. Take, for example, boundary hedges that might impact upon spaces beyond the immediate confines of one garden. Questions arise of to what extent a hedge should be allowed to grow into a neighboring property, who is entitled to cut it back if necessary, and so on. In these and other instances, descriptions of spaces are very much linked to constructions of the actions that are appropriate within these spaces. These constructions of space provide sites for the negotiation of neighbor relations, in terms of individual identities and entitlements. Good neighbors are viewed as people who carry out whatever activities they choose within their own homes, but who do not intrude upon the space of those around them. Bad neighbors, however, intrude upon the space of neighbors and impinge upon their range of choices (Stokoe & Wallwork, 2003).

Closely linked to considerations of space is the matter of noise. The sounds of the activities that individuals carry out within spaces often impact upon others in the close or not so close vicinity. Many of us, for example, will have heard the sounds of neighbors cutting the grass or doing other gardening activities. Ordinarily, we treat such sounds as unexceptional and as directly appropriate to the space in which they originate. Other sounds, however, are commonly treated as exceptional, and often complainable, issues. Excessive noise coming from a neighbor's late night party might not be accepted in quite the same way as the sound of daytime gardening, especially where it impacts upon activities such as sleeping, and might form the basis of a complaint to the neighbors or to the police if it persists. Sounds, like space, can be described as reasonable or unreasonable, according to the argument that is being made. Where individuals are making complaints to others on the basis of sounds coming from a neighbor's house, the complaint usually rests upon the sounds themselves and of the activities that might be inferred from them. Thus, for example where people report complaints to a child helpline, the complaint will often be based upon the occurrence of sounds that do not appear to reflect normal family activities and that therefore should be treated as legitimate grounds for concern (Stokoe & Hepburn, 2005).

Complaints about neighbors, on the basis of space or noise, usually construct the com-

plainer's actions as being entirely reasonable and unexceptional. Neighbors' actions, by contrast, are constructed as being unreasonable in not corresponding to activities that are reasonable in a neighboring context. Neighbor relations and disputes thus are bound up with issues of morality as to what being a neighbor actually should involve. Often, however, disputes between neighbors also bring in wider issues of morality and of what should be expected of people in a broader sense as members of a social order.

1 G: y'know it's getting– it's getting real serious this is (.) ↑but the
2 lad keeps getting away with it (.) unfortunately (.) his mother hasn't
3 got a bloke there (.) so she is talking in [front of the children
4 L: [she's not living there half
5 the time is she=
6 G: =no she's out at night and they are using it as a– a rendezvous for the
7 gang
[. . .]
8 G: that's the whole top [and bottom of it
9 L: [it's like the dustbin left out for a week (?) on
10 [the pavement
11 G: [IT's ALL TO DO with this one lad (.) right (.) we've had report– we've
12 got connections at the school (.) they said "what's the point of him
13 coming to school he knows nothing (.) he only causes trouble" (0.5) so
14 [they never bothered about him
15 L: [it's like they've had words with this woman and can't get through to
16 her from school you know [course (.) he's left now so
17 G: [(?)
[. . .]
18 G: (?) °no no° I mean the funny thing about this is that (.) in actual
19 fact (.) I mean the lady's got to be responsible (.) she's got to
20 be responsible [at the end of the day because [she's never there [she
21 E: [well she's never there is she
22 L: [( ) she's effing and
23 G: can't control him
24 E: yeah

(Stokoe, 2003, p. 326)

The extract above comes from a dispute mediation session, in which two married couples (Graham and Louise, Bob and Ellen) are discussing with a mediator a complaint about a family living in their street, specifically a complaint that children of the family have been vandalizing their properties. Although the complaint draws in issues of space and behavior, this complaint is set also in a context of family relationships between the children who are carrying out the vandalism and their mother. The actions of the children are constructed, first as unreasonable in themselves, and second as evidence of the moral failure of the mother to discharge adequately her obligations as a parent to her children. The actions that are complained of accordingly become presented as breaches of a moral order that extends well beyond immediate concerns of space and behavior into other aspects of identity and action (Stokoe, 2003).

Neighbor disputes can go even further beyond the immediate vicinity of proximate living, as seen below.

```
1   C:   An' a coupla times:since then. .pt .hhh
2   M:   Ye– racial abuse.
3   C:   Yep.
4   M:   °H:mm.°
5              (1.1)
6   C:   Uh: >I–I–< I'm Asian:: my Wes– my
                            [wife is] West
7   M:                     [Right. ]
8   C:   Indian:
9   M:   ↑Oh: o– [okay. (Mm.)]
10  C:          [.hhhh um:: ]
11            (0.9)
12  C:   Um: uh such as (.) Paki family: etcetera hhh
13  M:   Oh:::.
14            (0.2)
                  (Stokoe & Edwards, 2007, p. 361)
```

The grounds of this complaint, also being raised in a mediation context, rely upon reported instances of racism and of the identities of individuals in broad social terms. Group memberships can be as relevant to neighbor disputes as they are elsewhere and can thus come to form part of the context within which relationship of being neighbors and its difficulties are played out. These and the other findings considered here give some indication of the possible scope of such disputes, ranging from immediate contact or

presence to identity with the social groups that people belong to and possibly further. What such findings suggest is that there is no exhaustive list of possibilities by which neighbor disputes can go wrong. Moreover, when they do go wrong, they can go very wrong. It is perhaps not surprising, therefore, that neighbor relationships have provided such rich pickings for the makers of television programs, who can encourage us to laugh at some of the difficulties or to view with alarm the extent of the problems that can arise.

Family and relationship troubles

Many of the difficulties that arise within families are resolved in the context of the family itself: ongoing family processes, dinnertime conversations, and other interactions provide space for renegotiating dynamics and for the construction of meanings that can be collaborative and shared rather than conflicting. When, however, family problems cannot be resolved in such ways, ending of the problematic relationships usually is not a readily available option. A more recognized course of action to address such issues is for the family to seek external help to overcome the difficulties, often by means of consulting a counselor or therapist. In the course of therapy sessions, family members can raise topics that are constructed as problematic within the family and be guided by the therapist in attempt to rework meanings and understandings of their concerns. Not all family members, however, are able to contribute fully towards this reworking.

```
1   MUM:   Well. (.) 'e's pushed me do↓wn the
                   sta:irs twice
2   FT:                ↓Right.
3   MUM:   bruised me leg and .hh (.) me *arms
4   DAD:             Threatened 'er (.) <who did
                   he> [threaten with a knife
5           the oth↑er day?
6→  KEVIN:                            [Da:d?
7   NIC:    ((raises her hand))
8   LEE:               ↑Ye↓ah
9   MUM:   ↑Yea::h
10  FT:              Right.
                        (O'Reilly, 2006, p. 555)
```

The extract above comes from a session in which a couple are discussing with the therapist the behavior of their son Steve, behavior that is presented as being extreme and disruptive to family patterns. Another son, Kevin, attempts to break in to the discussion but his attempted contribution is ignored both by parents and by the therapist as the discussion proceeds. Whether that contribution would or would not been relevant to the discussion itself we can only surmise. On other occasions, parents do pick up on and respond to children's interruptions.

```
1  MUM:  And 'e got 'is hair off with that and
          >chucked it< on the
2                floor >and I says< we [ll
                 once ↓yo–
3  STEVE: [NO I Haven't I dropped *it on the
4                ↑flo:or
5  DAD:           <YOU [threw it> across the
                 livin' ro:om befo:re n↑ow
6  MUM:   [N– <YOU CHUCKED IT> .hh I was
          ↑there and seen ya
7                >and I says< once you break
                 that <you ARE NOT 'avin'
8                another one> because they're
                 not ↓cheap they are a lot of
9                money.
                        (O'Reilly, 2006, p. 562)
```

Here the interruption is immediately taken up as being relevant to the topic being discussed, that is, Steve's behavior. The response, however, is still a negative one, **undermining** Steve's denial that his behavior was extreme. In this way, the exchange confirms the construction of the complaint that is being advanced as indicative of the family problems that are under discussion (O'Reilly, 2006). Children therefore appear unsuccessful in attempting to contribute to family therapy sessions and to the working out of difficulties within the family, unless their contributions largely coincide with those being advanced by their parents. Even in such instances, children's contributions are more likely to be treated as indicative of the difficulties within the family rather than as part of a wider consideration of the issues that are being discussed.

Counseling and therapeutic settings also provide opportunities for the discussions of problems within marriages and partnerships. There are of

course other possibilities for seeking assistance. A highly influential source of possible assistance for couples comes in the form of self-help books, perhaps best exemplified by the top-selling book *Men are from Mars, women are from Venus* (Gray, 1992). Much of the advice provided in this popular text, however, comprises little more than a restatement of traditional understandings of gender roles within relationships, and places responsibility for achieving relationship harmony on female partners. This advice, although perhaps acceptable to many male spouses and relationship partners, is likely to prove unsatisfying in many respects to female partners, especially where prevailing understandings of gender are implicated in the difficulties within relationships (Crawford, 2004). Counseling thus offers a rather more interactive and potentially open way for both partners to explore relationship issues.

Couple counseling, however, is far from a neutral endeavor within which both parties attempt to put their relationship back on an even footing. We have already seen that the breakdown of heterosexual relationships is commonly treated as an accountable matter, in that it leads to the termination of a socially valued form of relationship. If accountability for relationship failure is an overriding consideration, then the apportionment of blame for such failure is likely to become all the more relevant in the presence of a third party. Thus, rather than being neutral supportive and investigative contexts, couple counseling sessions can easily become sites for attributing blame for the breakdown of relationships. Individuals accordingly provide descriptions of the relationship and its troubles in ways that account for their own actions and attribute blame to their partners (Edwards, 1995). In a classic study, Buttny (1993) examines the ways in which the partners of one particular couple account for their relationship troubles. (See 'Classic Study' box on p. 86.)

Just as understandings of relationships are located within broader social patterns, so are understandings of the breakdowns of these relationships. The termination of an established close relationship brings problems for the couple involved in that relationship, certainly, but can also have major repercussions for other relationships. Where children are involved in the family that is breaking up, they too will have to make sense of

Undermining Weakening or countering an argumentative position

CLASSIC STUDY: Accountability for relationship troubles

Buttny provides a detailed analysis of a couple counseling session involving an unmarried couple, Jenny and Larry, and their therapist, Sluzki. Within this consultation, Jenny and Larry describe at length problems encountered within their relationship. Each of the couple describes the problems so as to attribute responsibility for the relationship difficulties to the other, while at the same time negating their own potential blame and responsibility.

The couple's descriptions are addressed to the therapist rather than to each other. This sequence makes it more difficult for Jenny and Larry immediately to resist the accounts that the other provides, in that the therapist might take the next turn. The succeeding turn by Jenny or Larry consequently is likely to provide a counter-version of the earlier description that accounts for her or his own actions or dispositions. This counter-version provides an alternative version of the relationship problems that attributes blame to the other partner. Accounts in therapeutic settings can thus easily adopt a blame–defense pattern.

In this consultation, the therapist uses questions, interruptions, and evaluations to frame the unfolding descriptions of the relationship. The therapist's account of the interaction as a therapeutic intervention is available in its own right, published as Sluzki (1990). Here the therapist's turns can be understood as part of a collaborative construction of the meanings and patterns of the relationship, involving all three people present in the session.

The consultation therefore forms part of an ongoing process of negotiating the meanings of the relationship. Jenny's and Larry's constructions of their relationship follow what appears to be a familiar pattern of blame and defense. The therapist's contributions are designed to highlight the recurrence of these patterns and to provide scope for the couple's ongoing negotiations to take on different, and possibly less blame-oriented, forms.

Buttny, R. (1993). *Social accountability in communication* (pp. 66–84). London and Newbury Park, CA: Sage.

the termination of the relationship and of the somewhat changed family circumstances in which they find themselves. Again, the assistance of another might help to facilitate the negotiation of different understandings of past and ongoing family life. In contrast to family counseling sessions in which children often are unheard, counselors in these sessions are more likely to demonstrate that they are listening to children and hearing their concerns (Hutchby, 2005).

Marriage, as the most valued form of interpersonal relationship, requires more effort if it is to be dissolved fully. Divorce is a common legal procedure that marks the end of the relationship, albeit not usually in such a public manner as the commencement of a marriage. This process thus requires individuals who are seeking divorce to make sense of the breakdown of their relation-

ship in ways that will be recognizable by the courts (Wharton, 2006). Legal procedures require individuals to provide explicit grounds upon which they seek particular outcomes, and almost invariably necessitate attributions of blame. Attributions of blame and accountability for the termination of the relationship thus again assume a particular importance.

On the conclusion of divorce, however, the couple legally become separate individuals. Like those who have ceased to be in other close relationships, divorced individuals are then socially accountable in other ways, for the ending of the relationship and for now being single. At that point they, like others, can start again if they choose to do so, attempting to do attraction and seeking possibilities of entering into new and as yet unknown relationships.

Chapter summary

- Attraction is a collaborative outcome of interaction and depends upon initial communications and responses. For women, sexual attraction is problematic in that female sexual desire is often understood to be morally blameworthy.
- Heterosexual relationships remain highly valued and are often assumed to be the usual form of close relationship. Involvements in lesbian and gay relationships have to be made explicit. Individuals commonly have to account for being single and for the ending of previous close relationships.
- Traditional versions of parenting are less prominent but have not been superseded by different forms. Parents and families have to deal with tensions between divergent understandings of parental responsibilities and arrangements.
- Within families, young children acquire communication skills in their interactions with family members. Families also provide contexts for the introduction and negotiation of social practices.
- In playing with peers, children display understandings of relationships themselves and of the broader social order. Peer interactions can exclude rather than include individual children from full acceptance by their peers.
- Relationships can bring their own problems. Neighbor relationships, for example, can involve conflict based upon a wide range of grounds. Troubles within families and close relationships are usually treated as issues of blame, in counseling and legal settings, and terminations of close relationships bring expectations of new attractions and relationships.

Connections

The study of relationships is closely interlinked with many other topics discussed in this book. In particular, understandings of relationships are connected to identities (Chapter 2), attributions (Chapter 5), issues of counseling (Chapter 10), and organizational interactions (Chapter 11).

Activity

Consider one non-family relationship in which you are involved. How did you initially become attracted to the other person? In what ways does that relationship link to other aspects of your life, such as friends, family, work, or otherwise? Does that relationship follow a pattern that seems familiar in society more generally? How do or would you explain the relationship to other people?

If you prefer, try the exercise above in relation to a relationship in which you were involved but which has ended. How do you make sense of the termination of that relationship? Are you required to do so?

Further reading

Haney, L. & March, M. (2003). Married fathers and caring daddies: Welfare reform and the discursive politics of paternity. *Social Problems*, 50, 461–481. A good example of how policy-makers' understandings of social practices can diverge greatly from people's understandings of everyday social life.

Katz, J. R. (2004). Building peer relationships in talk: Toddlers' peer conversations in childcare. *Discourse Studies*, 6, 329–346. An example of the positive side of early relationships, and of the considerable skills that children as young as 3 years display in their interactions with each other.

Chapter 5

Social Cognition

Topics covered in this chapter

Knowledge of Others and Mental States
Knowing and mental models
Not knowing and the sequential structure of
  conversation
Knowing and not knowing: Beyond
  cognitive states

Social Memory

Impression Management

Attributions

Categorization

Key terms

Action-orientation
Attribution
Categorization
Category-bound activities
Cognitive agnosticism
Cognitive state
Cognitivism
Disclaimer
Dispreferred
Extreme case formulation
Footing
Impression management
Interactional implications
Interactional resource
Making available
Making relevant
Management of inferences
Marker
Mediating factor
Mental model
Metaphor
Minimal response
Mutual knowledge
Orienting
Participants' categories
Practical concern
Recursive
Rhetoric
Sequential pattern
Stake

In January 2007, the *New York Times* reported a spat between the CNN news agency correspondent Wolf Blitzer and US Vice-President Dick Cheney. In the report, Blitzer was described as questioning Cheney's unwillingness to comment on his lesbian daughter's pregnancy given that, in the past, he had apparently supported anti-gay legislation. The report goes on to describe how Vice-President Cheney responded angrily to Blitzer's question.

This little episode raises some interesting topics for the social psychologist. Both Blitzer and Cheney clearly had differing perceptions about the social interaction in which they were engaged. Blitzer reveals that he knows something about Cheney – that he has apparently anti-gay views – and uses that knowledge to frame a question which he views as appropriate within that interactional context. Cheney, on the other hand, views the question as inappropriate. Blitzer also demonstrates his beliefs about Cheney as a person, one of which involves the judgment that Cheney could be acting in an inconsistent manner by having promoted anti-gay legislation and yet not criticizing his daughter's status as a potential gay parent. Cheney, on the other hand, realizes that Blitzer holds those beliefs about him and demonstrates that he feels this is unfair. Part of the tension observable between the two men arises from the different forms of social categorization which might be placed on Cheney. One might infer, given Cheney's membership of the category "politician," that he would publicly defend any anti-gay views he held. But one might also infer, given his membership of the category "parent," that he would refrain from criticizing his own daughter on national television.

So what are we to make of this disagreement? Was Cheney acting as a duplicitous and inconsistent politician? Or was he acting as a concerned parent? This particular episode is unusual because it involved famous figures in a very public forum. But, at the same time, it is also the sort of interaction with which we are all familiar in everyday life. Most of us have had the experience of interactions in which we suddenly wonder whether a friend or family member really knows us in the way we have come to expect. These sorts of issues, such as how we characterize what we know about each other, how we form impressions of each other, and how we attribute meaning to one another's actions, and how we reconstruct our memories of those actions, form the social psychological research area known as "social cognition." At first sight it might seem odd that discursive researchers are interested in "social cognition" because the term seems to imply a theoretical preoccupation with individual mental structures and functions. And, indeed, it is true that experimental social psychologists often study processes of impression formation and meaning attribution in those terms. But although discursive researchers focus their research efforts on discourse rather than on cognitive processes, they nevertheless have an interest in understanding social processes such as how people form impressions of, or make attributions to, other people. Moreover, as we will see, there is a range of views within discursive research on the extent to which reference to cognitive states and processes is a useful adjunct to the study of such discursive phenomena.

Knowledge of Others and Mental States

Knowing and mental models

One of the most central questions in social cognition which discursive researchers have examined is the question of social knowledge: how do we get an idea of what other people know, and how do they know what we know that they know? In trying to understand this sort of phenomenon, discursive researchers who work within the critical discourse analysis tradition reply upon a notion of **cognitive states** which would be familiar to the traditional experimental cognitive psychologist. According to this view, human behavior, including discourse, is caused by, or is at least constitutively associated with, mental states such as knowing something, or having motivations or experiencing emotions. Indeed, Chilton (2005) argues that one of the major problems in contemporary critical discourse analysis is that this causal connection between language and prior mental states is not often enough recognized within critical discourse analysis literature.

Cognitive state A condition which the mind is in at a given moment

These cognitive states are sometimes viewed as **mediating factors** between social structures on the one hand and individual human behavior and talk on the other. Of course this leaves open the question of in what such mediation consists. Wodak (2006) refers to this question as the "mediation problem." In presenting a preliminary solution to this problem, she argues that phenomena such as perceptions, beliefs, and memories label cognitive processes which are themselves essential parts of discourse processes. Cognitive phenomena of this sort come to be represented within the individual as "**mental models**" of people and events. And socialization into a specific culture can be thought of, in part, as learning how to automatically apply the mental models which ground "everyday" or "common-sense" understanding within that culture. So at the individual level, experienced life events come to be represented and reproduced according to the relevant mental model within which perception of those events was subsumed. Wodak notes that this process can be understood as a **recursive** one in which mental models and mental representations in episodic and long-term memory guide comprehension of experience but are also continuously updated by experience. However, this is not just an account of individual cognition, because these mental models can become more socially widespread. This process is one in which cognitive phenomena such as stereotypes are reinforced by discursive phenomena such as the use of **metaphors** and stories. As one example of this, Wodak discusses the way in which anti-Semitic stereotypes become more widespread. Specific discursive terms such as "East coast" have become recontextualized so that whereas in original contexts the phrase was used to refer to the idea that New York was a center of "powerful Jewish lobbies," the term subsequently became a more generalized reference in anti-Semitic talk. Another example is the way in which the semantic concepts of "immigrant" and "asylum seeker"

have become merged in political discourse of the rights and entitlements of those seeking to emigrate to other countries. In this sense, then, recursive mental models represent a cognitive link between discourse and society, and these cognitive processes can be seen as playing important social and ideological roles in constraining what it is we think we know about the people and events which such models depict.

It is important to note that critical discourse analysis views the process of developing and deploying mental models as one in which participants actively deploy language. For example, in the next chapter, when we look at discourses of persuasion, we will see that van Dijk (2002, 2006a, 2006b) offers an example of persuasive political discourse which can be characterized as an attempt to develop a mental model in the minds of listeners. In another example, Koller (2005) uses a study of business media discourse to show how an author may actively strive to create a mental model of economic relations in the minds of others. In this study, Koller explored the links between discourse and cognition by examining the ideological functioning of metaphoric models at both cognitive and social levels. Koller describes ideology as an "interface" between the cognitive representations underlying discourse and the interests of social groups. Koller points out that metaphoric models are especially useful in studying the cognitive and ideological determinants of discourse, because metaphors link the cognitive structures which underlie discourse to the ideology that permeates it. In her study, one of the metaphoric models she identifies in business merger discourse is that of evolutionary struggle, which encompasses three sub-metaphors of fighting, mating, and feeding.

1   How mergers go wrong
2   It is important to learn the lessons from the failures and successes of past

Mediating factor Some thing or property which links two events or states

Mental model A representation in the mind which organizes experience of the external world

Recursive Having the property of repetitiveness in which an operation may repeatedly apply to itself

Metaphor A figure of speech used to refer to something not literally identified by means of similarities between it and the thing which is explicitly mentioned

3 mergers

4 They are, like second *marriages*, a triumph of hope over experience. A stream of

5 studies has shown that corporate mergers have even higher failure rates than the

6 liaisons of Hollywood stars. One report by KPMG, a consultancy, concluded that

7 over half of them had destroyed shareholder value, and a further third had made

8 no difference. Yet over the past two years, companies around the globe have

9 jumped into *bed* with each other on an unprecedented scale.

[. . .]

10 Most of the mergers we have looked at were **defensive**, meaning that they were

11 initiated in part because the companies involved were under threat. Sometimes,

12 the threat was a change in the size or nature of a particular market: McDonnell

13 Douglas merged with Boeing, for example, because its biggest customer, the

14 Pentagon, was cutting spending by half. Occasionally the threat lay in that

15 buzzword of today, globalization, and its concomitant demand for greater scale:

16 Chrysler merged with Daimler-Benz because, even as number three in the

17 world's largest car market, it was too small to prosper alone. Or the threat may

18 have come from another **predator**: Bayerische Vereinsbank sought a merger

19 with a Bavarian rival, Hypobank, because its management was scared of being

20 **gobbled up** by Deutsche Bank.

21 When a company merges to escape a threat, it often imports its problems into the

22 *marriage*. Its new *mate*, in the starry moments of *courtship*, may find it easier to

23 see the opportunities than the challenges. Hypobank is an egregious example: it

24 took more than two years for Vereinsbank to discover the full horror of its

25 partner's balance sheet.

[. . .]

26 Above all, personal chemistry matters every bit as much in mergers as it does in

27 *marriage*. It matters most at the top. No company can have two bosses for long.

28 [. . .] Without leadership from its top manager, a company that is being bought can

29 all too often feel like a **defeated army** in an occupied land, and will wage

30 guerrilla **warfare** against a deal. The fact that mergers so often fail is not, of itself,

31 a reason for companies to avoid them altogether. But it does mean that merging

32 is never going to be a simple solution to a company's problems. And it also

33 suggests that it would be a good idea, before they book their *weddings*, if

34 managers boned up on the experiences of those who have gone before. They

35 might begin with our series of briefs (see article).

(Koller, 2005, p. 211)

Koller notes that all three sub-metaphors appear in this extract, taken from the *Economist* journal. She argues that the text is designed to persuade the reader to frame the issue of business mergers in terms of the mating sub-metaphor, by inserting that metaphor at the beginning and end of the text. The negative implications of the title of the text, "How mergers go wrong," are developed in the text through the sub-metaphor of marriages which may lead to subsequent relationship breakdowns. The identification of business mergers with interpersonal relationships is further established by the subsequent explicit reference to "mating." The "feeding" and "fighting" sub-metaphors are worked up in the text by the references to predators and to entities being "gobbled up" and to descriptions of a company being akin to a "defeated army" and involved in "warfare." Koller also points to the way in which these sub-metaphors are interlinked. For example, she argues that the idea, drawn from the "feeding" sub-metaphor, of a predator gobbling up the competition is related to the notion drawn from the "fighting" sub-metaphor of companies facing a "threat" against which they must take "defensive" actions. Koller concludes that the deployment of the composite "evolutionary struggle" metaphoric model is an ideological move on the part of the author whose aim is to recast the reader's perceptions of business practices in terms of a neoliberal logic of economic activity as aggressive behavior.

Not knowing and the sequential structure of conversation

Discourse researchers have, then, been interested in understanding how discourse processes are bound up with social knowledge about people and events. However, lack of knowledge, or mis-understanding, has also proven to be of interest to discursive researchers, especially in the con-versation analytic field, because it seems to be an area in which the interests of the conversation ana-lyst overlap those of the cognitive researcher. For example, recently Schegloff (2006) has indicated that there are possible rapprochements between the conversation analyst's close attention to what is said and the neurocognitivist's goal of design-ing explanatory models of how interactions are cognitively processed. Schegloff complains that cur-rent cognitive science places an undue emphasis on individual mental states rather than on empirically grounded studies which explore the fine-grain detail of actual interaction. However, he suggests that more appropriate cognitive models could be developed which would explain the "workings and capacities" of interaction by showing how the resources of interaction are deployed in talk. This sort of cognitive science would provide generalized explanations which were capable of dealing with the wide variety of specific episodes that arise in genuinely empir-ical interactional data. As an example of this, Schegloff draws attention to the different ways in which everyday talk seems to be designed to encompass a number of speakers' "possible un-derstandings." Schegloff discusses a variety of data which typify occasions where participants treat an utterance as a "possible X" where X might be some conversational event such as a turn-completion or an invitation or an understanding.

1 ART: Which one::s are closed, an' which ones are open.
2 ZEL: ((pointing to map)) Most of 'em. This, this,
3   [this, this
4 ART: → [I don't mean on the shelters, I mean on the roads.
5 ZEL: Oh!

(Schegloff, 2006, p. 146)

In this extract, one of the participants is seeking to gather information from the other. Schegloff draws attention to the way in which the particip-ants deal with Zel's misunderstanding of what Art was referring to by "ones." Art corrects Zel's misunderstanding by specifying the referent of "ones" as roads, not shelters. This demonstrates

that both Art and Zel "entertained" at least two different possible understandings of the original utterance. In episodes such as this, Schegloff argues, participants must manage a number of tasks: they must address the number of different possible X's which the utterance might repre-sent; they must resolve that multiplicity of poss-ibilities into a determinate grasp of what was actually being said or done; they must display that grasp in their own actions in response to the initial utterance. Schegloff suggests that cognitive science may be a useful resource in explaining these capacities which underlie the ability to carry out these tasks. In entertaining possible X's such as possible understandings, the participants are pursuing possible understandings of talk along "multiple lines." This, says Schegloff, indicates that a neurocognitive model for processing of inter-action should be designed to account for the fact that people apparently utilize "multiple passes" of understanding an interactional episode in which these various possible understandings are given consideration.

In a similar vein, Drew (2005) has suggested that the notion of cognitive states such as mis-understanding plays an important role in con-versation analytic work. He draws attention to cases where cognitive states "manifestly come to the interactional surface" even though they are not overtly expressed, are not the focus of attributional references, and participants do not use the dis-play of cognitive states as interactional resources. In "cognitive moments" of this sort, Drew sug-gests that social action can be thought of as con-tingent upon a cognitive state. In these cases, the analyst's interest is in understanding the social organization of the conversational **sequential patterns** which routinely arise at these "cognitive moments." Although the cognitive state is not it-self manifested as an interactional resource by participants, there is still a sense in which it is interactionally generated in that one speaker's realization that another speaker is in some cognitive state or other is observable in the way that prior conversational turns and subsequent responses are designed. As an example of this sort

Sequential pattern The design of an episode in talk in terms of its turn-taking structure

of thing, Drew introduces episodes where the cognitive state of confusion arises in accounts.

```
1   LES:   .pk An' I got s'm nice cott'n to:ps:: I'm
2           Not g'nna[tell Skip    ].hhh
3   JOY:            [↑Oh did   ↓y]ou:
4   LES:   Ye::s. u–I meant (.) only to get one or
            two.hhh but
5           they're– (0.2) iyou kno:w I mean if I stock
            up ↓now
6           then I don't need t'do it again do I
7           hhe[h heh h]a–[: .hhhhh
8   JOY: + [Ye:↓ah.] [°Ri:ght,°
9   LES:   Yes.[°( ) °
10  JOY: +      [Oh weh:– what (.) duh–aa–ou:ter–:
            wear: tops you
11          mean
12  LES:   .hhh Well no: some I c'n wear under-
            neath::.
13  JOY:   ↑Oh:.
14  LES:   You see::? d–against my skin,hh
15  JOY:   Oh:[:'
16  LES:      [.hhh An' some ↓↓I c'n wear on
            top. ↓↓.hhh But the
17          ↑thing was I couldn't get eh:m .p.t I
            couldn't get a
18          (.) cott'n: (.) pettycoat or(p) (.) p-
            cott'n slip
19          any ↓where.
20  JOY:   Coul[↓d'n you[:
21  LES:       [.h h h [No: they're all: this
            polyester mos'ly,
                            (Drew, 2005, p. 176)
```

Lesley provides a report on events at lines 1 to 6 which ends with her seeking support for her actions by asking "do I." Instead of offering a supportive reply, however, Joyce offers two very minimal, quietly spoken utterances at line 8. Drew points out that this **minimal response**, coupled with the fact that she does not join in with Lesley's laughter, displays that Joyce has some sort of problem with what Lesley said. Drew then suggests that the reason for this surfaces at lines 9, 10, and 11, where it becomes clear that Joyce is uncertain about what Lesley bought. Lesley produces a confirmation, "Yes," despite the fact

---

Minimal response A conversational turn, produced in response to a prior turn, which is noticeably brief

---

that Joyce has indicated that there is something problematic in what has passed up to that moment. So by this point, Lesley and Joyce seem to have reached some sort of impasse, in that Lesley has sought a confirmation from Joyce and subsequently treats what Joyce said as though it was such a confirmation, while Joyce, on the other hand, seems to treat what Lesley originally said as some sort of conversational difficulty. Drew argues that the route out of this impasse for the two participants begins in Joyce's subsequent turn at line 10. By asking whether Lesley meant outerwear, Joyce can be seen to introduce a phase of the conversation in which her potential misunderstanding can be conversationally repaired. Her question displays to Lesley what her current understanding of her original comment is and this gives Lesley a conversational slot in which she can, if required, repair Joyce's misunderstanding. It is in this sense that Drew suggests that "cognitive moments" are also interactional phenomena, because Joyce's cognitive state of uncertainty has resulted in a sequential position in this unfolding interaction in which her uncertainty is exposed. It is this sequential turn which then opens up for Lesley the possibility of clearing up Joyce's confusion by explaining that she is talking about tops which can be worn "against the skin . . . You see?"

Knowing and not knowing: Beyond cognitive states

Other discursive researchers have been less willing to deploy cognitive states such as knowing or misunderstanding as explanatory phenomena. From the perspective of discursive psychology, Potter and te Molder (2005) define "cognition" in terms of a set of criterial features: cognition involves internal mental states which are directed to or about something. Cognition is therefore associated with the notions of perception, on the one hand, and knowledge on the other. Discursive social psychologists do not focus their analyses on examining or revealing mental states of this sort. Instead, they are interested in explaining social psychological phenomena in terms of discourse processes (Edwards, 2006a; Edwards & Potter, 2005). In this approach, cognitive issues are only relevant when they become matters of interest to participants themselves as revealed in their talk.

> In contrast to **cognitivism**, DP (discursive psychology) has a very different way of conceptualizing psychological issues. Instead of treating discourse as dependent upon, and explicable by way of, cognitive objects and processes, it starts by studying the way things appear as participants' concerns. That is, it treats mind, personality, experience, emotions, intentions and so on in terms of how they are constructed and oriented to in interaction.
>
> (Potter, 2006, p. 132)

> The key to DP (discursive psychology) is that it is primarily a way of analysing talk and text. It does not start with psychological questions, and does not offer a rival theory of mind. Nor does it deny the reality and importance of subjective experience. Rather, DP rejects the assumption that discourse is the product or expression of thoughts or intentional states lying behind or beneath it. Instead, mental states, knowledge, thoughts, feelings, and the nature of the external world, figure as talk's topics, assumptions and concerns.
>
> (Edwards, 2006a, p. 41)

In approaches of this sort, cognitive themes are revealed in talk as matters of interest to participants in at least two different ways: either in (1) participants' explicit use of cognitive terms or in (2) participants' **management of inferences** and implications about cognitive matters (Potter & Edwards, 2003).

(1) *Participants' use of cognitive terms.* When participants themselves make use of cognitive state terms such as "knowing," "wanting," or "remembering," the discursive analyst's social psychological interest is to understand how such terms are used interactionally and **rhetorically**. In other words, the analyst seeks to understand why these terms are deployed at a particular moment in conversation as opposed to alternative terms which could reasonably be viewed as relevant alternatives within the local conversational context.

(2) *Participants' management of cognitive implications and inferences.* Discursive research is also interested in a range of cases where participants themselves do not deploy cognitive terms but where cognitive themes become relevant. In these cases, discursive analyses of participants' talk reveal how participants' descriptions of actions, actors, and events are built in such a way that cognitive issues are **made available** as reasonable potential inferences on the part of hearers or are countered as being inappropriate potential inferences. For example, speakers may produce talk which is designed to have the characteristics of "mere" description or statement of fact. And in this talk, there may be no use of cognitive terms. But this descriptive statement might be formulated in such a way that the speaker makes available to hearers the inference that what is said is warranted by a cognitive state such as knowledge rather than, say, an alternative cognitive state such as guessing. On the other hand, the statement might be formulated to undermine potential inferences that what the speaker says derives from a cognitive state such as having a particular motivation or interest in making the statement.

We can turn to the topic of knowledge in order to see how this version of discursive research operates in practice by examining Edwards's (2004) study of the phenomenon of shared or **mutual knowledge**. This is the idea that when people talk to each other, on occasion an individual can be seen to attend to what it is about what is being said that the other person knows. Edwards points out that other forms of research such as psycholinguistics rely on explaining shared knowledge by characterizing the mental states of the participants, especially in terms of an individual's hunches or guesses about

---

Cognitivism An approach to explaining people's behavior in terms of their cognitive states

---

Management of inferences Dealing with issues which speakers might be taken to have implicitly introduced

---

Rhetoric The way talk is designed, e.g., through lexical choices, to perform actions within local contexts of talk

---

Making available Allowing a hearer to make an inference about something which is not explicitly stated by the speaker

---

Mutual knowledge Something known to some or all of the participants in an interaction

or mental models of what the other person knows. However, from the discursive psychologist's viewpoint, this sort of intersubjectivity is better thought of as a part of what participants are doing when they perform social actions through their talk.

```
1   E:  (. . .) I teach at uh:: North Cadb'ry a boy call'
2       Neville Cole?
3   L:  Oh:: [yes:,
4   E:       [over there, (perchance yo[u know im?=
5   L:                                  [hn
6   L:  =No I do:[n't
7   E:          [Uh::::m
8       (0.6)
9   L:  ['s lots of Coles.]
10  E:  [He's at Ansford as we] : ll.
11  L:  Hm:?
12  E:  He's at Ansford as we : ll
13  L:  hAh:.
14      (0.3)
15  E:  A::[nd
16  L:     [↑Oh  I   know:w  him:,  nuh–  nice
            fam↓ily.=
17  E:  =Neville Cole yeh.[( )
18  L:                    [↑Ye:s  ↑Gordon's  very
                           friendly
19      with ↓Ronald the older son.=
20  E:  =Right.
```
(Edwards, 2004, pp. 46–47)

In this extract, Ed is responding to a query from Lesley about whether he does "private teaching." Edwards points out that there is apparently something slightly odd about Lesley's conversational turns at lines 3 and 6. She appears to acknowledge that she does know the boy Ed mentions but then, moments later, appears to say that she does not know him. Edwards claims that, rather than attempt to understand the mental state or states which Lesley is in, it is more fruitful for the analyst to understand the sequential unfolding of the turns in the conversation. He points out that after Ed has offered, at lines 1 and 2, an opportunity for Lesley to produce a recognition response, Lesley does so. But she does so only in a very minimal form in that she does not go on to say anything about the boy which would develop the idea that she does know him. Edwards suggests that this minimal response is treated by Ed as some sort of indication that Lesley does not really know the boy, in

that Ed "pursues" Lesley's recognition response by making an explicit enquiry about whether Lesley does in fact know the boy. In other words, although Lesley indicates at line 3 that she does recognize the boy, both Lesley and Ed **orient** towards that recognition response as though it might indicate a lack of knowledge. It is in this sense, says Edwards, that the notion of Ed knowing or not knowing what Lesley knows or does not know becomes analytically relevant.

At lines 7 and 8, Ed demonstrates this difficulty which has arisen about what Lesley knows. Lesley subsequently produces an explanatory account for why she might not be able to recognize the boy, because there are a lot of Coles while, in overlapping talk, Ed goes on to give further information which Lesley might use to identify the boy. In this sense, both Lesley and Ed orient to what has been said up until then as though it indicates that Lesley may have insufficient information about the boy to identify him. Lesley responds to Ed's turns by indicating, at line 13, that what Ed has said is informative and then, at line 16, she produces an explicit statement of recognition. Edwards points to the way that in this statement, unlike that at line 3, Lesley goes on to provide further information about the boy as a means of showing or demonstrating that she does indeed recognize him. Edwards concludes that this shows the way in which the question of what Lesley knows is worked up interactionally by both Lesley and Ed. Moreover, Edwards argues, the analysis of the extract reveals that the analyst is in a position to account for a phenomenon such as intersubjective knowledge without recourse to mental or cognitive states. Instead, all that requires to be said about what Lesley and Ed know can be captured by examining the publicly available discourse which they use to negotiate that knowledge.

This idea, that there need be no analytic reference to cognitive states, is echoed in the work of some conversation analysts (McHoul & Rapley, 2003). From this perspective, Antaki (2006) has described the discursive approach here as one of being "agnostic" about cognition itself, focusing instead on how cognition is practically dealt with

Orienting Interpreting what is said in a specific way

by people in discourse. As an example, Antaki examines a conversation between a careworker and a client with a learning disability, Mal, about what Mal knows.

```
1     R   Um::::, >so Mal< where do you get your
          money from.
2         (1.8)
3→    M   I don't know
4         (3.0)
5     R   Where does it come from.
6         (1.5)
7→    M   °don' know r'lly°
8         (2.0)
9→    M   don't ↑know.
10        (2.1)
11    R   Have you got a job.
12        (.4)
13    M   eh?
14    R   Do you get a– I mean– a lot o' people,
          get money from, (.)
15        from th' jobs, is that °that how you get
          your money?°
16        (1.0)
17    M   (bank).
18        (1.2)
19    R   Ye:ah,
20        (2.5)
21    M   From the bank real [ly
22    R                     [°yeh°
23        (2.0)
24→   R   >Cos I mean<, y– you know who pays
          the rent, don't you cos y–,
25        y–, (jumm–) bt– when I >sd wh' ps the
          rent< you said >the
26        ↑council pays the rent< din'ya.
27    M   Yeah he does yeah=
28    R   =Yeah
```

(Antaki, 2006, pp. 10–11)

During the conversation, the careworker asks Mal what he knows about where his money comes from. Mal's answer is that he does not know. However, as Antaki reveals, the conversation unfolds with the careworker offering a variety of hints to the client about his financial resources to which the client offers limited agreements. Thus although the careworker could have accepted Mal's denial of knowledge at line

> **Practical concern** An issue which participants address through talk which has consequences beyond the talk itself

3, instead he goes on to reformulate his question at line 5 and then subsequently, at line 11, to provide Mal with a suggestion about where his money might come from. The careworker reinforces this hint at lines 14 and 15 but Mal's eventual response is dealt with by the careworker as in some way unsatisfactory, in that he provides only the most minimal of responses. So up to this point, the conversation reveals that Mal is being "disallowed" from not knowing where his money comes from, and from "knowing" falsely that it comes from a bank. Finally, the careworker offers yet another hint by telling Mal what he does know, that his rent is paid by the council. At a later point in this conversation beyond the segment which is presented here, the careworker concludes by attributing to Mal a "good understanding" of his own financial affairs. The point of this, says Antaki, is that it demonstrates that having a cognition such as knowing something is best understood as a **practical concern** for the conversational participants. Within a context in which a careworker is attempting to teach a client something about managing money, the question of whether that client knows something about his money turns on the specific features of that local conversational context, together with the practical outcomes which follow on from that. That is, given that the careworker is attempting to teach Mal something about money, the series of hints and reformulations of what Mal knows are best understood in a context in which teachers teach their pupils through a process of hinting and encouraging them to come up with appropriate answers. And within such a context, the issue of Mal's knowledge is just one **interactional resource** which is unpacked as the conversational sequence unfolds. To this extent, then, the issue of Mal's cognitive states of knowing or not knowing are of no direct relevance to the analyst. Elsewhere, Antaki (2004) has emphasized this **"cognitivist agnosticism"** by stressing that, for the

> **Interactional resource** An element of the discursive context which participants may deploy or draw on to accomplish a particular action or rhetorical effect

> **Cognitive agnosticism** In analysis, setting aside questions of whether cognitive states exist

CLASSIC STUDY: Discourse and cognition

In this text, Edwards begins by arguing that cognitive psychology has been overly influenced by the "mechanical" input–output model of stimulus–response behaviorism even though it was developed in opposition to behaviorist ideas. In response, Edwards introduces the notion of cognition as a discourse topic. In the subsequent chapter, Edwards describes the ways in which discourse-oriented researchers have tried to analyze notions such as factuality and reality by looking at the detail of how descriptive accounts are developed. He then takes the reader on a journey through conversation analytic research, emphasizing the conversation analyst's goal of explicating the role of discourse as an arena of social action. The book continues with an exploration of intersubjective knowledge of the sort which has been discussed in this present chapter. The book continues with a discussion of scripts, and

Edwards stresses the distinction between the way that cognitive scientists and conversation analysts utilize the idea of scripts. For the conversation analyst, unlike the cognitive theorist, scripts are worked up or challenged as just that, as routinized or structured ways of acting. In this sense, they are participants' accomplishments, rather than neutral features of events which people merely notice. In subsequent chapters, Edwards applies the same analytic approach to the study of other apparently prototypical cognitive states such as emotions, perceptions, and memories. Overall, the text represents one of discursive psychology's earliest fully worked-up accounts of the potential shortcomings of cognitive research and of the advantages of the turn to discourse.

Edwards, D. (1997). *Discourse and cognition.* London: Sage.

---

conversation analyst, when people report on their own mental states or those of others, their talk is treated as doing something, as accomplishing some sort of social action, rather than as referring to internal mental states.

Social Memory

In order to outline the various ways in which discursive research has sought to explore social cognition, we have focused till now on the issue of social knowledge. However, discursive researchers have also displayed interest in other areas of social cognition. One of these areas is social memory. Here, the aim of the discursive researcher is to reveal the ways in which claims about remembering or forgetting, or orientations to what is said as counting or not counting as appropriately remembered, carry **interactional implications** for participants (Howard & Tuffin,

> **Interactional implications** Consequences which may arise from a speaker's utterances and which are relevant to how the interaction proceeds

2002). For example, in Chapter 9, when we discuss discourse and the law, we will see how courtroom witnesses rely upon claims to remember or forget something as discursive maneuvers in the giving of evidence. The use of memory as a rhetorical resource in this way is highlighted in a study by Locke and Edwards (2003) of the testimony which President Bill Clinton provided to a Grand Jury about his relationship with the White House intern Monica Lewinsky.

8 C: I hav- (.) I hav– I know that Monica Lewinsky
9   (0.6) came to the gate (.) on (.) the sixth,
10   (0.5) and uh (.) apparently directly (.) called
11   in and wanted to see me (.) and couldn't, (.)
12   and was angry about it.
13   (0.9)
14 C: I know that.
15   (1.0)
16 Q: A:nd she expressed that anger to: (.) uh Betty
17   Currie over the teleph'one isn't that correct sir.
18 C: That– Betty told me that.

(Locke & Edwards, 2003, p. 242)

Immediately prior to this fragment of transcript, a Grand Jury questioner has asked Clinton whether he knew that Lewinsky was angry about not being admitted to see Clinton. Locke and Edwards note that, in his response, Clinton treats these events as problematic in terms of accurate recall. His response begins with truncated expressions and a reformulation from "I hav' to "I <u>know</u>." At line 10, he uses the **disclaimer** "app<u>a</u>rently," while at line 18 he produces a cut-off remark followed by a repair in which he states that his knowledge arose indirectly through something that Betty told him. These features, say Locke and Edwards, allow Clinton to focus on the way in which he is seeking to confirm only what he actually knows. They specify the limited nature of his knowledge claim while, at the same time, highlighting his own care and consideration in providing reliable testimony. In this way, Locke and Edwards argue, Clinton can be seen to draw upon memory and its limitations as a resource in dealing with the interactional issues which the Grand Jury testimony present for him.

Of course, the rhetorical force of appeals to memory is not restricted to courtroom encounters. Wooffitt (2005b), for example, has examined the ways in which the discourse of individuals' recollections of paranormal experiences displays structural similarities with verbal accounts of "flashbulb" memories. In cognitive psychology, flashbulb memories are taken to be memories about some significant or important event which someone has experienced and subsequently stored in memory in great detail.

1   I was mean a simple example which everybody's had
2   Something similar to hhhh I was living in uhm (.)
3   inglan years ago:
4   And all of a sudden
5 X I was sitting in bed one night (.)
6 ins Getting ready to go to sleep
7 Y And I decided to write to a friend I hadn't seen
8   For four years (.) in Massachusetts (.) a:and

> **Disclaimer** A phrase which is designed to prevent hearers from drawing otherwise potentially available inferences

9   I found myself congratulating her
10   On (.) the engagement of her oldest daughter
                          (Wooffitt, 2005b, p. 219)

Wooffitt draws this extract from a corpus of data in which people provide remembered accounts of paranormal experiences by using a specific "X happened," then "Y happened" format. In this format, a speaker refers to some activity, X, which was itself very commonplace or routine, but which then led on to an unusual, paranormal event, Y. Wooffitt's suggestion is that this format allows speakers to emphasize the mundane nature of the circumstances in which the remembered paranormal event occurred. Part of the reason for this particular design feature, according to Wooffitt, is that speakers are producing accounts of this sort in a context, that of talking about paranormal experiences, where hearers may be skeptical of or hostile to the claim which is being made. And so the X then Y format can be understood as in some ways a defensive strategy in which the speaker seeks to design the account so that it is less open to skeptical undermining.

In the present extract, the speaker claims to have been engaged in a commonplace activity, sitting in bed, when all of a sudden he or she acquired knowledge about a friend's daughter becoming engaged, although they had not spoken for a number of years. To this extent, the account fits the "X happened" then "Y happened" format. However, as Wooffitt points out, there is something particular about the mundane activity which the speaker has selected. Given that the speaker has described lying in bed, a skeptical hearer might infer that the supposedly paranormal event which followed was, in fact, merely a remembered dream. In the light of such possibly relevant skepticism, the speaker works up the memory as a remembered event by inserting additional information: the speaker was getting ready to sleep, and was therefore not actually asleep. Wooffitt suggests that in accounts of this sort, insertions are often added to the X then Y format. This further strengthens the account as an account of something remembered. It provides extra descriptive content, which makes the remembered story more vivid, but it also counters potential skeptical responses by dealing in advance with troublesome inferences which might otherwise arise from the mundane details provided in the "X" element of the story. In this way, Wooffitt argues, the structural features of his participants' accounts are selected by them in order to establish the authenticity of the memories which they are describing.

It is worthwhile noting that, as was the case with knowledge and misunderstanding, discursive research in the field of memory reveals a variety of approaches. For example, in one conversation analytic study of memory, Kitzinger (2006) follows Drew in emphasizing the way a cognitive state can become "manifest" in interaction. In contrast to Antaki's (2006) view of cognitive states, Kitzinger describes this position as being "non-agnostic" about memory. In her study, she suggests that although the participants are not analyzably designing their talk as claims about mental states, memory is generated and made relevant to the interaction during the course of other interactional business. In this study, Kitzinger examines a fragment of transcript taken from a telephone call made by a pregnant woman to a helpline for women experiencing problems with the planning of home births. In previous calls, the woman, Parvati, has discussed having a home birth despite medical advice to the contrary from her medical team. In the present extract, Parvati calls the helpline to reveal the news that she successfully gave birth at home.

```
01 CLT:  [We:ll I >think it] is marvellous<=And
          now
02        you can ring up the: (.) was it the au:nts
03        who said "are you having a caesarian
          section."
04        (.)
05 PAR:  Oh they're– they're already in the kno:w.
                              (Kitzinger, 2006, p. 79)
```

Kitzinger draws attention to the call-taker's (Clt) turn at lines 1 to 3, noting that this is a comment which both celebrates Parvati's success and functions as a first move towards closing the conversation. However it is, says Kitzinger, also a moment in the conversation where the call-taker's memory becomes manifest. In previous telephone calls, Parvati had mentioned her relatives and their expectation that she would have a caesarean delivery. In her current turn at lines 1 to 3, the call-taker refers to these aspects

of Parvati's previous telephone call, including reproducing the relatives' reported speech. Kitzinger notes that Parvati apparently accepts the call-taker's account as an adequate memory of what was said, in that her own turn moves on to a next action – informing the call-taker that "they" already know about the birth. Kitzinger concludes that this is clear evidence that the call-taker has a memory of the preceding telephone call, even though the question of the call-taker's memory does not arise as interactionally relevant for the participants. It is in this sense, says Kitzinger, that the call-taker's memory becomes "manifest" in the extract. So just as in the case of knowledge and misunderstanding, discursive research in the area of memory reveals that different discursive researchers hold different views on the status of memory as a mental state.

Impression Management

We all understand that in any social setting the people we are with not only perceive us but draw inferences or form judgments about us based on those perceptions. Indeed, we do the same thing ourselves. When we meet someone for the first time, we often rely upon basic clues such as mode of dress or speech and accent to form an impression of that person. For example, suppose you are attending a funeral. At the service, you see a scruffily dressed person who is loudly telling jokes to another person who is conservatively dressed and is quietly spoken. It is likely that you will form different impressions of these two individuals. Perhaps you will judge that the first person is insensitive in a way that the second person is not. Or you may infer that the two people have different ways of coping with sadness. Whatever the nature of your inferences, the basic process will be the same: you will form an impression of those people based on what you see and hear. But just because these processes are so prevalent, we have all, to a greater or lesser extent, become adept at managing the way we act and talk in order to manage or control the impressions which other people gain about us. It is this process of actively managing impressions, as opposed to regarding them as the passive outcome of social perceptions, in which discursive researchers have become especially interested.

The study of **impression management** dates back to the work of the sociologist Erving Goffman (1959), who analyzed the techniques that people use to control the impression of themselves that they give to others. Among those techniques, his work on **footing** (Goffman, 1979), the differing participants' roles which people may adopt in interaction, and framing (Goffman, 1974), the control of interpretative schemata to organize experience for rhetorical effect, has proven to be particularly influential in discursive research. As an example of "footing," consider the fragment of transcript below, which is taken from a discussion between a travel agent and a client (Ylänne-McEwen, 2004).

8	BETHAN:	looking forward to it?
9	MRS TAYLOR:	oh gosh yes I'm trying to think what to pack (.) when you have
10		this sort of weather it puts you off ((laughs))
11	BETHAN:	it's terrible isn't it I think you need one suitcase for the summer
12		clothes and then one suitcase for the winter clothes
13	MRS TAYLOR:	((smiling)) oh dear
14	BETHAN:	((quietly)) that's probably the best ((louder)) what you needed to
15		do is er to sign the bottom of that . . .

(Ylänne-McEwen, 2004, p. 524)

In this extract, the travel agent, Bethan, and the client, Mrs Taylor, begin by discussing the clothing requirements associated with Mrs Taylor's trip. During these conversational turns, Bethan can be thought of as adopting the role of friendly discussant, making small-talk about weather and clothes. However, Ylänne-McEwen notes that at line 14 Bethan switches footing in that she adopts the role of expert by issuing instructions to Mrs Taylor about how to complete a form.

Impression management Designing what is said in order to convey to others a picture or sense of what sort of person the speaker is

---

Footing A perspective which makes relevant properties of the speaker such as a range of normative actions or a set of social relationships

---

In the preceding example, Bethan's switch of footing might be regarded as a "bland" or everyday occurrence of impression management which arises out of the situational context in which Bethan, employed to give advice to holidaymakers, might be expected to routinely adopt this particular footing. However, discursive research reveals that impression management, as accomplished through discursive features such as footing, is often rhetorically employed in contexts where participants have a particular **stake** or interest in managing impressions. To see how impression management techniques are used in these more potentially controversial contexts, we can turn to a recent study by Condor and her colleagues (Condor, Figgou, Abell, Gibson, & Stevenson, 2006). The authors note that Goffman's original work on impression management implies that it is essentially a dialogical process. The emphasis on the interactive nature of such impression management, they say, reminds the researcher that management of this sort must be viewed as a collective accomplishment. That is, a potentially problematic inference about someone is only successfully managed by that person if the others with whom that person is interacting accept, rather than challenge, the forms of discourse through which the speaker is attempting to manage the relevant impression. There is, however, another consequence of the dialogical nature of impression management. Condor and her colleagues suggest that not only do people manage impressions on behalf of themselves, but they may also go further and attempt to manage the impressions of others. In particular, they demonstrate that people may not only attempt to manage the impression of themselves as prejudiced in some way, but they also seek to manage that impression of other people with whom they are interacting.

1	JACK:	[: : :] let's face it, it's not as if they're wanted here. We have enough low-
2		life here already without importing [other people's.
3	HILDA:	[Jack! ((to Susan)) I'm sorry about
4		that. He's not xenophobic. It's it's not=

Stake An interest in or concern with how what is said is interpreted by hearers

5 JACK: =it's not racist, no. We've never been
       racist, have we Hilda?
6 HILDA: No. We've got nothing against=
7 JACK: =nothing against the refugees. I have
       every sympathy for them. But you'd
8   be mad not to ask, why are they all
       coming <u>here</u>?
                      (Condor et al., 2006, p. 452)

At the start of this extract, Jack is concluding a statement about "illegal immigrants." Condor and her colleagues note that Jack's comment at line 1 is hearably xenophobic. However, his wife, Hilda, offers an apology to the interviewer and then attempts to defend Jack from a potential negative inference about his character by explicitly claiming that he is not xenophobic. Moreover, at line 5 Jack shifts footing to suggest that any imputation of this sort might be something that affected both himself and Hilda, rather than just himself, a shift in footing which Hilda accepts in her turn at line 6. So while Jack's initial statement might have given the impression that he is xenophobic, Hilda's comments work to defuse that potential inference about Jack, while both Jack and Hilda collusively adopt a footing switch which lessens Jack's own responsibility.

Another context in which the management of impressions is clearly bound up with controversial issues is the courtroom. In trials, lawyers for defense and prosecution are charged with the responsibility of providing summary statements, usually at the end of their presentations. Hobbs (2003a) has examined the way in which lawyers control this aspect of the trial by managing the impressions of themselves formulated by the trial jurors. In particular, Hobbs draws attention to the way that lawyers seek to convey an impression that they are in some respects similar to the jurors so that jurors are more ready to affiliate with the lawyer's point of view. In a case presented in a Detroit, Michigan, courtroom, a young black woman was accused of being part of a gang of women who beat and robbed an older white woman. Hobbs notes that 10 of the 12 jury members were black, as were the judge and the defense and prosecution lawyers. She describes the way in which the prosecution lawyer relies upon the use of African American Vernacular English in order to index a switch from the formal concerns of the courtroom to an affiliative stance

between herself and the members of the jury. One impression management technique which Hobbs observes in her study is the lawyer's use of a framing device of spontaneous talk. Hobbs notes that "improvisational performance" is regarded as a feature of African American Vernacular English. She suggests that the lawyer adopts this frame of reference in her speech to the jurors by adopting a conversational style in which a number of direct references to herself and to the jurors are employed. This allows her to manage the impression of herself which the jurors are likely to develop as a result of hearing what it is that she says.

What these last two examples reveal is that impression management is often bound up with other social actions in which participants are engaged. They may seek to manage impressions at the same time as they are expressing views on national identity or while they are seeking to persuade a jury in the courtroom. In other words, the management of impressions is associated with other discursive ends than mere self-presentation. For example, in their study of "show concessions," Antaki and Wetherell (1999) show how managing an impression can have argumentative consequences, by examining the ways in which people make a "show" of conceding an argumentative point. On occasion speakers display sensitivity to the question of whether a claim they are making is disputable. Somewhat surprisingly, Antaki and Wetherell show that speakers sometimes deal with this issue by conceding that there may be difficulties with the relevant claim. Indeed, Antaki and Wetherell argue that speakers may even make a "show" of conceding a point. A show concession has three structural elements. The first is an initial statement that might be interpretable as open to challenge. The second is some form of acknowledgment of that potentially problematic status which might include an indication of the grounds for the potential challenge. This acknowledgment is likely to include some sort of **marker** of concessions such as "alright" or "okay" or "fair enough." The third element is represented by

Marker An utterance, or a feature of an utterance, designed to draw the hearer's attention in some way

some sort of restatement of the initial claim. This is likely to be preceded with a contrastive conjunction such as "but" or "nevertheless."

In the present context, what is especially interesting about show concessions of this sort is the rhetorical effect which they can achieve. On the face of it, a show concession appears to convey the impression that an argumentative point is being conceded. However, far from representing a bland acceptance that their claim has been undermined, speakers who deploy show concessions use this structural device to undermine the potential criticisms which their initial claim might provoke. One of the ways in which show concessions accomplish this is through the use of what Antaki and Wetherell refer to as "Trojan horses." (Movie buffs who saw the 2004 epic *Troy*, very loosely based on Homer's *Iliad*, may remember that Greek soldiers were smuggled into the city of Troy in a large wooden horse.) In these cases the second part of the show concession "smuggles in" a caricatured version of the complaint which makes that complaint seem unacceptable. In this way, although the speaker acknowledges a potential problem with the initial claim being made, this very acknowledgment is used to weaken the evidence for the problem by making it seem trivial or absurd. In the present context, then, one way to interpret show concessions is to view them as conveying the impression of giving way on some potential argumentative point while, at the same time, undermining that point.

Another example of the ways in which managing impressions is bound up with other social actions is represented by a study conducted by Edwards and Fasulo (2006) of how "honesty phrases" such as "to be honest" are used in interaction. Edwards and Fasulo note that it is conventionally assumed that in everyday settings people are truthful in what they say and that this makes honesty phrases analytically interesting to the discursive researcher. If we are routinely taken to be telling the truth in everyday contexts (unlike, say, courtroom contexts), then the point or purpose of adding "to be honest" to a claim becomes analytically interesting. In their data, honesty phrases often appear "parenthetically," in that they are attached to something else that is said, which they refer to as the honesty phrase's "complement." They point to several types of

interaction in which such phrases and their complements have a particular role to play. One of these discursive contexts arises in question and answer sequences. Discursive researchers have long drawn attention to the fact that when someone asks a question, the speaker can be conventionally taken to prefer that the question be answered appropriately. Where this does not happen, the answer to the question can be described as a "**dispreferred**" response (Atkinson & Heritage, 1984). Edwards and Fasulo argue that when dispreferred responses are given to questions, the questioner may attribute a particular motive or attitude to the speaker, such as unwillingness or apathy, on hearing the dispreferred response. They suggest that honesty phrases and their complements are used to deal with this potential interactional difficulty.

```
1   LES:  Oh! Did they invoice you f'r carriage?
2   PHI:  We:ll I do:n't (.) think so because ih big
          or:der
3→        but I .hhh quite honestly I: I I don't
          kno:w: (0.4)
4         u–e– if they put yours on or ↑no:t.
5         (1.0)
6   PHI:  Uh::m (.) u–I uh sorry to be so va:
                        [gue b u t u h ]
7   LES:                [O h you've had]
8         other things from them have you:?
```
                        (Edwards & Fasulo, 2006, p. 349)

In this extract, Phil produces an honesty phrase together with its complement at line 3 ("quite honestly I: I I don't kno:w") following his negative response to Lesley's question, which is marked by "We:ll" at line 2. Edwards and Fasulo suggest that Phil is apparently accounting for being unable to answer Lesley's question because he provides an account, that the order is big, and also offers an apology at line 6. They suggest that this addresses a common feature of contexts in which honesty phrases arise: it is not just that Lesley asks Phil a question, but there is an implication that Phil ought to be able to provide an answer. It is within this context that Phil deals

> **Dispreferred** A conversational turn, designed as a response to a prior turn, in which what is said is taken to be potentially problematic for the recipient, e.g., turning down a request

with his accountability for giving a dispreferred response. They also note that the honesty phrase itself makes honesty relevant, while its complement refers to a mental state. This touches on another prevalent feature in the use of such phrases. The phrase and its complement address the implication in Lesley's question that Phil ought to be able to provide an answer by attending to Phil's responsibility in a particular way. Not only is honesty made relevant, but it is attached to a "private" mental state to which Phil is conventionally assumed to have special access. This, say Edwards and Fasulo, makes it especially difficult for Lesley to challenge Phil's account.

Attributions

Attribution research has traditionally focused on the experimental study of ways in which people explain the actions of others by attributing to them underlying causes for their behavior. However, discursive researchers have also studied this phenomenon (Anderson, Beattie, & Spencer, 2001; Breheny & Stephens, 2003; Horton-Salway, 2001b). This interest stems in part from the work of Edwards and Potter (1992, 1993), who have argued, in developing what they term the "discursive action model," that experimental studies of attribution have underestimated the complexity of this type of discursive interaction. Firstly, as in the case of impression management, when people make attributions the explanatory accounts they produce are, themselves, **action-oriented**. Attribution accounts typically arise in contexts where the speaker is doing something, e.g., refusing a request or defending a point of view. And the development of an attribution is itself an activity in which descriptions of people and events are carefully tailored to fit in with these surrounding discursive actions which the speaker is performing. Secondly, attribution accounts tend to be carefully designed. Any stake or interest the

> **Attribution** Explaining actions and events by ascribing causes to them

> **Action-orientation** The property of talk which directs it towards accomplishing specific outcomes or goals

speaker might be taken to have in giving just this explanation, as opposed to some other, is managed by designing the explanatory account as a factual statement or description. Thirdly, in attributions the speaker will attend to his or her own accountability in producing the explanatory account. We all understand that if we offer an explanation of what someone else has done, we are seen as being responsible for having given that explanation and for ensuring that it is accurate and we are also seen as responsible for any interactional consequences which follow on from having given it. So explanatory accounts are often designed with this accountability feature in mind. For example, we have noted that footing can be deployed in managing impressions of the self. In the context of making attributions, speakers may likewise attend to their own accountability by adopting particular footings. Thus, a speaker might for example distance himself or herself from giving an account by adopting a neutral footing in which the account is designed as a report emanating from some other source which the speaker is merely repeating.

In a study of success and failure on the sport field, Locke (2004) has applied the discursive action model to the way in which sport performance is accounted for.

```
1   INT:  um (.) how accountable did you personally
2         feel for the result in the race
3   TIM:  U:m (1.2) I was made to feel as though >it
          was um<
4         (1.8) as though I was quite accountable
          but u–
5         (0.2) no: I don't think >I was< (1.0) I
          think us
6         ones (0.2) >y'know are just< (0.8) being
          that age I
7         can't (1.0) compete in– in that (1.0) arena
          (0.8)
8         as well as I'd be able to in a few years
          time but
9         (1.6)
10        it wasn't down to me (1.2) °that we didn't
          do so
11        well (.) but°
                                    (Locke, 2004, p. 315)
```

In this extract, Tim, an international rower, is asked about an event in which his rowing crew were unsuccessful. At the start of the extract, the interviewer explicitly calls for a response in terms of management of blame. Locke notes that in his response Tim adroitly avoids being accountable for failure. Tim designs his response to make available the inference that there were others who "made" him feel "as though" he was accountable. However, he then goes on to categorize himself in terms of "us ones" for whom age is a relevant feature. He then associates his current age with an inability to compete, emphasizing this by indicating that this is a temporary state of affairs which will change within a "few years." So by establishing that his accountability is attributable to others, rather than something he acknowledges himself, and by categorizing himself in such a way that that accountability is not appropriate, Tim is able to warrant his conclusion that "it wasn't down to me."

Another example of how attributional processes arise in talk is found in a study of how vegetarians discuss the health consequences of adopting a vegan lifestyle (Sneijder & te Molder, 2005b). Vegans are sometimes described as "strict vegetarians" because they avoid the use or consumption of any animal products, including the consumption of dairy products, which vegetarians find acceptable.

12 As far as we know there is no
13 link between veganism and
14 osteoporosis. Osteoporosis occurs
15 mainly in western countries,
16 where a lot of dairy products and
17 protein-rich foods are consumed.
18 With a good vegan lifestyle you
19 won't get osteoporosis. [. . .]
20 Osteoporosis is thus a luxury
21 "disease"; if you have symptoms,
22 I'd say they were probably caused
23 by your vegetarian lifestyle.
24 Vegetarians eat far too many
25 dairy products, like cheese. [. . .]
                (Sneijder & te Molder, 2005b, p. 690)

In the above extract, a contributor to a website forum on veganism, Ronald, is discussing whether veganism is associated with the disease of osteoporosis. This contribution follows an earlier one in which another contributor to the forum, Melanie, indicated that she might be suffering from osteoporosis. Sneijder and te Molder note that Ronald is careful to provide a footing ("As far as we know") for his claim that veganism is not associated with osteoporosis while at the same time presenting himself as knowledgeable by producing supportive evidence (lines 14

Classic Study: Explaining and arguing

In this text, Antaki provides an in-depth examination of the sorts of interactional contexts which the discursive action model applies to. The book begins by reviewing "traditional" attributional research and the Edwards and Potter response as represented by their discursive action model. Having discussed a variety of features of causal talk from a conversation analytic perspective, Antaki moves on to consider how exonerating explanations work as accounts when the speaker faces an interactional difficulty such as being accused of something. He highlights the crucial role of conversation analysis in understanding this sort of process, emphasizing the ways in which speakers jointly produce sequential structures in conversation which open up conversational "slots" into which

accounts of this sort can be placed. In the following chapters, Antaki switches emphasis by considering the content of accounts by looking, for example, at the way specific discourses are adopted and organized within any specific account. The latter chapters of the book move from consideration of explanation itself to consider the related notion of how argument gets done in talk. After a discussion of argument in terms of informal logic and rhetoric, Antaki provides a number of examples of actual arguments and quarrels in order to highlight the way in which claims made within such contexts are rhetorically maintained and developed.

Antaki, C. (1994). *Explaining and arguing: The social organization of accounts.* London: Sage.

to 17). The authors also point that Ronald deals with attribution of responsibility in a particular way by stating that osteoporosis does not occur in a "good" vegan lifestyle. This implies that osteoporosis might arise if a vegan does not live a good lifestyle. In one sense, then, the contributor's account implies that if Melanie is suffering from osteoporosis then she is not living a good vegan lifestyle. (See 'Classic Study' box on p. 104.)

Categorization

One feature of social thought which has received close attention from discursive researchers is **categorization**, the process in which people, actions, or events are subsumed under or associated with category labels denoting more general types or sorts of phenomena. Within discursive research, the process of categorization is taken to have at least three important features.

The first of these is that categorization is an active, discursive process in which some particular category or other is **made relevant** to the current context. Authors such as Sacks (1992) and Schegloff (1997) draw attention to the fact that we have a certain amount of leeway in deploying categories. And this applies even to apparently "obvious" categorizations such as gender or race. Now this notion of leeway might strike one as rather odd. Surely someone just is male or female, or just is black or white, or just is blonde or red-headed? Surely an event just is a riot, or a war, or an accident, or it is not? Well, as both Sacks and Schegloff have pointed out, at any point in an interaction people, events, and contexts can be categorized in a multiplicity of ways. So someone who could be categorized in gender terms might equally well be categorized in terms of nationality, or age, or favorite foods, and so on. An episode in which a teacher berates a pupil might be categorized as an educational context, but it might equally be described as a bullying context. So what is to count as the "relevant" categoriza-

tion within an interaction is in some sense "up for grabs" during that interaction. It is in this sense that categorization can be viewed as allowing participants leeway in how they go about making specific categories relevant to people and events.

The second feature of categorization is that it treats categories themselves as the product of discursive activities. We have already said that speakers face a range of possibilities in the process of categorizing someone or something. But discursive researchers go further. They argue against the view that categorizations involve "factual" or "natural" categories which speakers observe and recognize in the world. So they reject the view that gender categorization, for example, involves observable, natural categories of men and women, and they likewise reject the view that racial categorization involves natural categories such as black, white, Latino, Chinese, and so on. Instead, discursive researchers emphasize the ways in which categorizations such as "male" or "female" are worked up and produced within discursive contexts. Some discursive researchers describe this process as one of social construction, in which relevant categorizations such as "male" or "white" are socially constructed during interactions. Edley and Wetherell (1997), for example, have argued that in gender categorizations, the notion of what counts as masculinity is not something which speakers merely observe from their social surroundings. Instead, notions of masculinity are worked up and developed by speakers as they are made relevant to the interactional context. Some researchers have gone even further and argued that categorization is so important that it is almost always a feature of discursive contexts. Thus it has been claimed, for example, that "the descriptive use of categories is an essential part of doing just about anything" (Potter, 1996b, p. 183). Potter's suggestion here is that categorization is a fundamental aspect of the way that discourse is used to formulate someone or something as being a particular sort of thing. On this view, it is the formulation of someone or something as a being a particular sort of thing which, to a large extent, underpins the ways in which we socially construct the world around us.

The third important feature of categorization which is bound up with these ideas of category

> **Categorization** Organizing experience by using terms which denote sorts or kinds of phenomena

> **Making relevant** Establishing that some feature of talk is appropriate to the local discursive context

relevance and category construction is that, like impression management and attribution, processes of categorization can become intertwined with other forms of social action. To see this, consider the case where participants are engaged in working up the nature and relevance of some specific categorization. From what has been said so far, we know that they are going to select from a range of possible categorizations and they are going to perform discursive work in establishing or socially constructing a version of the category. But what makes one categorization more relevant to a particular interaction than other potential candidates, and why is one particular version of a category worked up instead of some other version? How does one categorization or another, and one social construction or another, get chosen? According to some discursive researchers, the answer lies in what else is going on in the interaction. The choices which people make in categorizing someone or something will depend, in part, on the other social actions which they might currently be performing in that interaction. So, for example, someone might categorize their neighbors as "third world immigrants" in order to fill out a complaint they are currently making about the neighbor's taste in home decorations or lack of care in garden maintenance. Equally, of course, that same categorization might be deployed in an account designed to act as a compliment. For example, the neighbors might be complimented on their recycling skills and "green" ethos as a result of coming from a less industrialized background.

West and Fenstermaker (2002) neatly capture the complexity of categorization in their study of how speakers used gender and race categorizations to describe themselves at an official meeting held by the University of California's Board of Regents. At this meeting, the Board decided to end the University's policy of affirmative action in employment. West and Fenstermaker studied the ways in which the participants of the meeting oriented their conduct to issues of gender and race during the course of the meeting. The point of interest, they suggest, is the way in which their participants used categorization as a means of establishing or "doing" difference based on gender, race, and class. The complexity of categorization is also captured in Mallinson and Brewster's (2005) study of how restaurant

servers display prejudice against black patrons and against white patrons identified as "rednecks" or "bubbas" (both terms being derogatory labels associated with poor, white people from rural areas). They note that the servers draw on only one type of categorization, categorization by race, when talking of black patrons. However, they deploy a wider range of categorization, such as categorization by region and class, when talking of white patrons. They also point out that their participants, by establishing these particular sorts of categorization, establish both a relatively negative sense of "the other," these patrons, while, at the same time, establishing a relatively positive view of themselves. (Other examples of maintaining a positive sense of self while negatively characterizing "the other" can be found here in the chapter on prejudice, Chapter 7.) In the following extract, one of the restaurant servers, Nate, provides an extended description of "redneck" patrons.

18 NATE: Oh, overalls (laugh). John Deere hats, you know, Dale Earnhardt
19   shirts, things like that. . . .
20   Rednecks, they actually shock me sometimes, but for the most part 75 to 80
21   percent of the time rednecks are just terrible as far as, I don't like to listen to
22   them talk as far as, I mean, I have a bit of a country accent. I talk country
23   sometimes but I mean these guys are horrible and they seem so ignorant when
24   I'm talking to them. And on top of that of course you're going to get a rotten
25   tip and it just, you know.
                (Mallinson & Brewster, 2005, p. 794)

Mallinson and Brewster draw attention to the way that in his categorization of some patrons as "rednecks," Nate relies on stereotypes of rural white people in terms of their clothing preferences. Moreover, he does this in a way which indicates that he takes knowledge of such references to be cultural commonplaces. Mallinson and Brewster note that this categorization of some patrons as "rednecks" is bound up with a number of derogatory claims, with rednecks being described as "terrible," "horrible," and "ignorant." They also note that, at the same time, Nate can be seen to include some mitigating statements which can be heard as attending to the issue of whether he is presenting himself as prejudiced against rednecks. Thus at line 20 he softens his claims through the use of "sometimes" and by carefully selecting percentage numbers to indicate that his remarks apply to some but not all of the people he is categorizing in this way.

What this example reveals, then, is that categorizations are the sorts of activities which arise in talk along with, or as part of accomplishing, other social actions such as criticizing others. At this point, it is worthwhile stressing that some discursive researchers have emphasized the importance of developing analyses which are grounded in **participants' categories** and categorizations, rather than using researcher-defined categories (Edwards & Stokoe, 2004). For example, in a study of how Greek people view Albanian refugees in Greece, Figgou and Condor (2006) examined the way that their participants accounted for hostile acts towards Albanians. They note that their participants, in accounting for such actions, could have produced discourses of prejudice involving talk of irrationality or lack of integration. That is, they could have produced accounts which involved the sorts of theoretical categorizations that are common in social psychological studies of prejudice. However, instead their participants produced responses which relied upon a quite different form of categorization based on issues of risk and insecurity.

8　LIA:　What about these associations of people who have been robbed
9　　　　or this president of the village council in Pieria and things like
10　　　　that we have witnessed recently
11　MINOS:　Look (.) I think that the problem is that fear governs (.) let's
12　　　　take the case of the head of this village (.) some people in a
13　　　　remote village of Northern Greece (.) most of them old (.)
14　　　　because no young people live in these villages anymore (.) see
15　　　　the foreigners settling in their village (.) and becoming the majority (.)
16　　　　the Albanians are most probably the majority in places like that (.) and
17　　　　the old people hear that a few robberies have taken place by Albanians (.)
18　　　　which may not be true (.) or anything serious (.) but the old people
19　　　　become afraid that they will lose control (.) they feel threatened (.) they
20　　　　feel that they have to do something
　　　　　　　　(Figgou & Condor, 2006, p. 235)

This extract begins with Lia asking Minos a question. It incorporates what Figgou and Condor refer to as "emblematic examples of organized racism," including reference to an event in the county of Pieria previously reported in the Greek press. The report had revealed that the president of a local village council had prohibited Albanians from walking in the village streets at night in order to "protect" the Greek residents. Figgou and Condor note that Minos recasts anti-Albanian organizations as atypical and utilizes a number of categorizations to work up the view that their members are in a minority in Greece. They are categorized spatially as living in a remote place, and are categorized by age as being old, and this is emphasized by Minos's use of the **extreme case formulation** "no young people live in these villages anymore." This categorization of the people "in places like that" forms a contextual backdrop against which Minos introduces a further notion. These people are in fear of the circumstances in which they find themselves. Of course, the categorization of anti-Albanian actions as the fearful responses of old people cut off in remote communities is not the only action performed in this episode of talk. Figgou and Condor note, for example, that in producing this account Minos is careful to avoid the suggestion the he himself endorses the idea that Albanians are criminals. At line 17 this notion is introduced in an indirect form in which other people, not him, have merely heard of criminal events. Moreover, the criminality of these events is minimized by describing them as "a few robberies." In addition, Minos presents himself as

Participants' categories The discursive terms used to organize experience which are deployed by participants (in contrast to theoretical notions which a researcher might introduce)

Extreme case formulation A discursive construction which uses the strongest version of comparative terms or phrases

open-minded on the issue by suggesting that such reports might not be true.

This example demonstrates that categorization is a discursive process in which people describe other people, actions, or events by means of labels or other grouping terms. However, it also highlights the way in which the categorizations which are of interest to the discursive researcher are those which participants themselves develop and deploy. In addition, the discussion of this extract reveals an important element of the discursive analysis of categorization. The categories which participants themselves develop may be developed by them in order to allow them to perform other social actions, such as Minos's formulation of people acting in an apparently prejudiced manner only as a result of their own personal difficulties.

Within discursive research, especially within those forms of research influenced by the conversation analytic approach, one particular type of categorization has come to play an important role: membership categorization. Membership categorization analysis (Hester & Eglin, 1997; Hester & Francis, 2001b; D. R. Watson, 1978, 1997) argues that people routinely deploy "membership categories" in their talk, and when membership categories are put to use this can carry interactional implications (Sacks, 1992). Categories such as "mother" or "doctor" are "inference rich" in that we all have tacit knowledge about the normative expectations which are bound up with membership of those categories (e.g., mothers are caring, doctors are knowledgeable). According to this view, if someone is presumed to be a member of a category, but does not behave in accordance with normative expectations which are bound up with that category in common-sense understanding, then that individual will be viewed as in some way exceptional or deficient (e.g., an ignorant doctor) so that the common-sense knowledge about the category is preserved.

Associated with a category are "**category-bound activities**" which common sense takes to be especially characteristic of that category (e.g., sportspeople train, academics lecture).

Category-bound activities Forms of action which are conventionally associated with being a member of the relevant category

Categories can become activated by formulating someone's actions in terms of category-bound activities, and so an observer will use reports such as "the professor lectured" rather than "the male lectured" or "the Californian lectured." The idea here is that these interpretative practices are regulated by rules of application and their corollaries (Sacks, 1992, pp. 246–247). One of these is that if you hear a report on an action or event, you will interpret the episode and the actors in terms of the way it has been formulated. Another is that if you are yourself observing an action or event, then you draw on the categories and their bound activities in interpreting what is going on. So if you see a category-bound activity being done by someone who is potentially a member of the relevant category, then you see the person that way. For example, if you see someone offering a diagnosis, then if that person is of the appropriate sort you categorize that person as a "doctor." If, on the other hand, you see a member of a category acting in a way which is potentially describable in terms of the activities bound to the relevant category, then you see the activities that way. For example, if you see a doctor offering an explanation of illness then you describe that activity as "diagnosis." Taken together, sets of categories together with these rules can be thought of as "membership categorization devices." These ideas, which were developed by Sacks, were extended by Watson (1978) to include the idea of the "category-bound predicate." This broadens application of Sacks's views on category boundedness from a consideration of activities in particular to properties more generally understood.

One example of membership categories in action is Mäkitalo's (2003) study of interactions between job applicants and vocational guidance officers. Membership categorization analysis is often held to be particularly relevant to institutional contexts of this sort. The categories which are made relevant by an institutional setting are routinely associated with rights, duties, and entitlements which derive from the institutional roles which such categorizations pick out or assign. Within this particular institutional setting, then, we might expect that the participants will display an awareness of the sorts of activities and predicates which attach to the membership category of "job applicant." In the following extract, an applicant (A) and a guidance officer (V) are discussing whether an educational program would benefit the applicant in his search for a job.

597 V: have I understood you correctly or did– or am I
598 wrong?
599 A: that uh, no I thought of this as . . . I was just
600 explaining if, for instance I know that if I attend this course
601 V: yeah?
602 A: afterwards I will, there is no possibility for me
603 to be employed . . . it's just– I attend a course
604 and then the course is finished and then you* come out . . .
605 V: no
606 A: and you're* unemployed again
607 V: ((inaudible))
608 A: I'm almost certain of that ((laughs))
609 V: ((laughing:)) but if you don't attend now, I was thinking if you
610 don't try these educational opportunities then I thought
611 have you considered . . . what your situation would be like then
612 and what jobs you could apply for?
(Mäkitalo, 2003, p. 504)

In this extract, the applicant suggests at lines 599 to 604 that further education or training would not lead to employment. Mäkitalo points out that the guidance officer orients to this claim as being insufficient. First, at line 604, she interjects a negative response. Subsequently, at lines 609 to 612, she introduces a counter-argument. If A does not try educational opportunities, then his situation is indeterminate. What is of especial analytic interest here is Mäkitalo's indication that, in introducing this counter-argument, the guidance officer draws upon the normatively bound obligations which are associated with the category of job applicant. The officer does not ask A whether he should seek a job or not. Instead,

her question is formulated as though it is already a taken-for-granted aspect of being a job applicant that A will seek a job and the live issue for discussion is only what particular jobs he could apply for. This, Mäkitalo argues, points up the way in which the guidance officer and the applicant orient to the category-bound attributes which are normatively associated with being a job applicant.

In Conclusion

What this chapter has shown is that discursive research has displayed great interest in a number of themes which might traditionally be viewed as falling within the area of cognitive social psychology. Moreover, the topics covered in this chapter do not exhaust the variety of contributions made by discursive research. For example, discursive researchers have also been interested in the notion of scripts (Edwards, 1995, 2006b; Frith & Kitzinger, 2001) and in emotions (Barnes & Moss, 2007; Edwards, 1999; Hepburn & Brown, 2001; Howard, Tuffin, & Stephens, 2000; Morgan, Stephens, Tuffin, Praat, & Lyons, 1997). What is common across all of these discursive studies, however, is the view that the study of social cognition is best undertaken by understanding the importance of talk and other forms of discourse. The development of understanding or misunderstanding of others, the management of impressions, the attribution of characteristics to others, and the deployment of categorizations in describing people and their actions are all essentially discursive phenomena. And so to understand them, one must understand the discursive contexts in which they arise. As we have noted here, there are, however, differences among discursive researchers over the question of whether that understanding requires reference to cognitions as more typically understood in terms of mental entities. We explore this theoretical tension further in Chapter 12.

Chapter summary

- Discursive researchers have displayed a lively interest in a range of areas more traditionally associated with cognitive social psychology.
- Knowledge of the social world is represented by critical discourse analysts in terms of mental models which are conveyed by means of discourse. One important ideological function of discourse is this regard is the rhetorical manipulation of the mental models of others.
- Like knowledge, misunderstanding has also been studied by discursive researchers. Some conversation analysts, e.g., Drew (2005), have suggested that here, too, there may be a role for mental states as explanatory phenomena. But they also emphasize the importance of understanding how misunderstanding is equally a phenomenon which arises out of the sequential patterning of talk-in-interaction.
- Discursive psychologists have also studied knowledge and misunderstanding. However, they are more critical of the suggestion that cognitive states are useful explanatory notions. Some conversation analysts are sympathetic to this view (e.g., Antaki, 2006). From this perspective, knowledge and misunderstanding are essentially discursive phenomena which are made relevant and worked up in conversational interaction.
- Discursive researchers reveal the ways in which accounts of memory and forgetting are designed to accomplish rhetorical goals in interaction, especially those which arise in "controversial" settings such as courtrooms.
- Impression management is a process in which people attend to the sorts of inferences which can be drawn about them from what they say and how they act. Discursive researchers have shown how rhetorical devices such as footing switches are routinely used by speakers to manage these sorts of impression.
- Discursive researchers have also examined the process of attribution in which people attribute a reason or cause to someone in order to explain that person's behavior. Like impression management, this discursive process is seen to be a complex one in which speakers routinely accomplish a variety of social actions as they set out their attributional accounts.
- The social action-orientation of discourse is seen once again when processes of categorization are examined. People do use categorizations to allocate people and events to types or to describe them as being of one sort or another. But in doing this, speakers can be seen to routinely perform other social actions, such as defending a point of view or leveling an accusation.
- One aspect of categorization which discursive researchers have found to be especially important is the use of membership categorization devices in which inferences are drawn about the sorts of characteristics and actions which might normatively be expected from someone as a result of that person having been classed as belonging, or not belonging, to a given category of people.

Connections

A wide variety of social actions arise out of explanatory accounts and the development of categorizations. In this respect, the content of the present chapter is relevant to most of the other chapters in this book. Especially noteworthy is the relationship between categorization and the chapters on identity (Chapter 2) and prejudice (Chapter 7). Attributions as discussed here are an element of the interactions between people described in the chapter on attraction and relationships (Chapter 4). Aspects of impression management are relevant to Chapter 2 and to some of the material in the chapter on legal matters (Chapter 9).

Activity

Have you ever managed an impression of yourself when talking? Has anyone ever attributed characteristics to you which you did not agree with? Think of one of these episodes and decide how that episode was discursively managed.

Further reading

Schegloff, E. A. (2007). A tutorial on membership categorization. *Journal of Pragmatics*, 39, 462–482. This text, by one of the "founding fathers" of conversation analysis, provides a lively and up-to-date commentary on how membership categorization analysis ought to be carried out.

Wodak, R. (2006). Mediation between discourse and society: Assessing cognitive approaches in CDA. *Discourse Studies*, 8, 179–190. A brief but interesting account written from the perspective of a critical discourse analyst on the relationship between discourse and cognition. One of a series of papers in a special edition of *Discourse Studies* dedicated to exploring the way discursive researchers deal with cognitive issues. Readers may also with to look at the other papers that appeared in this issue, which are written by leading figures in the field.

Chapter 6

Attitudes and Persuasion

Key Terms

Argument by analogy
Attitude
Authoritative discourse
Category entitlements
Consensual
Conversational floor
Discursive mind control
Displaying sensitivity
Epistemological orientation
Factual description
Interest management
Irony
Listing
Objective
Opinion
Persuasion
Presupposition
Propositional attitude
Rhetorically self-sufficient
Self-qualifying segments
Self-repair
Subjective

Evil Saddam's last moments

The Sun, 1/1/2007

Saddam Hussein executed

The Guardian, 12/30/2007

On the morning of December 30, 2006, the ex-president of Iraq, Saddam Hussein, was executed. The headlines above are taken from two British newspaper stories which dealt with these events. Both headlines tell the reader about Saddam Hussein's death. But one of the differences which strikes the reader in looking at the headlines is that the *Sun* headline includes an evaluative term, "evil," while the *Guardian* headline does not. The reader immediately understands that the *Sun* journalist is conveying a particular point of view on Hussein. In other words, the reader already knows something about the *Sun* journalist's **attitudes**, merely from reading those four words of the headline. And knowing something about the journalist's attitudes allows the reader to predict the kinds of things that the journalist is likely to say about Hussein in the rest of the article.

One of the reasons that the study of attitudes is taken to be so important in social psychology is that we all understand that knowing about someone's attitudes allows us some understanding of how that person will behave. Moreover, because attitudes are important to us in this way, we have all become very adept at expressing (or concealing) our attitudes and at identifying others' attitudes from what they say and do. There is a long history in experimental social psychology of studying attitudes. The explanatory model which is used by the experimental social psychologist regards attitudes as internal mental states which are usually described as having several elements. According to one experimental model of attitudes, these states are held to have a "cognitive" component in that they represent beliefs about the attitudinal object. In the case of the *Sun* journalist, this would include beliefs about Hussein having been president of Iraq and beliefs about the actions he performed as president. Within the same model, attitudes are also

held to have an "evaluative" component in that a person's attitude towards an object involves placing that object on some sort of evaluative dimension (e.g., good–bad, pleasant–unpleasant). In the case of the *Sun* journalist, it is clear that he evaluates Hussein negatively. Attitudes are also described as having a behavioral component in that they are taken to cause behavior. (In some models, behavior is also taken to be a component part of the attitude.) The experimental social psychologist studies attitudes by observing behavior and then inferring something about the internal state which has caused that behavior. In the case of the *Sun* journalist, it is predictable that the newspaper article he produced under the headline was one in which Hussein was portrayed in a relatively unsympathetic light.

Discursive researchers, like their experimental counterparts, also have an interest in understanding the relationship between attitude and action. However, discursive research does not share the experimentalist's concerns with the structure and function of mental states. Instead, discursive researchers are interested in how attitudes come to be manifested through discourse. For some discursive researchers, this means understanding how attitudinal talk plays a role in wider ideological discourse. For others, it means analyzing the way people in talk-in-interaction display and orient towards their own and others' beliefs and in the evaluative practices which accompany the expression of those beliefs. In the two sections which follow, we will examine both of these perspectives.

Although "attitude" is the preferred term of use in experimental social psychology, the term "**opinion**" also sometimes appears. Where that term is used, it is often taken to be synonymous with "attitude," although other researchers, notably market researchers, prefer to use "opinion" to refer to expressed attitudes, thereby highlighting the difference between the inner, attitudinal, mental state and the overt expressions, the opinions, which that inner state causes. Some discursive researchers have also drawn a distinction between attitudes and opinions (van Dijk, 1995) with attitudes being

Attitude An evaluative belief about a social object

Opinion An evaluative view or belief

understood as complex clusters of opinions, and have emphasized that opinions, like attitudes, can be analyzed discursively (Xu, 2000).

Of course, attitudes are not static. We all understand that our own attitudes, and those of others, may change over time. Indeed, the salesman on the car showroom floor and the politician on the campaign trail both have vested interests in the idea that not only might your attitudes change, but that they can influence this change. It is this notion which lies at the heart of the social psychologist's interest in processes of **persuasion**. In the latter half of this chapter, we will examine persuasive talk and the ways in which the discursive researcher has examined this phenomenon. However, it will be evident from what follows that discursive researchers often do not rely on a strict distinction between the analysis of attitudes *per se* and the analysis of persuasive communication. Discursive researchers are interested in attitudes as elements of discourse, and attitudinal talk or text, unlike the expression of attitudes within a laboratory setting, is often implicitly or explicitly related to attempts to induce attitude change in the hearer.

Attitudes

Attitudes and control

Some forms of discursive research such as critical discourse analysis rely upon the notion of attitudes in explaining how discourse functions. However, critical discourse analysts differ from experimental social psychologists in the emphasis which they place on discourse processes, rather than on mental structure and function. Fairclough (2003) emphasizes this distinction in pointing out the potential shortcomings of analyses which rely upon "generalized" attitudes rather than specific statements and evaluations. If such analyses "abstract away" from the diversity of what is actually said or written, they may provide a misleading picture of how attitudes function. Another difference between the experi-

mentalist's approach to attitudes and that of the critical discourse analyst is that the latter draws connections between attitudes and other social phenomena such as ideologies. In his discussion of the critical discourse analyst's account of discourse and power, van Dijk (2001a, 2006a) suggests that socially dominant groups seek to ideologically control the attitudes (or opinions or social representations) that people should, or should not, have. Through a process of "**discursive mind control**," dominant groups attempt to control cognitive beliefs and the evaluations which attach to those beliefs. The discursive mechanisms through which this control functions range from the establishment of what is to count as the appropriate context for considering an issue to the development and maintenance of discursive structures such as global topics and locally available models of how to discuss such topics in specific interactions. Van Dijk suggests that the attitudinal aspects of this manipulation or control are long-term memory effects because the changes effected are alterations to stable social attitudes.

As an example of the way that dominant groups seek to manipulate attitudes, van Dijk (2006a) analyzes statements made by the British prime minister, Tony Blair, during a speech made in justification of his government's decision to take part in the war in Iraq. Van Dijk suggests that certain contexts are typical of manipulation. These are typified by one or more of the following properties of the person targeted by the manipulation: the target may have incomplete or lack of knowledge of the matter under discussion or may suffer from emotional vulnerability; the target may inhabit a social position or status that induces him or her to accept what is said by elite groups; or the manipulation may appeal to values or ideologies that the target cannot easily ignore. The successful manipulator, van Dijk argues, will focus on these properties of the target in developing the discourse through which manipulation takes effect. A number of these elements are, he says, identifiable in what Blair says in the following extract, taken from a speech

---

Persuasion The alteration of someone's beliefs or attitudes via communication

---

Discursive mind control A term employed by critical discourse analysis to represent the persuasive ideological effects of discourse

made to the British House of Commons (one of the two Houses of Parliament which comprise the British government).

> At the outset, I say that it is right that the House debate this issue and pass judgment. That is the democracy that is our right, but that others struggle for in vain. Again, I say that I do not disrespect the views in opposition to mine. This is a tough choice indeed, but it is also a stark one: to stand British troops down now and turn back, or to hold firm to the course that we have set. I believe passionately that we must hold firm to that course. The question most often posed is not "Why does it matter?" but "Why does it matter so much?" Here we are, the Government, with their most serious test, their majority at risk, the first Cabinet resignation over an issue of policy, the main parties internally divided, people who agree on everything else –
> [Hon. Members: "The main parties?"]
> Ah, yes, of course. The Liberal Democrats – unified, as ever, in opportunism and error.
> [Interruption.]
>
> (van Dijk, 2006a, p. 377)

Van Dijk notes that Blair begins by establishing a positive self-presentation as someone who supports the democratic principles of government ("the House") and the debate which such principles embody. He introduces an ideological polarization through his nationalistic talk of supporting "British troops" and the implicit distinction between Britain and democracy on the one hand, and the opponents of those troops on the other. Part of the manipulative effect of this polarization, van Dijk argues, is the further inference which it makes available to the hearer: if someone opposes Blair's view, then he or she is supporting the enemies of Britain and democracy. Blair, according to van Dijk, also makes relevant his own powerful status by his description of being placed in a position of someone who holds firm in the face of tough choices. Blair also lays stress on his own emotional commitment to what he says by reporting that he holds these beliefs passionately. Finally, Blair uses the interruption from other members of the House to undermine the status of opponents, the Liberal Democrats, as opportunists.

Another example of the sort of control which van Dijk describes is seen in a recent study of polit-ical discourse in press conferences. In this study Bhatia (2006) examines statements made by President George W. Bush of the United States and President Jiang Zemin of China during a number of press conferences held between 2001 and 2003. Bhatia notes that one of the concerns of political figures in such contexts is to minimize negative attitudes. They accomplish this, in part, by controlling the agenda of questions which reporters may put to them, or by offering vague or non-responsive answers to questions which stray outwith that agenda. Bhatia also notes that in such contexts, politicians may seek to deceive listeners by disguising the extent to which different attitudes are held by the different parties. During one press conference, President Bush makes the following claims:

> It is inevitable that nations of the size of the United States and China will have differences . . . we need to resolve our differences through mutual understanding and respect.
> My government hopes that China will strongly oppose the proliferation of missiles and other deadly technologies. President Jiang and I agreed that the United States and China could cooperate more closely to defeat HIV/AIDS.
>
> (Bhatia, 2006, p. 184)

Bhatia notes that Bush describes differences between the US and China as "inevitable" and argues that this description makes relevant the predictability and unavoidability of such differences, which are warranted by reference to a natural feature, the respective countries' sizes. Bhatia also argues that explicit reference to disagreements such as the countries' differing views on nuclear proliferation is balanced by reference to other topics on which the countries might be taken to agree. In this respect, Bhatia concludes, Bush attempts to disguise or diminish the way in which the two presidents hold conflicting attitudes.

So from this perspective, attitudes play a role in discourse in developing or maintaining an ideological viewpoint. It is, of course, not surprising that professional politicians are engaged in such practices, and critical discourse analysts are careful to point out that these practices are only problematic when politicians seek to manipulate the public in the support of ideologies that are unfair or coercive. However, critical discourse analysts also draw attention to the way that attitudes produce or reproduce ideologies in contexts other than the politician's overtly political pronouncements. Bergvall and Remlinger (1996), for example, demonstrate how the university classroom is a locus for such ideological activity. Heterosexist ideologies embody a number of attitudes towards women which characterize the difference between men and women in static terms and ignore the dynamic nature of actual social interactions. Bergvall and Remlinger show how these attitudes become manifest in classroom interactions. The discursive practices of male students are seen to be supportive of a view on gender roles in which men are expected to have control of **conversational "floor"** (Jones & Thornborrow, 2004), although Bergvall and Remlinger also draw attention to ways in which women students attempt to challenge this.

The preceding examples have used data which derive from spoken utterances. However, it is important to note that one of the stated aims of critical discourse analysts is to extend their analyses to other forms of discourse, including written text. For example, Achugar (2004) examined a series of editorials published in Uruguayan newspapers in the weeks following the September 11, 2001 attack on the United States which led to the destruction of the World Trade Center in New York. Achugar describes how these editorials negotiated attitudes towards the relevant social actors. She points out that one of the ways in which the editorial authors evoke attitudes towards these actors is through the use of social esteem and emotional discourses. Thus the attackers are described as expert but irrational, while the US is characterized as powerful. In a different dichotomy, the US is described in emotional terms as fearful and unhappy while the attackers are described as happy and satisfied. This, Achugar argues, allows the editorial authors to construct a version of the events in which the attackers are evaluated negatively while those attacked are evaluated positively.

The issue of how "the other" is represented through newspapers' discursive invocations of

attitudes is also pursued by Flowerdew, Li, and Tran (2002; Flowerdew, 2004). In a study of a large number of articles published in the *South China Morning Post*, they examine the discriminatory discourse which is used to transmit to readers negative attitudes towards mainland Chinese people who seek right-of-abode on the island of Hong Kong. In a taxonomy of discursive strategies, they identify: negative representations of mainland Chinese and "scare tactics" involving exaggeration of statistical evidence which are intended to evoke negative attitudes; the provision of warrants for discriminatory attitudes towards mainland Chinese people by "blaming the victim" for the social problems of integration; and delegitimation of mainland Chinese people by questioning the legality of their status and behavior or drawing on appeals to authoritative voices which question the legitimacy of the mainlanders' claims.

> Right of abode migrants could stir social unrest and bear the brunt of anger over jobs and welfare, it was claimed yesterday.... The Hong Kong Council of Social Service called on the Government to channel more resources into relieving potential grievances and reducing the gap with the migrants.... "Many people are unhappy because they fear the mainlanders will flood Hong Kong, crowd schools and compete with us for jobs and housing ... and there will be social unrest" [Council Director Hui Yin-fat said].
> (Flowerdew, Li, & Tran, 2002, p. 334)

Flowerdew, Li, and Tran point out the way in which texts such as this reproduce the government position that acceptance of mainland Chinese people would lead to social division and would harm the interests of Hong Kong locals. Such acceptance is depicted as leading to an unwanted burden on social welfare, as producing competition for education and housing, and as accentuating unemployment. In this way, Flowerdew, Li, and Tran argue, the underlying discriminatory attitudes of the Hong Kong administration are reproduced and supported by the newspaper's coverage.

So for the critical discourse analyst, the study of attitudes is essentially concerned with the analysis of spoken or written discourse. From this perspective, the analyst's task is to expose the underlying attitudes which are evoked or

---

Conversational floor Participants' understanding of the immediate conversational context, including appropriateness of next turn position

transmitted in talk and text and to understand the ways in which such discourse contributes to processes of attitude change. In many respects, then, the critical discourse analyst is broadly sympathetic to the experimental social psychologist's approach to attitude research except that whereas the experimentalist seeks to understand cognitive structure and function, the critical discourse analyst seeks to elucidate the ideological impact of attitudinal discourse. However, other discursive researchers have attempted a more radical reinterpretation of the attitude research paradigm, and it is to this work we now turn.

Constructing attitudes and evaluative practices

Discursive researchers from traditions such as discourse analysis and discursive psychology treat attitudes as the expression of evaluative judgments which arise during the performance of a variety of social actions in everyday interaction. Instead of studying the structure and function of inner mental phenomena, these discursive researchers are interested in discovering what evaluations arise, how they are produced, and the

social actions which accompany such production. There is, then, a difference in emphasis between the approaches of the discourse analyst and the discursive psychologist on the one hand, and the approach of the critical discourse analyst on the other hand, in that some discourse analysts and discursive psychologists are more critical of the experimental tradition. From their perspective, the action-oriented analysis of how descriptive and evaluative discursive practices are produced exhausts what the social psychologist can usefully say about how attitudes affect us, and further analysis of inner mental states adds nothing further to the social researcher's understanding.

In an early example of this sort of work, Potter and Wetherell (1987) argued that the discourse analyst's approach to the study of attitudes should focus on the variability and contextual relevance of attitude expressions and on the way in which such expressions formulate or construct a particular version of the attitudinal object. From this perspective, social objects are best considered as social constructions, and the idea of a "real" attitudinal object becomes less relevant to the analyst's concerns. In fact, the process of socially

---

CLASSIC STUDY: Discourse and social psychology: Beyond attitudes and behavior

This is the text which introduced many social psychologists to the world of discursive research. Published in 1987, the book outlines the main tenets of discourse analysis and its application to social psychology. The book begins with a brief survey of some historical precursors such as speech act theory and ethnomethodology. After discussing the limitations of these approaches, Potter and Wetherell introduce the reader to the discourse analytic perspective. They criticize experimental attitude research (and, in a later chapter, social representations research), arguing that it wrongly emphasizes the drawing of inferences about mental phenomena from behavior. This approach mistakenly ignores a number of features of everyday discourse, including context-relevance, variability,

and social construction. They go on to illustrate the way in which the discourse analytic perspective can be used to unpick the accounts and constructions of the self which are observable in the way people actually talk. They then introduce the reader to the different ways in which categories are deployed in discourse, and highlight what they see as shortcomings in the experimental psychologist's use of the notion of categories in areas such as prototype research. Overall, the book represents a key text in discourse analysis and two decades after its publication it is still referred to by researchers working in the discourse analytic tradition.

Potter, J. & Wetherell, M. (1987). *Discourse and social psychology: Beyond attitudes and behavior*. London and Thousand Oaks, CA: Sage.

constructing an object even blurs the distinction between what is to count as factual, descriptive talk and what is to count as evaluative talk. For one of the ways in which people evaluate an object is precisely by producing a social construction which carries evaluative implications. Subsequently, Potter has made similar constructionist points about the notion of opinions. He suggests that traditional perspectives on opinion surveys wrongly ignore the constructionist element of interaction, claiming that "descriptions are bound up with action and evaluation" (Potter, 1996b, p. 211). Lipari (2000) makes a similar constructionist claim about opinion polling, suggesting that opinion poll questions are akin to the questions raised in other interrogative settings such as the courtroom and so, like the questions of the lawyer, are susceptible to reformulation and reinterpretation in order to achieve local discursive aims.

Verkuyten (1998a) offers an example of the way that attitude objects are constructed through discourse in a study of a television panel discussion. The topic of the discussion was an annual fair which takes place in Utrecht, a city in the Netherlands. The theme of the fair was "lifestyle and eroticism," and the discussion panel included a representative of the fair's organizers, Mrs. Blom, and a representative of a "Christians for Life" group, Mr. Kunning.

42 KUNNING: We've been to the fair, we've seen what was shown there, as we
43 otherwise wouldn't know what we're talking about. They had, one of the things
44 they had, was a, a, a large X, sort of two wooden beams to which shackles with
45 sharp spikes were attached and on which a person could be hung with instruments
46 of torture. People were all dressed in black leather, that's not a, a normal way of
47 experiencing sex, that's perversity. It is very clearly pornography.
48 HOST: No, that's, that's got something to do with yourself, some people like that
49 sort of thing, others don't. Live and let live.
50 KUNNING: Of course, of course . . .
(Verkuyten, 1998a, p. 307)

Verkuyten draws attention to the way in which Kunning constructs a version of the fair as an episode in pornography. Kunning defines events

at the fair as "perversity" rather than normality. He supports this claim, says Verkuyten, by including in his utterance a **factual description** of what the fair organizers were exhibiting. Factual discourse of this sort is often used to make a claim appear to follow naturally from the way the world is, rather than being the subjective view of the speaker. Moreover, he precedes this with a justification for his claim by presenting himself and his colleagues as knowledgeable, in that they have visited the fair and so know what they are talking about. By presenting himself as knowledgeable, he thereby undermines potential counter-claims that, as a spokesperson for Christian values, he is not qualified to comment on the subject matter of the fair. Having carried out this discursive work, Kunning then draws his conclusion, using a relatively strong formulation, that the fair is "very clearly pornography."

Verkuyten contrasts this construction of the fair with a quite different version provided by Mrs. Blom.

32 BLOM: No, absolutely not, because we don't propagate free sex or so at this fair.
33 It's just a representation of what is accepted in society today. We've set up a fair
34 Which ties romance, eroticism and life-style together, particularly the latter, and
35 this just means that the people find this an excellent concept and also like going
36 there. In contrast to, exactly because it, erm, we have set a number of limits that
37 work very well. The people expect to find a number of things there and they do,
38 but we really think that we have kept pornography out and we absolutely want it
39 to stay that way . . . We, we are absolutely against hard and unacceptable things,
40 just like all right-minded people in this world.
(Verkuyten, 1998a, p. 309)

Blom's claim is that "we have kept pornography out." To establish this, she begins by making the fair a setting of ordinary activities, of what society today accepts. This is given emphasis by her claims that "the people" like going to the fair and

> **Factual description** A discursive formulation of something which emphasizes its literal qualities and its direct reference to the world

have expectations of the fair which are met. Her use of the general referring term "the people" also makes available the inference that the activities of the fair are the subject of **consensual** agreement, thereby undermining potential accusations that those involved with the fair are in some way deviant or unusual. Like Kunning, she also deploys relatively extreme formulations, describing the fair organizers as "absolutely" wanting to keep pornography out and being "absolutely" against "hard and unacceptable things." In this way, Blom is able to work up a quite different version of the fair from Kunning's pornography construction and, instead, present an idea of the fair as something which combines romance, eroticism, and lifestyle which "the people" find to be an excellent concept. What Verkuyten's study shows, then, is that discursive construction of "attitudinal objects" plays an important role in the way attitudes enter into talk. It is noteworthy in the above extract that both Kunning and Blom interweave descriptive talk with evaluative talk: Kunning's use of "perversity" carries a negative evaluation, while Blom's use of "excellent," her appeal to limits "that work very well," and her consensual invocation of "right-minded people" all express positive evaluations.

More recently, Puchta and Potter (2002, 2004) have examined the notions of attitudes and opinions within the context of focus group research and practice. Focus groups (Myers, 1998) are discussion groups in which the discussion is guided by someone who holds the formal status of moderator. Usually the moderator will have been trained in techniques for managing group discussions. The primary goal of these groups is to elicit from participants perceptions, beliefs, attitudes, or opinions towards a given topic. Puchta and Potter point out that focus group practice often relies upon a "traditional" social psychological model of attitudes. Puchta and Potter outline the discursive researcher's alternative approach to attitudes or opinions by drawing a distinction between attitudes as "preformed," the traditional perspective which views attitudes as inner mental states that cause behavior, and attitudes as "performed," the discursive researcher's

perspective. Puchta and Potter locate the idea of "performed" attitudes within Billig's work on rhetorical psychology (Billig, 1987, 1991), with its emphasis on discourse as a medium in which the expression of evaluations is, at least in principle, argumentative in that such expressions usually involve some consideration of counter-arguments to the evaluation which is produced. Puchta and Potter also point out that the action-orientation of discourse analysis and discursive psychology lends further weight to the "performed" nature of attitudes. Evaluation talk is produced in order to perform social actions such as making complaints or offering compliments, and evaluations are specifically designed to fit into local discursive contexts in order to achieve these aims. And, as was pointed out earlier, one important element of talk such as this is that it is often analytically fruitless to separate out "descriptive" talk, which might be taken to correspond to the traditional social psychologist's "cognitive" element, from evaluative talk. Edwards and Stokoe (2004) similarly argue that the process of identifying attitudes by focus group procedures may ignore the way that people construct versions of things and that this occurs in a context where the construction is action-oriented because it is produced in order to do something like making a complaint, offering praise, or working up a justification.

From this "performative" perspective on attitudes, then, the discursive researcher's task includes understanding how versions of the "target" of an attitude are constructed and how evaluations come to be associated with them. And a key element of this approach is the view that descriptive and evaluative practices are often woven together within a local context in which other social actions are being accomplished. Wiggins and Potter (2003), for example, have applied this general discursive perspective to the study of attitudes towards food.

1	BETH:	can I try some ↑wi:ne
2	LAURA:	°oh::: (0.2) (↑ mm-hm) °
3		(2.0)
4	BETH:	don't [↑ like red really
5	LAURA:	[its <u>very</u> nice:
6		(1.0)
7	LAURA	↑well=
8	BILL:	=how d'you <u>know</u> (0.8) have you ↑ever <u>tried</u> it

Consensual Having the property of being agreed upon by a set of relevant individuals

9   BETH: I've <u>tried</u> it about a ↑million times
10   I <u>hate</u> all red (.) it's too st<u>rong</u>
                (Wiggins & Potter, 2003, p. 520)

Wiggins and Potter note that the extract starts with Beth, the daughter, performing an action in making a request. They suggest that in performing this action Beth is acknowledging her status as "junior" in respect to her mother, Laura, as well as suggesting, through the use of "try," that her drinking would be in the nature of an experiment. Wiggins and Potter suggest that Laura, at line 2, can be heard as agreeing, albeit in a way which uses the extended "oh:::" and the short delay to display that this agreement is a considered one, and in the subsequent silence at line 3 begins to pour Beth some wine. However, at line 4, Beth then refuses Laura's offer by producing a negative evaluation of red wine. Wiggins and Potter emphasize the performative nature of this negative evaluation: Beth produces the evaluation in order to perform the action of refusing the wine. At line 5, Laura offers an alternative, positive evaluation, followed by a pause and then, at line 7, says "↑well" expressed with a questioning, rising intonation. Wiggins and Potter suggest that this might indicate that Laura is attempting to persuade Beth to have some wine. This is an indication of the way in which, in everyday language, expressions of attitude of this sort can become the focus of negotiation or argumentative rhetoric. This is also shown at line 8, where Beth's uncle, Bill, challenge's Beth's evaluation and asks for the grounds or warrant for her claim. Beth's response, at lines 9 and 10, consists in an extreme formulation of her experience: she has tried red wine about "a ↑million times," followed by an even stronger negative evaluation. What this reveals, say Wiggins and Potter, is the way that performative attitudes appear in discourse at points where practical actions are being accomplished. Beth uses her negative evaluation in order to avoid drinking the wine. However, the extract also shows that the practical outcomes

of evaluative practices are, at least potentially, moderated by the sorts of evaluative counter-strategies which others speakers may employ.

One of the features of this extract which Wiggins and Potter emphasize is that Beth's negative evaluation is of a specific sort. Beth refers to her own personal preferences. In doing so, her negative evaluation has a **subjective** character. This can be contrasted with Laura's evaluation at line 5, which is an **objective** evaluation of the properties of red wine, one of which is that red wine is "nice." One of the aspects of Beth's subjective evaluation which Wiggins and Potter draw attention to is that it allows Beth to offer her evaluation without implying that the others, who may evaluate red wine more positively, are wrong. The subjective nature of Beth's evaluation focuses accountability for her not drinking the wine on Beth, rather than focusing accountability on the others for wanting to drink it. This, together with the interplay between Beth and Bill at lines 8 to 10, indicates another way in which attitude talk in real-life contexts displays complexity. In providing her evaluation, Beth at the same time attends to her own accountability for producing her evaluation.

This issue of accountability for attitudes or opinions is also seen in a study by Mori (1999), who points out that one of the features of talk in which opinions are expressed is that speakers display a sensitivity to the issue of whether hearers will agree or disagree with the opinion. She points out that opinion expressions often include **self-qualifying segments**. For example, if the speaker is expressing an opinion about customs, he or she may include the qualification that such customs have changed or may be changing. Mori points out that this procedure is similar to conversational **self-repair** or hesitation where the speaker displays sensitivity to the potentially controversial nature of what is being said. Mori suggests that one of the useful features of such self-qualifications is that where an opinion is produced in a strong form, e.g., through the use of an

Subjective Pertaining to an individual's own view or perspective

Objective Pertaining to aspects of the world independently of any individual's view or perspective

Self-qualifying segments Episodes of talk in which the speaker reflexively comments on what he or she has said

Self-repair A correction of what is said instigated by the speaker, e.g., in displaying hesitancy

extreme case formulation, speakers may use self-qualification to exhibit awareness of the exaggerated nature of their opinion expression. What Mori's analysis shows, then, is that speakers locate episodes of descriptive and evaluative talk within contexts in which other social actions, such as justifying one's viewpoint, are also taking place. Jucker, Smith, and Ludge (2003) draw attention to a similar phenomenon in a study of the uses of vague referential terms. They point out that such expressions are often used to indicate what they refer to as the "**propositional attitude**" of the speaker. Thus expressions such as "I haven't been to see the movies since *probably* ... May" and "I plan on seeing it *probably* this weekend" include indicators of uncertainty which allow the speaker to reflexively comment on features such the accuracy or the depth of commitment implied by the statement.

What these studies show is that the discursive researcher is often interested not only in the attitudes towards something which are worked up in talk, but also in what the design of utterances reveals about the speaker's attitudes towards the talk itself. In a recent study of mundane domestic telephone conversations during which speakers make complaints, Edwards (2005b) examined the way in which speakers display a particular attitude or stance to the complaint which they make. Adopting a discursive psychological approach that applied the basic principles of conversation analysis, Edwards demonstrates a number of ways in which a complainer may indicate this stance or attitude. Edwards is careful to point out that this analysis does not imply participants are expressing underlying states of mind. The stances or attitudes which Edwards has in mind are discursive phenomena:

> ... these notions of investment, irony attitude, etc. indicate participants' practices and concerns, performed and oriented-to in how they talk.
> (Edwards, 2005b, p. 19)

For example, O'Halloran (2005), in his conversation analytic study of the conduct of meetings at Alcoholics Anonymous, notes the use of **irony** as a means of indicating stance. At one point, one of the speakers seeks to alter the views of members about the relationship Alcoholics Anonymous should have with other groups which tackle addiction.

> so (.) if I I could leave you with any particular point (.) it's the idea that maybe (.) just maybe we have to look at each programme as an individual programme (.)
> (O'Halloran, 2005, p. 549)

O'Halloran draws attention to the ironic status of the speaker's use of "maybe." He argues that "maybe" is not used here to indicate that the speaker has real doubt. The speaker is not reporting an inner mental state of confusion or indecision. Instead, "maybe" is used to indicate that the speaker's stance in making the suggestion is one of reasonableness and that the suggestion follows on from considered thought, as well as implying that the audience itself should begin to rethink its approach to other groups. In Edwards's own study, he examined "indirect complaints": complaints directed at something or someone other than the person to whom the complainer is speaking. In making complaints like this, speakers may announce that they are about to produce a complaint; they may incorporate laughter into the production of the complaint; they may "displace" the object of the complaint by focusing on incidental features of the event about which the speaker complains; they may deploy lexical choices such as "moan" or "whinge" to characterize the complainer in a specific way.

```
1  ROB: → ↑Well ↓and the other thing I wz dis-
            gusted b– I'm
2           ↓sorry you're getting'n earful'v this
            you couldn't'v:
3           phoned't a better ↑ti:me,hheh ↑he[h
4  LES:                                    [.hh ↑Oh that's
5           alri:ght,
6  ROB:     Well the ↑other thing ↓I've (.) found
            very strange
7           is ↑there weren't any dictionaries in
            the classroom
```

Propositional attitude A stance by means of which the speaker indicates what he or she thinks or feels about what is being said

Irony A discursive device in which what is said differs from what is actually meant

```
 8  LES:     .t.k.hhh[h
 9  ROB:          [Not actua[l
10  LES:               [↑No children's dih- e-w'l not
11          many children's dictionaries,hh
12  ROB:   W'l, they ↑have those little (.) booklety
        ↓things
```
                        (Edwards, 2005b, p. 9)

In the above extract, two schoolteachers, Robbie and Lesley, are discussing work and at this point in the conversation, Robbie announces a complaint at line 1 which she subsequently produces at line 7, using the extreme case formulation "weren't any" to emphasize the claim's status as a complaint. Edwards draws attention to the way that Robbie and Lesley jointly negotiate the production of Robbie's complaint. At line 2, Robbie inserts an apology for issuing a complaint, apparently one of a series, and then at line 3 makes a joke at her own practice of complaining, while at lines 4 and 5 Lesley acknowledges the apology. Edwards notes that Lesley's acknowledgment is somewhat unenthusiastic, and suggests that Robbie's downgrading of the complaint from "disgusted" (line 1) to "very strange" (line 6) **displays sensitivity** to this lack of enthusiasm. What this shows is that Robbie is careful to display her own attitude or stance to what she is saying, by apologizing for and joking about being about to make a complaint, and by softening the complaint in response to Lesley's equivocal receipt of her initial announcement that she is about to make a complaint about something.

One of the advantages of the discursive approach to attitudes is that it can help to make clear the indeterminate nature of some forms of attitude talk. While on some occasions participants may wish to construct a very explicit version of the attitude object under discussion, at other times they may appear to direct their attitudes towards that constructive process itself. For example, we have seen that irony is one recognizable form of talk in which the speaker indicates an attitude towards something. But, as Clift (1999) points out, the target of an ironic evaluation may be indeterminate. Indeed, evaluations

> **Displaying sensitivity** Implicit or explicit acknowledgment to the hearer that what one is saying is relevant to a specific issue or concern

of this sort may not even be easily categorized as dealing with an attitude object which participants have constructed or as referring to the speaker's talk itself.

Persuasion

Readers will have already noticed that in the examples of attitude research given above, the participants often seemed to be as concerned with undermining potential counter-positions as they were with establishing their own views. It is almost as though the expression of attitudes is, itself, at the same time a form of persuasive communication. This idea turns out to be crucial in separating out the study of persuasion as understood by experimental social psychology and the study of persuasion as viewed from the discursive perspective.

Experimental psychologists take persuasion to be the use of communication to alter someone's attitudes, understood as stable mental phenomena. This implies a model in which under certain conditions someone may hold stable attitudes, then be exposed to persuasive argument, and then hold a different set of stable attitudes (depending on the effectiveness of the persuasive message). So, just as the experimental social psychological model of attitudes separates out descriptions of cognitive beliefs from evaluative judgments in defining "attitude," it likewise separates out stable attitudes on the one hand from processes of persuasion on the other.

From a critical discourse analysis perspective, Pardo (2001) defines persuasion as the attempt to convince someone of something and argues that persuasion becomes manipulation or coercion depending on the extent to which the persuader relies upon power to accomplish the persuasive goal. However, we pointed out at the start of this chapter that the discursive researcher's interest in attitudes rests on the way that they appear in interaction as discursive accomplishments. And the examples of critical discourse analysis which were discussed revealed something about the dynamic nature of these accomplishments. Van Dijk's (2006a) emphasis on the expression of attitudes as an ideological process demonstrates well the way in which expression of attitudes is as much about manipulation and control as it is about the description of the speaker's inner mental states. To this extent, then, the notion of persuasion is already "built in" to the critical discourse analyst's account of attitudes. And persuasion is analyzed in terms of unfair manipulation or control on those occasions where the persuasive attempt to alter attitudes is supportive of an ideology which the analyst regards as, in some respect or another, unjust.

We saw earlier that other discursive analysts such as conversation analysts and discursive psychologists emphasize the fine-grain analysis of ways in which descriptive talk is seamlessly woven into evaluative talk in the construction of attitudinal objects. In a similar fashion, these discursive analysts also emphasize the way socially constructive processes of description and evaluation are themselves woven into rhetorical or argumentative discourse which allows the speaker to support his or her own attitudes while undermining counter-positions. So, across a broad spectrum of discursive approaches, analysts take the view that attitude and persuasion are interlinked, in that the expression of attitudes is often associated either with wider persuasive concerns of ideological manipulation or with the everyday persuasion that arises in situated social action.

Persuasion and ideology

One example of the critical discourse analyst's interest in ideological persuasion is Pinto's (2004) examination of a 1944 elementary school textbook that was in use in Spain during the rule of Francisco Franco. Franco's government was a coalition that included monarchist and fascist elements and emphasized strong central state control. Pinto argues that within such a context, school textbooks are an important locus for the transmission of the ruling elite's ideology. Drawing on the work of Bakhtin (1981), Pinto identifies an "**authoritative discourse**" throughout the school text which seeks to persuade the reader while disguising the structural mechanisms through which this persuasion takes place.

One of the means by which this is accomplished is the use, at a number of points in the text, of the first person plural "we."

> We, the subordinate ones, do not have any mission except obeying. We must obey without arguing.
>
> (Pinto, 2004, p. 656)

Pinto notes that this allows the author to establish that the present claim is a consensual view. Moreover, although the claim is expressed in the imperative, in the form of an order, the status of this command as a command is disguised by the suggestion that the author is making a general statement that includes himself. Among other persuasive techniques which Pinto describes are the use of **presuppositions**, the employment of slogans, and the use of **argument by analogy**. For example, he draws attention to claims within the text which embody presuppositions such as: "It is not enough that Spaniards live united and communicate among themselves" (Pinto, 2004, p. 660). Pinto notes that this claim presupposes that Spaniards are united, a presupposition which might be open to undermining if stated overtly, given that Spain had, a few years previously, experienced a three-year-long civil war. With reference to slogans, Pinto argues that their use is one of the most common of persuasive techniques. Drawing on Lu's (1999) analysis of slogans, Pinto locates their persuasive effect in the way they enable polarized thinking and in the ease with which they can be memorized. This reflects the critical discourse analyst's view that ideological effects take place in long-term memory. Pinto also refers to a number of different analogies in use throughout the text. For example, he notes that the authors draw an analogy between the child's relationship to the state and a young bird's relationship to its nest in order to persuade the reader that loving one's country is important and natural.

Presupposition An assumption which is implicitly or explicitly held as a prior basis for what is said

Authoritative discourse Talk in which a speaker is held to be especially privileged, e.g., as a result of status or role, in terms of the claims that are made

Argument by analogy Drawing similarities between two different phenomena in order to develop or defend a point of view

This use of rhetorical analogy is an interesting example of the "indirect" way in which persuasion may be accomplished. Persuasive argument need not rely upon logical inference from premise to conclusion, nor upon appeal to evidence and facts. For example, in their study of a sermon delivered by a religious preacher, Neuman and Levi (2003) point out the way in which the preacher draws an analogy between using threats to persuade a child to take medicine and using threats to persuade people to lead religious lives. In another study, which examined the use of parables in self-help books, Askehave (2004) notes that the authors of these texts often rely upon inserting brief narratives which present an analogical link between the events in the story and the persuasive message that the author intends to convey. Similarly, authors such as Charteris-Black (2006) and Santa Ana (1999) have drawn attention to the way in which metaphors are deployed persuasively to produce "cognitive frames" that provide a viewpoint on social issues. For example, Charteris-Black conducted an analysis of speeches and texts on immigration produced by politicians from the right wing of the political spectrum. One of the metaphors Charteris-Black identified in these texts was the metaphors of disaster as a result of flooding.

> A BNP government would accept no further immigration from any of the parts of the world which present the prospect of an almost limitless flow of immigration: Africa, Asia, China, Eastern and South Eastern Europe, the Middle East and South America would all be placed on an immediate "stop" list.
>
> We will also clamp down on the flood of "asylum seekers," the vast majority of whom are either bogus or can find refuge much nearer their home countries.
>
> We recognize that a reversal of the tide of immigration can only be secured by negotiation and consent, and that it is probably now too late to anticipate a return to the status quo ante 1948.
>
> (Charteris-Black, 2006, pp. 570–571)

Charteris-Black points out that the authors of these texts rely upon the metaphor of excessive flows of water through the use of terms such as "limitless flow," "flood," and "tide." These metaphors are politically persuasive, says Charteris-Black, because the authors employ them to draw upon common-sense understandings of the natural properties of water. The implication here is that just as the movement of water is a natural property which must be controlled if it becomes excessive, so too is the movement of peoples. Charteris-Black also points out that the metaphor of the flood is especially persuasive in a United Kingdom context, both because the United Kingdom is an island, and so areas of the country are susceptible to flooding, and because immigrants to the country are typically waterborne, in that they must cross a sea in order to enter the country. Although this metaphor is used to develop a persuasive representation of other people, immigrants, it is worth noting that metaphors can equally well be deployed in characterizing one's own group. Ricento (2003), for example, draws on the analysis of national identity by Wodak and colleagues (Wodak et al., 1999) in identifying a range of persuasive strategies, among which is the use of metaphor, in showing how texts by American authors develop the idea of what it is to be an American.

Discursive processes of persuasion such as the use of analogy and metaphor are of interest, then, in part because their persuasive effect does not rely upon what a logician would recognize as valid argument nor upon what the scientist would accept as the presentation of empirical evidence. Perhaps the most extreme form of this non-argumentative persuasion is what Wetherell and Potter (1992) refer to as "**rhetorically self-sufficient**" arguments, which are presented as principles that are to be taken as beyond question, such as "You cannot turn the clock backwards" and "You have to be practical." In this respect, rhetorically self-sufficient arguments function in a manner similar to proverbs. Gandara (2004) notes that proverbs are similarly regarded as unchallengeable and that because of this they are valuable tools in persuasive argument.

In a study of arguments mobilized by the Australian prime minister, John Howard, during an address to a convention which focused on the

Rhetorically self-sufficient A claim which speakers treat as though it stands in no need of additional justification

rights of Indigenous Australians, Augoustinos, LeCouteur, and Soyland (2002) examine the prime minister's use of rhetorically self-sufficient arguments to defend his government's views. One of the important issues associated with this social rights question was the issue of "reconciliation." This is a broadly defined term which became associated with attempts at building national consensus across the Australian population, partly as a result of the government setting up a "Council for Aboriginal Reconciliation." Another relevant issue was the question of whether the Australian government should issue a national apology to Indigenous Australians as a result of perceived abuses to human rights experienced by past generations. During his speech on these matters, Howard identified a number of potential threats to reconciliation.

P1 But this optimism, my friends, about the reconciliation process cannot be blind. We must be realistic in acknowledging some of the threats to reconciliation.

P2 Reconciliation will not work if it puts a higher value on symbolic gestures and overblown promises rather than practical needs of Aboriginal and Torres Strait Islander people in areas like health, housing, education and employment.

(Augoustinos, LeCouteur, & Soyland, 2002, pp. 120–121)

Augoustinos and her colleagues suggest that at P1 and P2 Howard is positioning himself as a realist who makes hard choices. Part of this is accomplished through his appeal to the rhetorically self-sufficient argument "We must be realistic." One of the consequences of this is that Howard is then able to make relevant a contrast between "symbolic gestures" and "practical needs." As someone who has positioned himself as being realistic, Howard is able to argue that practical issues of health, housing, education, and employment outweigh symbolic gestures. Augoustinos and colleagues suggest that Howard is thereby implicitly arguing in favor of his government's position, which is against the offering of a national apology as a symbolic gesture towards Indigenous Australians.

As might be expected from their ideological perspective, many critical discourse analyses of persuasion focus on the text and talk of powerful elites

such as politicians. However, Carranza (1999) has examined the persuasive discourse of people from non-powerful groups in order to show that people in those groups are able to utilize their own forms of persuasive discourse in ideological resistance. In analyzing an interaction between a Latino male, Fernando, and a police officer, Carranza refers to van Dijk's (1995, 2006a) analysis of ideology to argue that the interaction is partly structured by the police officer's ideologically informed belief that Latino males are an appropriate target for hostility.

36 And then he takes my wallet
37 and tells me "So you don't sell drugs? and what about this money? Where does it come from?"
38 I say "Just a minute.
39 I come from work
40 it was pay day today
41 I cashed my check
42 and I don't think anyone can tell me what to do with my money,
43 I'm the one who earned it.
44 I'm the one who sweated to earn it
45 so I don't see any reason for you to ask me to explain anything
46 why– what do I do with my money
47 where I put it where I don't put it"

(Carranza, 1999, p. 528)

In this episode, Fernando recounts an interaction with a police officer who approaches Fernando and his friends and accuses them of possessing drugs. Carranza points out that the use of reported speech adds to the verisimilitude of an account by providing detail of the encounter, thereby making an account more persuasive. Fernando begins his report of what he said with "Just a minute," which establishes for the hearer that in his response to the police officer, he began by disrupting the normative routine of question and answer which is typical of interactions between the police and citizens. Fernando does then develop an answer to the officer's question, but the reported speech format allows him to present an argumentative structure which makes relevant his right to carry money and to put that money wherever he wishes and also establishes as relevant the lawful manner in which the money was obtained. The effect of this, says Carranza, is that Fernando can be seen to resist the negative ideology of the police officer and to challenge it with a claim to the "competence, rights and values of the mainstream society" (Carranza, 1999, p. 537). Carranza suggests that one noteworthy feature of Fernando's account is the list-like structures involved. A number of discursive researchers have pointed out the persuasive effect of building accounts which rely on a **listing** structure. For example, in a critical discourse analysis of promotional literature for frequent flyer programs, Thurlow and Jaworski (2006) have also identified listing as a persuasive device. In the present example, Fernando first provides a description of a list of actions, "I come from work, it was pay day today, I cashed my check," which acts as a warrant for his claim that no one can tell him what to do with his money.

Mundane persuasion in everyday talk

Much of the modern interest among discursive researchers in the link between attitude and argument in discourse draws upon Billig's (1987) work on rhetoric. We have already seen, for example, the way Puchta and Potter (2002) draw on Billig's work in elucidating focus group processes. Billig draws attention to the way that expressions of attitude are publicly adopted positions located within current controversy. What this means is that expressing an attitude involves either implicitly or explicitly criticizing possible counter-positions. From this perspective, then, all attitude discourse is essentially rhetorical. Billig notes that one consequence of adopting this approach is that, if all attitude talk is essentially rhetorical, then notions such as argument and rhetoric become applicable in a whole range of contexts beyond those which are typified by the ideological persuasion observable in political speeches or the explicitly persuasive blandishments of the courtroom lawyer.

More recently, Potter (1996b) has argued that Billig's perspective can be applied to factual accounts. We noted earlier that the discursive perspective on attitudes emphasizes the way that attitude objects are socially constructed by the production of accounts which are designed to be heard

as factual statements. Potter draws on Billig's rhetorical approach to suggest that these factual accounts are also essentially argumentative. Potter is careful to point out, though, that treating factual accounts as essentially rhetorical does not rely upon a cognitive social psychology in which the efficacy of persuasion is measured by establishing whether the audience's mental state, e.g., the mental representations encoded within attitudes, have changed. Instead, the "antagonistic" relationship between different versions produced in factual accounts is better thought of in terms of "the traditional notion of 'suasive' rhetoric, which is discourse designed to elicit expressions of agreement from an audience" (Potter, 1996b, p. 108). In a similar vein, Woofitt (2005a) treats the terms "persuasive" and "factual language" as interchangeable. He argues that this approach provides the discursive analyst with a more sophisticated understanding of persuasive language use, because it allows the analyst to extend the range of analytic interests from narrowly defined discursive concerns to a broad range of interpersonal, inferential, and interactional matters.

In this respect the influence of argument and rhetoric transcends explicitly persuasive talk and becomes a feature of everyday interaction. Of course, discursively designing an account as factual is of use in explicitly persuasive contexts, as Muchnik (2005) shows in her description of the ways in which a Hebrew preacher seeks to persuade his congregation to repent. However, while some contexts such as the preacher's sermon or the politician's address might appear to be obvious examples of persuasion, we must bear in mind a different notion of what might be called "mundane persuasion" in which rhetorical strategies are woven into processes of social construction or other discursive activities in performing a wide range of social actions. Bearing this in mind helps to explain why discursive studies of attitude often generate analyses which identify persuasive elements of discourse. If the social construction of attitude objects incorporates the production of accounts and these accounts incorporate rhetorical design features, then it is hardly surprising that the analysis of attitudinal discourse often involves identifying the ways in which people persuasively justify their own attitude claims while undermining those of others.

Listing Talk which sequentially itemizes a series of things that are related in some way

CLASSIC STUDY: Arguing and thinking

Like *Discourse and social psychology: Beyond attitudes and behavior*, this text was to have enormous influence on the way that discursive research developed. Billig begins the book by making a plea for what he calls "antiquarian psychology" and emphasizing the importance to the social psychologist of the ancient study of rhetoric. He identifies for the reader a distinction between rhetoric understood as "tricks of the trade" of professional persuaders such as politicians and what he terms "the argumentative dimension." In subsequent chapters, Billig expands on what he means by "argumentative," contrasting the argumentative perspective with others which ignore the ways in which people routinely consider counter-arguments in their everyday talk. Billig applies these insights in a contemporary context by discussing the ways in which experimental social psychology has over-emphasized reasoning processes such as logical inference at the expense of other processes in which explicit or implicit argumentation or "witcraft" can be seen. Billig goes on to describe the ways in which processes of categorization seem to intrinsically involve processes of particularization in which speakers consider the variety of ways in which the applications of

categories may be limited in specific contexts. Drawing on these thoughts, Billig argues that attitudes, rather been viewed as stable clusters of internal mental phenomena, are better understood as positions which are taken in wider controversies and are, as a result, themselves inherently argumentative. At the end of the book, Billig discusses the argumentative nature of common sense and the ways in which common-sense expressions often seem to produce contradictions. This, says Billig, raises a false dilemma. If attitudes are the argumentative advocacy of a particular point of view, then this implies that people deploy argument to develop and maintain one-sided points of view. But if everyday common sense embraces contradiction, then people seem to be inherently disposed towards adopting multiple, potentially contradictory, points of view. Billig resolves this issue by drawing attention to the ways in which expressions of attitude demonstrate an ambiguity which reflects the underlying argumentative nature of attitudes themselves.

Billig, M. (1987). *Arguing and thinking: A rhetorical approach to social psychology*. Cambridge: Cambridge University Press.

Potter's (1996b) analysis of the way descriptions are worked up as factual statements relates in part to what he refers to as "defensive rhetoric." Defensive rhetoric is employed in order to forestall potential undermining of the version of the attitudinal object or other social phenomenon which the speaker is producing by constructing a description as a factual account. (Potter distinguishes defensive rhetoric from what he terms "offensive rhetoric," which is used to undermine alternative accounts.) The essence of defensive

rhetoric is that factual accounts display an **epistemological orientation** in that they are built up in a way which establishes their status as "mere" descriptions that merely tell the hearer how the world is. This epistemological orientation is displayed in a number of different ways in talk. One feature of such talk is **interest management**. Interest management refers to that property of talk in which speakers explicitly or implicitly acknowledge that they have a stake or interest in presenting the version of the attitude object,

Epistemological orientation A discursive stance or position towards some thing in which the speaker's state of mind towards that thing is made explicit

Interest management Attending through talk to issues or concerns which hearers might attribute to the speaker or other social phenomenon, that they develop. Another feature is the explicit or implicit use of **category entitlements**, in which categories of actors are treated as being entitled to know certain things, which lends their accounts particular credence. A third feature is the deployment of detail. Potter notes that detailed descriptions can be used to build up an account as factual because the account thereby produced conveys an impression that it is a report from someone who has an eyewitness-like grasp of the events with which the account deals.

Interest management

Stake or interest might be local to the specific conversational context: a speaker may wish, for example, to avoid appearing prejudiced. Interest management might equally be relevant to a wider context: in a courtroom, a defendant giving evidence might wish his statement to appear neutral, rather than influenced by the fact that if he is not believed he may be sent to jail. Speakers manage potential accusations of interestedness in a number of ways. One of these is to develop descriptions which are designed to forestall such accusation, through a process Potter (1996b) identifies as "stake inoculation." As one example of this process, Potter describes a newspaper account of a psychiatrist's claim that great artists are "tortured souls." The newspaper account begins by acknowledging that this is a stereotyped view of creative artists. However, the psychiatrist is depicted as being "initially skeptical" and as only coming to this conclusion after reviewing large numbers of case studies. Potter describes this as an attempt to inoculate the psychiatrist's account from accusations that it is merely a repetition of a well-worn stereotype by making relevant the psychiatrist's initial skepticism. In the study by Augoustinos, LeCouteur, and Soyland (2002) mentioned above, Howard was shown to rely on rhetorically self-sufficient arguments. However, at another point in his speech, Howard also draws on what Augoustinos and her colleagues describe as "a full blown attempt at stake inoculation."

Category entitlements Rights or privileges normatively associated with a classification of someone

---

Since the inception of the Council in 1991, the Coalition Parties have committed themselves to the reconciliation process and today, on behalf of the Liberal and National parties, I reaffirm that commitment.

(Augoustinos et al., 2002, p. 116)

In a context in which he has argued against "symbolic" displays such as the offering of a national apology to Indigenous Australians, Howard shows sensitivity to the question of whether he is seen as not supporting reconciliation. A potential criticism of his position is that he has a stake in preventing such national initiatives because he is unsympathetic to the cause of Indigenous Australians. Augoustinos and her colleagues point out that Howard counters these potential criticisms by explicitly avowing his commitment.

In a number of studies, Abell and Stokoe (1999, 2001) have analyzed the interactions that took place in an interview, broadcast on British television in 1995, between the late Diana, Princess of Wales, and a journalist, Martin Bashir. In Chapter 2 we examined some of the ways in which Diana constructed identities for herself during this interview process. However, Abell and Stokoe also point out that, in the course of the interview, Diana can be seen to attend to issues of stake or interest. At one point, Diana deals with the question of whether she is to blame for the press attention she received. Abell and Stokoe suggest that negotiating implications of blame is a sensitive matter. In particular, allocating blame involves speakers in the tricky task of accusing others of being blameworthy without appearing to be biased or to have a stake in that accusation.

BASHIR: some people would say (.) that in the early years of your marriage (.) you were partly responsible for encouraging the press interest (.) you danced with people like Wayne Sleep (.) you seemed to enjoy it (.) you had a very good and warm relationship (.) do you feel any responsibility (1) for the way the press (.) have (.) behaved towards you

DIANA: I've never (.) encouraged the media (1) er (.) there's (.) there was a relationship which worked (.) before (.) but now I can't tolerate it because it's become abusive (1) and it's harassment (.) but I don't want to be seen to (.) indulging in self pity I'm not (.) I understand they have a job to do (.) you could equate it to a soap opera really (.) it (.) goes on and on and on and the story never changes (2) and each time one enjoys oneself (.) albeit it's in a (.) di–different situation (.) you have to pay for it because people criticize (.) which (.) comes with the patch as I said previously (.) but I am a free spirit (2) unfortunately for some

(Abell & Stokoe, 1999, pp. 304–305)

Abell and Stokoe draw attention to Bashir's use of the expression "some people would say." In a context in which Diana is being asked about press intrusion into her life, Bashir's implication that some of this is Diana's own fault might be heard as being interested in that Bashir himself is a member of the press. Bashir deals with this potential problem by attributing the claim about Diana's own responsibility to some unspecified set of people. By deflecting ownership of this claim away to "some people," Bashir lessens both the role that he, as a journalist, plays and the role of journalists in general. Abell and Stokoe go on to argue that Diana also deals with issues of stake in her reply to the question. If Diana was to blame for the press intrusion, then she could be seen as having an interest in trying to shift that blame onto someone else. Abell and Stokoe note that Diana's reply employs a distinction between her "self," identified through the use of the first person singular pronoun "I" in "I've never (.) encouraged the media," and her role, that aspect of her life which "comes with the patch" and might well carry a requirement for interaction with the media. This is supported by Diana's explicit reference to self-pity, "I don't want to be seen to (.) indulging in self pity." Abell and Stokoe argue that this is an instance of stake inoculation. By negatively acknowledging this potential inference, she addresses and undermines the potential accusation that her claims about the press being responsible for intruding on her life arise merely because she feels sorry for herself.

Category entitlements

In his early work on conversation analysis, Sacks (1992) demonstrated that categories are "inference rich" in that when someone is categorized, this may be associated with a range of inferences

about that person grounded in culturally available knowledge and understandings of what members of that category are like. For example, in Chapter 9, when we examine discourse and the law, it will be seen that in courts of law medical "expert witnesses" are allowed special leeway to reformulate lawyer's questions and to produce conclusions This derives from the common-sense understanding that doctors know about medicine in a way that lawyers do not. As Sneijder and te Molder (2005a) have pointed out, such category entitlements may require to be worked up and established within a local conversational context. For example, in their discussions of evaluative practices towards food, Sneijder and te Molder examine the way in which people work up their identity as "gourmet," thereby establishing a right to claim expertise in producing evaluations of food. Moreover, the epistemological orientation implied by claims to category entitlement does not necessarily have to be attributed to oneself when dealing with issues of stake or interest. In a study of cancer patient support groups, Bishop and Yardley (2004) showed how group members used references to complementary medicine as a means of showing that they had an active participation in their own welfare. In the following extract, one of the group members delivers a positive evaluation of a complementary approach as "effective."

90 (. . .) And if I could just give you a quick snap-shot of

91 why I think it is effective, I saw my consultant last week a

92 consultant surgeon, and that was for my six-monthly regular

93 check-up: the first thing he tells me is how I'm getting on – the results

94 of my blood test, which were very encouraging, so he says, "to what

95 do you attribute your continuing success?" I said, "Well, without a

96 doubt I place lots of faith and credence in my diet and the

97 supplements I take." Bearing in mind he is a surgeon, he said, "I

98 couldn't agree more with you – definitely been playing a crucial part."

99 There's something good to get endorsement from a consultant.

(Bishop & Yardley, 2004, pp. 475–476)

Bishop and Yardley argue that Adam is attending to an issue of stake in reporting what his surgeon has said. In presenting a highly positive evaluation of complementary approaches, Adam might be taken to be insufficiently objective because his evaluation helps to demonstrate that he is active in caring for his own health and also, perhaps, that he has a vested interest in believing that the complementary approach is efficacious. Adam deals with this issue of stake by invoking the category entitlements of his own consultant, who is explicitly allocated to the category "surgeon," in support of his claim. One of the entitlements which is normatively bound to categories of medical "consultant" and "surgeon" is, of course, a knowledge of what counts as successful treatment. This helps to establish that his own evaluation of the complementary approach is not merely a matter of personal interest.

Deploying detail

Detail can be useful in establishing the factual nature of a claim because it helps the speaker to establish that a claim is grounded in a number of actual features of the actions or events which are being described. For example, in a study of students' disruptive behavior in the classroom, Verkuyten (2002) examines the way that detail is introduced into descriptions of behavior which are potentially identifiable as "disruptive."

> T: Will you stop talking. You're disturbing everybody else.
> S1: But Ms, we were talking about the assignment.
> S2: Yes, she asked me whether we, where we should fill in them words for the second question if we should . . .
> T: Nonsense, you're talking again.
>   (Verkuyten, 2002, pp. 110–111)

Verkuyten points out that following S1's claim to be working, S2 provides detail about what they are doing: S1 asked S2 a question about the task and identifies a specific element of the task, "the second question," and identifies this element as problematic in that S1 is unclear about where "them words" should be "filled in." This task-specific detail, says Verkuyten, helps to establish the claim made by the girls that they are working.

One of the ways in which accounts can be designed to build up factuality through the provision of detail is the inclusion of reported speech. In general, the citing of others as corroborators of what is said is a useful resource in persuasive communication (Dickerson, 1997). We noted earlier in discussing Carranza's (1999) study that Fernando deploys reported speech as a means of establishing the verisimilitude of the description he provides as a vivid and accurate representation of his interaction with the police officer. Similarly, in the example of the cancer support group, it is noteworthy that Adam used reported speech in establishing the factuality of his account. In his discussion of persuasion in *Conversation analysis and discourse analysis* (Wooffitt, 2005a, Ch. 5), Wooffitt likewise notes that one of the varied functions of reported speech is to attest to the facticity of an experience.

> Tha:t night: (1.5) I don't know what time it was: (1.3) my: husband (.) and I both woke up: (0.7) with the mo:st (.) dreadful (0.5) feeling of (1.7) hhh °well° being (nyrie) smothered (0.3) but the powerful smell ÿh and a blackness (o.3) that w's that was (0.2) blacker than black I can' describe it like (.) anything else (.) ÿhh it was the most penetrating (0.3) type of blackness ÿhh and there was this (1.7) what I assumed to be th– the shape of a man (.) in a cloak (2) it was the most (0.3) formidable (1.2) sight (1) my husband said "my God what is it" (.) an' I just said "now keep quiet and say the Lord's prayer"
>   (Wooffitt, 2005a, pp. 101–102)

In this excerpt, a speaker is recounting a paranormal experience, and uses reported speech to help establish that the evil spirit was not merely a figment of her imagination. Wooffitt notes that the description provides detail of the features of the experience: the smell, the "blackness" and the figure that appeared. In addition, the speaker reports what her husband said. The inclusion of this reported speech utterance, "my God what is it," establishes that the husband could also see the object. The strongly formulated nature of the husband's reported utterance also lends credence to the urgent and alarming nature of the experience as described by the speaker.

It is worth noting that discursive researchers have warned that the provision of detail in an account offers the hearer an opportunity to undermine that account by questioning some of its detailed elements. For this reason, somewhat paradoxically, the rhetorical effectiveness of an account may be improved by a systematic use of vagueness. As one example of this, Potter (1996b) notes the ways in which idiomatic expressions such as clichés and proverbs, such as "banging your head against a brick wall," may be used in accounts precisely because they are often very general in scope while, given their proverbial status, they are difficult to challenge.

In Conclusion

This chapter does not exhaust the ways in which discursive analysts have explored persuasion and argument. It has not explored the discourse analytic concern with discourses and repertoires as argumentative devices (Swan & McCarthy, 2003). Nor has it looked in detail at the way in which conversation analysts delineate argumentative processes through analysis of sequential organization. For example, in an analysis of one person's telephone requests to airlines seeking discounted air fares, Beach and Lockwood (2003) identify some of the sequential properties of persuasive talk. They note that at the beginning of a call the airline representative typically issues a formalized introduction which identifies the airline and other salient features. Upon receipt of this introduction, the caller responds by issuing the informal greeting "Hi" before going on to make his request. Beach and Lockwood argue that this greeting is designed by the caller to give the call a personalized character and to set up his subsequent requests in respect of a discounted air fare.

That said, it is nevertheless clear that discursive analysts have an ongoing interest in how we display our attitudes and how we seek to persuade others. Critical discourse analysts are broadly sympathetic to some of the concerns of the social cognitive psychologist, but emphasize the ideological functions which attitude expressions and persuasion serve. Other discursive researchers are more critical of the idea that attitudes should be construed as cognitive phenomena and that persuasion should be seen as a communicative process that results in changes to those inner states. However, there is broad agreement across the varied discursive approaches that attitudes are inherently action-oriented. The display of attitudes is a process in which the expression of beliefs is often commingled with evaluative practices in a socially constructive fashion. Moreover, attitude talk is essentially argumentative, in that speakers have routine persuasive concerns with ideological matters or with developing and maintaining their own accounts while at the same time undermining alternative versions.

Chapter summary

- In this chapter, we have outlined the way in which discursive researchers deploy the notions of attitude and persuasion.
- Some discursive researchers such as critical discourse analysts are in many ways sympathetic to the view that attitudes are cognitive phenomena. However, other discursive researchers are more critical of this "cognitivist" approach.
- Discursive research identifies a relationship between attitude talk and social control. One aspect of this relationship is the way in which attitudes can be deployed to address ideological concerns.
- Some discursive researchers, notably discursive psychologists, have emphasized the way in which attitudes are constructed as discursive entities. This is related to the distinction between "preformed" and "performed" attitudes.
- Discursive research on attitudes is closely associated with the study of persuasion, because many discursive researchers focus on the way in which attitudes are dynamically developed and maintained through persuasive discourse.

- Persuasive discourse, like discourse about attitudes, is associated with ideological concerns of speakers and hearers.
- However, discourse analysis also reveals that persuasion arises in contexts of a more everyday nature. "Mundane" persuasion can be seen to be a feature of normal talk which need not be associated with the special concerns of the courtroom lawyer or the professional politician.
- "Mundane" persuasion draws on rhetorical features such as interest management, category entitlements, and the deployment of argumentative detail.

Connections

In this chapter we have examined the way that the critical discourse analyst draws upon the notion of "attitude" in analyzing journalistic representations of the other. In Chapter 7, we discuss other forms of discriminatory discursive formulations of "the other." In Chapter 9 we will explore further the ways in which people manipulate discourse for persuasive ends during courtroom interactions.

Activity

Consider a recent speech made by a politician about some issue on which you have definite views. What discursive features can you identify in the politician's talk? Were your views altered? If they were, did these discursive features play a role? If they were not altered, what is it about the politician's talk (as opposed to the topic) which you find unpersuasive?

Further reading

Puchta, C. & Potter, J. (2004). *Focus group practice*. London: Sage. In this book, Puchta and Potter provide a critical introduction to a popular methodological technique for gathering qualitative data about attitudes and opinions. They point to a number of shortcomings of focus group techniques and provide readers with a set of "dos and don'ts" in utilizing this method.

van Dijk, T. A. (1998). *Ideology: A multidisciplinary approach*. London: Sage. This text sets out van Dijk's views on the relationships between cognitive states such as attitudes and beliefs and social structures and forces such as ideologies. He identifies the ways in which discourse is deployed with reference to ideological concerns in order to effect changes in cognition, including the use of persuasion.

Chapter 7

Prejudice

Key terms
Ageism
Banal nationalism
Discrimination
Dispositional state
Essentializing
Heterosexism
Human genome
Interpretative repertoires
Membership category features
Normalizing practices
Occasioned
Organizational features
Overtly prejudicial talk
Political correctness
Prejudice
Procedural relevance
Production features
Quantification
Racism
Reformulations
Script
Sexism

Few people would deny that **prejudice** is one of society's greatest social problems. Prejudice has not only been a focus of social research, but also has been much more widely acknowledged as a major challenge to contemporary society. Indeed, at the start of the twenty-first century it is difficult to identify an area of the world in which prejudice is not associated with disastrous social consequences, although the interaction between prejudice and the many other socioeconomic factors which generate societal conflict is often murky. In Africa, the Janjaweed armed militias are accused of trying to "ethnically cleanse" Sudan of its black African population. In the Middle East, the Israelis and their Arab neighbors seem perpetually on the brink of war. In the Far East, the Chinese castigate the Japanese for what they see as a refusal to admit to wartime atrocities. In Europe and America too, the effects of prejudice are felt across a wide spectrum, from the Basque separatists' campaign of violence against the government in Spain to the rise in concern within the US and the UK over the relationship between the state and its Muslim citizens.

A brief consideration of events like these shows that the study of prejudice is fraught with difficulty. Prejudice is often associated with **discrimination** or more generally negative actions. However, such actions always arise in a specific social, political, and historical context, and some researchers maintain that an understanding of such actions arguably requires an understanding of that context. Moreover, consideration of examples like this may mask the fact that experiencing prejudice is dynamic. During a lifetime, people may become the target of a form of prejudice which, at a different time, had not affected them. For example, most of us will grow old enough to become the potential target of **ageism**, or we may become infirm enough to suffer from prejudice against those with a disability. Some people will undergo changes in family circumstances, e.g., through marriage, so that newly

acquired racial or ethnic associations generate prejudice. In other words, prejudice is the sort of social problem which may lurk around the corner for anyone. At the same time, of course, other forms of prejudice can be more enduring throughout a person's life, being grounded in issues such as nationality, race, ethnicity, religion, gender, or sexual orientation.

It is important to note at the outset that prejudice need not be associated with blatant forms of prejudice talk or discriminatory action. The ethnic cleansing of a village in the Balkans or the Sudan is newsworthy, in part, because journalists understand that the majority of people will find such actions repugnant. More generally, most members of civil society have a good grasp on the codes and rules which circumscribe "social acceptability."

> Whites are aware of norms against "sounding prejudiced," so they design their talk to appear "reasoned" and their narratives to provide "evidence" for their positions.
>
> (Buttny, 2004, p. 101)

It follows that whenever someone has an interest in creating or maintaining a sense of self as an appropriately qualified societal member, that person is less likely to indulge in **overtly prejudicial talk** or action. So some forms of prejudice may be much more difficult to identify than those which are bound up with conflict or open social tension. However, this does not mean that prejudice of this kind does not, in its own way, generate problems for its targets.

In the following sections, we explore this phenomenon as it is understood from a discursive perspective, by focusing on two sorts of prejudice: **racism** and prejudice in respect of gender or sexual orientation. We will explore the ways in which the analysis of prejudice talk contributes

---

Prejudice Dislike of others who are described as different from oneself, e.g., in terms of category membership

Discrimination Unfair behavior directed at others as a result of prejudice

Ageism Prejudice towards others because of their age

Overtly prejudicial talk Talk designed by the speaker to be heard as prejudiced

Racism Prejudice towards others because of their race

to an understanding of prejudice as a phenomenon. We will also explore questions such as the following. How is prejudice talk managed in local interactional contexts where other interests are in play? How do individuals who might be positioned as the targets of prejudice attend to this problem? What do such analyses tell us about the ways in which prejudice as a pervasive social problem might be challenged? We begin by outlining the discursive research approach to prejudice, and then turn to look at how this perspective has been applied in the study of race, sex, and gender orientation.

Prejudice and Discourse

For some discursive researchers, the analyst's interest in prejudice lies in the way that prejudice is attended to, handled, and managed in talk and text (Edwards, 2005a). What this means is that the analyst wishes to unwrap the ways in which prejudice becomes apparent in talk such as accusations, disagreements, explanations, or descriptive formulations. Prejudice is understood as the sort of thing which is primarily a concern of participants, as shown up by what they say and by the way in which they display that the issue is of importance to them.

This approach has two useful benefits. First, it offers a method of analysis which is common across all sorts of mental states. For the discursive psychologist, the way to understand any mental state such as recognizing or forgetting is to understand what the participant is doing or accomplishing by making relevant such mental states in what they say (Edwards, 2003). This means that, instead of appearing as an aberrant form of interaction which requires special forms of explanation, prejudice can be placed within the same analytic framework as all other sorts of mental state. Second, the discursive approach to prejudice treats as analytically equivalent the issue of whether participants are engaged in expressing prejudice or in "covering up" prejudice. Within discursive psychology, there is no attempt to "read behind" what the participant says to some prior causal inner mental state. The analyst is therefore not concerned with dealing with the "problem" of a discrepancy between what participants say and what they "really

think." Instead, the analyst seeks to examine the situated actions which such talk is performing. In this respect the issue is not one of whether participants make explicit avowals of prejudice or not, but rather one of examining how participants orient to what it is that they are saying, for example by making prejudice a relevant concern.

Of course, the issue of whether prejudice is made a "relevant concern" is complex. In some cases, explicit avowals of prejudice may not appear, but explicit *disavowals* may appear through the use, for example, of disclaimers, which are forms of talk or text in which someone seeks to prevent potentially negative inferences or categorizations being drawn from what is said by explicitly denying that such inferences or categorizations are appropriate. Thus a speaker might begin a conversational turn by saying "I am not prejudiced, but. . . ." The social scientist's interest in disclaimers began over 30 years ago with the publication of Hewitt and Stokes's paper of the same name (Hewitt & Stokes, 1975). Since then, a number of discursive studies have illuminated the way in which disclaimers function in everyday speech. However, as Condor and her colleagues point out, such research often under-emphasizes the way in which the use of disclaimers is a dialogical accomplishment (Condor et al., 2006). In other words, if someone designs a conversational turn as a display of non-prejudice, whether it is taken as such depends, in part, on how hearers respond.

So for some researchers, the proper study of prejudice is to attend to episodes of talk in which participants explicitly deal with matters of prejudice, for example by producing avowals or disavowals, by issuing challenges, or by formulating corrections. But it is important to remember that other researchers emphasize the additional importance of the wider context in which such discourse arises. For example, in his discussion of the related notion of bigotry, Billig draws attention to its ideological basis and to the way in which ideologies are "instantiated within discursive actions" (Billig, 2002). Verkuyten (2001) makes a similar point when he says that the "wider ideological context is both inside and outside the talk." Wodak (Reisigl & Wodak, 2001; Wodak, 2002) goes further in pointing out that talk like anti-Semitic rhetoric is only understood by taking historical and sociopolitical factors into account. This, of course, highlights the sorts of issues that were mentioned briefly in Chapter 1 and are discussed more fully in the last two chapters. As will be argued there, a live issue within the discursive researcher's approach to prejudice is the question of how analysis of prejudice ought to take account of factors beyond talk (or text) itself.

Race

The definition of "race" has been hotly contested within the natural and social sciences. Indeed, following the completion of the draft map of the **human genome**, one of the major scientists associated with the Human Genome Project declared that race was not a "scientific concept" at all. However, as McCann-Mortimer and her colleagues point out (McCann-Mortimer, Augoustinos, & LeCouteur, 2004), scientific claims like this must be understood as discursive accomplishments in their own right. They draw on the work of Gilbert and Mulkay (1984) to show that scientific pronouncements of this sort are always open to rhetorical challenge. Gilbert and Mulkay demonstrated that scientists' talk often relies upon what they described as "**interpretative repertoires.**" These are linguistic registers which rely upon specific stylistic, grammatical, and lexical features in depicting someone's actions and beliefs as being of a certain sort. "Empiricist repertoire" talk, which can be found, for example, in formal research papers, emphasizes experimental data, impersonal procedures, and impersonal forms of description. "Contingent repertoire" talk draws on references to personal or social factors outside the realm of empirical data. Gilbert and Mulkay showed how contingent accounts were often drawn upon by scientists in explaining why theoretical opponents held the "wrong" view. McCann-Mortimer and her colleagues demonstrate that the same sorts of rhetorical strategies are deployed not only in scientists' constructions of "race" which minimize group differences, but also in those other scientists' constructions which maximize group differences. They conclude that:

> protagonists on both sides of this debate typically drew upon the rhetoric of science to legitimate their position, primarily by means of invoking the empiricist repertoire. In pursuit of their claims to scientific "truth," both sides employed "defensive" rhetorical devices such as **quantification** to warrant the "factual" nature of their position.
>
> (McCann-Mortimer et al., 2004, p. 428)

The work of McCann-Mortimer and her fellow researchers illustrates an important feature of the discursive approach to understanding forms of prejudice like racism. For some discursive researchers, there are no phenomena which stand outside of discourse itself that the analyst can usefully appeal to in providing an understanding of what people are doing when they exhibit prejudice. And this is as true of the scientists who take their business to be the identification and explication of fundamental concepts such as "race" as it is for anyone else. From this perspective, the proper way to understand the meaning of "racism" is to explore how racism is actually accomplished through talk.

One of the most important figures whose work has typified this discursive approach to racism is Verkuyten. He has emphasized the importance of this perspective in a series of studies of ethnic Dutch and ethnic minority adolescents and adults in the Netherlands (Verkuyten, 1998b, 2001, 2003). In these studies he examines the everyday meaning of racism as it appears in the focus group talk of his participants as they discuss and argue among themselves. For example, in his 2003 study of **essentializing**, Verkuyten argues that this notion is often assumed to be associated with racism. In turn, anti-racist, emancipatory discourse is often assumed to benefit from de-essentializing discourse. However, Verkuyten

---

Quantification Talk which relies on reference to numerical and other quantity references for rhetorical effect

---

Interpretative repertoires Forms of talk or text in which the content of what is said is organized via specific styles of speaking or writing

---

Essentializing Talk designed to depict group membership categories as inevitable or quasi-natural

reveals that the talk of both ethnic majority and ethnic minority members draws upon notions of essentialism. One conclusion to be drawn from these studies is that the discursive researcher must be careful not to begin with a prior theoretical definition of "racism" which may prevent him or her from understanding how racism is actually accomplished through everyday talk.

Of course, the discursive nature of fundamental constructs such as "race" is only half the story. The importance of understanding racism as talk is also revealed by examining the social scientist's practical methodologies for studying racism. Bonilla-Silva and Forman have demonstrated that participants' views as revealed by analysis of interview material were more racist than views expressed by means of a traditional survey instrument (Bonilla-Silva & Forman, 2000). They conclude that what they observed during their interviews was talk which exemplified a "new racial ideology" in which racism was described as the fault of a minority of white Americans and was compounded by shortcomings among black Americans. All of this was accomplished through careful construction of accounts in which the speaker produced versions of the "other" while attending to possible accusations of racism by a variety of means, such as incorporating "discursive elements into their answers that expressed social distance (indirectness) or projection (displacement)" (Bonilla-Silva & Forman, 2000, p. 76).

So, thinking about fundamental theoretical concepts associated with racism, and about the practical methodologies for its study, provides evidence to support Edwards's view that the researcher must pay close attention to how racism is worked up in discourse. And as the work of Verkuyten and others shows, one of the features of such talk which analysis reveals is the way in which (1) people craft discursive accounts of "the other" while (2) attending to the potential pitfalls of being seen as racist themselves. It is to these two notions that we now turn.

CLASSIC STUDY: Mapping the language of racism

Over a period of eight years from the mid-1980s onwards, Margaret Wetherell and Jonathan Potter collected and analyzed a dataset of 81 interviews conducted in New Zealand with ordinary New Zealanders. The participants were drawn from a range of sources such as voluntary groups, Rotary clubs, and local public and private schools. The study was an attempt to explore white New Zealanders' views on race relations and white New Zealanders' racism and discrimination against Maori people. They were asked questions about multiculturalism, integration, and affirmative action, about New Zealand's colonial experience, about Maori social protests, and about the controversial 1981 South African rugby tour of New Zealand and the public protests which followed. (South Africa was, at that time, still an apartheid state.) In a complex and interwoven set of analyses, Wetherell and Potter show that white New Zealanders sometimes draw on discourses of race, culture, and nation in talking about their relationship to their Maori neighbors. Their examples provide an illustration of the way in which categorization talk can be rhetorically deployed within racist talk. In subsequent chapters, they illustrate the ways in which accounts of social conflict or protest can be developed around talk of innocent majorities being swayed by culpable minorities; they also examine how other discourses such as talk of land rights and language barriers can be deployed for racist ends. They conclude with an extended analysis of the way that their participants talk about racism itself, and point out the ways in which people "protect" themselves from possible imputations of racism by carefully constructing the accounts they offer.

Wetherell, M. & Potter, J. (1992). *Mapping the language of racism: Discourse and the legitimation of exploitation*. London and New York: Harvester Wheatsheaf.

Constructing "the other"

In the years that followed the publication of *Mapping the language of racism*, a number of studies appeared which examined racism in the South Pacific region. For example, Augoustinos and her colleagues (Augoustinos, Tuffin, & Rapley, 1999; Augoustinos, Tuffin, & Sale, 1999) looked at the patterns of talk and the rhetorical arguments amongst white Australians as they discussed race relations with the Indigenous Australian population. As Wetherell and Potter had found in the case of New Zealand, these studies demonstrated that racist talk was often characterized by a complex mix of discourses which blended narratives of national history and discourses of economics and entitlement with descriptions of **membership category features** such as the "plight" of Aborigines and the collective nature of being "Australian."

One of the interesting aspects of such work is the way in which racist discourses are seen to rely in part on characterizing "the other" in a manner which is evident in many other studies. Just as white New Zealanders and Australians can be seen to be busily developing descriptions of the indigenous populations as in some way troubled or needy, so Verkuyten showed, half a world away in the Netherlands (Verkuyten, 2001), that his Dutch participants constructed a version of ethnic minorities as "abnormal." Similarly, van der Valk demonstrated how right-wing French politicians, during a series of official debates, relied upon characterizations of immigrants as numerous, causing unemployment, and being welfare-dependent (van der Valk, 2003).

Of course, one of the rhetorical consequences of this sort of talk is that descriptions like this can be used to accomplish specific social actions. In a recent paper, Tileagă concentrates on the position of Romanies in Romania (Tileagă, 2005). She argues that the end of communism in Central and Eastern Europe brought with it a rising tide of prejudice against minority groups and that Romanies were among those who suffered most. She looks at the detail of one specific case of

> **Membership category features** Descriptive traits or properties which are inferentially linked to a category label

Romanians talking about Romanies. (To avoid confusion, it should be noted that Romanians are natives of the country Romania, while Romanies, often referred to as "gypsies," are an ethnically diverse population which is found in many different countries.) Tileagă describes the way in which, following a section of the interview in which the interviewee has been characterizing Romanies as very different from other people, she moves on to actually blame the Romanies themselves for the prejudice they suffer from.

```
99   CHRIS  What do you think the causes of such
            discrimination that
100         you talked about are? (.) I don't know,
            for example, a
101         Romany can be easily refused a job
102         (1.2)
103  CARLA  °Because to me°– (.) >what can I say<
            (.) >what are the
104         causes<? (0.2) right? (.) I think that
            everything
105         happens because of them (.) because
            even they don't want
106         (.) they don't have the desire (0.4) I
            don't think that
107         they are accepting (.) so, they would like
            to (0.4) to
108         (.) so, >they don't really like to work<
            (.) so,
109         as far as I know, >they don't own land
            to cultivate, to
110         farm< and >when they were offered a
            place to stay or
111         something like that< (.) I saw it on
            televi[sion (.)
112  CHRIS                         [uh huh
113  CARLA  They've put their horses in (.) so (.)
            >even if there
114         were flats< (.) where they managed to
            or (0.4) so
115         (0.4) even them, what they receive,
            they ruin (.)
116         so, they don't (0.8) °they don't respect,
            that's the
117         thing° (.)
                                    (Tileagă, 2005, p. 615)
```

Tileagă notes the way in which Carla's talk is marked, at lines 103 and 104, by signs of hesitancy and difficulty such as pauses, mis-start, explicit acknowledgments of difficulty ("what can I say"), and **reformulations**. Marked speech of this sort is often used in accomplishing accusations and blamings to formulate what is said as something that the speaker is reluctant to say. In the present case, Tileagă notes that what follows next is an explicit blaming of Romanies: whatever happens, happens "because of them." This is then supported by a narrative of the way that Romanies are different. For example, they put horses in their flats. As Tileagă points out, such narratives are often understood by speakers and hearers as doing moral work. Here, the blaming which Carla has produced earlier is supported by the moralistic accusation of transgression in Carla's complaint about horses being put into flats. Tileagă concludes from this study that the reason why prejudice against Romanies can be reproduced in talk in this way, as part and parcel of the business of formulating complaints and accusations, is in part due to the extreme nature of the characterizations of Romanies which accompany such complaints.

Another example of this sort of process is seen in a recent text edited by van den Berg, Wetherell, and Houtkoop-Steenstra (2006). In this book, the editors set a fascinating task for a number of leading discursive researchers. Each was asked to provide an analysis of the same three research interview transcripts drawn from the dataset which Wetherell and Potter used in writing *Mapping the language of racism*. The following extract is a fragment of one of the episodes of talk that was analyzed by Edwards.

1 R: It's <u>norm</u>ally that– Okay <u>that</u> argument gets put in that Maoris never get
2   the jobs okay but you look. Hh when they turn up for an interview
3 I: Yes
4 R: <u>What's</u> he wearing <u>how's</u> he sitting
5 I: Yeah
6 R: How's he talking >ya'know what I mean< an' there's no
7   <u>point</u> in having a receptionist that picks up a phone "Yeah
8   g'day 'ow are ya" ((strong New Zealand accent))

> **Reformulations** Talk in which a partial or complete word or phrase is followed by a restatement in other words of what was just said

9   I: Ye:s (0.4) [mm mhm
10 R: [I mean they want someone that is– (0.4) that is
11   gonna put their clients at ea:se
12 I: Right (.) [mm mhm
13 R: [You don't wanna <u>shop</u> a– a <u>shop</u> assistant who's <u>smelly</u>
14 I: [Yes
15 R: [who's got un-<u>dirty</u> unkempt hair [an' tattoos all over your
16 I: [Mm mhm
17 R: arms [an' fingers all that sort of thing
                              (Edwards, 2003, p. 41)

Edwards points out that this extract begins with the speaker setting out what he is saying within a rhetorical context. The opening lines set up an argument (that Maoris never get the jobs). The speaker then uses a number of formulations which rely on the notion of a **script**: a known and predictable pattern of events associated with getting a job, such as turning up for an interview. Woven in with these is another set of formulations referring to **dispositional states** such as having a problematic accent or being tattooed. It is the juxtaposition of these in the speaker's account which attributes the lack of jobs as an accountable failure on behalf of the Maoris. Edwards also points out the details of talk which generalize what is said, such as "all that sort of thing," help to assign problematic characteristics to Maoris generally. This, Edwards suggests, is an example of the way that someone can accomplish a criticism of the Maoris in general by offering a description of what Maoris are like, how they behave, and even how they look. One further noteworthy feature of this example is that it displays a feature which is common in the findings of the other studies already discussed. The speaker characterizes "the other," in this case Maoris, in a certain way. But at the same time what is said is carefully formulated. It is presented as rationally

> **Script** A series of steps or elements which are conventionally related to one another in a sequential fashion

> **Dispositional state** Having the property of tending towards a particular action under given circumstances (e.g., sugar has the dispositional state of melting when placed in hot coffee)

inferred from the way the world is rather than as deriving from the speaker's own way of seeing things. And this, of course, works to undermine potential claims in response to what is said that the speaker is saying this because of anti-Maori prejudice. In the next section, we will examine this aspect of racism talk more closely.

Managing the self

As we saw at the start of this chapter, people are usually aware of the social norms against sounding prejudiced. An important feature of this kind of "self-presentation" is that it is the sort of thing which is routinely attended to in all kinds of everyday discourse where issues of prejudice such as racism might become relevant. Indeed, it is part of the way discursive researchers understand a notion like "racism" that talk should be considered as potentially racist precisely because the speakers perform this type of discursive work in managing inferences that can be drawn about them from what they say. In a study of immigrants in Vienna, Austria, Gotsbachner examined a conversation between two Viennese residents about the immigrants who worked as janitors in their respective buildings (Gotsbachner, 2001). Gotsbachner points out that, even though the conversations amounted to little more than gossip between acquaintances, the participants' talk was specifically designed to be heard as something other than "prejudiced slander."

One of the important ways in which people achieve this goal is by selecting **organizational features** which demonstrate the reasonableness of what they say. In a study of American undergraduate students, Kleiner (1998) showed that the students relied upon an organizational strategy which he described as "pseudo-argument." His participants were seen to jointly construct claims which were introduced as though they represented the views of someone else. By framing their talk as though it was argumentative (rather than, say, the expression of privately held views), his participants were able to present potentially controversial beliefs as though they were the inferential results of a process of reasoned argument. Verkuyten has also emphasized the importance of this sort of process. In his 1998 study in the Netherlands of conversations among ethnic Dutch people (Verkuyten, 1998b), he showed that they provide accounts in which they are presented as reasonable and moral people and that this is consistent with the sorts of talk about others which might otherwise be potentially seen as racist.

Another way in which speakers attend to the potential difficulty of being seen as racist is by sometimes displaying sensitivity to the sorts of interactional context they find themselves in. For example, in a study of the way English people approach the task of talking about their own country, Condor revealed that her participants treated talk of "this country" as a very sensitive matter, as though such talk might carry the same sort of opprobrium as overtly racist talk (Condor, 2000). In part, this sort of sensitivity derives from the way in which racism has come to be seen as particularly associated with other forms of talk such as nationalism. For example, in a study of young white South Africans, Lea (1996) demonstrated that participants who described themselves as "nationalist" deployed particular discourses of racial differences which appealed to racist "lay theories" such as biological discourses. In her study Condor showed, by examining the way in which her participants' talk was organized, that her respondents were unwilling to speak about their own country in categorical terms, and were unwilling to display explicitly nationalist talk (although they did rely on forms of "**banal nationalism**"). In an early part of her analysis she notes, for example, that some of her participants oriented to a question about what is different about England from other countries as though it were an invitation to express prejudiced views.

> RESP: Hm (.) I don't (.) y'know (.) I don't really think about (.) in terms of countries (.) or different nations or (.) whatever
>
> (Condor, 2000, p. 182)

Organizational features The structural properties of talk which allow a speaker to present that talk as being of a particular sort

---

Banal nationalism Nationalistic talk which relies upon everyday, commonplace forms of expression and which can be contrasted with extreme or overtly xenophobic forms of nationalism

By using **production features** such as pauses and false starts, and by raising a question about national categorization as a process, Condor's participant is able to signal hesitancy about the task of talking about "this country" and to question the very legitimacy of thinking about different countries.

Racist talk in context

It was pointed out above that racist talk can arise in many different sorts of social interaction and that such talk can also be deployed to accomplish a range of different conversational ends. However, discursive researchers have also shown interest in the extent to which talk about race may be especially relevant to specific contexts. One obvious example of this is where the local conversational context is in some way already relevant to discussion of race. Barnes and colleagues (Barnes, Palmary, & Durrheim, 2001) examined conversational contexts in post-apartheid South Africa which included interracial couples. They found that these were occasions in which race talk was introduced in a variety of ways. By relying on rhetorical moves such as humor and personal experience, speakers were able to deflect potential attributions of being racist in what they said.

Durrheim and Dixon have emphasized the relevance of a different sort of context in which racism arises: the relevance of space and place. In one study (Durrheim & Dixon, 2001) they draw from a large sample of newspaper articles and examine the way in which talk about the beachfront of Durban, in South Africa, offers people a discursive opportunity for racism. "Blacks" are portrayed as corrupting the beaches, either by supplanting "normal family activities" with politicized activities or with unmannerly and uncivilized conduct.

> I, my husband and our 13-year-old granddaughter had set up our umbrella and chairs on South Beach during the early morning of Boxing Day. By 10am hordes of blacks started arriving. By 11.30am our towels and cooler bags had been stolen after my husband and I had briefly turned our backs ... Despite the theft we continued our stay until the arrival of my daughter and son-in-law. During that time we witnessed the township dwellers' manners and dress codes – loud music, naked breasts, men's skimpy underpants, mobile hair salons, the eating of dirty tripe, even bound live chickens! Never in my life have I experienced such a fearful feeling after being swamped by so many unruly black youths who show absolutely no consideration for middleaged persons such as myself.
>
> (Durrheim & Dixon, 2001, pp. 445–446)

This text appeared in a letter to the editor of the newspaper. Durrheim and Dixon argue that in texts of this sort the representation of space, in this case a beach, has rhetorical effect. The narrative of "cosy domesticity" with which the extract begins is interrupted by the description of "township dwellers" and their actions which include theft, sexually inappropriate behavior, and unacceptable eating practices.

Indeed, for Durrheim and Dixon this interest in space as a context for racism goes even further. In their later writings (Durrheim & Dixon, 2005a, 2005b) they argue that an adequate account of racism must also provide an analysis of social practices which go beyond the study of language as represented by discursive psychology. They present a "case study" of a desegregated beach in South Africa which employs what they term a "dual empirical focus on linguistic and embodied spatio-temporal practices," with the latter being operationalized via a "mapping" exercise in which observations were recorded of the racial seating patterns of people who visited the beach.

Moving yet further away from the immediate conversational context, a number of other studies have examined the way that institutional settings provide frameworks in which racist talk takes place. In a study of African asylum seekers in Belgium, Blommaert (2001) noticed that official procedures placed many asylum seekers at a disadvantage. In particular, he noted that institutional practices such as summarizing, noting, creating files, interviewing, and translating were all part of a bureaucratic process in which applicants' narratives were recast through a process he called the "dynamic of entextualization." The

---

Production features Aspects of talk which are concerned with the way talk is produced, such as the use of repetitions or particular ways of speaking (e.g., adopting a "precise" form of delivery)

effect of this is to create power asymmetries in which asylum seekers fail to access appropriate levels of communicative control during their encounters with officialdom. Perhaps even more worryingly, Blommaert suggests that the processes and procedures which give rise to such problems are, in a sense, "invisible" because they are phenomena which are "normalized" for the middle-class members of society who are responsible for the creation of the formal structures within which the asylum applicants are enmeshed.

What the papers say

The work of Durrheim and Dixon demonstrates the importance of media other than the spoken word to the study of racism. That media such as newspapers are of interest to the discursive researcher is hardly surprising, given the important effect which the media have on cultural understanding. Discourse researchers have, accordingly, spent much time in examining the way that racism is accomplished in print media. In one study, Lynn and Lea (2003) examined a sample of letters sent to the editors of British national newspapers about the question of foreigners applying for asylum in the United Kingdom. Lynn and Lea identified discursive strategies which involve talk of citizenship, identity, and nationhood, all of which were deployed to construct a particular version of the "asylum seeker." In the following extract, a letter-writer draws on a distinction between "genuine" and "bogus" asylum seekers.

> Bad feeling occurs when refugees are housed ahead of homeless British citizens. No-one begrudges genuine refugees a home, but when bogus ones are housed within weeks and UK citizens, black and white, are left to rot in hostels, it does seem unfair.
>
> (Lynn & Lea, 2003, p. 433)

Lynn and Lea point out a number of the rhetorical features of this letter excerpt. First, the perceived inequality in housing is presented as common-sense fact (without, for example, any supporting argument or evidence). At the same time, the potential for claims of this sort to be undermined through accusations of racism is forestalled through the author's distinction between applicants who are "bogus" and "genuine" applicants. By making this distinction, the author is able to establish that it is only those applicants who fall into the common-sense (and unexplicated) category of bogus people that he is complaining about. The account is further strengthened through the contrast between Britons, who are described, through the use of an extreme case formulation as "left to rot," and refugees. Within this context, Lynn and Lea argue, the author's reminder that United Kingdom citizens might be black or white functions as a means of further establishing his non-racist credentials.

Although some analyses of newspaper articles rely on discourse analytic techniques of the sort used by Lynn and Lea, many others use the critical discourse analysis (CDA) approach. For example, from a CDA perspective, Erjavec (2001) argues that the themes and formal structures of news reports generate prejudice against the Roma in Slovenia. She argues that news journalists selectively use and misuse information in order to present a biased view of the Roma and that this is exemplified in the formal structure of their news reports. She analyzes reports of the way people in a Slovenian village prevented a Romani family from moving into a house which they had bought. In her analysis, she isolates the way in which the lead sentences of the relevant news reports position Slovenian villagers as protecting or guarding against something which is unwanted and draws attention to the way that few of these reports mention that the house legally belonged to the Romani family.

Another CDA study of racism in journalism is Peter Teo's analysis of what he describes as "subtle racism" against Asian immigrants to Australia in Australian newspapers (Teo, 2000). He examines nine newspaper reports about the activity of a Vietnamese gang, the "5T." One element of the newspapers' coverage which he identifies is the way in which lead paragraphs in the selected reports emphasize the "common-sense" view that the gang is a violent one. He then explores the way in which this "violence" discourse is progressively widened from the gang to encompass Vietnamese people and then Asians in general through phrases such as "groups of youth, many of South-East Asian appearance."

Although the emphasis in this section has been on studies of racism in the news, it is worth concluding by noting that other analyses of racist talk and text have focused on different media. In a more recent study, Lynn and Lea themselves cast their research net more widely by examining racist graffiti in Glasgow, Scotland (Lynn & Lea, 2005), while Gyasi Obeng (2000) conducted a similar study in Legon, Africa. In a more formal setting, Kirkwood, Liu, and Weatherall (2005) have explored the ways in which some of the submissions made in 2003 to the New Zealand government in connection with proposed land and sea legislation were formulated to exclude the rights of the indigenous population. And, of course, the Internet has proved a fruitful arena for research of this sort. For example, Billig (2001) carried out an analysis of race talk on Internet websites which support the Ku Klux Klan. Billig provides a sophisticated analysis of the "meta-discourse" behind the discourse of jokes which peppers these sites. He shows that such discourse demonstrates that the sites' racist jokes are presented as more than that, and that for the authors there is enjoyment to be had in their very use of extreme racist language. Moreover, the association of such talk with discussion of extreme violence suggests, says Billig, that such sites promote a linkage between racist talk and violent action.

Sex

The study of prejudice towards others on the basis of race has a long history in the social sciences. A more recent addition to the social analyst's field of research is consideration of the impact of gender and sexual orientation. To provide a picture of the way discursive research has examined prejudice in respect of these latter phenomena, we focus here on two themes: sexism and heterosexism.

> **Sexism** Prejudice against others in terms of their gender

> **Heterosexism** A point of view which lends priority to the assumption that heterosexual relationships are normative in society

Sexism

Most people will openly state that sexism is wrong. However, people often disagree as to what counts as sexism. For example, the hearty party goer telling "blue" jokes may not see himself as sexist, while female members of his audience may feel that he is. Indeed, debates as to whether sexism has occurred can arise in all sorts of everyday conversational interactions, with one participant leveling accusations of sexism and the other replying with accusations of **political correctness**. Weatherall (1998) has drawn attention to the subtle complexities of this sort of talk. In an analysis of discussions which took place during a television program, she described the way in which sex bias did appear differentially in the contributions of men and women. However, she noted that such differences did not the include forms of overt sexism that might have been expected in such a context. She concluded that such biases might have become routinized and so have become a part of our everyday language which it can be difficult to discern.

This tension is nicely encapsulated in a study by Beach (2000). He examined a number of interactions involving two men, W and T, gossiping about an absent woman, Melissa. The thrust of his study was an examination of the way in which the participants' turns were carefully constructed so that they were able to collaboratively develop a story or narrative structure through the use of conversational features such as invitation for collaboration. In this respect, his study was not fundamentally a study of sexism at all.

```
34              .hhh(sf) (.) So anyw[a:ys,]
35  1→  T:  >[I do]n't think she's that good loo:king
                do you?<=
36  2→  W:  =°Hm um. ° (hh)
37              (0.2)
38  3→  T:  >Sh:e'(s) got a nice litt:le– bo:dy,
                (("Southern Drawl"/SD))
39              ↓°[but that's ab]out it.°=((SD))
40  4→  W:  [Mm: h:m:,] =
41              = pt >(We–) an' she got cute little
                br[easts. ]< ((SD))
                                        (Beach, 2000, pp. 392–393)
```

> **Political correctness** The inappropriate use of explicitly non-prejudiced terms or phrases

Beach notes that T's comment at line 35 is a somewhat blunt and critical assessment and that W's subsequent response orients to this as potentially troublesome. In this context, Beach points out that W, by adopting a "Southern drawl," is able to accomplish both distancing himself from the claim on offer and an invitation to T to collaborate with him in an illusory episode in which the speakers pretend that what is said is being said by two gravelly-voiced Southerners.

Although the thrust of his paper is an examination of how episodes of talk such as this are managed, Beach points out that even a "cursory inspection" would lead many readers to conclude that the speakers are being sexist, even though the participants never orient to their talk in this way. However, he also points out that this is different from demonstrating analytically that issues of sexism have become **procedurally relevant** for the speakers. One way of analyzing what W and T say is that they are merely dealing with the everyday problems which are associated with being a competent conversational participant. In the present case, this requires them to display the ability to be evaluators of women as well as maintaining identities and relationships appropriate to the local conversational context. On this reading, their preoccupation with sexual matters might be understood as an artefact of the situational circumstances in which they find themselves.

Beach himself concludes by being somewhat equivocal on the point of whether this sort of analysis constitutes an analysis of sexism *per se*, although he does suggest that this might be one means of examining how the business of sexism is accomplished in talk. However, in our initial discussion of prejudice and discourse, we discussed the question of whether the discursive analysis of prejudice should be narrowly understood as a phenomenon of locally **occasioned** talk or more widely as involving broader social factors. And it is clear that other researchers would be more willing to draw firm conclusions about whether

Procedural relevance Contextually appropriate in terms of preceding sequences of talk

Occasioned The idea that the meaning of an utterance is bound up with the local discursive context in which it is uttered

sexism is being displayed in episodes such as those reproduced by Beach. For example Naples (2003) has emphasized, from what she describes as a "materialist feminist" standpoint, the relevance of extra-discursive factors:

> a materialist feminist analysis of discourse attends to the historical and structural patterns of domination and resistance to render visible the features of everyday life that are unspoken or unrepresented in discursive frames.
>
> (Naples, 2003, p. 106)

From a perspective of this sort, it is likely that the researcher would conclude that, whatever else W and T are doing, they are also being sexist in the way they talk about Melissa.

Prejudice in respect of gender is not, of course, a problem merely because of what is said. It is implicit in the discursive approach that talk is constitutive of social action. That is, what people say is intricately involved with how actions and events are construed by social actors. This action-orientation of discursive research can be clearly seen in a series of studies carried out by Riley (2001, 2002, 2003). In these studies, Riley interviewed a number of white, heterosexual, professional men. In her 2002 study, Riley examined a number of the interpretative repertoires that her interviewees generated. Riley noted that within the context of talking about equal opportunities in employment, her interviewees produced accounts which relied on repertoires constructing equality in terms of interchangeability (properties that could be interchangeably associated with either men or women) and individual ability. By presenting employment success as a matter of individual achievement, her interviewees were able to represent equal opportunity policies as in some way discriminatory. If success is largely a matter of individual attainment, then providing support through a social structural policy which benefits an entire group, irrespective of individual talents, is unfair. In other words, positive discrimination is just discrimination.

1 I can see the argument that there is a need for them (women's groups), to strengthen
2 women and make them more confident and all the rest of it . . . I disagree with it in fact, but
3 I can see the argument . . . I don't think that there should be separate women's groups

4 because they become just as sexist and exclusive
   as men's groups do . . . and as I said

5 before, I don't make a distinction, I don't say you
   would be a poorer solicitor because

6 you're a female than you would if you were a male
   . . . I think it comes down to the

7 qualities of the individual. If you're going to
   recognize that, then I think that whenever

8 you're saying "is there a need for groups of one
   sex or the other?" then I would say

9 "no."

(Riley, 2002, p. 452)

Riley notes that her participant relies upon an inter-changeability repertoire, in which being "sexist and exclusive" is something negative that could apply to groups of women or to groups of men. It is this aspect of women's groups that allows him to present individualism ("I don't make a distinction") as an appropriate response, which leads naturally to his claim for ability, the "qualities of the individual," as a deciding criterion.

Elsewhere, Riley also draws attention to the ways in which "traditional" gender roles are depicted as occurring through impersonal forces, such as biological pressures or socialization, and notes her participants draw distinctions such as that between individualistic equality and social structural inequality and between providers who are associated with the production of male identity and non-providers who are depicted in gender-neutral terms. Intriguingly, Riley finds that on some occasions her participants even embed their claims within explanatory accounts which draw in feminist arguments:

> I do think there's a need (for separate women's groups) but the need needs to be diluted slightly so that men are included men with open minds such as Philip. Men will believe men more than they'll believe women .. I would say .. if a woman comes up to a guy .. I don't want to generalize but .. and says you know "women's issues, women's issues" "oh bugger off!." I believe that there are societies are starting up now saying that white Anglo-Saxon men are the most discriminated against group, they don't believe it, they feel as if they've been ganged up against whereas if a guy comes up and says "look you know, get your finger out" I think they'll accept it a bit more (participant 8, accountant under 35).

(Riley, 2001, p. 64)

Riley argues that the participant's claim at the start of this extract, that separate women's groups are needed, functions in this case like a disclaimer, because the participant then goes on to represent men as the "power brokers" for passing on women's message to other men. This is contrasted with the alternative, which Riley describes as a "cartoon like" depiction of women saying "women's issues, women's issues." So this participant is able to position himself as someone who has no problem in agreeing with a feminist notion such as women-only groups, while at the same time undermining the feminists who might make that claim. One of the ironies implicit in this sort of sexism, says Riley, is that the very arguments propounded by feminists in support of equality for women are taken up by men in arguing against it. This feature of sexist talk has also been noted by Gough and Peace (2000) in their study of how male university students construct masculinity.

One noteworthy feature of these studies of sexism is that sexism appears to share some of the properties of racism. We pointed out earlier that racism may involve attempts both to construct the other and maintain the self. The participants in the studies of Beach and Riley seem to rely on similar types of talk. For example, in Beach's study as the two participants talk about Melissa, we can identify the same processes of constructing the other and maintaining the self that were seen in racist talk. A very particular "version" of Melissa, based on her physical attractiveness, is made relevant. But in doing so, W manages the impression of himself by ironically positioning himself as a stereotypical Southerner. Similarly, in Riley's study her interviewees attend to the possibility that what they say may be heard as sexist while criticizing women who have feminist views. For example, in the extract presented above, her participant constructs his criticism of women's groups through the use of a two-sided argument which allows him to present his negative conclusion as a reasoned outcome.

Heterosexism

When Millett's book *Sexual politics* was published at the start of the 1970s, its title was deliberately chosen to challenge assumptions that there could be no greater distance than that between the privacy of the bedroom and the

CLASSIC STUDY: Changing the subject

In the series of studies entitled *Changing the subject: Psychology, social regulation and subjectivity*, Henriques and his colleagues begin from the assumption that people are intrinsically social beings. Drawing on the work of French philosopher Michel Foucault, they describe a notion of "subjectivity" in which people's sense of self and others is influenced by the dominant discourses of their surrounding culture. One of the important aspects of this book was the wealth of debate which subsequently grew up around this "subjectivity" notion. In particular, theorists came to hold differing views of the nature of the "influence" that such discourses have. Some researchers claimed that this idea was overly deterministic and carried the implication that we had no choice but to see ourselves and others in terms of those dominant discourses. Other researchers disagreed, and cited the original emphasis which Henriques and colleagues had placed on rejecting the view that we are "simply the sum total of all positions in discourses since birth." Viewed in this light, subjectivity is better understood as a dynamic process in which people actively take up positions in discourse, even if the "range of options" open to someone is, itself, constrained by the nature of the discourses which constitute that person's social world. The general perspective taken in the book is well represented by the chapter written by Wendy Hollway, "Gender difference and the production of subjectivity." In this study of heterosexism, Hollway describes gender subjectivity as non-unitary, in that someone may view herself in terms of both masculine and feminine characteristics. She then goes on to look at the way different types of discourse exemplify gender differences which, she says, can produce gender subjectivity. Her suggestion is that each of these discourses establishes a difference between men and women in respect of sexuality. These differences then generate, for those men and women, a sexual identity or "subjectivity." These identities often place women at a disadvantage relative to men. Hollway identifies two sexuality discourses, both of which produce gender differentiation and, in consequence, generate an unequal notion of male and female sexual identity. The "male sexual drive" discourse presents men as biologically driven to have sex, and establishes for women the position as objects of that drive. The "have/hold" discourse emphasizes monogamy and partnership between man and woman and often establishes the woman as a person seeking a relationship which men do not need. Where the two discourses coexist, Hollway notes that their potential contradictions are seen as a problem which women should resolve: through the creation of two "types" or "category" of women. (She also describes a third discourse, the "permissive" discourse, which is similar to the "male sexual drive" discourse except that men and women are both depicted as having an interest in sex outside relationships.)

Henriques, J., Hollway, W., Urwin, C., Venn, C. & Walkerdine, V. (1984). *Changing the subject: Psychology, social regulation and subjectivity*. London: Methuen.

publicity of social and political debate. In the years that have followed, a range of researchers and activists have attempted to delineate the ways in which public understandings about men and women have conditioned the ways in which sexuality and the sexual roles of men and women are culturally understood.

More recently, discursive researchers such as Speer (2005) and Kitzinger (Kitzinger, 2005a; Land & Kitzinger, 2005) have drawn on the conversation analytic approach to examine the way in which heterosexuality is reproduced as normative through a range of conversational features such as unmarked topic talk and the use of referential terms that draw on the "normative" feature of heterosexuality. For example Kitzinger (2005b) studied the way in which heterosexism is produced as a situated, practical accomplishment in a number of telephone calls made by patients to their doctor and revealed that these interactions were designed to construct a version of the heterosexual family as the norm.

10 DOC: .hhh Oh right, ew: how old is your son?
11 CLR: Ah he was one last week, .hh[h
12 DOC: [B:right, an' an'
13   what's actually been happening to 'im =
//   ((61 lines of diagnostic questioning omitted))
75 DOC: [.hh Fine, <Any other children in your family?
76 CLR: Yeah, I've got another boy,
77 DOC: Ha– older or younger?
78 CLR: Ah– [older,
79 DOC: [Well, must be older, mustn't he?
80 CLR: Olde[r, yeah]
81 DOC: [.hhhh] ehhehm! Well, unless you're very
82   quick, sorry .hh
83   ah:m yeah has he had measles?
                            (Kitzinger, 2005b, p. 484)

In this fragment of an extract examined by Kitzinger, the doctor draws an assumption at line 79 that because the caller's other son is only one year old, her other son must be older. Kitzinger notes that the doctor apparently ignores a range of circumstances which might explain why a woman would have two children with less than a year's difference in age between them. These include adoption of one or both children, the caller and her partner bringing children from previous relationships into the current partnership, and the caller and partner being in a lesbian relationship in which both partners conceived and gave birth within months of each other. Kitzinger argues that the doctor's "must be" at line 79 indicates that these alternative circumstances are not oriented to by the doctor as possibilities. This, says Kitzinger, reproduces the mother and son relationship as one which is grounded in a biological relationship which thereby excludes other potential relationship forms such as adoptive parents, step-parents, and lesbian/gay parents.

Like Beach (2000), Kitzinger notes that one of the features of these interactions is the way in which participants *refrain* from explicit orientation to this pervasive way of talking as a potential conversational "trouble." Unlike Beach, however, she explicitly draws analytic conclusions about heterosexism from this fact. She points out that

the very fact that such routine adoption of heterosexist references and inferences passes unremarked is, in itself, evidence for the taken-for-granted or "normative" nature of hetero-sexism and of the way in which it permeates everyday interactions. Tainio (2003) provides an example of this sort of analytic conclusion in her study of a series of telephone calls between a male Member of the Finnish Parliament and a young schoolgirl. She points out that although the Member of Parliament was subsequently tried and found guilty of attempting to sexually abuse a child, there is little in the detail of their conversations that points to the sort of heterosexism which Kitzinger discusses. Tainio notes that the Member of Parliament repeats his invitation 15 times. She reminds the reader that Kitzinger (Kitzinger & Frith, 1999) characterizes men who claim not to have understood women's refusals of invitations as merely producing justifications for coercive behavior, on the grounds that socially competent actors will normally understand the normative consequences of having invitations repeatedly denied. However, as Tainio points out, her conclusions about the way the girl was harassed stand, in a sense, outside the detail of the conversational interactions she describes.

Gavey (2005) has explored some of the extreme consequences of heterosexism in her analysis of the cultural underpinnings of rape. She argues that the **normalizing practices** associated with dominant traditional variants of male sex drive discourse are bound up with women's sexual experiences. She describes a range of women's sexual experiences from episodes where women felt unhappy about the experience to those where they produced descriptions of apparently violent sex, even though the women themselves might actively avoid construing the experience as "rape."

ANN: . . . he was in bed with me, and I was being woken up with him sort of groping me, as it were, an I was quite disoriented, and thinking God, it's Ralph, you know, he's in bed with me . . . [gap] I mean it all happened quite

Normalizing practices Social processes, including discursive processes, which establish particular ways of viewing the world as commonplace

quickly really, but I remember thinking quite clearly, "Well if I don't– If I try and get out of the bed perhaps if I run away or something . . . he might rape me (pause) so I had better just . . .

NICOLA: If you try and run away you mean?

ANN: If I tried it, if I'd resisted, then he might rape me, you know. So he did it anyway, sort of thing, really, when you think about it, when I look back.

(Gavey, 2005, p. 161)

Gavey points out that our understanding of what is normal can readily encompass what she describes as an "obviously rape-like experience" within a notion of "normal" sex. She points out that although Ann later admitted the experience has left her bleeding and emotionally damaged, to the extent that she was "nervous within the house," Ann had come to construe the event as one which displayed her own shortcomings as someone who was "sexually uptight."

Of course, it is not suggested that heterosexist talk occurs within a discursive vacuum. One of the issues which makes heterosexist analyses complex is the way in which bland description of "normative" heterosexuality may be embedded within other forms of talk. For example, Praat and Tuffin (1996) have examined the ways in which discourses of homosexuality have been deployed in discussion with serving policemen of the employment of gay men in the police. As Riley revealed in respect of women employees, Praat and Tuffin showed that the responses on offer were carefully crafted to avoid inferences of prejudice while nevertheless accomplishing a variety of other actions such as criticizing and accusing. The police officers within the study relied upon discourses of effeminacy and deviance in order to represent the employment of gay men within the police force as somehow problematic. At the same time, a discourse of "conditional acceptance" was deployed in order to undermine potential ascriptions of homophobia. Praat and Tuffin conclude that, by contrasting gay men against a normative, heterosexist background, the police officers were able to establish that gay men would not make good officers while, at the same time, avoiding possible imputations of prejudice.

Heterosexism analyses have a long tradition in research on sexuality and gender. However, as the description of Henriques et al.'s *Changing the subject* showed, debate has arisen about the way in which heterosexism is understood as an analyst's perspective. For example, just as Beach argued that a discursive analysis is best thought of as revealing sexism as a practical activity embedded within the "ordinary yet finely coordinated achievements in everyday conversation," so Speer and Potter (2000) have argued that heterosexism is best understood as embedded within an entire set of flexible discursive practices such as discounting and displaying lack of understanding. In other words, if an overly simplistic form of analysis is applied to heterosexist talk, then the researcher is likely to produce simplified pictures of what participants are doing in their talk which relies on treating sexism or heterosexism like primitive causal attitudes that drive behavior. And the problem with this, as researchers such as Beach, Tainio, and Speer and Potter would argue, is that it disguises the complex way in which such phenomena make themselves apparent in everyday interactions. According to Speer and Potter, "derogatory" terms only become derogatory when they are "worked up" as such by participants, and whether a statement is prejudicial or not depends on the relevant interactional particulars. However, this does not mean that the researcher cannot talk of heterosexism occurring if the interactants do not attend to that issue during the interaction. But it does mean that the researcher must be clear about whether imputations of heterosexism are made at the level of what the participants take themselves to be doing or at the level of the researcher's conclusions:

> However, by decomposing heterosexist interaction, and exploring it from a participants' perspective, we are not implying that we cannot, as analysts, specify that such heterosexist interaction has occurred (when, or if the interactants do *not* seem to be attending to it as such). Rather, what it *does* mean is that it is important not to mix up the two analytic levels: on the one hand, what the participants take the interaction to mean (as derogatory and offensive, or perfectly acceptable, for example), and on the other hand, what we, as analysts, choose to make of that piece of interaction, over and above, or regardless of what its status is for the participants.
>
> (Speer & Potter, 2000, p. 563)

In Conclusion

One of the themes which emerges here is that the analysis of prejudice talk is a difficult challenge, partly because of the way in which it is seamlessly woven into everyday interaction. Condor (2006), for example, has drawn attention to this occasioned feature of racism talk. Expressions of racist positions may arise in a variety of local conversational contexts. But racist talk may also be used for a variety of conversational ends. Condor points out that such talk may be used to display intimacy or solidarity, or to shock, or to mark the identity one is claiming for oneself during the current conversational interaction. This is one of the reasons, she concludes, that prejudice is difficult to challenge.

Another complicating factor is that the natural tendency of researchers to focus on a single research question can blur the extent to which forms of prejudice interact. In 1999, Tannock demonstrated this in an analysis of an interaction between two members of an inner-city youth theater group, "TeenTalk," in which "insulting routines" were used by participants (Tannock, 1999). The participants were a white, middle-class female and a black, working-class male. Tannock showed that, as Condor pointed out, everyday interactions that were used to accomplish everyday functions such as the business of the theater group were, at the same time, arenas in which aspects of both gender inequality and racism were displayed. So not only did forms of prejudice talk appear as discursive practices situated within other conversational concerns, but the participants' talk represented an overlapping layering of both sexism and racism.

Another aspect of the complexity of prejudice is the wide extent of its targets. The focus here has been on race and sex. However, discursive analyses have revealed the cultural prevalence of other forms of prejudice. For example, McVittie, McKinlay, and Widdicombe (2003) showed that older workers suffer from similar forms of prejudice to those discussed by Riley in relation to women. Potential employers were shown to develop a number of accounting practices that managed the non-appearance of older workers in their workforce while, at the same time, avoiding potentially troublesome attributions of ageism.

So prejudice may be difficult to identify, and it can involve a range of targets. However, it is either explicit or at least implicit in many of the writings on prejudice within the discursive research field that prejudice ought to be challenged. One prevalent notion here is that the analyst's job is essentially to expose such prejudice. As Bonilla-Silva and Forman point out in their conclusions about "new racism" (Bonilla-Silva & Forman, 2000), this can be an achievement in itself. When racists themselves preface their statements with "I am not racist, but . . ." it can be sometimes difficult to see the racist wood for the disclaiming trees. However, Bonilla-Silva and Forman also conclude that the work of discursive researchers should inform political struggle against prejudice of this sort. From a CDA perspective, Teo (2000) also draws connections between the functions of analysis and political change. Indeed, drawing on van Dijk's work (van Dijk, 2001b), he points out that for proponents of CDA the very act of demonstrating how the discourse of societal elites reproduces and legitimates prejudice is at the same time a political critique of those responsible for perpetuating prejudice.

However, the issue of whether discursive researchers can make a more practical contribution to political change is perhaps less clear. One potential action implication of the discursive approach to prejudice is that, in some ways, people ought to be able to solve problems of prejudice for themselves. If people are sophisticated enough to carefully craft prejudice talk in such a way as to manage the inferences which hearers might draw about speakers, then it would seem likely that they are in a good position to recognize prejudice as it arises in talk and challenge it. Indeed, in drawing attention to the way in which prejudice talk is a collaborative achievement, in that it can be woven into the fabric of everyday conversation, Condor (2006) points out that where such talk arises it is the joint responsibility of all of the participants. And she notes that one consequence of this is that people can often be seen to "police" what is being said in order to suppress open expressions of prejudice. However, she also points to the practical difficulties of this. The co-participants in a conversational interaction face a normative expectation that they will display appropriate levels of responsibility as social actors for preventing potential interaction breakdowns and for maintaining apparent consensus. So someone in the habit of openly challenging what is said as the business of everyday, mundane conversation unfolds, on the grounds that it might constitute prejudice, runs the risk of being perceived as behaving inappropriately and this can have long-term consequences for his or her social relations.

Tannock (1999) also draws attention to the potential dangers of disrupting interactions in order to highlight prejudice in his discussion of how multiple forms of prejudice arise in the insulting routines observed in TeenTalk. Conversational participants may place a variety of interpretations on what is said during an interaction (although this range of interpretative choice is always likely to be situationally constrained in some way or other). An utterance in a conversation might be taken as an immediate response to the preceding turn, or it might be taken to be part of a broader activity (e.g., joking) or as part of an overall speech genre (e.g., gossiping or disputing). Tannock points out that when elements of prejudice talk appeared in his participants' insulting routines, one or other of the participants could have stopped the interaction then and there and reflexively discussed how and whether what they said constituted racism or sexism. However, as Tannock points out, this might in itself have had a negative impact. The aim of TeenTalk was to work towards a community built on diversity, and one of the ways the participants selected to achieve this was to rely upon the "play frame" of the insulting routine. So, somewhat paradoxically, deliberate attempts to challenge prejudice in moments of occasioned talk might have prevented some of the successes gained within the wider discursive context.

However, on a more positive note, Buttny and Williams (2000) point out that, in some respects, discourses are always being developed and redefined by the people who use them. They argue that the form of talk they observed, in which young African Americans utilize a form of reported speech that demands respect, is a discursive positioning which reflects a growing confidence among their participants.

In terms of a more directly activist approach, some discursive theorists have argued that researchers might become more involved in shaping cultural norms by, for example, influencing the media. Van Dijk (1997) has proposed an "applied discourse analysis" approach in which dis-cursive theorists work to apply discourse study to the way in which race and nationality are represented in the media. For example, Teo (2000) points out that news media can be a source for change as well as a source for reproduction, and argues that the media should be more open to the voices and faces of minority groups. Other researchers have argued for even broader attempts to influence society. In her discussion of how to prevent rape, Gavey (2005) emphasizes the importance of challenging the cultural background represented in normative assumptions of heterosexism. She includes in her discussion the importance of importing into educational spheres representations of girls and women that challenge heterosexist depictions of women as passive and non-aggressive. She also discusses other forms of challenge to normative heterosexism, such as "culture jamming" in which new "ways of seeing" men and women are released within different forms of popular culture.

Of course, the proponents of applied discursive analysis and other discourse-based forms of tackling prejudice are well aware of potential pitfalls. Precisely because discourse is such a complex and varied phenomenon, it leaves open, in its moments of situated talk, space for those who wish to resist attempts to reduce prejudice. We have already seen how discourses of equal opportunity could be reformulated to provide for continued forms of prejudice against women and older people in the workplace. Whitehead and Wittig (2004) have demonstrated similar findings in showing how student participants of a multicultural educational program generated a number of discursive strategies to resist the aims of the program while managing a sense of themselves as unprejudiced. These strategies included denials and normalization of prejudice and constructing segregation into diverse groups as in fact preventative of prejudice. This ironic adoption of discourses which ostensibly promote positive social values is also seen in the 2005 study by Augoustinos and colleagues of race relations in Australia (Augoustinos, Tuffin, & Every, 2005). Just as Riley's male executives counterposed discourses of equal opportunity to discourses of individual merit, so the participants of this study drew on discourses of individual merit to legitimate opposition to forms of affirmative action.

Chapter summary

- Prejudice and discrimination are prevalent in most contemporary societies. Most of us either have been or will be in a position where we may face prejudice at some point in our lives.
- Many qualitative psychologists approach the topic of prejudice from a discursive perspective. In this area, the question of whether such analyses should refer to extra-linguistic contexts is especially important.
- Discursive analyses of the concept of "race" have underlined its socially constructed nature.
- Some studies on racism have emphasized the ways in which prejudice involves the construction of "the other" as in some ways either deficient or responsible for being the target of prejudice.
- In common with many other forms of account construction, racist talk is often seen to be associated with displays of sensitivity towards being heard as racist.
- A number of studies have focused on racism within specific contexts, such as the media.
- Gender and sexual orientation are other areas in which prejudice arises. A number of studies have highlighted the way in which sexist talk is produced, although debate exists among qualitative researchers on whether the researcher is justified in treating such talk as sexist if the participants themselves do not orient to that talk as prejudiced.
- Studies of heterosexism have highlighted the way in which heterosexist assumptions underpin many everyday forms of discourse. More worryingly, research indicates that heterosexist discourses are associated with the "normalization" of violence or coercion in women's sexual experiences such that women fail to construct apparently coercive sexual encounters as rape.

Connections

Issues of prejudice are closely bound up with the self (Chapter 2) and with group membership (Chapter 3). The formulation of prejudice in talk is also bound up with the production of categorizations and explanatory accounts of the sort discussed in Chapter 5. In addition, aspects of prejudice talk are related to talk of "the other" (Chapter 6) and to aggression talk of the sort discussed in Chapter 8. Prejudice is also relevant to the problem of discrimination in the workplace (Chapter 11).

Activity

Think of the ways that different races and nationalities, or people of different genders or sexuality, are portrayed in the media. When you examine these portrayals closely, is there evidence that particular identities are being constructed "for" a particular race, nationality, gender, or sexual orientation?

Further reading

Durrheim, K. & Dixon, J. (2005). *Racial encounter: The social psychology of contact and desegregation*. London: Psychology Press. In this book, Durrheim and Dixon identify the discursive practices which white South Africans use to justify covert racism. The book also explores the authors' approach to extending discursive research by examining what they call "sociospatial" forms of desegregation.

Speer, S. A. (2005). *Gender talk: Feminism, discourse and conversation analysis*. London: Routledge. In this book Speer adopts a conversation analytic perspective to examine the ways in which a feminist discursive approach can make sense of dominant discourses of masculinity and heterosexism.

van den Berg, H., Wetherell, M. & Houtkoop-Steenstra, H. (Eds.) (2003). *Analyzing race talk: Multidisciplinary approaches to the interview*. Cambridge: Cambridge University Press. The editors bring together a number of the leading exponents of discursive research to provide analyses of a single corpus of material from a variety of discursive perspectives.

Chapter 8

Dispute and Aggression

MASCOT MAYHEM; BLUEBIRD AND BOBBIE SCRAP IN FOOTY FARCE

Two soccer club mascots were sent off after a touchline brawl which had to be broken up by seven stewards. Fans forgot the football to cheer on the punch-up between Bartley the Bluebird and Robbie the Bobbie. The pair clashed during a Nationwide League Division Two game between Bury and Cardiff City on Wednesday night. Robbie – dressed like the founder of British policing Sir Robert Peel – put on boxing gloves and began sparring with Bartley. Then Bartley – a 6ft high giant furry bluebird with a yellow beak – threw a punch on the chin of his rival mascot as Robbie tried to arrest him. The mascots crashed to the ground and wrestled on the touchline while the players carried on during the sec-ond half of Bury's 3–0 win. Stewards rushed to break up the pair – but it took seven to separate them and frogmarch them off the touchline at Bury's Gigg Lane ground.

*   Robbie – building worker Jonathan Pollard, 20 – said yesterday: "It wasn't my fault. I was just having a bit of a laugh when I was thumped in the face."*

The Mirror, November 19, 2001, p. 15

We are surrounded by media representations of **aggression** and violence. And official reports and statistics seem to demonstrate that their prevalence is not mere journalistic hyperbole. Recent UK government figures show that there were over 2.4 million violent incidents reported in England and Wales in the year 2005–2006 (Walker, Kershaw, & Nicholas, 2006). In the United States, there were over 465 violent crimes per 100,000 people in 2004 (Federal Bureau of Investigation, 2006). There are, of course, regional variations. United Nations statistics (2005) show that in 2002 there were 0.15 homicides in Germany per 100,000 people, while in the same year there were 25.34 homicides per 100,000 people in nearby Lithuania. But making sense of data like these can be a challenging task, in part because there are many different ways to categorize aggression and violence. For example, Archer (2000) distinguishes between acts of physical aggression that do not have damaging consequences and acts of violence that do. Moser (2004) separates out a wide variety of forms of violence that can arise in the urban setting, including political (e.g., paramilitary conflict), institutional (e.g., abuse by health or education workers), economic (e.g., robbery), and social (e.g., interpersonal abuse within the family). So although violence and aggression are phenomena which we can all readily recognize, providing definitions of,

and explanations for, this behavior represents a challenge to the social psychologist.

However, Bartley the Bluebird and Robbie the Bobbie have helpfully provided some clues. Episodes of **dispute** or aggression often arise out of other forms of social interaction. What counts as an episode of violence as opposed to, say, "having a laugh" is something which is open to discursive negotiation. And when they do arise, such episodes are often the sorts of things that subsequently call up explanatory accounts from those involved. In exploring some of these issues, discursive psychologists have sought to contribute to our understanding of this complex phenomenon by examining the ways in which discourse has played a role.

Disputes in Talk

Agreeing to disagree: The usefulness of disagreement

When we consider the forms of social interaction which can give rise to acts of aggression, it is obvious that aggressive acts are often preceded by instances of discursive interaction such as the exchange of insults or arguing. However, it is also common for such discursive actions to arise in

---

Aggression Behavior intended to cause harm

Dispute A disagreement or argument

non-aggressive contexts. For example, in a study of pre-adolescents' use of insults, Evaldsson (2005) notes that on occasion her participants' use of insults bordered on the production of physical aggression. However, her data revealed that even young children are adept at managing the boundaries of insults so that they are kept within an interactional context of playfulness. Mizushima and Stapleton (2006) have likewise shown that this use of insults as a form of teasing play also arises among adults. In a similar fashion, it has long been noted in discursive research that arguments serve a variety of functions other than that of introducing bouts of violence. Schiffrin (1984), for example, separated out the ideas of argument as engaging in dispute from argument as a sociable or enjoyable form of social interaction. Billig (1987) has also stressed the discursive richness of argument as a form of interaction. Placing rhetoric at the heart of social interactions, Billig suggests that establishing differences through argument is an important facet of the way that we understand the social world. By presenting opposing points of view, speakers are able to present, develop, and maintain contrasting discursive versions of the conversational topic under discussion. In this sense, disagreement is as important to the discursive formulation of the social world as is agreement. Antaki (1994) takes issue with Billig's analytic focus on rhetorical persuasion as a matter of formulating or reformulating a conversation's topic. However, he too draws attention to argument as a pervasive device in talk, especially in terms of how the structure of conversation routinely allows for turn positions in which what is said in an earlier turn can be disputed. Indeed, it is because disagreement and argument are so pervasive in everyday life that we have developed a range of interactional forms which help to manage it.

Some of the **fine-grain detail** of how disagreement is managed in conversation was revealed by Pomerantz (1984) in her examination of the way that disagreements, like other "dispreferred" next actions, are typified by features such as pauses, hesitancy, and reformulations. She con-

cludes that, even if disagreement is a regularly occurring activity in talk, speakers routinely orient to it as more unpleasant, difficult, and risking threat or insult or offense, and so in many contexts speakers produce disagreements in a careful way which indicates to hearers that what is being said is understood to have that potential status. As an example of what can happen when disagreement is not handled sensitively in this way, consider the following extract where two people are evaluating something.

> STEPHEN: I think it's functional <and> non-functional and I mean it looks very nice
> HARRY: I haven't seen anything quite so nasty for a long time
> STEPHEN: ↑No it isn't
> (McKinlay & McVittie, 2006, p. 803)

In this extract, Stephen produces his positive evaluation as the end-point of a three-part list structure: functional, non-functional, and looks nice. Harry's negative evaluation response at line 2 takes the form of a strong oppositional formulation: he has not seen anything so nasty for a long time. The problem posed for the participants is that Harry does not perform the conventionally expected work of orienting to his own turn as a dispreferred response, e.g., through the use of delay devices or weakly stated disagreement components. As Pomerantz points out, the absence of such turn features makes it more likely that the subsequent turn will take the form of an overtly stated disagreement. In this sense, then, there is no conversational place for them to go other than for Stephen to utter an outright rejection of Harry's claim.

The preceding extract occurred during a group discussion among members of an arts and crafts guild. The guild members were assessing the work of other artists and artisans who had applied to join the guild. The frequent occurrence of outright disputes between guild members would represent an interactional problem for them, in terms of both the cohesiveness of the guild as a collective and the more localized requirement that the guild members reach a decision on each of the applicants. However, as other extracts from their group discussion revealed, the guild members were adept at deploying conversational

---

Fine-grain detail Characteristics of talk examined at the level of construction of individual turns (e.g., lexical choice) and turn-by-turn sequences

resources in avoiding such disputes, as the next extract shows.

> SUE: Did Babs actually have any=
> BETTY: =Yes (.) she said that °she would vote against° (.) em (.) if we would take it as valid (.) her vote (.) not having (seen) them
> SUE: Yes
> PATRICK: With all due respect (.) I think if she hasn't seen them=
> BRIAN: =That's not fair
> PATRICK: I don't really feel she's entitled to=
> SUE: =>I think she is because< she can imagine however well painted they are (0.5) which is a bit how I'm feeling
> BETTY: So I did explain=
> SUE: =Yes (.) anyway let's see how we get on (.) mm (.) ?Betty (.) what about yourself
> BETTY: Well (.) I'm jus I'm gonna vote just in (2.0) just.

(McKinlay & McVittie, 2006, pp. 807–808)

At lines 1 to 3, Sue and Betty introduce discussion of Babs's opinion. At line 2, Betty introduces Babs's negative evaluation of the applicant: "She said she would vote against." Although Betty **hedges** this through a conditional "if" formulation at line 2, at line 4 Sue appears to state that the condition is met. This establishes the negative evaluation as being a relevant one. At lines 5 to 9, the participants display sensitivity to the potential for conversational disruption associated with the sorts of overt disagreement we saw in the preceding extract. In the turn which follows on from Sue's turn at line 4, Patrick challenges her acceptance that Babs's negative evaluation is admissible. However, he constructs this response in a way which suggests that he is aware of the potential interactional difficulties associated with rejecting Babs's view when Sue and Betty do not. He prefaces his negative remark with "With all due respect." This is hearable as either

a genuine or ironic reference to the potential interactional difficulty of having given an undermining response. After Brian and Patrick have worked this up, Sue, at lines 8 and 9, reiterates her opposing view. The stage is therefore set for the sort of potentially disruptive overt disagreements which were seen above. However, this is negotiated by Sue at line 11, where she **restarts** (Jefferson, 1984) the conversation via "Anyway, let's see how we get on." What is particularly noteworthy here is that Sue actually interrupts Betty in order to hand her back the conversational floor. By deploying this restart device, Sue is therefore able to avoid the sort of disruptive agreement which might otherwise have arisen.

So it turns out that aspects of talk that might be taken to be obvious precursors of aggression, such as arguments, in fact serve a variety of functions. And speakers have a variety of means at their disposal to ensure that even where argument arises out of genuine disagreement, the potentially negative social consequences of such disagreement are attended to. This complex social nature of arguing is highlighted in a study by Georgakopoulou (2001) of the sequencing and production of disagreements in the everyday talk of four young women discussing matters such as entertainment, appearance, and relationships. Georgakopoulou notes that in some respects, her participants' talk might be taken to resemble Schiffrin's findings that disagreement is a mundane element of sociability. But she draws attention to a particular feature of her own participants' discussions. The young women are discussing matters which have a social relevance to their own lives, especially in terms of making decisions about future actions and decisions. In this respect, their disagreements take on the aspect of genuine argument, rather than sociable argument for its own sake, because the women are using argument to try to formulate conclusions about what will, or ought to, happen in the future. However, Georgakopoulou also reveals that in her data, the participants do not mark their disagreements as "dispreferred" in the way that

Hedge An aspect of talk in which the speaker displays that what is to be said is potentially problematic, e.g., through the use of expressions of doubtfulness

Restart The production of an utterance which is designed to signal that the speaker is recommencing his or her utterance

Pomerantz's study would indicate. Instead, speakers introduce argumentative themes in a relatively indirect fashion through the use of stories which function as analogies for the issues currently under discussion.

F: Re let me tell you something, Irene's ((feelings)) go back to six years Tonia
T: Yes re Fotini but I'm telling you, as I made it clear, so she should do
F: She might not be so strong within herself to do that
T: But that's why I'm saying that she has to talk to him about this, Irene//I think
F: Shall I tell you something . . . same thing as Irene's happened to me in my mum's home town with a guy called Jannis, who had gone out with my cousin Katerina=
T: = Oh right, from Athens
F: They had been out twice, then they broke up, and then I started realizing that I liked the guy. I went and asked Katerina ((if she had a problem with that)), and she says don't be silly, and then came the real crush, you know. I saw him three years afterwards, and you know the flame was still there
T: I understand that
F: You can't imagine
T: I can understand that cause same thing happened to me with Dimitris, when I saw him every summer, when didn't see him I was fine.

(Georgakopoulou, 2001, p. 1889)

In this extract, Fotini and Tonia disagree about a course of action which Irene should follow in connection with her interpersonal relationship. Fotini argues that it is difficult for Irene to let go of her feelings, while Tonia argues that Irene should have a meeting with the man in question in order to make her feelings clear. At this point, Fotini introduces a story by means of an analogy, signaled through her use of "same thing as Irene's happened to me." Georgakopoulou notes that the telling of this story allows Tonia and Fotini to establish an agreement, indicated by Tonia's "I understand that," that love is a difficult thing, even though they disagree about Irene's future actions. So according to Georgakopoulou, producing these short-storied episodes as analogies affords speakers a relatively indirect means of managing disagreeing. On the one hand, the analogy introduces a potentially critical commentary on what is being said while, on the other, speakers are able to attribute this viewpoint to an actor in a story, rather than establishing the critical viewpoint as a locally available topic in the immediate conversational context.

We saw that in Billig's view, argumentation is a means of establishing a variety of versions of whatever it is that the conversation is about. A similar function appears to underpin the young women's use of argument. Georgakopoulou suggests that because the participants have close relationships and share a common interactional history, this provides their interactions with a number of implicit, rather than explicit, understandings. The effect of this is that within any given interaction, the speakers can rely upon such implicit understandings as taken-for-granted "norms" of argumentation. And they rely upon these norms to jointly take part in "collaborative perspective-building" in making sense of the range of alternative future actions which are open to them and their friends.

In everyday settings, then, it seems as though participants sometimes rely upon argument and dispute in order to accomplish conversational goals which are unrelated to aggression. Indeed, it has been shown that in certain specialized contexts, participants orient towards a norm of dispute, rather than towards norms of agreement and consensus. In a study of televised political interviews, Dickerson (2001) has shown how interviewees regularly challenge prior turns produced by the television interviewer. However, such challenges are of a specific type, in that they are designed to ensure that the challenge they raise is "boundaried." The challenge is restricted to only part of the interaction without becoming a generalized questioning of the interview as a whole.

JS [↑Can he do anything to] to put Mister Lamont off his ↓stride
EL (0.6) Well I think you must ask Mister La↑mont that > I mean I am not here as Mister Lamont's spokesman< (0.7) erm nut er (.) >you must °ask him that [question°<
JS [despite catching you on the end of our lens with him on the er (.) Terrace of (.) er the House of [Commons]
EL [well it's] no longer a crime ↑is it to >to (0.3) have a drink with a< (0.4) a friend and a colleague

(Dickerson, 2001, pp. 213–214)

In this extract the interviewer, JS, asks his politician interviewee, EL, what the British prime minister can do to prevent a challenge from another politician, Mr. Lamont. The interviewee refuses to provide an answer. However, Dickerson notes that in doing so, the interviewee provides a justification for not complying with the interviewer's question by stating that he is not Mr. Lamont's spokesman. When, in the next turn, JS attempts to provide a justification for asking his question, EL treats his comment ironically, thereby defusing it as a good reason for the question having been asked. What is interesting about this interaction, says Dickerson, is that EL is careful to establish that this is not the beginning of a general breakdown in their conversation. Although EL has refused to answer JS's question, he does so in a way which indicates that he is unable to answer rather than, for example, being unwilling to answer because he is refusing to cooperate in the interview process. In a similar study, Leon (2004) has shown how the participants in news interviews routinely attempt to deal with biased questions by subverting the original question even while demonstrating cooperation with the interview process by maintaining the appearance that the question is being answered.

Disagreement and dispute: Power and participants' orientations

There are, then, forms of talk such as producing insults or engaging in argument which might be taken to be conventionally associated with aggression. However, the discursive study of these sorts of interaction reveals that people have a range of complex discursive skills which allow the potentially negative behavioral consequences of such talk to be safely negotiated in its use (Bonito & Sanders, 2002; Clayman, 2002). So the discursive researcher who wishes to explore themes of aggression by examining discourse must take careful account of the ways in which discursive features such as insults or arguments pervade and are managed in everyday interactional contexts. In pursuing this goal, discursive researchers have emphasized two features: structural properties of interactions through which participants display some form of dominance, and the way in which participants' own orientations to what is said separate out genuine argument from other activities such as playful talk or argumentative social construction.

Itakura (2001) explains **conversational dominance** in terms of asymmetry. In asymmetrical interactions, talk arises in which there is an unequal distribution of entitlements and rights, such as the opportunity to introduce new topics, or to retain the conversational floor for extended periods. Itakura notes that this asymmetric form of interaction can be thought of as a form of conversational dominance in which one interactional partner controls the conversational contributions of the other. Shan (2000) has drawn attention to the way that monopolizing floor as a means of establishing interactional power is related to gender, in that it is a tactic more often pursued by men than by women. However, Goodwin (2002a, 2002b) has shown how power asymmetries of this sort can also be associated with domination within single-sex groups of young schoolgirls. Goodwin suggests that in this form of "relational aggression" (Currie, Kelly, & Pomerantz, 2007) the careful production of "dispreferred" responses which Pomerantz described is missing from the talk of these young girls. Instead, their talk seemed to display a preference for disagreement over agreement. One of the ways in which these power asymmetries played themselves out in the girls' talk was in the discursive development of social relationships and social boundaries.

5 SARAH: You're like a <u>tag</u>. You tag along. ((*left palm extended with arm bent towards Angela*))
6   Basically– Angela tags along.=
                                          [
7 ANGELA: So,
8 SARAH: That's it.=right?
9 ANGELA: So li ke– <u>Yeah</u>. ((*shoulder shrug*))
                     [
10 SARAH: Right Angela? Admit it. eh heh heh!
11 ANGELA: Yeah like– whatever.
                                [

> **Conversational dominance** Having rights or entitlements to talk and direct the talk of others which supersede those of other speakers

12 SARAH: ADMIT IT ANGELA!

13 SARAH: ADMIT IT! ((*extends arms palm up to Angela*))
            [

14 ANGELA: OKAY! ((*leaning towards Sarah*))

15 SARAH: Say it. "You:: (.) are:: (.) I: am a: (.)"
            ((*using hands as if conducting on each beat, then extends hands palm up towards Angela as if asking her to complete the utterance*))

16 ANGELA: I'M A TAG-ALONG °girl°! ((*jerks body in direction of Sarah*))
                                              (0.4)

17 SARAH: <u>Good</u> girl! eh heh!
                    (Goodwin, 2002a, pp. 723–724)

In this interaction, Sarah provides a description of Angela as someone who merely tags along and presses Angela to make a public confession of this status. Although Angela produces an agreement, Sarah treats this as inadequate, and produces a frame for Angela's next response by chanting rhythmically the content of what would count as an acceptable response. Goodwin suggests that this episode takes on the form of ritualized degradation, which is emphasized by the ironic positive comment which Sarah produces at line 17.

One important aspect of episodes of this sort, Goodwin argues, is that the "victims" of such rude activity can themselves be seen to orient to that activity as offensive.

RUTH: <u>Hi</u> Angela! <u>Bye</u> Angela! ((raising right hand, palm toward Angela))

LISA: Shoo <u>shoo</u>::!
        ((Angela walks away))
                    (Goodwin, 2002a, p. 725)

In this example, Angela has approached a group of girls. As she approaches, Ruth ironically draws upon the ritual forms of greeting by uttering a greeting and then immediately following this with a farewell expression:: Lisa then adopts a form of talk which is associated with people in authority or positions of superiority, such as teachers, in order to amplify Ruth's dismissal. In response, Angela clearly orients to what has just happened as rudeness by leaving the scene. Indeed, just as participants can react to the consequences of asymmetrical interactions, they can

also react to the asymmetrical nature of the interaction itself. In a study of interactions between service providers and their customers, Morales-Lopez and her colleagues (Morales-Lopez, Prego-Vazquez, & Dominguez-Seco, 2005) noted that conflict sometimes arose because some customers refused to acknowledge or accept the service provider's attempt to establish a conversational asymmetry by adopting a formal mode of speech.

So although some forms of talk can be used to display interactional dominance, it turns out that how people interpret or orient to what is said is also relevant to the issue of whether disagreement leads to interactional problems. This is clearly seen in a study by Dersley and Wootton (2001) of episodes in which arguments veer towards antagonistic dispute. They studied a set of encounters in which a pair of people leveled accusations at each other. They note that sequences of talk in which people present complaints to each other can produce confrontation and generate an interactional impasse in which, like Angela, one of the parties to the interaction unilaterally leaves the vicinity. The key to this sort of communication breakdown, they say, is that sometimes arguments escalate in such a way that one of the participants interprets what the other is doing or saying as not only wrong, but deliberately or willfully wrong.

113 MILLY: 'cause you're ↑still playing on the fact
            [that,=

114 CLARA: [NO

115 MILLY: =on [Sunday,

116 CLARA: [<u>I</u>:'M <u>NOT</u>,= ((slow, deliberate prosody))

117 MILLY: =you had an ↑argument ↑on camera an' so y're usin' it

118   a↑ga [in?

119 CLARA: [<u>WHAT</u> ↑ARE ↑YOU
                 [↑↑<u>TALK</u>↓<u>ING</u>= ((shrieking))

120 MILLY: [t' make you=

121 CLARA: =[<u>ABOU</u>:::T.

122 MILLY: =[look like a put down (.) little (.) kid=

123   =['n I'm <u>fed up</u> with it. ((then immediately begins to exit))

124 CLARA: =[<u>WHAT</u> ARE YOU TALK–

125   (.)

126 CLARA: <u>WHAT</u> ARE YOU <u>TALKING</u> A [BOUT.

127 MILLY: [you know what–

128   I'm talk [in' about. ((here with her
             back to Clara, on way to door))
129 CLARA: [NO I DON'T HAVE A ↓CLUE
             (Dersley & Wootton, 2001, p. 627)

In describing how relatively normal conversational contexts can transform into these sorts of antagonistic encounters, Dersley and Wootton note that their own data show up a particular feature of how arguments such as this are developed. In general, their data show that the participants relied, as might be expected, on responding to complaints both by issuing defenses and by offering counter-complaints. However, the participants' defenses against complaints directed towards them were weakened by the way in which complaints were designed. For example, in this current extract, Milly identifies a pattern of behavior in Clara's recent conduct and produces a description of it which highlights its offensive nature. One important aspect of this description, say Dersley and Wootton, is the way in which it not only establishes a pattern in Clara's behavior, but also locates her current behavior as an exemplar of that pattern. This turns out to be a powerful feature in the development of complaints and accusations. In Dersley and Wootton's study, complainers produced accusations which specified both general and ongoing deficiencies in the other speaker. Because complaints were framed in terms of general tendencies to behave in some problematic way or another, this made less available a defense that the behavior complained about was in some sense a one-off lapse or temporary mistake or aberration. However, the complainers also routinely introduced the idea that this generic bad behavior was instantiated by what the conversational partner was currently doing. And this seemed to lead up to the moment of impasse. In a number of cases, immediately prior to one of the participants leaving, the complainer would offer to the complainee an opportunity to desist from the problematic behavior, and it was the complainee's non-uptake of that opportunity which seemed to lead to the complainer leaving. In these cases, both participants placed interpretations on the interaction which provided them with what Dersley and Wootton referred to as "warrantable grounds for self-righteousness." In particular, the complainer could be seen as walking out in part because the

complainee was apparently determined to continue with behavior which typified a general, negative tendency or disposition even after being given the opportunity to "shape up."

Perhaps the most extreme case in recent history of participants interpreting another's actions as problematic in this way is the confrontation which arose between the American Federal Bureau of Investigation and the Branch Davidian religious community during the so-called "Waco standoff." This was an event in which a religious group came into conflict with the authorities and found themselves besieged in their compound for 51 days. The standoff ended in a horrific fire where more than 80 men, women, and children died. In a study of the discussions between the Branch Davidian leader, David Koresh, and FBI negotiators, Agne and Tracy (2001) have pointed to the way in which the negotiators interpreted Koresh's frequent references to his biblical beliefs as "Bible babble." Agne and Tracy suggest that the negotiators contributed to the breakdown of negotiations with the religious group by treating such talk as an impediment to achieving a peaceful solution.

So one particular participant's orientation which seems to mark out genuine dispute from more playful or socially constructive forms of talk is that produced by participants who interpret another speaker's actions as deliberately argumentative or problematic. This is highlighted in a study by Gruber (2001), who draws attention to the issue of whether participants in an interaction interpret what another speaker has said as having some sort of strategic goal. Gruber notes that conflict in discourse often arises after a preliminary conversational turn in which one of the speakers has outlined a particular point of view on some topic. The point or issue of conflict is introduced by another participant in the succeeding or "second" turn position within the conversational sequence. Interestingly, it turns out that such "second position" responses are often in the form of a question. These may be explicit, e.g., of the form "May I put the opposite view to you?," or they may be less direct, such as rhetorical questions which undermine the first speaker's claim. Whether explicit or implicit, these second position questions are framed so as to establish the current speaker's oppositional stance to what was said by the previous speaker. Of course, this could be accomplished by merely stating a disagreement. But, Gruber suggests, the employment of a question format has useful interactional benefits. Questions are normatively bound with the expectation that the hearer will produce a response. And a further normative expectation is that this response will take the form of an answer to the question which is appropriately relevant to the topic produced within the question. In this sense, then, the introduction of disagreement through the use of challenging questions imposes certain interactional constraints on the participant whose view is being challenged. Since disagreements can be formulated through the strategic use of this particular sequential device, speakers routinely display sensitivity to the issue of whether a question reflects this sort of strategic orientation.

One of the issues which separates out "arguments" from arguments thus turns out to be the way in which participants themselves interpret the actions of other speakers. But participants' orientations are not restricted to orientations towards other speakers. Saft (2004) has drawn attention to the way that participants also orient to the settings in which their interactions take place. In a study of arguments which arose in two different types of university faculty meeting in Japan, Saft draws attention to the way that differences between the institutional work being accomplished in these meetings were associated with differences in the way that members of the committee used argumentative practices. In meetings where the discussion focused on matters that were important to the administration of the university, the interactional organization militated against open argument, with participants routinely orienting to the chairperson of the meeting as someone whose permission was required before a contribution could be made. However, in other meetings, participants oriented to the setting as one in which they were entitled to directly address one another by interjecting comments on what another participant was currently saying.

CLASSIC STUDY: Conflict talk

In this text, a number of researchers explore the ways and contexts in which conflict talk arises. The book begins by examining how children develop the discursive capacity for argument in social settings such as the school playground and the street. For example, Goodwin and Goodwin utilize conversation analytic techniques to explore interactions among a group of boys preparing for a game in which they will fight with sling-shots. One of the features they draw attention to is the way that the sequential ordering of the boys' talk displays patterns of social dominance. The book then moves on to consider how conflict talk is managed among adults. Following an examination of conflict narratives, a number of chapters in the book focus on discourse analyses of different forms of dispute. The contexts in which these disputes arose include doctor–patient interactions in psychiatric settings, disputes within small-claims courts and within more formal legal settings, and interactions in the workplace. One example of these is O'Donnell's study of disputes between workers and management in an American city's public utility company. One of the features she draws out is the way that power differentials among participants underpin the structure of the disputes that take place. In a subsequent chapter, Schiffrin explores the sorts of "cooperative argument" which have been discussed in this chapter, noting that "conflict talk" can be delicately negotiated to ensure continuing social cohesion among participants. The book moves towards a close with Tannen's chapter on fictional texts and the way in which the portrayal of silence is used to depict interpersonal conflict.

Grimshaw, A. D. (Ed.) (1990). *Conflict talk: Sociolinguistic investigations of arguments in conversations.* Cambridge: Cambridge University Press.

Summary

It might seem obvious that some sorts of discourse, such as insults or argument, are precursors of aggression. But discursive research demonstrates that these forms of talk play a much wider role in social interaction. Insults can be bound up with playful teasing, and arguments can be used to establish sociability. Moreover, arguments may play a central role in allowing people to socially construct a joint understanding of the world around them. However, such forms of disputatious talk can result in interactional problems. Whether such problems arise depends in part on the nature of the interaction. If the interaction is one in which there is an unequal distribution of rights and entitlements, then the socially dominant participants may use this unequal position to victimize other participants. But participants' own orientations are also important. Interactional difficulties such as someone unilaterally breaking off communication arise in part because participants view one another as deliberately acting in a problematic way.

Accounting for Aggression

Aggressors' accounts

Up until now, we have discussed the way in which disputes arise or are avoided in talk. We have also looked at some examples where talk constituted forms of aggressive activity such as rudeness or bullying. However, a range of other discursive studies have focused on the different question of how acts of aggression are represented in accounts produced in the aftermath of violent episodes. At this point, it is important to note that accounts of this sort arise in contexts in which both speaker and hearer have a multiplicity of specific, localized interests in the production of those accounts (Trinch & Berk-Seligson, 2002). One of the ways in which such multiplicity arises is the circumstance in which people provide accounts of aggressive or violent events for which they themselves may potentially be held to have some kind of responsibility. In such contexts, it is commonplace that descriptions are produced in such a way as to manage that

responsibility. For example, McKenzie (2001) conducted interviews in 1992 with members of US and British diplomatic communities who were asked to talk about the Gulf War. McKenzie notes that in their discussions, the diplomats produced accounts of the causes of the war that were designed to manage issues of accountability for that armed conflict. The interviewees accomplished this by introducing into their responses a variety of different and competing plausible grounds for the outbreak of the war. In doing this, says McKenzie, his participants were "producing undecidability" as a way of managing accountability. The outcome of this was that the speakers were able to manage demands for expressions of their own accountability by implying that definitive answers about responsibility for the war and its aftermath were not practically available.

The multiplicity of interactional goals associated with accounts of aggression is also nicely illustrated by Presser (2004), who examined what she describes as "trajectories of the moral self" in which violent offenders produce narrative accounts of themselves as morally decent. In "return" narratives the offender differentiated between a previous, bad self and a current, good self, while in "stability" narratives offenders contrasted episodic incidents in which they performed a morally reprehensible act with their general characters as good people. Presser notes that in all of these accounts, her participants relied upon a general theme of struggle in which their own goodness had, or would, triumph over obstacles which they faced such as problematic inner attitudes or difficulties with other people or agencies. In this way, her participants were able to attend to issues of self-presentation and identity while providing accounts of the aggressive acts in which they had formerly engaged. Osvaldsson (2004) found a similar phenomenon in the talk of young female offenders in youth detention centers in Sweden.

Another interactional goal which may surface in aggressors' accounts is the attempt to establish that somehow the victim was responsible for the aggressors' actions. This is highlighted in Eglin and Hester's (1999) analysis of a statement made by the person who murdered 13 women on a university campus in Montreal in 1989. Prior to the killings, the murderer, Marc Lepine, is reported to have made the following announcement to his women victims:

> You're women. You're going to be engineers. You're all a bunch of feminists. I hate feminists.
> (Eglin & Hester, 1999, p. 255)

Eglin and Hester point out that Levine's announcement works, in part, as a means of establishing something about himself. In a context in which he is about to murder a number of people and then kill himself, a potential explanation for his actions could be that he is mentally ill. By performing this announcement as an explanation, Eglin and Hester suggest, Lepine demonstrates a concern with this possible interpretation by providing a statement which is designed as a "rational" account for what he is going to do. In addition, however, Lepine also provides a category label in identifying his victims as "feminists." In doing this, Lepine attempts to "anonymize" his victims by casting them as representatives of a political movement. In this sense, his statement aims to establish that his actions are directed not against specific individual human beings, but against exemplars of a problematic category. The statement begins by making two categories relevant: women and engineers. Eglin and Hester argue that this lays the ground for Levine's complaint, because the succeeding categorization, "feminists," then makes relevant the idea that these are women who wrongly intend to take up jobs as engineers, which is a stereotypically masculine occupation. The negative aspect of feminism is emphasized through Levine's use of the "You are all a bunch of Xs" formulation, which is hearable as a denunciation of the women. So within a few short words, Levine is able to depict his actions as the rational outcome of adopting a particular political perspective, rather than as the random acts of a madman. In addition, he draws into this description the inference that his actions are caused by the problematic behavior of his victims. Elsewhere in their study, Eglin and Hester address the extent to which similar features arose in the suicide message which Levine left behind him. In this respect, it is interesting to note that in their study of suicide messages, McClelland, Reicher, and Booth (2000) discovered

that over half of the notes left by those who had committed suicide dealt with the issue of blaming someone else.

Others' accounts

Aggressors are not the only people who deploy complex accounts of aggression in order to serve a variety of interactional goals. A similar interactional complexity can be observed in the way other people, such as victims or third parties, account for the aggressive actions of others. Of course, these accounts differ from aggressors' accounts in that the other interactional goals being pursued need not involve the account giver in managing his or her responsibility for the event. However, they are often similar to aggressors' own accounts in that they seek to offer an explanation of the aggression or violence which gave rise to the account. Moreover, just as aggressors' accounts contain self-characterizations, so the accounts and explanations of victims and third parties can contain their characterizations of the aggressor. But whereas the aggressors' self-characterizations are intended to deflect personal responsibility, others' characterizations of the aggressor are often deployed in order to attribute responsibility.

Rapley, McCarthy, and McHoul (2003) examined press accounts of an event which took place in Australia in which a lone gunman, Martin Bryant, shot 35 people. Using membership categorization analysis, they looked at the ways in which the gunman was portrayed as suffering from some sort of psychological disorder. (The routine nature of this sort of ascription is highlighted in the Eglin and Hester study mentioned earlier. Part of Levine's concern in making an announcement was precisely to avoid this sort of explanation of his actions.) In particular, Rapley and colleagues noted that these newspaper characterizations were designed to accomplish two potentially contradictory tasks: explaining the gunman's behavior while at the same time establishing his responsibility for that behavior. The newspaper accounts offered explanations for why someone would perform such an unusual, aberrant act which were based on the gunman's irrationality. However, since madness is a potential defense against attributions of responsibility, it might seem as though accounts that described the gunman as mad thereby excused him from his actions. But Rapley and colleagues point out that the characterizations of the gunman as "mad" were produced in such a way that the gunman's moral culpability for carrying out those acts was maintained.

> Martin Bryant, in the months following the Port Arthur tragedy, was examined by four psychologists and psychiatrists. They all concluded that, while he suffered from a personality disorder and was, according to intelligence tests, in the borderline range between intellectual disability and the "dull normal individual," he was not criminally insane, and did not suffer from serious mental illness, such as depression or schizophrenia. In other words, in the opinion of those psychologists and psychiatrists who examined him, Bryant was capable of distinguishing between right and wrong, and understood, in the words of Paul Mullen, a forensic psychiatrist from Monash University, "what it meant to be guilty and to be not guilty."
>
> (Rapley et al., 2003, p. 439)

In this extract, taken from the *Sydney Morning Herald*, the newspaper journalist reproduces both of the relevant category memberships. However, they are woven together in order to establish what Rapley and his colleagues describe as a "no man's land" of being both insane and yet morally culpable. Thus Bryant is depicted as "personality disordered" but not criminally insane and as intellectually disabled but also as borderline normal. By drawing on these determinations produced by psychologists and psychiatrists, the journalist is able to lead to the conclusion that Bryant was morally responsible for his own actions even while explaining those actions in terms of Bryant's mental incapacities.

As well as producing explanations for past actions, accounts of violence produced by victims and third parties can also be deployed as a means of justifying future actions. In this case too, descriptions of prior aggressive actions can be seen to be bound up with other interactional business such as characterization of the aggressor. Leudar, Marsland, and Nekvapil (2004) examined public responses to the attacks on the World Trade Center and the Pentagon in the United States on September 11, 2001. Using a membership

categorization analysis, they showed the way in which alternative representations of the events of September 11 are produced and used as justifications for past or future action. In their analysis, they emphasize the action-orientation of their participants' categorizations. In producing categorizations of self and others in terms of properties such as moral stance or religious persuasion, participants could, at the same time, be seen to be accomplishing actions such as rejecting a point of view or encouraging others to act in a specific way.

1 THE PRESIDENT: I have just completed a meeting with my national security
2 team, and we have received the latest intelligence updates.
3 The deliberate and deadly attacks which were carried out yesterday against our
4 country were more than acts of terror. They were acts of war.
5 This will require our country to unite in steadfast determination and
6 resolve. Freedom and democracy are under attack.
7 The American people need to know that we're facing a different enemy
8 than we have ever faced. This enemy hides in shadows, and has no regard
9 for human life. This is an enemy who preys on innocent and unsuspecting
10 people, then runs for cover. But it won't be able to run for cover forever.
11 This is an enemy that tries to hide. But it won't be able to hide forever. This is an
12 enemy that thinks its harbors are safe. But they won't be safe forever.
(Leudar et al., 2004, pp. 249–250)

In this extract, Leudar and colleagues present a section of the address which President Bush made on the day following the events of September 11. They note that Bush characterizes actors and events in specific ways, as being "deliberate and deadly" and as "acts of war." The attackers are characterized as the "enemy" and described in cowardly terms and in terms of lack of humanity, in that they are identified through the use of the impersonal pronoun "it." On the other hand, the thing which is being attacked is described positively through the use of the phrase "freedom and democracy." Leudar,

Marsland, and Nekvapil point out that through these characterizations, Bush is able to draw a distinction between "us" and "them" in which the lack of human qualities in "them" is emphasized.

In the preceding studies, we saw how aggressors' explanations of violent acts may incorporate characterizations of the victim which attribute responsibility. On occasion, characterization of victims also becomes interactionally relevant in the accounts of third parties. In a study of the phenomenon of male rape, Doherty and Anderson (2004) asked male and female couples to discuss a male rape event. In these discussions, Doherty and Anderson note, the participants routinely deployed a classification of rape victims based on gender and sexuality, separating out the experiences of women and gay men as victims from the experiences of heterosexual men. In part, this form of categorization was bound up in the participants' accounts with formulations of rape which stressed its similarity to consensual sexual intercourse. One consequence of this, say Doherty and Anderson, is that heterosexual male rape was described as more traumatic for the victim than other forms of rape. However, another consequence was that male rape victims were depicted as likely to suffer from charges that they, themselves, were in some way responsible for the rape, having failed to demonstrate appropriately masculine behaviors of defending themselves against aggression.

1 GARY: I mean it's like a thing where I reckon, I suppose it gets to a heterosexual man that, I mean for a woman to be raped by a man, it's, it's a heterosexual act, whereas for a man to be raped by another man it's a homosexual act and I don't know, it it, not only, it destroys yourself and, sexuality as well really, erm, I don't

2 SARAH: Puts your own sexuality in your own mind perhaps

3 GARY: Yeah, yeah, also mean in the rape of women I think that when a woman has been raped you can say all right, she's been raped by a man, sort of in most cases a man is bigger, stronger.

4 SARAH: Yeah, it's coming down to the ableness, the issue that men are stronger than women generally, and so it's, if you're raped by another man

5 GARY: Yeah, and so if you're raped by another man then you'd think, people would say, "you're a bloke why couldn't you fight them off, why couldn't you stop him from doing that." It's words that normally you'd say, I mean oh well, you know

(Doherty & Anderson, 2004, pp. 94–95)

Doherty and Anderson note the way that in this extract Gary makes sexuality and gender relevant to the discussion by distinguishing between the experiences of men and women and between homosexuality and heterosexuality. Homosexuality and heterosexuality are demarcated as clearly different forms of social identity and this distinction is used to suggest that rape is worse for heterosexual men than for homosexual men or women because it transcends conventional social boundaries. However, the participants then provide descriptions of men and women in which men are depicted as stronger and more able than women. This particular characterization of difference between the genders is then picked up by Gary in the last turn. The potentially controversial nature of what he is about to say is signaled by Gary through his reformulation of "you'd think" into "people would say." This self-repair indicates that Gary is sensitive to the issue of whether what he is about to say could be heard as "blaming the victim." What Gary does say is that male rape victims are potentially characterizable as failed males, as something other than "blokes," because they did not appropriately defend themselves. So although the plight of male rape victims is described as in some ways worse than that of other victims, the way in which this is established provides a discursive setting in which heterosexual men are depicted as potentially being held responsible for what happened to them.

Two further points are worth making. Gary's apparent association of rape with sexual activity is representative of a form of discourse which rape offenders themselves can be seen to employ (Lea & Auburn, 2001). On the other hand, the description produced by Gary and his other participants which associated defending oneself from aggression with specific gender roles has been thrown into question (Day, Gough, & McFadden, 2003). In a study of young women's talk about aggression that arises during "nights out," Day and colleagues noted that physical aggression can play an important role in the construction of working-class women's identities just as it can in the construction of masculine identities.

Summary

Episodes of aggression are often followed by accounts which seek to explain what has occurred. These accounts are often complex discursive achievements in which the account giver attends to a number of different interactional goals. When aggressors themselves are supplying these accounts, their explanations are often designed to attend to their own responsibility for what occurred. For example, aggressors seek to avoid culpability by presenting themselves as essentially good people, or by blaming the episode on the victim. When others, such as victims or third parties, produce accounts of aggression, the descriptions they offer are similarly complex. Thus accounts of someone behaving violently often seek both to explain the violence that was perpetrated and to establish the culpability of the perpetrator. Interestingly, third-party accounts sometimes rely on characterizations of the victim in a manner similar to that deployed by aggressors in their accounts.

Disguising Aggression

Denials

The preceding examples explored ways in which people account for aggressive or violent episodes. One common theme was that the accounts on offer all embraced an acceptance that aggressive acts had, in fact, occurred. However, other sorts of accounts are quite different. In a range of cases, accounts of events which could potentially be described as violent or aggressive are formulated in such a way as to deny that aggression took place. Perhaps the most obvious example of this is the case where aggressors' accounts are designed to accomplish this sort of denial. In the following extract, the participant, S, is taking part in an interview with a police officer, P, in connection with the theft of cigarettes from a shop.

```
6   S:  =Well then somebody else has done that
        mate.
7       I wouldn' I ↑wouldn't do that. No I'll admit to
8       stealin the ciggies, right .hh but they were on
        the
9       counter, .h I did not jump over no counter
        for them.
10      (0.3)
11  P:  NO I [Didn't say you jumped over a
        count[er.
12  S:       [I-          [I didn'
13      even go behind the counter for them.= I
        didn' push
14      the woman or nothin, (0.5) I really did not
        do
15      that.= I'm not that type of person y'know
        what I
16      me:an. .h Fair enough I stole the ciggies, (0.9)
17      I wouldn' hurt an old lady.
                            (Edwards, 2006b, p. 479)
```

Immediately preceding the turns reproduced in this extract, the police officer, P, had mentioned an accusation from the shopkeeper that S had pushed her, causing her to become bruised. At line 6, S invokes some other perpetrator in order to deny this accusation, while at lines 7 to 14 he offers a factual denial, summed up by the phrase "I really did not do that." One particular point of interest here is the way S relies on "wouldn't" as a "generalized, dispositional expression." Edwards (2006b) identifies S's use of "wouldn't" with the formulation of normative, generalized self-assessments. By using "wouldn't," S is able to establish what Edwards refers to as "back-dated predictability" by implying that if the participants were to travel back through time and observe S, then they would be able to predict that S would not perform a violent act. Another part of the generalizability of S's account, says Edwards, is the way in which it draws upon general categorization. By choosing the particular description of "an old lady," S implies that the alleged victim belonged to a category of people which is emblematic of people who should not be hit.

But aggressors are not the only people who seek to deny or minimize the occurrence of aggression. For example, in a study of lesbian and gay parents' accounts of homophobic bullying, Clarke, Kitzinger, and Potter (2004) noted that their participants either denied that such bullying took place at all, or sought to minimize its effects or consequences. Clarke and her colleagues point out that where children are raised in lesbian or gay families, homophobic bullying is used as a means of undermining families by those who oppose lesbian and gay parenting. The argument here is that if children are raised in such circumstances, then they will suffer from homophobic bullying, and so these forms of family arrangements should be opposed. Within this context, lesbian and gay parents face an interactional dilemma. Denying that bullying takes place may be heard as implausible. But admitting that it takes places leaves the parents accountable for their children's negative experiences.

```
11 SUSIE:  .hh And I mean one of the views we
           took (0.2) about
12         the whole thing was well (0.2) if they
           weren't
13         calling him names because his parents
           were lesbians,
14         they'd be calling him names because
           he's got big
15         ea:rs, or little ea::rs, or: a big nose, or
16         >whatever<,
17 ANNA:   Or his dad [(was) fat]
18 SUSIE:  [So chil– ]
19 ANNA:   or his mum looked old [or you know]
20 SUSIE:  [>Yeah so children<] I mean we
21         had to be careful not to blow it out of all
22         proportion and think "oh god we're
           awful we're
23         causing our children all these prob-
           lem:s"
24 INT:    mm
25 SUSIE:  er because children get picked on for all
           sorts of
26         reasons,
27 INT:    mm
28 SUSIE:  and (.) erm (0.2) that was just another
           reason.
                              (Clarke et al., 2004, p. 544)
```

In this extract fragment, the parents generalize bullying from a specifically homophobic event to a less particularized experience by producing lists of the causes for bullying, such as "big ears" or "little ears." Clarke and her colleagues note that Susie's use of "whatever" at line 16 indicates that the list could be extended, suggesting that the issue is even more general than the current listing of

items might imply. Moreover, her selection of both "big ears" and "little ears" conveys the idea that such prejudice is indiscriminate, rather than patterned or specific. In addition, both Anna and Susie draw upon mundane features of people such as the shape of facial characteristics or body type in order to build up a "normalized" picture of bullying episodes. These features of the parents' account help to establish a basis for the claim which Susie then makes at lines 25 and 26, that bullying arises for a range of reasons, a claim which blurs distinctions between homophobic bullying and other forms of bulling. In presenting this account, Susie attends to the potential interactional difficulty that it will be heard as trivializing a serious problem. She describes her position as "one of the views," which implies that she has other perspectives which can be introduced if she is challenged. In addition, she reports an imaginary complaint at lines 22 and 23 in relatively extreme terms. However she represents this extreme complaint as a case where the problem is being blown out of proportion. In this way, she forestalls potential criticism that she is ignoring the seriousness of homophobic bullying by providing an easily undermined version of that complaint. Clarke and her colleagues conclude that this normalization of bullying allows their participants to deal with the problems which their children face while at the same time managing the other interactional concerns that arise from their particular family circumstances. In this respect, they note, the parents' accounts of bullying are similar to accounts of bullying produced by teachers (Hepburn, 2000), who seek to minimize the impact of bullying as a means of managing implications about the social order of the classroom.

What we have seen, then, is that the accounts of aggressors and the accounts of third parties can be similar in that they are developed in such a way as to minimize the nature of the aggressive acts which they describe. Perhaps even more worryingly, discursive research throws up examples of cases where the victims of aggression themselves seek to deny that episodes of aggression have arisen. In a UK study of sexual abuse, Reavey, Ahmed, and Majumdar (2006) conducted a series of interviews with South Asian women who had been the victims of attacks. They noted that the social work professionals involved in helping these women faced a number of problems associated with cultural norms within the victims' communities. For example, Reavey and her colleagues noted that among South Asian communities, the importance of family relationships meant that the women victims were concerned about bringing shame to the family and adversely affecting the "honor" of their husbands. Another important feature of this study is that it underlines the importance of understanding the interrelationship between discourses of gender and race in developing an understanding of domestic violence (Burman, 2005) as well as questioning traditional perspectives on the responsibility that women have for such episodes (Lavis, Horrocks, Kelly, & Barker, 2005).

Making aggression invisible

Accounts which deny that aggression took place at least acknowledge the possible existence of aggression. A more subtle issue is where discourse makes the phenomenon itself invisible (Kettrey & Emery, 2006). For example, Coates and Wade (2004) have argued that some public forms of discourse about violence are designed in order to conceal it or to lessen the perceived responsibility of the perpetrators. They also claim that such violence discourse can be designed to conceal victims' resistance and to blame the victim. Indeed, just as victims themselves can be seen to deny the occurrence of aggression, they can also be seen to be involved in making aggression and violence invisible. Thus Berman (2000) has suggested that victims of violence may themselves employ forms of discourse which conceal that violence. Berman examines the narratives of violence produced by homeless youths in urban Indonesia. These stories were reproduced in a street bulletin called "Jejal," in which the children were able to share stories about their own experiences with other street children. By looking at the discursive features of these narratives, such as the interpretative repertoires selected and the ways in which the children position themselves within these narratives, Berman argues that the analyst is able to understand how these children socially construct or formulate their own reality. One area of emphasis is the exploration of the children's survival strategies for dealing with violence and abuse.

My name: Unyil Jangkung I was born in Jogja Wage market, Wonosari Street.
I left home because I had a problem and now live in Purwokerto.
To eat each day I go with homos and service them and I am given money and that money I use to eat.
So that's my daily job until one day after a date with a homo I got a dangerous disease called syphilis.

When I urinated it hurt and from my penis came out
pus and blood and I then went to Jakarta on the Cipuja train then I got off at Tasik and met mas Heri
who is good and I can write this story of my life.

Then I was helped and given medicine to cure my disease
and at the same time write my life story and so on.

(Berman, 2000, p. 155)

Berman points out that in this story, Unyil provides a spatial location as a context in which his original "problem" arose with the implication that Unyil's resolution of the problem was to move from that location. This emphasis on spatial orientation is repeated in the second part of Unyil's narrative where he describes the trip to Jakarta as the means of dealing with contracting an illness. In this sense, Berman argues, Unyil's narrative is designed around a series of cause and effect connections in which spatially and temporally specified events, rather than personal **agency**, cause the storyteller to act. The narrative contains no detail of social relationships either at home or on the street in Purwokerto other than the impact such relationships have on his physical survival. In this sense, then, the narrative can be construed as a story of events which contingently arise and cause Unyil to act in order to preserve his physical survival.

Berman notes that narratives of this sort do not fit neatly into categorizations of narrative structures identified in previous research on narratives. They do not contain story-like features such as plotting or rich imagery, and, although they are

---

Agency The property of being the source or cause of action or events

autobiographical, they do not display a reflexive or evaluative stance. Events, including violent events, are presented in a casual manner which, instead of emphasizing personal agency, describes temporal and spatial constructions and the social interactions with others that contingently arise at such times and places. Berman suggests that this emphasis on events as "just happening" and on others rather than the self allows the children to construct narratives which avoid discussing the "why" of the events that occurred. In doing this, the children are able to link their own activities to issues of material well-being, such as having enough food to eat. In this way, they present their own coping with violence strategies as ways of behaving which are aimed at mere physical survival.

Berman concludes that this displays a sense of identity which is at odds with that normally revealed by analysis of life stories. Instead of danger and violence being represented as important aspects of the storyteller's life, the children's narratives emphasize place and social relations and frame physical survival as the main concern of the story. The child's own perspective on his rights as an individual and the ways in which those rights might be violated largely disappears from the narrative. In a sense, then, the basic needs of physical survival are presented as outweighing the need to evaluate or reflect upon experience. In these stories, violence is understated because it is perceived as a norm. Berman describes these ways of talking as interpretative repertoires which are culturally shared among the children. The children interpret abusive or violent acts against them not in terms of their own rights but in terms of the range of responses available to them, which are essentially to do with changing location to avoid such acts. Because they live in a hierarchical social order in which they inhabit one of the lowest positions, violence and abuse are seen as necessary aspects of their low status and hence not as areas for evaluation or reflection.

Summary

One of the difficulties associated with the study of aggression is that the very question of whether aggression has or has not occurred is itself open to debate. Perhaps unsurprisingly, we can see that aggressors rely upon accounts in which the occurrence of violence is denied. More surprisingly, the same sorts of denials can arise in the accounts of third parties and even in the accounts of victims themselves. The situation is compounded by the fact that overt denials do not always arise in such circumstances. Instead, accounts can be developed in which aggression and violence are made invisible, in that it never surfaces as an element in the accounts which are being produced.

In Conclusion

It is evident from the range of examples presented here that discourses of dispute and aggression are complex affairs. There are, of course, other aspects to these discourses which cannot be covered here. For example, in Goodwin's study we saw that discourse takes on an aggressive aspect when it is used to perform social exclusion. It is important to note that this use of discourse as a means of marginalizing or excluding others is not restricted to the school playground. Wilson and Stapleton (2005), for example, have shown how locals discursively construct "versions" of the anniversaries and celebrations that play an important symbolic role in the life of Northern Ireland. Northern Ireland is a country which has a long history of violence and aggression that centers on the divisions between its Protestant and Catholic inhabitants. Wilson and Stapleton argue that one of the consequences of these constructive efforts is the reproduction of forms of social exclusion in which Protestants or Catholics negotiate differences between themselves and those from the alternative tradition.

Discursive studies show that it can be difficult for social policy to address issues of aggression and violence, because such episodes are discursively bound up with other participants' concerns. Phillips (2007), for example, has demonstrated that in some respects bullying must be understood as a part of masculine identity. But this very discursive property may offer some hope for improvement. Hollander (2002) has pointed to prevailing discourses which socially construct women as vulnerable to men's aggression. However, she also describes the variety of discursive resources which women deploy in order to challenge this social construction of women as helpless in the face of male aggression. This does not, of course, imply that potential victims of aggression can readily be taught how to "talk their way" out of trouble. As Kitzinger and Frith (1999) have pointed out, educational campaigns designed to help potential victims by teaching them what to say in dangerous situations often underestimate the discursive complexity of aggressive contexts. However, the research reviewed in this chapter does suggest that a closer attention to discursive practices will provide the social researcher with a clearer understanding of how aggressors and their victims understand such events in their own terms.

Chapter summary

- The aim of this chapter has been to introduce the ways in which discursive research has examined the problems of dispute and aggression.
- It is clear from what has been said that researchers must be careful to separate out different occasions in which potentially disputatious talk arises.
- In some contexts forms of talk which are apparently problematic, such as insults or arguments, can be shown to have positive interactional roles.
- In some other contexts, where there is an asymmetry of power, the same sorts of talk can represent genuine instances of verbal aggression.
- One of the aspects of talk that determines whether argument results in contentious disputation is the interpretation that participants place on what is said.
- This flexible aspect of argumentative talk extends, in a sense, to episodes of aggressive behavior too, in that such episodes are often followed by accounts produced by aggressors, their victims, and third parties.
- These accounts are complex, in that the account giver often attends to several different interactional tasks, such as both explaining the episode of aggression and attending to issues of culpability.
- Aggressors' accounts are sometimes designed to minimize personal responsibility while attributing blame to the victim, while the accounts of others are often designed as explanations which, at the same time, attribute blame to the aggressor.
- Denials feature in the accounts of aggressors, but they also feature in others' accounts. In some accounts, the account giver goes further and produces accounts which make the violence and aggression "invisible."

Connections

Aspects of argumentative discourse are also relevant to the discussion of discourse in the law presented in Chapter 9. In addition, the material in this chapter on aggressors' accounts and on denying aggression is also relevant to issues of prejudice as discussed in Chapter 7.

Activity

Newspaper accounts of aggression and violence, such as the extract used at the start of this chapter, arise almost every day. Select several of these and decide what is "going on." Is the account offering an explanation? Is it doing anything else, e.g., producing characterizations of aggressor or victim? If so, how does the account provider combine these different interactional goals within a single account?

Further reading

McKenzie, K. (2001). Fact and the narratives of war: Produced undecidability in accounts of armed conflict. *Human Studies, 24,* 187–209. In this paper, McKenzie introduces some extended extracts (which are too long to reproduce here) taken from the talk of members of the diplomatic community. In these extracts, the diplomats can be seen to negotiate their own moral accountability for the Gulf War. This is an enjoyable and instructive look at how professional diplomats wield language in the provision of extenuating explanations when their own responsibility is in question.

Mizushima, L. & Stapleton, P. (2006). Analyzing the function of meta-oriented critical comments in Japanese comic conversations. *Journal of Pragmatics, 38,* 2105–2123. This paper, drawing on interactions among Japanese adults, is a fascinating insight into the way playful teasing can be developed by means of ritualistic patterns of discourse. Talk which in other contexts might lead to interactional difficulties is seen to be skillfully negotiated by the participants. The authors draw attention to the way in which Japanese culture embodies a degree of unspoken understanding among participants, which may help to explain their adroitness.

Chapter 9

Social Psychology, Law, and Order

It was one of the most publicized trials of the new century. In January 2005, jurors were selected in the case of Michael Jackson who was accused of child molestation. Emotions in the case were heightened by the fact that a previously broadcast television documentary, *Living with Michael Jackson*, had included scenes in which Jackson had defended his practice of sharing his bed with children. During the period of the trial, journalists pored over every moment of witness testimony and cross-examination. Television "experts" opined on the practices and procedures of the court. Six months later, Jackson was acquitted of all ten counts. The Jackson case is an intriguing reminder of the ways in which courtroom participants negotiate versions of actions and events. In the court, accounts from witnesses of what they had seen and heard were exhaustively reanalyzed by both prosecuting and defense counsel during direct and cross-examination. These reformulations were brought into play again as closing speeches were made. The trial jurors were left to deliberate on the evidence in an atmosphere which one juror said "reeked of hatred."

As we have pointed out elsewhere in this text, it is important for the discursive researcher to keep in mind the occasioned nature of discursive constructions. Participants can produce a variety of formulations of events to suit the immediate discursive context by organizing descriptions in different ways. Participants may draw upon mobilizations of everyday knowledge or cultural understandings to achieve specific rhetorical effects. The upshot of this is that "unremarkable" aspects of discourse such as social categorizations have to be thought of as social accomplishments rather than as prelinguistic givens. Because of this, the analyst of courtroom discourse does not assume that talk will usefully be compartmentalized into **pre-analytic categories** such as "lawyers' accusations" or "witnesses' statements of fact." A lawyer's question or a witness's testimony may be shaped by the discursive contexts

in which it is given. And the situation is made more complex by the fact that what the witness and the lawyer say is often designed for an overhearing audience – the jury or the judge (Drew, 1985).

So what are the discursive processes which constitute legal interactions of this sort? One key element is the study of what happens before a citizen enters the courtroom: the police investigation. Once a trial is underway, the roles of the lawyer, the witness, and the judge all become important. Trial outcomes are determined in part through the way in which segments of questions and answers which make up **direct** and **cross-examination** are structured to fit local conversational goals such as persuasion or undermining. Another factor is the way in which counsel's closing arguments and the judge's summing-up present "packaged" versions of what has been said. Finally, there is the important question of how discursive processes play a role in the determination and effectiveness of trial outcomes. Jackson was acquitted, but many others are found guilty. What are the features of talk about legal penalties which determine the eventual outcome for the criminal?

Police Investigations

Legal processes do not begin at the courthouse steps. Before a criminal trial takes place, the police must carry out a process of investigation to establish whether a crime has taken place, to understand its nature, and to identify those responsible. Of course, part of the difficulty in police investigations is that criminals are often aware of the fact that they are under investigation. Mason (2004) has explored this phenomenon in a study of undercover surveillance recordings made of conversations between alleged members of the Colombian Cali drugs cartel. Mason points out that according to **Grice's maxims** (Grice, 1975), the norms of conversation

---

Pre-analytic categories Typologies produced by an analyst before the analysis has been performed

Direct examination The questioning of witnesses by the lawyer representing the party who has called the witness

Cross-examination The questioning of witnesses by the lawyer not representing the party who has called the witness

Grice's maxims A set of rules for cooperation in conversation described by Paul Grice

require that one try to be informative in talking with someone else. However, in a case where criminals suspect that their conversations may be overheard by the police, they may strive for concealment by making ambiguous or vague references to people and places. The tension between these two different conversational goals, Mason suggests, can lead to interactional problems such as difficulties in establishing referents, and these, in turn, can lead the participants to initiate conversational repairs.

1. SP1: Do you know something about the young
         guy?
2. SP2: About whom?
3. SP1: The young guy.
4. SP2: Yes from there where we were.
5. SP1: Yes.

(Mason, 2004, p. 1151)

The above extract nicely captures the problems which these alleged criminals face. On the one hand, SP1 wishes to refer to someone in gaining information from SP2. On the other hand, neither SP1 nor SP2 wish to use an obvious reference that would allow overhearing listeners to identify that person. In this case, the problem is resolved by SP1 through the repetition of the phrase "the young guy." This acts as a prompt to SP2 that he should utilize their shared knowledge to infer the identity of the person to whom SP1 refers. The success of SP1's strategy is signaled by SP2 at line 4, where he indicates that he now grasps the identifying term's referent.

Of course, police surveillance is not the only way in which the authorities are notified of crimes. In many cases, victims of crimes report directly to the police or other agencies themselves. Imbens-Bailey and McCabe (2000) examined this process in a study of emergency telephone calls to a police department in a North American town. Utilizing narrative analysis techniques, the authors identify a problematic tension in the caller's need to convey relevant information quickly and efficiently while at the same time adapting what they say to everyday norms of social interaction. In particular, Imbens-Bailey and McCabe suggest, callers tended to rely upon narrative conventions which required them to produce relatively dense descriptions of events, rather than merely to state a need for help

together with a location. However, the authors do note that, in comparison with everyday narratives, emergency calls to the police tended to use more abbreviated narratives. The interactional complexity of calls of this sort is also revealed by Hepburn (2005) in a study of the way that calls to a national children's helpline are dealt with. She points out that during such calls the question of whether the child's complaint will be referred to the police is determined, in part, by a complex process of interaction in which the children are faced with having to provide warrants and explanations that deal with their motivations in making the call.

One important aspect of the investigatory process is the interaction between police officers and their suspects once the police are in a position to confront their suspects with the evidence they have gathered. It is important to remember that such interactions are set within **formal contexts** which establish the rights and responsibilities of participants. Under certain circumstances police officers are formally empowered to detain civilians and ask a range of questions which would normally be considered inappropriate or impolite. Because they have this formal position, police officers also benefit from the informal conversational advantages of setting the conversational agenda and steering the conversation along topical paths which they wish to follow. Thornborrow has referred to this mixture of formal institutional role (e.g., police interrogator or suspect) and informal discursive role (e.g., question asker or answer giver) as a form of interaction in which what people do "is produced, overall, as a result of this interplay between their interactional and discursive role and their institutional identity and status" (Thornborrow, 2002, p. 5).

In a study of the warnings which police officers give to motorists during traffic stops, Ho Shon (2005) shows that the coercive power of the police is accomplished and negotiated in the mundane details of these interactions. He points out that interactions of this sort differ markedly from the "egalitarian" discourse found in everyday talk. In particular, threats and warnings

Formal contexts Scenes of interaction which are typified by rules of proceeding established by the relevant authority

produced by police officers in police–citizen interactions occur in situations where the practical relationship between the two participants is asymmetrical. Ho Shon points out that if a citizen denies a request made by a police officer, then this raises practical difficulties, such as physical coercion, which do not normally arise in everyday conversation when requests are rejected. However, as Ho Shon points out, even in these highly asymmetrical settings, where the police officer has a formally powerful position and is adopting a discursive footing of being a threat-maker, these interactions are co-constructed by both participants. This allows the police officer, for example, to attend to issues of impression management by accomplishing threats or warnings while at the same time undermining potential inferences of impoliteness.

Police interviews

One important aspect of police–citizen interactions is that they occur within formally and informally asymmetric relationships. Johnson (2006) has highlighted this aspect of police work in the distinction between processes of "interrogation," where the police officer relies upon power deriving from official status, and the "interview," in which the police officer is less accusatory and more enquiring. However, even the interview process is one in which the skilled police officer is able to exert influence on how the interaction progresses. For example, drawing in part upon narrative analysis, Johnson notes that the narratives which police interviewers generate during the questioning of suspects have "built-in" evaluations.

I I mean did he look the type that were going to cause trouble?

A Well, no but . . .

I 'Cause other people have said that he had the stool but he didn't have it above his head in a threatening manner, he were just holding the stool.

A He didn't, he'd, he'd lifted it up and that's why I jumped up and hit him before he had chance to swing it.

I Do you agree that, er, you could have just grabbed the stool and stopped him swinging it down?

A May be so. I don't know.

I You, you'd be younger and stronger than he was, do you accept that?

A Mhm, yeah.

I I mean it, I accept in the heat of the moment we do silly things, don't we?

A Mhm.

I But do you agree that, erm, looking back, you should've just grabbed hold of the stool and restrained the fellow, preventing him from hitting your brother?

A Yeah, now I do, but it's too late now, isn't it. It's already happened.

(Johnson, 2006, p. 9)

Here, the police officer and the suspect jointly produce a narrative of events which lead up to the suspect admitting hitting the victim. Woven in with this narrative is the police officer's evaluation of the victim's behavior as "silly" together with the formulation of a more desirable course of action ("you should've just grabbed hold"). In a similar fashion, Komter (2003) analyzed the sequential nature of a police interrogation and showed that, during questioning, the suspect is presented with two contrasting versions of events. One, attributed to her, is characterized as lacking an appropriate warrant while the alternative version proposed by the police officer is depicted as "logical." These formulations are then used to lead up to an invitation to the suspect to admit that she had been lying. This joint adoption of evaluative discourse is also seen in the study by Auburn, Drake, and Willig (1995) of the way in which police interviews rely on particular discourses such as discourses of "disorderly" violence versus "justificatory" violence.

Although these studies have emphasized the relatively powerful formal role of the police interviewer as someone who asks questions and determines topics and forms of discourse, it is important to note that the sequential unfolding of conversational turns of this sort is a site for the co-construction of interaction. Seen from this perspective, the suspect under questioning is not as "helpless" as a consideration of the formal and informal roles of the police officer might suggest. This has been by shown by Haworth (2006) in a fascinating study of police interviews with the British mass murderer Dr. Harold Shipman, who was eventually determined to have murdered an estimated 260 people. Employing a mixture of CA and CDA techniques,

Haworth explores the way in which Shipman is able to take an active part in the development of the interaction.

P: . . . there's one or two points we'd like to pick up
        [on from]
S: [errr] can I clarify something first.
P: yeah
S: I've had the chance to mull over the questioning this morning, (.) and perhaps I've made clear what ha– happened when Mrs (.) Grundy asked me to witness the will. . . .
                                    (Haworth, 2006, p. 745)

Haworth notes that in this example Shipman ("S") interrupts the police officer ("P") as he is about to introduce a new topic and, instead, inserts a topic of his own. This indicates that the formal power of the police officer to set the interview agenda is, in this one instance, limited by what actually occurs in interaction. Moreover, the normatively expected sequential structure of question–answer is, in this instance, disrupted by the way in which Shipman volunteers a new topic without waiting for a relevant question. Haworth notes that in part this is accomplished within the conversation by Shipman orienting to what he is saying as though it *is* a breach of such normative expectations in that he issues a "request to speak" by asking whether he can "clarify something first."

Police calls

This kind of delicate negotiation between officer and citizen can be seen in other types of setting in which the two interact. Tracy and her colleagues (Tracy & Agne, 2002; Tracy & Anderson, 1999) have examined citizen calls to the police in which close relatives of the citizen are the focus of the complaint. There are some similarities and some differences between this type of interaction and the police interview. In the police call setting, as in the interview setting, police officers are expected to ask questions and the citizen callers are expected to provide information. However, calls to the police, unlike police interviews, are initiated by the citizen, and usually will incorporate some form of request. In these police–citizen calls Tracy has noted the way in

which both police officers and citizens are required to deal with a number of **interactional troubles**. On the one hand, the officer must identify the nature of the call and establish whether the police can help with the complaint. If not, the officer must negotiate the resultant request refusal in a context-sensitive manner. On the other hand the citizen, through the act of calling the police, makes inferable a range of identity-relevant implications about himself which are negative in character, such as being the kind of person whose relatives get into trouble with the police. So although such scenarios differ in some respects from interview settings, it can be seen that calls to the police, like police interviews, display an apparent asymmetry in formal power invested in the police officer and the citizen. But at the same time police calls, like interviews, display a more equal balance in terms of the actual conversational normative expectations which both parties face.

Lawyers in the Courtroom

Once the police have carried out their duties, the suspect may end up having to answer to his or her alleged crimes in court. Even apart from understandable concerns about crime and punishment, the ordinary citizen is liable to find a courtroom encounter a strange and even disconcerting experience. Just as interactions between police officers and suspects have formally circumscribed rules, so talk within a formal courtroom setting is quite different from the everyday communication with which the average citizen is familiar. In a courtroom, witnesses and defendants are placed in the position of answering questions over which they have no influence, and lawyers will often have a prearranged agenda of questions which witnesses must answer. Moreover, there is a formally established asymmetry between witnesses and lawyers. Legal procedures ensure that witnesses and defendants are not free, for example, to demand answers to questions which they may pose to the lawyers. On the other hand,

Interactional troubles Elements of an episode of talk in which participants orient to what is being said as though it is problematic

CLASSIC STUDY: Order in court

In this study, *Order in court: The organization of verbal interaction in judicial settings*, Atkinson and Drew begin by arguing that previous sociological studies of the courtroom have not appropriately considered the interactional detail of the court proceedings. In remedying this, they draw attention to the way that normal features of everyday conversation are constrained by court settings. For example, turn-taking, and the types of turn which are permissible, are determined by court procedures in a fashion which is quite different from normal talk, with a greater emphasis on adjacency pairs such as question and answer and accusation and rebuttal. They also note that one aspect of courtroom proceedings is their relative formality, which arises partly from the multiparty nature of the court. Thus turns such as "Be upstanding in court," for example, are introduced into

proceedings in order to formally establish opening sequences in the commencement of a hearing. The authors present analyses of the proceedings of a coroner's court and of the interactions that took place during a tribunal which was instigated by the British government. The Scarman Tribunal had been convened to examine riots which took place in 1969 in Northern Ireland. The analyses show that the questioning which arose was used to accomplish a variety of interactional goals, such as the imputation of blame or the construction of shared versions of actions and events. The book explores the ways in which accusations are managed and justifications and excuses produced under cross-examination.

Atkinson, J. M. & Drew, P. (1979). *Order in court: The organization of verbal interaction in judicial settings*. London: Macmillan.

whether the witness or defendant answers a lawyer's questions, and the relevance of those answers, is taken to be assured by the formal power which the courtroom context invests in both lawyers and the judge. In addition, unlike everyday conversations, witnesses and defendants are formally treated as having little or no control over the initiation of new discursive topics and the closure of existing topics. All of these formal aspects of legal proceedings are designed to allow the courtroom professionals to have a controlling interest in what is said in testimony.

The role of the lawyer in cross-examination

One important element of the courtroom process is the evidential part of a trial in which witnesses and defendants say what happened. This trial phase is often crucial in determining the trial outcome. In many instances, due to the adversarial nature of trial proceedings, witnesses and lawyers are concerned to achieve strategic goals in the presentation of their cases. The most obvious examples of this are those occasions where a lawyer is questioning a witness in cross-examination in

order to discredit that witness's **testimony**. In these cases, the lawyer may seek to damage the witness's credibility in front of the judge or jury by raising questions about the witness's truthfulness or by seeking to attribute other unflattering or morally dubious properties to the witness or to the witness's testimony. In addition, the cross-examining lawyer will seek to make relevant those elements of the case which are most damaging to the witness's testimony and will carefully design descriptions of those elements to enable the jury or judge to draw inferences which support the lawyer's position.

In emphasizing the nature of courtroom interactions as a site of adversarial discursive negotiation, one strand of research on the discourse of witness testimony has revealed the way in which what witnesses say is *controlled* by the context of the courtroom (Danet, Hoffman, Kermish, Rahn, & Stayman, 1980). And given the formal constraints on how witnesses may contribute to

Testimony A statement which a witness provides and affirms to be true (e.g., by swearing an oath)

proceedings, it is hardly surprising that cross-examination allows the lawyer some useful advantages. For example, Ehrlich (2001, 2002) examined the way in which lawyers manage the construction of actions and events in a Canadian criminal trial in which the defendant was accused of sexual assault on one of the witnesses, Connie. In the extract presented below, Connie has been describing to the defendant's counsel, during cross-examination, how the defendant lay on top of her.

SC: Right. Did you try to push him off?

CD: Yes, I did.

SC: You weren't able to?

CD: No, I wasn't.

SC: Is that because you weren't able to get your arms free or because he was on top of you?

CD: I couldn't get my arms free and I couldn't push him off.

SC: At one point you were naked?

CD: Yes.

SC: At what point was that?

CD: I can't even pinpoint a specific time.

SC: *Well, your shirt came off first as a result of the fondling of your breasts, right?*

CD: Yes.

SC: *And your arms still in the same position above your head and crossed over and being held by one hand?*

CD: Yes. I am not sure at what point exactly he let go of them.

(Ehrlich, 2002, p. 740)

Ehrlich notes that the lawyer offers a reformulation of the witness's description of events in which the defendant's agency is diminished. The witness has described trying unsuccessfully to push the defendant off. However, in the italicized turns, the lawyer can be seen to offer a reformulation in which the defendant's actions are made less relevant. The lawyer states "your shirt came off" and describes contact between the defendant and witness as "the fondling" rather than using an alternative, more action-oriented construction such as "the defendant fondling you." Similarly, "your arms still in the same position above your head and crossed over" is less indicative of action than a formulation such as "he held your arms above your head" and the only indication of action, "being held by one hand," is a passive construction which refers to a disembodied hand rather than to the defendant himself.

In another study, Matoesian (2001, 2005) looked at court transcripts from the trial of the late President John F. Kennedy's nephew, William Smith, in 1991. Matoesian points out that trial discourse typified by cross-examination can be thought of as oppositional talk between adversaries in which both parties are engaged in negotiating what is to count as "truth." One of the significant elements of this process is what Matoesian refers to as "nailing down" (ND) an answer. This is an interactive process which:

> represents a sequential and embodied struggle of identity, implicated forms of participation and power strategically forged in a constellation of legal linguistic ideologies (ideas about legal language and discourse) and legal epistemologies (constitution of legally relevant forms of knowledge), cultural practices unfolding incrementally, contingently and interactively over a lengthy exchange between defense attorney and witness in cross-examination.
>
> (Matoesian, 2005, p. 735)

As an example of ND, Matoesian reproduces a fragment of cross-examination testimony in which the defense council (RB) asks a witness (AM) about whether she had had discussions with the alleged victim (Patty) about whether and when AM could sell her story to the media.

051 RB: Well you and Patty had a conversation, didn't you? Your friend Patty.

052   (2.6)

053 AM: We might have talked about it yes

054   (.)

055 RB: Well

056   [

057 AM: But that doesn't mean that we collaborating.

058   (.)

059 RB: Let's– *hold it* (.) you say "we *might* have talked." *Isn't* it a *fact* that you

060   *did* talk?

061   (3.0)

062 AM: Probably yes.

063   (.)

064 RB: Well– (.) Not *probably*. Isn't it *true* that you and Miss Bowman *talked*

065   about *you giving a statement.*

066   (2.3)

067 AM: Yes

(Matoesian, 2005, pp. 747–748)

Matoesian points out that RB's use at line 51 of "Patty" is designed to make relevant a relational identity between the witness and the alleged victim which is emphasized by RB's use of the relatively informal "Patty" in comparison with alternative available forms of identification such as "Patricia" or "the complainant." At line 59, RB then pursues the **epistemological stance** which AM has produced at line 53, where her "yes" was qualified with the phrase "We might have." Matoesian here points out RB's use of the implicit contrast between the epistemic "might" used by AM and the emphatic "did" and also draws attention to the way that this is upgraded through RB's use of the phrase "*Isn't* it a *fact.* . . ." This allows RB to introduce a distinction between a possible state of affairs and the facts of the matter. Matoesian suggests that this is an indication of the way in which RB accomplishes a local conversational goal by making AM's "might" formulation the relevant part of her conversational turns rather than the denial of collaboration. Although AM tries to reintroduce a modal operator indicating possibility through the use of "probably," she eventually agrees with RB's negative reformulation.

The role of the lawyer in direct examination

The preceding examples illustrate the way in which lawyers accomplish rhetorical effects during hostile interrogation by the use of varied discursive strategies and by making use of their formally privileged position which enables them to ask questions and reformulate answers. However, the issue of control extends beyond the courtroom drama of a lawyer interrogating a hostile witness. Trials usually involve the presentation of a series of witnesses, and at certain points in a trial a witness may be questioned by the lawyer representing the party who has called that witness to give evidence. This is referred to as the direct examination or evidence-in-chief portion of the trial. However, even in cases where a lawyer accepts the evidence given in testimony,

his or her control over what the witness says is still a vital part of the trial process. Harris (2001) has examined this process in a study of the testimony given in the trial of a famous ex-sportsman, O. J. Simpson, who was accused of murdering his wife (Cotterill, 2003). In the following extract, the prosecuting council is questioning a police witness.

Q: What did you say to Mr Simpson
A: I told him who I was – I was Detective Ron Philips of the Los Angeles Police Department and that I had some bad news for him – and he said something about what's that – and I said I got some bad news – your ex-wife Nicole Simpson had been killed
Q: What happened next
A: He – I think the first words out of his mouth were something to the effect – oh my God Nicole is killed – my God she's dead – and then he got very upset on the telephone
Q: And then what happened
A: I kept trying to calm him down – and he continued to be upset – and I finally said Mr Simpson please try and get a hold of yourself – I have your children at the West Los Angeles police station and I need to talk to you about that – and he stopped and he said what do your mean you have my children at the police station – why are my kids at the police station and I said because we had no place else to take 'em – they're there for safe-keeping – I need to know what to do with your children – and at that time he said well I'm going to be leaving out of Chicago and the first available flight – I'll come back to Los Angeles is Arnell there – I said yes she is – and he said let me talk to Arnell – and I gave the phone back to Arnell
Q: Did Mr Simpson ask you how she was killed
A: No
Q: Did he ask you when she was killed
A: No
Q: Did she – did he ask you if you had any idea who had done it
A: No
Q: Did he ask you where it had occurred
A: No
Q: Did he ask you anything about the circumstances about how his ex-wife had been killed
A: No

(Harris, 2001, p. 67)

Epistemological stance A perspective on what is said which makes relevant a mental state such as "doubt" or "belief"

In this example, the lawyer may be taken to be working in a collaborative fashion with the witness, in that his task is not to cross-examine what he says but merely to elicit the witness's account. However, the lawyer still exerts control over the nature of the testimony provided. Drawing on a modified version of Labov's work on the analysis of narratives (Labov, 1972), Harris describes the first part of this extract as a "core narrative." Narratives recapitulate prior events, often in a temporally ordered fashion. From the start of the extract, up to his description of handing the telephone back to Arnell, the police officer provides a set of descriptive statements couched in the past tense which function as a non-evaluative account of the actions and events that arose during the telephone call. Following this, the prosecutor then formulates a series of questions which, says Harris, are designed to provide an implicit evaluative context in which the "point" of the description offered within the narrative is made clear. The effect of the prosecutor's repetitive questions, according to Harris, is to make hearable to the jury the **implicature** that Simpson might reasonably have been expected to show some interest in the circumstances under which his wife was killed.

Although the preceding description has emphasized the way in which lawyers deliberately control witnesses, it is important to remember that the influence of the courtroom context on witness testimony can also arise in more subtle ways. In a study of Australian Aboriginal witnesses, Eades (2000) examined episodes of questioning during the examination-in-chief portion of a trial. Although examination-in-chief is a process in which lawyer and witness might be taken to be cooperating in presentation of the evidence, Eades revealed that lawyers and judges used a variety of means to prevent Aboriginal witnesses from "telling their story," including interruptions, **metalinguistic** comments such as "that is not an answer," and preventing witnesses from talking about Aboriginal culture in explanation.

So even though this was not a context in which clever lawyers strategically sought to manipulate what was said in testimony, Eades demonstrated that the witnesses in her study were still constrained in the presentation of their evidence. This indicates that one of the difficulties which witnesses face in court is that witnesses and legal experts may have differing understandings of what courtroom discourse is. Barton (2004) has referred to this phenomenon as the discursive construction of legal consciousness. Lay constructions of legal interactions emphasize the importance of social entitlement and so lay witnesses rely upon discourses in which the particular details of their social lives are foregrounded, whereas expert legal discourse relies upon an asocial, rule-based understanding of the law. For Eades's Aboriginal witnesses, then, there is a clash between the way they try to develop their own accounts in evidence and the way in which the officers of the court orient to what they are saying, and the consequence of this is what Eades refers to as "silencing" the witness.

In a similar vein, Englund (2004) has examined whether the rights of courtroom participants are preserved by formal frameworks. He points out that, from the discursive perspective, rights talk is a specific form of institutionalized discourse. Somewhat surprisingly, his study of clients in a legal aid clinic demonstrates that this institutional framework can sometimes work against their interests. The legalistic orientations of the legal advisors' discourse and the detailed narratives of the clients represent what Englund refers to as a "contest of contexts." In part, this contest involves clients resisting the legal advisors' attempts to frame their complaints within legal discourse. This resistance takes a variety of forms such as trying to avoid the abstract, decontextualized form of talk that the advisors adopt through the use of idiomatic forms of talk.

Witnesses in the Courtroom

Witness testimony

There is, then, evidence to suggest that the formal structure of the courtroom offers lawyers a degree of control over what is said by witnesses and how what is said is to be taken by judge and

Implicature The inferences which an utterance makes available

Metalinguistic Talk which refers to the discursive properties of other talk

jury. However, in a study of the trial of an eminent Italian businessman who was accused of illegal financing of political parties in Italy, Gnisci and Pontecorvo (2004) argue that actual interactions between witnesses and lawyers are more "emergent" than this formal distribution of rights and entitlements might suggest. Both lawyers and witnesses rely upon a set of linguistic resources which are employed to achieve particular pragmatic purposes. And so interrogation of a witness by a lawyer can more accurately be thought of as a process of co-construction of facts. Gnisci and Pontecorvo point out that witnesses and lawyers deploy different strategies in these dynamic interactions. Lawyers, for example, ask questions which are designed to control the features of the subsequently produced answer. Witnesses, on the other hand, utilize elaborations which are designed to accomplish effects such as the minimization of blame. Gnisci and Pontecorvo draw out the ways in which participants craft their interactional turns so that they are hearable as contextually relevant. In addition, outright dispute is often avoided in favor of alternative constructions of facts which, though dissimilar, are not contradictory. Thus witnesses, in presenting an alternative construction of actions or events, may focus their replies on a peripheral topic raised during the preceding question. In this way, they are able to present elaborated responses which fit their own pragmatic ends while respecting the formal requirement to provide a relevant answer to the question posed.

This suggests that witnesses, in response to hostile questioning or difficult interactional circumstances, may adopt discursive strategies of their own. They may construct alternative versions of the actions and events which are made relevant in the questions or otherwise seek to manage the potentially damaging attributions and inferences arising out of a lawyer's questioning. They may also align specific identities to meet local conversational goals. For example, in the following extract, the witness attempts to deal with the consequences of a common courtroom construction of witnesses as individuals who must know what happened, because they were present at the time of the relevant actions and events.

NIELDS: Did you suggest to the Attorney General that maybe the diversion memorandum and the fact that there was a diversion need not ever come out?

NORTH: Again, I don't recall that specific conversation at all, but I am not saying that it didn't happen.

NIELDS: You don't deny it?

NORTH: No.

NIELDS: You don't deny suggesting to the Attorney General of the United States that he just figure out a way of keeping this diversion document secret?

NORTH: I don't deny that I said it. I'm not saying I remember it either.

(North & Schorr, 1987)

The above extract is taken from the testimony of Lieutenant Colonel Oliver North to the Select Committee of House and Senate hearings on the Iran–Contra affair. This was a political scandal in which North was accused of illegally selling arms to Iran in order to fund the Contras in their fight against the Sandinista government in Nicaragua. Lynch and Bogen (2005) argue that this is a good example of a witness who makes himself "practically unavailable" through the use of constructions such as "I don't remember." Replies such as this neither confirm nor deny the facts or events which are at issue. What this shows is that questions about whether **eyewitness testimony** is, for example, accurate or inaccurate often underestimate the complexities of giving evidence. Instead, testimony of this sort is seen to be an arena in which the discursive practices of lawyer and witness are crucial in determining the outcome of a trial.

Another possible formulation which witnesses may adopt under hostile questioning is what might be termed "doing being vague." Janney (2002) argues that vagueness is not necessarily an identifiable property of a single interactional turn within a courtroom exchange considered in isolation. Instead, the vagueness of what is said is often only specifiable by considering a particular turn in relation to its immediate interactional context. In a study of the O. J. Simpson trial, Janney points to the ways in which Simpson,

> **Eyewitness testimony** Testimony provided by someone who was present at the time and place relevant to the events which are under consideration

under hostile questioning, relied on a number of strategies in formulating answers to questions.

> P: So you didn't leave that hotel room with those blue pants on, right?
> S: I don't think so.
> P: And those blue pants had blood on them, right?
> S: Whatever. Whatever. [...] My memory is that I changed before I left the hotel [...]
> P: Where are the gloves you're wearing in the photograph? [...]
> S: I don't know where any of my gloves are.
> (Janney, 2002, p. 468)

Janney suggests that what examples such as these reveal is the way in which witnesses craft their responses to questions in order to achieve a specific rhetorical effect. But this effect, of evading potential blame by being vague, is only understandable by locating the witness's response within the sequence in which it appeared. For example, if a question contained a specific noun, such as "blood," Simpson's reply might contain an indefinite pronoun such as "whatever," which counts as being vague because it ignores the specificity of the question raised in the prior element of the interactional sequence. If a question contained a definite article, such as "the," Simpson's answer might contain an indefinite quantifier such as "any," which is a vague response precisely because it references not just the gloves the questioner has asked about in the preceding turn but all of the gloves which Simpson owns.

The "expert" witness

Although the "normal" witness clearly has discursive resources at hand in order to manage interactions within the courtroom, another means by which witnesses may gain control of their own testimony is when they are treated by participants as "expert" scientific witnesses. By definition, these witnesses present testimony to the court which is "privileged" in that it deals with

> **Expert witness** A witness whose testimony is produced on the basis of his or her skills or knowledge

matters about which the witness is positioned as having knowledge and understanding that may not be available to others, including the lawyers who are questioning the witness. Stygall (2001) has argued, from a CDA perspective, that this represents the intersection of two different forms of "discourse of elites": the legal and the scientific. In explicating how these two different discourses are represented within the courtroom, Stygall draws out two features of expert testimony which differ from the testimony of a "lay" witness. One element is the way in which such witnesses use the contrastive marker "well" in order to identify that the question asked by a lawyer is in some way insufficient. Thus, expert witnesses, unlike lay witnesses, are positioned as being able to undermine questions which lawyers may ask during direct examination or cross-examination. Moreover, expert witnesses can be seen to make regular use of the marker "so" in order to make relevant issues to do with professional procedures and practices. This allows expert witnesses to introduce conclusions into their statements in a way which it is difficult for lay witnesses to manage.

Matoesian (1999) has also examined this clash between the adversarial nature of legal discourse in which lawyers seek to advocate their own case and what Matoesian describes as the "objective practices of science." He argues that when expert witnesses present conclusions in their evidence, this raises potential interactional difficulties for the lawyer who wishes to present the client's strongest case while preventing witnesses from introducing evidence which is potentially damaging to the client. Matoesian examines an example of this sort of interaction which occurred during the trial of a physician who was accused of second-degree sexual battery. An important aspect of the evidence was whether the alleged victim had suffered from a rib contusion. Matoesian notes how the doctor produces his evidence in a way which relies upon footing shifts:

> 095 ML: (OK) and Doctor Prostko stated in her medical
> 096   opinion (1.5) she observed a <u>rib contusion</u>
> 097   on (Patty Bowman) on March thirtieth,
> 098   Nineteen Ninety-One (0.7) What is your
> 099   explanation of <u>HOW SHE SUSTAINED THAT INJURY?</u>
> 100   (4.4)

101 WS: Doctor Prostko (1.0) eh– eh– you're asking me
102   my explanation. As I said (0.2) all I can tell you
103   is what happened that night.
104   (0.5)
105 ML: OK
106   [[
107 WS: Now– (0.5) Doctor Prostko testified (1.0) that
108   she had a rib contusion (1.0) I also recall (1.7)
109   that early (.) on (0.8) before charges were filed (1.9)
110   before my name was even released I believe (1.6) that
111   there were some medical reports (1.6) released from
112   that hospital (1.6) which indicated (1.2) that Patty
113   Bowman had a broken rib
114   (1.5)
115 ML: Well
116   [[
117 WS: I HAVE heard (0.5) two people testify (1.0) that she
118   did not have a broken rib (1.0) I also heard (1.2)
119   her own orthopaedic surgeon (1.0) testify (1.3) that she
120   had (0.6) bilateral tenderness (1.5) If Patty Bowman
121   had a rib contusion (0.9) on March thirtieth I would
122   expect that finding (0.4) to be noted by her orthopaedic
123   surgeon one week later (0.7) A rib contusion does
124   not become bilateral rib tenderness in one week.
                        (Matoesian, 1999, pp. 499–500)

Matoesian argues that the prosecutor's utterance at lines 95 to 99 could have been taken by the witness as an implicit accusation. However, WS begins his response with a metalinguistic description of what the prosecutor has just said which formulates the prosecutor's turn as a request for information ("you're asking me my explanation"). This produces an interactional context in which WS can produce an expert formulation of the alleged victim's medical status which is hearable as responsive, relevant, and on-topic. So on the one hand, the witness is able to produce a denial of responsibility through a defendant footing which emphasizes his localized knowledge of what happened at that particular time ("all I can tell you is what happened that night"). But subsequently, the witness is able to manipulate his participant footing in a second way by drawing upon the quite different footing of medical expert. At line 107, WS begins his utterance with the discourse marker "now," which Matoesian identifies as functioning to indicate that the preceding and following utterances are different parts of his discourse and to register the speaker's stance towards the information being presented. In other words, he is laying the groundwork for a footing shift. Matoesian then describes how WS "animates and authors" diagnoses of "that hospital," "two people," and "her own orthopaedic surgeon." The sequential nature of this account allows WS to construct a dynamic interplay of competing medical voices through which a variety of competing diagnoses are made relevant. Matoesian argues that this has the rhetorical effect of potentially undermining the diagnosis of Dr. Prostko. Moreover, WS's emphasis on the status of the alleged victim's own orthopaedic surgeon as a surgical expert, and as the alleged victim's *own* surgical expert, provides that diagnosis with what Matoesian describes as "epistemological superiority." By organizing his turn in this way, WS is able then to shift footing in an unremarkable way to defendant-as-expert in providing the expert conclusion "A rib contusion does not become bilateral rib tenderness in one week." Matoesian concludes that this sequential organization of footing allows the witness both to deny the accusation from the perspective of someone who was there and to offer an alternative explanation for evidence about the alleged victim's injuries based on medical expertise.

The Role of the Judge

So far, we have looked at the way in which lawyers and witnesses have engaged in discursive strategies in the presentation of evidence to the court. However, courts involve interactions beyond those in which lawyers interrogate witnesses. For example, in some legal or pseudo-legal

CLASSIC STUDY: Reproducing rape: Domination through talk in the courtroom

In this text, Matoesian uses conversation analytic techniques to show how cross-examination within the courtroom recasts the violence of rape within the context of everyday consensual sex. He begins by presenting evidence on the prevalence of rape and then considers a number of potential explanatory models such as psychopathological and feminist accounts. He argues that each in turn has problematic aspects. For example, he suggests that feminist accounts of women as victims may in fact obscure the ways in which language in the courtroom works against women. After presenting several chapters on the techniques and theoretical concerns of conversation analysis, he turns to a consideration of how conversation analysis can be applied to the courtroom. In his main empirical chapter, he draws on thousands of pages of court transcriptions from three separate rape trials. He uses this material to explore the way that courtroom talk, especially cross-examination, reproduces ideologies of rape as a sexual activity. One example of this is the way in which courtroom lawyers use discursive techniques to combat witnesses' accounts. The format of question and answer within the courtroom allows the lawyer to ask "loaded" questions. As we have seen in this chapter, witnesses have a number of resources at their disposal to challenge the underlying assumptions embedded in such questions. But Matoesian points out that lawyers in their turn are able to rely upon the formulaic nature of courtroom enquiry to overcome these attempts. The outcome of these interactions is that the courtroom becomes a context in which patriarchal ideologies are used as framing devices in making sense of what witnesses say. From this perspective, for example, it becomes questionable whether it makes sense to consider men and women ever being together for purely platonic reasons rather than for purposes associated with sexual motivations. Towards the end of the book, Matoesian broadens his consideration of power relations within the courtroom to examine the ways in which fine-grain conversation analyses might intersect with broader forms of analysis such as Giddens's theory of structuration.

Matoesian, G. M. (1993). *Reproducing rape: Domination through talk in the courtroom*. Chicago: University of Chicago Press.

settings those who perform the role of judge may take part in direct questioning of witnesses. Ehrlich (1998, 1999) examined this process in a study of the workings of a university disciplinary tribunal dealing with a sexual harassment case in which a male student faced complaints of "date rape" from two female students. Ehrlich argues that members of the tribunal constructed a "model" of communicative interaction in which the women were positioned as being deficient in their ability to signal non-consent to the accused. In her later paper, Ehrlich looks in particular at the way in which two of the tribunal members, who were responsible for determining the outcome of the case, reconstruct the events in question as consensual sex by adopting an interpretative frame which minimizes the complainants' resistance against the advances of the accused. Ehrlich emphasizes what she describes as the "ideological work" that is accomplished by the questions of the tribunal members.

> BW: Could you explain that? Because we've heard that twice and in your story the only time you mention about being scared of Matt was with the eavesdropping incident . . . that he was very scary. He was insisting that you tell him. Were there other things that he did or is it a general demeanor? What do you mean by he's very scary?
>
> MK: He's . . . the way he . . . it seems to me if his way . . . it's either his way or no way. The

way he was talking to Bob like even his friend Bob when I asked Bob to come to the bathroom, Matt said "No, don't go." And Bob hesitated not to go which sort of led me to believe that Bob was scared of Matt and maybe Bob knows a history of [Matt

BW: [Well, let's just stick to what you know. The two times in that evening that you found Matt scary would be the eavesdropping incident and with Bob . . . how insistent he was about Bob. You saw a side of him that scared you. Anything else than those two things?

MK: No.

(Ehrlich, 1999, p. 246)

Ehrlich argues that in this extract, the tribunal member can be seen to attempt to isolate specific instances of behavior that the accused produced which counted as threatening. By drawing out a relative paucity of specific features in this way, the tribunal member is, Ehrlich argues, thereby minimizing the extent to which the complainant was actually in a state of fear, which is an inference made available by the complainant's description of the accused as "very scary."

Of course, one of the primary functions of the judge within the courtroom is to come to a judgment in the case if the trial does not involve a jury. In looking at how judgments of guilt and innocence arise in court, MacMartin (2002; MacMartin & Wood, 2005) has studied judges' discourse in the context of child sex abuse cases that were presented in Canadian criminal courts. One of the features of such cases is that the issue of whether a crime took place can sometimes hinge on the nature of the social interactions between the alleged victim and the accused after the point in time at which the alleged crime took place. If sexual abuse took place, the defense lawyer's argument runs, then one would expect the victim to avoid all subsequent social contact with the perpetrator. MacMartin suggests that this rhetorical contrast between a child's negative reception of sexual advances and subsequent neutral or positive engagement in social interaction with the perpetrator can be deployed as a warrant or ground for raising doubt that the crime took place at all. MacMartin analyzes how the judges in these cases describe the relevant events and then provide reasons for the decision to

acquit or convict. She notes that the judges' descriptions make available inferences about what the child complainants could reasonably be expected to have done within the circumstances. For example, the judgments which MacMartin examined used extreme case formulations (Pomerantz, 1986) in depicting the relevant actions and events. MacMartin notes that extreme case formulations are sometimes deployed to rhetorically strengthen the claim being made, but, in other cases, are used to create an account which is susceptible to irony or doubt. As an example of this latter sort of extreme formulation, MacMartin demonstrated that sometimes judges formulated descriptions in an extreme way in order to make available the inference that, had the form of abuse been as extreme as the description suggested, then the victim could not reasonably have been expected to continue social contact with the alleged abuser. Since other evidence suggested that such contact did persist, the judge therefore draws upon this apparent contradiction as a warrant for an acquittal.

Not all judgments that arise in court are based on a trial process. Plea bargaining is an alternative to trial procedures in which a defendant agrees to plead guilty in order to receive concessions on the penalties imposed. In an interesting study of plea bargaining by Lee (2005), he points out that the judge's role in this process is equivocal. On the one hand, the judge will be interested in maximizing the efficiency of courtroom processes while, on the other, he or she must maintain a stance of impartiality. In a study of misdemeanor cases in a Californian court, Lee shows that the judge both facilitates the bargaining process between prosecuting and defending lawyers and moves the parties towards a resolution. In addition, the judge also displays what Lee refers to as "stance." For example, in one case, the judge indexes a sympathetic attitude towards the defendant during the process of identifying him to the court. He indexes this sympathetic attitude by providing characterizations of him as pitiable and as someone who has already had to spend a long time in court that day in order to have his case tried. Lee notes that this sympathetic characterization of the defendant is then referenced by both the public defender and the district attorney. At a number of points throughout the bargaining process the judge's characterization of the defendant is picked up by the public defender while the district attorney attempts to disaffiliate himself from it. Lee argues that the judge is thereby able to accomplish two tasks. He promotes the efficiency of the courtroom by guiding defense and prosecution lawyers in the way they should approach the plea bargain. But at the same time, he maintains a position of neutrality by embedding what he says within a formal identification of the defendant as the defendant, which of course is an unexceptional action for the judge of a courtroom to engage in.

It is interesting to note that just as the requirements of impartiality and efficient disposal of a case can leave judges in an equivocal position during the plea bargaining process, so others who perform a similar function face a similar difficulty. Garcia (2000) has outlined the equivocal status of mediators within the quasi-legal setting of mediation hearings. In these contexts the mediator, like the judge, must appear impartial. However, in order to present possible resolutions of the difficulties under mediation, the mediator may be required to adopt a position that is in conflict with one or even both of the parties to the mediation (Conley & O'Barr, 1998). Garcia notes that when a mediator solicits a suggestion for resolving the conflict from the disputants, this is sometimes performed in an open fashion. He suggests that these open solicits are similar to general **topic initial elicitors** such as "What do you know?" or "Anything else to report" of the sort described by Button and Casey (1984). However, other forms of solicit are more focused in that they embed some form of specific suggestion which may be at odds with the position that one or other disputant has established. So, for example, if a mediator solicits from one disputant what it might cost to purchase an item under dispute, that question carries with it the implication that purchase of the item is a potential resolution of the problem.

Treatment of Offenders

If legal processes do not begin at the courthouse steps, nor do they end as the convict is led out of the courtroom. Just as courtroom processes are preceded by a prior investigatory phase, they in turn may precede an outcome phase, if the defendant is found guilty. In this outcome phase of the legal process, the guilty person undergoes punishment, or rehabilitation, or some combination of the two. Here too, discursive researchers have shown that the way talk is accomplished by participants has a crucial role in determining the nature of relevant social interactions and their outcomes. Rehabilitation requires effort on the part of the guilty person, and one element of this effort is coming to accept that the crimes committed were wrong. But O'Connor (2000) has pointed to the ways in which prisoners, when describing their crimes, often attempt to diminish the agency of their accounts through the use of **passive constructions** such as "I caught that charge" instead of more active constructions such as "I committed that robbery." A clear example of this process is demonstrated by Auburn and Lea (Auburn, 2005; Auburn & Lea, 2003), who looked at one particular type of punishment outcome in which offenders were required to attend a sex offender treatment program. At one point in the treatment offenders were required to provide an account of the offense they had committed. Auburn and Lea show how offenders produced these accounts in a manner that both emphasized the way such offenses followed on from everyday concerns and offered some mitigation. In his later study, Auburn shows how the offenders make use of narrative **reflexivity** to manage normative inferences by providing hearers with counter-inferences.

```
1   Off °twennyone twentytwo° (1.4)
2        >↑no she wasn't< she was nineteen (1.3)
3        >yeh she was nineteen=
4        =cuz I was twentyone<
5        (3.2)
6        a::nd (1.3) I 'ad this ↑jacket on (0.3)
7        and I said to 'er=
8        =I said (0.3)
9        she said what do you want now,=
10       =I said ↑well (0.2) don't know
```

Passive construction Talk which uses features such as the grammatical passive voice in order to counter potential attributions of agency to the speaker

Reflexivity Discourse which is designed to make relevant properties of the discourse itself

11   I said uh (0.3) lets do it shall we=
12   =and she said well ↑yeah: OK (0.5)
13   and I– (0.2)
14   she was petrified
15   I know that now↓ (0.8)
16   and I took my jacket off (0.2)
17   and laid it down (0.4) for her (1.2) to ↑lie
      on↓
18   (2.3)
19   >it's important to say that cuz the jacket
      comes
20   into it in a moment<
21   (0.4) a:nd she got on the ↑jacket

                              (Auburn, 2005, p. 708)

Auburn points out that the narrative seems to imply that this was an interaction between two equally willing partners. However, in the context of a sex offender treatment program, the offender is meant to be describing a coercive assault. He orients to this through his depiction of his victim's mental state as one of "being petrified." Of course, this makes available to hearers the inference that the offender coerced a terrified person into sex. He deals with this through his reflexive comment "I know that now↓." Auburn argues that this helps the offender to display a level of awareness of the victim's state of mind which is normatively required within the current context. Moreover, by indexing this knowledge to the present moment, the offender is also able to mitigate in that he makes available the inference that although he knows this now, he did not know that then.

This sort of subtle conversational work gives some indication of the difficulties which rehabilitation programs face. Many contemporary approaches to rehabilitation have focused on correcting "cognitive deficiencies" in prisoners, but Mayr (2003) has argued from a CA and CDA perspective that these approaches rely upon a range of ideological assumptions which mean that such programs tend to be seen by prisoners as coercive. Mayr suggests that these ideological assumptions, manifested through such structural processes as turn-taking and topic control, are embedded within interactions which take place between prison officers and offenders during therapeutic sessions. Mayr points out that prisoners display awareness of, and resistance to, these interactional phenomena. This suggests that not only do prisoners have discursive resources to introduce mitigation

into their descriptions of what they have done, but that they also engage in discursive resistance against attempts to introduce alternative discursive frameworks which set their actions in a more blameworthy evaluative dimension.

However, O'Connor (2000) has, on a more positive note, identified the ways in which prisoners who give accounts of their criminal actions often embed what she describes as "frame breaks" into their narratives. She points out that these constitute interactional moments in which the speaker indicates a readiness to think more deeply about what he has done and the consequences of his actions. Similarly, in a study of the life narratives of prisoners, McKendy (2006) points to the fact that some of the prisoners found the process of reproducing their life narratives to be an enjoyable experience. He also points to the way in which the production of these life narratives offered the prisoners a chance to rethink their own actions and the events which made up their histories. The suggestion is that this is a locus for prisoners to develop new understandings of their behavior as a first step towards changing their lives in the future.

In Conclusion

This chapter has shown that discursive practices within legal settings play an important role in determining the nature of interactions between the citizen and the officers of the state. Police officers, lawyers, judges, and prisoner treatment officials all, in some respects, occupy positions which can be characterized as formally powerful. The citizen's interactions with people who occupy these roles are normatively constrained by the legal rights and entitlements which are bound up with such roles. There is, therefore, seemingly an asymmetry between the requirement that the citizen respond appropriately in such interactions and the entitlements of police officers and lawyers to set the agenda by asking questions, choosing conversational topics, and producing evaluative characterizations of what the witness says. And the roles of judges and prisoner treatment officials are bound up with the entitlement to produce summary accounts of actions and events which can have real-life consequences for the citizen who is the focus of such discursive work.

However, examination of the discursive elements which arise out of, and are constitutive of, such interactions shows a somewhat different story. The talk of suspects, witnesses, and offenders shows that in important respects the nature of their actions is determined through a collaborative process of co-construction between citizen and representative of the state. In this process, the suspect or witness can display discursive resources which mean that, within the informal structures of actual interaction, he or she is able to exert a perhaps surprising level of influence on the outcomes of talk.

Finally, it is worthwhile picking out some themes in this area which have not been touched on in this chapter, but which are relevant to an understanding of the way discursive psychology approaches the topics of law and order. The first of these is the issue of cultural specificity. Most of the examples reproduced here derive from the English-speaking world. However, as Chang (2004) has pointed out, courtroom procedures may vary across different cultures in important ways. In China, for example, courtroom questioning is often used to accomplish a range of discursive ends which would be unfamiliar in a US courtroom. Lawyers and judges often employ questions to invoke confessions, using discursive mechanisms such as constant repetition of questions, asking unanswerable questions, and asking questions which are designed to accomplish a criticism of the witness.

One important aspect of cultural differences is the question of whether witnesses are competent speakers of the language which the court uses in its work. If witnesses have to give testimony in a language other than the official language of the court, this can raise problems associated with translation. The question of appropriate translation practices within the courtroom has received much attention from language researchers. For example, in a study of translation from Spanish to English of statements made by witnesses in court, Hale (2002) points out that the outcome of translation is often subtly different from what witnesses originally said. For example, the hedges and fillers which witnesses used to convey uncertainty were omitted from the translated version while extra pauses and hesitations were often added by the translators where, for example, a phrase was difficult to translate. Hale

warns that this has an effect on how members of the court or jury evaluate these witnesses and what they say, although, ironically, the overall effect of these two processes probably canceled one another out in terms of overall effect on **speech style**. Hale argues that the elements of the original Spanish testimony which the translator omitted, such as hedges and fillers, are often associated by hearers with a "powerless" style of speech which has been shown to be less persuasive in the courtroom. However, the additional pauses and hesitations added in by the translators also mark speech as "powerless," so in this one respect the two effects of translation cancel one another out.

It is also important to remember that legal processes take place within a wider social context. For example, Gavey and Gow (2001) have drawn attention to the way in which media such as magazine articles produce interpretations of legal matters. They analyze a magazine article on rape and demonstrate that the article constructs a particular notion of false allegations of rape which is supportive of arguments against gains made by women in challenging rape-supportive discourses. This is an important reminder of the fact that legal discourses arise within a broader, societal-level framework and that when courtroom discourse draws upon the everyday or the commonplace, it may well be drawing upon these discursive accomplishments established within that broader discursive framework.

Finally, it must be noted that the discursive processes outlined in this chapter should not be thought of as arising in a "discursive vacuum." The sorts of discourse which are discussed elsewhere in this book in terms of identity, prejudice, group affiliation, and so on all arise within the confines of the court as well. For example, in the study by Ehrlich (2002) mentioned earlier, there was evidence that discursive formulations of gender were an important aspect of the way in which the judges came to their conclusion. As another example, readers may care to turn back to Chapter 2, where Willott and Griffin's (2004)

Speech style Form of talk which is designed to be appropriate to a given context, e.g., selection of level of formality or carefulness of production

study of convicted criminals' accounts of masculinity in terms of "male breadwinners" was described in the context of discursive identity. Theoretical and empirical overlaps of this sort are indicative of the way in which discursive representations of self and the other can be selectively drawn upon in a wide variety of interactional contexts.

Chapter summary

- Studies of interactions between police officers and citizens have shown that differences in their social roles give police officers formal entitlements in structuring discursive interactions, although police officers can be seen to perform discursive work to manage potentially damaging inferences, such as perceived impoliteness, which can arise from this formal asymmetry.
- Police officers' talk during interviews is a subtle blend of description and evaluation which is designed to make conversationally relevant offenders' acceptance of their own guilt.
- The formal entitlements which are normatively associated with the role of police officer can be undermined in the sequential unfolding of the interview if the accused person adopts particular locally occasioned footings within the conversation.
- Like police officers, lawyers hold a social role which is normatively associated with discursive rights and entitlements.
- However, in both direct testimony and cross-examination, witnesses can be seen to engage in a variety of discursive strategies which limit the practical outcome of the lawyer's entitlement to discursive control.
- Expert witnesses occupy a role which is associated with its own entitlements, and this allows expert witnesses greater flexibility in controlling their discursive interactions with the lawyers who are questioning them.
- Judges often produce extended descriptions to warrant their judgments. In doing this, judges deploy discursive devices such as rhetorical contrasts and making inferences available in order to warrant the decisions they produce.
- In non-trial courtroom interactions, the role of judges can be equivocal: their utterances are designed to display impartiality but, at the same time, often function as a means of introducing suggestions as to the nature of the outcome of the interaction between opposed lawyers.
- Studies of offenders' discourse demonstrate that offenders build carefully designed accounts of their own actions which minimize their responsibility for those actions, e.g., through the use of passive constructions.

Connections

Impression management techniques of the sort discussed in Chapter 5 are clearly of importance within the courtroom context. In addition, the lawyer's use of persuasive discourse is related to aspects of persuasion that were discussed in Chapter 6. As might be expected, the role of argumentative discourse as discussed in Chapter 8 is also important in legal discourse.

Activity

Suppose you were the defendant in a criminal trial. What sorts of discursive devices might you expect the prosecutor to deploy against you? What discursive resources would you have?

Further reading

Ehrlich, S. (2001). *Representing rape: Language and sexual consent.* London: Routledge. In this book, Ehrlich examines the way in which dominant discourses such as one which emphasizes extreme forms of resistance to assault are deployed in the courtroom. These framing devices, she argues, are often crucial in determining the outcome of the trial.

Matoesian, G. M. (2001). *Law and the language of identity: Discourse in the William Kennedy Smith rape trial.* Oxford: Oxford University Press. This text analyzes the discursive strategies of courtroom participants in a rape trial. Matoesian shows how lawyers rely upon techniques such as developing inconsistencies in what witnesses have said. He also examines the role of reported speech and the dynamic nature of the "expert witness" identity.

Thornborrow, J. (2002). *Power talk: Language and interaction in institutional discourse.* Harlow: Longman. Thornborrow provides an analysis of talk within institutional settings which demonstrates that power is a dynamic phenomenon that arises out of locally negotiated interactions rather than from the discursive entitlements "bestowed" by social role.

Chapter 10

Social Psychology and Health

Key terms

Aetiology
Assessment
Case notes
Co-constructed accounts
Community care
Community resistance
Contested condition
Diagnosis
Entitlement to speak
Expertise
External evidence
"Fakers" and "haters"
Formulation
Gendered condition
Health behavior
Health initiative
Health professionals
Health status
Illness identity
Individual pathology
Lay knowledge
Moral imperative
Quasi-objective evidence
Stoical

> *Doc Morrissey:*   *Do you find you can't finish the crossword like you used to, nasty taste*
> *in the mouth in the mornings, can't stop thinking about sex, can't start*
> *doing anything about sex, wake up with a sweat in the mornings, keep*
> *falling asleep during* Play For Today?
> *Reginald Perrin:*   *That's extraordinary, Doc! That's exactly how I've been feeling.*
> *Doc Morrissey:*   *So have I. I wonder what it is. Take two aspirins!*
>
> (Nobbs & Gwenlan, 1976)

Issues of health and well-being are central to our daily lives. Not only do concerns with health impact upon our sense of who we are as individuals, but they also bear upon many of our interactions with other people and upon our locations within a broader social realm. During periods of ill-health our routine activities are often disrupted. Instead of conducting daily life in the usual ways, we may find ourselves interacting with doctors and/or other health practitioners in looking to recover the health that we previously enjoyed.

One (fictional) interaction between an individual and a health practitioner is seen in the excerpt above. This excerpt is taken from an episode of the television comedy series *The Fall and Rise of Reginald Perrin*, first broadcast on British television in 1976. We see the title character, Reggie, consulting a doctor employed by the organization for which they both work. Unfortunately for Reggie, and indeed for other employees of the organization, the doctor (Doc Morrissey) consistently displays little, if any, medical knowledge and fails to provide useful advice when he is called upon to do so. The consultation proceeds to a conclusion that is unsatisfying for Reggie, as do many similar examples. While this particular instance is designed to amuse, and not to exemplify typical medical practice, it does illustrate two aspects of health interactions that are of greater concern to us here.

The first point to note is the matter of **health status**. Health is not simply a matter of inspecting and reporting individual states of being, but rather involves the interpretation of experience and the description of that experience in terms that

are recognized by others. Where described experience does not match up with recognized health terms, health or ill-health can remain uncertain and open to further interpretation, as happens here. Alternatively, the relevance of what is described may be challenged instead of accepted, leading to health or ill-health being taken up as matters of contestation and negotiation.

A second point of interest is the form of the interaction. Interactions between individuals and health professionals typically differ from everyday interactions; the conversational topics tend to be circumscribed rather than emergent, and the identities of those involved bring expectations of particular actions. For example, a disavowal of relevant knowledge might be accepted in a conversation with a friend or neighbor; explicit denial of health knowledge is not an action that would usually be associated with a doctor. We expect doctors and other health practitioners to display knowledge and not to describe their own difficulties and uncertainties.

Everyday understandings of health are closely linked also to descriptions of health across numerous contexts. For instance, media coverage of health matters potentially reflects or influences how we understand our own health and that of others. The Internet too generates much talk of health through a diverse range of discussion boards and groups that allow individuals to share their experiences with those who might have similar experiences. The descriptions of health found in these and other contexts might or might not accord with those of practitioners but inevitably will impact upon how we make sense of health. Such constructions and the negotiation of health and illness across diverse contexts have provided much fertile ground for discursive researchers, and it is these that we explore in this chapter.

Health status The construction of individual experience in terms of health or illness

What is Health?

Health is a realm of **expertise**, within which professional understandings of relevant matters are privileged over those coming from other sources. Medical understandings of health are presented in different formats and different contexts, each version being tailored to meet the demands of a different anticipated audience. While research articles and medical textbooks are likely to be most accessible, physically and conceptually, to people with specialized understanding, communications between doctors and patients assume rather less familiarity with finer details of health and medicine (MacDonald, 2002). The extent to which individuals access reports of medical research or textbooks, instead of seeking advice from professionals, depends largely on their familiarity with different genres of medical discourse.

Of course, health advice and information come to us in many forms other than the dissemination of medical knowledge. Psychological theories of health, literature, media, the Internet, and interactions with family, friends, and others, offer a diverse range of ways of understanding individual health. In an interview study conducted with health coordinators (senior health teachers) working in secondary schools in New Zealand, Tuffin and colleagues (Tuffin, Tuffin, & Watson, 2001) examined how individuals used different versions of health to make sense of their everyday experiences. A major part of the teachers' roles, as school health coordinators, was to identify possible mental health problems of students and where appropriate to refer students for treatment, and they found themselves, in effect, in the frontline of health practice. When they were asked about mental health, the coordinators often talked about mental illness, as seen below.

INTERVIEWER: When you talk about mental health, what are you talking about?

PATSY: Well, really, when I think about it . . . we talk about depression and stress and I think that we probably just talk about it, you

> **Expertise** Specialized understanding of, and practice within, a particular field of activity

know, mental health like stress management.

(Tuffin et al., 2001, p. 481)

At such times, the teachers did not mention positive aspects of health, instead referring only to possible difficulties that might arise. However, in other parts of the interviews, when the coordinators did talk about mental health they equated it with mental well-being.

PEGGY: I think of mental health, I think of sort of mental well-being. Not sort of mental *ill* health but mental health in the sense of mental well-being, of being in tune with yourself, knowing your culture, your origins, having a good self esteem, just feeling good about things.

(Tuffin et al., 2001, p. 482)

These descriptions of mental health as mental well-being referred to a range of positive individual attributes, and to how these attributes led to positive life experiences. Usually the health coordinators talked about mental health in some detail. By contrast, when talking at other times about mental illness, the coordinators described mental illness in brief ways and as comprising malfunction or slippage from ideal mental health.

PEGGY: So that mental ill health or you're not mentally well is, is something one of those [well-being] things has sort of gone wrong.

(Tuffin et al., 2001, p. 484)

As can be seen, the coordinators' descriptions of mental health and mental illness were not consistent throughout the interviews: mental health could be equated with mental illness or described more positively as well-being, while mental illness varied between being a specific condition, such as depression, and a general malfunction of mental health. These varying constructions provided the health coordinators with different ways of making sense of the mental health of their students and of their own responsibilities. According to Tuffin and her colleagues, these forms of talk also reflected versions of health and illness found more widely in the media, in medicine and psychology, and in terms of health promotion. For example, the media commonly report health in negative ways, referring to illness and injury rather than positive health. It is therefore unsurprising that a negative emphasis on mental illness was found in the health coordinators' discussions of mental health. Similarly, talk of specific forms of mental illness, such as stress or depression, is common within medicine and psychology, with similar references being found in the health coordinators' descriptions. The availability of these specialized understandings of illness allowed the health coordinators to display expertise in describing the mental illness of their students. Accordingly, the different elements found within the health coordinators' descriptions of students' health and of their own responsibilities can be seen to reflect broader social understandings of health and illness.

One point that we should note here is the complexity of the relationship between health and illness. Often we think of health and illness as being polar opposites, the absence of one constituting the other. As we can see, however, this is not necessarily so. Health can be described as the absence of illness and vice versa, but equally descriptions of illness can be used to talk about health, or illness to discuss health. It is not therefore that a person is simply healthy or ill. Health and illness are parts of broader patterns of sense-making, within which individuals locate themselves and other people.

A second point to note is the variation in the health information that is derived from different sources. It is not just that the media and other sources of information provide more accessible content than medical expertise, but rather that different sources of advice offer varying and inconsistent versions of what it means to be healthy or to be ill. The versions of health that, for instance, we find in the media might well conflict with those found in medical books or offered to us by doctors. We can think of conditions such as myalgic encephalomyelitis (ME), for which support groups offer advice that diverges widely from that often provided by health practitioners. Similarly, information relating to particular behaviors, such as the immunization of children, may vary markedly according to the source from which it comes. Contexts of health and illness comprise an array of differing and competing constructions within which we have to negotiate what it means to be healthy or ill.

The ideology of health

Many analysts, including social constructionists and critical discursive researchers, argue that everyday experiences of health and illness are largely shaped by prevailing social discourses. Willig (2000) for example, taking a Foucauldian discourse analytic perspective, argues that everyday talk about health and illness is the outcome of dominant discourses of expertise. On this view, overarching expert discourses of health and illness provide a range of subject positions, such as doctor, patient, nurse, healthy person, and so on. These subject positions, or identities, are immediately recognizable to us as lying within the realms of health and illness and provide for us a framework within which we understand our own experiences. As a result our subjective experiences of being healthy or ill, of being a healthy person or a patient, arise as a consequence of our being positioned within prevailing discourse: our health is always located within broader social patterns and practices.

Moreover, from this viewpoint, expert discourses place certain individuals in more powerful positions than others. **Health professionals** are empowered to make decisions about the health and illness of other individuals, and to determine what outcomes are relevant. Patients, in contrast, are not usually regarded as having the necessary expertise, even in relation to their own experiences, to advise professionals on appropriate health care. Health and illness are thus ideological practices, empowering certain individuals while granting less power to others.

Although broadly accepting that health and illness are ideological matters, many discursive researchers are skeptical that individual experience is determined to the extent that is suggested above. Conversation analysts, discursive psychologists, and others prefer to view health and illness not as outcomes of power relations but as interactional concerns. Consider, for example, the greeting "How are you?" that we commonly exchange with people that we meet. Typically, this greeting is met with a response of "fine," "okay," or similar. In giving responses of this type, people

Health professionals People who are employed within health-oriented disciplines to deal with the health or illness of other individuals are not really describing their current health but are responding to greetings in social recognizable ways. These responses allow conversations to turn to other matters. Where people give responses that differ from those that are anticipated, they usually also offer some fuller explanation of health status, such as an account of illness, a visit to a health professional, or a report of similarly recognizable health-related activities.

In examining the accounts of health that individuals provide, Radley and Billig (1996) note that these accounts commonly orient more to what people should do to be healthy than to mere descriptions of individual health. Health accordingly is as much a matter of what people should be as it is of what they are. Accounts of health sustain a moral order within which speakers are concerned with being ordinary, normal people. Within this moral order, good health is treated as routine and acceptable; being healthy is taken to be the ordinary and normal course of events. Illness, however, constitutes a breach of the moral order, and individuals are required to account for any such breaches. To do so, those who describe themselves as being ill are expected to produce evidence to warrant the illness, and to demonstrate that they are coping with illness or attempting to overcome it. Failure to account in these ways is likely to lead to those concerned being regarded as feigning illness, malingering, or otherwise being morally culpable. Discussions of health and illness therefore are not just neutral contexts within which broad ideology operates. Rather, such contexts are ideological occasions, in and of themselves, that sustain a **moral imperative** to be healthy.

An example of the morality of health in action is provided by Breheny and Stephens (2003) in a study of middle-aged women's descriptions of the menopause. Often, the menopause is seen as a complex time for women, when physical changes can lead to health difficulties. A common medical response to menopausal symptoms is the prescription of hormone replacement therapy, designed to enable women to avoid or to address difficulties in experience. Many women of course

go through the menopause without seeking hormone replacement therapy or without reporting problems. Breheny and Stephens found that the women in their study accounted for menopausal experience in ways that avoided the necessity of seeking help. The women either described themselves as being able to maintain their health through diet and exercise, or claimed that they could overcome any difficulties by adopting a "get-on-with-it" approach to life. They accordingly constructed themselves as being able to surmount, or to accept, any health difficulties that they might have encountered, and thus identified themselves as individuals who met their moral obligations.

Being ill

Being ill is no straightforward matter. We have already seen the moral imperative that accompanies health and the requirement for individuals to account for any lapses from health. Moreover, not just any account is likely to be accepted by professionals, or possibly by other people. Describing ill-health that is vouched by **external evidence**, such as injury or physical symptoms, is one thing; to claim ill-health based upon factors that are known or knowable only to the person making the claim is quite another. People making claims of ill-health have an interest in having their claims accepted: any claims of ill-health are immediately open to potential challenge on grounds of the stake of the maker of the claim. Accounts of illness that are based solely or primarily upon subjective experience will therefore be difficult to sustain.

One condition that is difficult to warrant through external evidence is depression. Depression, although subjectively debilitating, is not immediately visible and experiences of depression cannot be warranted by reference to external markers. Changes in individual behavior, although perhaps visible, might be attributed to factors other than depression in itself. As a result, individuals reporting depression face the possibility that their experiences will not be recognized as sufficient grounds for illness and that they will be viewed as morally culpable. Achieving acceptance of the

---

Moral imperative An obligation to act in certain accepted ways, here an obligation to be healthy and to stay healthy

External evidence Evidence that is visible to other individuals

condition is accordingly problematic within a framework of biomedicine that emphasizes the importance of external evidence (Lafrance, 2007).

Where no external evidence is available, speakers might draw upon less direct evidence to warrant being ill. Consider, for example, the condition of chronic obstructive pulmonary disease (COPD), of which the major recognized symptom is dyspnoea (difficulty in breathing). Dyspnoea is not associated with any precise physical mechanism and there is no external evidence that might be produced in support of the illness. Instead, therefore, of describing dyspnoea in itself, individuals can describe symptoms, particularly anxiety and poorer emotional functioning, that are accepted as being associated with this condition. Such symptoms are manifest to a greater extent and are consistent with subjective accounts of COPD (Bailey, 2004).

There are conditions where both the meaning of subjective experience and the relevance of particular symptoms are widely contested. One such **contested condition** is ME, otherwise known as chronic fatigue syndrome (CFS). Commonly, individuals with ME report symptoms that include debilitating fatigue, pain, and reduced social functioning. However, no established **aetiology** for the condition exists, the symptoms that are commonly reported are knowable only to the individuals involved, and these symptoms are open to differing interpretations. Given the absence of external evidence and of symptoms that are widely recognized, a claim to be suffering from ME is problematic. Individuals claiming to be suffering from ME consequently face the possibility of being treated as morally culpable, either in claiming to have an illness that does not exist, or in failing to make appropriate efforts to overcome difficulties that have no physical basis. For sufferers, to negotiate ME as a verifiable condition and an **illness identity** presents considerable challenges. In a classic study, Mary Horton-Salway (2001a) examines how indi-

viduals can make sense of ME as an illness and of their own identities.

The accounts of individuals suffering from ME frequently involve descriptions such as those seen in Angela's narrative above. By narrating their experiences in these ways, sufferers construct the condition as one that has a physical explanation, even if that explanation is not yet recognized (Tucker, 2004). The moral upshot of such arguments is that sufferers are not accountable for their suffering and for medical failure to identify the physical (and consequently legitimate) origins of the illness.

Establishing, then, that one is ill is difficult in situations where neither subjective experience nor described symptoms will necessarily be accepted as constituting a recognized medical condition. Certainly, individuals can provide accounts similar to that of Angela and Joe in which they counter potential challenges. Whether such accounts will be accepted by health professionals, or indeed by others, or whether such accounts will remain open to challenge, is another matter.

Health and gender

Even where illness is medically recognized, not all illnesses are recognized similarly. Take the example of influenza. Flu is understood to be an illness that can affect men and women, young and old alike, and which is not specific to certain individuals or groups. Other health conditions, however, are viewed somewhat differently. For example, anorexia nervosa is taken to be a condition mostly relevant to adolescent girls and young women, who account for about 90 percent of all diagnoses (Andersen & Holman, 1997; Robb & Dadson, 2002). Anorexia nervosa is thus a **gendered condition** in a way that flu is not.

In order to understand the relationship between gender and health, let us start by reconsidering gender identities. As noted in Chapter 2, traditional feminine identities include a concern with beauty and appearance, slenderness, individuality,

---

Contested condition A claimed medical condition that is not recognized, or that is challenged, either by individuals or by health professionals

Aetiology Recognized cause or origin of disease

Illness identity An identity of being ill through no fault of one's own

Gendered condition A condition that is understood to affect, only or mainly, individuals of one gender

---

CLASSIC STUDY: Management of personal accountability in talk about ME

Horton-Salway examines in detail the account of the experiences of one person, Angela, suffering from ME. The account is given in the course of an interview conducted with Angela and her husband, Joe. During the interview, Angela and Joe describe Angela's condition in a range of ways.

Angela and Joe attribute the onset of Angela's difficulties to a specific time and event, namely an outing to local swimming baths. This attribution provides Angela's condition with a clear and recognizable origin. Further, this origin is consistent with the accepted causality of another condition, namely polio, that is medically recognized as potentially being associated with swimming. By comparing the causality of ME with that of polio, Joe argues that a similar scientific mechanism is involved in the transmission of ME.

The couple also describe the problems that Angela routinely faces, for example that of being unable to complete everyday household tasks. They contrast her current experiences with her experiences of life before she became ill. Angela is said to be unable to engage in activities that she used to enjoy greatly, suggesting that there is no motivation for her to feign illness.

In addition, Angela and Joe describe how Angela received unsound health advice, in being told to push herself to continue as before. The outcome of attempting to follow this advice has been a delay in recovery. Attributing delay in recovery to poor advice shifts responsibility for the delay away from Angela, and counters any suggestion that she is not making sufficient efforts to overcome the illness.

Angela and Joe also refer to statements of other people, such as Angela's mother, who have witnessed her struggle. (This process is known as "active voicing" [Wooffitt, 1992]). This reference indicates that the effects of the condition are knowable to other people and that Angela's claims, as supported by Joe, do not solely depend upon her subjective account.

Drawing upon these various elements, the joint narrative works to construct ME as a verifiable condition and to construct Angela as a morally virtuous and bona fide patient.

Horton-Salway, M. (2001a). Narrative identities and the management of personal accountability in talk about ME: A discursive psychology approach to illness narrative. *Journal of Health Psychology, 6,* 247–259.

---

and self-control. Although individuals negotiate other feminine identities, this version of femininity remains prevalent in our current culture. For example, media coverage of female role models commonly associates slenderness with success, and body-size is often a matter of discussion among women who are looking to achieve an ideal thin body-image (Guendouzi, 2004).

In the context of health, this gender identity presents something of a paradox. Public health messages aimed at discouraging excess weight often promote slim body-size as important for good health. Yet, the same emphasis on maintaining thin body-size is found in the accounts of women diagnosed as suffering from bulimia nervosa, and these accounts are used to justify

eating practices that would be considered anything but healthy (Burns & Gavey, 2004). Constructions of ideal femininities accordingly can appear consistent with both healthy and unhealthy eating practices (Brooks, LeCouteur, & Hepworth, 1998; Burns, 2004).

Of course, the numbers of women who are diagnosed with eating disorders are relatively small. However, for those who are diagnosed, attention falls on health rather than on aspects of femininity: women who practice unhealthy eating are viewed as having breached the moral imperative to be healthy and therefore as morally blameworthy (Brooks et al., 1998). In such ways, the potential conflicts between meeting the requirements of ideal femininity and the maintenance of good health become leveled at individual women (Hepworth, 1999; Hepworth & Griffin, 1990, 1995). Conflicts of identities are subsumed into the realms of medicine and psychiatry, leading to them becoming matters of **individual pathology**. The conditions that reflect such difficulties in turn are constructed by medicine and psychiatry as gendered disorders (Hepworth, 1999). Anorexia nervosa is thus constructed both as individual pathology and as a gendered disorder, and these constructions are reflected in the ways in which we make sense of the condition on an everyday basis (Benveniste, LeCouteur, & Hepworth, 1999).

Masculine identities can be equally problematic in relation to health. In Chapter 2 we saw that hegemonic masculine identities construct men as being all-powerful and invulnerable to difficulties. Although such identities might sit well with the moral imperative to maintain health, they fit less comfortably with illness. In situations of illness, men are commonly described as being **stoical**, enduring problems that cannot readily be overcome, and refraining from seeking appropriate medical help (Hodgetts & Chamberlain, 2002). Often, as a result, men have poorer health outcomes than women. For example, young men experiencing mental health problems may have difficulty in reconciling expected patterns of masculine behavior with their own life stories, leading to mental distress (McQueen & Henwood, 2002). Even where men are presented with messages that might promote better health, they resist and rework these messages in ways that are more compatible with hegemonic masculinities and behaviors (Hodgetts & Chamberlain, 2002).

The consequences of hegemonic masculinity for the health of individual men are often critiqued. However, such critiques are found in contexts that simultaneously sustain or are complicit in sustaining notions of male invulnerability. For example, the media frequently criticize men for not displaying emotion or vulnerability but simultaneously undermine versions of masculinity that might be alternative to the hegemonic ideal (Coyle & Morgan-Sykes, 1998). Doctors and nurses similarly critique typically masculine health behaviors, but describe men who adopt

alternative behaviors as deviant (Seymour-Smith, Wetherell, & Phoenix, 2002). On a similar note, female partners encourage men to describe emotional aspects of health that they would otherwise neglect, doing so, however, in ways that do not challenge hegemonic masculinities (Seymour-Smith & Wetherell, 2006).

The relationship between both femininities and masculinities and health can be seen in a study by McVittie and colleagues (McVittie et al., 2005) of male university students' understandings of anorexia nervosa. In the course of focus group discussions, the participants described the condition in terms of prevailing medical understandings.

MARTIN: It's like it (.) happens (.) maybe with girls or something, because (.) there must be a (.) a gender thing (.) and probably if (.) uh it's around all the same age.

I: Yeah.

MARTIN: Maybe like (.) uh ei:ghteen to.

PETER: See, I think that e:h (.) the whole (.) girls' magazines kinda (.) model (.) culture has (.) I don't yeah like.

(McVittie et al., 2005, p. 415)

The references to gender and to age reflected available constructions of anorexia nervosa as a gendered condition, restricted to women within specific age groups. Later on in the discussion, these descriptions were challenged when the participants were asked to account for diagnoses of anorexia nervosa in men.

COLIN: New age men, basically (.) they've got to be (.) sort of .hh more feminine in a way ... the same time they are getting (.) .hh possibly more (.) emotional, and what have you, as opposed to hiding (.) things which may've (.) basically tended to do in the past so they wouldn't cry out for help (.) so they wouldn't necessarily suffer from AN.

(McVittie et al., 2005, p. 415)

In responses such as that seen above, the participants distanced anorexia nervosa in males from mainstream male identities. Males who were diagnosed with the condition were described as being

Individual pathology Illness or disorder that is attributed to origins lying within an individual

Stoical Accepting misfortune, without complaint or indication of difficulty

"feminine," mentally weak, or simply different. These accounts sustained both the prevailing view of anorexia nervosa as a female condition and the masculine identity of being invulnerable to illness, especially to a feminine illness. Males who might be seen to have anorexia nervosa were constructed both as failing to display hegemonic masculine behavior and as accountable for weakness and behaviors that were specifically feminine.

From such findings we can see that issues of gender are often closely interlinked with the ways in which we understand health and illness. The moral imperative of health is not a discrete and separable part of experience, but rather part of a broader network of social relations and identities. The discursive negotiation of health, illness, and behaviors therefore implicates many other aspects of our everyday lives that we take to be equally central to experience.

Professional expertise

Professionals also have to negotiate issues of health and illness, displaying expertise in their chosen fields. Think back to the fictional interaction at the start of this chapter. Part of the amusement, and apparent difficulty, of that interaction is that the doctor fails to display expertise in matching up clearly identified and accepted symptoms with medical understandings of illness. Expertise, then, is not simply a property that people have; instead it can be understood as a practice that professionals do within health-care contexts. Professional expertise is negotiated discursively in a range of settings, including interactions between practitioners and patients, among practitioners themselves, and communications with other health professionals (Candlin & Candlin, 2002).

A major part of doing expertise is to communicate in ways that are consistent with health professional identities. Much of this communication is with fellow professionals, and practitioners will be expected to adhere to the forms of communication that are associated with such practice. For doctors, information relating to patient care is commonly recorded and transmitted by way of **case notes**. Case notes are designed to circulate

Case notes Notes used by health professionals that record a patient's health status and care

between practitioners, who are not co-present during instances of patient care, information of potential relevance to a patient's progress. Hobbs (2003b), however, notes that case notes do more than simply record and convey information; these notes construct versions of the patient's health status and of the relevant factors. Such notes are organized in two ways: first, temporally, according to the dates on which information is recorded, and second, grammatically, detailing different sorts of available information and the source of the information. Conventionally, the grammatical organization is reflected in a "SOAP (Subjective, Objective, Assessment, and Plan)" structure that allows practitioners readily to view and make sense of the information being presented. Within this structure, information that is reported by the patient and that relies upon subjective experience is clearly marked. For example:

(2) Pt states that she is doing well except for some leg swelling.
(3) Denies discomfort at this time.
(Hobbs, 2003b, p. 464)

In examples such as those above the content is clearly attributed to the patient, and the use of active voice signals the patient's role in providing the information. By contrast, objective notes are attributed to external evidence that is not dependent upon any individual.

(7) H: RRR. [Heart: regular rate and rhythm.]
(8) VS [vital signs]: [blood pressure] 150/80 [temperature] 992 [pulse] 82
(Hobbs, 2003b, p. 467)

The evidence available from subjective and objective sources provides the basis for the assessment and plan in the subsequent part of the case notes. For example:

23 suggestive
24 A/P: increased jitteriness. The movements are not ^ of
25 classical seizure activity. These movements need to
26 be followed very closely and investigated in case of
27 persistence. For now lytes and Ca, Mg, P04 will be
28 done to rule out abnormalities. In case of persistence

29 of the problem CNS need then to be investigated for
30 possible injury or bleed. Withdrawal reaction is always
31 a possibility. Dr. Walters agreed on the plan and
32 will follow.

(Hobbs, 2003b, p. 470)

In assessments such as that above, there is no explicit mention of the basis of the assessment. Instead, the medical grounds are taken to be common knowledge among professionals and are not specified. The plan, while hedged with terms such as "possible," is presented as an obvious outcome of the patient's health status as recorded and is stated as being agreed with another practitioner. The assessment and plan thus appear to follow directly from the preceding evidence.

Progress notes of this sort display some of the ways in which professional practice gets done among practitioners. The reporting structure both reflects and accords with conventional expectations of practice, including the weighting of available evidence and the production of conclusions. In training, medical residents increasingly become familiar with the reporting of health information in this format and in demonstrating their expertise to other professionals (Hobbs, 2004).

Similar forms of expert communication are found across a range of health professions. Medical interpreters, for instance, instead of simply translating patients' words, may define their role to include the determination and transmission to doctors of information that accords with medical understandings. Where interpreters take on this role, patient details that are taken to be subjective or irrelevant to medicine are filtered out in the translation process (Bolden, 2000). Nurses working in palliative care similarly make sense of their practices by drawing upon shared understandings of patient identities (Li & Arber, 2006). Displays of shared understandings are equally important within professions such as pharmacy and dietetics, in which examples of communication that are deemed to be effective and to display expertise can be used to train other practitioners (Pilnick, 2001; Tapsell, 2000).

As well as involving communication in conventional ways with fellow professionals, doing expertise is reflected in other discursive forms. One

part of doing expert practice involves the construction of what is relevant or not relevant to that practice. Health professionals almost invariably prefer external evidence to subjective accounts, and accord greater relevance to the former in forming assessment and treatment plans where appropriate. The quality of available evidence and what is to count as external evidence are thus almost entirely determined by the practitioner. Images obtained through technologies such as magnetic resonance imaging are routinely treated as direct evidence of the physical body, notwithstanding the human, and potentially subjective, processes involved in the use of such technologies (Joyce, 2005). Moreover, whenever external evidence is required, patients are expected to cooperate in the production of that evidence. Expectant mothers, for instance, might be offered a choice between different antenatal screening procedures rather than a choice between participation and non-participation in the process of obtaining screening results (Pilnick, 2004). However, the production of external evidence is also a matter largely determined by health professionals. When patients attempt to call for specific tests, professionals may refuse these requests, especially where the carrying out of the test is regarded as being an unnecessary drain on health-care resources (Teas Gill, 2005).

Health professionals, while prioritizing conventionally recognized forms of communication and evidence, orient also to alternative versions of health and illness. In an interview context, for instance, doctors might accept that a condition such as depression can have social rather than individual origins. Medical practice, however, continues to emphasize the individual aspects of the condition, consistent with the prevailing understandings of individual-based medicine (Thomas-MacLean & Stoppard, 2004). Similarly, doctors do display an awareness of the different accounts that patients give for contested conditions. These accounts, though, are treated somewhat differently from the ways anticipated by patients themselves. Rather than being taken as evidence of illness identities, any such accounts can be used as providing opportunities for professionals to do skepticism. The differentiation of health from illness is a core part of doing expertise, and accounts of contested conditions, such as ME, offer particular contexts in which this expertise can be demonstrated (Horton-Salway, 2002). Patients, of course, need not necessarily accept health expertise in practice, and, as we shall below, often resist or challenge the determinations of health professionals. To resist or challenge professional constructions of evidence or of illness, however, brings its own risks: individuals who persistently refuse to accept professional constructions can be identified as intransigent people, whose problems lie beyond the remit of professional expertise (McVittie & Tiliopoulos, 2007).

Coping and Support

The support of others can offer a valuable source of support in the negotiation of health status. For one thing, the production of external evidence of illness may be unimportant to people with whom we interact frequently and who usually accept our accounts of subjective experience. In a similar way, subjective experience is perhaps less likely to be contested by those who claim similar experience in a context of support than by potentially skeptical health professionals. However, it should not be assumed that, even in these contexts, all accounts of health and illness will go unchallenged; other forms of negotiation may be required for illness identities to be accepted.

Coping as an individual

One form of support arises in the fine details of the interactions in which issues of health status arise. Consider the condition of schizophrenia. Schizophrenia is a condition that is recognized in medical terms as encompassing a range of individual deficits, preventing sufferers from conversing as fully competent speakers. In contexts where chronic schizophrenics interact with mental health professionals, schizophrenics encounter conversational difficulties, in that professionals do not accept the unwarranted claims that they make and indeed treat any such claims as further evidence of the illness (McCabe, Leudar, & Antaki, 2004).

Let us contrast such interactional outcomes with those found in a study by Kremer-Sadlik (2004) of everyday interactions involving other individuals with potential communicative dif-

ficulties. These interactions involved children who had been diagnosed as having autism, another condition that is widely accepted as encompassing a lack of communicative competence. Below we see details of a family mealtime interaction between a child, Anthony, who has been diagnosed as autistic, and his grandma.

→ GRANDMA: After dinner, we can (.) paint the butterflies.
Did you want any more butterflies (.) drawn on there?   **(Question #1)**
ANTHONY: Yeah.
→ GRANDMA: Do you know which ones?
(Question #2)
ANTHONY: I really wanna get another– any other tall one.
→ GRANDMA: Do you want the two tall candle sticks?   **(Question #3)**
ANTHONY: Candle (.) stick holders?
GRANDMA: mmhm
ANTHONY: Yeah.
MOTHER: (xxx) need to do one. [(xxx)–
→ GRANDMA: [So you can– so you can put more butterflies on, is that it?
(Question #4)
ANTHONY: ((*nods*))
→ GRANDMA: Or do you have something else you want on the second one?
(Question #5)
ANTHONY: Butterflies. >Butterflies butterflies butterflies.<
(Kremer-Sadlik, 2004, p. 198)

Kremer-Sadlik notes that grandma's turns, involving repeated questions, are designed to allow Anthony to participate effectively in the interaction. Instead of taking the minimal responses that Anthony initially provides as indications of lack of competence, grandma pursues the topic to a point where Anthony is able to communicate effectively his desire for butterflies. This competence does not simply come from Anthony himself but is instead negotiated by both parties involved. Accordingly, this framing of the question–answer sequence supports Anthony to a point where he can display his communicative competence and be identified as an ordinary healthy participant.

Support, of course, is not always immediately forthcoming. Often, individuals run into difficulties in negotiating acceptance of health or illness and look elsewhere for advice on how to understand their condition. One source of such assistance is that of self-help books. The increasing popularity of self-help books in recent times suggests that these do indeed offer support that people can draw upon in making sense of their own experiences. Much of this support comes through explicit recognition of particular conditions and advice on how they might be reworked in order to achieve greater understanding. Advice along these lines is especially useful where the condition is not readily recognized in conventional health settings. In the case, for example, of fibromyalgia syndrome, a condition that has no accepted organic cause or visible abnormality, self-help books can draw together otherwise disparate threads and provide an explicit illness identity for those who read them to draw upon (Barker, 2002). This is not altogether a one-way process: commonly the information provided in sources such as this describes the experiences of other sufferers. The support offered thus reflects and makes available possibilities for those who share similar experiences.

Support groups

Other potential sources of support are more overtly interactive. Support groups have become increasingly popular contexts, offering the opportunity for people to discuss health and illness with others who appear to share similar illness identities.

Support found within such groups can take various forms. In some instances, interactions between members of the group are structured in ways that facilitate explicit displays of support in interactional sequences. For example, meetings of Alcoholics Anonymous routinely have a highly structured format in which individual members take extended individual turns, comprising monologues that do not anticipate interruptions by other members. Speakers complete their turns by expressing gratitude to the organization or to other members, and in so doing orienting to their moral responsibility for their health. Subsequent speakers reformulate the monologue and align themselves with the first speaker. These reformulations display understanding and acceptance of the account, and commonly propose some resolution of the problems that have

been narrated, thus providing support for the first speaker (Arminen, 2001, 2004b).

More frequently though, support group interactions are less structured than those considered above. In consequence, support tends to come either by way of specific agreement with what has been said or the implicit acceptance of individuals' accounts within collective constructions of the meaning of their experiences. Usually, the process of sharing experiences is most important for the individuals who have these experiences; support groups come into being commonly through the efforts of those who are directly affected, especially in seeking support for contested conditions. This, however, is not always so. In Sweden, for example, patient schools have been set up by hospital clinics. These schools provide patients suffering from ME with opportunities to discuss, and to learn more about, their experiences within a broader perspective of illness. Sufferers who attend the patient schools are consequently better equipped to manage their condition (Bulow & Hyden, 2003). Bulow (2004) shows how, within this context, groups of sufferers produce **co-constructed accounts** of their experiences.

01	CLARA:	sometimes my husband says he is [. . .]
		.h shall we do this or that? What about going to the
		movies today?
		No but I can't *go* see a film today.
		No but why not?
28		No but I– today– I *can't*.
		It's like a *huge* effort for me (Carol: mm) to go see a movie.
		Oh– yes. So I don't *do* that.
08	P:	°No°
09	CLARA:	I did that before.
		And then I felt *terrible* (P: °mm°) of course. Now I don't *do* it.
11	CATHY:	but that's probably the important thing.
12	CLARA:	yes, it's important. (PP: mm) I think so.
13	CAROL:	and then like you say, too, you– .h if you're going to do something,
		you can *do* things anyway. (Clara: yes) like babysitting.

Co-constructed accounts Accounts that are shared and produced by more than one individual in the course of conversation

.h (Clara: yes) but it's just that you have
to plan (it) (Clara: yes) because you
can't stand to
have it be a *must*

17 CLARA: no. [(and then–)
18 CAROL: [because– then it gets so bothersome
(and) then you give up right [away. It just
doesn't *work*.
20 CATHY: [mm
21 PP: no
22 CLARA: this stress tol[erance, you know
23 CAROL: [oh it's *very* important [that you get the
people around you [to understand that.
24 CLARA: [yes [mm
25 CLARA: .h yes but you can do a lot.
(you know) I can wash the windows, and
everything.
And I– I can clean.
I think that things like that are fun to do
at home.
.h but I have to do it at my own speed,
you know. (PP: mm) peace and quiet, like
.h (Carol: .hm) (.) not so that somebody
comes oh now let's do this. [and oh: no
[God.
31 CAROL: [mm [mm
32 CINDY: but then I think that it also feels a little
like if you're really going to do
something that you
know is going to take– require a lot of
energy. .h then it's usually very
important too to plan the coming
hours then and the days (PP: mm)
afterwards there I'm
free. (PP: mm yes)
then I don't do *anything*. (PP: mm yes
mm) ((many voices at the same time))
then [I just lie down and sleep.
38 CAROL: [there is constant prioritizing
(Bulow, 2004, p. 46, extract
abbreviated)

In discussions such as that above, what starts
as a personal account becomes a shared account
of similar experiences contributed by various
participants. What emerges, as a result of indications of approval, completions of others' claims,
and reformulations, is a co-produced narrative that
is based upon jointly constructed experience.
Individual sufferers can make sense of their own
experiences by comparing them to the illness as
jointly constructed. In doing so, and regardless
of whether or not individual experience cor-

responds exactly with the joint version, sufferers
receive support through the process of sharing
experience with those who give similar accounts.

However, group contexts of support do not
in themselves resolve all issues associated with
the management of illness. In some groups,
co-constructed accounts of illness can serve to
reinforce the problems of the group members.
For example, in cancer support groups, uncertainties relating to responsibility for overcom-
ing the illness and to the use of different forms
of treatment can simply resurface as group issues
without any resolution being achieved (Bishop
& Yardley, 2004). Further, even where support
groups accomplish joint understandings of their
illness, these understandings might simply focus
their disagreements with other groups, such as
health professionals. The meanings of illness produced within cancer support groups, for instance,
might diverge widely from those used by oncolo-
gical social workers, even where each group acts on
the basis that the other group shares its understanding of the illness (Kacen & Bakshy, 2005).

Other individual difficulties can also reappear
in the context of support groups. We have
already seen that, in circumstances where illness
is not recognized, sufferers may find their illness
identities contested. Illness identities are equally
open to challenge within groups. In such instances,
it is not the validity of subjective experience as a
source of evidence but rather the form of experience as narrated that is likely to be challenged.
Here, individuals must have their experiences
accepted as being similar to those of other group
members, and only by doing so are they likely
to be accepted as bona fide sufferers. In relation,
for example, to the contested illness of ME,
group members are required to display sufficient
relevant subjective experience for them to be
accepted as people who are entitled to speak to
the condition (Horton-Salway, 2004). Individual
entitlement to be ill can be accepted, challenged,
or undermined by others in support group settings as is can elsewhere.

Issues of acceptance or rejection by other
group members are more likely, if anything, to
arise in Internet-based support groups. In these
settings, individuals have no external evidence
available to them and are less certain of the entitlements of others who claim to have experienced
particular conditions. Joint constructions of the

illness in question are often similar to those found in the interactions of face-to-face groups. The question of who is entitled to speak to the condition, however, can be a matter of ongoing contention, with challenge, negotiation, and possible rejection by other group members being a live issue for all involved (Guise, Widdicombe, & McKinlay, 2007).

Entitlement to speak is likely to be fiercely contested in settings where group constructions of health and health behaviors diverge widely from more common understandings. We noted above how anorexia nervosa and bulimia have come to be recognized by health professionals and by lay individuals as specific forms of illness. However, these constructions of illness can be rejected by those who are diagnosed as having either condition. Over recent years, there has been a proliferation of Internet support sites, known as "pro-ana" sites, that promote a diagnosis of anorexia nervosa as a virtuous identity to which site users should aspire. Behaviors consistent with the condition are encouraged, and medical constructions of anorexia nervosa as a disorder are frequently challenged or rejected. In such contexts, accepted users treat with suspicion any accounts of individuals that do not appear fully to accept the prevailing versions of anorexia nervosa that are found on the site. Contributors who do not demonstrate sufficient personal experience of the condition, or who contest accepted meanings, come to be seen as **"fakers"** or **"haters"** rather than as entitled users. In these ways the sites maintain their own internal logics of health and illness, logics that support their claimed identities and reported behaviors but which are totally inconsistent with wider prevailing understandings of health, morality, and identity (Giles, 2006). Support for individuals from such groups will be forthcoming only on terms that are recognized by other group users.

Entitlement to speak Acceptance by others, who claim the same illness identities, that one legitimately describe the experience of that illness

"Fakers" and "haters" Individuals who are constructed by accepted site users as resisting or challenging support group understandings

Professional/Patient Encounters

Interactions between professionals and patients provide a meeting point for the negotiation not just of health itself but also of professional health expertise. Professionals, in doing expertise, display specialized understandings of health and illness and of the application of these to the circumstances of individual patients. Patients are expected to be able to produce accounts that can be recognized within professional constructions of health. However, commonly, professionals look to patients to display not just external evidence of illness but also some understanding of the operation of health in practice. How patients orient to such expectations, as much as their individual accounts, will have consequences for how the encounter will proceed.

Consider, for example, common medical procedures such as the taking of temperature or measurement of blood pressure. Procedures such as these are not usually treated as specialized techniques. The inferences to be drawn from the readings that are obtained may be taken to be within **lay knowledge**, and often such results are given to patients with little or no expansion. Patients, of course, may or may not be sufficiently familiar with medical procedures to draw appropriate inferences. How they respond to the introduction of such results will influence the level of information that they subsequently receive from health professionals during an encounter (Pomerantz & Rintel, 2004).

Other forms of medical information, however, are treated as lying beyond lay knowledge. Often health interactions include descriptions of risk, such as those associated with particular diseases or drugs. Scientific assessments of risk are somewhat more difficult to grasp than descriptions that rely upon everyday perceptions of risk. Doctors and nurses accordingly tailor the sorts of information about risk that they provide to the demands of the immediate patient context (Linell, Adelsward, Sachs, Bredmar, & Lindstedt, 2002). Other types of medical information might simply be too specialized for patients reasonably to comprehend. Where information appears

Lay knowledge Understandings of practices and procedures that do not require expertise

too abstract, patients prefer practitioners to use examples, metaphors, scenarios, or other concrete descriptions that make the information relevant to everyday life. In these ways, the relative expertise of the professional and non-expertise of the patient are played out in the course of the interaction (Gulich, 2003).

Patients, of course, do not always accept the levels of understanding that are accorded to them by professionals. When patients do demonstrate the levels of expertise that are attributed to them, their interactions with professionals are likely to produce joint constructions of health and of future courses of action. By contrast, where patients do not display the understanding that is attributed to them, or do not show that they are sufficiently compliant with professional advice, doctors will often adopt a more authoritative stance and the interaction will become asymmetrical (Barton, 2000). In this, as in other matters, individuals can resist or challenge professional constructions of health and outcomes; doing so in a context of professional expertise, however, is in turn likely to be met with challenge and further appeals to expertise from the professionals involved.

Assessments

Assessments provide an opportunity for the production and evaluation of evidence that can be used in determining the health status of the individual who is being assessed. Often, this will not in itself constitute an identifiably separate segment of the encounter and will be combined with diagnosis or the determination of outcome. However, in some instances, assessment constitutes the main focus of an interaction between a health professional and patient. Usually in these cases, assessments are conducted in order to obtain further evidence that can be used in subsequent management of the patient's care.

One common use of assessments is found in relation to quality of life. Quality of life is a construct that is central to many aspects of the delivery of health care and frequently offers a basis

for judgments as to what interventions might be appropriate or inappropriate, successful or unsuccessful. The usual means by which quality of life is assessed is through the use of a standardized instrument, possibly completed in an interview setting, and the resulting measure is routinely accepted by professionals as providing **quasi-objective evidence** of the health status of the patient. Accordingly, the results of such assessments are preferred to any subjective accounts of the patient that describe quality of life in more variable terms.

However, the evidence of quality of life produced by such assessments can be highly artificial. Antaki and Rapley (1996a, 1996b) note that quality of life interviews, in themselves, set up a highly unnatural form of social interaction. To inquire about someone's well-being is a common part of everyday life; to ignore or preclude the responses that individuals ordinarily give to such inquiries is, however, far removed from usual interaction. Interviewers may deal with this mismatch of expectations by altering the standardized wording of questions and by reinterpreting interviewees' responses in ways that are compatible with the standard instrument. The outcomes of these interviews become joint products of highly unnatural interactions rather than meaningful assessments of interviewees' quality of life. Quality of life assessments conducted with individuals belonging to particular groups, such as people regarded as having learning disabilities (mental retardation in North American terminology), can both be disempowering for the individuals concerned and produce misleading evidence (Antaki, 1999). Ironically, subjective and natural evidence of quality of life is discarded, while artificial but supposedly objective evidence is retained and used as a basis for future action (McHoul & Rapley, 2002).

Formulations

Whereas assessments are commonly used to produce further evidence, formulations orient to accounts and evidence that are already available.

Assessment Production or evaluation of evidence, usually conducted by a professional

Quasi-objective evidence Evidence that is not external and objective but which is treated as being objective

A **formulation** comprises a selective summary of what has previously been discussed, in terms of the gist of the preceding talk or of the implications of what has been said. Formulations thus offer professionals and patients means of displaying their understandings of the point that an encounter has reached and of how it should go forward. Of course, these summaries in themselves can be matters of agreement or disagreement. Where formulations display agreement and are accepted by the other party, the encounter will proceed as one of joint construction. In cases, however, where formulations are disputed, subsequent conversational turns are likely to appear as instances of professional decision-making and patients' attempt to resist these (Gafaranga & Britten, 2004).

Formulations of preceding talk are particularly common in interactions where subjective accounts provide both the main focus of the interaction and the only evidence available for discussion. Common instances of such interactions are psychotherapeutic encounters, in which individual accounts of difficulties are narrated to professional therapists who offer interpretations of the difficulties and proposals for how they should be addressed. An example of how psychotherapeutic interactions commonly proceed is provided by Hodges (2002) in a study of telephone calls to a radio phone-in slot. During this slot, designated as "counseling hour," individuals call in to the radio program to discuss a problem with a counselor and to receive advice as to how they should address the problem. One such call comes from Belinda, who reports that she is experiencing difficulties in her relationships with other family members ("C" = caller, "A" = advisor).

```
13    right well my problem is erm it's a grand-
      mother [clicks tongue]
14    I have=
15
16 A: =not a mother-in-law
17
18 C: well i–yes it is a mother-in-law [laughs]
19    [
20 A: a grandmother-in-law
21
```

> **Formulation** A summary that offers the gist of what has been said previously or of what should happen following that talk

```
22 C: a grandmother-in-law
23
24 A: and a mother-in-law at the same time
25    [
26 C: and well it's yes it's the whole
27    it's the whole in-law family.hhh or basically
      [laughs]
28    grandmother
```
(Hodges, 2002, p. 468)

This call follows a pattern that is common to many of those that are made to the phone-in. Belinda describes her problems as involving relationships with particular other people. Subsequent to this, she goes on to give more detailed descriptions of the people and of the specific difficulties. However, in offering a formulation of Belinda's problem, the counselor adopts a rather different focus.

```
187 A: Belinda you (1) you sound like somebody
       who,
188    likes to please people and who doesn't like
       to let them down
189    and I think what we've got in here hidden
       away in this
190    [
191 C: [sighs]
192
193    very complex story is what I call guilt and
       what we all know
194    [
195 C: Mm
196
197    as guilt.hh you feel (.75) guilty about the
       grandmother (y-)
```
(Hodges, 2002, p. 469)

In contrast to Belinda's description, the counselor formulates the problem as one that belongs to the caller herself. There is no reference to wider aspects of the relationships and attention comes to focus on Belinda and her possible inner emotions, particularly guilt. Further, the counselor undermines Belinda's account by suggesting that it is based on a partial view, in failing to acknowledge hidden material. The counselor's subsequent advice follows this formulation.

```
215 A: well well th– th– this this is a the
216 is an issue of not going.hh on being Mrs Nice
       for the rest of
217 your life.hh and that sometimes
```
(Hodges, 2002, p. 469)

The outcome is that both the problem and its potential solution are attributed to Belinda herself. The formulation removes the context of the difficulties that were narrated, and emphasizes Belinda's moral imperative to be healthy and to be responsible for maintaining her own health.

This emphasis on individual responsibility, and the formulation of problems in such terms, permeates much of psychotherapeutic practice. Factors that individuals report as relevant, but not as personally situated, can become interpreted as symptoms of their personal difficulties (Hak, 1998). Therapeutic formulations thus often represent clients' words and their implications in terms that are compatible with therapeutic interpretations (Antaki, Barnes, & Leudar, 2005a). Where clients describe experiences from different episodes of their lives, such as early childhood and current experiences, much therapeutic work focuses on the identification and formulation of apparent similarities across the range of experiences. In this process, the contexts of experience are omitted and attention becomes directly focused on the client and on individual responsibility for addressing life difficulties (Perakyla, 2004; Perakyla & Vehviläinen, 2003). Client accounts of lived experience are thus of subsidiary interest, or are made relevant only insofar as contributing towards analytic reworking of the problems (Shakespeare, 2006).

There are, though, specific instances where clients are encouraged to play a more active role in the formulation of issues. Interestingly, such cases also can be understood as part of the professional framing of the encounter. For example, in HIV prevention counseling, clients are encouraged to ask questions about risks and behavior. When clients do ask these questions, the counselor can respond by giving information, allowing the interaction to appear less one-sided than it might do otherwise. Such structures accordingly can be seen as part of professional practice and its impact upon the design and conduct of the interaction (Kinnell, 2002).

Often in psychotherapeutic interactions, as in Belinda's call to the counselor above, the client and therapist provide different formulations of the problem. Clients commonly attribute problems externally, while therapists attribute problems internally to the particular clients. Where these different attributions persist throughout the course of therapy, and the client continues to resist professional formulations of the issues, the outcome of the therapeutic process is likely to be an unsuccessful one in which no agreement is reached (Madill, Widdicombe, & Barkham, 2001).

Diagnoses

Diagnostic formulations, like formulations in general, provide summaries of the preceding interaction and of how matters should proceed. Although psychotherapeutic formulations are based primarily upon narrated subjective accounts, formulations in other forms of health encounter more commonly proceed on the basis of evidence then available from all sources. **Diagnosis** is the point of the encounter where a summary is required of all relevant information and of how that information relates to established knowledge of health. Diagnoses accordingly come from doctors or other professionals who are expected to display the expertise on which to form a construction of the health status of the individual patient.

As with other aspects of health, and indeed other formulations, the diagnoses that professionals produce are open to negotiation in the interactions in which they occur. Patients can and do respond to diagnostic formulations proposed by doctors in various ways, including explicit agreement, minimal responses, and outright disagreement (Perakyla, 2002). Disagreement is most likely to occur in cases where the evidential basis for the diagnosis has not been agreed between the parties. If the subjective evidence offered by a patient is ignored or overruled, the diagnostic outcome is unlikely to be a straightforward matter of agreement between those involved. Alternatively, there may be cases where the health professional produces a diagnosis without making explicit the evidential basis on which it is offered. Maynard (2004) notes that at such times individuals are likely to treat the diagnosis as presumptive and unwarranted. We see below an example encounter, in which a pediatrician is

Diagnosis Summary of available evidence and of how that evidence relates to professional understandings of health and illness

offering to patients a diagnosis of their 7-year-old son's condition.

```
1   Dr D:   And I admire both of you really and (0.8)
               an' (2.2) as
2               hard as it is (0.4) seeing that there is
               something that
3               is the matter with Donald, he's not like
               other kids (0.2)
4   →        he is slow, he is retarded.
5               (0.2)
6   Mrs R:  HE IS NOT RETAR[DED!]
7   Mr R:   [Ellen.]
8   Mrs R:  HE IS NOT RETARDED!=
9   Mr R:   =Ellen.
10              (0.3)
11  Mr R:   Uh plea:s::e
12  Mrs R:  NO::!
13  Mr R:   May– look– (0.6) it's their way of::
               I'oh'know.
14  Mrs R:  hhhhh HE's NOT RETAR:(ghh)DED!
               ((sobbing))
                        (Maynard, 2004, pp. 58–59)
```

In instances such as that above, the doctor proposes a diagnosis for which no prior evidence has been cited. Here, the mother of the child being discussed does not accept the diagnosis, and strongly contests it in repeated straightforward rejections. The interaction accordingly proceeds to confrontation rather than agreement as to the health status of the child. This type of sequence can be contrasted with that seen below.

```
1   Dr B:   Well (0.5) No we– we: would (0.4) we
               feel that (0.2) the
2               problem is that he ca:n't (.) yet.
3               (0.9)
4   Dr B: → And that he– (0.2) all our exams show
               that he is (.) quite
5       →    retarded.
6               (1.2)
7   Dr B:   Have– have you (0.7) h– heard this
               word before? And thought
8               of it in relation to him?
9   Mrs M:  Retarded? . . .
                        (Maynard, 2004, pp. 59–60)
```

Above is an example of a somewhat different sequence. The doctor starts by agreeing with a prior observation by the mother that her son cannot talk and then cites the relevant evidence, namely

"exams." This is followed by a qualified diagnosis which is then pursued. Although the mother of the child in question does not explicitly accept this diagnosis of her son, there is no confrontation similar to that in the previous extract and the parties appear to be moving towards some agreement.

Of course, some diagnoses are more likely to be contested than others. A diagnosis of influenza, for example, can be matched against lay knowledge of symptoms and individual experience. In addition, treatment for the illness is widely known and accepted. Such a diagnosis therefore probably will be very rarely contested. Contrast this example with a diagnosis of a rather more controversial condition, attention-deficit/hyperactivity disorder (ADHD). Rates of diagnosis of ADHD, especially among boys, have increased markedly in recent years. Diagnosis of ADHD is, however, based primarily upon subjective interpretations of observational evidence, and there is considerable public skepticism regarding the aetiology and existence of the condition. In addition, the recognized treatment for ADHD is medication, directed at the individual child and aimed at changing his behavior. This treatment, together with the lack of an external evidential base for the diagnosis, make diagnosis of ADHD an outcome that parents often attempt to resist. McHoul and Rapley (2005a) present a detailed study of one particular diagnostic session, involving a young boy (Alan), his parents, and a pediatrician. In the extract below, which comes some way into the interaction, the pediatrician explicitly proposes that Alan should be diagnosed as having ADHD.

```
Dr:  Because (y'see) then he goes on to say erm
       they they did thee child behavior checklist
       >he did it and his teacher did it< erm and
       he
       was er positive for >anxious, depressed,
       social
       problems, attention problems, delinquent
       behavior,
       'n aggressive behavior< on your thing and
       on the
       teacher's report um areas of clinical
       significance
       are social problems, delinquent behavior and
       aggressive behavior
       (.)
```

Dr: Bu:t on the other hand th– ob– observations
   in the classroom showed Alan to be restless
   non-attentive and very seldom in his seat >his
   pers'nal bound'ri– bound'ries were poorly
   defined and he w's largely non-compliant<
      (.)
Dr: h a:nd then they gotchu and his teacher to
   fill
   out >fill out that questionnaire< ↑yeh (.) an
   both of them rated er both rated (.) the
   ratings
   from each are significant in inattention and
   hyperactivity (.) so they say A– Alan's a
   child
   whose behavior is >severely hampering his
   education
   and social development< .h in in spite of
   having
   fairly intensive behavioral interventions
   he continues to behave in >ways that are
   detrimental
   to his progress< .h and it was recommended that
   Alan be sent for paediatric assessment to
   confirm
   an ADHD .h diagnosis possibly with
   >oppositional
   defiant disorder< so .hh
      (McHoul & Rapley, 2005a, pp. 429–430)

In this extract, the pediatrician explicitly states what she takes the purpose of the session to be, that is the confirmation of a diagnosis of ADHD. She sets out the evidential basis for such a diagnosis, which comprises a summary of findings included in the school psychologist's report. That report in turn is stated to be based upon assessment by the psychologist and questionnaires that were completed by the schoolteacher and the parents. However, Alan's mother in turn contests the validity of the psychologist's report and, in consequence, the evidential weight that it should carry in diagnosis.

Mo: (hh) um he:'s (grabbing at all) stuff ↓too
Dr: Is he
Mo: He::: (uh.h)
Dr: This guy °↑yeh mm°
Mo: He– he's one 'v those people th't (1.0)
   makes th– like th– say the diagno[sis=
Dr: [Mm
Mo: =themselves
Dr: Mm hm

Mo: and then expects ev'rybody to agree with
   [him
Dr: [Mm=
Dr: =Mm hm, mm hm
Mo: E:rm that questionnaire th't he w's talking
   about
   I filled that out
Dr: ↑Ye: s
   ((Child enters; short inaudible exchange))
Fa: Knock on the door next time
Mo: I– it w's all based on (.) ↓school
Dr: Mm [Mm
Mo: [The questions were what's he like in
   the [cla:ss[room
Dr: [Mm [Mm
Dr: Mm
Mo: I can't answer that [as a parent=
Dr: Mm yes
Mo: =because I'm not in the cla:ssroom
      (McHoul & Rapley, 2005a, p. 431)

Here, Alan's mother challenges the methods that were used to produce the report, on the grounds that the psychologist has simply anticipated compliance rather than being rigorous in interpreting the relevant evidence. She backs up this challenge by offering an example of how the questionnaires could not produce accurate evidence, in that they required her to comment on matters of school conduct that clearly lie beyond her knowledge as a parent. The effect of this challenge is to put in doubt (at least potentially) the evidential value of a report that is itself based upon questionable interpretations. By implication, the diagnosis that is produced in the interaction seen above thus is unsupported by sufficient evidence. Following the challenge, and a number of subsequent somewhat curious twists, the session reaches an inconclusive outcome in which the diagnosis remains potentially relevant and is to be confirmed or refuted following a trial course of treatment.

Contestation of medical diagnoses therefore, as with other challenges to professional expertise, can produce inconclusive and messy outcomes. Health professionals are likely to respond to challenges with further attempts to negotiate acceptance of the diagnosis and with production of further evidence if possible. It is unlikely that professionals will readily be persuaded to recognize illnesses that cannot be vouched in their terms; equally, however, they will not be easily persuaded to abandon professional constructions of illness that lay individuals would seek to contest. Even in circumstances of controversial professional constructions, patients cannot readily overcome professional expertise in practice. More commonly, professional expertise will prevail, with individuals being brought under the auspices of illness or excluded from illness, according to the prevailing constructions of professional practice.

Health Behaviors and Change

In this final section, we turn to topics of health behavior and change. We have already seen how the meanings of health and illness are managed across a diversity of contexts. As with identities more generally (see Chapter 2), the negotiation of identities in contexts of health and illness is closely linked to consequences for social action, for example in challenges to contested conditions, in seeking support from others, in arguing for or against medical procedures, and so on. What we do is thus inextricably bound up with who we claim to be in health terms. Often therefore the primary focus of interest, for individuals and for health professionals alike, is not health in itself but rather individual **health behaviors** and their potential relevance for future health or illness.

Moreover, many **health initiatives** are targeted beyond the individual and instead seek to influence behavior at the level of social groups or indeed communities. When health professionals extend their horizons to the broader context of health, a range of other considerations become relevant. In these contexts, professional expertise in health is no longer the only point of reference. Realms such as politics, morality, and other forms of expertise all provide alternative understandings of social life. In broader contexts, the negotiation of health moves from being an individual concern to a social one, in which the role of health as a form of expertise and practice itself

comes under potential challenge from different and differing sets of social understandings.

Health and individual behavior

Broadly speaking, individual behaviors are taken to be healthy insofar as they accord with professional expertise and professional constructions of health. Where individual experiences differ from professional views, professional understandings are likely to have the greater impact upon the construction of behaviors that exemplify health. For example, one instance where individual experience of health might diverge from professional expertise is that of pregnancy. Individual women's stories of pregnancy narrate a wide range of different experiences, emphasizing the subjective elements of individual pregnancies. However, health professionals including doctors and other health professionals commonly construct pregnancy as a standardized set of behaviors (Freed, 1999). Professional practice again is thus less concerned with subjective experience than with the application of recognized expertise to the individual.

Often, however, individual behavior is treated as being directly in conflict with professional understandings and consequently as unhealthy. In such instances, professional attention is directed at changing the behavior in question. Consider, for example, the campaigns that are frequently promoted through the media, and through health professionals, to encourage particular forms of behavior, such as vaccination of children, smoking cessation, and weight loss, among numerous potential examples. Possible subjective factors, such as right of choice, enjoyment, or skepticism of the content of such messages, usually are dismissed or receive little acknowledgment. Instead, attempts to change behavior more commonly refer only to professionally constructed understandings of health and appropriate behaviors, and, often, to the moral imperative to be healthy.

One instance of an emphasis on moral aspects of health can be seen in the treatment of drug addicts. Commonly, drug addiction is constructed as behavior that is degrading, dirty, solitary, and savage. Treatment programs accordingly require addicts to accept personal responsibility for their behavior, with "a good deal of treatment discourse [being] taken up with inducing and

---

Health behavior A behavior that impacts upon or results from health status

---

Health initiative An attempt to change the health behaviors of a social group or community

offering confessions of the depths to which one's disease has forced one to sink" (Weinberg, 2000, p. 611). Explicit references to moral responsibility and moral failure are common to many different forms of treatment programs; variations in the forms of treatment provided by different programs, therefore, may be less important than the common moral framework within which these treatments are located (Arminen, 2004a).

Other attempts to change individual behaviors also focus upon individual responsibility. One focus of health promotion, for example, has been to encourage safe sexual behavior whereby condoms are used to prevent potential transmission of disease. Recently, the responsibility for the use of condoms within heterosexual relationships has been primarily directed at women. Many women, however, appear to resist or not to accept this responsibility, persisting in what, in health terms, is constructed as unsafe sexual behavior. Here, it is the meaning of such behavior that is open to debate, as health comes into conflict with other aspects of individual experience. For, heterosexual activity, although a concern for health, is relevant also to relationships and to gender identities. These other realms of experience offer understandings of sexual behavior that are somewhat different from those provided by health professionals. Individual women, in consequence, negotiate their sexual behavior in relation to conflicting understandings of sexual behavior in heterosexual relationships. Specifically, traditional understandings of femininity can lead to women taking up relatively passive roles within relationships, as a consequence of which female partners are poorly placed to argue as to how sex should take place (Gavey & McPhillips, 1999). In addition, relationships bring their own expectations, particularly the expectation that one should trust one's partner. Trust, of course, can be constructed in different ways; one common effect, however, of the expectation of trust of sexual partners is to construct insistence upon condom use as indicating a lack of trust (Willig, 1997). Women accordingly often are disempowered from taking responsibility for behavior that might be viewed as safe, but which is incompatible with the behavior associated with a trusting relationship.

Ironically, where women do take responsibility for condom use within heterosexual encounters, behavior that is seen to be healthy can impact upon other understandings of that experience. Gavey and colleagues (2001) found that, where women described using condoms in sexual encounters, such encounters were regarded as having little meaning in relationship terms.

SALLY: It's like condoms are about more casual kinds of encounters or mean– I mean, I'm kind of – um they are kind of anti-intimacy at some level.

NICOLA: And so if you'd used condoms with him, that would've meant –

SALLY: Maybe it would have underscored its temporariness or its– yeah, its lack of perma-nence, I don't understand that. What I've just said really particularly. It doesn't [seem] very rational to me. [laughter]

NICOLA: [laughter] No it very rational and I–

SALLY: [indistinguishable] it seems to be coming out of you know, somewhere quite deeper about um– I think it goes back to the business about ideals stuff. And I think that's one of the things about not saying no, you know. And that the ideal woman and lover– the ideal woman is a good lover and doesn't say no. Something like that. And it is incredibly counterproductive [softly] at my present time in life. [sigh/laugh]

(Gavey, McPhillips, & Doherty, 2001, p. 926)

Gavey and colleagues noted that many of their participants described condom use as relevant only to sexual encounters that were temporary, and that involved no ongoing personal commitment. In addition, some participants also described condom use within sexual encounters as being an inevitable precursor to full sexual intercourse, even where this was not the participant's immediate wish. For many women therefore, responsibilities of health come into conflict with other sets of meanings and can have consequences that are unforeseen and disempowering.

Conflicts of health and gender arise also in relation to masculine identities. Many of the health promotion campaigns aimed at men emphasize the importance to them of seeking professional help when it is required. Such messages of course, as noted above, conflict with prevailing constructions of masculinities that emphasize invulnerability and discourage help-seeking behaviors. Direct statements of appropriate health behavior do little to resolve this tension, and often are simply resisted by individual men (Hodgetts & Chamberlain, 2002). A perhaps more useful health strategy would be to recognize the transitions in identity that are required for men to seek professional help, and to facilitate these transitions, rather than simply to highlight the changes in behavior that are expected (McVittie & Willock, 2006).

Many individuals experience difficulties in negotiating the demands of health and of other elements of experience. Frequently, these subjective difficulties lead to non-engagement with health behaviors. In other instances, however, non-adoption of healthy behaviors goes beyond this. Persisting with behaviors that are taken to be unhealthy offers individuals one way of resisting the constructions of health and behavior that are promoted by health professionals. Unhealthy behavior can also become a way of doing identities that resist broader social understandings of identities and identity practices. For example, gay men commonly ignore messages that encourage condom use among the gay community and continue to have unprotected sex. In these cases, continuation of sexual practices that are deemed risky or unsafe provides a means of rebelling, not just against health messages but also against cultural norms in general (Crossley, 2004). Where subjective experience and behavior cannot meaningfully be reconciled with professional constructions of health, negotiation of identity can perhaps only be achieved by seeking to engage with wider social realms of experience that routinely are excluded from narrow constructions of health, and thus stepping out of the domain of health entirely (Guilfoyle, 2001).

Health in the community

Although much of health and illness in practice is concerned with the individual, there are other occasions when health practice looks to engage at a broader level. Initiatives that are designed to promote health, or to influence behavior, can take as their focus particular social groups or communities. In such contexts, the practice of health takes on forms that differ from those found in individual-oriented contexts, such as professional–patient encounters. For, at a broader level, emphasis on individual responsibility becomes of lesser relevance as the meanings of health have to be negotiated, and possibly accepted or contested, alongside a diverse range of other social elements.

One health initiative, in many parts of the world, has been the promotion of **community care** to address the health and social needs of people diagnosed as having mental health problems. Many people, within the populations of countries where such initiatives are in place, are however skeptical of community-based mental health schemes, and of the motivations of the policymakers who introduce them. Accordingly, it cannot be assumed that communities will fully endorse the operation of these schemes, or the inclusion within the community of individuals diagnosed with mental health difficulties. Tuffin and Danks (1999), in a study of community care in New Zealand, found that Wellington residents expressed views that could be described, at best, as ambivalent.

> KIM: Well I think you can look at it from two angles. You can look at it from their point of view and from the community's point of view. Now from the patients (.) you know (.) in quotes (.) point of view, obviously that's going to be a very positive step because obviously they need to be reintroduced back into society.
>
>   (Tuffin & Danks, 1999, p. 293)

In extracts such as that seen above, local residents appeared sensitive to the needs of patients living within community settings. However, such patients were also described as being outside the community rather than being part of it (McKinlay & McVittie, 2007). As a result, the local population was constructed as comprising dual communities, a construction that resisted the social inclusion of those with mental health problems and which reinforced existing divisions. Mental health patients were described as

---

Community care Health initiative designed to allow people with mental health needs to live fully within the community

having conditional rights to community life, and as having disorders that varied between being inconvenient and being unpredictable. A common response from local residents to community care was one of patronization of the mentally disordered who lived among them.

> BEV: I suspect, from what I glean from papers, news and so on that what has happened that people have been let out and they've been put in circumstances in the community where they're not capable of looking after themselves, as as you or I might quite comfortably do, and they need a <u>large</u> amount of help to do this, if they're <u>not</u> given that help I think (.) I think I think they're better off in an institution, if that help is not available.
>
> (Tuffin & Danks, 1999, p. 297)

In these ways, established community residents constructed those living with mental health problems as less than full members of the communities in which they resided. Such constructions, although to some extent tolerating aspects of community care, resisted the behavioral consequences of the scheme. Constructions of health and health care at the community level, therefore, can meet with **community resistance**. As with matters of individual health, community health initiatives become open to negotiation.

Community resistance is also found where attempts to promote health within communities simply conflict with alternative community practices and understandings. One recent form of health initiative has been the introduction of programs to address increasing rates of sexually transmitted infections, in particular HIV/AIDS, in many parts of the world. Often, however, sexual health programs are incompatible with local understandings of sexual health and sexual behavior. For example, in South Africa, community views of sexually transmitted infections diverge widely from Western biomedical understandings. Onset of infection is often attributed to causes that include bewitchment and the use of prescription medication, while treatments

include the use of self-inflicted physical interventions and the consumption of disinfectant, potassium permanganate, or Jeyes Fluid (toilet cleaner). Such community understandings of sexual health clearly are at odds with accepted medical views of sexual health, and pose considerable challenges for health service providers (Shefer et al., 2002). However, even in contexts where biomedical understandings of health are widely accepted, constructions of HIV/AIDS and of appropriate treatments may come up against community resistance. In contexts where recommended treatments change over time, any such changes can be used to highlight apparent inconsistencies in health practice and so to undermine the application of professional expertise within the community (Newman, Persson, & Ellard, 2006).

Health practices can not only be resisted within the community, but also may be challenged. In the context of the wider community, groups might seek to open up to scrutiny and challenge health practices that otherwise would lie within the remit of health practitioners. If such practices are brought into the public domain, they become open to negotiation in terms of alternative understandings of social life. One such case is that of abortion. Although the circumstances in which abortions may be carried out change over time and vary from country to country, abortions under some circumstances are allowed in many parts of the world. Insofar as abortions are managed within the remit of health, the responsibility for carrying out or refusing abortions rests with individual health practitioners. When, however, abortion becomes open to public debate, it is no longer health expertise that primarily settles issues of morality and of interpretation of evidence. Instead, alternative constructions can be mobilized to challenge outright current health practices in relation to such matters (Hopkins, Zeedyk, & Raitt, 2005).

Finally, let us return to the issue with which we began this chapter, namely, health in the workplace. The intersection of health and employment provides one instance where health expertise is not resisted or challenged, but instead is widely accepted within the community. However, this acceptance does not necessarily come on the terms of health practitioners. Organizations provide contexts for the practice also of other forms

---

Community resistance Collective resistance at the level of the community, not the individual

of expertise, most notably managerial expertise. Different forms of expertise may offer quite inconsistent understandings of practice and call for rather different behaviors. Workplace health programs, for example, commonly include elements such as health and safety procedures, intended to safeguard and promote the health of individual employees. Health and safety are, however, open to construction in different ways, and indeed can vary considerably according to the logics of different versions of expertise. A study of practices within one international company operating across the Asia-Pacific region (Allender, Colquhoun, & Kelly, 2006) found that, across the organization, health could be constructed either as safety or as lifestyle. These two versions of health were respectively organized around professional concerns with organizational practices or with lifestyle choices and health behaviors. As such, the two constructions of health reflected tensions between managerial expertise and health expertise. Neither version of expertise, however, allowed any active role in health for company employees, and the effect of the two constructions taken together was to make all aspects of employees' lives, whether work-related or not, available for inspection by the organization. It is difficult enough for individuals to contest one form of expertise; seeking to contest two different forms of expertise presents an almost insurmountable challenge.

In professional terms, the tensions between different forms of expertise become most salient when the same person is responsible for doing expertise in both realms. Iedema and colleagues (2004) provide the example of a doctor-manager (physician-executive in North American terminology) working in a publicly funded hospital in Sydney, Australia. The individual is required to do professional expertise with fellow health professionals, but is at the same time expected to meet policy-makers' expectations of managing the delivery of services within the hospital. Doing managerial expertise in this setting involves ensuring delivery of health care within budgets and managing operational practices in order to deliver such care efficiently. The doctor-manager thus is required to demonstrate health expertise to medical colleagues who are skeptical of organizational practices, while also arranging for such practices to operate to best effect. Iedema and colleagues note that, in meetings with colleagues, the post-holder often attempts to negotiate these competing demands by means of a buffer position.

> "[It is important] on behalf of the institution that we recognize what we're up to. I think it's a very useful conversation I'm hearing and it's important that we're at this point in thinking."
> (Iedema, Degeling, Braithwaite, & White, 2004, p. 25)

Buffer statements such as that seen above and similar formulations allow the doctor-manager to defer resolution of the potential conflicts between health expertise and managerial expertise. The potential conflict is thus presented as a reasonable engagement of divergent forms of understanding, with the indication that at some point in the future the requirements of each form of expertise will become more closely aligned and amenable to resolution. The difficult health choices are thus postponed to another day.

The statement seen above, "it's a very useful conversation I'm hearing," enables the doctor-manager to display understanding of the talk of fellow organizational employees while offering no conclusive outcome. Now, you might well argue that this formulation is, in practical terms, no more committal than the statement ("I wonder what it is") that we saw the fictional Doc Morrissey produce in the excerpt that began this chapter. Indeed, these two statements have similar effect, in that neither offers any conclusive understanding of health in practice. What these two statements, taken from very different contexts, demonstrate, however, as do the many other examples that we have considered in this chapter, is that health, its meanings and consequences, are matters of ongoing negotiation across the many contexts that go to make up the "long conversation" (Dixon & Wetherell, 2004) of social life.

Chapter summary

- Issues of health and illness are negotiated across a range of contexts, including encounters with health professionals, support groups, and everyday interactions.
- Individuals are morally bound to be healthy or to produce recognizable accounts for illness, in constructing illness identities. Illness identities have to be negotiated and are open to acceptance, challenge, undermining, and so on.
- Health is also linked to gender, with certain conditions and behaviors being constructed as mainly relevant either to men or women.
- Support for illness identities is available in different forms, including communicative support, self-help literature, and support groups. Often individuals have to negotiate within groups illness identities that entitle them to support.
- Health professionals routinely display expertise in health in their communications with individuals and with other professionals. In their encounters with individuals, professionals emphasize the individual and moral aspects of health, using assessments, formulations, and diagnoses.
- Professional expertise also has to be negotiated. It is difficult for individuals successfully to challenge this expertise, and resistance to professional constructions of health or illness will be met with further displays of expertise.
- Attempts to change health behaviors emphasize individual behavior and moral responsibility, and have little regard for conflicts of identity, particularly those of health and gender identities.
- Community health initiatives can be resisted, challenged, or accepted within the community. The outcomes of tensions between health and other social understandings may be inconclusive and open to future negotiation.

Connections

Much of the material in this chapter is closely linked to the negotiation of identities, seen in Chapter 2. The work on support groups and communication within groups is relevant also to the study of group processes more generally, covered in Chapter 3. Communicative support is connected to issues of communication within relationships, covered in more detail in Chapter 4.

Activity

Consider one time in your life when you have experienced illness. What impact did that illness have on your experiences? Was your ill-health readily accepted by family, friends, or health professionals? What support, if any, did you receive and from where? How did you make sense of the experience?

Further reading

Hepworth, J. (1999). *The social construction of anorexia nervosa.* London: Sage. This text provides a useful historical analysis of how the condition became constructed in terms of gender and individual pathology.

Horton-Salway, M. (2001). Narrative identities and the management of personal accountability in talk about ME: A discursive psychology approach to illness narrative. *Journal of Health Psychology, 6,* 247–259. A clear example of how individuals seek to negotiate contested illness and to have their illness identities accepted.

McHoul, A. & Rapley, M. (2005). A case of attention-deficit/hyperactivity disorder diagnosis: Sir Karl and Francis B. slug it out on the consulting room floor. *Discourse & Society, 16,* 419–449. A comprehensive analysis of one diagnostic session in which individuals challenge professional expertise in practice.

Chapter 11

Social Psychology and Organizations

> *At Microsoft, success comes from our passion for creating value – value for customers, shareholders, and partners; value for our employees and the communities around the world where we do business. Underlying our success is an approach to corporate governance that extends beyond simple compliance with legal requirements. I believe that corporate governance must provide a framework for establishing a culture of business integrity, accountability, and responsible business practices.*
>
> *Strong corporate governance at Microsoft starts with a Board of Directors that is independent, engaged, committed, and effective. Our Board establishes, maintains, and monitors standards and policies for ethics, business practices, and compliance that span the company. Working with management, we set strategic business objectives, ensure that Microsoft has leadership that is dynamic and responsive, track performance, and institute strong financial controls. We believe in strengthening investor confidence and creating long-term shareholder value so we can continue to deliver technology innovations that provide opportunities for customers and for Microsoft.* — Bill Gates, Microsoft Chairman
> (Microsoft Corporation, 2007)

The extract above comes from a public statement on corporate governance of Microsoft, one of the largest organizations in the world. This particular message appears under the subheading "Message from our Chairman," and ends with the name of Bill Gates as Microsoft Chairman. In itself, the message seems pretty unexceptional, referring to the corporation, and to a range of individuals and groups that are relevant to Microsoft and its success.

Let us consider the various people that are included in this description, namely "customers," "shareholders," "partners," "communities around the world," and "a Board of Directors." Add to that list "our Chairman" from whom the message comes. Certainly, these individuals and groups are those that we might expect to be closely involved with the organization as it conducts its business. However, if we subtract all such people from consideration, we are left with the question of what, more precisely, is the corporation and who are the "we" that appear to comprise it?

The above message refers also to the operations of Microsoft, for instance, in relation to the "culture" of the organization, "business practices," and "leadership." One might ask of Microsoft, as indeed of any other organization, how such operations are carried out within the organization. For example, to what extent and in what ways are its activities managed by the Board of Directors, or influenced by other employees, or by people

such as customers who are external to Microsoft? Organizations such as Microsoft are immediately recognizable to us as entities in their own right; yet, as we look more closely, organizations become inseparable from the human activities that present them to us on a recurring basis.

Talk and Organizations

Often we talk about organizations as distinct objects. We can, for example, scan daily newspapers for share prices and other financial information relating to companies and profit-making organizations. Other kinds of organizations, such as the United Nations, the World Bank, or the UK National Health Service, also feature heavily in much of the media coverage that we hear and read. Numerous similar references produce a picture of a world inhabited by objects that for their existence are somehow distinct from any dependence upon people. However, for any organization to function, it requires action on the part of individuals within the organization and of others. The more that we look at what organizations do and are, the more that we see that they are inseparable from human action in some form or another. Rather, therefore, than treating organizations as being discrete and anonymous entities, Watson (1996, p. 295) encourages a somewhat different view, as follows:

[O]rganizations [are] ongoing and ever changing patterns of human interactions, meanings, negotiations, conflicts and ambiguities. The organization is not so much a "thing" which we can see or touch as sets of stories or practical fictions which help shape relationships within which work tasks get done.

This view usefully directs our attention to the central role of interaction and the construction of meaning in organizational activities. However, the more precise relationship between interactions and organizations potentially remains unclear. We might ask whether interactions in themselves enact and construct organizations or whether interactions in organizational contexts are the effects of social patterns and processes. On the former argument, interactions that make relevant an organization or organizational practices bring into being the organization as an immediate concern for those involved. Writ large, the recurring conversations relating to a corporation such as Microsoft daily present to us an image of Microsoft as an independent organization. The opposing view is that our understandings of organizations and any single organization result from broader social patterns that promote organizations as a form of social practice. The practices of organizations such as Microsoft thus are not dependent upon the immediate concerns of individuals but instead reflect prevailing social meanings and ideologies. You will by now not be surprised to learn that discursive researchers take up widely divergent positions on these matters, and that for many researchers the issues are by no means as clearly defined as this simple distinction might suggest.

Institutional talk

For conversation analysts, organizations are a meaningful topic of inquiry only insofar as they can be shown to be relevant to individuals in the details of everyday interactions. Rather than studying organizations, it is talk that is the topic of interest. For such reasons, conversation analysts in considering the work of organizations have focused their efforts on examining whether or not talk in institutional settings differs from ordinary talk-in-interaction, and if so, in what ways it differs. Setting here refers to the interaction

rather than to the physical location; institutional talk need not necessarily occur within places that we recognize as being institutions but rather can be found in many interactions, for example home visits to patients by health professionals, people's telephone calls to emergency services, and so on. The question is whether talk found in exchanges between professionals and lay individuals has features that mark it out as being **institutional talk** instead of commonly occurring talk. In a classic text, Drew and Heritage (1992) set out features that might be distinctive to institutional talk.

Adopting a focus on institutional talk, analytic interest lies in how interactions are managed in order to accomplish institutional activities. By close study of the details of interactions, we should be able to identify features that are specific to particular institutions and practices and that comprise the "fingerprints" that distinguish one institution or organization from another. Further, in institutional talk individuals use pronouns that develop their identities and those of institutions. References to pronouns such as "we" or "us" display individuals' alignments with institutional identities and enhance the identities of institutions themselves (Drew & Sorjonen, 1997). The categories that are found within institutional talk thus are linked with issues of identity and of activities that are relevant to the work of an institution or organization (Psathas, 1999). Examination of particular instances of institutional talk also can reveal patterns of asymmetry, displaying the relative power of an institution in its dealing with other people (Hutchby, 1996b, 1999). We can therefore see the work of specific organizations being achieved by and through individual interactions (Psathas, 1999).

In pointing to how work is accomplished in talk and the features of talk that appear to be specific to particular institutions, conversation analysis offers one approach to studying organizations and organizational practices. Practical applications of this sort are required if conversation analysis is to offer insights that are socially meaningful and to provide possibilities for critiquing social life (ten

---

Institutional talk Talk found in institutional settings and which differs from everyday conversation

---

CLASSIC STUDY: Talk at work

Although it can be found in physical work-based settings, institutional talk is not limited to these settings. Institutional talk can be found in any instances in which professional identities and concerns are relevant. Drew and Heritage, in this edited collection, present a collection of studies of institutional talk-in-interactions from legal, health, and other contexts.

These studies demonstrate how talk is both implicated in and constitutive of institutional practices. In contrast to ordinary talk, which is relatively unconstrained, institutional talk typically focuses more narrowly on topics and identities that are immediately relevant to the institution.

According to Drew and Heritage, institutional talk differs from ordinary conversation in the following ways:

- there may be special turn-taking rules, e.g., who is allowed to speak in a courtroom,
who asks questions in doctor–patient consultations, etc.;
- specific conversational structures may apply;
- the participants orient towards specific tasks or goals;
- there may be restrictions on what is "allowable," i.e., on what individuals may say;
- the institutional context may be reflected in specific lexical terms or vocabulary;
- the interactions are often asymmetrical, with one participant having greater power or knowledge than the other, e.g., employer/ employee interactions.

Through use of these features, specific forms of talk can become specific to particular institutions. A particular form of talk can thus provide, in effect, a "fingerprint" for institutional practices.

Drew, P. & Heritage, J. (Eds.) (1992). *Talk at work: Interaction in institutional settings.* Cambridge: Cambridge University Press.

Have, 1999, 2001). Not all conversation analysts, however, agree that the approach should be used in this way, and many are skeptical that institutional talk can be readily differentiated from ordinary talk. For example, some researchers argue that institutional concerns will not be continuously relevant in people's interactions with professionals (Zimmerman & Boden, 1991), and that we should not treat institutional structures of talk as existing beyond the boundaries of the specific conversations in which they are found (Hester & Francis, 2000, 2001a). Primarily, such doubts stem from the core principle of conversation analysis that the researcher must not take context and setting to be relevant to individuals in their interactions with others unless that relevance can be demonstrated in the talk (Schegloff, 1991). In the present case, this principle presents difficulties in that, if it were applied strictly, there would appear to be no obvious or immediate grounds for distinguishing institutional talk from ordinary talk.

One way of dealing with such difficulties comes from Arminen (2005). Arminen argues that

conversation analysis can only work at all on the basis of a researcher's initial understanding of the context of talk; without some competence in making sense of what is going on, research would be a futile pursuit. The conversation analyst's task, therefore, is one of "reverse engineering," seeking evidence from the data to show that the initially assumed context is indeed relevant to the participants. In the case of institutional talk, therefore, it is reasonable to go forward on the basis that we understand institutional talk to differ from ordinary talk, but we should indicate where institutional features become relevant. Rather than assuming that talk about organizations or work practices has particular features, researchers should point to the features of talk that specifically deal with the organizational issues in question.

Organizations and culture

For other discursive researchers, the use of context to understand organizational discourse is unproblematic, and moreover is necessary in order to understand organizational discourse meaningfully as a social phenomenon. In recent years, a number of journal special issues (e.g., Grant & Hardy, 2004; Iedema & Wodak, 1999; Oswick, Keenoy, & Grant, 2000) have been devoted to the study of organizational discourse as instances of social practices. From this perspective, greater attention is paid to the effects of language in particular social and historical contexts than to the detail of language in use. Accordingly, interest lies in power and the ideological effects of language in advancing and sustaining particular understandings of organizations, organizational practices, and identities. The social context of discourse thus offers analysts a useful and necessary way of interpreting the language found in specific organizational instances. Take, for example, politeness. A number of studies of organizations have explored politeness as a main concern in organizational communications. Organizational forms of politeness, from this approach, are not restricted to particular individual organizations but rather are linked to cultural expectations of behavior. Displays of politeness vary from culture to culture, certainly between Western and Eastern cultures, and in more nuanced ways between different Eastern cultures. To understand politeness within organizations, therefore, we need to look not just at the words that people use within organizations, but also at the cultural context within which the discourse and the organizations are located (Bargiela-Chiappini & Gotti, 2005; Bargiela-Chiappini et al., 2007). The relationship between organizational discourse and social practices is thus open to study both at social and organizational levels (Alvesson & Karreman, 2000).

The study of organizational discourse is in itself a somewhat diverse field. To date, work on this topic has come from two very different traditions (Grant & Iedema, 2006). One tradition, as might be expected, is the study of organizations as an important element of social life, and discursive researchers have applied methods similar to those used to investigate other topics of social interest. This strand can usefully be termed **organizational discourse analysis**. A second strand of

work has derived mainly from researchers working in the fields of organization theory and management theory. Researchers within this tradition have increasingly come to study discourse as a means of understanding organizations that goes beyond previous models of organizational systems or cultures. Work within this tradition is termed **organizational discourse studies**. Unsurprisingly, given their different origins and development, these two strands differ in some respects, mainly in the emphases that they place upon discourse analysis in its own right rather than as a means of understanding organizational practices, and upon identifying commonalities rather than diversities in organizational discourse. Thus, this far, there has been relatively little cross-referencing of work within the two traditions. The *Sage handbook of organizational discourse* (Grant, Hardy, Oswick, & Putnam, 2004), for example, provides a comprehensive coverage of organizational discourse studies research while offering little mention of organizational discourse analysis work. Such existing differences, however, are primarily matters of emphasis, not principle, and it appears likely that commonality of interests will lead to future cross-fertilization of research that addresses organizational discourse in a broad sense.

One example of the relationship between organizational discourse and social practices can be seen in relation to retirement. Whereas it was once regarded as a period of relative inactivity, often accompanied by decline, retirement has become viewed widely as a time for active leisure and choice, allowing the possibility of active and positive aging. Changing understandings of retirement have, in various countries, led to the development of retirement villages that offer lifestyle choices in older age within a managed environment. The extent of these choices, though, is not always clear. In a study of retirement villages in New Zealand, Simpson and Cheney (2007) noted that village organizations did promote some choice and participation on the part of residents. For example:

> Experience new activities "I had never bowled before I moved into the village." (Metlifecare, n.d.)

Organizational discourse analysis The use of discourse analysis to study organizations as a social topic

Organizational discourse studies Studies of organizations that focus on organizational discourse

For some quiet time, browse through a selection of books or newspapers, or relax in front of the library. (Vision Senior Living, n.d.)

Becoming a Metlifecare resident is much like joining an exclusive club . . . including access to common facilities . . . such as community centre, swimming pool, bowling green, and restaurant. (Metlifecare, n.d.)

(Simpson & Cheney, 2007, pp. 202–204)

These extracts are taken from the organizations' promotional literature. The first extract explicitly links resident participation with active leisure in the form of the activities that the organization makes available. This participation is only one of the options available to residents, as we see in the second extract. In the third extract, we see clearly the comparison drawn between the village organization and possible members' clubs, in terms of the choice of activities and the importance of leisure. All such marketing descriptions thus encompass widely held expectations of active leisure, choices, and participation in older age.

These descriptions, however, in setting out available possibilities, also circumscribed the extent of residents' participation. Treating residents as club members rather than as home-owners does not readily allow for participation in other aspects of retirement village life, such as being involved in the running of the village.

I believe a retirement village – especially after this "spout" we got from [Board member] right at the beginning – that the residents are the most important thing in this village that's my belief and I think the residents' interests have to be paramount and they are not paramount – they are not paramount and I think we are gradually getting them to understand more and more especially as they're spreading their wings into other places and they are getting more comfortable with their financial mood I think they're listening more and more but we have still got a way to go. (Resident, Focus Group)

(Simpson & Cheney, 2007, p. 212)

When residents sought to participate in financial management or other operational aspects of the village organizations, these attempts led to friction between residents and staff. Whereas residents presented such claims as being a reasonable part of their entitlements to participation, staff took such requests to be unreasonable as falling beyond the limits of resident participation and sought to maintain their own control over the operation of the village. Discourse within the village thus became the site of competing versions of participation and its meaning within the organization.

What studies of organizational discourse offer, then, are accounts of how broader social practices come to be taken up within organizations in their operations. Social understandings are by no means uniform; we can see how divergent constructions, for example of retirement and participation, can easily lead to the contestation of issues within the organizational context. In many cases, potential claims may be marginalized while other versions are privileged and prevail. Understanding organizations from this perspective, however, requires us to engage with the broader social realm in which an organization is to be found, and the range of ways in which social constructions are taken up within an organization as those involved make sense of ongoing organizational practices.

Behavior at Work

Often we might consider work to be a fairly specific set of task-oriented activities. Certainly there are times when what we do at work seems marked out as being separate from other aspects of our lives. Any such separation, however, can be problematic, as in the following example provided by Drew (2002) of what can happen when work considerations come into unexpected contact with other more personal issues.

1	JERRY:	Wichitaw'(bluepri:nt)
2	LINDA:	Hey Jerry?
3		(.)
4	LINDA:	.h[h
5	JERRY:	[Ye:[s.
6	LINDA:	[hHi:. .h[h
7	JERRY:	[HI:[:.
8	LINDA:	[He:y– you don'haftuh bring'ny
9		paper plates I think ah'll jus:t use the plates ah'v
10		go::t,hh
11	JERRY: +	Who's thi:s.
12	LINDA: +	↑Linda.ehh[hhhkhhh
13	JERRY:	[↑OH(h):.
14	LINDA:	°henh°

15 JERRY: H[i::.
16 LINDA: [Wuhdihyou mean uwho(h)'s[this,
17 JERRY: [heh heh .hh
18   (.)
19 LINDA: [.hhhhhhhhhhh
20 JERRY: [Hm::, huh hu-eh .hu::[:h.
21 LINDA: [khh[hh
22 JERRY: [Oh::: yeah fine? En you?

(Drew, 2002, p. 484)

In this extract, we see an excerpt of a telephone conversation between Jerry, who is at work, and his wife, Linda. As is apparent from his question at line 11, Jerry fails during the earlier part of the conversation to recognize his wife's voice. This failure of recognition arises from the preceding turns that orient to different concerns, with Jerry treating the call as being work-related and Linda proceeding on the basis that her voice has been recognized and that discussion of domestic issues has become appropriate. These differing understandings come into sharp relief when Linda refers to preparations for a party that they are to attend that evening, leading to Jerry's request for identification. The conversation therefore requires numerous turns before Jerry treats the call as relating to domestic arrangements and thus as not being work-related.

Now, one might argue that the above excerpt represents an extreme case situation. Many individuals will expect their spouses, partners, or friends to recognize their voices, even in a workplace setting! Indeed, it frequently appears difficult meaningfully to separate out our working activities from other aspects of our lives. We have already noted that some discursive researchers argue that we cannot assume that all talk in apparent work settings will necessarily be related to work. Rather, such talk potentially might in some ways resemble talk found in everyday conversations. Further, organizations and work are set within a broad framework of social life. This framework has implications not just for work but for how we understand all aspects of our lives. Work, social, and personal issues are not readily separable. For example, our conversations with work colleagues will often include references to personal issues or other matters that are not directly task-related. This is not to say that such talk has no bearing on work activities; far from it. In such cases, sharing personal experiences with work colleagues can help to foster good relationships and so to promote effective collaboration within the workplace (Holmes, 2005b; Marra & Holmes, 2004). What all of this points to is that it is not solely work practices that have to be negotiated in the workplace; the workplace provides a setting for the discussion and management of personal experiences and relationships as well as work itself.

Working relationships

One difficulty for any attempt to separate out work-related activity and discourse from other discourse is that often both are found together in close proximity. Koester (2004) notes that much of the interaction in work settings draws on task-related and more personal and social elements. There are, of course, instances that are solely directed towards accomplishment of work tasks. For example:

1 DAVE Basically I've used their o:ld. price list,
2 VAL Right,
3 DAVE And . . . I've made a few changes.
4 VAL Yeah,

(Koester, 2004, p. 1406)

Commonly though, interactions between colleagues involve both work-related and other matters. Consider the following extract.

Making arrangement (Proposing)	1 JIM	I was wondering if . . . you an' I could possibly this week, at about eleven o'clock on Thursday morning, *reinforce* each other half an hour on– just to *look* through [name of journal] and see where we are
Relational sequence	2 LIZ	[Yes [it's– it's on my mind *terribly*, in fact →
	3 JIM	[yeah
	4 LIZ	I've been dreaming about it all night.
	5 JIM	Well *I* had a dream about it as *well*.
	6 LIZ	[So–
	7 LIZ	I've got to get i– because it's on my mind so much I–
	8 JIM	[It's funny [a really guilty conscience about it =
	9 LIZ	= Yes, I am, so I *must* . . . get on and do it.

Making	10 LIZ	So yes, Thursday at eleven will be fine.
arrangement		
(Accepting)	11 JIM	[Heheheh
Finalizing/	12 JIM	Ok, we'll just review where we
specifying		are: an' ...
arrangement		what's ... urgent and what's um ... →
	13 LIZ	[yeah um
	14 JIM	perhaps not so urgent to do.
	15 LIZ	[Ok. [...]

(Koester, 2004, p. 1419)

In this exchange, Jim and Liz arrange a meeting to discuss issues relating to a journal of which Jim is editor. A number of turns are required in order to make this arrangement. However, in addition to completing the task, the participants introduce into the conversation personal elements that are not strictly necessary to arrange the meeting. This personal talk is closely connected with work talk in that it takes the task of arranging the meeting to be relevant for the duration of the conversation. However, by introducing personal matters, Jim and Liz develop an interpersonal understanding that displays affiliation in their working relationship. Relational talk of this kind offers possibilities for individuals to show solidarity and build relationships with colleagues in the course of accomplishing work. Work activities and relationships thus become closely intertwined, with relational talk forming an important part of organizational discourse.

Interactions with work colleagues offer considerable scope for introducing and discussing social and personal concerns and promoting cohesion in the workplace (Cheepen, 2000; Coupland, 2003; Mirivel & Tracy, 2005). Choice of topic, though, is not the only way of enhancing workplace solidarity. A common feature of many workplace interactions is humor. Individuals often use humor to display friendliness and their support of colleagues. Holmes and Marra (2002a) provide an example taken from a planning meeting of colleagues within a New Zealand government department.

1	ELLEN:	Grace you're gonna chair next week
2	RUTH:	it must be my turn soon
3	ELLEN:	and Kaye can scribe
4	XF:	so it's at three /(isn't it)\
5	SALLY:	/I must\ be due for a turn at chairing too+

6		and I'll put in my apologies now
7		[general laughter]
8	KAYE:	no you're not you're not at all sorry [laughs]

(Holmes & Marra, 2002a, p. 1689)

Although workplace humor is not always explicitly supportive, other uses of humor can also contribute towards effective working relationships within an organization (Holmes, 2006). One use of humor, for example, is to avoid explicit references to power or status of different employees. By using humor, a manager can instruct more junior colleagues without recourse to the overt use of authority.

Context: Manager, Beth, to administrative assistant, Marion, who is chatting to a secretary.

1	BETH:	OK Marion I'm afraid serious affairs of state will have to wait
2		we have some trivial issues needing our attention
3		[All laugh]

(Holmes, 2000, p. 172)

Working relationships can be enhanced by directing humor at practices beyond the organization itself.

Context: Jacob is a member of an American company working on a project in New Zealand.

| JACOB: | [Specialists] for some reason are rare in New Zealand no matter what |
| ERIC: | it's because we train them so highly and then they bugger off overseas. [General laughter] |

(Holmes & Marra, 2002b, p. 74)

The instances and uses of humor in workplace interactions vary between and within organizations. Over time, the instances found within any group of workers can become patterned, with the emerging patterns distinguishing particular groups from other groups and organizations (Holmes & Schnurr, 2005). The same can be said of the use and frequency of social talk and the ways in which working relationships are negotiated between specific individuals. Other elements too contribute towards work group understandings. For example, the use of expletives such as "fuck," although often considered offensive, might well be taken in certain groups to be acceptable and indeed to be a part of the solidarity of the group itself (Daly, Holmes, Newton, & Stubbe, 2004). In such ways, the recurring practices of work groups develop their own logics, or micro cultures, that provide meanings for activities in the workplace.

Established cultures of particular work groups do, however, have their downside. Newcomers looking to enter a highly cohesive work group might well experience difficulty in being accepted by existing members, particularly if incomers do not share the understandings that have developed. What is one person's expression of solidarity might to someone else be little more than an unnecessary and offensive expletive. Nor might newcomers share established patterns of humor (Rogerson-Revell, 2007), or social talk (Holmes & Marra, 2004), that have developed over time in highly specific ways. Gaining acceptance presents considerable difficulties for individuals who are less skilled conversational participants, such as people with intellectual disabilities, and who are less likely to contribute to ongoing patterns of interaction (Holmes, 2003). The developed cohesion of groups in specific settings thus can provide benefits for those involved in the group but simultaneously presents hurdles for anyone looking to enter an existing workplace and its culture.

Working activities

In work settings, people commonly interact not just with other workers but also with physical environments of space and equipment. Where work is carried out within an office, we would expect to find people using computers and files; in production plants, individuals use specialized machinery; and so on. In settings such as the control center for the London Underground, or a BT Restoration Control Office, many of the working activities will be centered around the use of monitors and attention to information from different sources. Individual employees in the course of their work select out relevant items of information for discussion and processing with work colleagues (Heath & Hindmarsh, 2000; Hindmarsh & Heath, 2000). Other types of work may require interactions with physical equipment and colleagues, and with recipients of the work services. The delivery of anesthesia,

for instance, involves medical staff in the use of appropriate medical instruments, collaboration with other members of the team, and interaction with the patient (at least for the initial part of the procedure!). Medical teams are thus required to coordinate a range of tasks, referring at relevant points to physical items and activities and to the patient, for the procedure to be successful (Hindmarsh & Pilnick, 2002).

On occasions, physical equipment in the workplace setting may itself become the focus of work activities. The output of a manufacturing plant, for instance, depends upon the interactions of employees with the machines that produce the end product. When a machine fails to act as expected, attention is likely to shift from the manufacturing output to the operation of the machine. Kleifgen (2001; Kleifgen & Frenz-Belkin, 1997) provides an example, from a circuit board manufacturing company located in Silicon Valley, California, of interaction surrounding a machine malfunction. The extract below marks the beginning of an exchange between two Vietnamese immigrant employees of the company, Tran, a machine operator, and Du, his supervisor. This sequence follows an observed malfunction in the assembly machine, in which the machine has failed to place the required number of sockets (four) on a circuit board.

10:17:16 DU:	MIS-PICK–	((robotic arm has tried and failed to pick a component from the feeder))
10:18:16 TRAN:	Oo: : : h.	
10:22:17		((*presses stop*))
10:25:23	°One two three°.	((*counts on fingers, gazing at board*))
10:35:04		((*presses start*))
10:35:25		((*presses button for slow motion*))
10:35:45		((*begins gaze directed at pick point*))
10:38:25	°Hai cái.° *Two.*	
10:39:22	°Ba cái.° *Three.*	
10:42:19		((*machine comes to a stop on initiating third pick try*))

10:45:15 DU: Có phái chinh con ôc' o duoi
              không?
              Need to fix the screw underneath?
10:47:28 TRAN: Ù.
              Yeah.
              (Kleifgen & Frenz-Belkin, 1997, p. 164)

Following Du's initial announcement of the malfunction, the attention of both workers focuses on the assembly machine. Tran counts the actions of the machine, as both Tran's and Du's hand movements and gaze are directed to what they take to be the problem. This joint activity displays shared knowledge of how the machine should operate and of the problem that has arisen. The sequence thus displays collaborative activity between Tran and Du, focusing on the work task that now has to be carried out.

A noteworthy feature of this interaction lies in the positioning of Tran and Du. As Tran's supervisor, Du is the more senior employee. More than this, however, both employees are Vietnamese. The Vietnamese language has a wide range of pronouns that index the relative status of individuals. An interaction between a worker and manager often would be marked by explicit displays of **referential status**. Such markers are noticeably absent in the extract above and, indeed, as the sequence continues, Tran gives his superior what might be taken to be directives.

10:58:04 TRAN: Duoc, cho nó di.
              Okay, let it go.
12:51:01 TRAN: Phái cân dên' muoi hai.
              [We] must set it to twelve.
              (Kleifgen, 2001, p. 290)

Although these utterances might be taken as (inappropriate) indications of unequal status between the workers, Du does not treat them in this way. Instead, with each worker's attention directed towards a different aspect of the operation of the assembly machine, the statements form part of the collaborative activity of diagnosing the malfunction and repairing the machine. It is only at the end of this collaborative exchange that Du reestablishes his seniority.

Referential status An individual's social status relative to another individual

---

15:27:55 DU: Chút nùa phái cho nó hai muoi bôn.
              After this [we] must give it twenty-four.
15:29:27   Hai muoi bôn' che sô' tám che làm
              ba cái.
              *Twenty-four divided by number eight
              is three.*
15:39:00   Yeah nó se che ba cái.
              Yeah, it divides into three.
              (Kleifgen, 2001, p. 298)

What the exchange between Tran and Du demonstrates, as do the earlier examples, is the role of physical objects in many working activities. Physical environments, and the items found within them, do not simply provide the backdrop to work activities but rather can form an integral part of these activities. Effective working practices may depend as much upon the interactions of individuals with all elements of work settings as they do upon the interactions with work colleagues. Collaboration with colleagues, however, is equally central to successful work outcomes. Different employees have different roles and often unequal positions within organizations. Nonetheless, it falls to individual employees to negotiate control of and responsibility for the work practices that are carried out within any organization.

Leadership and Decision-Making

The ways in which decisions are made within organizations are linked to cultural expectations of leadership and participation. For example, cultural understandings of politeness influence the style of leadership found within particular organizations (Schnurr, Marra, & Holmes, 2007). In addition to the style of decision-making, however, there is the question of how control of organizational decisions is negotiated. Broadly speaking, we can contrast organizations in which decisions are made primarily by individuals of higher status, as managers or leaders, with those in which the decision-making process is more democratic and inclusive in its procedures.

Where organizations operate on an inclusive basis, scope is provided for all employees with an interest in an operational decision to have some influence over the decision that is made. Discourse designed to elicit the participation of employees is likely to be encouraging, to use questions to promote involvement in discussions of the issues, and to display alignment between managers, subordinates, and the organization itself. The emphasis thus is placed on the process of participation rather than on any predetermined outcome (Yeung, 2004). This principle of **participatory decision-making**, however, often appears to be rather more of a theoretical ideal than a reflection of processes that operate in practice. Within many organizations, there is a tension between competing discourses of dynamic growth on the one hand, and economic control on the other. It is through the use of these two discourses that managers and senior employees make sense of their own experiences within the organization (T. J. Watson, 1997). These discourses provide for different levels of participation by more junior employees. Whereas discourse of dynamic growth might suggest inclusion and facilitative inclusion of subordinates in organizational decision-making, discourse of economic control provides for the continuing authority and power of senior managers and limited involvement by subordinates. In practice, it is often discourse of economic control that prevails.

Management control can be exercised by more or less visible means. When employees share and do not question the accepted operating procedures of the organization, control need not be exerted overtly and can operate in unobtrusive ways. More commonly, issues of control arise explicitly at times when subordinate employees question or disagree with management understandings. Yeung (2004), in a study of bank practices in Australia and Hong Kong, observes that participatory decision-making in these organizations can amount to little more than explicit management attempts to bring employees' understandings into line with existing organizational practices.

(Manager)
Ngodei moukchin jauhaiwaa, hou choungfouk, hou chaamhei
We at present that is to say, very repetitive, very irritably repetitive
"Our present situation is this: To do it [this way] is very repetitive and very irritably repetitive,"

hui jou, houchi yansau hou saai dou hai yui heui jou. Gaam nigo
to do seem manpower very waste still EMP must EMP do ADV this
"it seems to be a waste of manpower that we still have to do it."

daaiyat moukbyui ne, jauhaiwaa mmhou cheutcho houngjaai daak yimaat
primary target PT that is not make mistake control ADV tightly
"So, this is to say that the [company's] primary objective is not to make any mistakes and to have tight control."

(Yeung, 2004, p. 94)

The extract above follows a lengthy argument between the manager and bank employees regarding the procedures used to check foreign exchange remittances. Earlier in the discussion, the employees have suggested and argued for a simplified method of carrying out this task. Although he acknowledges the issues raised by staff members, namely the repetitive and wasteful aspects of existing procedures, the manager terminates the discussion with a restatement of the organizational logic that underlies these procedures. The final decision as to the method of performing the task thus reflects management control and takes little account of the employees' expressed concerns.

Similar tensions between management control and empowerment of employees run through many aspects of organizational processes. For example, **mentoring** is designed to be a process whereby senior employees can provide advice and guidance to more junior employees within an organization, enabling the junior employees to gain experience and to develop their future careers. Holmes (2005a) notes that, in practice, mentoring can take various forms, depending upon the emphasis that the mentor places on organizational concerns or on employee development.

1 JILL: where's that part two again + well see
2 KIWA: but I /mean would you–\ do you um do you agree with me here
3 JILL: /what it– what\
4 KIWA: it may be better for her

Participatory decision-making Involvement of all interested employees in the making of organizational decisions

Mentoring Advice and guidance given by senior employees to more junior employees

5		if she doesn't take on as much project work next year
6		as she did in the last two years +
7		making a conscious decision to curtail product development
8		and concentrate concentrate more on policy response ++
9		do you think
10	JILL:	yes see th– see this is why I botched this

(Holmes, 2005a, pp. 1786–1787)

Above we see an exchange between a male manager, Kiwa, and his female subordinate, Jill. This interaction forms part of a review of Jill's performance over the preceding year and is designed to establish her goals for the year to come. The focus of the review, however, is on securing Jill's agreement to what is already written on the review form rather than on discussing her further development within the organization. This interaction contrasts with that in the example below.

1	JAN:	well what are you going to do with this information
2	KIWA:	well um I think we'll have to use the information now
3		in our in our discussions with the Ministry of [name]
4		about what policies what you know more /interventionist\ type
5	JAN:	/right\
6	KIWA:	/policies\
7	JAN:	/you'll be\ bri– briefing the Minister of– the Ministry of [name]
8	KIWA:	yep
9	JAN:	and what about our Minister . . .

(Holmes, 2005a, pp. 1793–1794)

This exchange comes from a meeting between a senior manager, Jan, and Kiwa as one of her section leaders. Jan's turns comprise questions that invite her subordinate to provide suggestions as to future action, which Jan subsequently approves at line 5. Rather than seeking compliance with existing aims, therefore, the emphasis is on indirect coaching and the review focuses on the employee's proposed actions and development. Mentoring in this instance thus operates in a reciprocal and facilitative manner, rather than comprising attempted control and direction seen in the previous extract.

Discourses of control and of empowerment and growth run through many organizational practices. The use of each discourse varies from organization to organization and from setting to setting within the same organization. Commonly, management control features more frequently than the participation of employees in the operation of the organization. Imposition of strict demands of control, however, can seriously restrict the capacity of an organization to amend its practices when necessary. In times of changing market conditions, organizations that place less emphasis on control and have substantial flexibility in their procedures are more likely to adapt successfully to changing contexts in which they find themselves (Menz, 1999).

Employment and Non-Employment

We have seen how individuals negotiate work activities and construct working relationships with colleagues. One question that we might usefully ask at this point is that of how people come to be in particular jobs and work settings. How do organizations and individuals negotiate the process of employment? Directly related to this question is the issue of non-employment, and of how people who are not employed and organizations that do not employ make sense of these outcomes. Let us consider these issues in more detail.

Career choices

Historically, jobs have been viewed largely as slots to be filled by individuals who have the necessary attributes or qualifications. It is commonplace to see in the media job advertisements that detail the requirements of particular jobs and that describe desired employees. Recruitment thus is often viewed as a process of matching people to opportunities that are available. This notion of matching people and jobs, however, is less to do with the essential elements of employment than it is to do with social understandings of the relationship between individuals and society. As Hollway (1984) notes, it becomes impossible on close examination meaningfully to describe any particular job without some reference to a potential person or persons. Jobs always have some social context. On the reverse side, people seldom, if ever, describe themselves solely in terms of personal attributes. Even those in particular forms of employment, or who are pursuing vocationally related qualifications, often explain their employment choices without reference to specific personal features. For individuals, making sense of employment is less a matter of describing matching processes than it is of providing accounts that are socially recognizable (Moir, 1993).

Achieving success in employment, then, is primarily a process of negotiating accounts of employment choices and desires that are likely to be accepted by prospective employers and by others. In many countries, people seeking to enter the labor market can undergo career guidance counseling in which they discuss their plans with a trained counselor who facilitates individual career planning. Counselors are trained to encourage self-reflection and planning of their clients rather than to offer specific advice. When clients explicitly seek counselors' advice, counselors typically refrain from providing specific comment, or reframe the issue raised as one that should be jointly explored in the course of the session (Vehviläinen, 2003). By requiring clients to display their own intentions and career plans, counselors are able to provide evaluations of these plans and to discuss the likely merits of the clients' accounts in an employment context (Vehviläinen, 2001).

Of course, for job-seekers the most important audience for their accounts is that of prospective employers. Scheuer (2001), in a study of job interviews conducted within major Danish companies, notes that there are various features that mark out successful ("felicitous") interviews as different from unsuccessful ("infelicitous") interviews. Commonly, in interviews that lead to success, applicants make substantial contributions to the interaction and do not leave control totally with the interviewers.

1 A I'll just repeat some of my written application. (laughing)
2 C That's okay, you just do what you feel like.
3 C Yes.
5 A I am still, obviously, 27 years of age, right.
6 C Yes.
7 C (laughter)
8 A Graduated from the political science study about a year ago (pause), and more or less by coincidence I'm working at (political organization). A friend of mine working there grabbed

the phone and called me, because they needed a secretary and they knew that I was about to graduate. And she knows that I would like to have something to do. (i.e. work)
9 C Yes.
10 C Yes.
11 A That is, sort of, the reason why I ended up in there, and not some other place I might have come up with.
12 C Yes.
13 A (pause) It, since I started working in there most of my time has been spent on working, cause
14 C Yes.
15 A it's not the most predictable work place.
16 C No.
17 A I would imagine yours isn't either . . . (i.e. your work place is not very predictable either)
18 C (indistinguishable)
19 C No. Not always.
20 C (laughter)
21 A When the same gentlemen I rely on (i.e. the politicians), gents and ladies, come up with brand new games . . .
24 C Yes.
25 C It's probably worse in there (i.e. in the political organization). But it is bad here too.
26 A Yes.
27 A But I would imag–, you feel, after all you feel the effect and have to start working.(clears her throat)
28 C Yes. Yes.
29 C Absolutely right.
30 A And . . . (pause) I do not practise all sorts of sports activities. It is more activities that can take place at home: good books and (pause) needlework and that sort of thing. (pause) So I am not the kind of person that rushes off to handball (huge sport in Denmark) every night or what else one might think of. I'm better at watching a little TV.
32 C (laughter)
33 C Yes?
34 C (laughter)

(Scheuer, 2001, pp. 229–230)
(C = organizational committee member, A = applicant)

In this interview, the applicant herself introduces the topics to be discussed and provides the majority of the content. Her topics and description meet with approval from the interviewing committee, as marked by the positive responses and laughter at several points of the interview. The interview thus displays a symmetrical shape, with control shared between interviewers and interviewee. Unsuccessful interviews, by contrast, display a rather less symmetrical shape.

1 A (laughter) well I finished my Master at the business school last September and have been applying for job after job after job, and I've been to at least . . . (lengthy pause) And I am 27 years old. (in a quiet voice) (pause)

2 C Mm.

3 A During my Master I did *Human Resources* and *Organizational Development* as, primarily, that was what I found most interesting after high school (pause) and (pause) What else are we to talk about? (laughter)

5 C Mm.

6 C Yes.

7 C Did you always know that you were going to specialize in, yeah okay I'm gonna use the term organizational theory, right? (pause) in, in your Master, right? You know, that you were going to go in that direction (i.e. organizational theory) from elementary school and through the rest of your education till now?

9 A No, that was something I found out during business school, right?

10 C Yes.

11 A You know, in business school one did *Accounting* as well as *Finance* and *Organizational Studies* as well. And that was what I found most exciting, simply.

12 C Yes. Yes.

13 C Aha.

14 C But if you try to go back a little further, right? (pause)

15 A Mm.

16 C You, you graduated from high school in (city) I see? (looking at written curriculum) (pause)

17 C Yes. (high school) in (city).

18 A Yes. (high school), yes.

19 C Yes.

20 A Yes. (pause)

(Scheuer, 2001, p. 232)
(C = organizational committee member,
A = applicant)

Here, the turns of the job applicant are somewhat shorter than those found in successful interviews, and the applicant fails to introduce new topics for discussion. As the interview progresses, the majority of the turns comprise questions to the applicant by members of the committee, these questions being met with brief, often monosyllabic responses. The interview thus increasingly takes on a highly asymmetrical shape with control of the interaction and its progress remaining with the interviewing committee. There is no indication of approval of the limited information that comes from the applicant herself.

Successful and unsuccessful interviews differed also in other ways. For example, unsuccessful job applicants relied mainly on fairly technical and work-related responses to questions put to them by interviewers. Successful applicants, however, mixed such talk with a range of topics that included also personal and social elements. Such talk, unsurprisingly, worked to enhance affiliation between interviewers and interviewees, as might commonly be found in organizational contexts. Display of understandings of work in a broad sense, taken together with the production of convincing career accounts, thus marked out the differences between success and failure in securing employment.

Employment difficulties

Of course, it is not only individual job applicants that experience difficulties in an employment context. Problems can arise also when individual workers do not appear to fall into recognized patterns of work and employment. For example, numerous organizations offer opportunities for flexible working in order to allow employees to negotiate their own balance between work and home life. These opportunities are commonly constructed as being primarily applicable to female employees with domestic responsibilities. Flexible working accordingly is largely a gendered rather than work-oriented practice, and male employees may experience difficulty in negotiating flexible working arrangements (Smithson & Stokoe, 2005). Part-time working, similarly, is commonly viewed as primarily relevant to women, and is not easily recognized as an appropriate working pattern for male workers (Smithson, 2005).

A different set of issues arises in relation to people who are not in employment at all. Individual job-seekers, as we have seen, may well be unemployed as a result of their failure to convince employers to employ them. Being in work, however, is treated as a moral imperative, and as a result, individuals are expected to account for not being employed (McVittie, McKinlay, & Widdicombe, 2008). A lack of gainful employment is all the more accountable when individuals are receiving benefit for being unemployed. Registered claimants commonly are called upon to convince others, such as employment office officials, that their unemployment is not due to intention or an absence of effort in seeking work but that it results from external market forces, including the supply of and demand for labor (Mäkitalo, 2003).

There are, though, circumstances in which unemployment potentially becomes less attributable to individual factors. Where employment difficulties are common to numerous members of a particular social group, their lack of employment might well result from that group membership than from an accumulation of individual instances of failure. In short, a lack of employment opportunities for women, people from minority ethnic backgrounds, people with disabilities, older people, or other identifiable groups makes available the inference that employers are systematically discriminating against people belonging to these groups.

Overt discrimination is, of course, now illegal in many parts of the world, in relation to employment and other social practices, and on numerous grounds that include race, gender, age, and disability among other factors. Employers thus face potential legal liability should their employment practices be deemed to be discriminatory. Equally importantly, though, employers are treated as socially responsible for their practices, and are required to account for employment outcomes that might be taken to indicate the unfair or discriminatory treatment of job applicants or potential employees.

Commonly, employers account for ostensibly unfair outcomes by attributing these outcomes to factors that lie beyond their control. One way of doing so is to distinguish what is desirable in terms of fairness from what can effectively be achieved in employment practice. This distinction between theory and practice enables individuals to appear equitable while justifying outcomes that appear far from equitable (Wetherell, Stiven, & Potter, 1987). Here, factors beyond employers' control can include the attributes and actions

of non-employed people themselves and wider considerations. For example, controllers within local radio stations attribute an absence of female disc jockeys to the characteristics or job-seeking activities of women or to the expectations of the audience of the radio station (Gill, 1993). On a similar note, a recent study of employment practices towards migrant workers in Australia found that employers either avoided the issue of migrant employment or distanced the outcomes from their organizations. Again, non-employment of group members was attributed to the attributes and actions of migrants themselves or to the requirements of others, including existing staff, customers of the organizations, and the employment market (Tilbury & Colic-Peisker, 2006). In these and other instances, employers attribute the lack of employment of individuals from specific social groups to factors over which they as employers do not have control.

As well as accounting for unequal employment outcomes, these attributions allow employers to claim explicitly that their practices are fair. For example, McVittie and colleagues (McVittie, McKinlay, & Widdicombe, 2003) examined how human resources managers and personnel managers within organizations accounted for organizational practices towards older workers. One question asked about the age balances within the organizations.

> CM: It's something that we've touched on before but (.) what sort of age balance is there in [organization name] between say younger workers and over 40s?
>
> JJ: I would say that predominately that people in their twenties um (.) people from, I would say about 23 to about 27. I can get you some stats and I can send them to you about where our age group lies but I'd say uh, probably (.) probably about 70% are within that age range. Um (.) maybe that's 65, I would say about 65 to 70% I'd say or that range. And the rest are then spread (.) upwards from that.
>
> (McVittie et al., 2003, p. 601)

Although descriptions of this sort did not provide details of the age composition of the workforces, these responses suggested a low representation of older workers. Managers were asked to account for this age balance.

CM: Why is there that age balance, do you think?

PA: I don't think it has anything to do with the way they come through the recruitment process because as soon as we receive an application age isn't considered and it is not considered right the way through the process. So it has to be something before then that is stopping people applying to us. Either that or the things that we are rejecting people throughout the process on the basis of is indirectly maybe sometimes linked to age, I don't know whether that might be experience, erm, or technology, being able to use a computer, I don't know what, but it could be something like that indirectly affecting it.

(McVittie et al., 2003, p. 605)

In their accounts, the managers distanced themselves and their organizations from any action or knowledge of elements that might disadvantage older workers. In this, these accounts negated any inference of discrimination within the organizations. Alongside these descriptions, the managers explicitly claimed that their organizations operated equitably, in that the organizations were committed to equal opportunities in employment.

CM: Could you tell me what form your equal opportunities policy takes?

LL: We have an equal opportunities policy statement, e::m, and we are in the process of forming it into a full-blown policy etc. but I do say that we do we won't discriminate against ethnic origin, etc. etc. We don't include age at the moment, we're sort of, we are revising our handbook at the moment, we are inserting age and some other issues, to make it up front (.) I don't think we have discriminated against age per se in the past, but I do want it to be up front anyway.

(McVittie et al., 2003, p. 599)

These explicit claims rhetorically emphasized the theoretical aspects of fair employment practices, aligning the managers and organizations with equity in the ways in which they operated. Strengthening the commitment to theory of fair employment opportunities, while also accounting for why these were not achievable in practice,

thus justified the existing outcomes in these organizations.

Increasingly employers are drawing upon other forms of apparently egalitarian discourse in accounting for employment outcomes. Discourse of **diversity** is becoming prominent within the employment realm. Although diversity usually is taken to indicate differences in the attributes of individuals, it equally can be used to construct certain groups as lacking abilities relative to other employees. Thus, diversity, although suggesting equity, can be used to account for differential treatment of different social groups (Zanoni & Janssens, 2004). Employers, therefore, use discourse of diversity similarly to discourse of equal opportunities, constructing themselves as acting fairly and reasonably towards all prospective employees. The distinction between theory and practice is especially marked, emphasizing the bona fide intentions of organizations as employers while negating the need for any change in existing practices. Accountability for the non-employment of individuals or groups becomes a matter for those seeking employment, or simply one element of the employment context within which both individuals and organizations find themselves.

Organizations and Society

The discourse circulating within organizations may well take on patterns that are specific to specific organizations and to forms of activity. This discourse nonetheless both reflects and influences discourse circulating more widely throughout society. Talk of equal opportunities or diversity, for example, is inherently linked to prevailing understandings of what is fair and equitable in our actions towards other people. As social practices change over time, however, so too do the contexts within which organizations are located and it falls to them to adapt to changing conditions if their activities are to continue to make sense. Organizations and their employees have to make sense also to others external to the organization. For example, international organizations working with local agencies in the delivery of health

Diversity Bringing together individuals with a range of different attributes

services will need to assure these agencies that they are not at risk as a result of international intervention (Cooren, Matte, Taylor, & Vasquez, 2007). Most commonly, though, organizations have to interact with those to whom they provide goods or services, and in doing so, will have to negotiate organizational understandings of practices in wider contexts. Communication of our understandings of organizations and work go somewhat further than this. The meanings of work can permeate much of our everyday lives, even when we are not at work, such as in discussions of events with our families and friends. Contexts such as these not only provide opportunities for us to make sense of what we do at work; they also provide opportunities for others, such as children, to acquire social competence in making sense of social practices in the world in which they live.

Organizations and change

Organizations conduct their operations within a social context that is continually in flux. Although organizations develop practices that enable them to operate within such contexts, such practices will need to be responsive and attuned to social understandings for an organization to continue to operate effectively. In so doing, organizations will require both to negotiate internally changes in relation to a wider audience and to negotiate internally changes that reflect changing social conditions. Take, for example, the instance of a hospital that requires renovation against a backdrop of expectations of health and its delivery. The initial plans for such a renovation will originate within the practices of the health-care provider and in the interactions of the individuals involved in making such a decision and negotiating its acceptance by others. As the proposed change progresses, however, the plans will have to be presented to people, such as architects and planners, who are external to the organization and not party to initial discussions of the proposed change. Discussions and presentations thus will take on different forms as the organization progressively negotiates implementation of the proposal, finally leading to its enactment in the form of bricks and mortar in a physical and material context (Iedema, 1999).

In many instances, initially anticipated changes may lead an organization to review a wide range of previous practices. Take the example of the Internet. The Internet has become commonplace in everyday life, and we now usually expect organizations on their websites to provide a wealth of readily accessible information. In the case of Microsoft, with which we began this chapter, the website offers extensive details of the corporation itself, its products and how to obtain these, its relations with external parties, and so on. For an organization setting up a website, however, the question of which information to provide and how it should be presented is by no means clear-cut. The negotiation of how a website is constructed, therefore, may well be interlinked with wider discussions of the priorities and the use of information within an organization, particularly one already engaged in processes of organizational change (Lemke, 1999).

When the impetus for change originates beyond the organization, the process of achieving change will not necessarily be a smooth one. Decisions on changes in practices, like other organizational decisions, are open to contestation and involve greater or lesser levels of participation of employees of an organization. In large part, it is managers that influence understandings of change for themselves and for others, using available discourse as a strategic resource (Dunford & Jones, 2000). They can, in order to do so, draw upon prevailing understandings of management that are available in a range of texts that describe how such changes should be managed and understood (Chiapello & Fairclough, 2002). Often, in the accomplishment of changes, subordinate employees will enjoy relatively little participation. During the process of change, the constructions of senior managers are likely to prevail while other viewpoints are marginalized and have little influence on the subsequent actions of the organization (Hardy, Palmer, & Phillips, 2000).

Dealing with clients/customers

We will all be familiar with oft-quoted sayings such as "the customer is always right" or "the customer is king." Although not literally true, this logic is commonly taken to underpin much of current organizational practice. Usually it is assumed that such talk reflects understandings that customers are of paramount importance to the business of organizations and should be treated accordingly. The effects of this discourse in use appear rather different. For instance, discourse of the client is prevalent within major professional services firms, whose recruitment literature and everyday talk make frequent references to clients and clients' requirements. Client discourse, however, is directed primarily at employees of the firms. Within the firms, the constructed importance of clients is used to justify organizational practices that require employees to prioritize work over other life activities, engaging in (unpaid) overtime hours when required to do so. The constructions of clients therefore are more to do with maintaining the operational logics of the organizations than with the relationships between the firms and their clients (Anderson-Gough, Grey, & Robson, 2000).

Customers or clients of any organization are of course usually unfamiliar with the internal operations of the organization. They thus, in their interactions with organizations, draw upon the communicative resources of the culture in which they live and on common understandings of organizational practices. Employees of an organization also have access to these resources. However, employees, regardless of the extent of their input into the development of practices, also have access to the organizational meanings and understandings of their operations. Third parties accordingly are often at a relative disadvantage in their dealings with organizations, being poorly positioned to argue for their desired outcomes. Organizational employees can thus disarm the arguments of customers, not simply through the use of organizational discourse, but also through switches between such discourse and shared communicative resources as required (Prego-Vazquez, 2007). Customers or clients seeking services or assistance from particular organizations thus have to rely heavily upon the conversational resources that are available to them. Thus, for example, customers draw upon culturally recognizable forms of politeness that are more likely to lead to subsequent requests being accepted (Márquez Reiter, 2006).

Often the expectations of customers may conflict with organizational logics, of which they are unaware. Such conflicts are all the more likely in contexts where organizational practices have changed and customers have little under-

standing of the changes. A common outcome is that customers contest the ways in which the organization now operates. Morales-Lopez and colleagues (2005) provide one such example from customer interactions with a private company that manages the urban water supply in Galicia, northwest Spain. The company has recently changed from being a publicly owned enterprise to being a private company, and this change has been accompanied by increased charges for water and changes in the bills sent to local residents.

50 C1: Well, so first you should say
51 E2: [I'm not going to re–
52 C1: "Look, [I'm going to check."
53 E2: [I'm not going to read] the meters, eh.
54 C1: Of course not, but first you should [say to me xx "I'll check for you."
55 E2: [I'm telling you what the readings are.
56 C1: I'll ch–, you mean,
57   You can tell me what's on the bill,
58   I can see what's on the bill,
59   I can see that it's not right.
60   Hey?
61 E2: Uh: twenty thousand nine hundred and twenty-two.
62   That's not being arrogant,
63   it's obvious that–
64 C1: But you're saying to me:
65   "Look, no, no, no, if you want I'll explain it to you."
66   Yes, no, you should say to me:
67   "Well, look, I'll check."
68 E2: Look,
69   The first [thing,
70 C1: [Eh . . .
71 E2: you were angry before you started
72 C1: Yes, [yes I was,
73 E2: [so you don't even let me
74 C1: because [with a bill for twenty-two thousand pesetas . . .
75 E2: [xx Well, then just calm down
76   and we'll explain it all to you,
77   there's no need for any fuss,
78   [the excess consumption.
79 C1: [Look,
80   I'm speaking to you correctly,
81   politely,
82   I'm speaking properly,
83   like you're talking to me.
84   Now,
85   you should say to me,

86   "Well look,
87   we'll check," eh?
88   because there could be a mistake,
89   couldn't there?
         (Morales-Lopez et al., 2005, pp. 244–245)

In interactions such as that above, company employees typically attempt to retain control over the exchange by adopting a depersonalizing strategy. Within this, employees' efforts were directed at presenting the company's operations as being efficient and as comprising a modern and transparent process. In doing so, they avoided affiliating with customers or opening up the practices of the company to contestation. Customers resisted this depersonalization, making requests for personal services, such as checking of individual bills, and contested the infallibility of the company's practices. Many interactions therefore largely comprised cross-talk in which employees were inflexible in their depersonalization of customers while customers continued to seek personalized responses, especially in relation to queries that referred to changes between previous and current practices.

There are some organizations for which employees and customers are in effect the same people. Network marketing organizations operate on the basis of selling their products directly to individuals who in turn promote the products to other people in their social networks. This blending of expectations places a central focus on the role of individual consumers. Consumers who fail to achieve the benefits that the organizations promise are likely to experience greater disillusionment and dissatisfaction with the organizations than individuals in their dealings with other forms of organization (Kong, 2001).

Learning about organizations

Throughout this chapter, we have noted that work and other aspects of work cannot easily be separated. Elements of personal and social life commonly are incorporated into our conversations with work colleagues as we develop working relationships and collegiality with them. Even the same conversation, as we have seen, can move in and out of work-related topics. The overlap between work and the rest of our lives is not of course a one-way process. Just as social talk impinges upon work, so too does work talk enter into our lives beyond work. For example, the client discourse found in professional services inevitably must impact upon individual choices beyond the world of work. Consider also the question that we frequently in social gatherings ask of people with whom we are unacquainted, namely, "what do you do?" This question clearly anticipates a work-related response. In these and other ways, we make sense of work in many settings that occur beyond the limits of the workplace.

One obvious setting is that of home. In the course of our relationships with spouses, partners, and children, the topic of work often can arise in direct or less direct forms. Consider the following extract, from a study by Paugh (2005) of dinnertime conversations within middle-class working families in Los Angeles.

Schultz family (2 children present, Lucy [9 years] and Chuck [6 years]):

1   FATHER: And we were fortunate I think in that uh: – we –
managed to keep – the meeting which started out as: – supposedly a workers' meeting=
2   MOTHER: Hm hmm?
3   FATHER: =as a workers' meeting. It's gone through – several –
(flavors/layers) of change since then but it – it's back to a workers' meeting which is good.
4   MOTHER: Mm (this [is when it's)
5   FATHER: [(It's always)
6   FATHER: It's always nice to actually get something done
without the managers –
7   MOTHER: Being around?
8   MOTHER: [(Wh–)
9   FATHER: [(Rather than/or) getting in the way.
         (Paugh, 2005, p. 66)

The above extract forms part of a family dinnertime interaction between two spouses, in which the two children of the family are present. As we can see, much of this comprises a description by the father of the family of events occurring in the course of his work and of employees in an organization negotiating work activities. The children do not participate in this exchange: nonetheless they are party to the discussions of work that occur within the family context.

Often, however, children in the course of such dinnertime interactions go beyond listening to active participation. In so doing, they display their developing understandings of the topics under discussion.

Barnes family (involving two children, Sonya [10 years] and Bess [8 years])

1	SONYA:	**But wasn't that lady the grumpy one?**
2	FATHER:	No, that was a different lady with a=
3	SONYA:	Oh.
4	FATHER:	=pretty fancy resume. Um no. This lady was very nice.
5	SONYA:	**You should pick her.**
6	FATHER:	That's – what I wrote – in my – in [evaluation.
7	BESS:	[**Is she good?**
8	FATHER:	Yeah. Well – I mean it's kind of hard to tell I only got to talk to her for twenty minutes or so. But based on – the things that she's done before –and: just based on her personality that came across in the twenty minutes I talked to her I thought she'd be good.
9	SONYA:	**What position?**
10	FATHER:	Uh: staff attorney.

(Paugh, 2005, p. 71)

Children therefore receive much information about organizations and work in the course of routine interactions at family mealtimes and possibly on other occasions. The discussions that take place within the family can cover numerous issues associated with organization and work, including work practices, relationships with colleagues, opportunities for participation, encounters with clients or customers; in fact, the whole range of work-relevant topics that we have explored in the course of this chapter. Children thus become acquainted with the numerous ways in which organizations and work are constructed and of how these relate to other aspects of our lives. As they become more actively involved in such discussions, children display their developing understandings and acquire social competence in the realm of organizations and work. With this competence, they are then equipped to display and negotiate their own understandings across a range of other potential interactions. It is in these ways that children come to make sense of organizations and work, developing their understandings until in time it becomes their turn to enter the realm of work and organizations and to negotiate with prospective employers, work colleagues, customers, and others.

Chapter summary

- There are various features, such as an orientation to specific tasks or goals, that can distinguish talk in institutional settings from ordinary talk. These features should be identifiable in the details of interactions between professionals and other participants.
- Discourses used within organizations reflect social understandings and practices, for example cultural understandings of politeness. Social understandings, however, are taken up in divergent ways, leading to some organizational discourses being privileged while others are marginalized.
- In the workplace, people use humor and personal social talk to construct working relationships with colleagues. Displays of affiliation are often interlinked with constructions of work activities. Over time, meanings and patterns of interaction become specific to relationships and groups. It may be difficult for newcomers to enter highly cohesive groups.
- Often in an organization, there is a tension between management control of operations and employee participation in decision-making processes. Usually it is management control that prevails, although more flexible processes allow greater scope for organizations to adapt to changing external contexts.
- In job interviews, successful job applicants produce convincing accounts of their career plans and personal experiences, and affiliate with prospective employers. Unsuccessful applicants give unpersuasive accounts and offer little information about social or personal topics.

- Unemployed people commonly have to convince others that they are not responsible for their unemployment. Employers are treated as being accountable for not employing people in circumstances where the marginalization of social groups might imply discrimination. Typically, employers attribute unequal employment outcomes to attributes or actions of the group itself or to external factors beyond their control.
- Managers usually manage change within organizations with little participation from subordinate employees. The employees, however, have to negotiate the practices of the organization in dealing with clients or customers. Clients and customers are likely to contest employees' constructions in contexts where they do not understand changes in practices.
- Much talk about work occurs in family settings, especially in family dinnertime conversations. Children hear and participate in these discussions. By doing so, they develop their own understandings of organizations and work.

Connections

Group identities, such as those of marginalized groups, are covered in more detail in Chapter 2. Work groups are an instance of the discursive construction of groups, seen in Chapter 3. The negotiation and construction of working relationships display many features common to relationships in general, discussed in Chapter 4. Discrimination in the employment context is intrinsically linked to inferences of prejudice, covered in Chapter 7.

Activity

Consider an organization in which you study or work. Do your conversations with people in the organization mainly resemble or differ from other conversations that you have? What aspects of your working relationships are most important to you and how do they influence your interactions with colleagues and others? Do you have opportunities to participate meaningfully in the ways in which the organization operates? If you were to give an account of your current work and future career plans to other people, how would you make that account convincing, particularly to others who are unfamiliar with the practices of the organization?

Further reading

Arminen, I. (2005). *Institutional interaction: Studies of talk at work*. Aldershot: Ashgate. This text provides a comprehensive coverage of conversation analytic and ethnomethodological work on institutional talk.

Grant, D. & Iedema, R. A. M. (2006). Discourse analysis and the study of organizations. *Text, 25*, 37–66. A useful discussion of organizational discourse analysis and organizational discourse and of potential collaboration between these approaches.

Paugh, A. L. (2005). Learning about work at dinnertime: Language socialization in dual-earner American families. *Discourse & Society, 16*, 55–78. This article offers interesting insights into how children learn about the world of work.

Chapter 12

Debates Within the Discursive Tradition

The aim of this book has been to demonstrate the ways in which discursive analysis contributes to an understanding of the central areas of social psychology. In order to accomplish this, we have selected from a range of recent writings in the discursive research field and tried to show their relevance to social psychology. In doing so, we have set to one side the theoretical and methodological differences in view which are contained within the discursive approach. However, at the start of this book, we presented a set of "thumbnail sketches" of the different versions of discursive research which this book draws upon. At that time, we mentioned that towards the end of the book we would explore some of the differences which those sketches glossed over. This is the purpose of the present chapter. As we will see, even within discursive research, there is a wide disparity of view on how best to understand and explain social interaction. Accordingly, in this chapter we delve into some of the debates which have arisen within the discursive tradition.

The "External Context" Debate

One of the issues which has caused debate among discursive researchers is the question of whether it is appropriate for an analyst to refer to knowledge that he or she possesses about the external context in which a discursive episode takes place. By "external" we mean details of time or place or location. But we also mean socially relevant information such as the social roles or status of the participants, their life histories, and the social and historical background in which the participants find themselves. This might include the analyst referring to broader social or political positions such as feminism. Some discursive researchers, notably those within the critical discourse analysis tradition, view information of this sort as vital to the analytic enterprise. Other discursive researchers, especially those from the area of conversation analysis which emphasizes the sequential organization of turn-taking structures, claim that appeals to external context are mistaken. Instead, they argue that the analyst should restrict analytic claims to those which are demonstrably concerns of the participants as revealed by the data. One way, then, to explore this debate is to proceed by outlining the basic

tenets of conversation analysis and critical discourse analysis and to show how those basic ideas lead to a theoretical disagreement about external contexts. Accordingly, we will begin this section with descriptions of conversation analysis and critical discourse analysis. By this stage in the book, the reader will be aware that, for discursive researchers, description is never "mere" description. The descriptions of conversation analysis and critical discourse analysis presented below are partial, drawing on the work of a few key exponents, and many conversation analysts and critical discourse analysts will no doubt bridle at the way in which what seem to them key intratheoretical insights have been glossed over. So readers should bear in mind that these descriptions are produced with the aim of introducing the "external context" debate and that on other occasions, for other purposes, quite different descriptions might have been worked up.

Conversation analysis

A number of points in this book have referred to conversation analytic research. But conversation analysis is not social psychology, and the fundamental aims of social psychology and conversation analysis are quite different. Conversation analysis has little, if any, direct analytic interest in psychological questions of social identity or discrimination or attitudes or emotional issues such as anger, happiness, or self-esteem. This is not meant to imply that conversation analyses cannot produce important knowledge about such phenomena. But the analytic means by which this knowledge arises is a concentration on the detail of the patterned ways in which sequences of utterances are interactionally organized. However, given that both social psychology and conversation analysis have an explicit interest in interaction, it is not surprising that some social psychologists working within the discursive approach have drawn upon conversation analysis in their work.

Conversation analysis offers a formal analysis of the organization of interaction. It is the emphasis on interaction which provides for conversation analysis its focal concern with social action understood as activities conducted through talk. A central question for the conversation analyst is: given that social interaction appears orderly and intelligible to its participants, what are the underlying competencies which those participants possess which allow them to engage successfully in such interaction? The answer which conversation analysis provides is that people produce and reproduce behaviors in interaction, and respond to the behaviors of others, by means of a set of procedures which are susceptible of description, usually provided in a relatively formal way. The formalization of this set of procedures not only describes the participants' procedures but also represents an explanation of the interpretative practices on which the participants' interactions are based. Participants themselves, through their actions, demonstrate that they take these procedural properties of interaction to be normative. That is, one of the elements of interaction is the display, by participants, that they hold themselves accountable to these normative procedures. For the conversation analyst, then, the description of structured processes within interaction, together with evidence that these processes recur consistently, is the means by which the interpretative structures of social life are laid bare, as long as it is remembered that "interpretative" refers not to analytic fiat but to the sense-making practices of participants themselves. One of the advantages of this approach, according to conversation analysts, is that there is a "two-for-one" advantage here. In the first place, the proper description of interactions will reveal the way participants themselves are making sense of the interaction. In particular, where some normative expectation is breached in an interaction, the participants will display that this occurs, either by accounting for such a breach or otherwise demonstrating that such an account is sequentially appropriate. In the second place, the fact that participants display to each other their interpretations of what is taking place within the interaction can be used by the analyst as a "proof procedure." An analyst's interpretative claim about an interaction can be held to be supported just if the participants themselves display, through how they behave, that that is how they interpret the interaction.

An understanding of the force of this emphasis on sequential organization can be gained by examining one of the most important papers in the development of conversation analysis, "A simplest systematics for the organization of turn-taking for conversation" (Sacks et al., 1974). Sacks and colleagues set out to describe an analytic approach which makes sense of the observable fact that conversation is structured in terms of organized turns. They state that the organizational features they are interested in are context-free, in that the structural properties they describe do not rely on particularities of identity or situation but are, in a sense, generalizably abstract. Indeed, it is this abstract property which allows participants to design their turns to fit in with the immediate, localized context of the ongoing interaction. Turns involve "recipient design" in which a subsequent speaker displays an orientation to other participants, thereby displaying a particular, local context-specific interpretation of what is being accomplished within a specific general turn-taking structure. Sacks, Schegloff and Jefferson identify a range of empirical observations which constrain any successful model of interactions. These observations include: people take turns in conversation; they rarely speak simultaneously but gaps between turns are usually very short; conversation is undetermined in that the sizes of a conversation and its component turns are not predetermined and the order and distribution of turns are not fixed; what is said in turns is not specified in advance; talk can be continuous or discontinuous and the number of participants can vary; the structure of a conversation is determined by participants in part through the use of turn-allocation techniques and "turn-constructional units"; turn-taking errors and violations may result in the use by participants of repair mechanisms. Sacks, Schegloff, and Jefferson produce a model based on two components: a turn-construction component and a turn-allocation component. Turn construction involves the speaker in selecting types of conversational unit such as single words, phrases, or sentences. The conclusion of a unit is a transition-relevant place where another speaker may take over the conversation. The model includes a relatively small set of rules which conversational participants appear to follow in generating the observable features of interaction. The rules specify that, within a turn, when a transition-relevant place is reached, a current speaker may either continue to talk or select another speaker or another speaker may self-select. These rules provide a basic description for what Sacks, Schegloff, and Jefferson describe as a "locally managed" system in that it emphasizes single turns and their subsequent transitions, thereby emphasizing the importance of ongoing management of the interaction by its participants. The fact that subsequent turns display speakers' orientations to what has already been said provides, for the analyst, a means of establishing that analytic interpretations match those of the participants themselves.

Although this text is now over 30 years old, and conversation analysis has developed a great deal during this time, this paper is still relevant today because it outlines clearly the importance of organizational structure to the "founders" of conversation analysis. In a more recent paper, Schegloff (2004) emphasizes the current importance of the same sorts of organizational concerns.

> I mean the various organizations of practice that deal with the various generic organizational contingencies of interaction without which it cannot proceed in an orderly way: (1) The "turn-taking" problem: Who should talk next and when should they do so? How does this affect the construction and understanding of the turns themselves? (2) The "sequence-organizational" problem: How are successive turns formed up to be "coherent" with the prior turn (or *some* prior turn), and what is the nature of that coherence? (3) The "trouble" problem: How should one deal with trouble in speaking, hearing and/or understanding the talk such that the interaction does not freeze in place, that intersubjectivity is maintained or restored, and that the turn and sequence and activity can progress to possible completion? (4) The word selection problem: How do the components that get selected as the elements of a turn get selected, and how does that selection inform and shape the understanding achieved by the turns' recipients? (5) The overall structural organization problem: How does the overall structural organization of an occasion of interaction get structured, what are those structures, and how does placement in the overall structure inform the construction and understanding of the talk as turns, as sequences and so on?
>
> (Schegloff, 2004, p. 207)

Critical discourse analysis

The term "critical discourse analysis" covers a range of different approaches. There are, however, common themes across a number of these. Critical discourse analysis tries to understand how language functions as a part of social processes, and embeds its analyses in contexts of social action. Fairclough (2003, 2005) views language as one form of semiosis, the imparting of meaning through the use of signs. The concept of semiosis is broader than language since it also encompasses non-linguistic phenomena such as visual images and nonverbal behavior. Critical discourse analysis is explicitly interdisciplinary in that its analytic focus is on social issues which are also of concern to other social theorists. The "critical" element of critical discourse analysis refers to the fact that critical discourse analysis attempts to reveal linkages between language and social action which may be hidden, such as the way language functions in social relations of power and domination. Critical discourse analysts also view it as their task to challenge unfair social relations by advocating progressive social change.

Some critical discourse analysis draws upon the work of Marxist theorists, especially Antonio Gramsci, and their characterization of hegemony as a social arrangement in which the ideas and representations of powerful elites become the taken-for-granted, common-sense way of viewing the world. From other theorists such as Althusser, Habermas, and Foucault, critical discourse analysts draw the ideas that ideological phenomena are associated with both language and communication and social practices and that these have a historical nature, in that systems of communication, or discourses, develop as systems of knowledge (e.g., medicine, penal policy) across time. From Mikhail Bakhtin, critical discourse analysis developed the ideas that texts can only be fully understood in relation to other texts and that different types of texts, e.g., conversations, speeches, business meetings, could be viewed as "genres" of discourse.

Within these societal arrangements, critical discourse analysts identify social practices as "more or less stable and durable forms of social activity" (Fairclough, 2005, p. 77). Social practices comprise elements such as social identities, activities, social relations, contextual elements of time and place together with semiotic elements such as language or visual representation. All of these elements are regarded as being different but interrelated so that, for example, the critical discourse analysis of a social event will focus on its semiotic dimension or "text" but will also draw upon other elements such as social identities and relations. These social practices are themselves "networked" into more complex social arrangements or "social orders." These articulated networks of social practices include large-scale social phenomena such as the law or a society's educational structures as well as more particularized organizational entities such as a business or governmental department.

The fact that social practices are described in this way, as comprising interrelated semiotic (e.g., language) and non-semiotic elements (e.g., social identities and relations) is what underlies the critical discourse analyst's view that discourse is only properly analyzed in relation to social processes and social action. In particular, semiotic elements such as language must, on this view, be understood as being both a part of social activity (e.g., the courtroom lawyer uses language in a particular way) and as representational. As social actors take part in social practices through their use of language, for example, they represent to themselves and others both their own practices and other social practices. This emphasis on discourse as representational highlights the critical discourse analyst's partially realist social perspective. Discrete social events on the one hand, and large-scale social structures on the other, exist in a real social world. However, social practices mediate between social events and social structures and, because they include representational semiosis, they are in this sense socially constructive in that such representations shape the social processes which are being represented.

The semiotic part of social activity is constituted by genres which are different ways of socially interacting, e.g., having a meeting or taking part in a political interview. "Discourse," on the other hand, refers to the representation (to oneself or to others) of social practices. As an example of this, Fairclough notes that the lives of poor people will be represented differently through alternative discourses in the social practices of medicine, law, and government. This shows that different discourses "position" people (e.g., as doctors or patients or as lawyers or clients) in

different ways and that people positioned in one way will represent the world to themselves and others differently from someone positioned in a different way. Just as social practices can be considered as networked together into social orders, so genres and discourses can be viewed as networked together into "orders of discourse." These larger-scale social structures of semiotic activity can be viewed as the semiotic element of social orders. And these larger social structures demonstrate hegemonic properties, in that there tend to be dominant or prevalent ways in which discourse is ordered.

External contexts

It is clear that there are many differences between conversation analysis and critical discourse analysis. One debate centers on the question of whether analysts are in a position to refer to social phenomena which are not themselves either explicitly mentioned or implicitly oriented to by interactional participants. Some of these ideas were elucidated by Schegloff in a paper entitled "Whose text? Whose context?" (Schegloff, 1997). In this paper, Schegloff suggests that an approach which lays emphasis on political perspectives, such as critical discourse analysis, runs the danger of allowing analysts to deploy terms which "preoccupy them" in describing and explaining events and texts at the expense of participants' own orientations. What this means is that the analysts get to superimpose their own "theoretical apparatus" on the actions, events, or texts being analyzed instead of allowing these matters to be explicated by using the terms of reference of the participants themselves. As an example, Schegloff reproduces a fragment of transcribed interaction of a telephone conversation between a man and woman, and notes that the data show occasions in which the man interrupts the woman while she is speaking. Schegloff claims that this episode might be analyzed in terms of gender-relevant power or status relationships. However, he goes on to argue that such an analysis would miss out on exactly those elements which are analytically relevant, i.e., the elements of the data which display the participants' own orientations to what is happening during the interaction. His conversation analytic analysis leads to the conclusion that the interruptions are associated with the organizational structure of the episode, which is described in terms of a succession of assessments. Schegloff concludes that this demonstrates the importance of conversation analytic analysis to critical discourse analysis and argues that critical discourse analysts must, therefore, always embed any critical analysis in a prior analytic process of conversation analysis. It is noteworthy that he suggests that nothing in his argument necessarily undercuts critical discourse analysis; all that is demonstrated is that "serious" critical discourse analysis needs to employ the methods of conversation analysis. However, he also draws attention to the possibility that, once a conversation analytic process has been undertaken, the analyst may discover that a consequent critical discourse analysis is "no longer in point" (Schegloff, 1997, p. 174).

The critical analyst's response

Fairclough himself has responded to Schegloff's claim by denying that conversation analysis should take up this analytically prior position. He argues that such a view misses out the importance of interdisciplinary insights which draw on factors outside the analysis of texts:

> Textual description and analysis should not be seen as prior to and independent of social analysis and critique – it should be seen as an open process which can be enhanced through dialogue across disciplines and theories, rather than a coding in the terms of an autonomous analytical framework or grammar.
> (Fairclough, 2003, p. 16)

So the critical discourse analyst's fundamental concern is that the conversation analyst is sacrificing socially relevant analysis in order to comply with the demands of an atheoretical "methodologism" (Chouliaraki & Fairclough, 1999).

In one of the immediate responses to Schegloff's article, Wetherell's paper "Positioning and interpretative repertoires: Conversation analysis and post-structuralism in dialogue" (Wetherell, 1998) attempts to deal with this fundamental concern. The paper outlines a perspective which has been termed "critical

discursive psychology" (Edley, 2001; Wetherell, 1998). From this perspective, Wetherell agrees that a poststructuralist discursive psychology can benefit from the fine-grain techniques of conversation analysis.

> I suggest that although the terms of engagement between post-structuralism and ethnomethodology/conversation analysis need revisiting, a stance which reads one in terms of the other continues to provide the most productive basis for discourse work in social psychology, in much the same way, for example, as cultural anthropologists and ethnographers of communication have found an eclectic approach to be the most effective.
> (Wetherell, 1998, p. 388)

However, critical discursive psychology argues that the sequential patterns of organization in talk must be viewed as embedded within a cultural and historical context. People perform social actions in talk partly as a result of the discourses or interpretative repertoires of talk which they are afforded by their own history. In the context of critical discursive psychology, Edley (2001) argues that there is little difference between "interpretative repertoire" and "discourse," although he does, like Wooffitt (2005a), note that "discourse" as a term used by other forms of discursive research, notably critical discourse analysis and Foucauldian discourse analysis, implies a more "monolithic" quality indicating a large-scale, ideological phenomenon representative of entire institutions, e.g., medicine or the judiciary.

From the critical discursive analysis perspective, not only are discourses culturally and historically determined, but those which are culturally dominant are likely to be especially influential in people's social constructionist practices. In this respect, then, social action should not be thought of as solely the result of talk designed for the immediate conversational occasion, but should also be understood as the consequence of the ways in which available discourses or interpretative repertoires structure our understanding within wider social forces. For example, Edley and Wetherell (Edley, 2001; Edley & Wetherell, 1997; Wetherell, 1998) agree with Fairclough's critical discourse analytic claim that one impact of ideology is that it establishes specific identities for people by influencing the way that people think about, and experience, themselves and their social world. So one consequence of discourse is that we become positioned as kinds or categories of subject. These "subject positions" represent an element of external context, in that it is the wider discourse which does the positioning (e.g., medical discourse might position someone as either a "patient" or a "doctor").

Conversation analysts frequently refer to the question "why that now" in isolating the idea that a participant's utterance is always designed to fit within the locally managed context. And Wetherell's claim is that, ironically, conversation analysis cannot fully answer its own question without recourse to critical reflection on external contexts. In response, Schegloff (1998) rejects the idea that conversation cannot appropriately answer this "why that now" question. "That" and "now" are intended, says Schegloff, to be indexical terms whose relevance is exhausted by the local context. In particular, the question does not presuppose that there is some analytically prior position from which referents for "that" or "now" can be established. It follows that the conversation analyst need not provide some description of those analytically prior referents which must draw upon external context in a critical sense. Of course, says Schegloff, the researcher may well go beyond conversation analytic concerns to questions of cultural constructions or ideological formations. But, in line with his original paper, he claims that this would best be accomplished by asking questions of that sort only once a prior conversation analysis process is completed.

It is clear from this that critical discursive psychology, while acknowledging the strengths of conversation analysis, maintains its disagreement with the conversation analyst's view that analysis should not refer to external factors. However, critical discursive psychologists do accept that such positionings are worked out within local interactional contexts, and so many of the techniques and findings of conversation analysis continue to be relevant. In some respects, Schegloff agrees with this, although he claims that conversation analysis should be regarded as a prior step in the explication of matters of culture or ideology.

The rhetorical psychology response

In his original paper, Schegloff appeared to argue that claims about the impact of gender, status, and power were shown to be inappropriate, as a means of construing the examples he presented, in the light of a close conversation analytic reading of his data. This might suggest that conversation analysis has little to say about broader social analytic concerns of power, control, etc. In another response to Schegloff's paper, Billig, in his paper "Whose terms? Whose ordinariness? Rhetoric and ideology in conversation analysis" (1999b), draws attention to this potential shortcoming. Billig uses the dramatic instrument of an imagined episode of rape, and argues that a conversation analysis of such an episode would fail to explain it because the resultant analysis would focus on turn-taking issues at the expense of talking about phenomena of power and violence which are relevant to rape. He argues that conversation analytic practices mean that the analyst cannot direct analytic attention to matters which participants do not overtly discuss. So, instead, the analyst would discuss features, such as turn-taking phenomena, using terminology unfamiliar to participants themselves. And in doing this, the analyst would miss out the sorts of concerns which critical analysts would view as essential, such as feminist concerns with power relationships.

> The irony is that to follow Schegloff's recommendations – and ostensibly to observe the participants in "their own terms" – the analyst would end up speaking about the things that the participants do not speak of, using a set of terms which the participants do not use. But to speak of the same things as the participants do, the analyst would run the risk of being accused of imposing her own categories on the analysis.
>
> (Billig, 1999b, p. 548)

Billig is careful to point out elsewhere in this paper that he views conversation analysis as a useful methodology within psychology. However, there are at least three issues which concern Billig here. The first issue is that conversation analysis uses a terminology with which participants are unfamiliar, and this seems at odds with the conversation analyst's goal of relying on participants' interpretations. The second issue is that conversation analysis imputes a spurious egalitarian perspective to interaction, with each participant being allocated an active role in determining the turn-by-turn nature of the sequential unfolding of conversation. This appears to be an unrealistically egalitarian view of interaction, at least in the context of the example which Billig sets out. The third issue is that conversation analysis prohibits the use of references to external features such as social control or power except where these are explicitly oriented to by participants. So if the participants in Billig's imaginary example do not explicitly talk about the violent episode in terms of power or violence, then neither can the analyst.

In responding, Schegloff disagrees with each of these aspects, suggesting that Billig has mischaracterized the conversation analytic program. In respect of the first issue Schegloff (1999b) argues that even though participants do not deploy terms which are in use by conversation analysis, these terms do describe practices which participants orient to and so conversation analysis remains true to its aim of exploring participants' interpretations. With regard to the second issue, Schegloff (1999a) points out that even in the early formulation of conversation analysis (Sacks et al., 1974), it was explicitly acknowledged that participants might have differing levels of control in conversation as a result of external factors. Sacks, Schegloff, and Jefferson note that everyday conversation is only one of a wide diversity of forms of speech, and that other forms, e.g., ceremonial discourse, may involve different rules. In taking up these points, some discursive researchers have explored ways in which role, status, and power have an influence on turn-taking structure. They have explored, for example, the sorts of constraints on conversational structure imposed by more formalized settings such as courtrooms. Recently Wooffitt (2005a), in discussing this debate, has pointed out that Hutchby (1996a) addressed precisely this issue in his discussion of interactions between presenters and callers to radio "phone-in" programs. Indeed, Hutchby argues that part of the analyst's job is precisely to identify those properties of sequential structures which show that participants have unequal access to discursive resources. For example, Hutchby suggests that one of the reasons why

radio program hosts are in a powerful position, relative to those who call in to the program, is that the host inevitably occupies the "first position" slot in the ensuing interaction (Hutchby, 2006).

In respect of the third question, Schegloff (1999a) suggests that social phenomena, even of the most episodic and violent sort, are best understood as the outcome of social processes, as "intricated into the texture of everyday life" (Schegloff, 1999a, p. 561), and so a proper understanding of such episodes requires that the analyst show how they arise out of the sequential structures of ordinary interaction. Although Billig (1999a) accepts this claim, he still insists that a conversation analysis of an actual episode of violence of the sort he described in his paper would nevertheless mislead because it would not appropriately capture the elements of power and control which would typify such an episode. At this point, it is interesting to note that researchers with strong conversation analysis leanings have voiced similar concerns. For example, earlier in this book, in Chapter 7, we discussed problems of prejudice and noted that occasions seem to arise in which the analyst might be tempted to accuse participants of being prejudiced even though the participants themselves did not orient to their own talk as prejudicial (Beach, 2000). Kitzinger has addressed this issue from a conversation analytic perspective:

> Insofar as conversation analysis has focused on social problems . . . these have been treated in the form of "trouble" as oriented to by participants in interaction. . . . However, from the point of view of many social activists, and others concerned with social problems – indeed, including Sacks, the founder of conversation analysis himself, in his early lectures . . . social problems can also be produced, and reproduced, by social actors who are not oriented to any trouble in their interactions. A social problem exists only for us, as analysts eavesdropping on their talk, who see in it the untroubled reproduction of a heterosexist (or racist or classist or otherwise oppressive) world.
>
> (Kitzinger, 2005b, p. 479)

Kitzinger argues that it is not necessary for the conversation analyst to isolate those episodes in which participants orient to issues of power as some sort of interactional "trouble." Indeed, it is the very unremarkedness of certain forms of talk which can produce social problems. In her analysis of heterosexist talk, Kitzinger argues that it is the commonplace or "quotidian" nature of heterosexist talk which represents a social challenge to lesbian and gay people. Her claim is that the analyst must address such cases where social norms have become embedded within everyday talk by examining how they are deployed in action. This approach deals with the analytic concern that prejudice might occur through talk in which prejudice is not "noticed" or dealt with by participants themselves. However, the consequence is, of course, that the conversation analyst's "proof procedure," the identification of the analyst's claims with participants' interpretations displayed through orientations, may no longer be available. Moreover, critical discourse analysts might well feel that the identification of forms of talk in which norms are deployed in action without explicit orientation to them is, in many respects, close to their own notion of the function of ideological discourses. In this respect, then, the differences between some contemporary forms of conversation analysis and critical discourse analysis may be less clear than Schegloff asserts.

Discursive psychology

Most of the researchers mentioned above have all, albeit in different ways, suggested that the appropriate response to Schegloff's critique is to combine conversation analytic fine-grain analysis with insights drawn from the critical perspective. However, before leaving this issue, it is worthwhile noting that this is not a unanimous response. Other discursive researchers have taken the different view implied by Schegloff that conversation analysis does indeed represent a method by means of which broader social psychological questions can be answered without a critical discourse analytic appeal to external context. Perhaps the clearest example of this is the discursive psychology of analysts such as Edwards and Potter (Edwards, 2005a; Edwards & Potter, 2005) which sees itself as "closely allied" (Edwards, 2006a, p. 43) to the conversation analysis approach:

Work in discursive psychology has been profoundly influenced by conversation analysis (CA) which offered the most analytically powerful approach for dealing with interactional materials.

(Potter, 2006, p. 132)

From a conversation analytic perspective, Wooffitt (2005a) has suggested that it is hard to distinguish the methodology of discursive psychology from conversation analytic methodology, although its founders suggest that discursive psychology also has other influences such as social constructionism, the sociology of scientific knowledge tradition, and ethnomethodology (Edwards, 2006a; Potter, 2006). In some respects, then, discursive psychology may be taken to have broader interests than those of conversation analysis itself:

While drawing heavily on the principles and methods of conversation analysis, it is also a particular feature of discursive psychology to explore the close, mutually implicative nature of subject–object relations, as a managed feature of discourse of various kinds.

(Edwards, 2005b, p. 6)

Beyond methodology, what distinguishes the theoretical aims of discursive psychology from those of conversation analysis is that discursive psychology is concerned with psychological states and characteristics. It reclassifies many of the traditional psychologist's research interests (e.g., memory, attitudes, and attributions) as practical accomplishments achieved through discourse. In part, though not exclusively, this means that the discursive psychologist is especially interested in examining interactional episodes where psychological terms describing emotions, judgments, beliefs, and so on are drawn upon in interaction. In addition, even when explicit psychological references are not involved, the discursive psychologist wishes to understand how descriptions developed in interactions make available (or undermine) inferences about psychological states such as intent, agency, doubt, or prejudice. However, the analyst refrains from drawing on the sorts of political or cultural knowledge which those of a more critical persuasion utilize, and this differentiates the discursive psychology approach from more critically oriented approaches, leaving it more closely aligned to the conversation analytic approach.

Summary

The pragmatic consequences of the debate about external context are therefore mixed. The weakness of the critical analysis approach, seen from the perspective of the conversation analyst, is that critical analysts rely upon insights which are unwarranted by the data. The weakness of the conversation analysis approach, from the perspective of the critical analyst, is that conversation analysts ignore important aspects of the world in analyzing social interaction. In consequence, some discursive researchers have argued that conversation analysis, while occasionally useful, represents a number of dangers for the pursuit of critical analysis, including an overemphasis on what is actually contained in text and a refusal to appropriately consider interdisciplinary explanations (Parker, 2005). Other discursive researchers have adopted a dual approach, drawing on both conversation analytic and external critical or cultural insights (Edley, 2001; Wetherell & Edley, 1999). For example, in the paper on identity discussed in Chapter 2, Abell and Stokoe (2001) argue that a conversation analytic approach to identity must be integrated with other elements of cultural knowledge. Indeed, they suggest that in a conversation analysis of a televised interview between a media journalist and the late Princess of Wales which did not also include cultural reference, "something important would be missed from the analysis" (Abell & Stokoe, 2001, p. 421). Other researchers have developed positions in which conversation analytic method is employed with little or no reliance on critical methodology (Edwards, 2005a; Potter, 2006). As to the question of whether one perspective is theoretically or methodologically more sound, it is clear that debate is still ongoing. The approach taken in this book has been one of unapologetic inclusion: we have tried to show how researchers from each of these various different perspectives have all contributed to the project of developing a discursive approach to the study of social psychological phenomena.

The "Membership Categorization Analysis" Debate

In Chapter 5, we saw that categorization is a form of social thought to which discursive researchers have devoted a lot of attention. In particular, we saw that those researchers interested in membership categorization analysis (Hester & Eglin, 1997; Hester & Francis, 2001b; D. R. Watson, 1978, 1997) have been especially interested in the ways that people categorize one another. Membership categorization analysis is probably best regarded as a sub-area of conversation analysis, because the notion itself derives from the work of Sacks. It does, however, display distinct differences from the "sequential" style of analysis of the sort described earlier and, in addition to its conversation analytic roots, membership categorization analysis arguably places even more emphasis on ethnomethodological issues, drawing heavily on the work of Garfinkel (1967), than does its sequential cousin. According to this approach, when someone is allocated in talk to a category of person, this is associated with inferences about that person which are grounded in the sorts of common-sense knowledge we hold about the members of that category. Thus mothers are conventionally held to be caring, and so if someone is categorized as a mother and revealed to be uncaring, this may be bound up in an account of that person in which she is depicted as deficient or morally culpable.

Membership categorization analysis and "sequential" conversation analysis

A number of discursive researchers have suggested that an exclusive focus on sequential organization wrongly ignores the important role, specified by Sacks, of membership categorization analysis. Watson himself, for example, argues that one area of enquiry in which membership categorization analysis is a prerequisite is institutional talk. He claims (D. R. Watson, 1997) that a sequential analysis is insufficient to explain institutional talk because within such contexts members make sense of the sequential nature of their inter-action in terms of membership categorization processes. In this respect, it is interesting to note that even those researchers who lay priority on sequential conversation analysis have likewise taken issue with the idea that sequential propert-ies alone are sufficient for the analysis of institu-tional talk. For example, Schegloff (1991) claims that an analyst's argument for the relevance of institutional context must provide details in the participants' talk as a warrant. In response, Arminen (2005) argues that even within a sequential conversation analytic approach, this sort of claim must be understood as relying on the ana-lyst already having relevant competencies which allow the analyst to "connect the interactional patterns to the institutional activities" (Arminen, 2005, p. 37). The idea here, then, is that in some senses members' categories are "built in" to any analysis which takes place, and so there may be no relevant explicit talk in the data which a more sequential approach might demand. As an example of this, Hester (1998) discusses the institutional relevance within an educational setting of teachers' talk about problematic schoolchildren. Such children are often referred to educational psychology services, and Hester notes that one might expect teachers to make explicit references to educational psychologists and their services in their talk of referring school-children. However, Hester points out that this rarely occurs in his data. In explanation, he sug-gests that where the teachers' talk categorizes schoolchildren as having serious problems, this is, in itself, also an indication that educational psychologists should be called in.

> In this regard, the categorizations can be under-stood to invoke the predicated professional expertise of educational psychology. In so far as it is a predicate of educational psychologists to deal with some children – those deemed to have "special educational" needs and problems – then the categorization can be heard to implicate intervention.
>
> (Hester, 1998, p. 148)

Membership categorization analysts are, though, careful to point out that such devices can also appear outwith contexts in which there is a relatively formal institutional setting. In an exam-ination of a newspaper account of the murder of 14 women in Canada, Eglin (2002) notes the way in which the newspaper article describes women as speaking of the murders as symbolic and symptomatic of societal misogyny:

> What I am saying, then, is that the specific actions predicated of "women" in this sentence are themselves category-bound activities of the category "feminists." In accordance with Sacks's (1974: 225) first "viewer's maxim" – "If a member sees a category-bound activity being done, then if one can see it being done by a member of a category to which the activity is bound, then: see it that way" – one may see this category-bound activity as making the category to which it is bound, namely feminists, pro-grammatically relevant without it being actually mentioned.
>
> (Eglin, 2002, p. 822)

So one of the advantages claimed for membership categorization analysis is that it can deal with the broader issues of social structures in a way which sequential conversation analysis allegedly finds difficult. Stokoe (2006), for example, has suggested that membership categorization analysis allows the feminist analyst to reveal the "mundane gender-ing of interaction." If correct, then this would resolve some of the issues of the sort described above such as Billig's claim that conversation analysis is unable to properly address feminist concerns.

Membership categorization analysis and warranting claims

However, it is at this point that an analytic ten-sion between "sequential" conversation analysis and membership categorization analysis arises. Some sequential conversation analysts worry that membership categorization analysis proceeds by drawing on common-sense or everyday cultural knowledge rather than relying on particip-ants' interpretations as displayed in the data. In other words, the data do not support or warrant the claims being made. In this respect, the disagreement between the sequential conversa-tion analyst and the membership categorization analyst resembles the debate about external context. The claim here is that the membership categorization analyst might feel entitled to step outside the data in order to draw upon knowledge about external factors such as what is culturally understood or known in a commonplace way. Schegloff (2007) argues that, if this occurs, then it is a mistake. It is the analyst's job to make sense of the way in which the participants in interaction draw upon and make relevant the ways in which they utilize "obvious" knowledge in this way, not to draw on that knowledge themselves as analysts.

> The "obviousness" of it is not the investigator's resource, but the investigator's problem. And this, the subsequent literature – especially in so-called membership categorization analysis – has too often failed to notice, has failed to take seriously, has failed to be constrained by. It can thereby become a vehicle for promiscuously introducing into the analysis what the writing needs for the argument-in-progress.
>
> (Schegloff, 2007, p. 476)

In discussing these issues, Schegloff (2007) points out that Sacks's membership categorization rules and their corollaries are "relevance rules." Some categories are general, in that they are applicable to all people at all times (e.g., sex and age). It follows that when a category is applied to someone, this always involves selection, in that there will be at least one other category which might have been deployed in place of the category that was actually used. So the fact that someone belongs to a category is not sufficient grounds for categorizing that person by using that category. There have to be other grounds for interactional co-participants, beyond mere membership of the category, which establish the relevance of the use of that category, as opposed to some other category, at that interactional moment. So the multiplicity of categories means that category relevance, and the question of how categories become relevantly oriented to, is of prime importance. And so a crucial part of the analyst's job is to show how talk is managed so that categorization devices are made relevant. Moreover, a categorization device may be possibly relevant to an episode even if it is not articulated. A categorization like "woman" may possibly be relevant even if none of the participants uses an explicit formulation like "speaking as a woman" (Schegloff, 2007,

p. 474). However, even in these cases, the analyst must also be able to demonstrate how participants' orientations can be used to support the analytic claim that particular categories are in play even when participants themselves do not offer explicit formulations of such categories.

Summary

This is clearly an important issue for discursive research in social psychology, since membership categorization analysis is a common resource for explicating social interaction in discursive research. Sequential conversation analysts such as Schegloff suspect membership categorization analysis of illegitimately "smuggling" external references into conversation analyses. Membership categorization analysts suggest that reference to categorization matters beyond sequential organization is a prerequisite, both in institutional settings and in more everyday contexts. In line with our inclusive approach mentioned earlier, we leave it to readers to decide which of these two positions is acceptable. In concluding, though, it is useful to point out that some researchers claim the tension between sequential conversation analysis and membership categorization analysis is more apparent than real. For example, Wowk and Carlin point out that Watson, one of the founders of the modern developments in membership categorization research, himself aimed at demonstrating how membership categorization analysis and sequential analysis are compatible:

> Watson is concerned to illustrate that (membership categorization analysis) can be combined with "sequential" (conversation analysis) . . . Furthermore these two aspects of his analyses are not simply co-present in his papers but are always examined for their reflexive (inter)relatedness.
>
> (Wowk & Carlin, 2004, p. 70)

In a slightly different vein, Housley and Fitzgerald (2002) have argued that the appeal to common-sense knowledge about categories and their bound activities need not represent any form of appeal to external context on the analyst's part, since membership categorization analysis can, in a manner consistent with Schegloff's views, restrict itself to those elements of category talk to which participants themselves orient.

The "Social Constructionism" Debate

Another debate which has become associated with the discursive approach is the question of the relative merits of social constructionism and realism. Some discursive researchers, especially some critical discourse analysts, view their position as profoundly realist, in that they take themselves to be describing the effects on social interaction of a real world which exists independently of discourse. Others are suspicious of this claim, and argue that social phenomena should only be considered as analytically available as they are worked up, or socially constructed, through discourse. Readers will have noticed that this bears some relevance to the question, pursued above, of whether analysts should draw upon explanatory factors which are external to the local discursive context. In fact, some (though by no means all) of those who argue for appeals to extra-discursive context do so precisely because they view these external contexts as real in this sense.

In order to separate out some of the issues which arise between the realist and the social constructionist, we focus here on three issues which arose in a debate between Hammersley and Potter in the pages of the journal *Discourse & Society* (Hammersley, 2003a, 2003b, 2003c; Potter, 2003a, 2003b). We select this particular debate because it highlights some of the more important aspects of reactions to social constructionism.

Covert realism

In the initial paper which sparked the debate, Hammersley (2003a) discusses some of the consequences which social constructionism has for discourse analysis. The example of discourse analysis which he relies upon is Wetherell and Potter's work on racism in New Zealand (Wetherell & Potter, 1992). (Potter (2003a) begins his subsequent reply by distinguishing discourse analysis from discursive psychology, and locates much of the rest of his response to Hammersley in terms of discursive psychology's concerns.) Hammersley draws attention to the way in which discourse analysis treats its phenomena of interest as dis-

cursive products, rather than as features of the world which are caused by psychological or social forces. However, Hammersley argues that, despite this explicit claim to be following a discursive, socially constructive approach, discourse analysis in fact draws in an explanatory fashion upon notions of social phenomena "as they are" rather than as social constructions. Hammersley complains that this is inappropriate within a perspective which treats phenomena in general as socially constructed. In replying to this point, Potter (2003a) interprets Hammersley's point here as the complaint that Wetherell and Potter's analyses depend on a "realist history" of New Zealand society and on identifying particular social groupings such as the "white settler community" (Hammersley, 2003a, p. 764). Potter agrees that "versions" of these are important for understanding why the analyses produced are significant and also for understanding how the analyses relate to societal conflicts, but denies that they are analytic "prerequisites" for many of the claims themselves. Hammersley (2003b) rejects this claim, insisting that these realist notions are "integral" to Wetherell and Potter's analytic claims. Potter's subsequent response (Potter, 2003b) is that the way in which these matters become "integral" to the analysis is as themselves social constructions, not as realist phenomena.

Disappearance of the person

One of the criticisms which Hammersley (2003a) makes is that discourse analysis regards social actors as essentially concerned with formulating persuasive accounts, and this ignores the variety of other ways in which aspects of the person and of social life in general may be relevant. In response, Potter (2003a) suggests that in one sense this "thin" notion of the human actor is exactly what discursive psychology needs. Since discursive psychology, unlike traditional social psychology, focuses on discourse, it explicitly rejects the notion that some more substantive view of the person could be introduced into analyses as an explanatory mechanism. Indeed, even appeal to a "thin" notion might be misconstrued, says Potter, if it is supposed that the "thin" model of the person is in some ways a model of the person which competes with, but is otherwise similar in background assumptions about personhood to, "thicker" models. Hammersley's rejoinder (2003b) is that the "thin" notion of actor is "thicker" than Potter might accept, since there is at least some notion of personhood bound up with discourse analytic claims about matters such as stake inoculation, which imply that people deploy discursive strategies for reasons and to fulfill motives.

Reflexivity

Hammersley also complains that the discursive practices which Wetherell and Potter locate in their data are treated as though they, themselves, are ontologically real and are not themselves merely discursive constructions. In other words, they illegitimately imply that their own analysts' accounts describe something in the real world in a way that their participants' accounts do not. His complaint is, then that "what they write is suffused with a commitment to documenting the reality of discursive practices" (Hammersley, 2003a, p. 765). The logical consequence of this, says Hammersley, is that discourse analysis ought to apply its own procedures to itself, and this would be to commit it to an infinite loop of reflexive self-characterizations which would vitiate its ability to say anything useful about social issues. In response, Potter points out that discourse analytic approaches have taken issues of reflexivity more seriously than has "conventional social science." He concludes that, even if the discourse analytic response to these problems of reflexivity is "far from ideal," it is better than the response of other social scientific approaches.

Summary

Hammersley suggests that discourse analysis trades on an implied realism about the world and about its own discursive claims, while providing an unrealistic account of the person. Potter responds that this critique mistreats discourse analytic claims by imputing a realist slant to material which is intended to be taken discursively. Both agree that the question of whether discourse analytic processes should be applied to its own claims is relevant, although Potter claims that discourse analysis has fared better in this respect than traditional social science approaches.

In concluding, it is worth noting that throughout his responses, Potter demonstrates an uneasiness with what he sees as Hammersley's identification of social construction with philosophical idealism. For a discourse analyst, "to deny the 'objective reality' of phenomena . . . would be as realist a move as endorsing that reality" (Potter, 2003a, p. 787). In other words, the discourse analyst wishes to stress that claims such as the denial of "objective reality" are, themselves, accomplished in discourse and should be understood in discursive terms. This present account does not exhaust the nature of the Hammersley–Potter debate. For example, both authors note that the realism–social constructionism debate is, itself, closely associated with debates about realism versus relativism. We do not pursue this matter here since the arguments involved are probably of more interest to the philosopher of social science and therefore bear little direct relevance for this book's goal of demonstrating how discursive research has contributed to social psychology. However, readers who wish to explore questions of relativism in detail might like to refer both to the original Hammersley and Potter papers and to the text Social constructionism, discourse and realism (Parker, 1998).

In Conclusion

In concluding this chapter, we should draw readers' attention briefly to two other live issues within the discursive tradition. Our intention in this last section is not to explore these issues in depth. Instead, we merely wish to use these two topics, one theoretical and one methodological, to alert readers to the fact that discursive research includes other areas of ongoing discussion beyond those we have already mentioned.

Cognitivism

One of the topics which we would like to mention briefly is the theoretical question of cognitivism. Cognitivism can be defined in the first instance as that approach to empirical research which relies upon a theoretical background in which cognition is a central element. However, Edwards notes that "cognitivism is both more and less than cognition" (Edwards, 1997, p. 27). It is more than cognition in that it addresses issues beyond cognitive states of memory or reasoning to encompass social psychological features such as social relationships and emotions. It is less than cognition in that its emphasis on psychological inner states precludes consideration of the impact on cognition of wider, cultural factors. It is in these terms that discursive researchers find themselves in disagreement as to the usefulness of cognitivism as a theoretical approach.

Van Dijk (2001a, 2006a), from a critical discourse analytic position, suggests that cognitive effects are important in understanding short-term memory discourse processes. He also suggests that cognitive phenomena such as attitudes and social representations are relevant to the critical discourse analysis program because these phenomena represent mental models upon which discursive actions have an effect. In this respect, cognition is the "crucial interface" between individual discourse on the one hand and social structure on the other (van Dijk, 2001a). In a similar vein, Wodak (2006) suggests, in the context of prejudiced stereotypes, that "sociocognitive" models are useful to critical discourse analysis in explaining why prejudice is difficult to eradicate.

As we described earlier in Chapter 5 when discussing social cognition, discursive psychologists such as Edwards and Potter argue strongly against adopting cognitivism as a means of explaining interactional phenomena. According to discursive psychologists, in its explanation of interactional phenomena cognitivism adopts a mistaken theoretical model in which the meaning of psychological terms derives from their reference to inner mental states. The proper analysis of such terms, according to the discursive psychologist, is to adopt a conversation analytic understanding of the way in which such terms come to appear as participants' concerns as displayed in their talk. This does not mean that all and every attempt to employ a cognitivist account is mistaken. Potter, for example, notes that cognitivism "grapples with some interesting and challenging questions, some of which would be hard to address from different perspectives" (Potter, 2000, p. 34). However, the discursive analyst's view is that cognitivist explanations routinely make the mistake of ignoring the detail

of how talk-in-interaction gets done by wrongly assuming that it is the internal terrain of mental states which gives such talk its point.

However, this debate cannot be categorized merely as a dispute between critical discursive researchers who emphasize the social concomitants of discourse such as ideologies and those other researchers such as discursive psychologists who emphasize the importance of finely grained analyses of actual talk. We saw in Chapter 5 that conversation analysis, the approach which discursive psychologists regard as foundational in their own work, is not necessarily opposed to the introduction of cognitive or mental state terms as explanatory terms. For example, the conversation analyst Paul Drew (2005) has suggested that a conversation analytic, fine-grained analysis of talk reveals "cognitive moments" which partly explain people's actions. From a similar conversation analytic perspective, Kitzinger (2006) has suggested that cognitive phenomena such as memories are clearly "manifested" in the sequential details of talk-in-interaction. In their different ways, both authors are careful to circumscribe the extent to which such cognitive manifestations become analytically relevant to the discursive researcher. Equally, however, both emphasize that this is a genuine area of debate between conversation analysis and discursive psychology. Drew even goes as far as to suggest that the analyst's preferred notion of participants "orienting" to what others have said might in fact be a covert reference to mental states. In a broader vein, Kitzinger implies that the discursive psychological project of criticizing cognitive social psychology by attacking its theoretical cornerstone, the cognitive state, might be an enterprise in which conversation analysts should have little interest or involvement.

Interviews

The second, methodological, topic we wish to mention is the question of whether interview methodology is appropriate in discursive research. Van den Berg, Wetherell, and Houtkoop-Steenstra (2003) point out that the research interview is a methodology commonly utilized in the social sciences and that this practice ranges from structured "survey" interviews to more open-ended "qualitative" interviews. Indeed, it is evident from the other chapters in this book that many discursive researchers have relied upon the interview technique in order to gather their data. However, van den Berg, Wetherell, and Houtkoop-Steenstra point out that both qualitative and quantitative researchers often underemphasize the constructed nature of interviews, in that interview data are the result of a joint sense-making effort of both the interviewer and the interviewee within the highly specific context of the interview situation. The complaint here is that some researchers wrongly assume that an interviewee's talk can be unproblematically taken to be a relatively simple report on how the world is as they see it.

This view of the interviewee's responses as an unproblematic "window on the world" is, van den Berg, Wetherell, and Houtkoop-Steenstra say, a perspective which discursive research seeks to challenge. From the discursive perspective, interviewee responses are thought of as being locally constructed and so the interaction between interviewee and interviewer itself becomes an appropriate topic of research for the discursive researcher. For example, the researcher must give attention to whether what the interviewee says in the interview context is the sort of thing that he or she would say in other contexts. The researcher should also take into account that he or she is a part of the social world under investigation and so may play a role in the outcome of the interview process. In consequence, the discursive researcher faces the responsibility of avoiding the temptation to treat interviews as decontextualized talk.

> The interview is, of course, a highly specific discursive situation where the interviewer's own discourse and construction of the issues is influential in setting the local context. Complete analysis needs to be attentive to this and other immediate contextual and interactional features. We contend, however, that the broad methods of self accounting we identify here have a generality outside the interview context and in this sense are robust phenomena.
>
> (Wetherell & Edley, 1999, p. 339)

In considering these issues, discursive researchers have, in practice, tended to adopt one of two procedures. Many discursive researchers follow Wetherell's suggestion that interviewing is an appropriate methodology for the discursive research, as long as the researcher bears in mind the sorts of caveat mentioned above. Other discursive researchers, notably those from the conversation analysis tradition, have expressed more suspicion about the validity of interviewing as a method, and have argued for the methodological priority of gathering "naturally occurring" talk from contexts other than the interview setting.

Problems or opportunities?

In outlining these debates about context, members' categories, and construction, we wanted to provide readers with a lively sense of the ways in which discursive research continues to develop. In some respects, these are unresolved tensions within discursive research as a whole. However, the creation of tension can often produce new ideas. We therefore want to conclude by suggesting that it would be a mistake to draw the inference that discursive research is in crisis or faces insoluble problems in respect of these debates. In his editorial introduction to the debate between Billig and Schegloff, van Dijk (1999) points out that debates between scholars from different fields do not imply that those fields are in conflict or are in some way incompatible. He points to the way in which all discursive researchers have, to a greater or lesser extent, some interest in the close and fine-grain analysis of the details of interactional talk. He draws attention to the fact that both critical discourse analysis and conversation analysis have an interest in viewing talk as a locus for interaction while acknowledging that such talk is context-dependent. He concludes that both approaches represent viable means of analyzing socially situated interaction in terms of "doing-social-analysis-by-doing-discourse-analysis." The "take-home message" from this is that debate within a field such as discursive research can be a fruitful way to proceed, and it is in this light that we trust readers will take the present chapter.

Chapter 13

Social Psychology in the Twenty-First Century

Social psychology aims to explain how people are influenced in what they say and do by actual or potential interaction with other people. Social psychologists want to understand, for example, how people make sense of their own social identities in relation to other people. They also want to understand how processes such as ascribing an identity to oneself or to others might have interactional consequences such as the development of prejudice or discrimination or the creation of feelings of linking or solidarity. Social psychologists understand that interactional outcomes of this sort may derive from phenomena other than those associated with identity. They are bound up with other ways of thinking about the world, such as attitudes towards relevant social objects such as governments or political standpoints. They are also related to other ways in which individuals take part in, and are influenced by, social interaction, whether that interaction arises in interpersonal relationships or through engagement with social groups. The social psychological view is that all of these sorts of social processes require an understanding of the ways in which social interaction influences psychological processes such as judgment and experiencing emotions.

Stated in this way, it appears that the central questions of social psychology should be amenable to both discursive and experimental analysis. One might suppose, then, that there is a busy and fruitful interchange of ideas between discursive researchers who are, for example, interested in processes of prejudice and their experimental counterparts. Such is not the case. Instead, it is probably fair to say that the prevalent relationship between the discursive and experimental forms of social psychology is well represented in Longfellow's poem "A theologian's tale: Elizabeth":

> Ships that pass in the night, and speak each
>   other in passing,
> Only a signal shown and a distant voice in
>   the darkness;
> So on the ocean of life we pass and speak
>   one another,
> Only a look and a voice, then darkness
>   again and a silence.
>
>   (Longfellow, 2004)

There are many reasons for the "silence" between discursive and experimental social psychology. As social psychologists, we can predict that some

of these reasons have to do with social psychological issues such as intergroup phenomena and the development and maintenance of self and identity. Both experimental and discursive social psychologists, for example, make sense of themselves partly in terms of their own occupational roles as researchers. And as the findings of discursive and experimental social psychology research reveal, such self-identifications are often associated with characterizations of "the other" as not only different but as, in some ways, problematic or negative. Moreover, as the discussion of Kuhn and Feyerabend below demonstrates, science can be viewed as a field of contest in which competing paradigms become involved in a struggle which relies upon sociological and ideological factors as well as the pursuit of "truth."

However, many proponents of discursive and experimental social psychology take the position that there are substantive theoretical reasons for preferring one approach over the other. In this respect, these proponents would characterize the discursive/experimental "silence" as a good thing, in that they view their own approach as correct and the alternative approach as incorrect. More recently, other researchers have argued the opposite, and taken the position that the two approaches can learn from each other. In this final chapter, we want to explore the relationship between discursive research and experimental social psychology by examining these two positions, which we term "research independence" and "research integration."

Research independence

The first position is one in which the two research approaches, discursive and experimental, are viewed as independent of one another. At least two variants of this independence position can be observed in the research practices of social psychology. The first variant, which might be termed "benign neglect," is exemplified by researchers from one approach who merely ignore research generated in the other approach. In the second variant, which might be termed "research competition," researchers view their own approach as correct and criticize the other as incorrect. The benefit of adopting a research independence position is that it respects the strength of the underlying differences, which are discussed below, between the two approaches.

The weakness of this position is that it prevents discursive and experimental researchers within a particular field such as identity or prejudice from benefiting from one another's research findings.

Research integration

The second position is one in which researchers argue that the findings derived from discursive and experimental research could usefully be combined. The research integration position often relies upon the development of multilayered models of social psychology which identify different layers of interaction with different research approaches. These models are then used to show how research at one level might be integrated with research at a different level. The benefit of adopting a research integration position is that it enables discursive and experimental researchers within a particular field to pay attention to and possibly benefit from one another's research findings. The weakness of this position is that it runs the risk of ignoring important differences between the discursive and experimental approaches.

The aim of this chapter, then, is to explore the research independence and the research integration positions. We begin by setting out some of the underlying differences in the discursive and experimental approaches which lie at the heart of the research independence position. We consider the differences in the underlying philosophical assumptions and in the practical methodological approaches that separate discursive from experimental social psychology. We then go on to examine the ways in which researchers from the research integration position are currently attempting to build bridges between the two approaches. We end by setting these discussions against the question of where social psychology is headed as we move further into the twenty-first century.

Arguments for Research Independence

Philosophical differences between discursive and experimental research

Our aim in this section is to describe the sorts of differences which exist between discursive and experimental social psychology and which motivate the research independence position. In order to set out these differences, we focus here on two issues: (1) underlying philosophical assumptions about realism and the views of science that arise out of, or can be associated with, those assumptions, and (2) the methodological issues that follow on from such views. One caveat though: we do not suggest here that all discursive researchers hold one set of views about issues such as realism or the nature of science while all experimental social psychologists hold the opposite view. Instead, we are merely attempting to set out the disparity in views which seem, to the diligent reader, to typify the perspectives held by many proponents of these two different approaches and which seem to encourage the adoption of a research independence position.

Philosophical presuppositions about realism

Towards the end of the last chapter, we mentioned that discursive researchers sometimes find themselves in disagreement over the incompatibility of social constructionism and realism. This tension also arises when we compare some forms of discursive research and experimental research. In thinking about this issue, it is useful to separate out some of the different notions of realism that appear in philosophical discussion. Metaphysical or ontological realism is the view that an external world exists independently of us. Epistemological realism is usually taken to be the view that we have knowledge of this independent reality, although the expression has also been used (Williams, 1996) to denote a quite different claim: that the objects of epistemological inquiry, the structures of knowledge, are real. In terms of the debate between experimental social psychologists and discursive researchers, perhaps the most important brand of realism to consider is realism about meaning or semantic realism (Wright, 1993). Realism about meaning is the view that the meaning of propositions is best described in terms of the conditions which must obtain in the world for those propositions to be correctly uttered. Scientific realism is usually taken to be a commitment to all or most of these forms of realism, especially the ontological commitment to the view that unobservable theoretical entities exist.

Implicit or explicit adherence to a particular realist view plays a role in distinguishing the discursive approach from the experimental approach. Experimental social psychologists often appear to implicitly accept, if not explicitly avow, a realist position on all these issues. Discursive researchers often do not. Given what was said in the last chapter about reactions against cognitivism, it is not surprising that some discursive researchers have expressed reservations, or at least agnosticism, about the experimental psychologist's apparent commitment to scientific realism as it applies to cognitive theoretical entities such as stereotypes or attitudes. More broadly, it has also been argued (Devitt, 1996) that there is a tension between the sort of poststructuralist social constructionism represented by discursive approaches and the "ontological" realism described above. Emphasizing the notion of "independence" which is foundational in this variety of realism, Devitt argues that the idea of an external reality which is independent of human thought is abandoned by perspectives such as the discursive approach. Discursive and experimental social psychologists can also be usefully thought of as, at certain times, varying in their commitments to epistemological and semantic realism. For example, a number of discursive researchers appeal to participants' own interpretations or to the framing effect of ideologies with the intention of supporting a view of understanding meaning which is in many ways antithetical to the realist position. These brief thoughts suggest, then, that one of the ways in which discursive and experimental approaches to social psychology vary is in the extent to which practitioners embrace or abandon a commitment to realism.

Discursive researchers frequently make reference to the work of Ludwig Wittgenstein (1953), especially his comments on rule-following. For example, of the journal articles referred to in Chapter 5 of this book alone, 19 make some reference or other to Wittgenstein and his work. In many cases, references such as these express the view that the discursive analyst's attention to participants' own concerns is justified by reference to the Wittgensteinian slogan that "meaning is use." Similarly, appeals to participants' contextualized social actions are often justified by reference to Wittgenstein's notion of "language games." This fondness for referring to Wittgenstein may, in part, be bound up with Wittgenstein's apparent rejection of a realist view of meaning, as represented by the swingeing critique of the "picture theory of language" with which he opens his book *Philosophical Investigations*. This marks out a further philosophical difference between discursive research and experimental social psychology, in that experimentalists rarely feel the need to address the philosophical issues which Wittgenstein raised.

The nature of science

In the first chapter of this book, we set out a preliminary description of social psychology which largely relied upon what is commonly referred to as the "positivist" view of science and then went on to point out that many discursive researchers take issue with that account. The background to this lies in the way in which philosophy of science developed in the twentieth century. "Positivism" (the term derives from the work of the nineteenth-century philosopher Auguste Comte), when applied to science, is the view that science comprises logically related sets of statements at least some of which are testable through empirical investigation. The process of testing scientific statements relies upon the neutral and objective nature of the claims being made, and the successive discovery of successful and unsuccessful claims constitutes scientific progress. Somewhat ironically, given his rejection of the label (Hacking, 1983), positivism has come to be associated with the hypothetico-deductive model outlined by Popper (1959) which sets out the ways in which science relies upon the formulation of testable hypotheses in order to support or discard theories through a process of falsificationism in which defeasible hypotheses are tested to see whether or not they are false. This view was criticized by Kuhn (1962), who deployed a number of historical examples to show that "normal" science does not proceed by challenging theories. Indeed, scientists often go to considerable lengths to adjust existing theories to take account of new empirical discoveries. Theoretical challenge and change, far from being a feature of "normal" science, only arises at "crisis" points in the history of a discipline such as when the number of anomalies faced by the prevalent theory grows at a time when a new, competing theoretical perspective becomes available. Feyerabend (1993) also criticized Popper's views, emphasizing instead that distinctions such as theoretical terms on the one hand and observational terms on the other cannot be usefully drawn. The "radical" philosophy of science views of authors such as Kuhn and Feyerabend emphasize the fact that scientific claims are essentially imbued with theory and that, as a consequence, a given scientific claim may be preserved in the face of potentially disconfirming evidence by making adjustments elsewhere in the theory. It follows from this that scientific change and theoretical upheaval are not a direct consequence of discovering how the world is, but rather an outcome of the struggle between competing theoretical perspectives. In Kuhn's view, ordinary science is conducted from within one of these perspectives, and the changeover to a quite different perspective only arises as a consequence of a revolutionary shift in the way scientists think about a problem or issue.

The question of how best to characterize science bears relevance to the divide between discursive and experimental social psychologists. Many discursive researchers endorse a view of science which emphasizes its socially constructed nature. In part, this provides a rationale for the development of the discursive approach: discursive research is sometimes portrayed as a radical advance on experimental social psychology analogous to the sort of "paradigm shift" which Kuhn identified with scientific revolutions. In addition, discursive researchers of a more critical bent sometimes refer to the work of the radical philosophers of science in arguing that science is not, as positivists might picture it, "value free" but instead embodies social phenomena such as heterosexism or racism. Many experimental social psychologists, on the other hand, are content to view their own scientific work from a broadly positivist perspective. However, as a reminder of the caveat introduced towards the start of this section, readers are encouraged to look at the recent endorsement of Feyerabend's ideas presented by one of the leading exponents of the experimental study of stereotypes, Anthony Greenwald (Greenwald, 2004).

Methodological differences between discursive and experimental research

Positivism, understood as associated with the hypothetico-deductive model, leads naturally to a predisposition towards adopting the experimental method. Proponents of the experimental social psychological approach point to the advantages which this approach has over the discursive approach. They suggest that experiments allow for levels of control which strengthen the scientist's ability to test specific predictions. In contrast, discursive research seems, from the experimentalist's perspective, to rely over much on mere description and redescription of actual events and this prevents the discursive researcher from formulating testable hypotheses.

The logic of experimentation

The familiar image of an experiment is one that is derived from the natural sciences. We envisage a laboratory setting in which an impartial scientist (the experimenter) carefully manipulates the objects of study for purposes of investigation. The general aim of experimental manipulation is to ascertain causal relationships between the different elements that are involved in the study. In order to do this, the experimenter will alter the behavior of one variable (the independent variable) in particular ways to examine the effects of this action on the behavior of another variable (the dependent variable). A physicist, for example, wishing to investigate the behavior of physical particles following collision, might vary the masses of the particles prior to impact and measure their velocities following impact. The outcomes of the investigator's actions in varying the particles' masses, the intervention(s), will be carefully monitored and noted. Behaviors observed following collision can be compared against particle behavior in other cases where no intervention has been made, that is, behavior arising in a "control" condition.

Across all conditions, the scientist will endeavor to ensure so far as possible that factors considered irrelevant to the study are eliminated from having any influence. Experimental equipment will be designed to minimize the possibility of there being any unwanted movement that might affect particle behavior and to exclude from possible intervention other particles that are not under investigation. Where potentially confounding factors cannot be excluded altogether, their effects will be kept constant across the different conditions. Temperature, for instance, obviously cannot be wholly excluded from any setting; there will inevitably be a temperature of some level, even if it is absolute zero. For experimental purposes, however, temperature can be maintained at an even level within and between the different conditions throughout the study. It is thus assumed that the effect of ambient temperature will be similar for the experimental condition and the control condition and that differences in temperature will not therefore be responsible for any differences in particle behavior that may be observed. The same principle of experimental control of unwanted influences can be applied to all known potentially confounding variables.

Following the exclusion of or control for unwanted sources of variability, the scientist is then able to argue for the basis of any differences in behavior that are seen to occur. Where changes in behavior of the particles are observed in the experimental condition, and are absent from the control condition, it is plausible to suggest that such changes are the result of the intervention that has been made. We therefore can observe a change in the behavior of the independent variable (a cause) leading to a change in the behavior of the dependent variable (an effect).

The logic of experimentation is well recognized throughout the natural sciences and can present a plausible argument for the cause–effect relationship that is being advanced in any particular instance. The experimental social psychologist's view is that, with appropriate changes suitable to the field of study, the same logic applies to the study of social psychological phenomena. And according to this view, it is precisely because discursive research abandons this set of procedures that it is condemned to mere redescription of events or merely concerns itself with talk instead of examining "real" social phenomena.

The artificiality of context

The discursive researcher's response is to point out that applying the logic of experimentation to social disciplines, including social psychology, is inappropriate. The sources of variability in each of our lives are not necessarily open to experimental control in the same way as variables such as temperature, and human participants act and respond differently to inanimate objects of study, such as physical particles. Inanimate objects do not look to make sense of their experiences of taking part in an experimental study or of the experimenter's actions towards them. Let us consider each of these in turn.

According to the discursive researcher, a first difficulty in applying experimental techniques in social psychology is that of bringing to the laboratory context precisely what is intended to be the object of study. This difficulty becomes immediately apparent when we start to reflect upon the matters that are of greatest interest to social psychologists. Suppose that, by way of example, we consider the study of relationships, a topic that is included in any mainstream textbook. Usually, we would take a relationship to involve at least two people, and to comprise not just their individual contributions but also some elements of social contact and mutual engagement. To study such a phenomenon in a laboratory setting, however, immediately raises two issues: (1) the availability of a relationship for study in this way and (2) the elimination from the experiment of elements of a relationship that are extraneous to investigation and that might otherwise affect outcomes.

Typically, in experimental social psychology, the response to the first issue, the availability of the phenomenon, is described as operationalization. By operationalization, we mean the way in which objects of interest are conceptualized and designed in order to make them amenable to experimental investigation. Staying with the example of relationships, the discursive researcher would argue that it is challenging to develop a definition of a relationship that encompassed all potential aspects and that at the same time provided the precision required for experimental purposes. Thus, in order to proceed, the experimentalist has to conceptualize the object of study rather differently. Although it is difficult to submit a relationship itself to close experimental examination, we could investigate related phenomena in attempting to gain insights into the relationships that people have. For example, individual perceptions allow for study in ways that the social practices do not. Instead, therefore, of aiming to consider relationships themselves, we can opt to look at individuals' views of their relationships to other people. The matters of investigation thus come primarily to be individual representations of or responses to social phenomena, not the phenomena themselves.

From the discursive perspective, this is a major weakness in the experimentalist approach.

The response of the experimentalist to the second issue, the elimination of unwanted elements from an experiment, essentially comes down to control. Taking the same example as before, if we aimed experimentally to study individuals' perceptions of relationships, we would probably not wish our participants to bring to the experimental context any direct reminders of their existing relationships. The histories, interactions, and meanings that link each of us to broader social networks, for the experimenter, become unwanted sources of noise that might interfere with the very restricted points of interest to the setting. In experimental terms, the aim is one of removing the variability between individuals and for individuals that goes to make up much of what we do in our interactions with other people. Accordingly, the underlying assumption is that social topics can most usefully be studied in isolation from the contexts in which they routinely occur. But, argues the discursive researcher, this abstraction from context is another problem. In the words of Wetherell and Maybin (1996, p. 222), in this experimental approach "the best view of the self is obtained when the social context is 'switched off' so that influences from other people do not complicate the picture."

So from the discursive perspective, the application of the experimental approach within social psychology thus necessitates, first, the study of topics of interest at the level of individuals, and second, the elimination from consideration of unwanted social variables. It is inevitable that these elements taken together will impact upon the knowledge that is thereby produced. Over time, social psychological knowledge of a topic such as relationships becomes based not on relationships themselves but instead on individual perceptions. Relationships as relationships disappear from view. Instead of deriving knowledge of what people do in their social lives, we are left only with the limited understandings that come from the perspectives of lone individuals, even on topics such as this that would appear to be social through and through (Pancer, 1997; Pepitone, 1981; Senn, 1989). Similar concerns arise in relation to a whole range, if not the whole range, of social psychological topics. In treating its objects of study as individuals only, and as entirely separable from the contexts in which they commonly occur, social psychology loses touch with everyday social practices that might reasonably be expected to provide its central concerns.

The "subjects" of study

From the discursive perspective, another concern is that the experimental emphasis on individuals has further implications for the pursuit of social psychology. Think back to the experimental procedures found in a natural scientific study as outlined earlier. For the physicist, the objects of study are quite clearly defined, in terms of particles, matter, or similar physical bodies. Objects of this kind are inanimate and lack intention; for most, if not all, purposes they can be treated as simply being present in the laboratory, waiting for the experimenter to act upon them. Clearly, the same lack of intentionality and consciousness cannot be attributed to human beings who participate in experimental studies.

Yet, the discursive researcher argues, it is exactly this view of human participants that pervades much experimental work. Those who take part in experimental research are commonly termed "subjects," although often being treated as objects that are not entirely dissimilar from inanimate particles awaiting the interventions of the researcher. As subjects, they are expected to be and are treated as being compliant and submissive, taking no initiative of their own. In addition, the control that is ever present in the experimental setting is likely to preclude much by way of possible action usually open to them. The range of possibilities left available will be largely predetermined and restricted to a specific range of options that are included as variables within the experimental design. The prevailing (implicit) assumption is that individuals who participate in such studies are there to do no more than follow the instructions that the researcher gives to them and thereby produce the data that are sought.

As noted above, the operationalization of social topics for study predominantly leads to these topics being located at the level of the individual, in terms of his or her perceptions, responses, or otherwise. When we add to this procedure the assumption that research participants are simply passive throughout the experimental process, the discursive researcher's claim is that the result is a somewhat curious picture of the individual.

Individuals come to be treated, if not altogether viewed, as little more than the containers of possible responses, not dissimilar to inanimate bodies awaiting investigation. As social psychology has moved increasingly towards an emphasis on social cognitions, so the individual has been seen as even more fragmented than this. Participants become in effect "atomized" in research terms, seen as collections of processes of recall, recognition, categorization, stereotyping, and so on, any of which processes can be isolated by the experimenter for study as and when required. Any holistic view of the individual as a social being is lost; the possibility of examining social context and social processes has long disappeared from view.

Another complaint which the discursive researcher makes is that this view of the individual in experimental terms, artificial in itself, has also led to a further consequence that increases the overall artificiality of experimental findings. If individuals are to be regarded as simply passive and compliant collections of units for the purposes of experimentation, then it matters little who actually takes part in psychology experiments: any passive and decontextualized human is much like another. Suppose, however, that we ask the question of who exactly does take part in psychology experiments. In recruiting participants for experimental studies, the main concern often lies in finding sufficient numbers of participants rather than on who these people might be at other times. Researchers thus frequently look for their numbers to those who are easiest to find and least resistant to taking part. A look through the social psychology literature tells the reader that a considerable quantity of experimental work has for its participants relied on undergraduate psychology students. In many cases, students are induced either through financial reward or course credit to participate in the research of other psychologists. You might indeed yourself be familiar with this method of recruitment! Now, consider the implications of conducting research primarily with participants drawn from such a population. Undergraduate students tend to be more educated, have better cognitive skills, be less attached to social groups, be more compliant, come from a narrower age range, and be wealthier than the population in general (Sears, 1986). No doubt, students are well able to take part in experiments and to fulfill the requirements of

the tasks with which they are confronted. The question, though, is to what extent knowledge that is derived from such a narrow selection of experimental participants can usefully and representatively tell us about the social actions of the wider population. When narrow sampling is combined with a focus restricted to very limited aspects of individual behavior, it adds a further dimension of artificiality to that inevitably produced by experimental control.

Deception and ethics

Discursive researchers have also voiced concerns about the question of deception in experimental studies. People are not the passive and submissive research subjects that are often assumed. Unlike physical particles, human participants look to make sense of the experiences in which they are involved. A further issue therefore for the experimenter in attempting to control the context is that of ensuring that participants' understandings of the situation do not affect the behavior that the experiment has been designed to study. It is for such reasons that experimenters have often attempted to minimize the effect of participants' understandings on performance of the experimental task by concealing the aims of a study, either through deception or by providing little information of what is expected. Of course, the American Psychological Association (2002) and the British Psychological Society (2006) now provide strict ethical codes of conduct that govern the conduct of research and that preclude studies of the sort outlined above in almost all circumstances. Most experimental studies involve deception in ways that are not obviously harmful, and experimental participants are expected to be fully debriefed at the end of an experiment. However, studies of compliance, obedience, and group processes have frequently been presented under cover stories of examining learning, memory, perception, or similar. This form of deception has been widely used within social psychology precisely in order to minimize participants' understandings of the study and possible (unwanted) influences on their behaviors. Such use of deception, even in relatively harmless ways, does raise the further question of what impact it might have on research outcomes. In everyday life, people do not ordinarily expect to be deceived; if we discover that we have been deceived by others, we are more likely than not to complain of such treatment. We certainly do not expect to be deceived by those with whom we regularly interact on a social basis. Introducing deception within the experimental context therefore again marks out such procedures as being at odds with usual social expectations. In what is already a highly controlled and artificial setting, experimenters' use of deception removes the context still further from that of everyday social experience.

Experimental interaction and knowledge

So the discursive researcher's complaint is that the very elements that are intrinsic to experimental procedures give rise to a range of problematic issues when researchers look to apply the approach within social psychology. Attempts to eliminate social variables together with the operationalization of social practices at the level of individuals or parts of individuals produce a setting that is both highly artificial and distanced from everyday social experiences. Further, the view of individuals that results from this treatment is inconsistent with everyday experience and experimental attempts to maintain this view through deception produce an experience that cannot really be said to be social in any meaningful way.

A further complaint of the discursive researcher is that experimental procedures do not occur in a vacuum. The interactions of research participants with experimenters and with experimental procedures, although they do not reflect more usual encounters, do set up specific and marked forms of interaction in their own ways. Consider again the encounter between the experimenter and the participant. In the experimental setting, the participant is expected to do little more than to accept the information given and to follow the instructions that are provided along the way. Language used to convey information and instructions is assumed to be value free and simply to convey necessary details between the parties. In this, the procedure takes language at "face value" (Tuffin, 2005) rather than considering any other elements of communication that might be taking place between those concerned. This assumption, together with the assumption that participants are compliant and submissive, provides an appearance of experimental objectivity in directing attention away from extraneous matters. This, however,

should not be taken to indicate that other interactional elements are missing. Rather, experimental procedures introduce particular forms of interaction, interaction that is, however, removed from the gaze of the experimenter.

According to the discursive researcher, three features mark out the experimental encounter as being a distinctive interaction in its own right. First is the inherent imbalance of power present in the encounter, reflecting the expectation that the participant will follow the instructions given and act as required. Little room is allowed for the questioning of or deviation from these instructions if the experiment is to proceed as anticipated. Second, the control imposed on the scope of the interaction provides a context that is largely static, unlike the fluid nature of much of everyday life. Third, the language that is used in this context is treated simply as a medium for transferring information between experimenter and participant. Other elements of language use, such as conversation or displays of affiliation, are excluded or discarded. To these interactional features the experimenter is effectively "blind," regarding them as no more than the procedures demanded by objectivity and procedure. For the participant, however, these considerations are likely to be experienced as distinctive features that are peculiar to this form of interaction. It is therefore unsurprising that the knowledge that results from such a setting is atypical of social exchanges more generally. This knowledge cannot unproblematically be taken to be equivalent to an understanding of everyday social life.

Summary

It is clear, then, that there are fundamental differences between the discursive and experimental approaches to the study of social psychology. Discursive and experimental researchers often differ in their underlying assumptions about the reality of their subject of study. They adopt different views of the nature of the science in which they are engaged in studying that subject. They hold different views on the advisability of employing the experimental method. The experimentalist views the control and precision of the experiment as a benefit, the discursive researcher feels that such procedures abstract away all that is of interest in social interaction. From this, it might seem as though the "silence" between the two approaches will continue into perpetuity. However, a number of influential thinkers from within both approaches have offered an alternative vision, and it is to that vision we now turn.

Arguments for Research Integration

Notwithstanding the apparently irreconcilable differences between the two approaches, the response of some theorists to the division in social psychology between discursive and experimental traditions has been to argue that this split is both undesirable and unnecessary. In this section, we want to explore why and how this response has been developed. Before doing this, it is worthwhile revisiting the underlying philosophical differences which are supposed to separate the experimentalists from discursive researchers. If such differences do not really exist, or are not as important as they might at first appear, then this clears away a lot of conceptual brushwood in preparation for establishing a common field. That said, readers who do not have a philosophical turn of mind can happily skip the following section without losing the thread of the overall argument.

Rethinking philosophical differences

Realism

We said above that in terms of the debate between experimental social psychologists and discursive researchers, perhaps the most important brand of realism to consider is realism about meaning or semantic realism (Wright, 1993). In order to assess the extent to which experimental and discursive researchers really are in disagreement on this issue, it is necessary to "unpack" exactly what this realism entails.

According to a popular philosophical view on discourse, the philosopher's task in explaining meaning is to provide a theory of how language works. To do this, the language theorist must establish which element of language represents its central theoretical entity by reducing the complexity of language to its component "atoms" or "molecules." The range of options here includes "truth condition," "verification condition," and "falsification condition." These can be thought of as different kinds of assertibility condition. That

is to say they each, in different ways, represent conditions under which it would be correct to assert a particular sentence. The idea here is that particular utterances of any given sentence are but "tokens" of one and the same sentence "type." By characterizing the conditions under which it is appropriate to utter instances of this sentence type, the theory is supposed to give an account of the meaning of that sentence within the language.

On some accounts this means that the actual truth value ascribed to a particular utterance (sentence token) depends on what the world is actually like and on what the language theory says about the truth conditions attached, in virtue of its meaning, to the relevant sentence type. The meaning realism debate as to which notion ought to play the role of central concept in a theory of meaning then centers on the status of the term "true" and on the consequences such status has for the explanation of meaning. The realist language theorist depicts the sense of a sentence as being determined by its truth conditions. These are the conditions under which an assertion made by means of that sentence would be true, where "truth" is understood according to the following formula: "each statement is to be regarded as determinately true or not true in a fashion which may transcend our abilities to establish that truth value, whose nature, in turn, is settled by an objective reality which is, likewise, independent of our thought."

The anti-realist views the sense of a sentence as being determined by those conditions under which it would be recognizably appropriate to affirm it. On this view, the language theorist's central concept is in an important way epistemically constrained. This constraint can take two forms. In the first, which can be termed "verificationist anti-realism," the central concept is a condition which is always (at least in principle) verifiable – a verification condition. In the second, which can be termed "defeasible anti-realism," the central concept is a condition which, though acting as a warrant for the relevant statement, leaves open the possibility that the statement might be false – a defeasible assertibility condition.

The verificationist anti-realist denies that the notion of evidence-transcendent truth which is involved in the realist's account ought to be the central concept in a theory of meaning. Originally, this denial was expressed by saying that the central concept in the theory of meaning is not "truth" but instead must be the ability to recognize whatever is counted as verifying a statement. To understand one of the expressions which make up a statement is to understand its role in determining what is to count as a verification of the statement. More recently, this same thesis has come to be expressed in a different way. The contemporary verificationist anti-realist accepts that the notion of truth ought to be the central concept in a theory of meaning but he retains his hostility to realism by arguing that the notion of truth involved must be a recognizable, non-transcendent affair. On this view, a statement's truth conditions just are its verification conditions. In both cases, grasp of meaning is explained in terms which are essentially linked to our epistemic capacities for conclusively establishing the truth of a statement. (It should be noted that this simple formula, however expressed, is contentious. The anti-realist's opponent might want to know, for example, what constitutes "conclusive" verification and whether this relies on "in principle" verifiability – we may not actually have verified the statement here and now, but we possess an effective procedure whereby we could, with suitable idealization, do so if pressed – or on "in practice" verifiability – we actually have the means to verify the statement.)

On this verificationist anti-realism formulation, it is important to keep clear the distinction between two quite separate capacities. The first capacity is the ability to recognize whatever counts as verifying the relevant statement – the ability to recognize whatever conclusively establishes the statement as true. The second capacity is the ability to recognize whether the statement is true or false. Now whenever we have an effective procedure for bringing whatever it is that establishes the statement as true within the scope of our cognitive faculties (e.g., having a mechanical procedure for generating a proof), these two capacities will coincide. If someone has the capacity to recognize whatever establishes a statement as true, and he possesses an effective procedure for bringing that which establishes the statement as true within the scope of his cognitive faculties, then he has the capacity to recognize whether the statement is true or false. However, where he lacks such an effective pro-

cedure, he will be unable to recognize the truth or falsity of the statement even when he possesses the capacity to recognize that which establishes the statement as true.

For the verificationist anti-realist, there is no commitment to the idea that the individual who understands a statement will always be able actually to verify that statement – he will not always have the capacity to recognize whether the statement is true or false. All that is required is that the individual be capable of recognizing a verification of the statement should one arise, and this ability is quite different from the capacity to recognize the statement's truth or falsity. It follows that, for the verificationist anti-realist, in cases where there can be no verification of a statement (all the relevant evidence may be long gone, for example), we may be unable to determine whether the statement is true or false. But the verificationist anti-realism formula still offers an account of what that statement means – an account which is given in terms of our practical capacities. The meaning of the statement is given in terms of what we know when we understand it. What we know is given in terms of the capacity which such knowledge provides us with. This capacity is the capacity to recognize what counts as verifying the statement – the capacity to recognize what counts as conclusively establishing its truth. What we do not have, in cases where there is no effective verification procedure, is the further capacity to recognize the truth or falsity of that statement.

The defeasible anti-realist likewise denies that the realist's notion of truth ought to be the central concept. Although he also accepts that the notion of truth is important, for the defeasible anti-realist, the central concept must be defeasible warrant for an assertion. The notion of defeasible assertibility condition which is thereby introduced as the language theorist's central concept relies on the idea of defeasible evidence – we may not be able to verify the statement here and now or in the future either, but we are able to determine whether the evidence is strong enough to warrant assertion of the statement. It seems obvious that for some types of statement, there can be no conclusive verification (e.g., statements about the remote past or about regions of outer space which are beyond the ken of astronomers). In such cases, there will be no capacity for recognizing when verification conditions obtain, since there will be no evidential state which guarantees the absolute truth of the relevant sentence. It follows that as far as recognition is concerned, the notion of defeasible evidence must take over from the idea of verification.

The assertion conditions of both the realist and the anti-realist have features to recommend them as the central concept of a theory of meaning and features which weaken their claim to such a role. The proponent of realist truth conditions is able to claim a direct link between that which makes a statement true and what the language theory says about the meaning of that statement. Such a link seems desirable as soon as the intuitive appeal of the equivalence thesis (the thesis that for any sentence A, A is equivalent to "It is true that A") is noted. In particular, the realist is able to present an uncluttered view of truth – that truth is determined by the world, irrespective of what anyone thinks or believes – and link this to his account of meaning. The weakness of this approach (in the eyes of its opponents) is that the conception of meaning offered is one which irreparably severs meaning from our practical capacities to use language. In contrast, the strength of the anti-realist position is that it directly links an account of meaning to our abilities. Its weakness (in the eyes of its opponents) is that it provides too thin a notion of truth.

Now that we have a clearer view about what meaning realism is, we can address the question of whether experimental and discursive researchers really are committed to differing views on it. To begin with, it is useful to point out the difference between philosophical accounts of meaning and empirical questions about what someone meant by a particular utterance. The philosopher wants to understand how a series of sounds represented in speech or a string of characters represented in text can, in principle, carry meaning. The discursive researcher addresses the quite different question of what, in practice, participants actually understood other people to be saying and doing in interaction. So it may be that the identification of discursive research with the rejection of realism at the semantic level is a step which discursive researchers need not take. Moreover, the debate between the realist and the anti-realist appears to require the philosophical apparatus of a meaning-theoretic approach to semantics. It could be argued that the philosopher's use of meaning-theoretical entities such as "sentence tokens" and "verification conditions" is antithetical to the discursive research program in general. This is especially so since such tokens and conditions are associated with a reductive program in which the various activities of discourse, such as warning, questioning, accusing, and so on, are treated as "secondary" to the notion of underlying "propositions." So, because realism is a philosophical thesis which does not address itself to the practical concerns of the empirical researcher and because it relies upon a heavily theorized perspective on language, it may well be that discursive researchers would be better advised to drop their concern with whether or not language use exhibits realism.

Wittgenstein

Above, we noted the way that discursive researchers, unlike experimentalists, have a predilection for referring to Wittgenstein's work, especially his comments on rule-following. However, this distinction between the two approaches is clouded by the fact that discursive researchers rarely spell out what they mean when they refer to meaning as use or to language games. A difficulty here is that Wittgenstein's remarks on rule-following are deep and dangerous waters for psychologists to paddle in. As an example of this, we can briefly consider two quite different philosophical accounts of what those remarks mean.

In his book *Wittgenstein on rules and private language*, Kripke (1982) argues the proper way to take Wittgenstein's remarks on rule-following is to see those remarks as formulating a challenge which can be cast in a skeptical light. They are taken to show that having a grasp of the rule for the use of an expression cannot be regarded as involving some kind of commitment as to one's future use of that expression. Any use can be made out, on some interpretation, to accord with the rule, and so one can never be said to know what the future correct use of an expression will be. Consequently, there is no content to the idea that one must do so-and-so if one is to employ the expression correctly, where "correctly" is taken to mean "according to a standard of correctness represented by the rule." The best that one can do, by way of prediction, is to assert that the question of which use will be correct on some given date in the future is an issue which will be settled, somehow or other, by appeal to the subjective inclinations of those in the community.

The key to this skepticism is the idea that claims about meaning suffer from a chronic lack of justification. For example, claims about what I meant in the past (e.g., as recovered from some past explanation) are seen as inadequate justification for regarding some current use of an expression as correct. Even if a variety of introspective facts are admitted as evidence together with whatever shows up in the behavioral record, the Kripke-skeptic's claim is that there is nothing about the totality of such facts to establish that some present application of a term is determined as correct by what I meant in the past, in a way that some other is not. In this sense, there is just no fact about what I meant. And since the strength of the evidence about what I meant in the past has been approximated to that of contemporary evidence, the Kripke-skeptic's conclusion is that the justificatory shortfall also extends to current claims about what I mean now by some expression. In effect, then, there is no fact of the matter as to what we mean by any expression. However we go along in our usage just is what is meant.

Now a short reply to this kind of skepticism would be that it ignores Wittgenstein's idea of grammatical linkage between rule and explanation. Kripke tries to raise a doubt about what is to count as the correct present application of a rule-guided term, even given a full range of explanation. There is, he says, no evidence strong enough to prove that such and such an explanation really meant that we should follow one rule rather than another. But if explanations of an expression are grammatically linked to the rules for the use of that expression, there could not be, nor is there any need for, any form of final support or justification for the claim that "if he is to follow the rule for the use of this expression, he will do so-and-so" which stands external to such applications. And so it makes no sense to talk here of a shortfall in justification. For conditionals such as this, the notion of external evidence is completely misplaced. Of course there is still doubt as to whether any particular individual or group of individuals will stick to this correct usage. But this is not the same thing as saying that there is no such standard of correctness.

But it will be replied that this answer misses the point. It might fairly be said that the worry is not: "even given that we know what explanation we were following in the past, how can we be sure about what the appropriate present usage is," but rather: "it makes sense to wonder whether some present usage is in accord with the rule we were following in the past, as 'grammatically' determined by some explanation, so we can never be certain which rule we were following then." On this latter formulation, even if it is accepted that the correct way to take talk of rule-following is to see it as the claim that rule and explanation are "grammatically" related, a skeptical worry remains. For it might be said that nothing in the past or in our current usage settles the issue as to whether, in the past, we intended to follow the rule/explanation which forbids our present applications or another rule/ explanation which allows them – nothing in the present or past guarantees that we were following one rule rather than another. So we can never be sure that our current applications are correct with respect to the rule which, historically, we might be said to have been following.

The bite in this version of the argument is that it undermines the whole idea that our use of an expression can be understood in terms of our being in conformity with a rule in precisely the way Kripke suggests. If it ever makes sense to doubt whether present use is in conformity with a given rule said to be previously grasped, then there can be no evidence strong enough to prove that we were, in the past, following one rule rather than another. The only alternative is to claim that no such doubt about current usage will arise. But now there seems no difference in content between the claim that we feel confident about applying the relevant expression in such-and-such circumstances and the claim that we are confident that we are following the rule. If any occasion arises in which we are not confident that so-and-so is the correct way to go on in the employment of some expression, nothing about the appeal to the rule for the use of that expression will help resolve matters. But this leaves matters in the same position as before: normativity, of the sort we might usually associate with rule-following, seems to have been abandoned.

The problem is, then, that we seem to face a dilemma: either it makes sense to question whether present usage is in accord with past usage or it does not. If the question does make sense, then this opens up a skeptical doubt: no evidence is strong enough to settle the question. If it does not make sense then the kind of guarantee required for rule-following normativity, the idea that communal usage is somehow responsible to a standard of correctness, cannot be made out. In either case, it seems that a proper account must, as Kripke suggested, do without rule-following understood as a normative exercise.

A very different account of Wittgenstein's rule-following remarks is provided by Baker and Hacker (1980, 1985). According to these authors, we talk correctly of the rule as determining what steps to take. But we are inclined to misconstrue this idiom as if the rule in some mysterious way already contained all its applications independently of us. The truth is that we fix these steps as what we count as being in accord with the rule. When it is correct to talk of a rule determining future steps, it is, in virtue of that fact, equally correct to talk of our fixing what is to be regarded as the correct step. To understand how such seemingly disparate accounts of correctness come together in this way, say Baker and Hacker, it must be realized that the essence of a rule-following account is its use of the notion of "internal relations." Such relations have a number of features: (1) if an internal relation holds at all, it holds necessarily; (2) if A and B are internally related, it is inconceivable that they should not be thus related; (3) this relation is not open to analysis, in that it is not possible to consider breaking down the internal relation between two entities into a pair of relations each of which holds between one of those entities and a common third.

Much of what Baker and Hacker say about rule-following can be understood by concentrating on this third aspect of internal relations. On their view, it is correct to say that a rule determines what is to be the correct future use of an expression – but "determines" here must not be misconstrued. All that is implied is that the rule determines its applications in the same way that the presentation of the obverse of a coin determines that the other side of the coin is the reverse. When one describes a set of activities by saying that the participants are following such

and such a rule, the description does not work through the identifying of some entity (the rule) which is in principle separable from those activities. In particular, Baker and Hacker urge, it must not be thought that the rule and its applications are separable to the extent that they require to be related by a third entity such as an interpretation or inductive step, for this would result in a kind of fracturing of the internal relation which might lead to an infinite regress. Of course, it does not follow from this that a rule and an application of that rule are the same thing (any more than it follows, from saying that obverse and reverse are two sides of the same coin, that the two sides of a coin are the same thing). A rule is a standard of correctness while the practice of applying the rule (e.g., in explaining it or correcting others in its use) is the use of the rule-governed term in actual discourse.

This appeal to practice is not, however, a reference to foundational matters upon which talk of rules and applications rests. The difference between a practice and a regularity of occurrences is that the actions which constitute a practice exhibit normative regularity. The only actions which possess this normative regularity are those which are carried out with the intention, on the part of the agent, of sticking to the pattern which is discernible in those actions. If an individual is to satisfy us that his actions constitute a practice, those actions must demonstrate that he understands the technique involved in applying a rule – that he recognizes the criteria of correctness associated with that technique. (It is for this reason that we are unwilling, typically, to describe a set of behaviors as rule-following unless they are embedded within a relatively complex context of explanations, exemplifications, and so on.) The practices of using a particular rule, of correcting others in its use and so on, are, then, themselves internally related to that rule. And the chain of internal relations which holds between rule, application, practice, and so on forms a circle of normative concepts which cannot be broken. It would be a mistake, therefore, to think that when we say "we fix what is to count as accord with the rule" we are grounding what is to count as an explanation of the correct application of a rule by appealing to the "majority verdict" or whatever. All that the reference to communal practice tells us is that one can recast talk of rule-following in terms of talk of following a practice.

This is a very brief excursion into the complex world of Wittgenstein's philosophy. However, it should already be apparent that philosophers do not hold a unified view on the correct way to interpret Wittgensteinian remarks about meaning as use or language games. Accordingly, it can be difficult to discern what exactly it is that discursive researchers mean when they refer to these Wittgensteinian notions. So although discursive researchers clearly differ from experimental social psychologists in their fondness for referring to Wittgenstein, it is, perhaps, less clear whether this distinction is one which really matters.

Rethinking methodological differences

At the start of this section, we pointed out that in recent times a number of researchers have argued that experimental and discursive research should be integrated. Of course, even if there are no genuine philosophical differences between the two approaches, there are clearly methodological differences about how psychology as a science ought to be conducted. However, as we will see below, one response to this has been to claim that these methodological differences do not constitute a fundamental divide between discursive and experimental research. Instead, they are better thought of as different levels of study which can usefully be combined.

In part, some of the motivation for this integrationist position derives from what has come to be known as the "crisis" in social psychology. Forty years ago, Kenneth Ring (Ring, 1967) wrote a swingeing critique of social psychology and its practices which represented one of the key texts associated with the so called "crisis":

Social psychology today, it seems to me, is in a state of profound intellectual disarray. There is little sense of progress; instead one has the impression of a sprawling, disjointed realm of activity where the movement is primarily outward not upward. We approach our work with a kind of restless pioneer spirit: a new (or seemingly new) territory is discovered, explored for a while, and then usually abandoned when the going gets rough or uninteresting. We are a field of many frontiersmen, but few settlers. And to the degree

that this remains true, the history of social psychology will be written in terms not of flourishing inter-locking communities, but of ghost towns.

(Ring, 1967, pp. 119–120)

It is perhaps testament to the early insights of Ring into the limitations of social psychology, or a reflection of the ongoing failure of social psychology to address these limitations, that some 30 years later writers continued to echo his concerns:

[s]ocial psychology as it is practised today seems not to have changed very much from its "crisis" period of the 1960s and 1970s. Many of the concerns of that day apply to the social psychology of today. In some respects, the difficulties have become more pronounced.

(Pancer, 1997, p. 160)

In the same year as Pancer was bemoaning the continuing crisis in social psychology, a group of senior leading American social psychologists were meeting at Yosemite National Park, California. This group comprised a number of well-known figures in social psychology, individuals who more than others had been responsible for the development of social psychology over the second half of the twentieth century. The purposes of their meeting were twofold: first, to reflect upon their individual involvements in the field over the preceding decades, and second, to consider the achievements of social psychology during that time. Some of the views expressed at that meeting and published two years later, coming from many of the leading figures in the discipline, suggest that as the twentieth century drew to a close, the "crisis" in social psychology was alive and well. Pepitone (1999), for example, noted that, over the course of a century of development, schools of research in social psychology had simply come and gone. There appeared to have been no intradisciplinary attempts to integrate the knowledge that resulted from different perspectives and social psychology had been left without any enduring body of knowledge to show for its endeavors. Zajonc (1999) similarly argued that social psychology had developed little cumulative knowledge over this time. In his view, one could randomly shuffle the chapters of a standard social psychology text without it having any meaningful impact on the content. In short, he could see no history of progress.

It is against this historical background that some researchers have argued that social psychology in the twenty-first century must seek to integrate insights from both the discursive and the experimental approaches. For example, in a recent text, Martha Augoustinos and her colleagues draw attention to the question of whether the "crisis" has ever really gone away, as opposed to being merely ignored by social psychology. In consequence, they argue that:

> We maintain the premise that a theoretically adequate social psychology must integrate the different positions afforded by the social cognitive, social identity, social representations and discursive perspectives.
>
> (Augoustinos et al., 2006, p. 301)

Augoustinos and her colleagues draw on Doise (1986) in developing a four-level model of social psychology's empirical and conceptual concerns which comprises intraindividual, interindividual, intergroup, and collective levels. Augoustinos and her colleagues suggest that social cognition researchers focus on the intraindividual level and social identity theorists on the intergroup level, while discursive researchers are concerned with the interindividual, intergroup, and collective levels. They suggest that the intellectual task which faces social psychology is to develop a means of integrating insights developed at each of these levels. For example, they point out that both the work by Macrae and colleagues on stereotypes (Macrae, Milne, & Bodenhausen, 1994) and Wetherell and Potter's work on racist discourses tell us something about prejudice. It is, say Augoustinos and her colleagues, up to social psychology as a discipline to understand how those disparate findings illuminate one another.

Another leading exponent of this research integration view is Maykel Verkuyten. In discussing the "crisis," he points to the current divisions between discursive and experimental social psychology and notes:

> Each of these positions is not so much wrong as it is limited. In an either/or approach, an opposite is created in which the other kind of analysis is dismissed as inadequate. Discursive

psychologists tend to take a strong anticognitivist stance, and cognitive psychologists ignore or reject the turmoil of everyday life. Either the one *or* other has to be right, and with that the possibility that both are useful disappears.

> (Verkuyten, 2005c, p. 24)

Like Augoustinos, Verkuyten (2005c) develops a multilevel model which depicts the different ways in which social psychology (and other areas of research) seek to make sense of the social world. He uses this model, adapted from House (1977), both to identify three different levels of analysis – individual, interactional, and societal – and to demonstrate how they are interrelated.

Individual

The individual level refers to intra-individual processes and personal characteristics, and social psychological researchers focusing on this level, such as researchers in the social cognition tradition, typically are concerned with cognitive structures and analyses of the self and identity.

Interactional

The interactional level refers to the dynamics of everyday interaction, and social psychological researchers focusing on this level, such as discursive psychologists, are concerned with discursive phenomena through which participants' concerns such as situated identities are made relevant.

Societal

The societal level refers to "broader" phenomena such as ideologies and cultural factors, and social psychological researchers focusing on this level, such as critical discourse analysts, are concerned with the ways in which ideologies are reproduced and challenged through discourse.

Verkuyten identifies a number of important factors associated with this model. The first is the model's presupposition that the interactional level mediates between the individual and societal levels. On the one hand, societal phenomena such as ideologies only exist insofar as there are interactions among people through which those ideologies are manifested. On the other hand, individual phenomena such as a sense of self arise out of the interactions that an individual has with others. The second factor is that the model also assumes these levels are not reducible to each other.

Although the levels are interdependent, in that the interactional level mediates between the other two, the analyses which are appropriate for one level cannot be used to reduce that level to one of the others. The third factor is that the model provides the researcher with a means of understanding how social phenomena arising at each of the three levels are interrelated. For example, a "top-down" approach to the model suggests that ideological and cultural issues from the societal level constrain the ways in which identities are developed and maintained at the interactional level, and these interactional outcomes in turn constrain the ways in which one understands oneself in terms of the individual level. A "bottom-up" approach to the model suggests that one's sense of self and how we present that self to others influences and structures interactions. The interactions themselves produce, in a social constructionist sense, the social actions, practices, and understandings through which societal phenomena such as institutions and ideologies are created. Verkuyten offers a practical example of how these differing perspectives can be combined through the use of both discursive and experimental methods in his study of discourses of choice in discourse about immigration (Verkuyten, 2005b).

This sense that there are interactions across the phenomena studied by both discursive and experimental researchers is echoed by other researchers whose work lies within the mainstream of experimental social psychology. For example, Jost and Kruglanski (2002) argue that the developing awareness of the "crisis" in social psychology was in part a consequence of the rise in social constructionist thought, and suggest that a resolution of the crisis involves, at least in part, a reconciliation between the experimental approach and social constructionist perspectives such as the discursive approach. As we have seen throughout this book, many researchers within the discursive research field adopt a social constructionist approach to their topic area. It follows that many of Jost and Kruglanski's arguments apply equal well to the divide between discursive and experimental approaches.

Jost and Kruglanski refer to Gergen's (1973, 1999) seminal contributions to the development of social constructionism and point out that the social constructionist movement has criticized the experimental approach on a number of levels. However, despite this apparent antagonism, Jost and Kruglanski argue that social psychology could benefit from the theoretical and conceptual ideas which social constructionism embraces. Jost and Kruglanski argue that social constructionism and experimental social psychology share the same disciplinary roots. In particular, they point out that both approaches share an interest in "the power of construal" and the "power of the situation" in that experimentalists, as much as social constructionists, are often interested in how cognitive processes such as attribution are part of an active, constructive process in which people shape their own reality. Both approaches also share an interest in understanding how such processes result in bias in the social actor. Jost and Kruglanski do acknowledge that, as was pointed out earlier in the discussion of realism, the two approaches diverge in their understandings of "truth" as it relates to scientific enterprise. However, they suggest that there are useful parallels between the notion of "truth" as used by the experimentalist and analogous notions as they appear in social constructionism. They point out, for example, that a discursive psychologist such as Potter still makes some use of the idea that participants themselves will orient to some discursive construction as, in some sense or another, valid or problematic. Jost and Kruglanski also note that the two approaches diverge in their perspective on language. However, they argue that the forms of social construction which the analyses of the discursive psychologist reveal are similar in relevant respects to the experimentalist's view of communication as a form of expressing shared representations.

Jost and Kruglanski suggest that experimental psychology has already benefited from its relationship with social constructionism. For example, they locate the growth in social identity research in the way that experimentalists interested in self and identity took to heart some of the anti-individualist criticisms of the social constructionist. They also note the ways that some attitude theorists and those concerned with collective representations such as social representation theorists have emphasized the constructive elements that arise in such processes. They go on to suggest that there are other areas in which the two approaches might usefully interact. Among these are the joint study of the historical and ideological development of human behavior as an integrative alternative to sociobiology. Jost and Kruglanski also point to the possibilities for mutual engagement which lie in the different approaches that social constructionists and experimentalists take to questions of content and process of phenomena such as beliefs.

Of course, the notion that experimental studies of cognitive phenomena are consonant with discursive approaches is already a key idea in some forms of discursive research. Many critical discourse analysts are explicit in their assumption that processes of ideology are mediated by cognitive phenomena. For example, in a recent paper, Wodak (2006) emphasizes the way that stereotypes and prejudicial beliefs represent "frames" which are embedded within culture. However, a similar emphasis on the potential usefulness of stereotypes as an explanatory construct also appears in recent work from the conversation analytic perspective:

> Now, there is no question that the stereotypes do not come near to capturing the details of actual occurrences. But if anything like what I've proposed here actually holds up, then it may be that these stereotypes are crude expressions, and products, of a sort of tacit, working sense of a whole complex of regularities . . . These stereotypes might then be seen to be reflecting, referring to, constituting a "gloss" for that complex of regularities.
>
> (Jefferson, 2004a, p. 131)

What most of these authors suggest, then, is that progress in social psychology depends on integrating the discursive and experimental approaches, in part as a means of addressing the "crisis" in social psychology. In closing this section, we thought it might be useful for readers to consider two brief extracts from research papers, one drawn from the discursive tradition and one from the experimental tradition, and to examine them in this integrationist spirit. The first paper is Schegloff's paper on membership categorization analysis (Schegloff, 2007), the second is Maurer, Park, and Rothbart's paper on stereotyping (Maurer, Park, & Rothbart, 1995). At one point in his paper, Schegloff notes that one facet of membership categorizations is that they are "protected against induction":

> The common-sense knowledge organized by reference to membership categories is protected against induction. If an ostensible member of a category appears to contravene what is "known" about members of the category, then people do not revise that knowledge, but see the person as "an exception," "different," or even a defective member of the category.
>
> (Schegloff, 2007, p. 469)

The experimental social psychologist will be immediately struck by this notion, which lies at the heart of the conversation analyst's understanding of membership categorization. For it bears strong resemblance to what stereotype theorists refer to as "subtyping":

> Subtyping refers to the process by which group members who disconfirm, or are at odds with, the group stereotype are mentally clustered together and essentially set aside as "exceptions to the rule." Subtyping as a process may serve to insulate the stereotype from change.
>
> (Maurer et al., 1995)

From these two excerpts, it would appear that the discursive researcher's concerns with categorization and the experimental social psychologist's concerns overlap. Both are interested in understanding the causes and consequences of the ways in which our categorizations are, in some respects, supervenient upon our actual experiences of other people. The integrationist position would suggest that researchers from these two quite different approaches, conversation analysis and experimental stereotype research, might well have interesting things to say to one another. For example, Maurer, Park, and Rothbart distinguish between the subtyping process and a related process they refer to as "subgrouping," in which different clusters of individuals may be created even though all of those individuals conform to the same stereotype. As a result of subgrouping, an individual perceives greater variability among the members of a class who might otherwise have been viewed as stereotypically similar to one another. An integrationist thought here would be that membership categorization analysis might benefit from an examination of whether naturally occurring conversation displays subgrouping as well as subtyping phenomena.

The Future of Social Psychology

From what has been said above, it is clear that the future direction that social psychology will or should take is unclear. Some researchers will no doubt be persuaded by the arguments put forward by proponents of research integration. Many others, however, will continue to adopt the research independence position. It is worthwhile noting that researchers from the latter position do acknowledge that difficulties of the sort identified 40 years ago by Ring persist. However, contrary to the research integrationists, they argue that the resources of their own approach alone, discursive or experimental, are sufficient in themselves to allow such problems to be resolved.

From within the experimental approach, for example, two eminent researchers in the area of social identity research, Haslam and McGarty (2001), draw attention to some of the current problems of experimental social psychology, which they partly locate in tendencies towards reduction of methodological uncertainty as an end in itself together with a tendency to ignore the creative aspects of uncertainty:

> We argue that these tendencies have become more pronounced as social psychology has progressed, and that while this has played a major role in normalizing social psychology as a science, it has also made that science increasingly more conservative, more safe and more dull.
>
> (Haslam & McGarty, 2001, p. 10)

But Haslam and McGarty argue that any continuing "crisis" of social psychology only arises from the fact that too many experimentalists have used the experimental method to test trivial or uninteresting ideas. Accordingly, they suggest that the "crisis" can be resolved by performing experiments that are non-trivial and which aim to explain important aspects of social life.

Also within the experimental approach, Anthony Greenwald, one of the founding figures in contemporary automaticity of stereotyping research, criticizes what he views as the prevailing opinion in experimental social psychology that empirical evidence is only valuable if it contributes to theoretical advances (Greenwald, 2004). The danger of this, he argues, is that the

experimental social psychological approach places heavy emphasis on explanatory internal mental phenomena which are inferred from the outward evidence of behavior. This emphasis on internal mental phenomena makes it easy for researchers to attack empirical evidence which seems to undermine their own preferred theory, and as a result there is often little fruitful cross-fertilization of ideas from different or competing theoretical perspectives. But Greenwald suggests that the problem of reinterpreting experimental data in terms of a "favored" theory could be resolved by encouraging researchers to consider ways in which their empirical data might illuminate relationships among different or even competing theories.

Within the discursive approach, researchers have also recently issued warnings about the state of discursive research. In a recent article, four of the most eminent practitioners of discursive research, Charles Antaki, Michael Billig, Derek Edwards, and Jonathan Potter, warn that such research can often be problematic:

> work continues to be produced, submitted to journals and sometimes published that embodies basic problems. When we compared notes from our experience of refereeing journal submissions across a wide range of discourse and social psychology journals we noticed that a particular range of shortcomings appeared with great regularity.
>
> (Antaki, Billig, Edwards, & Potter, 2002)

Antaki and his colleagues identify a number of problems with many instances of discursive research. These are associated with under-analysis of the data presented, the circularity of arguing from data extracts to the existence of a discursive phenomenon whose existence is then warranted by appeal to the same extract, the making of unwarranted general or universal claims, and the mere identification or "spotting" of discursive features without reference to an underlying analytic rationale. But, like their experimental social psychology cousins, Antaki and colleagues similarly argue that successful research can be accomplished from within their own approach. Successful research merely requires, they argue, that the researcher focus on the meaning and significance of the analyses produced, as well as ensuring that such analyses are grounded in a close engagement with the text.

Each of these positive suggestions can be thought of as representing the research independence position. The message here is that the researcher already has the tools at hand, either experimental or discursive. All that is required is that the researcher ensures that the work performed in using those tools is genuinely important and socially relevant. However, as noted above, it has been claimed that social psychologists in the twenty-first century also have available a further means of ensuring that their analyses are relevant and important. This research integration position holds out the promise that, by combining insights from both the discursive and experimental approaches, the integrationist researcher can eliminate many of the difficulties represented by social psychological research.

Whether in future the research independence position continues to predominate, or whether it is supplanted by the research integration position, is, then, an open question in the early part of the twenty-first century. However, as Reicher and Taylor have noted in a recent article about integrating discursive and experimental approaches, whatever the future status of these two positions, it is important for both experimental and discursive researchers to at least acknowledge that such methodological and conceptual issues are worthy of constructive debate:

> It depends upon, firstly, listening to and respecting different traditions; secondly, understanding the coherence and rigour of each tradition within its own terms (although we need not necessarily agree with those terms); and therefore, thirdly, respecting others not in order to agree but as a condition for clarifying differences constructively.
>
> (Reicher & Taylor, 2005, p. 549)

Moreover, against this backdrop, the message from the leaders in the field seems clear. Whether one is an experimentalist or a discursive researcher, or both, and whether one is in favor of research independence or research integration, the most important thing that a social psychology researcher can do is to avoid the trivial fetishism of methodology by ensuring that his or her studies are aimed at solving important and socially relevant questions. In this book, we have tried to show the variety of ways in which discursive research has met this challenge. We hope that readers have found this both informative and intellectually stimulating, and will take away from this book a lively appreciation of the ways in which social psychology can, in the future, help us to understand ourselves and others.

Glossary

Accountability: Responsibility, especially in relation to the speaker's responsibility in providing a particular account.

Action-orientation: The property of talk which directs it towards accomplishing specific outcomes or goals.

Aetiology: Recognized cause or origin of disease.

Ageism: Prejudice towards others because of their age.

Agency: The property of being the source or cause of action or events.

Aggression: Behavior intended to cause harm.

Agony aunt: Person employed by magazine or similar to respond to readers' personal letters.

Apartheid: A political and legal system of social separation based on race.

Archive research: The collection of data from existing sources such as official records.

Argument by analogy: Drawing similarities between two different phenomena in order to develop or defend a point of view.

Assessment: Production or evaluation of evidence, usually conducted by a professional.

Asymmetrical interactions: Episodes in which participants differ in socially relevant ways, e.g., formal position or status.

Attitude: An evaluative belief about a social object. See **opinion**.

Attribution: Explaining actions and events by ascribing causes to them.

Authoritative discourse: Talk in which a speaker is held to be especially privileged, e.g., as a result of status or role, in terms of the claims that are made.

Banal nationalism: Nationalistic talk which relies upon everyday, commonplace forms of expression and which can be contrasted with extreme or overtly xenophobic forms of nationalism.

Behavior: What people do, including the production of verbal utterances.

Case notes: Notes used by health professionals that record a patient's health status and care.

Case study: An in-depth observational study of a single event or context.

Categorization: Organizing experience by using terms which denote sorts or kinds of phenomena.

Category-bound activities: Forms of action which are conventionally associated with being a member of the relevant category.

Category entitlements: Rights or privileges normatively associated with a classification of someone.

Co-constructed accounts: Accounts that are shared and produced by more than one individual in the course of conversation.

Cognitive: Pertaining to states of cognition such as beliefs.

Cognitive agnosticism: In analysis, setting aside questions of whether cognitive states exist.

Cognitive state: A condition which the mind is in at a given moment.

Cognitivism: An approach to explaining people's behavior in terms of their cognitive states.

Collaborative identification: Identification of an individual through the turns of two or more people.

Community care: Health initiative designed to allow people with mental health needs to live fully within the community.

Community resistance: Collective resistance at the level of the community, not the individual.

Confabulation: An unintentionally false statement about the world, usually resulting from pathological disorder.

Consensual: Having the property of being agreed upon by a set of relevant individuals.

Contested condition: A claimed medical condition that is not recognized, or that is challenged, either by individuals or by health professionals.

Context: The setting, surroundings, and other background elements relevant to the data that are being collected.

Conversation analysis: The collection and analysis of naturally occurring talk, emphasizing its sequential properties and the actions performed.

Conversational dominance: Having rights or entitlements to talk and direct the talk of others which supersede those of other speakers.

Conversational floor: Participants' understanding of the immediate conversational context, including appropriateness of next turn position.

Conversational identities: Identities that individuals take up when interaction occurs.

Conversational power: Power to shape the progress of a conversation, such as in taking of conversational turns.

Conversational repair: An element of a conversational sequence which addresses problems of mis-speaking, mis-hearing, or misunderstanding.

Correlation: The strength and direction of the relationship between two variables.

Critical discourse analysis: The analysis of discourse with an emphasis on the way it is affected by power and ideology.

Cross-examination: The questioning of witnesses by the lawyer not representing the party who has called the witness.

Cultural and interpretative framework: Broad social and historical context in which individual identities are located.

Dependent variable: A variable whose values are compared by the experimenter across the levels of the independent variable.

Diagnosis: Summary of available evidence and of how that evidence relates to professional understandings of health and illness.

Direct examination: The questioning of witnesses by the lawyer representing the party who has called the witness.

Disclaimer: A phrase which is designed to prevent hearers from drawing otherwise potentially available inferences.

Discourse analysis: The collection and analysis of verbal material, spoken or written, which emphasizes properties such as structure and variability and focuses on action.

Discrimination: Unfair behavior directed at others as a result of prejudice.

Discursive action: That which people do or accomplish through talk.

Discursive mind control: A term employed by critical discourse analysis to represent the persuasive ideological effects of discourse.

Discursive psychology: The use of discursive techniques to analyze talk of psychological states and the application of those analyses to real world settings.

Displaying sensitivity: Implicit or explicit acknowledgment to the hearer that what one is saying is relevant to a specific issue or concern.

Dispositional state: Having the property of tending towards a particular action under given circumstances (e.g., sugar has the dispositional state of melting when placed in hot coffee).

Dispreferred: A conversational turn, designed as a response to a prior turn, in which what is said is taken to be potentially problematic for the recipient, e.g., turning down a request.

Dispute: A disagreement or argument.

Diversity: Bringing together individuals with a range of different attributes.

Double standard: Evaluation of behavior that differs according to the actor rather than the behavior.

Entitlement to speak: Acceptance by others, who claim the same illness identities, that one legitimately describe the experience of that illness.

Epistemological orientation: A discursive stance or position towards some thing in which the speaker's state of mind towards that thing is made explicit. See also **epistemological stance**.

Epistemological stance: A perspective on what is said which makes relevant a mental state such as "doubt" or "belief." See also **epistemological orientation**.

Essentializing: Talk designed to depict group membership categories as inevitable or quasi-natural.

Evaluation: Talk which situates the relevant topic in a comparative frame indicating features such as levels of goodness or worth.

Experiment: A set of observations collected under controlled conditions in order to test a hypothesis.

Expert witness: A witness whose testimony is produced on the basis of his or her skills or knowledge.

Expertise: Specialized understanding of, and practice within, a particular field of activity.

External evidence: Evidence that is visible to other individuals.

Extreme case formulation: A discursive construction which uses the strongest version of comparative terms or phrases.

Eyewitness testimony: Testimony provided by someone who was present at the time and place relevant to the events which are under consideration.

Factual description: A discursive formulation of something which emphasizes its literal qualities and its direct reference to the world.

"Fakers" and "haters": Individuals who are constructed by accepted Internet site users as resisting or challenging support group understandings.

Feminism: The view that men and women should be treated equally.

Fine-grain detail: Characteristics of talk examined at the level of construction of individual turns (e.g., lexical choice) and turn-by-turn sequences.

Focus group: A group organized by a researcher to discuss issues relevant to the research topic.

Footing: A perspective which makes relevant properties of the speaker such as a range of normative actions or a set of social relationships.

Formal contexts: Scenes of interaction which are typified by rules of proceeding established by the relevant authority.

Formulation: A summary that offers the gist of what has been said previously or of what should happen following that talk.

Foucauldian discourse analysis: A form of discourse analysis which relies on the work of Foucault and emphasizes the historical and ideological aspects of discourse.

Frame: A term deriving initially from Goffman to indicate participants' organization of their experiences into recognizable activities.

Gendered condition: A condition that is understood to affect, only or mainly, individuals of one gender.

Grice's maxims: A set of rules for cooperation in conversation described by Paul Grice.

Grounded theory: A method of categorizing qualitative data in which categories are developed out of the data.

Health behavior: A behavior that impacts upon or results from health status.

Health initiative: An attempt to change the health behaviors of a social group or community.

Health professionals: People who are employed within health-oriented disciplines to deal with the health or illness of other individuals.

Health status: The construction of individual experience in terms of health or illness.

Hedge: An aspect of talk in which the speaker displays that what is to be said is potentially problematic, e.g., through the use of expressions of doubtfulness.

Hegemonic masculinity: Socially prevailing view of ideal form of masculine identity.

Heterogeneity: A term used to describe a collection or group of people or things whose members are not similar.

Heterosexism: A point of view which lends priority to the assumption that heterosexual relationships are normative in society.

Homogeneity: A term used to describe a collection or group of people or things whose members are similar.

Human genome: The totality of the hereditary information encoded in human DNA.

Hypothesis: An empirically testable statement about relationships among theoretical entities.

Ideology: An organized set of ideas which typifies the thinking of a group or society.

Illness identity: An identity of being ill through no fault of one's own.

Implicature: The inferences which an utterance makes available.

Impression management: Designing what is said in order to convey to others a picture or sense of what sort of person the speaker is.

Independent variable: A variable whose different levels are assigned to experimental participants by the experimenter.

Individual pathology: Illness or disorder that is attributed to origins lying within an individual.

Institutional talk: Talk found in institutional settings and which differs from everyday conversation.

Interactional implications: Consequences which may arise from a speaker's utterances and which are relevant to how the interaction proceeds.

Interactional resource: An element of the discursive context which participants may deploy or draw on to accomplish a particular action or rhetorical effect.

Interactional troubles: Elements of an episode of talk in which participants orient to what is being said as though it is problematic.

Interest management: Attending through talk to issues or concerns which hearers might attribute to the speaker.

Interpretative phenomenological analysis: A research method focusing on participants' experiences as they interpret them.

Interpretative repertoires: Forms of talk or text in which the content of what is said is organized via specific styles of speaking or writing.

Interview: An interaction between a researcher and a participant in which the researcher asks questions relevant to the research topic.

Invited guessing: Overt request that a listener correctly guesses information known to the speaker.

Irony: A discursive device in which what is said differs from what is actually meant.

Lay knowledge: Understandings of practices and procedures that do not require expertise.

Linguistics: The scientific study of the system and structure of language.

Listing: Talk which sequentially itemizes a series of things that are related in some way.

Making available: Allowing a hearer to make an inference about something which is not explicitly stated by the speaker.

Making relevant: Establishing that some feature of talk is appropriate to the local discursive context.

Management of inferences: Dealing with issues which speakers might be taken to have implicitly introduced.

Marker: An utterance, or a feature of an utterance, designed to draw the hearer's attention in some way.

Mediating factor: Some thing or property which links two events or states.

Membership category features: Descriptive traits or properties which are inferentially linked to a category label.

Mental model: A representation in the mind which organizes experience of the external world.

Mentoring: Advice and guidance given by senior employees to more junior employees.

Metalinguistic: Talk which refers to the discursive properties of other talk.

Metaphor: A figure of speech used to refer to something not literally identified by means of similarities between it and the thing which is explicitly mentioned.

Micro context: The immediate surroundings of an interaction, including time and place.

Minimal response: A conversational turn, produced in response to a prior turn, which is noticeably brief.

Moral imperative: An obligation to act in certain accepted ways.

Mutual knowledge: Something known to some or all of the participants in an interaction.

Narrative analysis: The analysis of talk in terms of its story-like elements.

National identities: Descriptions of individuals as members of distinct national communities.

Naturally occurring talk: Talk between or among people which is unprompted but recorded by the researcher.

New father: Father who participates actively in all aspects of parenting and domestic life.

New woman: Woman who has full opportunities to enjoy a successful career and family life.

Norm: A standard or rule which applies to human behavior.

Normalizing practices: Social processes, including discursive processes, which establish particular ways of viewing the world as commonplace.

Noticing: Making some feature of the environment salient or relevant to the present discursive context.

Objective: Pertaining to aspects of the world independently of any individual's view or perspective.

Observation: Collecting and recording empirical data to answer a research question.

Occasioned: The idea that the meaning of an utterance is bound up with the local discursive context in which it is uttered.

Operationalization: The process of identifying variables within a hypothesis with measures of observable events.

Opinion: An evaluative view or belief. See **attitude**.

Organizational discourse analysis: The use of discourse analysis to study organizations as a social topic.

Organizational discourse studies: Studies of organizations that focus on organizational discourse.

Organizational features: The structural properties of talk which allow a speaker to present that talk as being of a particular sort.

Orienting: Interpreting what is said in a specific way.

Overtly prejudicial talk: Talk designed by the speaker to be heard as prejudiced.

Participants' categories: The discursive terms used to organize experience which are deployed by participants (in contrast to theoretical notions which a researcher might introduce).

Participatory decision-making: Involvement of all interested employees in the making of organizational decisions.

Passive construction: Talk which uses features such as the grammatical passive voice in order to counter potential attributions of agency to the speaker.

Patriarchy: Set of social practices that favors men over women.

Persuasion: The alteration of someone's beliefs or attitudes via communication.

Place-identities: Constructions of places and of the relationships of individuals to these.

Political correctness: The inappropriate use of explicitly non-prejudiced terms or phrases.

Positioning: Adopting a stance or voice normatively associated with a category of person.

Positivism: The view that explanations of empirical events must be scientific.

Practical concern: An issue which participants address through talk which has consequences beyond the talk itself.

Pre-analytic categories: Typologies produced by an analyst before the analysis has been performed.

Prejudice: Dislike of others who are described as different from oneself, e.g., in terms of category membership.

Presupposition: An assumption which is implicitly or explicitly held as a prior basis for what is said.

Procedural relevance: The property of being contextually appropriate in terms of preceding sequences of talk.

Production features: Aspects of talk which are concerned with the way talk is produced, such as the use of repetitions or particular ways of speaking (e.g., adopting a "precise" form of delivery).

Propositional attitude: A stance taken towards one's own mental states.

Qualitative data: Observations (often verbal material) which are not represented by numerical values.

Quantification: Talk which relies on reference to numerical and other quantity references for rhetorical effect.

Quantitative data: Observations which are represented by numerical values.

Quasi-objective evidence: Evidence that is not external and objective but which is treated as being objective.

Racism: Prejudice towards others because of their race.

Recursive: Having the property of repetitiveness in which an operation may repeatedly apply to itself.

Referential status: An individual's social status relative to another individual.

Reflexivity: Discourse which is designed to make relevant properties of the discourse itself.

Reformulations: Talk in which a partial or complete word or phrase is followed by a restatement in other words of what was just said.

Reported speech: Discourse in which the speaker deploys actual (or apparent) literal repetition of previously made statements.

Restart: The production of an utterance which is designed to signal that the speaker is recommencing his or her utterance.

Rhetoric: The study of rhetoric can be traced back to Aristotle. Modern discursive approaches to rhetoric emphasize the way talk is designed, e.g., through lexical choices, to perform actions within local contexts of talk.

Rhetorical psychology: The application of discursive techniques to the study of persuasive language and, more broadly, the view that talk is inherently argumentative.

Rhetorically self-sufficient claim: A claim which speakers treat as though it stands in no need of additional justification.

Role-play: Interactions in which individuals play roles that differ from their own identities.

Science: The method of studying our world which relies upon the systematic, theory-led gathering of data.

Script: A series of steps or elements which are conventionally related to one another in a sequential fashion.

Second stories: Conversational turns which have a narrative element and which follow on from, and are oriented to, stories produced in preceding turns.

Self-qualifying segments: Episodes of talk in which the speaker reflexively comments on what he or she has said.

Self-repair: A correction of what is said instigated by the speaker, e.g., in displaying hesitancy.

Sequencing: The ordering of turns within a conversation.

Sequential pattern: The design of an episode in talk in terms of its turn-taking structure.

Sexism: Prejudice against others in terms of their gender.

Social constructionism: The view that social phenomena are best understood as the outcome of discursive interaction rather than as extra-discursive phenomena in their own right.

Social psychology: The study of how what people say and do is influenced by social interaction.

Sociology: The study of people interacting in social groupings and other social formations.

Speech style: Form of talk which is designed to be appropriate to a given context, e.g., selection of level of formality or carefulness of production.

Stake: An interest in or concern with how what is said is interpreted by hearers.

Stoical: Accepting misfortune, without complaint or indication of difficulty.

Subjective: Pertaining to an individual's own view or perspective.

Survey: The collection of data via interview or questionnaire from a sample of a population.

Talk-in-interaction: Discourse which reflects and is constitutive of the local context of a particular social interaction.

Testimony: A statement which a witness provides and affirms to be true (e.g., by swearing an oath).

Theory: An explanatory model used to explain a phenomenon by positing relationships between or among the theory's constructs.

Topic initial elicitors: Words or phrases which are conventionally deployed to indicate the appropriateness of producing a new conversational topic.

Turn: The basic unit of conversation in which one speaker talks.

Undermining: Weakening or countering an argumentative position.

Variable: A changeable property of the experimental context.

Virtual identities: Forms of identity that people take up in online communications and communities.

Warrant: A reason or rationale for making a claim.

Worked up: Designing what is said in order to achieve an interactional goal.

References

Abell, J. & Stokoe, E. H. (1999). "I take full responsibility, I take some responsibility, I'll take half of it but no more than that": Princess Diana and the negotiation of blame in the "Panorama" interview. *Discourse Studies, 1,* 297–319.

Abell, J. & Stokoe, E. H. (2001). Broadcasting the royal role: Constructing culturally situated identities in the Princess Diana Panorama interview. *British Journal of Social Psychology, 40,* 417–435.

Abu-Akel, A. (2002). The psychological and social dynamics of topic performance in family dinnertime conversation. *Journal of Pragmatics, 34,* 1787–1806.

Achugar, M. (2004). The events and actors of 11 September 2001 as seen from Uruguay: Analysis of daily newspaper editorials. *Discourse & Society, 15,* 291–320.

Agne, R. R. & Tracy, K. (2001). "Bible babble": Naming the interactional trouble at Waco. *Discourse Studies, 3,* 269–294.

Al-Ali, M. N. (2006). Religious affiliations and masculine power in Jordanian wedding invitation genre. *Discourse & Society, 17,* 691–714.

Allender, S., Colquhoun, D., & Kelly, P. (2006). Competing discourses of workplace health. *Health, 10,* 75–93.

Alvesson, M. & Karreman, D. (2000). Varieties of discourse: On the study of organizations through discourse analysis. *Human Relations, 53,* 1125–1149.

Andersen, A. E. & Holman, J. E. (1997). Males with eating disorders: Challenges for treatment and research. *Psychopharmacology Bulletin, 33,* 391–397.

Anderson, I., Beattie, G., & Spencer, C. (2001). Can blaming victims of rape be logical? Attribution theory and discourse analytic perspectives. *Human Relations, 54,* 445–467.

Anderson-Gough, F., Grey, C., & Robson, K. (2000). In the name of the client: The service ethic in two professional service firms. *Human Relations, 53,* 1151–1174.

Antaki, C. (1994). *Explaining and arguing: The social organization of accounts.* London: Sage.

Antaki, C. (1998). Identity ascriptions in their time and place: "Fagin" and "the terminally dim." In C. Antaki & S. Widdicombe (Eds.), *Identities in talk* (pp. 71–86). London: Sage.

Antaki, C. (1999). Interviewing persons with a learning disability: How setting lower standards may inflate well-being scores. *Qualitative Health Research, 9,* 437–454.

Antaki, C. (2001). "D'you like a drink then do you?" Dissembling language and the construction of an impoverished life. *Journal of Language and Social Psychology, 20,* 196–213.

Antaki, C. (2004). Reading minds or dealing with interactional implications? *Theory & Psychology, 14,* 667–683.

Antaki, C. (2006). Producing a "cognition." *Discourse Studies, 8,* 9–15.

Antaki, C., Barnes, R., & Leudar, I. (2005a). Diagnostic formulations in psychotherapy. *Discourse Studies, 7,* 627–647.

Antaki, C., Barnes, R., & Leudar, I. (2005b). Self-disclosure as a situated interactional practice. *British Journal of Social Psychology, 44,* 181–199.

Antaki, C., Billig, M., Edwards, D., & Potter, J. (2002). Discourse analysis means doing analysis: A critique of six analytic shortcomings. Discourse Analysis Online [Online]. Available: extra.shu.ac.uk/daol/articles/v1/n1/a1/antaki2002002.html.

Antaki, C., Condor, S., & Levine, M. (1996). Social identities in talk: Speakers' own orientations. *British Journal of Social Psychology, 35*, 473–492.

Antaki, C. & Rapley, M. (1996a). "Quality of life" talk: The liberal paradox of psychological testing. *Discourse & Society, 7*, 293–316.

Antaki, C. & Rapley, M. (1996b). Questions and answers to psychological assessment schedules: Hidden troubles in "quality of life" interviews. *Journal of Intellectual Disability Research, 40*, 421–437.

Antaki, C. & Wetherell, M. (1999). Show concessions. *Discourse Studies, 1*, 7–27.

Antaki, C. & Widdicombe, S. (Eds.) (1998). *Identities in talk*. London and Thousand Oaks, CA: Sage.

Archer, J. (2000). Sex differences in aggression between heterosexual partners: A meta-analytic review. *Psychological Bulletin, 126*, 651–680.

Arminen, I. (2001). Closing of turns in the meetings of Alcoholics Anonymous: Members' methods for closing "sharing experiences." *Research on Language and Social Interaction, 34*, 211–251.

Arminen, I. (2004a). On the weakness of institutional rules: The case of addiction group therapy. *Discourse & Society, 15*, 683–704.

Arminen, I. (2004b). Second stories: The salience of interpersonal communication for mutual help in Alcoholics Anonymous. *Journal of Pragmatics, 36*, 319–347.

Arminen, I. (2005). *Institutional interaction: Studies of talk at work*. Aldershot: Ashgate.

Askehave, I. (2004). If language is a game – these are the rules: A search into the rhetoric of the spiritual self-help book *If Life Is A Game – These Are The Rules*. *Discourse & Society, 15*, 5–31.

Atkinson, J. M. & Drew, P. (1979). *Order in court: The organization of verbal interaction in judicial settings*. London: Macmillan.

Atkinson, J. M. & Heritage, J. (1984). *Structures of social action: Studies in conversation analysis*. Cambridge: Cambridge University Press.

Auburn, T. (2005). Narrative reflexivity as a repair device for discounting "cognitive distortions" in sex offender treatment. *Discourse & Society, 16*, 697–718.

Auburn, T., Drake, S., & Willig, C. (1995). You punched him, didn't you: Versions of violence in accusatory interviews. *Discourse & Society, 6*, 353–386.

Auburn, T. & Lea, S. J. (2003). Doing cognitive distortions: A discursive psychology analysis of sex offender treatment talk. *British Journal of Social Psychology, 42*, 281–298.

Augoustinos, M., LeCouteur, A., & Soyland, A. J. (2002). Self-sufficient arguments in political rhetoric: Constructing reconciliation and apologizing to the Stolen Generations. *Discourse & Society, 13*, 105–142.

Augoustinos, M., Tuffin, K., & Every, D. (2005). New racism, meritocracy and individualism: Constraining affirmative action in education. *Discourse & Society, 16*, 315–340.

Augoustinos, M., Tuffin, K., & Rapley, M. (1999). Genocide or a failure to gel? Racism, history and nationalism in Australian talk. *Discourse & Society, 10*, 351–378.

Augoustinos, M., Tuffin, K., & Sale, L. (1999). Race talk. *Australian Journal of Psychology, 51*, 90–97.

Augoustinos, M. & Walker, I. (1995). *Social cognition: An integrated introduction*. London: Sage.

Augoustinos, M., Walker, I., & Ngaire, D. (2006). *Social cognition: An integrated introduction* (2nd ed.) London: Sage.

Bailey, B. (2000a). Communicative behavior and conflict between African-American customers and Korean immigrant retailers in Los Angeles. *Discourse & Society, 11*, 86–108.

Bailey, B. (2000b). Language and negotiation of ethnic/racial identity among Dominican Americans. *Language in Society, 29*, 555–582.

Bailey, P. H. (2004). The dyspnea-anxiety-dyspnea cycle – COPD patients' stories of breathlessness: "It's scary when you can't breathe." *Qualitative Health Research, 14*, 760–778.

Baker, G. P. & Hacker, P. M. S. (1980). *Wittgenstein: Understanding and meaning*. Oxford: Blackwell.

Baker, G. P.& Hacker, P. M. S. (1985). *Wittgenstein: Rules, grammar and necessity*. Oxford: Blackwell.

Bakhtin, M. M. (1981). Discourse in the novel. In M. Holquist (Ed.), *The dialogic imagination* (pp. 259–422). Austin: University of Texas Press.

Bangerter, A. (2000). Self-representation: Conversational implementation of self-presentational goals in research interviews. *Journal of Language and Social Psychology, 19*, 436–462.

Bargiela-Chiappini, F. & Gotti, M. (2005). *Asian business discourse(s)*. Bern: Peter Lang.

Bargiela-Chiappini, F., Chakorn, O. O., Chew Chye Lay, G., Jung, Y., Kong, K. C., Nair-Venugopal, S., et al. (2007). Eastern voices: Enriching research on communication in business: A forum. *Discourse & Communication, 1*, 131–152.

Barker, K. (2002). Self-help literature and the making of an illness identity: The case of fibromyalgia syndrome (FMS). *Social Problems, 49*, 279–300.

Barnes, B., Palmary, I., & Durrheim, K. (2001). The denial of racism: The role of humor, personal experience, and self-censorship. *Journal of Language and Social Psychology, 20*, 321–338.

Barnes, R., Auburn, T., & Lea, S. J. (2004). Citizenship in practice. *British Journal of Social Psychology, 43*, 187–206.

Barnes, R. & Moss, D. (2007). Communicating a feeling: The social organization of "private thoughts." *Discourse Studies, 9*, 123–148.

Baron, A. (2004). "I'm a woman but I know God leads my way": Agency and Tzotzil evangelical discourse. *Language in Society, 33*, 249–283.

Barton, E. L. (1999). Informational and interactional functions of slogans and sayings in the discourse of a support group. *Discourse & Society, 10*, 461–486.

Barton, E. L. (2000). The interactional practices of referrals and accounts in medical discourse: Expertise and compliance. *Discourse Studies, 2*, 259–281.

Barton, E. L. (2004). The construction of legal consciousness in discourse: Rule and relational orientations toward the law in a disability support group. *Journal of Pragmatics, 36*, 603–632.

Beach, W. A. (2000). Inviting collaborations in stories about a woman. *Language in Society, 29*, 379–407.

Beach, W. A. & Lockwood, A. S. (2003). Making the case for airline compassion fares: The serial organization of problem narratives during a family crisis. *Research on Language and Social Interaction, 36*, 351–393.

Benveniste, J., LeCouteur, A., & Hepworth, J. (1999). Lay theories of anorexia nervosa: A discourse analytic study. *Journal of Health Psychology, 4*, 59–70.

Benwell, B. & Stokoe, E. H. (2006). *Discourse and identity*. Edinburgh: Edinburgh University Press.

Bergmann, J. R. (1993). *Discreet indiscretions: The social organization of gossip*. New Jersey: Aldine Transaction.

Bergvall, V. L. & Remlinger, K. A. (1996). Reproduction, resistance and gender in educational discourse: The role of critical discourse analysis. *Discourse & Society, 7*, 453–479.

Berman, L. (2000). Surviving on the streets of Java: Homeless children's narratives of violence. *Discourse & Society, 11*, 149–174.

Bhatia, A. (2006). Critical discourse analysis of political press conferences. *Discourse & Society, 17*, 173–203.

Billig, M. (1987). *Arguing and thinking: A rhetorical approach to social psychology*. Cambridge: Cambridge University Press.

Billig, M. (1991). *Ideologies and beliefs*. London: Sage.

Billig, M. (1995). *Banal nationalism*. London: Sage.

Billig, M. (1999a). Conversation analysis and the claims of naivety. *Discourse & Society, 10*, 572–576.

Billig, M. (1999b). Whose terms? Whose ordinariness? Rhetoric and ideology in conversation analysis. *Discourse & Society, 10*, 543–558.

Billig, M. (2001). Humour and hatred: The racist jokes of the Ku Klux Klan. *Discourse & Society, 12*, 267–289.

Billig, M. (2002). Henri Tajfel's "Cognitive aspects of prejudice" and the psychology of bigotry. *British Journal of Social Psychology, 41*, 171–188.

Bishop, F. L. & Yardley, L. (2004). Constructing agency in treatment decisions: Negotiating responsibility in cancer. *Health, 8*, 465–482.

Bishop, H. & Jaworski, A. (2003). "We beat 'em": Nationalism and the hegemony of homogeneity in the British press reportage of Germany versus England during Euro 2000. *Discourse & Society, 14*, 243–271.

Blommaert, J. (2001). Investigating narrative inequality: African asylum seekers' stories in Belgium. *Discourse & Society, 12*, 413–449.

Blommaert, J., Creve, L., & Willaert, E. (2006). On being declared illiterate: Language-ideological disqualification in Dutch classes for immigrants in Belgium. *Language & Communication, 26*, 34–54.

Blum-Kulka, S., Huck-Taglicht, D., & Avni, H. (2004). The social and discursive spectrum of peer talk. *Discourse Studies, 6*, 307–328.

Blum-Kulka, S. & Snow, C. E. (2004). Introduction: The potential of peer talk. *Discourse Studies, 6*, 291–306.

Bolden, G. B. (2000). Toward understanding practices of medical interpreting: Interpreters' involvement in history taking. *Discourse Studies, 2*, 387–419.

Bonilla-Silva, E. & Forman, T. A. (2000). "I am not a racist but . . .": Mapping white college students' racial ideology in the USA. *Discourse & Society, 11*, 50–85.

Bonito, J. A. & Sanders, R. E. (2002). Speakers' footing in a collaborative writing task: A resource for addressing disagreement while avoiding conflict. *Research on Language and Social Interaction, 35*, 481–514.

Bowker, N. & Tuffin, K. (2002). Disability discourses for online identities. *Disability & Society, 17*, 327–344.

Breheny, M. & Stephens, C. (2003). Healthy living and keeping busy: A discourse analysis of mid-aged women's attributions for menopausal experience. *Journal of Language and Social Psychology, 22*, 169–189.

Britsch, S. J. (2005). The multimodal mediation of power in the discourses of preschool story designers. *Text, 25*, 305–340.

Brooks, A., LeCouteur, A., & Hepworth, J. (1998). Accounts of experiences of bulimia: A discourse analytic study. *International Journal of Eating Disorders, 24*, 193–205.

Brown, G. & Yule, G. (1983). *Discourse analysis*. Cambridge: Cambridge University Press.

Bucholtz, M. (1999). "Why be normal?": Language and identity practices in a community of nerd girls. *Language in Society, 28*, 203–223.

Bulow, P. H. (2004). Sharing experiences of contested illness by storytelling. *Discourse & Society, 15*, 33–53.

Bulow, P. H. & Hyden, L.-C. (2003). Patient school as a way of creating meaning in a contested illness: The case of CFS. *Health, 7*, 227–249.

Bunzl, M. (2000). Inverted appellation and discursive gender insubordination: An Austrian case study in gay male conversation. *Discourse & Society*, *11*, 207–236.

Burman, E. (2005). Engendering culture in psychology. *Theory & Psychology*, *15*, 527–548.

Burman, E. & Parker, I. (1993). Introduction – discourse analysis: The turn to the text. In E. Burman & I. Parker (Eds.), *Discourse analytic research: Repertoires and readings of texts in action* (pp. 1–13). London: Routledge.

Burns, M. (2004). Eating like an ox: Femininity and dualistic constructions of bulimia and anorexia. *Feminism & Psychology*, *14*, 269–295.

Burns, M. & Gavey, N. (2004). "Healthy weight" at what cost? "Bulimia" and a discourse of weight control. *Journal of Health Psychology*, *9*, 549–565.

Butler, C. & Weatherall, A. (2006). "No, we're not playing families": Membership categorization in children's play. *Research on Language and Social Interaction*, *39*, 441–470.

Buttny, R. (1993). *Social accountability in communication*. London and Newbury Park, CA: Sage.

Buttny, R. (1999). Discursive constructions of racial boundaries and self-segregation on campus. *Journal of Language and Social Psychology*, *18*, 247–268.

Buttny, R. (2004). *Talking problems: Studies of discursive construction*. Albany: State University of New York Press.

Buttny, R. & Williams, L. S. (2000). Demanding respect: The uses of reported speech in discursive constructions of interracial contact. *Discourse & Society*, *11*, 109–133.

Button, G. & Casey, N. (1984). Generating topic: The use of topic initial elicitors. In J. M. Atkinson & J. Heritage (Eds.), *Structures of social action: Studies in conversational analysis* (pp. 167–189). Cambridge: Cambridge University Press.

Candlin, C. N. & Candlin, S. (2002). Discourse, expertise, and the management of risk in health care settings. *Research on Language and Social Interaction*, *35*, 115–137.

Carranza, I. E. (1999). Winning the battle in private discourse: Rhetorical-logical operations in storytelling. *Discourse & Society*, *10*, 509–541.

Chang, Y. (2004). Courtroom questioning as a culturally situated persuasive genre of talk. *Discourse & Society*, *15*, 705–722.

Charmaz, K. (2006). *Constructing grounded theory: A practical guide through qualitative analysis*. London: Sage.

Charteris-Black, J. (2006). Britain as a container: Immigration metaphors in the 2005 election campaign. *Discourse & Society*, *17*, 563–581.

Cheepen, C. (2000). Small talk in service dialogues: The conversational aspects of transactional telephone talk. In J. Coupland (Ed.), *Small talk* (pp. 288–311). London: Longman.

Chiapello, E. & Fairclough, N. L. (2002). Understanding the new management ideology: A transdisciplinary contribution from critical discourse analysis and new sociology of capitalism. *Discourse & Society*, *13*, 185–208.

Chilton, P. (2005). Missing links in mainstream CDA: Modules, blends and the critical instinct. In R. Wodak & P. Chilton (Eds.), *A new agenda in (critical) discourse analysis* (pp. 19–51). Amsterdam: John Benjamins.

Chouliaraki, L. & Fairclough, N. L. (1999). *Discourse in late modernity: Rethinking critical discourse analysis*. Edinburgh: Edinburgh University Press.

Clarke, V. (2002). Sameness and difference in research on lesbian parenting. *Journal of Community & Applied Social Psychology*, *12*, 210–222.

Clarke, V. & Kitzinger, C. (2004). Lesbian and gay parents on talk shows: Resistance or collusion in heterosexism? *Qualitative Research in Psychology*, *1*, 195–217.

Clarke, V., Kitzinger, C., & Potter, J. (2004). "Kids are just cruel anyway": Lesbian and gay parents' talk about homophobic bullying. *British Journal of Social Psychology*, *43*, 531–550.

Clayman, S. E. (2002). Disagreements and third parties: Dilemmas of neutralism in panel news interviews. *Journal of Pragmatics*, *34*, 1385–1401.

Clift, R. (1999). Irony in conversation. *Language in Society*, *28*, 523–553.

Coates, J. (1996). *Women talk*. Oxford: Blackwell.

Coates, J. (2007). Talk in a play frame: More on laughter and intimacy. *Journal of Pragmatics*, *39*, 29–49.

Coates, L. & Wade, A. (2004). Telling it like it isn't: Obscuring perpetrator responsibility for violent crime. *Discourse & Society*, *15*, 499–526.

Condor, S. (2000). Pride and prejudice: Identity management in English people's talk about "this country." *Discourse & Society*, *11*, 175–205.

Condor, S. (2006). Public prejudice as collaborative accomplishment: Towards a dialogic social psychology of racism. *Journal of Community & Applied Social Psychology*, *16*, 1–18.

Condor, S. & Antaki, C. (1997). Social cognition and discourse. In T. A. van Dijk (Ed.), *Discourse as structure and process: A multidisciplinary introduction* (Vol. 1, pp. 320–347). London: Sage.

Condor, S., Figgou, L., Abell, J., Gibson, S., & Stevenson, C. (2006). They're not racist . . . Prejudice denial, mitigation and suppression in dialogue. *British Journal of Social Psychology*, *45*, 441–462.

Conley, J. M. & O'Barr, W. M. (1998). *Just words: Law, language and power*. Chicago: University of Chicago Press.

Connell, R. (1987). *Gender and power*. Cambridge: Polity.

Connell, R. (1995). *Masculinities*. Cambridge: Polity.

Conroy, T. M. (1999). "I don't want to burst your bubble": Affiliation and disaffiliation in a joint accounting by affiliated pair partners. *Human Studies, 22*, 339–359.

Cook, G., Pieri, E., & Robbins, P. T. (2004). "The scientists think and the public feels": Expert perceptions of the discourse of GM food. *Discourse & Society, 15*, 433–449.

Cooren, F., Matte, F., Taylor, J. R., & Vasquez, C. (2007). A humanitarian organization in action: Organizational discourse as an immutable mobile. *Discourse & Communication, 1*, 153–190.

Cotterill, J. (2003). *Language and power in court: A linguistic analysis of the O. J. Simpson trial*. London: Palgrave Macmillan.

Coupland, J. (1996). Dating advertisements: Discourses of the commodified self. *Discourse & Society, 7*, 187–207.

Coupland, J. (2003). Small talk: Social functions. *Research on Language and Social Interaction, 36*, 1–6.

Coyle, A. & Morgan-Sykes, C. (1998). Troubled men and threatening women: The construction of "crisis" in male mental health. *Feminism & Psychology, 8*, 263–284.

Crawford, M. (2004). Mars and Venus collide: A discursive analysis of marital self-help psychology. *Feminism & Psychology, 14*, 63–79.

Croghan, R. & Miell, D. (1999). Born to abuse? Negotiating identity within an interpretative repertoire of impairment. *British Journal of Social Psychology, 38*, 315–335.

Crossley, M. L. (2004). Making sense of "barebacking": Gay men's narratives, unsafe sex and the "resistance habitus." *British Journal of Social Psychology, 43*, 225–244.

Currie, D. H., Kelly, D. M., & Pomerantz, S. (2007). "The power to squash people": Understanding girls' relational aggression. *British Journal of Sociology of Education, 28*, 23–37.

Daiute, C. & Lightfoot, C. G. (2003). *Narrative analysis: Studying the development of individuals in society*. London: Sage.

Daly, N., Holmes, J., Newton, J., & Stubbe, M. (2004). Expletives as solidarity signals in FTAs on the factory floor. *Journal of Pragmatics, 36*, 945–964.

Danet, B., Hoffman, K., Kermish, N., Rahn, J., & Stayman, D. (1980). An ethnography of questioning in the courtroom. In R. Shuy & A. Shnukal (Eds.), *Language use and the uses of language* (pp. 222–234). Washington, DC: Georgetown University Press.

Davies, J. (2003). Expressions of gender: An analysis of pupils' gendered discourse styles in small group classroom discussions. *Discourse & Society, 14*, 115–132.

Day, K., Gough, B., & McFadden, M. (2003). Women who drink and fight: A discourse analysis of working-class women's talk. *Feminism & Psychology, 13*, 141–158.

de Cillia, R., Reisigl, M., & Wodak, R. (1999). The discursive construction of national identities. *Discourse & Society, 10*, 149–173.

Dersley, I. & Wootton, A. J. (2001). In the heat of the sequence: Interactional features preceding walkouts from argumentative talk. *Language in Society, 30*, 611–638.

Devitt, M. (1996). *Realism and truth*. Princeton, NJ: Princeton University Press.

Dickerson, P. (1996). Let me tell us who I am: The discursive construction of viewer identity. *European Journal of Communication, 11*, 57–82.

Dickerson, P. (1997). "It's not just me who's saying this": The deployment of cited others in televised political discourse. *British Journal of Social Psychology, 36*, 33–48.

Dickerson, P. (2000). "But I'm different to them": Constructing contrasts between self and others in talk-in-interaction. *British Journal of Social Psychology, 39*, 381–398.

Dickerson, P. (2001). Disputing with care: Analysing interviewees' treatment of interviewers' prior turns in televised political interviews. *Discourse Studies, 3*, 203–222.

Dixon, J. A. & Durrheim, K. (2004). Dislocating identity: Desegregation and the transformation of place. *Journal of Environmental Psychology, 24*, 455–473.

Dixon, J. A. & Durrheim, R. (2000). Displacing place-identity: A discursive approach to locating self and other. *British Journal of Social Psychology, 39*, 27–44.

Dixon, J. A. & Wetherell, M. (2004). On discourse and dirty nappies: Gender, the division of household labour and the social psychology of distributive justice. *Theory & Psychology, 14*, 167–189.

Doherty, K. & Anderson, I. (2004). Making sense of male rape: Constructions of gender, sexuality and experience of rape victims. *Journal of Community & Applied Social Psychology, 14*, 85–103.

Doise, W. (1986). *Levels of explanation in psychology*. Cambridge: Cambridge University Press.

Drew, P. (1985). Analyzing the use of language in courtroom interaction. In T.A. van Dijk (Ed.), *Handbook of discourse analysis* (pp. 133–137). New York: Academic Press.

Drew, P. (2002). Out of context: An intersection between domestic life and the workplace, as contexts for (business) talk. *Language & Communication, 22*, 477–494.

Drew, P. (2005). Is confusion a state of mind? In H. F. M. te Molder & J. Potter (Eds.), *Conversation and cognition* (pp. 161–183). Cambridge: Cambridge University Press.

Drew, P. & Heritage, J. (Eds.) (1992). *Talk at work: Interaction in institutional settings.* Cambridge: Cambridge University Press.

Drew, P. & Sorjonen, M. (1997). Institutional dialogue. In T. A. van Dijk (Ed.), *Discourse as social interaction* (pp. 92–118). London: Sage.

Drewery, W. (2005). Why we should watch what we say: Position calls, everyday speech and the production of relational subjectivity. *Theory & Psychology, 15,* 305–324.

Drury, J. (2002). "When the mobs are looking for witches to burn, nobody's safe": Talking about the reactionary crowd. *Discourse & Society, 13,* 41–73.

Drury, J. & Reicher, S. D. (2000). Collective action and psychological change: The emergence of new social identities. *British Journal of Social Psychology, 39,* 579–604.

Dunford, R. & Jones, D. (2000). Narrative in strategic change. *Human Relations, 53,* 1207–1226.

Durrheim, K. & Dixon, J. A. (2001). The role of place and metaphor in racial exclusion: South Africa's beaches as sites of shifting racialization. *Ethnic and Racial Studies, 24,* 433–450.

Durrheim, K. & Dixon, J. A. (2005a). *Racial encounter: The social psychology of contact and desegregation.* London: Psychology Press.

Durrheim, K. & Dixon, J. A. (2005b). Studying talk and embodied practices: Toward a psychology of materiality of "race relations." *Journal of Community & Applied Social Psychology, 15,* 446–460.

Eades, D. (2000). I don't think it's an answer to the question: Silencing Aboriginal witnesses in court. *Language in Society, 29,* 161–195.

Edley, N. (2001). Analysing masculinity: Interpretative repertoires, ideological dilemmas and subject positions. In M. Wetherell, S. Taylor, & S. J. Yates (Eds.), *Discourse as data: A guide for analysis* (pp. 189–228). London: Sage.

Edley, N. & Wetherell, M. (1995). *Men in perspective: Practice, power and identity.* Hemel Hempstead: Harvester Wheatsheaf.

Edley, N. & Wetherell, M. (1997). Jockeying for position: The construction of masculine identities. *Discourse & Society, 8,* 203–217.

Edley, N. & Wetherell, M. (1999). Imagined futures: Young men's talk about fatherhood and domestic life. *British Journal of Social Psychology, 38,* 181–194.

Edley, N. & Wetherell, M. (2001). Jekyll and Hyde: Men's constructions of feminism and feminists. *Feminism & Psychology, 11,* 439–457.

Edwards, D. (1995). 2 to tango: Script formulations, dispositions, and rhetorical symmetry in relationship troubles talk. *Research on Language and Social Interaction, 28,* 319–350.

Edwards, D. (1997). *Discourse and cognition.* London: Sage.

Edwards, D. (1999). Emotion discourse. *Culture & Psychology, 5,* 271–291.

Edwards, D. (2003). Analyzing racial discourse: The discursive psychology of mind–world relationships. In H. van den Berg, M. Wetherell, & H. Houtkoop-Steenstra (Eds.), *Analyzing race talk* (pp. 31–48). Cambridge: Cambridge University Press.

Edwards, D. (2004). Shared knowledge as a performative category in conversation. *Rivista di psicololinguistica applicata, 4,* 41–53.

Edwards, D. (2005a). Discursive psychology. In K. L. Fitch & R. E. Sanders (Eds.), *Handbook of language and social interaction* (pp. 257–273). Mahwah, NJ: Lawrence Erlbaum.

Edwards, D. (2005b). Moaning, whinging and laughing: The subjective side of complaints. *Discourse Studies, 7,* 5–29.

Edwards, D. (2006a). Discourse, cognition and social practices: The rich surface of language and social interaction. *Discourse Studies, 8,* 41–49.

Edwards, D. (2006b). Facts, norms and dispositions: Practical uses of the modal verb would in police interrogations. *Discourse Studies, 8,* 475–501.

Edwards, D. & Fasulo, A. (2006). "To be honest": Sequential uses of honesty phrases in talk-in-interaction. *Research on Language and Social Interaction, 39,* 343–376.

Edwards, D. & Middleton, D. (1986). Joint remembering: Constructing an account of shared experience through conversational discourse. *Discourse Processes, 9,* 423–459.

Edwards, D. & Middleton, D. (1987). Conversation and remembering: Bartlett revisited. *Applied Cognitive Psychology, 1,* 77–92.

Edwards, D. & Middleton, D. (1988). Conversational remembering and family relationships: How children learn to remember. *Journal of Social and Personal Relationships, 5,* 3–25.

Edwards, D. & Potter, J. (1992). *Discursive psychology.* London: Sage.

Edwards, D. & Potter, J. (1993). Language and causation: A discursive action model of description and attribution. *Psychological Review, 100,* 23–41.

Edwards, D. & Potter, J. (2005). Discursive psychology, mental states and descriptions. In H. F. M. te Molder & J. Potter (Eds.), *Conversation and cognition* (pp. 241–278). Cambridge: Cambridge University Press.

Edwards, D. & Stokoe, E. H. (2004). Discursive psychology, focus group interviews and participants'-categories. *British Journal of Developmental Psychology, 22,* 499–507.

Egbert, M. (2004). Other-initiated repair and membership categorization: Some conversational events that trigger linguistic and regional membership categorization. *Journal of Pragmatics, 36,* 1467–1498.

Eglin, P. (2002). Members' gendering work: "Women," "feminists" and membership categorization analysis. *Discourse & Society*, 13, 819–825.

Eglin, P. & Hester, S. (1999). "You're all a bunch of feminists": Categorization and the politics of terror in the Montreal massacre. *Human Studies*, 22, 253–272.

Ehrlich, S. (1998). The discursive reconstruction of sexual consent. *Discourse & Society*, 9, 149–171.

Ehrlich, S. (1999). Communities of practice, gender, and the representation of sexual assault. *Language in Society*, 28, 239–256.

Ehrlich, S. (2001). *Representing rape: Language and sexual consent*. London: Routledge.

Ehrlich, S. (2002). Legal institutions, nonspeaking recipiency and participants' orientations. *Discourse & Society*, 13, 731–747.

Englund, H. (2004). Towards a critique of rights talk in new democracies: The case of legal aid in Malawi. *Discourse & Society*, 15, 527–551.

Erjavec, K. (2001). Media representation of the discrimination against the Roma in Eastern Europe: The case of Slovenia. *Discourse & Society*, 12, 699–727.

Evaldsson, A. C. (2005). Staging insults and mobilizing categorizations in a multiethnic peer group. *Discourse & Society*, 16, 763–786.

Fairclough, N. L. (1995). *Critical discourse analysis: The critical study of language*. Harlow: Longman.

Fairclough, N. L. (2003). *Analysing discourse: Textual analysis for social research*. London: Routledge.

Fairclough, N. L. (2005). Critical discourse analysis. *Marges Linguistiques*, 9, 76–91.

Federal Bureau of Investigation (2006). *Crime in the United States 2004*. Washington, DC: US Department of Justice.

Feyerabend, P. (1993). *Against method* (3rd ed.). London: Verso.

Fielding, H. (1997). *Bridget Jones's diary: A novel*. London: Picador.

Figgou, L. & Condor, S. (2006). Irrational categorization, natural intolerance and reasonable discrimination: Lay representations of prejudice and racism. *British Journal of Social Psychology*, 45, 219–243.

Fina, A. D. (2000). Orientation in immigrant narratives: The role of ethnicity in the identification of characters. *Discourse Studies*, 2, 131–157.

Finlay, W. M. L. & Lyons, E. (2005). Rejecting the label: A social constructionist analysis. *Mental Retardation*, 43, 120–134.

Fiske, S. T. (1998). Stereotyping, prejudice, and discrimination. In D. T. Gilbert, S. T. Fiske, & G. Lindzey (Eds.), *The handbook of social psychology* (4th ed., pp. 357–411). Boston: McGraw-Hill.

Flowerdew, J. (2004). Identity politics and Hong Kong's return to Chinese sovereignty: Analysing the discourse of Hong Kong's first chief executive. *Journal of Pragmatics*, 36, 1551–1578.

Flowerdew, J., Li, D. C. S., & Tran, S. (2002). Discriminatory news discourse. *Discourse & Society*, 13, 319–345.

Foucault, M. (1980). *Power/Knowledge*. Brighton: Harvester.

Foucault, M. (2002). *The archaeology of knowledge*. London: Routledge.

Freed, A. F. (1999). Communities of practice and pregnant women: Is there a connection? *Language in Society*, 28, 257–271.

Frith, H. & Kitzinger, C. (2001). Reformulating sexual script theory: Developing a discursive psychology of sexual negotiation. *Theory & Psychology*, 11, 209–232.

Gafaranga, J. (2001). Linguistic identities in talk-in-interaction: Order in bilingual conversation. *Journal of Pragmatics*, 33, 1901–1925.

Gafaranga, J. & Britten, N. (2004). Formulation in general practice consultations. *Text*, 24, 147–170.

Gandara, L. (2004). "They that sow the wind . . .": Proverbs and sayings in argumentation. *Discourse & Society*, 15, 345–359.

Garcia, A. C. (2000). Negotiating negotiation: The collaborative production of resolution in small claims mediation hearings. *Discourse & Society*, 11, 315–343.

Garfinkel, H. (1967). *Studies in ethnomethodology*. Englewood Cliffs, NJ: Prentice-Hall.

Gavey, N. (2005). *Just sex? The cultural scaffolding of rape*. London: Routledge.

Gavey, N. & Gow, V. (2001). "Cry wolf," cried the wolf: Constructing the issue of false rape allegations in New Zealand media texts. *Feminism & Psychology*, 11, 341–360.

Gavey, N. & McPhillips, K. (1999). Subject to romance: Heterosexual passivity as an obstacle to women initiating condom use. *Psychology of Women Quarterly*, 23, 349–367.

Gavey, N., McPhillips, K., & Doherty, M. (2001). "If it's not on, it's not on" – or is it? Discursive constraints on women's condom use. *Gender & Society*, 15, 917–934.

Georgakopoulou, A. (2001). Arguing about the future: On indirect disagreements in conversations. *Journal of Pragmatics*, 33, 1881–1900.

Georgakopoulou, A. (2002). Narrative and identity management: Discourse and social identities in a tale of tomorrow. *Research on Language and Social Interaction*, 35, 427–451.

Gergen, K. J. (1973). Social psychology as history. *Journal of Personality and Social Psychology*, 26, 309.

Gergen, K. J. (1999). *An invitation to social construction*. London: Sage.

Gibson, S. & Abell, J. (2004). For Queen and Country? National frames of reference in the talk of soldiers in England. *Human Relations*, 57, 871–891.

Gilbert, G. N. & Mulkay, M. J. (1984). *Opening Pandora's box: A sociological analysis of scientists' discourse*. Cambridge: Cambridge University Press.

Giles, D. (2006). Constructing identities in cyberspace: The case of eating disorders. *British Journal of Social Psychology*, 45, 463–477.

Gill, R. (1993). Justifying injustice: Broadcasters' accounts of inequality in radio. In E. Burman & I. Parker (Eds.), *Discourse analytic research: Repertoires and reading of texts in action* (pp. 75–93). London: Routledge.

Glaser, B. G. (1992). *Emergence vs. forcing: Basics of grounded theory analysis*. Mill Valley, CA: Sociology Press.

Glaser, B. G. & Strauss, A. L. (1967). *The discovery of grounded theory: Strategies for qualitative research*. New York: Aldine de Gruyter.

Gnisci, A. & Pontecorvo, C. (2004). The organization of questions and answers in the thematic phases of hostile examination: Turn-by-turn manipulation of meaning. *Journal of Pragmatics*, 36, 965–995.

Goffman, E. (1959). *The presentation of self in everyday life*. New York: Doubleday.

Goffman, E. (1974). *Frame analysis: An essay on the organization of experience*. New York: Harper & Row.

Goffman, E. (1979). Footing. *Semiotica*, 25, 1–29.

Goodwin, M. H. (2002a). Building power asymmetries in girls' interaction. *Discourse & Society*, 13, 715–730.

Goodwin, M. H. (2002b). Exclusion in girls' peer groups: Ethnographic analysis of language practices on the playground. *Human Development*, 45, 392–415.

Gordon, C. (2002). "I'm Mommy and you're Natalie": Role-reversal and embedded frames in mother–child discourse. *Language in Society*, 31, 679–720.

Gordon, C. (2003). Aligning as a team: Forms of conjoined participation in (stepfamily) interaction. *Research on Language and Social Interaction*, 36, 395–431.

Gordon, C. (2006). Reshaping prior text, reshaping identities. *Text & Talk*, 26, 545–571.

Gotsbachner, E. (2001). Xenophobic normality: The discriminatory impact of habitualized discourse dynamics. *Discourse & Society*, 12, 729–759.

Gough, B. & Peace, P. (2000). Reconstructing gender at university: Men as victims. *Gender and Education*, 12, 385–398.

Grant, D. & Hardy, C. (2004). Introduction: Struggles with organizational discourse. *Organization Studies*, 25, 5–13.

Grant, D., Hardy, C., Oswick, C., & Putnam, L. (2004). *Sage handbook of organizational discourse*. London and Thousand Oaks, CA: Sage.

Grant, D. & Iedema, R. A. M. (2006). Discourse analysis and the study of organizations. *Text*, 25, 37–66.

Gray, J. (1992). *Men are from Mars, women are from Venus: How to get what you want in your relationships*. New York: HarperCollins.

Greenwald, A. G. (2004). The resting parrot, the dessert stomach, and other perfectly defensible theories. In J. T. Jost, M. R. Banaji, & D. A. Prentice (Eds.), *Perspectivism in social psychology: The yin and yang of scientific progress* (pp. 275–285). Washington, DC: American Psychological Association.

Grice, H. P. (1975). Logic and conversation. In P. Cole & J. L. Morgan (Eds.), *Syntax and semantics*. Vol. 3: *Speech acts* (pp. 41–58). New York: Academic Press.

Grimshaw, A. D. (Ed.) (1990). *Conflict talk: Sociolinguistic investigations of arguments in conversations*. Cambridge: Cambridge University Press.

Gross, H. & Pattison, H. (2001). Pregnancy and working: A critical reading of advice and information on pregnancy and employment. *Feminism & Psychology*, 11, 511–525.

Gruber, H. (2001). Questions and strategic orientation in verbal conflict sequences. *Journal of Pragmatics*, 33, 1815–1857.

Guendouzi, J. (2004). "She's very slim": Talking about body-size in all-female interactions. *Journal of Pragmatics*, 36, 1635–1653.

Guilfoyle, M. (2001). Problematizing psychotherapy: The discursive production of a bulimic. *Culture & Psychology*, 7, 151–179.

Guise, J., Widdicombe, S., & McKinlay, A. (2007). "What is it like to have ME?": The discursive construction of ME in computer-mediated communication and face to face interaction. *Health*, 11, 87–108.

Gulich, E. (2003). Conversational techniques used in transferring knowledge between medical experts and non-experts. *Discourse Studies*, 5, 235–263.

Gyasi Obeng, S. (2000). Speaking the unspeakable: Discursive strategies to express language attitudes in Legon (Ghana) graffiti. *Research on Language and Social Interaction*, 33, 291–319.

Hacking, I. (1983). *Representing and intervening: Introductory topics in the philosophy of natural science*. Cambridge: Cambridge University Press.

Hak, T. (1998). "There are clear delusions": The production of a factual account. *Human Studies*, 21, 419–436.

Hale, S. (2002). How faithfully do court interpreters render the style of non-English speaking witnesses' testimonies? A data-based study of Spanish–English bilingual proceedings. *Discourse Studies*, 4, 25–47.

Halliday, M. A. K. (1985). *Spoken and written language*. Oxford: Oxford University Press.

Hammersley, M. (2003a). Conversation analysis and discourse analysis: Methods or paradigms? *Discourse & Society*, 14, 751–781.

Hammersley, M. (2003b). Doing the fine thing: A rejoinder to Jonathan Potter. *Discourse & Society*, 14, 795–798.

Hammersley, M. (2003c). The impracticality of scepticism: A further rejoinder to Potter. *Discourse & Society*, 14, 803–804.

Hanak, I. (1998). Chairing meetings: Turn and topic control in development communication in rural Zanzibar. *Discourse & Society*, 9, 33–56.

Haney, L. & March, M. (2003). Married fathers and caring daddies: Welfare reform and the discursive politics of paternity. *Social Problems*, 50, 461–481.

Hansen, A. D. (2005). A practical task: Ethnicity as a resource in social interaction. *Research on Language and Social Interaction*, 38, 63–104.

Hardy, C., Palmer, I., & Phillips, N. (2000). Discourse as a strategic resource. *Human Relations*, 53, 1227–1248.

Harris, S. (2001). Fragmented narratives and multiple tellers: Witness and defendant accounts in trials. *Discourse Studies*, 3, 53–74.

Haslam, S. A. & McGarty, C. (2001). A 100 years of certitude? Social psychology, the experimental method and the management of scientific uncertainty. *British Journal of Social Psychology*, 40, 1–21.

Haworth, K. (2006). The dynamics of power and resistance in police interview discourse. *Discourse & Society*, 17, 739–759.

Heath, C. & Hindmarsh, J. (2000). Configuring action in objects: From mutual space to media space. *Mind, Culture & Activity*, 7, 81–104.

Heatherton, T. F., Macrae, C. N., & Kelley, W. M. (2004). What the social brain sciences can tell us about the self. *Current Directions in Psychological Science*, 13, 190–193.

Henriques, J., Hollway, W., Urwin, C., Venn, C., & Walkerdine, V. (1984). *Changing the subject: Psychology, social regulation and subjectivity*. London: Methuen.

Henwood, K. & Procter, J. (2003). The "good father": Reading men's accounts of paternal involvement during the transition to first-time fatherhood. *British Journal of Social Psychology*, 42, 337–355.

Hepburn, A. (2000). Power lines: Derrida, discursive psychology and the management of accusations of teacher bullying. *British Journal of Social Psychology*, 39, 605–628.

Hepburn, A. (2005). "You're not takin' me seriously": Ethics and asymmetry in calls to a child protection helpline. *Journal of Constructivist Psychology*, 18, 253–274.

Hepburn, A. & Brown, S. D. (2001). Teacher stress and the management of accountability. *Human Relations*, 54, 691–715.

Hepworth, J. (1999). *The social construction of anorexia nervosa*. London: Sage.

Hepworth, J. & Griffin, C. (1990). The discovery of anorexia nervosa: Discourses of the late 19th century. *Text*, 10, 321–338.

Hepworth, J. & Griffin, C. (1995). Conflicting opinions? "Anorexia nervosa," medicine, and feminism. In S. Wilkinson & C. Kitzinger (Eds.), *Feminism and discourse* (pp. 68–85). London: Sage.

Heritage, J. (1984). *Garfinkel and ethnomethodology*. Cambridge: Polity Press.

Hester, S. (1998). Describing "deviance" in school: Recognizably educational psychological problems. In C. Antaki & S. Widdicombe (Eds.), *Identities in talk* (pp. 133–150). London: Sage.

Hester, S. & Eglin, P. (1997). *Culture in action: Studies in membership categorization analysis*. Lanham, MD: University Press of America.

Hester, S. & Francis, D. (2000). Ethnomethodology, conversation analysis and "institutional talk." *Text*, 20, 391–413.

Hester, S. & Francis, D. (2001a). Is institutional talk a phenomenon? Reflections on ethnomethodology and applied conversation analysis. In A. McHoul & M. Rapley (Eds.), *How to analyse talk in institutional settings* (pp. 206–217). London: Continuum.

Hester, S. & Francis, D. (2001b). Institutional talk institutionalised? *Text*, 20, 319–413.

Hewitt, J. P. & Stokes, R. (1975). Disclaimers. *American Sociological Review*, 40, 1–11.

Higgins, M. (2004). Putting the nation in the news: The role of location formulation in a selection of Scottish newspapers. *Discourse & Society*, 15, 633–648.

Hindmarsh, J. & Heath, C. (2000). Embodied reference: A study of deixis in workplace interaction. *Journal of Pragmatics*, 32, 1855–1878.

Hindmarsh, J. & Pilnick, A. (2002). The tacit order of teamwork: Collaboration and embodied conduct in anesthesia. *Sociological Quarterly*, 43, 139–164.

Ho Shon, P. C. (2005). "I'd grab the S-O-B by his hair and yank him out the window": The fraternal order of warnings and threats in police–citizen encounters. *Discourse & Society*, 16, 829–845.

Hobbs, P. (2003a). "Is that what we're here about?": A lawyer's use of impression management in a closing argument at trial. *Discourse & Society*, 14, 273–290.

Hobbs, P. (2003b). The use of evidentiality in physicians' progress notes. *Discourse Studies*, 5, 451–478.

Hobbs, P. (2004). The role of progress notes in the professional socialization of medical residents. *Journal of Pragmatics*, 36, 1579–1607.

Hodges, I. (2002). Moving beyond words: Therapeutic discourse and ethical problematization. *Discourse Studies*, 4, 455–479.

Hodgetts, D. & Chamberlain, K. (2002). "The problem with men": Working-class men making sense of men's health on television. *Journal of Health Psychology, 7,* 269–283.

Holland, S. (2004). *Alternative femininities: Body, age and identity.* Oxford: Berg.

Hollander, J. A. (2002). Resisting vulnerability: The social reconstruction of gender in interaction. *Social Problems, 49,* 474–496.

Hollway, W. (1984). Fitting work: Psychological assessment in organizations. In J. Henriques, W. Hollway, C. Urwin, C. Venn, & V. Walkerdine (Eds.), *Changing the subject: Psychology, social regulation and subjectivity* (pp. 26–59). London: Methuen.

Holmes, J. (2000). Politeness, power and provocation: How humour functions in the workplace. *Discourse Studies, 2,* 159–185.

Holmes, J. (2003). Small talk at work: Potential problems for workers with an intellectual disability. *Research on Language and Social Interaction, 36,* 65–84.

Holmes, J. (2005a). Leadership talk: How do leaders "do mentoring," and is gender relevant? *Journal of Pragmatics, 37,* 1779–1800.

Holmes, J. (2005b). Story-telling at work: A complex discursive resource for integrating personal, professional and social identities. *Discourse Studies, 7,* 671–700.

Holmes, J. (2006). Sharing a laugh: Pragmatic aspects of humor and gender in the workplace. *Journal of Pragmatics, 38,* 26–50.

Holmes, J. & Marra, M. (2002a). Having a laugh at work: How humour contributes to workplace culture. *Journal of Pragmatics, 34,* 1683–1710.

Holmes, J. & Marra, M. (2002b). Over the edge? Subversive humor between colleagues and friends. *Humor, 15,* 65–87.

Holmes, J. & Marra, M. (2004). Relational practice in the workplace: Women's talk or gendered discourse? *Language in Society, 33,* 377–398.

Holmes, J. & Schnurr, S. (2005). Politeness, gender and humour in the workplace: Negotiating norms and identifying contestation. *Journal of Politeness Research, 1,* 121–149.

Holt, M. & Griffin, C. (2005). Students versus locals: Young adults' constructions of the working-class other. *British Journal of Social Psychology, 44,* 241–267.

Hopkins, N. & Kahani-Hopkins, V. (2004a). Identity construction and British Muslims' political activity: Beyond rational actor theory. *British Journal of Social Psychology, 43,* 339–356.

Hopkins, N. & Kahani-Hopkins, V. (2004b). The antecedents of identification: A rhetorical analysis of British Muslim activists' constructions of community and identity. *British Journal of Social Psychology, 43,* 41–57.

Hopkins, N., Reicher, S. D., & Kahani-Hopkins, V. (2003). Citizenship, participation and identity construction: Political mobilization amongst British Muslims. *Psychologica Belgica, 43,* 33–54.

Hopkins, N., Zeedyk, S., & Raitt, F. (2005). Visualising abortion: Emotion discourse and fetal imagery in a contemporary abortion debate. *Social Science & Medicine, 61,* 393–403.

Horton-Salway, M. (2001a). Narrative identities and the management of personal accountability in talk about ME: A discursive psychology approach to illness narrative. *Journal of Health Psychology, 6,* 247–259.

Horton-Salway, M. (2001b). The construction of ME: The discursive action model. In M. Wetherell, S. Taylor, & S. J. Yates (Eds.), *Discourse as data: A guide for analysis* (pp. 147–188). London: Sage.

Horton-Salway, M. (2002). Bio-psycho-social reasoning in GPs' case narratives: The discursive construction of ME patients' identities. *Health, 6,* 401–421.

Horton-Salway, M. (2004). The local production of knowledge: Disease labels, identities and category entitlements in ME support group talk. *Health, 8,* 351–371.

House, J. S. (1977). The three facets of social psychology. *Sociometry, 40,* 161–177.

Housley, W. & Fitzgerald, R. (2002). The reconsidered model of membership categorization analysis. *Qualitative Research, 2,* 59–83.

Howard, C. & Tuffin, K. (2002). Repression in retrospect: Constructing history in the "memory debate." *History of the Human Sciences, 15,* 75–93.

Howard, C., Tuffin, K., & Stephens, C. (2000). Unspeakable emotion: A discursive analysis of police talk about reactions to trauma. *Journal of Language and Social Psychology, 19,* 295–314.

Huls, E. (2000). Power in Turkish migrant families. *Discourse & Society, 11,* 345–372.

Hutchby, I. (1996a). *Confrontation talk: Arguments, asymmetries and power in talk radio.* Mahwah, NJ: Lawrence Erlbaum.

Hutchby, I. (1996b). Power in discourse: The case of arguments on a British talk radio show. *Discourse & Society, 7,* 481–497.

Hutchby, I. (1999). Beyond agnosticism? Conversation analysis and the sociological agenda. *Research on Language and Social Interaction, 23,* 85–93.

Hutchby, I. (2005). "Active listening": Formulations and the elicitation of feelings-talk in child counselling. *Research on Language and Social Interaction, 38,* 303–329.

Hutchby, I. (2006). *Media talk: Conversation analysis and the study of broadcasting.* Maidenhead: Open University Press.

Hutchby, I. & Wooffitt, R. (1998). *Conversation analysis: Principles, practices and applications*. Oxford: Polity Press.

Iedema, R. A. M. (1999). Formalizing organizational meaning. *Discourse & Society*, 10, 49–66.

Iedema, R. A. M. & Wodak, R. (1999). Introduction: Organizational discourses and practices. *Discourse & Society*, 10, 5–20.

Iedema, R., Degeling, P., Braithwaite, J., & White, L. (2004). "It's an interesting conversation I'm hearing": The doctor as manager. *Organization Studies*, 25, 15–33.

Imbens-Bailey, A. & McCabe, A. (2000). The discourse of distress: A narrative analysis of emergency calls to 911. *Language & Communication*, 20, 275–296.

Itakura, H. (2001). Describing conversational dominance. *Journal of Pragmatics*, 33, 1859–1880.

Jackson, S. M. (2005). "I'm 15 and desperate for sex": "Doing" and "undoing" desire in letters to a teenage magazine. *Feminism & Psychology*, 15, 295–313.

Jackson, S. M. & Cram, F. (2003). Disrupting the sexual double standard: Young women's talk about heterosexuality. *British Journal of Social Psychology*, 42, 113–127.

Janney, R. W. (2002). Cotext as context: Vague answers in court. *Language & Communication*, 22, 457–475.

Jaworski, A. & Coupland, J. (2005). Othering in gossip: "You go out you have a laugh and you can pull yeah okay but like. . . ." *Language in Society*, 34, 667–694.

Jefferson, G. (1984). On stepwise transition from talk about a trouble to inappropriately next-positioned matters. In J. M. Atkinson & J. Heritage (Eds.), *Structures of social action* (pp. 191–222). Cambridge: Cambridge University Press.

Jefferson, G. (2004a). A note on laughter in "male–female" interaction. *Discourse Studies*, 6, 117–133.

Jefferson, G. (2004b). Glossary of transcript symbols with an introduction. In G. H. Lerner (Ed.), *Conversation analysis: Studies from the first generation* (pp. 13–31). Amsterdam: John Benjamins.

Jingree, T., Finlay, W. M. L., & Antaki, C. (2006). Empowering words, disempowering actions: An analysis of interactions between staff members and people with learning disabilities in residents' meetings. *Journal of Intellectual Disability Research*, 50, 212–226.

Johnson, A. (2006). Police questioning. In K. Brown (Ed.), *The encyclopaedia of language and linguistics* (2nd ed., pp. 661–672). Oxford: Elsevier.

Jones, R. & Thornborrow, J. (2004). Floors, talk and the organization of classroom activities. *Language in Society*, 33, 399–423.

Jost, J. T. & Kruglanski, A. W. (2002). The estrangement of social constructionism and experimental social psychology: History of the rift and prospects for reconciliation. *Personality and Social Psychology Review*, 6, 168–187.

Joyce, K. (2005). Appealing images: Magnetic resonance imaging and the production of authoritative knowledge. *Social Studies of Science*, 35, 437–462.

Jucker, A. H., Smith, S. W., & Ludge, T. (2003). Interactive aspects of vagueness in conversation. *Journal of Pragmatics*, 35, 1737–1769.

Kacen, L. & Bakshy, I. (2005). Institutional narratives in the discourse between oncology social workers and cancer patients' self-help organization. *Qualitative Health Research*, 15, 861–880.

Kahani-Hopkins, V. & Hopkins, N. (2002). "Representing" British Muslims: The strategic dimension to identity construction. *Ethnic and Racial Studies*, 25, 288–309.

Kangasharju, H. (2002). Alignment in disagreement: Forming oppositional alliances in committee meetings. *Journal of Pragmatics*, 34, 1447–1471.

Katz, J. R. (2004). Building peer relationships in talk: Toddlers' peer conversations in childcare. *Discourse Studies*, 6, 329–346.

Kendall, S. (2006). "Honey, I'm home"! Framing in family dinnertime homecomings. *Text & Talk*, 26, 411–441.

Kettrey, H. H. & Emery, B. C. (2006). The discourse of sibling violence. *Journal of Family Violence*, 21, 416.

Kiesling, S. F. (2005). Homosocial desire in men's talk: Balancing and re-creating cultural discourses of masculinity. *Language in Society*, 34, 695–726.

Kinnell, A. M. (2002). Soliciting client questions in HIV prevention and test counselling. *Research on Language and Social Interaction*, 35, 367–393.

Kirkwood, S., Liu, J. H., & Weatherall, A. (2005). Challenging the standard story of indigenous rights in Aotearoa/New Zealand. *Journal of Community & Applied Social Psychology*, 15, 493–505.

Kitzinger, C. (2000). Doing feminist conversation analysis. *Feminism & Psychology*, 10, 163–193.

Kitzinger, C. (2005a). "Speaking as a heterosexual": (How) does sexuality matter for talk-in-interaction? *Research on Language and Social Interaction*, 38, 221–265.

Kitzinger, C. (2005b). Heteronormativity in action: Reproducing the heterosexual nuclear family in after-hours medical calls. *Social Problems*, 52, 477–498.

Kitzinger, C. (2006). After post-cognitivism. *Discourse Studies*, 8, 67–83.

Kitzinger, C. & Frith, H. (1999). Just say no? The use of conversation analysis in developing a feminist perspective on sexual refusal. *Discourse & Society*, 10, 293–316.

Kleifgen, J. A. (2001). Assembling talk: Social alignments in the workplace. *Research on Language and Social Interaction*, 34, 279–308.

Kleifgen, J. A. & Frenz-Belkin, P. (1997). Assembling knowledge. *Research on Language and Social Interaction, 30*, 157–192.

Kleiner, B. (1998). The modern racist ideology and its reproduction in "pseudo-argument." *Discourse & Society, 9*, 187–215.

Koester, A. J. (2004). Relational sequences in workplace genres. *Journal of Pragmatics, 36*, 1405–1428.

Koller, V. (2005). Critical discourse analysis and social cognition: Evidence from business media discourse. *Discourse & Society, 16*, 199–224.

Komter, M. (2003). The interactional dynamics of eliciting a confession in a Dutch police interrogation. *Research on Language and Social Interaction, 36*, 433–470.

Kong, K. C. C. (2001). Marketing of belief: Intertextual construction of network marketers' identities. *Discourse & Society, 12*, 473–503.

Kong, K. C. C. (2003). "Are you my friend?": Negotiating friendship in conversations between network marketers and their prospects. *Language in Society, 32*, 487–522.

Kremer-Sadlik, T. (2004). How children with autism and Asperger syndrome respond to questions: A "naturalistic" theory of mind task. *Discourse Studies, 6*, 185–206.

Kripke, S. (1982). *Wittgenstein on rules and private language.* Oxford: Blackwell.

Kuhn, T. S. (1962). *The structure of scientific revolutions.* Chicago: University of Chicago Press.

Labov, W. (1972). *Language and the inner city: Studies in the Black English vernacular.* Oxford: Blackwell.

Laforest, M. (2002). Scenes of family life: Complaining in everyday conversation. *Journal of Pragmatics, 34*, 1595–1620.

Lafrance, M. N. (2007). A bitter pill: A discursive analysis of women's medicalized accounts of depression. *Journal of Health Psychology, 12*, 127–140.

Lafrance, M. N. & Stoppard, J. M. (2006). Constructing a non-depressed self: Women's accounts of recovery from depression. *Feminism & Psychology, 16*, 307–325.

Land, V. & Kitzinger, C. (2005). Speaking as a lesbian: Correcting the heterosexist presumption. *Research on Language and Social Interaction, 38*, 371–416.

Lauerbach, G. (2006). Discourse representation in political interviews: The construction of identities and relations through voicing and ventriloquizing. *Journal of Pragmatics, 38*, 196–215.

Lavis, V., Horrocks, C., Kelly, N., & Barker, V. (2005). Domestic violence and health care: Opening Pandora's box – Challenges and dilemmas. *Feminism & Psychology, 15*, 441–460.

Lawes, R. (1999). Marriage: An analysis of discourse. *British Journal of Social Psychology, 38*, 1–20.

Lazar, M. (2000). Gender, discourse and semiotics: The politics of parenthood representations. *Discourse & Society, 11*, 373–400.

Lea, S. J. (1996). "That ism on the end makes it nasty": Talking about race with young white South Africans. *South African Journal of Psychology-Suid-Afrikaanse Tydskrif Vir Sielkunde, 26*, 183–190.

Lea, S. J. & Auburn, T. (2001). The social construction of rape in the talk of a convicted rapist. *Feminism & Psychology, 11*, 11–33.

LeCouteur, A., Rapley, M., & Augoustinos, M. (2001). "This very difficult debate about Wik": Stake, voice and the management of category memberships in race politics. *British Journal of Social Psychology, 40*, 35–57.

Lee, S. H. (2005). The scales of justice: Balancing neutrality and efficiency in plea-bargaining encounters. *Discourse & Society, 16*, 33–54.

Leeds-Hurwitz, W. (2006). Making marriage visible: Wedding anniversaries as the public component of private relationships. *Text, 25*, 595–631.

Lehtinen, E. (2005). Achieved similarity: Describing experience in seventh-day Adventist Bible study. *Text, 25*, 341–371.

Lemke, J. L. (1999). Discourse and organizational dynamics: Website communication and institutional change. *Discourse & Society, 10*, 21–48.

Leon, J. (2004). Preference and "bias" in the format of French news interviews: The semantic analysis of question–answer pairs in conversation. *Journal of Pragmatics, 36*, 1885–1920.

Leudar, I., Marsland, V., & Nekvapil, J. (2004). On membership categorization: "Us," "them" and "doing violence" in political discourse. *Discourse & Society, 15*, 243–266.

Leudar, I. & Nekvapil, J. (2000). Presentations of Romanies in the Czech media: On category work in television debates. *Discourse & Society, 11*, 487–513.

Li, S. & Arber, A. (2006). The construction of troubled and credible patients: A study of emotion talk in palliative care settings. *Qualitative Health Research, 16*, 27–46.

Linell, P., Adelsward, V., Sachs, L., Bredmar, M., & Lindstedt, U. (2002). Expert talk in medical contexts: Explicit and implicit orientation to risks. *Research on Language and Social Interaction, 35*, 195–218.

Lipari, L. (2000). Toward a discourse approach to polling. *Discourse Studies, 2*, 187–215.

Locke, A. (2004). Accounting for success and failure: A discursive psychological approach to sport talk. *Quest, 56*, 302–320.

Locke, A. & Edwards, D. (2003). Bill and Monica: Memory, emotion and normativity in Clinton's Grand Jury testimony. *British Journal of Social Psychology, 42*, 239–256.

Longfellow, H. W. (2004). The theologian's tale: Elizabeth. In *Tales of a wayside inn* (pp. 211–225). Whitefish, MT: Kessinger.

Lu, X. (1999). An ideological/cultural analysis of political slogans in Communist China. *Discourse & Society, 10*, 487–508.

Lynch, M. & Bogen, D. (2005). "My memory has been shredded": A non-cognitivist investigation of "mental" phenomena. In H. te Molder & J. Potter (Eds.), *Conversation and cognition* (pp. 226–240). Cambridge: Cambridge University Press.

Lynn, N. & Lea, S. (2003). "A phantom menace and the new apartheid": The social construction of asylum-seekers in the United Kingdom. *Discourse & Society, 14*, 425–452.

Lynn, N. & Lea, S. J. (2005). "Racist" graffiti: Text, context and social comment. *Visual Communication, 4*, 39–63.

MacBeth, D. (2004). The relevance of repair for classroom correction. *Language in Society, 33*, 703–736.

MacDonald, M. N. (2002). Pedagogy, pathology and ideology: The production, transmission and reproduction of medical discourse. *Discourse & Society, 13*, 447–467.

MacMartin, C. (2002). (Un)reasonable doubt? The invocation of children's consent in sexual abuse trial judgments. *Discourse & Society, 13*, 9–40.

MacMartin, C. & LeBaron, C. D. (2006). Multiple involvements within group interaction: A video-based study of sex offender therapy. *Research on Language and Social Interaction, 39*, 41–80.

MacMartin, C. & Wood, L. A. (2005). Sexual motives and sentencing: Judicial discourse in cases of child sexual abuse. *Journal of Language and Social Psychology, 24*, 139–159.

MacMillan, K. & Edwards, D. (1999). Who killed the Princess? Description and blame in the British press. *Discourse Studies, 1*, 151–174.

Macrae, C. N., Milne, A. B., & Bodenhausen, G. V. (1994). Stereotypes as energy saving devices: A peek inside the cognitive toolbox. *Journal of Personality and Social Psychology, 66*, 37–47.

Madill, A., Widdicombe, S., & Barkham, M. (2001). The potential of conversation analysis for psychotherapy research. *Counseling Psychologist, 29*, 413–434.

Mäkitalo, Å. (2003). Accounting practices as situated knowing: Dilemmas and dynamics in institutional categorization. *Discourse Studies, 5*, 495–516.

Mallinson, C. & Brewster, Z. W. (2005). "Blacks and bubbas": Stereotypes, ideology, and categorization processes in restaurant servers' discourse. *Discourse & Society, 16*, 787–807.

Mandela, N. (1994). *Long walk to freedom: The autobiography of Nelson Mandela*. London: Little, Brown.

Márquez Reiter, R. (2006). Interactional closeness in service calls to a Montevidean carer service company. *Research on Language and Social Interaction, 39*, 7–39.

Marra, M. & Holmes, J. (2004). Workplace narratives and business reports: Issues of definition. *Text, 24*, 59–78.

Mason, M. (2004). Referential choices and the need for repairs in covertly-taped conversations. *Journal of Pragmatics, 36*, 1139–1156.

Matoesian, G. M. (1993). *Reproducing rape: Domination through talk in the courtroom*. Chicago: University of Chicago Press.

Matoesian, G. M. (1999). The grammaticalization of participant roles in the constitution of expert identity. *Language in Society, 28*, 491–521.

Matoesian, G. M. (2001). *Law and the language of identity: Discourse in the William Kennedy Smith rape trial*. Oxford: Oxford University Press.

Matoesian, G. M. (2005). Nailing down an answer: Participations of power in trial talk. *Discourse Studies, 7*, 733–759.

Matoesian, G. M. & Coldren, J. R. (2002). Language and bodily conduct in focus group evaluations of legal policy. *Discourse & Society, 13*, 469–493.

Maurer, K. L., Park, B., & Rothbart, M. (1995). Subtyping versus subgrouping processes in stereotype representation. *Journal of Personality and Social Psychology, 69*, 812–824.

Maynard, D. W. (2004). On predicating a diagnosis as an attribute of a person. *Discourse Studies, 6*, 53–76.

Mayr, A. (2003). *Prison discourse: Language as a means of control and resistance*. Basingstoke: Macmillan.

McCabe, R., Leudar, I., & Antaki, C. (2004). Do people with schizophrenia display theory of mind deficits in clinical interactions? *Psychological Medicine, 34*, 401–412.

McCabe, S. & Stokoe, E. H. (2004). Place and identity in tourists' accounts. *Annals of Tourism Research, 31*, 601–622.

McCann-Mortimer, P., Augoustinos, M., & LeCouteur, A. (2004). "Race" and the Human Genome Project: Constructions of scientific legitimacy. *Discourse & Society, 15*, 409–432.

McClelland, L., Reicher, S. D., & Booth, N. (2000). A last defense: The negotiation of blame within suicide notes. *Journal of Community & Applied Social Psychology, 10*, 225–240.

McHoul, A. & Rapley, M. (2001). Culture, psychology and "being human." *Culture & Psychology, 7*, 433–451.

McHoul, A. & Rapley, M. (2002). "Should we make a start then?": A strange case of (delayed) client-initiated psychological assessment. *Research on Language and Social Interaction, 35*, 73–91.

McHoul, A. & Rapley, M. (2003). What can psychological terms actually do? (Or: if Sigmund calls, tell him it didn't work). *Journal of Pragmatics, 35*, 507–522.

McHoul, A. & Rapley, M. (2005a). A case of attention-deficit/hyperactivity disorder diagnosis: Sir Karl and Francis B. slug it out on the consulting room floor. *Discourse & Society, 16*, 419–449.

McHoul, A. & Rapley, M. (2005b). Re-presenting culture and the self: (Dis)agreeing in theory and in practice. *Theory & Psychology, 15*, 431–447.

McIlvenny, P. (2002). Researching talk, gender and sexuality. In P. McIlvenny (Ed.), *Talking gender and sexuality* (pp. 1–48). Amsterdam and Philadelphia: John Benjamins.

McKendy, J. P. (2006). "I'm very careful about that": Narrative and agency of men in prison. *Discourse & Society, 17*, 473–502.

McKenzie, K. (2001). Fact and the narratives of war: Produced undecidability in accounts of armed conflict. *Human Studies, 24*, 187–209.

McKinlay, A. & Dunnett, A. (1998). How gun-owners accomplish being deadly average. In C. Antaki & S. Widdicombe (Eds.), *Identities in talk* (pp. 34–51). London: Sage.

McKinlay, A. & McVittie, C. (2006). Using topic control to avoid the gainsaying of troublesome evaluations. *Discourse Studies, 8*, 797–815.

McKinlay, A. & McVittie, C. (2007). Locals, incomers and intra-national migration: Place-identities and a Scottish island. *British Journal of Social Psychology, 46*, 171–190.

McKinlay, A. & Potter, J. (1987). Social representations: A conceptual critique. *Journal for the Theory of Social Behavior, 17*, 478.

McKinlay, A., Potter, J., & Wetherell, M. (1993). Discourse analysis and social representations. In G. Breakwell & D. Canter (Eds.), *Empirical approaches to social representations* (pp. 134–156). Oxford: Oxford University Press.

McQueen, C. & Henwood, K. (2002). Young men in "crisis": Attending to the language of teenage boys' distress. *Social Science & Medicine, 55*, 1493–1509.

McVittie, C., Cavers, D., & Hepworth, J. (2005). Femininity, mental weakness, and difference: Male students account for anorexia nervosa in men. *Sex Roles, 53*, 413–418.

McVittie, C., McKinlay, A., & Widdicombe, S. (2003). Committed to (un)equal opportunities? "New ageism" and the older worker. *British Journal of Social Psychology, 42*, 595–612.

McVittie, C., McKinlay, A., & Widdicombe, S. (2008). Passive and active non-employment: Age, employment and the identities of older non-working people. *Journal of Aging Studies* (in press).

McVittie, C. & Tiliopoulos, N. (2007). When 2–3% really matters: The (un)importance of religion in psychotherapy. *Mental Health, Religion & Culture, 10*(5), 515–526.

McVittie, C. & Willock, J. (2006). "You can't fight windmills": How older men do health, ill health, and masculinities. *Qualitative Health Research, 16*, 788–801.

Menz, F. (1999). "Who am I gonna do this with?": Self-organization, ambiguity and decision-making in a business enterprise. *Discourse & Society, 10*, 101–128.

Meyer, M. (2001). Between theory, method and politics: Positioning of the approaches to CDA. In R. Wodak & M. Meyer (Eds.), *Methods of critical discourse analysis* (pp. 14–31). London: Sage.

Microsoft Corporation (2007). Corporate governance: Message from our chairman [Online]. Available: www.microsoft.com/about/companyinformation/corporategovernance/default.mspx.

Miller, J. M. (2000). Language use, identity, and social interaction: Migrant students in Australia. *Research on Language and Social Interaction, 33*, 69–100.

Millett, K. (1970). *Sexual politics*. New York: Ballantine Books.

Mirivel, J. C. & Tracy, K. (2005). Premeeting talk: An organizationally crucial form of talk. *Research on Language and Social Interaction, 38*, 1–34.

Mitchell, R. W. (2001). Americans' talk to dogs: Similarities and differences with talk to infants. *Research on Language and Social Interaction, 34*, 183–210.

Mizushima, L. & Stapleton, P. (2006). Analyzing the function of meta-oriented critical comments in Japanese comic conversations. *Journal of Pragmatics, 38*, 2105–2123.

Moir, J. (1993). Occupational career choice: Accounts and contradictions. In E. Burman & I. Parker (Eds.), *Discourse analytic research: Repertoires and readings of texts in action* (pp. 17–34). London: Routledge.

Morales-Lopez, E., Prego-Vazquez, G., & Dominguez-Seco, L. (2005). Interviews between employees and customers during a company restructuring process. *Discourse & Society, 16*, 225–268.

Morgan, M., Stephens, C., Tuffin, K., Praat, A. C., & Lyons, A. C. (1997). Lawful possession: A constructionist approach to jealousy stories. *New Ideas in Psychology, 15*, 71–81.

Mori, J. (1999). Well I may be exaggerating but . . . : Self-qualifying clauses in negotiation of opinions among Japanese speakers. *Human Studies, 22*, 447–473.

Moscovici, S. (1984). The phenomenon of social representations. In R. Farr & S. Moscovici (Eds.), *Social representations* (pp. 3–69). Cambridge: Cambridge University Press.

Moscovici, S. (2000). *Social representations*. Cambridge: Polity.

Moser, C. O. N. (2004). Urban violence and insecurity: An introductory roadmap. *Environment & Urbanization, 16*, 3–16.

Muchnik, M. (2005). Discourse strategies of maxzirim bitshuva: The case of a repentance preacher in Israel. *Text, 25*, 373–398.

Muhlhausler, P. & Peace, A. (2001). Discourses of ecotourism: The case of Fraser Island, Queensland. *Language & Communication, 21*, 359–380.

Myers, G. (1998). Displaying opinions: Topics and disagreement in focus groups. *Language in Society, 27*, 85–111.

Naples, N. A. (2003). *Feminism and method: Ethnography, discourse analysis, and activist research.* London: Routledge.

Neuman, Y. & Levi, M. (2003). Blood and chocolate: A rhetorical approach to fear appeal. *Journal of Language and Social Psychology, 22*, 29–46.

Newman, C., Persson, A., & Ellard, J. (2006). "We just don't know": Ambivalence about treatment strategies in the Australian community-based HIV media. *Health, 10*, 191–210.

Nobbs, D. W. & Gwenlan, G. D. (1976). "Reggie visits Doc Morrissey." *The Fall and Rise of Reginald Perrin.* London, British Broadcasting Corporation.

Norrick, N. R. (2004). Humor, tellability, and conarration in conversational storytelling. *Text, 24*, 79–111.

North, O. L. & Schorr, D. (1987). *Taking the stand: The testimony of Lieutenant Colonel Oliver L. North.* New York: Pocket Books.

O'Byrne, R., Rapley, M., & Hansen, S. (2006). "You couldn't say 'No,' could you?": Young men's understandings of sexual refusal. *Feminism & Psychology, 16*, 133–154.

O'Connor, P. E. (2000). *Speaking of crime: Narratives of prisoners.* Lincoln: University of Nebraska Press.

O'Halloran, S. (2005). Symmetry in interaction in meetings of Alcoholics Anonymous: The management of conflict. *Discourse & Society, 16*, 535–560.

Ohara, Y. & Saft, S. (2003). Using conversation analysis to track gender ideologies in social interaction: Toward a feminist analysis of a Japanese phone-in consultation TV program. *Discourse & Society, 14*, 153–172.

Oktar, L. (2001). The ideological organization of representational processes in the presentation of us and them. *Discourse & Society, 12*, 313–346.

O'Reilly, M. (2006). Should children be seen and not heard? An examination of how children's interruptions are treated in family therapy. *Discourse Studies, 8*, 549–566.

Orulv, L. & Hyden, L. C. (2006). Confabulation: Sense-making, self-making and world-making in dementia. *Discourse Studies, 8*, 647–673.

Ostermann, A. C. & Keller-Cohen, D. (1998). "Good girls go to heaven; bad girls . . ." learn to be good: Quizzes in American and Brazilian teenage girls' magazines. *Discourse & Society, 9*, 531–558.

Osvaldsson, K. (2004). I don't have no damn cultures: Doing normality in a deviant setting. *Qualitative Research in Psychology, 1*, 239–264.

Oswick, C., Keenoy, T. W., & Grant, D. (2000). Discourse, organizations and organizing: Concepts, objects and subjects. *Human Relations, 53*, 1115–1123.

Pancer, S. M. (1997). Social psychology: The crisis continues. In D. Fox & I. Prilleltensky (Eds.), *Critical psychology: An introduction* (pp. 150–165). London and Thousand Oaks: Sage.

Paoletti, I. (2001). Membership categories and time appraisal in interviews with family caregivers of disabled elderly. *Human Studies, 24*, 293–325.

Paoletti, I. (2002). Caring for older people: A gendered practice. *Discourse & Society, 13*, 805–817.

Pardo, M. L. (2001). Linguistic persuasion as an essential political factor in current democracies: Critical analysis of the globalization discourse in Argentina at the turn and at the end of the century. *Discourse & Society, 12*, 91–118.

Parker, I. (1992). *Discourse dynamics: Critical analysis for social and individual psychology.* London: Routledge.

Parker, I. (1998). *Social constructionism, discourse and realism.* London: Sage.

Parker, I. (2005). *Qualitative psychology: Introducing radical research.* Maidenhead: Open University Press.

Paugh, A. L. (2005). Learning about work at dinnertime: Language socialization in dual-earner American families. *Discourse & Society, 16*, 55–78.

Peace, P. (2003). Balancing power: The discursive maintenance of gender inequality by wo/men at university. *Feminism & Psychology, 13*, 159–180.

Pepitone, A. (1981). Lessons from the history of social psychology. *American Psychologist, 36*, 827–836.

Pepitone, A. (1999). Historical sketches and critical commentary about social psychology in the golden age. In A. Rodrigues & R. Levine (Eds.), *Reflections on 100 years of experimental social psychology* (pp. 170–199). New York: Basic Books.

Perakyla, A. (2002). Agency and authority: Extended responses to diagnostic statements in primary care encounters. *Research on Language and Social Interaction, 35*, 219–247.

Perakyla, A. (2004). Making links in psychoanalytic interpretations: A conversation analytical perspective. *Psychotherapy Research, 14*, 289–307.

Perakyla, A. & Vehviläinen, S. (2003). Conversation analysis and the professional stocks of interactional knowledge. *Discourse & Society, 14*, 727–750.

Petraki, E. (2005). Disagreement and opposition in multigenerational interviews with Greek-Australian mothers and daughters. *Text, 25*, 269–303.

Phillips, D. A. (2007). Punking and bullying. *Journal of Interpersonal Violence, 22*, 158–178.

Pichler, P. (2006). Multifunctional teasing as a resource for identity construction in the talk of British Bangladeshi girls. *Journal of Sociolinguistics, 10*, 225–249.

Pilnick, A. (2001). The interactional organization of pharmacist consultations in a hospital setting: A putative structure. *Journal of Pragmatics, 33*, 1927–1945.

Pilnick, A. (2004). "It's just one of the best tests that we've got at the moment": The presentation of nuchal translucency screening for fetal abnormality in pregnancy. *Discourse & Society, 15*, 451–465.

Pinto, D. (2004). Indoctrinating the youth of post-war Spain: A discourse analysis of a fascist civics textbook. *Discourse & Society, 15*, 649–667.

Pleck, J. H. (1993). Are "family-supportive" employment policies relevant to men? In J. C. Hood (Ed.), *Men, work and family* (pp. 217–237). London and Newbury Park, CA: Sage.

Pomerantz, A. (1984). Agreeing and disagreeing with assessment: Some features of preferred/dispreferred turn shapes. In J. M. Atkinson & J. Heritage (Eds.), *Structures of social action: Studies in conversation analysis* (pp. 57–101). Cambridge: Cambridge University Press.

Pomerantz, A. (1986). Extreme case formulations: A way of legitimizing claims. *Human Studies, 9*, 219–229.

Pomerantz, A. & Rintel, E. S. (2004). Practices for reporting and responding to test results during medical consultations: Enacting the roles of paternalism and independent expertise. *Discourse Studies, 6*, 9–26.

Popper, K. R. (1959). *The logic of scientific discovery*. New York: Harper Torchbacks.

Potter, J. (1996a). Attitudes, social representations, and discursive psychology. In M. Wetherell (Ed.), *Identities, groups and social issues* (pp. 119–173). London and Thousand Oaks, CA: Sage.

Potter, J. (1996b). *Representing reality: Discourse, rhetoric and social construction*. London: Sage.

Potter, J. (1997). Discourse analysis as a way of analysing naturally occurring talk. In D. Silverman (Ed.), *Handbook for qualitative research methods for psychology and the social sciences* (pp. 144–160). London: Sage.

Potter, J. (2000). Post-cognitive psychology. *Theory & Psychology, 10*, 31–37.

Potter, J. (2003a). Discursive psychology: Between method and paradigm. *Discourse & Society, 14*, 783–794.

Potter, J. (2003b). Practical scepticism. *Discourse & Society*, 799.

Potter, J. (2006). Cognition and conversation. *Discourse Studies, 8*, 131–140.

Potter, J. & Edwards, D. (1999). Social representations and discursive psychology: From cognition to action. *Culture & Psychology, 5*, 447–458.

Potter, J. & Edwards, D. (2003). Rethinking cognition: On Coulter on discourse and mind. *Human Studies, 26*, 165–181.

Potter, J. & te Molder, H. F. M. (2005). Talking cognition: Mapping and making the terrain. In H. F. M. te Molder & J. Potter (Eds.), *Conversation and cognition* (pp. 1–54). Cambridge: Cambridge University Press.

Potter, J. & Wetherell, M. (1987). *Discourse and social psychology: Beyond attitudes and behavior*. London and Thousand Oaks, CA: Sage.

Praat, A. C. & Tuffin, K. (1996). Police discourses of homosexual men in New Zealand. *Journal of Homosexuality, 31*, 57–73.

Prego-Vazquez, G. (2007). Frame conflict and social inequality in the workplace: Professional and local discourse struggles in employee/customer interactions. *Discourse & Society, 18*, 295–335.

Presser, L. (2004). Violent offenders, moral selves: Constructing identities and accounts in the research interview. *Social Problems, 51*, 82–101.

Priola, V., Smith, J. L., & Armstrong, S. J. (2004). Group work and cognitive style: A discursive investigation. *Small Group Research, 35*, 565–595.

Psathas, G. (1999). Studying the organization in action: Membership categorization and interaction analysis. *Human Studies, 22*, 139–162.

Puchta, C. & Potter, J. (2002). Manufacturing individual opinions: Market research focus groups and the discursive psychology of evaluation. *British Journal of Social Psychology, 41*, 345–363.

Puchta, C. & Potter, J. (2004). *Focus group practice*. London: Sage.

Pudlinski, C. (2005). Doing empathy and sympathy: Caring responses to troubles tellings on a peer support line. *Discourse Studies, 7*, 267–288.

Radley, A. & Billig, M. (1996). Accounts of health and illness: Dilemmas and representations. *Sociology of Health & Illness, 18*, 220–240.

Rapley, M. & Antaki, C. (1996). A conversation analysis of the "acquiescence" of people with learning disabilities. *Journal of Community & Applied Social Psychology, 6*, 207–227.

Rapley, M., Kiernan, P., & Antaki, C. (1998). Invisible to themselves or negotiating identity? The interactional management of "being intellectually disabled." *Disability & Society, 13*, 807–827.

Rapley, M., McCarthy, D., & McHoul, A. (2003). Mentality or morality? Membership categorization, multiple meanings and mass murder. *British Journal of Social Psychology, 42*, 427–444.

Reavey, P., Ahmed, B., & Majumdar, A. (2006). "How can we help when she won't tell us what's wrong?" Professionals working with South Asian women who have experienced sexual abuse. *Journal of Community & Applied Social Psychology*, 16, 171–188.

Reicher, S. D. & Taylor, S. (2005). Similarities and differences between traditions. *The Psychologist*, 18, 547–549.

Reisigl, M. & Wodak, R. (2001). *Discourse and discrimination: Rhetorics of racism and anti-Semitism.* London: Routledge.

Rendle-Short, J. (2005). "I've got a paper-shuffler for a husband": Indexing sexuality on talk-back radio. *Discourse & Society*, 16, 561–578.

Reynolds, J. & Wetherell, M. (2003). The discursive climate of singleness: The consequences for women's negotiation of a single identity. *Feminism & Psychology*, 13, 489–510.

Ricento, T. (2003). The discursive construction of Americanism. *Discourse & Society*, 14, 611–637.

Riley, S. C. E. (2001). Maintaining power: Male constructions of "feminists" and "feminist values." *Feminism & Psychology*, 11, 55–78.

Riley, S. C. E. (2002). Constructions of equality and discrimination in professional men's talk. *British Journal of Social Psychology*, 41, 443–461.

Riley, S. C. E. (2003). The management of the traditional male role: A discourse analysis of the constructions and functions of provision. *Journal of Gender Studies*, 12, 99–113.

Ring, K. (1967). Experimental social psychology: Some sober questions about some frivolous values. *Journal of Experimental Social Psychology*, 3, 113–123.

Robb, A. S. & Dadson, M. J. (2002). Eating disorders in males. *Child and Adolescent Psychiatric Clinics of North America*, 11, 399–418.

Rogerson-Revell, P. (2007). Humour in business: A double-edged sword. A study of humour and style shifting in intercultural business meetings. *Journal of Pragmatics*, 39, 4–28.

Rosenberg, A. (2005). *Philosophy of science: A contemporary introduction* (2nd ed.). London: Routledge.

Rumelhart, D. E. (1980). Schemata: The building blocks of cognition. In R. J. Spiro, B. Bruce, & W. F. Brewer (Eds.), *Theoretical issues in reading comprehension* (pp. 33–58). Hillsdale, NJ: Erlbaum.

Rutter, J. (2000). The stand-up introduction sequence: Comparing comedy compères. *Journal of Pragmatics*, 32, 463–483.

Sacks, H. (1992). *Lectures on conversation*. Oxford: Blackwell.

Sacks, H., Schegloff, E. A., & Jefferson, G. (1974). A simplest systematics for the organization of turn-taking for conversation. *Language*, 50, 696–735.

Saft, S. (2004). Conflict as interactional accomplishment in Japanese: Arguments in university faculty meetings. *Language in Society*, 33, 549–584.

Sandel, T. L. (2004). Narrated relationships: Mothers-in-law and daughters-in-law justifying conflicts in Taiwan's Chhan-chng. *Research on Language and Social Interaction*, 37, 365–398.

Sandfield, A. & Percy, C. (2003). Accounting for single status: Heterosexism and ageism in heterosexual women's talk about marriage. *Feminism & Psychology*, 13, 475–488.

Santa Ana, O. (1999). "Like an animal I was treated": Anti-immigrant metaphor in US public discourse. *Discourse & Society*, 10, 191–224.

Saussure, F. de (1983). *Course in general linguistics.* London: Duckworth.

Schegloff, E. A. (1988). Goffman and the analysis of conversation. In P. Drew & A. J. Wootton (Eds.), *Erving Goffman: Exploring the interactional order* (pp. 89–135). Cambridge: Polity Press.

Schegloff, E. A. (1991). Reflections on talk and social structure. In D. Boden & D. H. Zimmerman (Eds.), *Talk and social structure* (pp. 44–70). Cambridge: Polity Press.

Schegloff, E. A. (1997). Whose text? Whose context? *Discourse & Society*, 8, 165–187.

Schegloff, E. A. (1998). Reply to Wetherell. *Discourse & Society*, 9, 413–416.

Schegloff, E. A. (1999a). "Schegloff's texts" as "Billig's data": A critical reply. *Discourse & Society*, 10, 558–572.

Schegloff, E. A. (1999b). Naiveté vs. sophistication or discipline vs. self-indulgence: A rejoinder to Billig. *Discourse & Society*, 10, 577–582.

Schegloff, E. A. (2004). Putting the interaction back into dialogue. *Behavioral and Brain Sciences*, 27, 207–208.

Schegloff, E. A. (2006). On possibles. *Discourse Studies*, 8, 141–157.

Schegloff, E. A. (2007). A tutorial on membership categorization. *Journal of Pragmatics*, 39, 462–482.

Scheuer, J. (2001). Recontextualization and communicative styles in job interviews. *Discourse Studies*, 3, 223–248.

Schiffrin, D. (1984). Jewish argument as sociability. *Language in Society*, 13, 311–335.

Schiffrin, D. (2002). Mother and friends in a Holocaust life story. *Language in Society*, 31, 309–353.

Schnurr, S., Marra, M., & Holmes, J. (2007). Being (im)polite in New Zealand workplaces: Maori and Pakeha leaders. *Journal of Pragmatics*, 39, 712–729.

Scott, K. D. (2000). Crossing cultural borders: "Girl" and "look" as markers of identity in black women's language use. *Discourse & Society*, 11, 237–248.

Sears, D. O. (1986). College sophomores in the laboratory: Influences of a narrow data base on social psychology's view of human nature. *Journal of Personality and Social Psychology, 51*, 515–530.

Senn, D. J. (1989). Myopic social psychology: An overemphasis on individualistic explanations of social behavior. In M. R. Leary (Ed.), *The state of social psychology: Issues, themes and controversies* (pp. 45–52). Newbury Park, CA: Sage.

Seymour-Smith, S. & Wetherell, M. (2006). "What he hasn't told you...": Investigating the micropolitics of gendered support in heterosexual couples' co-constructed accounts of illness. *Feminism & Psychology, 16*, 105–127.

Seymour-Smith, S., Wetherell, M., & Phoenix, A. (2002). "My wife ordered me to come!": A discursive analysis of doctors' and nurses' accounts of men's use of general practitioners. *Journal of Health Psychology, 7*, 253–267.

Shakespeare, P. (2006). Embodiment and bodily description: Common sense data in expert accounts. *Qualitative Research in Psychology, 3*, 59–69.

Shakespeare, P. & Clare, L. (2005). Focusing on task-oriented talk as a way of exploring the interaction between people with early-onset dementia and their carers. *Qualitative Research in Psychology, 2*, 327–340.

Shan, S. (2000). Language, gender and floor apportionment in political debates. *Discourse & Society, 11*, 401–418.

Shefer, T., Strebel, A., Wilson, T., Shabalala, N., Simbayi, L., Ratele, K. et al. (2002). The social construction of sexually transmitted infections (STIs) in South African communities. *Qualitative Health Research, 12*, 1373–1390.

Shim, Y. H. (2001). Feminism and the discourse of sexuality in Korea: Continuities and changes. *Human Studies, 24*, 133–148.

Simpson, M. & Cheney, G. (2007). Marketization, participation, and communication within New Zealand retirement villages: A critical–rhetorical and discursive analysis. *Discourse & Communication, 1*, 191–222.

Sirota, K. G. (2004). Positive politeness as discourse process: Politeness practices of high-functioning children with autism and Asperger Syndrome. *Discourse Studies, 6*, 229–251.

Sirota, K. G. (2006). Habits of the hearth: Children's bedtime routines as relational work. *Text & Talk, 26*, 493–514.

Sluzki, C. E. (1990). Therapeutic conversations: Systemic blueprints of a couple's conversation. In R. Chasin, H. Grunebaum & M. Herzig (Eds.), *One couple, four realities: Multiple perspectives on couple therapy* (pp. 106–127). New York: Guilford Press.

Smith, J. A. (1997). Developing theory from case studies: Self-reconstruction and the transition to motherhood. In N. Hayes (Ed.), *Doing qualitative analysis in psychology* (pp. 187–200). Hove: Psychology Press.

Smithson, J. (2005). "Full-timer in a part-time job": Identity negotiation in organizational talk. *Feminism & Psychology, 15*, 275–293.

Smithson, J. & Stokoe, E. H. (2005). Discourses of work–life balance: Negotiating "genderblind" terms in organizations. *Gender Work and Organization, 12*, 147–168.

Sneijder, P. & te Molder, H. F. M. (2005a). Disputing taste: Food pleasure as an achievement in interaction. *Appetite, 46*, 107–116.

Sneijder, P. & te Molder, H. F. M. (2005b). Moral logic and logical morality: Attributions of responsibility and blame in online discourse on veganism. *Discourse & Society, 16*, 675–696.

Solomon, O. (2004). Narrative introductions: Discourse competence of children with autistic spectrum disorders. *Discourse Studies, 6*, 253–276.

Speer, S. A. (2002). What can conversation analysis contribute to feminist methodology? Putting reflexivity into practice. *Discourse & Society, 13*, 783–803.

Speer, S. A. (2005). *Gender talk: Feminism, discourse and conversation analysis*. London: Routledge.

Speer, S. A. & Potter, J. (2000). The management of heterosexist talk: Conversational resources and prejudiced claims. *Discourse & Society, 11*, 543–572.

Staske, S. (2002). Claiming individualized knowledge of a conversational partner. *Research on Language and Social Interaction, 35*, 249–276.

Sterponi, L. (2003). Account episodes in family discourse: The making of morality in everyday interaction. *Discourse Studies, 5*, 79–100.

Sterponi, L. (2004). Construction of rules, accountability and moral identity by high-functioning children with autism. *Discourse Studies, 6*, 207–228.

Stokoe, E. H. (1998). Talking about gender: The conversational construction of gender categories in academic discourse. *Discourse & Society, 9*, 217–240.

Stokoe, E. H. (2000). IV. Toward a conversation analytic approach to gender and discourse. *Feminism & Psychology, 10*, 552–563.

Stokoe, E. H. (2003). Mothers, single women and sluts: Gender, morality and membership categorization in neighbour disputes. *Feminism & Psychology, 13*, 317–344.

Stokoe, E. H. (2004). Gender and discourse, gender and categorization: Current developments in language and gender research. *Qualitative Research in Psychology, 1*, 107–129.

Stokoe, E. H. (2006). On ethnomethodology, feminism and the analysis of categorial reference to gender in talk-in-interaction. *Sociological Review, 54*, 467–494.

Stokoe, E. H. & Edwards, D. (2007). "Black this, black that": Racial insults and reported speech in neighbour complaints and police interrogations. *Discourse & Society, 18,* 337–372.

Stokoe, E. H. & Hepburn, A. (2005). "You can hear a lot through the walls": Noise formulations in neighbour complaints. *Discourse & Society, 16,* 647–673.

Stokoe, E. H. & Smithson, J. (2001). Making gender relevant: Conversation analysis and gender categories in interaction. *Discourse & Society, 12,* 217–244.

Stokoe, E. H. & Wallwork, J. (2003). Space invaders: The moral-spatial order in neighbour dispute discourse. *British Journal of Social Psychology, 42,* 551–569.

Strauss, A. L. & Corbin, J. (1990). *Basics of qualitative research: Grounded theory procedures and techniques.* London: Sage.

Stygall, G. (2001). A different class of witnesses: Experts in the courtroom. *Discourse Studies, 3,* 327–349.

Sun, H. (2002). Display and reaffirmation of affect bond and relationship: Invited guessing in Chinese telephone conversations. *Language in Society, 31,* 85–112.

Sun, H. (2004). Opening moves in informal Chinese telephone conversations. *Journal of Pragmatics, 36,* 1429–1465.

Sunderland, J. (2000). Baby entertainer, bumbling assistant and line manager: Discourses of fatherhood in parentcraft texts. *Discourse & Society, 11,* 249–274.

Swan, D. & McCarthy, J. C. (2003). Contesting animal rights on the Internet: Discourse analysis of the social construction of argument. *Journal of Language and Social Psychology, 22,* 297–320.

Szymanski, M. H. (1999). Re-engaging and disengaging talk in activity. *Language in Society, 28,* 1–23.

Tainio, L. (2003). "When shall we go for a ride?" A case of the sexual harassment of a young girl. *Discourse & Society, 14,* 173–190.

Tannen, D. (2004). Talking the dog: Framing pets as interactional resources in family discourse. *Research on Language and Social Interaction, 37,* 399–420.

Tannen, D. (2006). Intertextuality in interaction: Reframing family arguments in public and private. *Text & Talk, 26,* 597–617.

Tannock, S. (1999). Working with insults: Discourse and difference in an inner-city youth organization. *Discourse & Society, 10,* 317–350.

Tapsell, L. (2000). Using applied conversation analysis to teach novice dietitians history taking skills. *Human Studies, 23,* 281–307.

Taylor, S. & Wetherell, M. (1999). A suitable time and place: Speakers' use of "time" to do discursive work in narratives of nation and personal life. *Time & Society, 8,* 39–58.

Teas Gill, V. (2005). Patient "demand" for medical interventions: Exerting pressure for an offer in a primary care clinic visit. *Research on Language and Social Interaction, 38,* 451–479.

ten Have, P. (1999). *Doing conversation analysis: A practical guide.* London: Sage.

ten Have, P. (2001). Applied conversation analysis. In A. McHoul & M. Rapley (Eds.), *How to analyse talk in institutional settings* (pp. 3–11). London: Continuum.

Teo, P. (2000). Racism in the news: A critical discourse analysis of news reporting in two Australian newspapers. *Discourse & Society, 11,* 7–49.

Thomas-MacLean, R. & Stoppard, J. M. (2004). Physicians' constructions of depression: Inside/outside the boundaries of medicalization. *Health, 8,* 275–293.

Thornborrow, J. (2002). *Power talk: Language and interaction in institutional discourse.* Harlow: Longman.

Thornborrow, J. (2003). The organization of primary school children's on-task and off-task talk in a small group setting. *Research on Language and Social Interaction, 36,* 7–32.

Thurlow, C. & Jaworski, A. (2006). The alchemy of the upwardly mobile: Symbolic capital and the stylization of elites in frequent-flyer programmes. *Discourse & Society, 17,* 99–135.

Tilbury, F. & Colic-Peisker, V. (2006). Deflecting responsibility in employer talk about race discrimination. *Discourse & Society, 17,* 651–676.

Tileagă, C. (2005). Accounting for extreme prejudice and legitimating blame in talk about the Romanies. *Discourse & Society, 16,* 603–624.

Timor, U. & Landau, R. (1998). Discourse characteristics in the sociolect of repentant criminals. *Discourse & Society, 9,* 363–386.

Todd, S. & Shearn, J. (1995). *Family secrets and dilemmas of status: Parental management of the disclosure of "learning disability."* Cardiff: Welsh Centre for Learning Disabilities, Applied Research Unit.

Todd, S. & Shearn, J. (1997). Family dilemmas and secrets: Parents' disclosure of information to their adult offspring with learning disabilities. *Disability & Society, 12,* 341–366.

Toerien, M. & Durrheim, K. (2001). Power through knowledge: Ignorance and the "real man." *Feminism & Psychology, 11,* 35–54.

Torras, M. C. & Gafaranga, J. (2002). Social identities and language alternation in non-formal institutional bilingual talk: Trilingual service encounters in Barcelona. *Language in Society, 31,* 527–548.

Tracy, K. & Agne, R. R. (2002). "I just need to ask somebody some questions": Sensitivities in domestic dispute calls. In J. Cotterill (Ed.), *Language in the legal process* (pp. 75–90). Basingstoke: Palgrave Macmillan.

Tracy, K. & Anderson, D. L. (1999). Relational positioning strategies in police calls: A dilemma. *Discourse Studies*, 1, 201–225.

Trinch, S. L. & Berk-Seligson, S. (2002). Narrating in protective order interviews: A source of interactional trouble. *Language in Society*, 31, 383–418.

Tucker, I. (2004). Stories of chronic fatigue syndrome: An exploratory discursive psychological analysis. *Qualitative Research in Psychology*, 1, 153–167.

Tuffin, A., Tuffin, K., & Watson, S. (2001). Frontline talk: Teachers' linguistic resources when talking about mental health and illness. *Qualitative Health Research*, 11, 477–490.

Tuffin, K. (2005). *Understanding critical social psychology*. London and Thousand Oaks, CA: Sage.

Tuffin, K. & Danks, J. (1999). Community care and mental disorder: An analysis of discursive resources. *British Journal of Social Psychology*, 38, 289–302.

Turkle, S. (1995). *Life on the screen: Identity in the age of the Internet*. New York: Simon & Schuster.

Ulrich, M. & Weatherall, A. (2000). Motherhood and infertility: Viewing motherhood through the lens of infertility. *Feminism & Psychology*, 10, 323–336.

United Nations (2005). The eighth United Nations survey on crime trends and the operations of criminal justice systems (2002–2003). www.unodc.org/crime_cicp_survey_eighth.html. [Online].

Vallis, R. (2001). Applying membership categorization analysis to chat-room talk. In A. McHoul & M. Rapley (Eds.), *How to analyse talk in institutional settings* (pp. 86–99). London: Continuum.

van den Berg, H., Wetherell, M., & Houtkoop-Steenstra, H. (2003). Introduction. In H. van den Berg, M. Wetherell, & H. Houtkoop-Steenstra (Eds.), *Analyzing race talk: Multidisciplinary approaches to the interview* (pp. 1–10). Cambridge: Cambridge University Press.

van den Berg, H., Wetherell, M., & Houtkoop-Steenstra, H. (2006). *Analyzing race talk*. Cambridge: Cambridge University Press.

van der Valk, I. (2003). Right-wing parliamentary discourse on immigration in France. *Discourse & Society*, 14, 309–348.

van Dijk, T. A. (1987). Structures and strategies of discourse and prejudice. In J. P. van Oudenhoven & T. M. Willemsen (Eds.), *Ethnic minorities: Social psychological perspectives* (pp. 115–138). Amsterdam: Swets & Zeitlinger.

van Dijk, T. A. (1995). Discourse, opinions and ideologies. *Current Issues in Language and Society*, 2, 115–145.

van Dijk, T. A. (1997). Applied discourse studies. *Discourse & Society*, 8, 451–452.

van Dijk, T. A. (1998). *Ideology: A multidisciplinary approach*. London: Sage.

van Dijk, T. A. (1999). Critical discourse analysis and conversation analysis. *Discourse & Society*, 10, 459–460.

van Dijk, T. A. (2001a). Critical discourse analysis. In D. Tannen, D. Schiffrin, & H. E. Hamilton (Eds.), *The handbook of discourse analysis* (pp. 352–371). Oxford: Blackwell.

van Dijk, T. A. (2001b). Principles of critical discourse analysis. In M. Wetherell, S. Taylor, & S. J. Yates (Eds.), *Discourse theory and practice: A reader* (pp. 300–317). London: Sage.

van Dijk, T. A. (2002). Knowledge in parliamentary debates. *Journal of Language and Politics*, 2, 93–109.

van Dijk, T. A. (2006a). Discourse and manipulation. *Discourse & Society*, 17, 359–383.

van Dijk, T. A. (2006b). Discourse, context and cognition. *Discourse Studies*, 8, 159–177.

Vehviläinen, S. (2001). Evaluative advice in educational counseling: The use of disagreement in the "stepwise entry" to advice. *Research on Language and Social Interaction*, 34, 371–398.

Vehviläinen, S. (2003). Avoiding providing solutions: Orienting to the ideal of students' self-directedness in counselling interaction. *Discourse Studies*, 5, 389–414.

Verkuyten, M. (1997). Discourses of ethnic minority identity. *British Journal of Social Psychology*, 36, 565–586.

Verkuyten, M. (1998a). Attitudes in public discourse: Speakers' own orientations. *Journal of Language and Social Psychology*, 17, 302–322.

Verkuyten, M. (1998b). Personhood and accounting for racism in conversation. *Journal for the Theory of Social Behavior*, 28, 147–167.

Verkuyten, M. (2001). "Abnormalization" of ethnic minorities in conversation. *British Journal of Social Psychology*, 40, 257–278.

Verkuyten, M. (2002). Making teachers accountable for students' disruptive classroom behavior. *British Journal of Sociology of Education*, 23, 107–122.

Verkuyten, M. (2003). Discourses about ethnic group (de-)essentialism: Oppressive and progressive aspects. *British Journal of Social Psychology*, 42, 371–391.

Verkuyten, M. (2005a). Accounting for ethnic discrimination: A discursive study among minority and majority group members. *Journal of Language and Social Psychology*, 24, 66–92.

Verkuyten, M. (2005b). Immigration discourses and their impact on multiculturalism: A discursive and experimental study. *British Journal of Social Psychology*, 44, 223–240.

Verkuyten, M. (2005c). *The social psychology of ethnic identity*. Hove: East Sussex.

Verkuyten, M. & de Wolf, A. (2002). Being, feeling and doing: Discourses and ethnic self-definitions among minority group members. *Culture & Psychology*, 8, 371–399.

Verkuyten, M. & Steenhuis, A. (2005). Preadolescents' understanding and reasoning about asylum seeker peers and friendships. *Journal of Applied Developmental Psychology*, 26, 660–679.

Walker, A., Kershaw, C., & Nicholas, S. (2006). *Home Office statistical bulletin: Crime in England and Wales 2006/06*. London: Home Office.

Wallwork, J. & Dixon, J. A. (2004). Foxes, green fields and Britishness: On the rhetorical construction of place and national identity. *British Journal of Social Psychology*, 43, 21–39.

Walton, C., Coyle, A., & Lyons, E. (2004). Death and football: An analysis of men's talk about emotions. *British Journal of Social Psychology*, 43, 401–416.

Walton, M., Weatherall, A., & Jackson, S. M. (2002). Romance and friendship in pre-teen stories about conflicts: "We decided that boys are not worth it." *Discourse & Society*, 13, 673–689.

Watson, D. R. (1978). Categorizations, authorization and blame-negotiation in conversation. *Sociology*, 12, 105–113.

Watson, D. R. (1997). Some general reflections on "categorization" and "sequence" in the analysis of conversation. In S. Hester & P. Eglin (Eds.), *Culture in action: Studies in membership categorization analysis* (pp. 49–76). Washington, DC: University Press of America.

Watson, T. J. (1996). Managing work – managing self. In M. Wetherell (Ed.), *Identities, groups and social issues* (pp. 293–298). London: Sage.

Watson, T. J. (1997). Language within languages: A social constructionist perspective on multiple managerial discourses. In F. Bargiela-Chiappini & S. Harris (Eds.), *The languages of business: An international perspective* (pp. 211–227). Edinburgh: Edinburgh University Press.

Weatherall, A. (1998). Women and men in language: An analysis of seminaturalistic person descriptions. *Human Communication Research*, 25, 275–292.

Weedon, C. (1997). *Feminist practice and poststructuralist theory* (2nd ed.) Oxford: Blackwell.

Weinberg, D. (2000). "Out there": The ecology of addiction in drug abuse treatment discourse. *Social Problems*, 47, 606–621.

Welton, D. (1999). *The essential Husserl: Basic writings in transcendental phenomenology*. Bloomington, IN: Indiana University Press.

West, C. & Fenstermaker, S. (2002). Accountability in action: The accomplishment of gender, race and class in a meeting of the University of California Board of Regents. *Discourse & Society*, 13, 537–563.

Wetherell, M. (1996). Life histories/social histories. In M. Wetherell (Ed.), *Identities, groups and social issues* (pp. 299–342). London: Sage/Open University Press.

Wetherell, M. (1998). Positioning and interpretative repertoires: Conversation analysis and poststructuralism in dialogue. *Discourse & Society*, 9, 387–412.

Wetherell, M. & Edley, N. (1999). Negotiating hegemonic masculinity: Imaginary positions and psycho-discursive practices. *Feminism & Psychology*, 9, 335–356.

Wetherell, M. & Maybin, J. (1996). The distributed self: A social constructionist perspective. In R. Stevens (Ed.), *Understanding the self* (pp. 219–275). London and Thousand Oaks, CA: Sage.

Wetherell, M. & Potter, J. (1992). *Mapping the language of racism: Discourse and the legitimation of exploitation*. London and New York: Harvester Wheatsheaf.

Wetherell, M. & Potter, J. (1998). Discourse analysis and the identification of interpretative repertoires. In C. Antaki (Ed.), *Analysing everyday explanations: A casebook of methods* (pp. 163–183). London: Sage.

Wetherell, M., Stiven, H., & Potter, J. (1987). Unequal egalitarianism: A preliminary study of discourses concerning gender and employment opportunities. *British Journal of Social Psychology*, 26, 59–71.

Wetherell, M., Taylor, S., & Yates, S. J. (2001). *Discourse as data: A guide for analysis*. London: Sage.

Wharton, S. (2006). Divide and rule: The power of adversarial subjectivities in the discourse of divorce. *Text & Talk*, 26, 791–814.

Whitehead, K. A. & Wittig, M. A. (2004). Discursive management of resistance to a multicultural education programme. *Qualitative Research in Psychology*, 1, 267–284.

Widdicombe, S. & Wooffitt, R. (1995). *The language of youth subcultures: Social identity in action*. Hemel Hempstead and New York: Harvester Wheatsheaf.

Wiggins, S. & Potter, J. (2003). Attitudes and evaluative practices: Category vs. item and subjective vs. objective constructions in everyday food assessments. *British Journal of Social Psychology*, 42, 513–531.

Williams, M. (1996). *Unnatural doubts: Epistemological realism and the basis of scepticism*. Princeton, NJ: Princeton University Press.

Willig, C. (1997). The limitations of trust in intimate relationships: Constructions of trust and sexual risk taking. *British Journal of Social Psychology*, 36, 211–221.

Willig, C. (2000). A discourse-dynamic approach to the study of subjectivity in health psychology. *Theory & Psychology*, 10, 547–570.

Willott, S. & Griffin, C. (1997). "Wham bam, am I a man?": Unemployed men talk about masculinities. *Feminism & Psychology, 7*, 107–128.

Willott, S. & Griffin, C. (1999). Building your own lifeboat: Working-class male offenders talk about economic crime. *British Journal of Social Psychology, 38*, 445–460.

Willott, S. & Griffin, C. (2004). Redundant men: Constraints on identity change. *Journal of Community & Applied Social Psychology, 14*, 53–69.

Willott, S., Griffin, C., & Torrance, M. (2001). Snakes and ladders: Upper-middle-class male offenders talk about economic crime. *Criminology, 39*, 441–466.

Wilson, G. B. & MacDonald, R. A. R. (2005). The meaning of the blues: Musical identities in talk about jazz. *Qualitative Research in Psychology, 2*, 341–363.

Wilson, J. & Stapleton, K. (2005). Voices of commemoration: The discourse of celebration and confrontation in Northern Ireland. *Text, 25*, 633–664.

Wingard, L. (2006). Parents' inquiries about homework: The first mention. *Text & Talk, 26*, 573–596.

Wittgenstein, L. (1953). *Philosophical investigations.* Oxford: Blackwell.

Wodak, R. (2001a). The discourse-historical approach. In R. Wodak & M. Meyer (Eds.), *Methods of critical discourse analysis* (pp. 63–94). London and Thousand Oaks, CA: Sage.

Wodak, R. (2001b). What CDA is about: A summary of its history, important concepts and development. In R. Wodak & M. Meyer (Eds.), *Methods of critical discourse analysis* (pp. 1–13). London: Sage.

Wodak, R. (2002). Friend or foe: Defamation or legitimate and necessary criticism? Reflections on recent political discourse in Austria. *Language & Communication, 22*, 495–517.

Wodak, R. (2006). Mediation between discourse and society: Assessing cognitive approaches in CDA. *Discourse Studies, 8*, 179–190.

Wodak, R., de Cillia, R., Reisigl, M., & Liebhart, K. (1999). *The discursive construction of national identity.* Trans. A. Hirsh & R. Mitten. Edinburgh: Edinburgh University Press.

Wooffitt, R. (1992). *Telling tales of the unexpected: The organization of factual discourse.* London and New York: Harvester Wheatsheaf.

Wooffitt, R. (2005a). *Conversation analysis and discourse analysis: A comparative and critical introduction.* London: Sage.

Wooffitt, R. (2005b). From process to practice: Language interaction and "flashbulb" memories. In H. F. M. te Molder & J. Potter (Eds.), *Conversation and cognition* (pp. 203–225). Cambridge: Cambridge University Press.

Wowk, M. T. & Carlin, A. P. (2004). Depicting a liminal position in ethnomethodology, conversation analysis and membership categorization analysis: The work of Rod Watson. *Human Studies, 27*, 69–89.

Wright, C. (1993). Realism: The contemporary debate – W(h)ither now? In J. Haldane & C. Wright (Eds.), *Reality, representation and projection* (pp. 63–84). Oxford: Oxford University Press.

Xu, S. (2000). Opinion discourse: Investigating the paradoxical nature of the text and talk of opinions. *Research on Language and Social Interaction, 33*, 263–289.

Yamaguchi, M. (2005). Discursive representation and enactment of national identities: The case of Generation 1.5 Japanese. *Discourse & Society, 16*, 269–299.

Yeung, L. (2004). The paradox of control in participative decision-making: Facilitative discourse in banks. *Text, 24*, 113–146.

Ylänne-McEwen, V. (2004). Shifting alignment and negotiating sociality in travel agency discourse. *Discourse Studies, 6*, 517–536.

Zajonc, R. B. (1999). One hundred years of rationality assumptions in social psychology. In A. Rodrigues & R. Levine (Eds.), *Reflections on 100 years of experimental social psychology* (pp. 220–214). New York: Basic Books.

Zanoni, P. & Janssens, M. (2004). Deconstructing difference: The rhetoric of human resources managers' diversity discourses. *Organization Studies, 25*, 55–74.

Zimmerman, D. H. (1998). Identity, context and interaction. In C. Antaki & S. Widdicombe (Eds.), *Identities in talk* (pp. 87–106). London: Sage.

Zimmerman, D. H. & Boden, D. (1991). Structure-in-action: An introduction. In D. Boden & D. H. Zimmerman (Eds.), *Talk and social structure* (pp. 3–21). Cambridge: Polity Press.

Author Index

Subject Index